CHARACTER
AND
CONFLICT

An Introduction to Drama

SECOND EDITION

CHARACTER AND CONFLICT

An Introduction to Drama

SECOND EDITION

ALVIN B. KERNAN

YALE UNIVERSITY

HARCOURT, BRACE & WORLD, INC.

New York / Chicago / San Francisco / Atlanta

ACKNOWLEDGMENT   The eight lines from William Butler Yeats' "In Memory of Major Robert Gregory" in the introduction to Synge are reprinted with permission of The Macmillan Company, Mr. M. B. Yeats, and The Macmillan Company of Canada from *Collected Poems* by William Butler Yeats. Copyright 1919 by The Macmillan Company renewed 1946 by Bertha Georgie Yeats.

COVER PHOTO   *Angus McBean, London.* Hamlet instructs the players in Act III, Scene 2, of a Stratford-on-Avon production.

ISBN: 0-15-506271-9

Library of Congress Catalog Card Number: 70-79934

Printed in the United States of America

CONTENTS

CONTENTS

PART III
GLOSSARY

CHARACTER
AND
CONFLICT

An Introduction to Drama

SECOND EDITION

INTRODUCTION

The plays in this volume are drawn from all the great periods of the theater. There is a Greek tragedy from the fifth century B.C., a late medieval morality play, a work from the English Renaissance, a comedy from the baroque theater in France, several examples of modern realism, and a number of plays from our own century in which the dramatists have broken out of traditional forms in order to express the modern consciousness of the world. This collection therefore offers a panorama of the development of the theater in the West and a history of the way in which the dramatists have adapted and exploited the resources of the play to show, as Hamlet puts it, "the very age and body of the time his form and pressure."

The plays included here were chosen not only because they are great drama, or because they represent a particular theatrical period, but because each provides a particularly clear and well-defined instance of the use of one fundamental element of drama. For example, a playwright creates characters; *Hedda Gabler,* according to one critic, is "a character study pure and simple. . . . The poet does not even pass judgment on his heroine; he simply paints her full-length portrait with scientific impassivity. But what a portrait! How searching in insight, how brilliant in coloring, how rich in detail!" *Hedda Gabler,* of course, is not all character; the play has a plot and it shows us a great deal of the world in which Hedda lives, but it is the character of Hedda Gabler that stands out and that is most carefully developed. The play is, therefore, an ideal place to begin the study of the ways in which a dramatist creates his characters and the uses he makes of them.

In *Mother Courage* the characters, interesting as they are, are less real and less important finally than the world, or environment, in which they live and act, and in *Antigone* the plot of the play stands out with unusual clarity. *Hamlet* has at its very center an examination of the nature of drama, its meaning, and what it means to present man and the world in the form of a play.

Each of these plays, except for *Hamlet,* is followed and supplemented by a second play, which stresses in a different manner the dramatic element prominent in the first, or reveals one way in which a dramatist can handle his material from another angle. *Hedda Gabler* is followed by *Everyman,* whose anonymous author was as relentlessly interested in presenting character as was Ibsen. But the *Everyman* author, instead of presenting his character in a realistic manner, simply breaks into the mind of Everyman and presents the various elements of thought as individual characters. *Mother Courage* is followed by Thornton Wilder's *The Skin of Our Teeth,* in which the world is a surrealistic compound of all times and places, from the ice age to suburban New Jersey, where men have struggled against extinction and death. This play is also a comic treatment of the situation Brecht treats tragically. Since Wilder's dramatic world is among other things a theater—that is, he, like Shakespeare, uses the metaphor of stage and play to reveal the meaning of life—a comparison with *Hamlet* can be helpful. In *Antigone* the plot is made up primarily of external, physical events. In order to help the student see that a plot may also be made up of mental events, of a series of thoughts and psychological changes, *Antigone* is followed by Strindberg's *The Stronger,* a short play with a very definite psychological plot but almost no external movement.

The "Plays for Further Reading," which comprise Part II, provide variety and additional examples of the dramatic techniques discussed in Part I. In some cases, a teacher may prefer to use plays in this part to present some aspect of dramatic theory. Chekhov's *The Cherry Orchard* employs various simple, realistic devices to reveal with fine skill the depths of character; and at the same time, even while focusing on character, it shows the helplessness of human beings in shaping a world made up of forces which though scarcely seen are relentless and powerful. *Riders to the Sea* is not only a perfect example of tragedy in miniature, but a play in which the sea, the wind, and the harsh conditions of life very nearly overwhelm and destroy character. The sea, though never visible, is a particularly sharp image of that part of drama which I have called the "world of the play." *The Misanthrope,* besides being one of the world's great comedies, is a dramatized confrontation of the tragic and comic views of existence. It may profitably be paired with *Hamlet,* for in both plays the leading character believes that his world is "out of joint" and that it is up to him to set it right. But Hamlet's Elsinore and the fashionable Paris salons in which Alceste lives are very different "worlds," and in the first play, the action moves inevitably to tragedy, while in the second, it turns equally inevitably to comedy. *Tiger at the Gates* is a play of uncanny appropriateness for our own moment in history, and it makes its point by emphasizing plot. Nowhere in Western drama does the difference between what the major characters want to happen and what actually happens appear so powerfully and clearly. Considered from one angle, *Tiger* is almost an academic demonstration of what plot is and of the traditional supremacy of plot in drama. *Picnic on the Battlefield* provides a good short example of the type of drama known as "the absurd," and is a particularly clear, exaggerated form of the expressionistic technique.

The selection of plays offered in this volume, then, can be approached in a number of ways, and the critical discussions, the introductions, and the glossary provide materials that will be of use to anyone who wishes to deal with the historical development of the drama, the nature of comedy and tragedy, or dramatic modes such as expressionism, realism, naturalism, and poetic drama. But the focus of the book is critical. By means of the selections, the critical discussions that precede seven of the plays, and the questions that follow all of the plays, this book aims to provide what might be called "a grammar of the play." Just as a grammar of language deals with such fundamentals as the parts of speech, definitions of words, and syntax, so this grammar of the play deals with such fundamentals as character, setting, plot, and meaning, with the constituent parts of each of these, and with the ways in which the components of the play can be connected and related to produce the whole. In other words, the purpose of the editorial material is to present as clearly and as simply as possible the elements, not the refinements, of drama.

The material printed before *Hamlet* makes use of that play to raise certain questions about literary genre. Specifically, the ways in which drama is fundamentally different from narrative and lyric are discussed, and the meaning inherent in the form of drama is explored.

If the approach to drama offered here were shining new and the invention of one critic's mind, it would be highly suspect. But the critical material in this book presents in a condensed and simplified form the methods of analysis now used in the majority of college classrooms where an effort is made to describe the dynamics of a play and get down to its basic elements. Any reader familiar with the literary criticism of the last thirty or forty years will also recognize that the theory of drama offered here is an attempt to gather together and to apply to the study of drama at an introductory level the work of many modern critics—T. S. Eliot, William Empson, Kenneth Burke, R. P. Blackmur, Francis Fergusson, Alan Downer, W. K. Wimsatt, and Northrop Frye, to name a few—who have tried to get close to the nature of literature and to construct an effective vocabulary for criticism.

The major categories of dramatic art discussed in this book, far from being new, ultimately derive from the first piece of dramatic criticism: Aristotle's *Poetics,* written in the fourth century B.C. Aristotle says that "all tragedy must necessarily contain six parts," and these are "fable, manners, diction, sentiments, decoration, and music." The fable (*mythos*) is roughly what we call "plot." Manners (*ethos*) refers in part to what is now known as "character." Diction (*lexis*) is the language used in the play. (I have, in agreement with modern criticism, chosen not to consider language as a separate element of drama but as a component of character and setting.) Sentiment (*dianoia*) apparently refers to the "theme" of a play, the ideas in it, and this I have enlarged to the topic "The Nature of Drama." By decoration (*opsis*) Aristotle means the scenery—he considered it unimportant— which I have expanded, following the practice of working dramatists since Aristotle's time, to cover all that part of creation represented by scenery, the "world" around man, his environment. Music (*melos*), which refers to the dances and chanting of the chorus in Greek tragedy, is no longer an important part of drama other than opera, though plays still have a "rhythm of action," and the language of poetic drama is still metrical.

Having said what this book tries to do, it now remains to say briefly what it does not try to do. First of all, it avoids as much as possible any analysis of a play before it is read. The one exception to this rule comes in the material introducing *Hamlet,* but there I have restricted discussion to the use of the theatrical metaphor and its meaning in the play. Each section of critical commentary discusses dramatic principles pertinent to the play that follows and draws examples from a number of other plays. But the play is not interpreted. The questions that follow each play ask the student to consider the play in the light of the general discussion and to examine the way it exploits various dramatic possibilities. Similarly, the introduction to each play provides general information, not an interpretation.

Second, no attempt has been made to present here a complete catalogue of the dramatic techniques developed over the last 2,500 years. Examples are offered of the basic ways in which a dramatist works, and it is then left to the reader to discover the variation and extension of techniques introduced in the plays printed here.

PART
I

CRITICISM
AND
PLAYS

CHARACTER IN DRAMA

When we see a play our attention first focuses on character. We are interested in the people on the stage, and we want to know more about them: What moves them to act as they do? What happens to them? Why does it happen? Are they responsible? These are legitimate interests, because a play is valuable only insofar as it tells us something about human nature and about the way the world goes for men. The characters are a dramatist's primary images of human nature; they are his statements in speech and gestures about the elusive creature man. The character Hamlet, for example, can be thought of as a *dramatic proposition,* similar to one philosopher's definition of man as "a featherless biped," or to the economist's definition of human beings as "consumers and producers of goods and services." Hamlet, featherless biped, consumers and producers—all are attempts to sum up, to find an adequate image for, the essential quality of man. Obviously, however, the character Hamlet is more complex than these other definitions. A summary statement about him must take into account, for example, his sorrow over the death of his father and the lust of his mother, his disturbed preoccupation with change and death, his suit of black clothes, his staging of a play, and, finally, his killing of a king. Besides being too simple to encompass the complex actions and feelings of Hamlet, the philosopher's and economist's definitions are also too abstract, too general, for the specific terms of the play. Hamlet is the Prince of Denmark, the lover—perhaps—of Ophelia, the son of Gertrude, the man who as a child was carried on the shoulders of Yorick, whose skull has been turned up by a gravedigger in making room for Ophelia's body.

The degree of complexity and the amount of detail are not the only ways in which these definitions differ. The philosopher's and the economist's definitions *fix* man, place him in a static condition. No matter what happens, he will always be two-footed and without feathers, always a user or producer of articles and work. But in drama man is dynamic, a restless seeker of some particular end. The forces at work within him—his *motives*—drive him forward to do or to attempt to do some particular thing in the outer world: to achieve freedom, control nature, or create order and stability from chaos and change. If we are to understand a character in a play we must think of him not as a static collection of qualities—a still portrait—but as a doer. Our aim as readers should not be the fine analysis of a fixed character; it should be an attempt to discover the fundamental motive that finds expression in everything the character does. Because dramatists conceive of their characters as doers or as attempters, every detail of costume and figure, every movement and gesture, every statement, is a partial expression of the basic motive of the character. As the play progresses, this motive, lightly sounded in the opening movements of the play, takes more obvious form in a major goal such as to bring peace to Rome, to marry Juliet, or to become the master of the world. The immediate obvious goal the character seeks is not itself, however, to be thought of as his basic motive. It is only one of the ways he seeks the realization of his motive, one expression of some more fundamental desire that in its less heroic forms is common to all men.

Since a character's actions and speech express his motive, it follows that we must look carefully at *all* he says and does. The simplest scheme to follow in our discussion of the components of character is to look at the visible elements of dramatic character—physical features, clothing, movements, and gestures. From there we can move inward to consider other expressions of character, such as thought and language. This movement from the external to the internal should strike us as natural, for it approximates the manner in which we come to know not only characters in plays but also people in actual life. In life, however, some details are irrelevant; it may be, for example, no indication of a person's character that he has a humpback, or thin hair, or is enormously fat. But in a play these physical details express character. In Shakespeare's *Richard III*, crookbacked Richard's motive is to twist and destroy; this motive is expressed as much in his deformed back as it is in the disorders he contrives in his family, his society, and his kingdom. Hedda Gabler's thin hair and her desire to pull out another woman's luxurious hair mark her as a woman who not only lacks vitality but also actively seeks the lifeless, a woman whose motive is to kill. Falstaff's great belly shows that he seeks a purely physical existence. To think of physical traits in this manner may at first require some readjustments, for nowadays we assume— or so we say—that a physical characteristic is an accident. But in plays, though there are a few exceptions, physical features are usually expressions of motives. Even such obvious physical attributes as youth and old age, beauty and ugliness, should be taken in this way. Juliet's extreme youth—she is only thirteen—and her startling beauty are physical realizations of her innocence.

Though playwrights have always made use of the theory that the outer man expresses the inner one, they have often dramatized circumstances in which appearance and reality do not square. As Duncan says in *Macbeth*, "There's no art to find the mind's construction in the face." Oedipus' deformed foot shows that for all his grandeur—King of Thebes and the greatest of living men—he is flawed, but no physical traits reveal that Iago in *Othello* is not the honest and trustworthy officer he seems, or that Claudius, the usurping king in Hamlet, is not the wise and efficient ruler he appears to be. Wherever physical appearance, actions, or words conceal rather than express directly the "mind's construction" we have *irony*. The word has many shades of meaning, but basically *irony* is used to describe circumstances in which what seems to be and what actually is are in some way opposed: for example, where a devil seems to be a god, where death masquerades as life, or where slavery presents itself as freedom.

The fact of irony complicates but does not invalidate our general point that physical appearance helps us understand the basic nature of a character. In the simplest kind of irony there is a direct and obvious contradiction between appearance and reality, between body and mind. The contradiction sets up a contrast, and a contrast is almost as useful as a similarity in defining something. White may be defined by black as well as by other instances of white. The "well compact dimensions," the straight, powerful, handsome bodies, of such hypocrites as Edmund, in *King Lear,* and Iago both conceal and reveal their twisted, ugly minds. The straightness of body defines by contrast the crookedness of mind. Irony complicates character in many ways by creating ambivalent or complex motives, but for the present it is only necessary to remember that the physical attributes of a dramatic character are never mere accidents. They are symbols or indexes, direct or ironic, of his basic nature.

Clothing—costume—also makes visible a character's motives. The realization of motive in clothing may be direct and obvious, as it is in Tennessee Williams' *A Streetcar Named Desire,* where the bright, pri-

mary colors worn by the men in the play express their brutal direct-
ness, their emotional simplicity, and their reduction of life to elemental
appetites. Clothing may also express more subtle motives. In the same
play Blanche DuBois' longing to disguise the crude, painful facts of
life is represented by the cosmetics (make-up may be considered part
of costume), fake furs, and costume jewelry with which she attempts
to veil her loss of youth, money, and social status. Correct but unremarkable clothing may suggest that a character is proper, that his
basic drive is to do the accepted thing.

Since clothing often manifests the man, a change of clothing
may signify a radical inner change. In *King Lear,* Lear first appears
clad in rich robes and wearing a golden crown, secure and certain of
his worth as a man and ruler. Two acts later, on the stormy heath,
when he comes to doubt his own value, his changed condition is reflected in his attempt to strip himself naked so that his outward appearance will conform to his new-found knowledge that man is no
more than "a poor, bare, forked animal." Clothing, like physical appearance, may also be employed in an ironic manner to reveal the
distinction between what a man is and what he pretends to be. Blanche
DuBois' cheap furs and Macbeth's kingly garments, which "hang loose
about him, like a giant's robe upon a dwarfish thief," provide grim
comments on the inadequacy of these characters to live up to their
pretensions. The key to understanding the function of costume in the
theater is to remember that dress is seldom decorative or realistic detail, but is an expression of the wearer's motives.

Just as a character's motives are visible in his person and in his
clothing, so his gestures and movements are an acting out of his motives. Care must be exercised to catch the meaning of deceptively
simple and ordinary movements such as pacing a room, breaking free
from an embrace, turning away from a conversation, frequently withdrawing from the stage, or retiring to an isolated corner. In a well-
written play, every stage action, no matter how trivial, expresses motives, but dramatists usually provide more obviously significant actions
to manifest the primary drives of their characters. In Shakespeare's
Antony and Cleopatra, for example, everything passes away in time—
love, friendship, power, beauty, wealth, youth, all disintegrate. Caught
up in the ceaseless change, the major characters' motive is to create
some kind of permanence, to hold together something that they value.
They express this motive by their frequent attempts to hold something
or to embrace someone: firm handshakes to seal bargains, tight em-

braces to bind love to love, buckling the body into armor to preserve reputation and to hold the empire together.

In attempting to understand dramatic characters, we must focus first on what they try to do, not on what they succeed in doing. In the plays of Anton Chekhov, for example, the characters often have a simple aim: to go to Moscow, to buy a farm. They are, however, ineffective people who fail to achieve what they want. Chekhov illustrates their basic ineffectiveness by showing their consistent failure to achieve smaller aims as well: they stumble when they try to walk, bump into furniture and knock things over when they try to move gracefully, fall down when they attempt to dance, and go to sleep when they intend to stay awake. To understand them, however, we must first see what they try to do and then discover the way in which these motives combine with what they actually do to make up their total characters.

The greatest dramatists use action in such a skillful fashion that stage movements often provide a summary of the entire play and an insight into the basic motives of all the major characters. In the duel between Hamlet and Laertes, which comes at the close of *Hamlet,* what appears to be a polite fencing match is in fact deadly serious, for Laertes' rapier is poisoned. The combatants occupy the foreground of the stage, while Claudius stands waiting behind them with a cup of poison. To one side stand the Queen and courtiers, apparently without knowledge of what is actually taking place. When the duel begins, Hamlet proves a far better fencer than he was thought to be. After Hamlet has hit Laertes several times, a scuffle occurs, the rapiers are dropped, and by chance Hamlet picks up the one with the poisoned tip. These actions are endlessly suggestive, but they obviously summarize in visual terms the principal activities of the major characters throughout the play. First of all, the weapons are fencing foils, and the rapid thrust and parry of these light, flexible swords duplicates the quick interplay of the minds of Claudius and Hamlet as each has sought during the play to counter the attacks of the other and in turn to open his antagonist up for the fatal thrust. (Obviously a duel using battle-axes or lances would not fit the situation here.) Claudius' position behind Laertes restates his method of working throughout the play: he has never attacked Hamlet directly but has always gotten at him through an agent—the Queen, Polonius, Ophelia, or Rosencrantz and Guildenstern. His major source of dupes has been Polonius and his family, and now he is using the last of them. Whenever Claudius has dealt with Hamlet, he has masked his true intentions behind a pretense of honest concern and fair dealing; his method is reflected in the pretense that the duel is no more than honest exercise, a courtly game involving a small wager. But behind Claudius' pretenses of honesty, he has always been a poisoner—he has metaphorically poisoned the kingdom and literally poisoned its king—and so the poisoned rapier and cup. The Queen and courtiers innocently looking on establish visually their simple-minded acceptance of all that has gone on in Elsinore and demonstrate that the majority of men look but do not see. The chance exchange of rapiers and the deaths of Laertes, Gertrude, and Claudius condense into a few swift actions the role that fate has played in the drama, the inevitable deaths of the stupid and innocent, who stumble between "the pass and fell-incensed points of mighty opposites," and the frequent recoil of the invention on the inventor. Finally, Hamlet's death shows once again the cost of ridding the court of Claudius. Not many dramatists employ actions as effectively as Shakespeare does in *Hamlet,* but in most plays action tells us a great deal about character.

Important as "visual language" may be, playwrights seldom provide us with much physical description of their characters, nor do they often elaborate on costume and action. A few swift, strong strokes of the descriptive brush in a stage direction or in a speech make the necessary point; it is up to the reader or the director to enlarge upon these hints. Dramatists write with the theater in mind—actors, costumes, movement, scenery, placement, gesture, sound. The text of the completed play is thus a kind of musical score that does not finally exist as a play until it is produced on a stage. This does not mean that it is futile to read plays; it only means that we must read in a special way, that we must stage the play in our heads as we read, providing form and voice for the actor, costumes, makeup, scenery, and movement. We must read as if we were directors placing the characters on stage for the maximum effect, directing them in their gestures and movements, providing the correct tone for a given line, telling them what to do during awkward intervals when they remain on stage without lines to speak. Only by reading in this way can we hope to arrive at something approximating an ideal "performance." Some readers—Charles Lamb is the most famous of them—have preferred never to go to the theater, insisting that a live performance can never match the magnificent acting and superb effects of the theater of the imagination.

But a word of caution is necessary here. Reading the text of a play in this fashion is not an invitation to rewrite the play. We are not free to costume the characters in any fashion that appeals to us, nor are we free to have them do anything that strikes our fancy. Costumes, action, and all other details of the production must be controlled by the play as we have it in the text. When the author does not provide specific directions, our theatrical additions must be material images of the fundamental ideas of the text. For example, while Shakespeare provides no directions about the physical appearance of Macbeth, it would clearly be inappropriate to make him thin and supple. His brutal doggedness in battle, his determination to control the kingdom by any means once he has committed himself to this course, and the ponderous quality of his speech and mind dictate that he be powerful and heavy-set in body, slow and steady in movement, deep and peremptory in voice.

Some historians of the theater maintain that drama began with miming, that is, the wordless acting out of rituals. Many modern men of the theater have used this theory to argue that the play is essentially, as well as originally, a visual art that makes its statements primarily by means of costume, scenery, and action. No great play fails to make use of these and other forms of visual expression, but our greatest drama has always had a verbal dimension as well, and it is difficult to understand how characters could convey their intricacies through their bodies, clothing, and actions alone. The visual and verbal elements of a play are not in opposition. Rather, they are complementary; motives expressed in visual terms will be echoed and refined by language. The lines spoken by a character are, in the best plays, not flat statements of fact; they are living language taut with effort. Bertolt Brecht, the German playwright, once described the nature of dramatic language—*language that is action*—by pointing out that the sentence "Pluck out the eye that offends thee" is essentially still and undramatic; but the sentence "If thine eye offend thee, pluck it out" is fully dramatic because it contains and compels an action. Brecht called this kind of language *gestisch*, or "gestural." In other words, in dramatic speech the speaker accomplishes or tries to accomplish with words what he also tries to accomplish with his hands and feet. Words, after all, can wound as well as a knife, nourish as well as food. Making and breaking, forming and separating, soaring and falling, covering and uncovering, and other such basic actions take place constantly in dramatic language, even when no visual objects are handled or no physical action takes place. A character's physical actions provide us with rough estimates of his motive, but his language confirms these estimates and provides more delicate shadings.

Motive as expressed in language is most obvious in what we may call *thought*. This term refers to the ideas of a character, his expressed opinions on any subject, his general pronouncements, his statements of values. Most people express a good many random ideas in their conversation, and it is difficult to trace a simple pattern in their thought; but a playwright, working under very severe demands of economy, gives many of his characters only one central idea, one unchanging motive. This idea will be expressed in a variety of ways and will appear in what the character says about such diverse subjects as the weather, foreign affairs, the latest novel, or the condition of the garden. The basic thought is obvious enough in the comic character who reduces every topic of conversation to food or turns always to the subject of money. It is nearly as apparent in a character like Parson Manders in Ibsen's *Ghosts*, who in the course of the first act discusses a great many topics: Which of the latest books should be read? Are the artists living in Paris moral? Should a child be sent away from his family to school? Should an orphanage be insured against fire? No matter what the subject, Manders argues that conventional ways of thinking should guide conduct. This simple pattern of thought reveals Manders as a spokesman, almost a *personification,* of propriety, a man whose rather undistinguished motive is to do what is generally thought to be correct.

The thought patterns of more interesting characters than Manders are usually more difficult to establish. For example, it is difficult for the audience to determine by his language what a character like Cassius in *Julius Caesar* is trying to do. Cassius talks about whether or not the heavens have any effect on human destiny, he describes Caesar, he persuades Brutus to join a conspiracy, he argues about a battle plan, and he discusses the necessity of wringing taxes from captive provinces. But when we look closely at what he has to say on each of these points we discover that his motive, while it is always half-hidden, is in every case to manifest his belief that he is the master of his own destiny, that no other man or force is superior to him or controls him. In the attempt to understand a character, one of the first steps should always be to see if a single idea runs through all of his statements. Since playwrights do not attempt to hide the nature of their characters, they will usually state their central idea succinctly and openly at some point in the play. Cassius' central motive is revealed perfectly in his famous lines,

> The fault, dear Brutus, is not in our stars,
> But in ourselves, that we are underlings.

Because they lack variety and depth, characters like Parson Manders who have only one simple value to which they predictably return are known as *type* or *flat characters.* This kind of character is found in all drama but is the staple of *comedy,* for in the comic vision of life character is not very diverse or complicated. Comic characters usually fall into well-known types—the young lover, the clever servant, the old merchant, the pedantic doctor; and these types mechanically and laughably seek their one goal—money, a particular young woman, food, or mischief. What happens to these characters in comedy is equally predictable: the young lovers overcome the obstacles of birth and fortune; the old merchant is cuckolded and robbed; and the world goes merrily on its way, not because the direction of events has been shaped very much by character, but simply because this is the way of the comic world.

In *tragedy,* however, the major characters are usually more complex, for tragedy emphasizes the inner life of man with all its conflicts, its ambiguities, its crosscurrents of value. Characters with conflicting motives, who sustain internal struggles, are often described as *rounded* or *three-dimensional,* meaning that they show some of the complexity that is believed to exist in actual men. But in the drama the most complex character seldom embodies more than two or three conflicting values, though this conflict will be expressed in a variety of ways. Hamlet is the perfect example: "To be or not to be," to act or to remain passive, to revenge his father or to let the opportunity go by, to love or not to love Ophelia, to accept the corruption of the world or to strike out at it. Even this variety has at its center a continuing concern for whether a man properly acts to change the world or accepts it as it is given to him.

In tragedy this conflict of thought may be realized in several ways. One way—the way used by Shakespeare in *Hamlet*—is for the character himself to be aware of the conflicts within him and to express his duality of motive directly. An equally common technique uses irony to create a character who is not self-aware, who is not conscious of the conflict within himself. He thinks that he is single-minded and that since he knows his own mind he can move to assert his principal value in a direct and uncomplicated fashion. But his language, actions, and dress make it clear that other, less obvious forces are at work within him, complicating his character. Let us take, for example, the case of Brutus in Shakespeare's *Julius Caesar.* Brutus thinks of himself as a cool rationalist who approaches all problems, whether they be as trivial as where he placed a book he was reading or as important as the decision to kill the prospective dictator Julius Caesar, in a purely objective manner. Yet the play reveals in subtle ways that Brutus is moved, in part at least, by common human passions such as pride, envy, fear, and hatred. Brutus remains throughout the play totally unaware of the division in his character, and he is unified, we might say, only in being consistently divided. Like most men, he acts at once rationally and passionately.

In most drama, man "ever but slenderly knows himself," as Goneril says of her father in *King Lear,* and the motives of the greatest characters are not easily understood. Below the level of consciousness expressed directly as thought lie the ranges of character where the irrational and the rational meet and where motives originate. Long before psychologists demonstrated the existence of the unconscious mind and its role in human speech, dramatists had created characters who said far more than they consciously knew they were saying—whose actions and words expressed aims and conflicts of which they were unaware. A great actor is often able to reveal these depths by the most subtle gestures and facial expressions, but the playwright relies on language, on poetry, to give us brief glimpses of the depths of being.

A characteristic speech pattern may manifest deeper motive. A character who habitually begins sentences bravely enough but trails off without finishing his thought because he realizes that no one is listening has verbalized both his desire to accomplish some aim and his despair of achieving it in the face of the world's indifference. The repetition of stock phrases at crucial moments is a realization in words of an unoriginal and inflexible mind, a mind that does the same thing again and again. Long pauses or a slow, involved speech express a hesitant and tangled mind; quick, flowing lines express a mind moving rapidly and with assurance toward a goal.

Carefully controlled *rhythms* of speech provide some of the most subtle and acute effects of this order. Macbeth's lines,

> Tomorrow, and tomorrow, and tomorrow
> Creeps in this petty pace from day to day,
> To the last syllable of recorded time, . . .

make audible in the long, slow, dragging, regular movements—coupled with the repetition of words—the flatness, the emptiness, the profound boredom with sameness, which lie at his center.

A character may also express his motives in his *imagery*—the general term for *comparisons, metaphors,* and *similes*. When Romeo sees Juliet in the Capulet garden he compares her to brilliant, distant things: to the sun, to a bright angel, to a rich treasure, and to the stars in the heavens. All this, of course, is perfectly standard love imagery, but it nonetheless reveals that Romeo, like other lovers, is seeking, and realizes his aspiration for a magical instant in language, to reach and be one with the highest, the transcendent. Juliet is for him, for at least this one moment, not a flesh-and-blood woman but the symbol of an unearthly ideal toward which he strains upward in his language just as he strains upward with his body from the ground to the balcony on which Juliet stands. Metaphor may move in the reverse direction as well. Iago in *Othello* regularly compares men and women to animals —a black ram, a dog, a white ewe, a Barbary horse, a fly; and he reduces all human actions, such as love or friendship, to physical functions—disgorging, disrelishing, feeding, eating, and tasting. His images express his constant wish to diminish life to no more than animal activity.

In the case of Iago, two *strains of imagery,* or *image patterns,* those of animals and those of physical functions, combine to suggest the same motive. Ordinarily a character uses a variety of images, but usually the images have a common element which comes to focus in some quality that provides insight into what a character is trying to do. Sometimes though, a character's images jar against one another. The imagery of a complex character will also be complex, for it will express his mixed motives. When Hamlet describes man as "this quintessence of dust," his reverence for man and his wish to glorify him appear in "quintessence," while his fear and sense of human weakness are carried by the word "dust." Dramatists use imagery in a great many ways to express character, but the general rule holds that the images a character uses are expressions in language of either his basic motive or his unresolved conflict of motives.

Patterns, rhythms, and images are but three components of *style;* a character's style—the *way* he puts things—is in each of its details an enunciation of his motives. Consider, for example, the following speech from Congreve's *The Way of the World*. Mirabell is explaining to a friend the ways he tried to gain the confidence of an old lady so that she would permit him to marry her ward.

I did as much as a man could, with any reasonable conscience; I proceeded to the very last act of flattery with her, and was guilty of a song in her commendation. Nay, I got a friend to put her into a lampoon, and compli-

ment her with the imputation of an affair with a young fellow, which I
carried so far that I told her the malicious town took notice that she was
grown fat of a sudden; and when she lay in of a dropsy, persuaded her she
was reported to be in labor.

Leaving aside its sprightly and irreverent humor, the most impressive
quality of the speech is its breath-taking speed, its swift, certain, un-
hesitating forward movement. Yet despite its steady advance the lines
are nicely balanced—phrase is played off against phrase and sentence
against sentence—so that the over-all effect is one of both force and
order. The *diction,* i.e., the choice of words, is adequate and precise
without being ornate, and there are no figures of speech. The lines
dramatize a perfectly functioning, naturally keen, powerful, realistic,
and ordered mind.

At the other end of the scale is a speech such as this from the same
play:

Come, come, you are malicious now, and would breed debates. Petulant's
my friend, and a very honest fellow, and a very pretty fellow, and has a
smattering—faith and troth, a pretty deal of an odd sort of a small wit:
nay, I'll do him justice. I'm his friend, and I won't wrong him neither.
And if he had any judgement in the world, he would not be altogether
contemptible.

These lines of Witwoud's progress slowly and haltingly with painful
breaks and hesitations. They are filled with deadwood, with needless
repetition that only darkens the sense of what Witwoud is trying to
say. The diction is vague and imprecise. The several mild exclamations,
such as "Come, come" and "faith and troth," emphasize the slow-
ness, the eddying drift, the lack of sense with which his mind is working.

These few examples are not intended as a catalogue of the stylistic
resources of the dramatist; they only suggest the kind of linguistic
devices he may use to bring his characters to life. Grammar, figures
of speech, and even so humble a device as punning tell a great deal
about character, and the dramatist who wishes to do so can use all
of the stylistic techniques developed in rhetoric and poetry over the
last 2,000 years. Dramatic speech in all its details serves as gesture,
and an understanding of a character must be based on a close examination of at least the main features of his style. In poetic drama, where
the language is stretched to maximum expressiveness, style will, of
course, be more complex and precise in what it says about a character; but good prose speech, while not as packed and taut as poetry,

makes use of the same stylistic devices that poetry does. The difference between good poetry and good prose is one of degree, not of kind.

Up to this point we have considered only those ways in which a character expresses *himself,* but playwrights often throw oblique light on their dramatis personae by relating them to objects, places, and people outside themselves. An association with some *prop* (stage property) often suggests some deep-lying interest. The unshaded, harsh electric light that hangs in the center of Stanley Kowalski's house in *A Streetcar Named Desire* is *his* light, the physical image of his unblinking way of looking at people and things. Both the light and the man expose pretense and cruelly reveal the objective truth. Light and man are finally joined when Stanley thrusts the bare bulb into the face of a woman who has been pretending to be younger than she is, revealing every wrinkle, every sign of age in her painted face. Props used in this way are called *symbols,* and they should always be approached with a good deal of care. In the case of the bare light, for example, it should be noticed that it is an "artificial" light, a man-made way of "looking at things." Stanley would be quite a different kind of person if he were identified with the sunlight and used it to expose Blanche's age.

A great deal may be revealed by a character's preference for a particular place; the nature of the place may establish his primary concerns. Willy Loman in Arthur Miller's *Death of a Salesman* gives form to his fierce desire to grow something in the world—sons, friends, dignity, reputation—by his frequent references to gardens and by his return to a barren, backyard garden to plant seeds in the middle of the night after his world has collapsed around him. Alceste in Molière's *The Misanthrope* gives symbolic statement to his desire for isolation and total self-dependence by his reiterated decision to leave the polite drawing rooms of Paris for the wilds of the desert.

What one character says about another often provides crucial information, though it is wise to remember that such descriptions may be biased or incomplete. Claudius' statements about Hamlet's motives are revealing, but they scarcely tell the whole story. One character's comments on another character usually result in a *double perspective;* the first tells us something about the second, but he also tells us a good deal about the way he himself thinks. When Gertrude, for example, attributes her son's melancholy to the death of his father and to her "o'er hasty marriage," she provides a partial and rather obvious insight into the character of Hamlet, but she reveals her own feelings of guilt as well.

Minor characters frequently serve as both commentators and *reflectors* of forces at work within the major figures. The calm, stoic Horatio, who so often stands silent behind Hamlet, makes visible the unruffled acceptance of a confused and evil world that Hamlet, in one part of his complicated being, himself longs to achieve. In Ibsen's *Ghosts,* Parson Manders is apparently a figure of the utmost respectability, who argues that men should always accept traditional moral standards because they are right and because they lead ultimately to happiness. The grotesque figure of the carpenter Engstrand, whose oily platitudes about duty and right are simply obvious attempts to mask his greed and selfish interests, reflects Manders' character. Manders is not the conscious hypocrite that Engstrand is, but in all that he says and does there is a concern for being well thought of by other people; it is this hidden, self-seeking part of his nature that is constantly reflected by the *parody figure* of Engstrand. The identification is ultimately objectified when after Engstrand has done Manders a favor they shake hands and Manders says with great feeling that from this time they "will travel together."

Formal relationships such as the partnership of Engstrand and Manders usually provide significant clues to the characters involved. Blood kinship frequently represents metaphorically a more essential kinship of nature. King Lear has three daughters, two of them evil, grasping materialists, the other the soul of kindness and love. While each daughter remains a character in her own right, each at the same time projects some of Lear's attitudes and values. The daughters act out for us—somewhat in the manner of an allegorical play—the struggle in Lear's mind between the forces of good and evil, and their words and actions show the full meaning of certain choices that Lear makes. All relationships—between master and servant, king and subject, husband and wife, father and child, sister and brother, friend and friend— should be examined closely. They are used by the dramatist to reveal the nature of the characters involved. In a play, even more than in life, a man is known by the company he keeps.

Since playwrights make their points by *contrast* as well as by *similarity,* a play will often contain characters whose radically different natures help to define one another. Iago's hatred for man and his attempts to destroy everyone around him are more distinct and more meaningful because he appears in the same play with Desdemona, whose nature is to love and be concerned for the welfare of everyone. The stark, brutal realism of Stanley Kowalski in *A Streetcar Named Desire* is set off by the vague, fumbling romanticism of Blanche

DuBois; the practical vision of Oedipus stands in direct contrast to the spiritual vision of the prophet Teiresias. The latter contrast is reinforced by the ironic fact that Teiresias is literally blind while Oedipus' physical vision is excellent.

Here then are a few of the techniques playwrights have used to construct dramatic characters. It will be useful at this point to sum up the general principles that have emerged from our discussion. First of all, let us consider the status of a character in a play. Dramatic characters, such as Oedipus, Falstaff, and Hamlet, often seem more "real," more vital, more essentially alive than do most people one meets. That a fictional character should seem more alive than a human being results from the dramatist's ability to concentrate and sustain in his characters those qualities that we consider the essence of life: perfect expression of self in language and action, fullness of thought, intensity of feelings, and relentless movement toward the realization of basic goals.

The "genuineness" of the more interesting dramatic characters is further established by the fact that they have about them an ultimate air of mystery. Here we arrive at one of the fundamental peculiarities of the dramatic form. In a novel or lyric poem the author is free to tell us the true nature of a person, the springs of character can be laid open directly. But in the more traditional realistic drama there can be no such thing as absolute certainty about character. We see, as in life, only the outside of the person, hear what he says, watch what he does, listen to what others say about him, and we proceed to make informed guesses about what kind of person he finally is. We attempt to define the unknown and invisible principle of being from the known and visible, and we can do so with considerable certainty in the case of such simple characters as Macduff in *Macbeth,* Cassio in *Othello,* and Polonius in *Hamlet.* But the great figures of the stage—Oedipus, Lear, Hamlet—defy our efforts to pluck out the heart of their mystery. Even when they speak directly of the currents that stir the bottoms of their souls, their words manage only to suggest areas of being and motives that cannot be explicitly stated, for which the character himself cannot find adequate language.

Dramatic characters for all their "realness" are not finally living people but artistic constructions in which form, voice, and movement give life to the playwright's vision of human nature. Dramatic characters possess *no qualities or attributes other than those the author en-*

dows them with, and we are not free to guess about the existence of other unstated qualities as we might be in trying to understand a real human being. For example, if a character in a play shows constant feelings of inferiority we should not conjecture that in childhood he had dominating parents and a superior brother. He is an invented character, and as such he had no childhood except that which the playwright may have given him. There is no point in trying to imagine what a character does before the play opens or after it closes, unless the author provides pertinent information.

This distinction between what we may call the *symbolic* and *realistic* theories of dramatic character might seem to be critical hair-splitting without practical value for understanding a play, but it is in fact a crucial matter. If we approach the characters as real people, we risk taking the details of the play for granted and thus missing their meaning. Drama becomes for us a mere imitation of life, which intrigues us because, like the photograph, it duplicates reality. Using the realistic approach we might conclude that King Lear has three daughters simply because he is a man who happens to have three daughters, and that Oedipus has a deformed foot simply because of an unfortunate childhood accident.

If, on the other hand, we approach characters not as real people, but as symbolic forms, like the images painters create, designed to present in a schematic fashion the essential qualities of human nature as the playwright perceives it, then our eye for detail and meaning is sharpened, and we are alert to the subtle portrayal of character presented. Our work as readers is to see *all* there is in the play, but no more.

The second major point to be made is that dramatic character is *coherent.* Characters are made up of many different details: physical features, clothing, movements, opinions, statements, and ways of speaking. These details are not a random collection of unrelated fragments but a focused whole in which each of the linked components points toward a central motive and at the same time gives it shadings and fullness of expression. As a result, a dramatic character is unified: what his clothes tell us about him in one way, his movements and his words will tell us in another way. This unity in variety will be most apparent in a *flat* or *type* character, but even the more complex characters are consistent in their particular kind of complexity. In ironic situations, where the character is not what he seems to be, his duality will be implicit in everything that pertains to him. To understand a dramatic character, we therefore must always attempt to find the com-

mon denominator of his being, the unstated motive implicit in all the ways in which he expresses himself.

This brings us to the third main point. Drama by its very nature presents man as an actor, a doer; not a static, unmoving object. To understand a dramatic character we must therefore think of him as dynamic, as always on the way to some goal, to the realization of some motive. Every aspect of him—appearance, movements, and language—is an arrow, not pointed inward to a still center of consciousness, but shot outward toward a target. In the majority of cases the dramatic character follows his fate to its inevitable conclusion, to the point where the meaning of his motive finally becomes clear in action. Classically, the point at which this occurs has been known as the *recognition scene*. But while the identification of man's fate with his character, fixed and incapable of change until it is too late, is closely associated with drama, there are plays in which the characters do change under the pressure of existence, and a reader should always be alert to this possibility. Such changes are usually signaled by a change in appearance, in clothing, and in style of speech.

HEDDA GABLER

BY

HENRIK IBSEN

In the 1870's, when Henrik Ibsen (1828–1906) began to write the realistic drama for which he is most famous, the standard theatrical fare in most European theaters consisted of melodramas: plays that show little concern for the realities of human nature and deal instead with sensational materials such as young officers falsely accused of betraying their country and being entangled with fascinating female spies, or honest and beautiful women who by some mistake are thought to be adulteresses and are banished from their homes and children. Usually both officer and wife are saved in the end by some trusting, warm-hearted admirer who has believed in them all along. A mechanical formula even existed for plotting such plays to maintain maximum suspense and extract the last tear.

Ibsen borrowed some of the conventions of this theater, such as withholding the key piece of information until late in the play, but he revolutionized its subject matter. Beginning with *The Pillars of Society* (1875) and continuing with such plays as *A Doll's House* (1878), *Ghosts* (1881), *An Enemy of the People* (1882), *The Wild Duck* (1883), *Hedda Gabler* (1890), and *The Master Builder* (1891), he brought to the stage frank, penetrating discussions of such real human problems as the struggles of just men with corrupt societies, the confinement of women to their homes, the effects of lies and pretenses on human relations, the desperate need of weak men for illusion, and the human failings that prevent men from achieving freedom.

Not only did Ibsen revolutionize the subject matter of the drama, but he also reformed methods of dramatic construction and the mode of presentation. Gone from his plays were the faraway castles and snow-covered, moonlit mountains of romantic melodrama. In their place were realistic sets of nineteenth-century middle-class homes, of business offices, and of town halls. To take the place of fantastic heroes and heroines with their outsize gestures and language, Ibsen created characters who act, talk, and think like human beings. For the type of construction designed to exploit the audiences' feelings, Ibsen substituted careful workmanship and detailed plotting in which each event of the play is the inevitable result of what has gone before. The illusion of reality is carefully maintained, entrances and exits are convincingly motivated, and at no point are characters allowed to do anything that they might not reasonably do in real life.

We take this kind of play to be the theatrical norm, but it is, nonetheless, a very new kind of play. No one had written quite like this before the nineteenth century. However, the fashion seems already to be passing. Dramatists today are seeking new, more openly theatrical forms that do not bind the playwright to recreating life as it commonly appears to the eye but allow him to present the world as man experiences it in his mind.

It would be a mistake to think, however, that Ibsen did no more than dramatize actual social problems in a manner as much like ordinary life as possible. He was not a photographer; his realistic method merely guarantees fidelity to the truth of life. Beneath the commonplace realities of his sets and the ordinary manners of his characters lie age-old energies and desires; within an everyday problem, such as a woman's boredom with her lot, enduring human questions and ancient antagonisms come once again to life. But so smooth and unexceptional is the surface of a play like *Hedda Gabler* that it may be difficult at first to see that its petty, commonplace movements and flat, unadorned speeches express primal powers. To see the meaning of such simple matters as Hedda's thin hair, the pistols she inherits from her father, or the placement of her writing desk, requires even more care and sensitivity than is necessary to interpret the brief words and acts by which people reveal themselves in actual life. Ibsen's realism, the normality of his surfaces, intensifies the violent powers thrusting up from beneath and forced, until the inevitable explosion, to express themselves in the polite prose and confined gestures of Victorian propriety.

CHARACTERS

GEORGE TESMAN
HEDDA TESMAN, *his wife*
MISS JULIANA TESMAN, *his aunt*
MRS. ELVESTED
JUDGE BRACK
EILERT LÖVBORG
BERTA, *servant at the Tesmans'*

The scene of the action is Tesman's villa, in the west end of Christiania.

ACT I

~~~ Scene: *A spacious, handsome, and tastefully furnished drawing room, decorated in dark colors. In the back, a wide doorway with curtains drawn back, leading into a smaller room decorated in the same style as the drawing room. In the right-hand wall of the front room, a folding door leading out to the hall. In the opposite wall, on the left, a glass door, also with curtains drawn back. Through the panes can be seen part of a verandah outside, and trees covered with autumn foliage. An oval table, with a cover on it, and surrounded by chairs, stands well forward. In front, by the wall on the right, a wide stove of dark porcelain, a high-backed armchair, a cushioned footrest, and two footstools. A settee, with a small round table in front of it, fills the upper right-hand corner. In front, on the left, a little way from the wall, a sofa. Farther back than the glass door, a piano. On either side of the doorway at the back a whatnot with terra-cotta and majolica ornaments. Against the back wall of the inner room a sofa, with a table, and one or two chairs. Over the sofa hangs the portrait of a handsome elderly man in a General's uniform. Over the table a hanging lamp, with an opal glass shade. A number of bouquets are arranged about the drawing room, in vases and glasses. Others lie upon the tables. The floors in both rooms are covered with thick carpets. Morning light. The sun shines in through the glass door.*

MISS JULIANA TESMAN, *with her bonnet on and carrying a parasol, comes in from the hall, followed by* BERTA, *who carries a bouquet wrapped in paper.* MISS TESMAN *is a comely and pleasant-looking lady of about sixty-five. She is nicely but simply dressed in a gray walking costume.* BERTA *is a middle-aged woman of plain and rather countrified appearance.*

MISS TESMAN (*stops close to the door, listens, and says softly*). Upon my word, I don't believe they are stirring yet!

BERTA (*also softly*). I told you so, Miss. Remember how late the steamboat got in last night. And then, when they got home!—good

Lord, what a lot the young mistress had to unpack before she could get to bed.

MISS TESMAN. Well, well—let them have their sleep out. But let us see that they get a good breath of the fresh morning air when they do appear. (*She goes to the glass door and throws it open.*)

BERTA (*beside the table, at a loss what to do with the bouquet in her hand*). I declare there isn't a bit of room left. I think I'll put it down here, Miss. (*She places it on the piano.*)

MISS TESMAN. So you've got a new mistress now, my dear Berta. Heaven knows it was a wrench to me to part with you.

BERTA (*on the point of weeping*). And do you think it wasn't hard for me too, Miss? After all the blessed years I've been with you and Miss Rina.

MISS TESMAN. We must make the best of it, Berta. There was nothing else to be done. George can't do without you, you see—he absolutely can't. He has had you to look after him ever since he was a little boy.

BERTA. Ah, but, Miss Julia, I can't help thinking of Miss Rina lying helpless at home there, poor thing. And with only that new girl, too! She'll never learn to take proper care of an invalid.

MISS TESMAN. Oh, I shall manage to train her. And of course, you know, I shall take most of it upon myself. You needn't be uneasy about my poor sister, my dear Berta.

BERTA. Well, but there's another thing, Miss. I'm so mortally afraid I shan't be able to suit the young mistress.

MISS TESMAN. Oh, well—just at first there may be one or two things——

BERTA. Most like she'll be terrible grand in her ways.

MISS TESMAN. Well, you can't wonder at that—General Gabler's daughter! Think of the sort of life she was accustomed to in her father's time. Don't you remember how we used to see her riding down the road along with the General? In that long black habit—and with feathers in her hat?

BERTA. Yes, indeed—I remember well enough—! But good Lord, I should never have dreamt in those days that she and Master George would make a match of it.

MISS TESMAN. Nor I. But, by-the-bye, Berta—while I think of it: in future you mustn't say Master George. You must say Dr. Tesman.

BERTA. Yes, the young mistress spoke of that too—last night—the moment they set foot in the house. Is it true, then, Miss?

MISS TESMAN. Yes, indeed it is. Only think, Berta—some foreign university has made him a doctor—while he has been abroad, you understand. I hadn't heard a word about it, until he told me himself upon the pier.

BERTA. Well, well, he's clever enough for anything, he is. But I didn't think he'd have gone in for doctoring people too.

MISS TESMAN. No, no, it's not that sort of doctor he is. (*Nods significantly.*) But let me tell you, we may have to call him something still grander before long.

BERTA. You don't say so! What can that be, Miss?

MISS TESMAN (*smiling*). H'm—wouldn't you like to know! (*With emotion.*) Ah, dear, dear—if my poor brother could only look up from his grave now, and see what his little boy has grown into! (*Looks around.*) But bless me, Berta—why have you done this? Taken the chintz covers off all the furniture?

BERTA. The mistress told me to. She can't abide covers on the chairs, she says.

MISS TESMAN. Are they going to make this their everyday sitting room then?

BERTA. Yes, that's what I understood—from the mistress. Master George—the doctor—he said nothing.

> [GEORGE TESMAN *comes from the right into the inner room, humming to himself, and carrying an unstrapped empty portmanteau. He is a middle-sized, young-looking man of thirty-three, rather stout, with a round, open, cheerful face, fair hair and beard. He wears spectacles, and is somewhat carelessly dressed in comfortable indoor clothes.*]

MISS TESMAN. Good morning, good morning, George.

TESMAN (*in the doorway between the rooms*). Aunt Julia! Dear Aunt Julia! (*Goes up to her and shakes hands warmly.*) Come all this way—so early! Eh?

MISS TESMAN. Why of course I had to come and see how you were getting on.

TESMAN. In spite of your having had no proper night's rest?

MISS TESMAN. Oh, that makes no difference to me.

TESMAN. Well, I suppose you got home all right from the pier? Eh?

MISS TESMAN. Yes, quite safely, thank goodness. Judge Brack was good enough to see me right to my door.

TESMAN. We were so sorry we couldn't give you a seat in the carriage. But you saw what a pile of boxes Hedda had to bring with her.

MISS TESMAN. Yes, she had certainly plenty of boxes.

BERTA (*to* TESMAN). Shall I go in and see if there's anything I can do for the mistress?

TESMAN. No, thank you, Berta—you needn't. She said she would ring if she wanted anything.

BERTA (*going towards the right*). Very well.

TESMAN. But look here—take this portmanteau with you.

BERTA (*taking it*). I'll put it in the attic. (*She goes out by the hall door.*)

TESMAN. Fancy, Aunty—I had the whole of that portmanteau chock full of copies of documents. You wouldn't believe how much I have picked up from all the archives I have been examining—curious old details that no one has had any idea of——

MISS TESMAN. Yes, you don't seem to have wasted your time on your wedding trip, George.

TESMAN. No, that I haven't. But do take off your bonnet, Auntie. Look here! Let me untie the strings—eh?

MISS TESMAN (*while he does so*). Well, well—this is just as if you were still at home with us.

TESMAN (*with the bonnet in his hand, looks at it from all sides*). Why, what a gorgeous bonnet you've been investing in!

MISS TESMAN. I bought it on Hedda's account.

TESMAN. On Hedda's account? Eh?

MISS TESMAN. Yes, so that Hedda needn't be ashamed of me if we happened to go out together.

TESMAN (*patting her cheek*). You always think of everything, Aunt Julia. (*Lays the bonnet on a chair beside the table.*) And now, look here—suppose we sit comfortably on the sofa and have a little chat, till Hedda comes.

> [*They seat themselves. She places her parasol in the corner of the sofa.*]

MISS TESMAN (*takes both his hands and looks at him*). What a delight it is to have you again, as large as life, before my very eyes, George! My George—my poor brother's own boy!

TESMAN. And it's a delight for me, too, to see you again, Aunt Julia! You, who have been father and mother in one to me.

MISS TESMAN. Oh, yes, I know you will always keep a place in your heart for your old aunts.

TESMAN. And what about Aunt Rina? No improvement—eh!

MISS TESMAN. Oh, no—we can scarcely look for any improvement in her case, poor thing. There she lies, helpless, as she has lain for all these years. But heaven grant I may not lose her yet awhile! For if I did, I don't know what I should make of my life, George—especially now that I haven't you to look after any more.

TESMAN (*patting her back*). There, there, there——!

MISS TESMAN (*suddenly changing her tone*). And to think that here you are a married man, George!—And that you should be the one to carry off Hedda Gabler, the beautiful Hedda Gabler! Only think of it—she, that was so beset with admirers!

TESMAN (*hums a little and smiles complacently*). Yes, I fancy I have several good friends about town who would like to stand in my shoes—eh?

MISS TESMAN. And then this fine long wedding tour you have had! More than five—nearly six months——

TESMAN. Well, for me it has been a sort of tour of research as well. I have had to do so much grubbing among old records—and to read no end of books too, Auntie.

MISS TESMAN. Oh, yes, I suppose so. (*More confidentially, and lowering her voice a little.*) But listen now, George—have you nothing—nothing special to tell me?

TESMAN. As to our journey?

MISS TESMAN. Yes.

TESMAN. No, I don't know of anything except what I have told you in my letters. I had a doctor's degree conferred on me—but that I told you yesterday.

MISS TESMAN. Yes, yes, you did. But what I mean is—haven't you any —any—expectations——?

TESMAN. Expectations?

MISS TESMAN. Why, you know, George—I'm your old auntie!

TESMAN. Why, of course I have expectations.

MISS TESMAN. Ah!

TESMAN. I have every expectation of being a professor one of these days.

MISS TESMAN. Oh, yes, a professor——

TESMAN. Indeed, I may say I am certain of it. But my dear Auntie—you know all about that already!

MISS TESMAN (*laughing to herself*). Yes, of course I do. You are quite right there. (*Changing the subject.*) But we were talking about your journey. It must have cost a great deal of money, George?

TESMAN. Well, you see—my handsome traveling scholarship went a good way.

MISS TESMAN. But I can't understand how you can have made it go far enough for two.

TESMAN. No, that's not so easy to understand—eh?

MISS TESMAN. And especially traveling with a lady—they tell me that makes it ever so much more expensive.

TESMAN. Yes, of course—it makes it a little more expensive. But Hedda had to have this trip, Auntie! She really had to. Nothing else would have done.

MISS TESMAN. No, no, I suppose not. A wedding tour seems to be quite indispensable nowadays. But tell me now—have you gone thoroughly over the house yet?

TESMAN. Yes, you may be sure I have. I have been afoot ever since daylight.

MISS TESMAN. And what do you think of it all?

TESMAN. I'm delighted! Quite delighted! Only I can't think what we are to do with the two empty rooms between this inner parlor and Hedda's bedroom.

MISS TESMAN (*laughing*). Oh, my dear George, I dare say you may find some use for them—in the course of time.

TESMAN. Why of course you are quite right, Aunt Julia! You mean as my library increases—eh?

MISS TESMAN. Yes, quite so, my dear boy. It was your library I was thinking of.

TESMAN. I am specially pleased on Hedda's account. Often and often, before we were engaged, she said that she would never care to live anywhere but in Secretary Falk's villa.

MISS TESMAN. Yes, it was lucky that this very house should come into the market, just after you had started.

TESMAN. Yes, Aunt Julia, the luck was on our side, wasn't it—eh?

MISS TESMAN. But the expense, my dear George! You will find it very expensive, all this.

TESMAN (*looks at her, a little cast down*). Yes, I suppose I shall, Aunt!

MISS TESMAN. Oh, frightfully!

TESMAN. How much do you think? In round numbers?—Eh?

MISS TESMAN. Oh, I can't even guess until all the accounts come in.

TESMAN. Well, fortunately, Judge Brack has secured the most favorable terms for me—so he said in a letter to Hedda.

MISS TESMAN. Yes, don't be uneasy, my dear boy. Besides, I have given security for the furniture and all the carpets.

TESMAN. Security? You? My dear Aunt Julia—what sort of security could you give?

MISS TESMAN. I have given a mortgage on our annuity.

TESMAN (*jumps up*). What! On your—and Aunt Rina's annuity!

MISS TESMAN. Yes, I knew of no other plan, you see.

TESMAN (*placing himself before her*). Have you gone out of your senses, Auntie! Your annuity—it's all that you and Aunt Rina have to live upon.

MISS TESMAN. Well, well, don't get so excited about it. It's only a matter of form you know—Judge Brack assured me of that. It was he that was kind enough to arrange the whole affair for me. A mere matter of form, he said.

TESMAN. Yes, that may be all very well. But nevertheless——

MISS TESMAN. You will have your own salary to depend upon now. And, good heavens, even if we did have to pay up a little——! To eke things out a bit at the start——! Why, it would be nothing but a pleasure to us.

TESMAN. Oh, Auntie—will you never be tired of making sacrifices for me!

MISS TESMAN (*rises and lays her hands on his shoulders*). Have I had any other happiness in this world except to smooth your way for you, my dear boy? You, who have had neither father nor mother to depend on. And now we have reached the goal, George! Things have looked black enough for us, sometimes; but, thank heaven, now you have nothing to fear.

TESMAN. Yes, it is really marvelous how everything has turned out for the best.

MISS TESMAN. And the people who opposed you—who wanted to bar the way for you—now you have them at your feet. They have fallen, George. Your most dangerous rival—his fall was the worst. And now he has to lie on the bed he has made for himself—poor misguided creature.

TESMAN. Have you heard anything of Eilert? Since I went away, I mean.

MISS TESMAN. Only that he is said to have published a new book.

TESMAN. What! Eilert Lövborg! Recently—eh?

MISS TESMAN. Yes, so they say. Heaven knows whether it can be worth anything! Ah, when your new book appears—that will be another story, George! What is it to be about?

TESMAN. It will deal with the domestic industries of Brabant during the Middle Ages.

MISS TESMAN. Fancy—to be able to write on such a subject as that.

TESMAN. However, it may be some time before the book is ready. I have all these collections to arrange first, you see.

MISS TESMAN. Yes, collecting and arranging—no one can beat you at that. There you are my poor brother's own son.

TESMAN. I am looking forward eagerly to setting to work at it; especially now that I have my own delightful home to work in.

MISS TESMAN. And, most of all, now that you have got the wife of your heart, my dear George.

TESMAN (embracing her). Oh, yes, yes, Aunt Julia. Hedda—she is the best part of all! (Looks towards the doorway.) I believe I hear her coming—eh?

> [HEDDA enters from the left through the inner room. She is a woman of nine-and-twenty. Her face and figure show refinement and distinction. Her complexion is pale and opaque. Her steel-gray eyes express a cold, unruffled repose. Her hair is of an agreeable medium brown, but not particularly abundant. She is dressed in a tasteful, somewhat loose-fitting morning gown.]

MISS TESMAN (going to meet HEDDA). Good morning, my dear Hedda! Good morning, and a hearty welcome.

HEDDA (holds out her hand). Good morning, dear Miss Tesman! So early a call! That is kind of you.

MISS TESMAN (with some embarrassment). Well—has the bride slept well in her new home?

HEDDA. Oh yes, thanks. Passably.

TESMAN (laughing). Passably! Come, that's good, Hedda! You were sleeping like a stone when I got up.

HEDDA. Fortunately. Of course one has always to accustom one's self to new surroundings, Miss Tesman—little by little. (*Looking towards the left.*) Oh—there the servant has gone and opened the verandah door, and let in a whole flood of sunshine.

MISS TESMAN (*going towards the door*). Well, then, we will shut it.

HEDDA. No, no, not that! Tesman, please draw the curtains. That will give a softer light.

TESMAN (*at the door*). All right—all right. There now, Hedda, now you have both shade and fresh air.

HEDDA. Yes, fresh air we certainly must have, with all these stacks of flowers—— But—won't you sit down, Miss Tesman?

MISS TESMAN. No, thank you. Now that I have seen that everything is all right here—thank heaven! I must be getting home again. My sister is lying longing for me, poor thing.

TESMAN. Give her my very best love, Auntie; and say I shall look in and see her later in the day.

MISS TESMAN. Yes, yes, I'll be sure to tell her. But by-the-bye, George —(*feeling in her dress pocket*)—I have almost forgotten—I have something for you here.

TESMAN. What is it, Auntie? Eh?

MISS TESMAN (*produces a flat parcel wrapped in newspaper and hands it to him*). Look here, my dear boy.

TESMAN (*opening the parcel*). Well, I declare! Have you really saved them for me, Aunt Julia! Hedda! isn't this touching—eh?

HEDDA (*beside the whatnot on the right*). Well, what is it?

TESMAN. My old morning shoes! My slippers.

HEDDA. Indeed. I remember you often spoke of them while we were abroad.

TESMAN. Yes, I missed them terribly. (*Goes up to her.*) Now you shall see them, Hedda!

HEDDA (*going towards the stove*). Thanks, I really don't care about it.

TESMAN (*following her*). Only think—ill as she was, Aunt Rina embroidered these for me. Oh, you can't think how many associations cling to them.

HEDDA (*at the table*). Scarcely for me.

MISS TESMAN. Of course not for Hedda, George.

TESMAN. Well, but now that she belongs to the family, I thought——

HEDDA (*interrupting*). We shall never get on with this servant, Tesman.

MISS TESMAN. Not get on with Berta?

TESMAN. Why, dear, what puts that in your head? Eh?

HEDDA (*pointing*). Look there! She has left her old bonnet lying about on a chair.

TESMAN (*in consternation, drops the slippers on the floor*). Why, Hedda——

HEDDA. Just fancy, if any one should come in and see it.

TESMAN. But Hedda—that's Aunt Julia's bonnet.

HEDDA. Is it!

MISS TESMAN (*taking up the bonnet*). Yes, indeed it's mine. And what's more, it's not old, Madame Hedda.

HEDDA. I really did not look closely at it, Miss Tesman.

MISS TESMAN (*trying on the bonnet*). Let me tell you it's the first time I have worn it—the very first time.

TESMAN. And a very nice bonnet it is too—quite a beauty!

MISS TESMAN. Oh, it's no such great thing, George. (*Looks around her.*) My parasol——? Ah, here. (*Takes it.*) For this is mine too—(*mutters*)—not Berta's.

TESMAN. A new bonnet and a new parasol! Only think, Hedda!

HEDDA. Very handsome indeed.

TESMAN. Yes, isn't it? But Auntie, take a good look at Hedda before you go! See how handsome she is!

MISS TESMAN. Oh, my dear boy, there's nothing new in that. Hedda was always lovely. (*She nods and goes towards the right.*)

TESMAN (*following*). Yes, but have you noticed what splendid condition she is in? How she has filled out on the journey?

HEDDA (*crossing the room*). Oh, do be quiet——!

MISS TESMAN (*who has stopped and turned*). Filled out?

TESMAN. Of course you don't notice it so much now that she has that dress on. But I, who can see——

HEDDA (*at the glass door, impatiently*). Oh, you can't see anything.

TESMAN. It must be the mountain air in the Tyrol——

HEDDA (*curtly, interrupting*). I am exactly as I was when I started.

TESMAN. So you insist; but I'm quite certain you are not. Don't you agree with me, Auntie?

MISS TESMAN (*who has been gazing at her with folded hands*). Hedda is lovely—lovely—lovely. (*Goes up to her, takes her head between both hands, draws it downwards, and kisses her hair*). God bless and preserve Hedda Tesman—for George's sake.

HEDDA (*gently freeing herself*). Oh! Let me go.

MISS TESMAN (*in quiet emotion*). I shall not let a day pass without coming to see you.

TESMAN. No you won't, will you, Auntie? Eh?

MISS TESMAN. Good-by—good-by!

> [*She goes out by the hall door.* TESMAN *accompanies her. The door remains half open.* TESMAN *can be heard repeating his message to Aunt Rina and his thanks for the slippers.*
>
> [*In the meantime,* HEDDA *walks about the room raising her arms and clenching her hands as if in desperation. Then she flings back the curtains from the glass door, and stands there looking out.*

[*Presently* TESMAN *returns and closes the door behind him.*]

TESMAN (*picks up the slippers from the floor*). What are you looking at, Hedda?

HEDDA (*once more calm and mistress of herself*). I am only looking at the leaves. They are so yellow—so withered.

TESMAN (*wraps up the slippers and lays them on the table*). Well you see, we are well into September now.

HEDDA (*again restless*). Yes, to think of it! Already in—in September.

TESMAN. Don't you think Aunt Julia's manner was strange, dear? Almost solemn? Can you imagine what was the matter with her? Eh?

HEDDA. I scarcely know her, you see. Is she often like that?

TESMAN. No, not as she was today.

HEDDA (*leaving the glass door*). Do you think she was annoyed about the bonnet?

TESMAN. Oh, scarcely at all. Perhaps a little, just at the moment——

HEDDA. But what an idea, to pitch her bonnet about in the drawing room! No one does that sort of thing.

TESMAN. Well you may be sure Aunt Julia won't do it again.

HEDDA. In any case, I shall manage to make my peace with her.

TESMAN. Yes, my dear, good Hedda, if you only would.

HEDDA. When you call this afternoon, you might invite her to spend the evening here.

TESMAN. Yes, that I will. And there's one thing more you could do that would delight her heart.

HEDDA. What is it?

TESMAN. If you could only prevail on yourself to say *du*[1] to her. For my sake, Hedda? Eh?

HEDDA. No, no, Tesman—you really musn't ask that of me. I have told you so already. I shall try to call her "Aunt"; and you must be satisfied with that.

TESMAN. Well, well. Only I think now that you belong to the family, you——

HEDDA. H'm—I can't in the least see why——

[*She goes up towards the middle doorway.*]

TESMAN (*after a pause*). Is there anything the matter with you, Hedda? Eh?

HEDDA. I'm only looking at my old piano. It doesn't go at all well with all the other things.

TESMAN. The first time I draw my salary, we'll see about exchanging it.

HEDDA. No, no—no exchanging. I don't want to part with it. Suppose we put it there in the inner room, and then get another here in its place. When it's convenient, I mean.

[1] *Du*—thou, the familiar form of the pronoun *you.*

TESMAN (*a little taken aback*). Yes—of course we could do that.

HEDDA (*takes up the bouquet from the piano*). These flowers were not here last night when we arrived.

TESMAN. Aunt Julia must have brought them for you.

HEDDA (*examining the bouquet*). A visiting card. (*Takes it out and reads.*) "Shall return later in the day." Can you guess whose card it is?

TESMAN. No. Whose? Eh?

HEDDA. The name is "Mrs. Elvsted."

TESMAN. Is it really? Sheriff Elvsted's wife? Miss Rysing that was.

HEDDA. Exactly. The girl with the irritating hair, that she was always showing off. An old flame of yours, I've been told.

TESMAN (*laughing*). Oh, that didn't last long; and it was before I knew you, Hedda. But fancy her being in town!

HEDDA. It's odd that she should call upon us. I have scarcely seen her since we left school.

TESMAN. I haven't seen her either for—heaven knows how long. I wonder how she can endure to live in such an out-of-the-way hole—eh?

HEDDA (*after a moment's thought says suddenly*). Tell me, Tesman— isn't it somewhere near there that he—that—Eilert Lövborg is living?

TESMAN. Yes, he is somewhere in that part of the country.

[BERTA *enters by the hall door.*]

BERTA. That lady, ma'am, that brought some flowers a little while ago, is here again. (*Pointing.*) The flowers you have in your hand, ma'am.

HEDDA. Ah, is she? Well, please show her in.

[BERTA *opens the door for* MRS. ELVSTED, *and goes out herself.* MRS. ELVSTED *is a woman of fragile figure, with pretty, soft features. Her eyes are light blue, large, round, and somewhat prominent, with a startled, inquiring expression. Her hair is remarkably light, almost flaxen, and unusually abundant and wavy. She is a couple of years younger than* HEDDA. *She wears a dark visiting dress, tasteful, but not quite in the latest fashion.*]

HEDDA (*receives her warmly*). How do you do, my dear Mrs. Elvsted? It's delightful to see you again.

MRS. ELVSTED (*nervously, struggling for self-control*). Yes, it's a very long time since we met.

TESMAN (*gives her his hand*). And we too—eh?

HEDDA. Thanks for your lovely flowers——

MRS. ELVSTED. Oh, not at all—— I would have come straight here yesterday afternoon; but I heard that you were away——

TESMAN. Have you just come to town? Eh?

MRS. ELVSTED. I arrived yesterday, about midday. Oh, I was quite in despair when I heard that you were not at home.

HEDDA. In despair! How so?

TESMAN. Why, my dear Mrs. Rysing—I mean Mrs. Elvsted——

HEDDA. I hope that you are not in any trouble?

MRS. ELVSTED. Yes, I am. And I don't know another living creature here that I can turn to.

HEDDA (*laying the bouquet on the table*). Come—let us sit here on the sofa——

MRS. ELVSTED. Oh, I am too restless to sit down.

HEDDA. Oh no, you're not. Come here. (*She draws* MRS. ELVSTED *down upon the sofa and sits at her side.*)

TESMAN. Well? What is it, Mrs. Elvsted?

HEDDA. Has anything particular happened to you at home?

MRS. ELVSTED. Yes—and no. Oh—I am so anxious you should not misunderstand me——

HEDDA. Then your best plan is to tell us the whole story, Mrs. Elvsted.

TESMAN. I suppose that's what you have come for—eh?

MRS. ELVSTED. Yes, yes—of course it is. Well then, I must tell you—if you don't already know—that Eilert Lövborg is in town, too.

HEDDA. Lövborg——!

TESMAN. What! Has Eilert Lövborg come back? Fancy that, Hedda!

HEDDA. Well, well—I hear it.

MRS. ELVSTED. He has been here a week already. Just fancy—a whole week! In this terrible town, alone! With so many temptations on all sides.

HEDDA. But my dear Mrs. Elvsted—how does he concern you so much?

MRS. ELVSTED (*looks at her with a startled air, and says rapidly*). He was the children's tutor.

HEDDA. Your children's?

MRS. ELVSTED. My husband's. I have none.

HEDDA. Your step-children's, then?

MRS. ELVSTED. Yes.

TESMAN (*somewhat hesitatingly*). Then was he—I don't know how to express it—was he—regular enough in his habits to be fit for the post? Eh?

MRS. ELVSTED. For the last two years his conduct has been irreproachable.

TESMAN. Has it indeed? Fancy that, Hedda!

HEDDA. I hear it.

MRS. ELVSTED. Perfectly irreproachable, I assure you! In every respect. But all the same—now that I know he is here—in this great town —and with a large sum of money in his hands—I can't help being in mortal fear for him.

TESMAN. Why did he not remain where he was? With you and your husband? Eh?

MRS. ELVSTED. After his book was published he was too restless and unsettled to remain with us.

TESMAN. Yes, by-the-bye, Aunt Julia told me he had published a new book.

MRS. ELVSTED. Yes, a big book, dealing with the march of civilization —in broad outline, as it were. It came out about a fortnight ago. And since it has sold so well, and been so much read—and made such a sensation——

TESMAN. Has it indeed? It must be something he has had lying by since his better days.

MRS. ELVSTED. Long ago, you mean?

TESMAN. Yes.

MRS. ELVSTED. No, he has written it all since he has been with us— within the last year.

TESMAN. Isn't that good news. Hedda? Think of that.

MRS. ELVSTED. Ah, yes, if only it would last!

HEDDA. Have you seen him here in town?

MRS. ELVSTED. No, not yet. I have had the greatest difficulty in finding out his address. But this morning I discovered it at last.

HEDDA (*looks searchingly at her*). Do you know, it seems to me a little odd of your husband—h'm——

MRS. ELVSTED (*starting nervously*). Of my husband! What?

HEDDA. That he should send you to town on such an errand—that he does not come himself and look after his friend.

MRS. ELVSTED. Oh no, no—my husband has no time. And besides, I—I had some shopping to do.

HEDDA (*with a slight smile*). Ah, that is a different matter.

MRS. ELVSTED (*rising quickly and uneasily*). And now I beg and implore you, Mr. Tesman—receive Eilert Lövborg kindly if he comes to you! And that he is sure to do. You see you were such great friends in the old days. And then you are interested in the same studies—the same branch of science—so far as I can understand.

TESMAN. We used to be, at any rate.

MRS. ELVSTED. That is why I beg so earnestly that you—you too— will keep a sharp eye upon him. Oh, you will promise me that, Mr. Tesman—won't you?

TESMAN. With the greatest of pleasure, Mrs. Rysing——

HEDDA. Elvsted.

TESMAN. I assure you I shall do all I possibly can for Eilert. You may rely upon me.

MRS. ELVSTED. Oh, how very, very kind of you! (*Presses his hands.*) Thanks, thanks, thanks! (*Frightened.*) You see, my husband is very fond of him!

HEDDA (*rising*). You ought to write to him, Tesman. Perhaps he may not care to come to you of his own accord.

TESMAN. Well, perhaps it would be the right thing to do, Hedda? Eh?

HEDDA. And the sooner the better. Why not at once?

MRS. ELVSTED (*imploringly*). Oh, if you only would!

TESMAN. I'll write this moment. Have you his address. Mrs.—Mrs. Elvsted.

MRS. ELVSTED. Yes. (*Takes a slip of paper from her pocket, and hands it to him.*) Here it is.

TESMAN. Good, good. Then I'll go in—— (*Looks about him.*) By-the-bye—my slippers? Oh, here. (*Takes the packet, and is about to go.*)

HEDDA. Be sure you write him a cordial, friendly letter. And a good long one too.

TESMAN. Yes, I will.

MRS. ELVSTED. But please, please don't say a word to show that I have suggested it.

TESMAN. No, how could you think I would? Eh? (*He goes out to the right, through the inner room.*)

HEDDA (*goes up to* MRS. ELVSTED, *smiles, and says in a low voice*). There. We have killed two birds with one stone.

MRS. ELVSTED. What do you mean?

HEDDA. Could you not see that I wanted him to go?

MRS. ELVSTED. Yes, to write the letter——

HEDDA. And that I might speak to you alone.

MRS. ELVSTED (*confused*). About the same thing?

HEDDA. Precisely.

MRS. ELVSTED (*apprehensively*). But there is nothing more, Mrs. Tesman! Absolutely nothing!

HEDDA. Oh, yes, but there is. There is a great deal more—I can see that. Sit here—and we'll have a cosy, confidential chat. (*She forces* MRS. ELVSTED *to sit in the easy chair beside the stove, and seats herself on one of the footstools.*)

MRS. ELVSTED (*anxiously, looking at her watch*). But, my dear Mrs. Tesman—I was really on the point of going.

HEDDA. Oh, you can't be in such a hurry. Well? Now tell me something about your life at home.

MRS. ELVSTED. Oh, that is just what I care least to speak about.

HEDDA. But to me, dear——? Why, weren't we schoolfellows?

MRS. ELVSTED. Yes, but you were in the class above me. Oh, how dreadfully afraid of you I was then!

HEDDA. Afraid of me?

MRS. ELVSTED. *Yes*, dreadfully. For when we met on the stairs you used always to pull my hair.

HEDDA. Did I, really?

MRS. ELVSTED. Yes, and once you said you would burn it off my head.

HEDDA. Oh, that was all nonsense, of course.

MRS. ELVSTED. Yes, but I was so silly in those days. And since then, too—we have drifted so far—far apart from each other. Our circles have been so entirely different.

HEDDA. Well then, we must try to drift together again. Now listen! At school we said *du* to each other; and we called each other by our Christian names——

MRS. ELVSTED. No, I am sure you must be mistaken.

HEDDA. No, not at all! I can remember quite distinctly. So now we are going to renew our old friendship. (*Draws the footstool closer to* MRS. ELVSTED.) There now! (*Kisses her cheek.*) You must say *du* to me and call me Hedda.

MRS. ELVSTED (*presses and pats her hands*). Oh, how good and kind you are! I am not used to such kindness.

HEDDA. There, there, there! And I shall say *du* to you, as in the old days, and call you my dear Thora.

MRS. ELVSTED. My name is Thea.

HEDDA. Why, of course! I meant Thea. (*Looks at her compassionately.*) So you are not accustomed to goodness and kindness, Thea? Not in your own home?

MRS. ELVSTED. Oh, if I only had a home! But I haven't any; I have never had a home.

HEDDA (*looks at her for a moment*). I almost suspected as much.

MRS. ELVSTED (*gazing helplessly before her*). Yes—yes—yes.

HEDDA. I don't quite remember—was it not as housekeeper that you first went to Mr. Elvsted's?

MRS. ELVSTED. I really went as governess. But his wife—his late wife—was an invalid—and rarely left her room. So I had to look after the housekeeping as well.

HEDDA. And then—at last—you became mistress of the house.

MRS. ELVSTED (*sadly*). Yes, I did.

HEDDA. Let me see—about how long ago was that?

MRS. ELVSTED. My marriage?

HEDDA. Yes.

MRS. ELVSTED. Five years ago.

HEDDA. To be sure; it must be that.

MRS. ELVSTED. Oh, those five years——! Or at all events the last two or three of them! Oh, if you[2] could only imagine——

HEDDA (*giving her a little slap on the hand*). De? Fie, Thea!

MRS. ELVSTED. Yes, yes, I will try—— Well if—you could only imagine and understand——

HEDDA (*lightly*). Eilert Lövborg has been in your neighborhood about three years, hasn't he?

MRS. ELVSTED (*looks at her doubtfully*). Eilert Lövborg? Yes—he has.

HEDDA. Had you known him before, in town here?

MRS. ELVSTED. Scarcely at all. I mean—I knew him by name of course.

HEDDA. But you saw a good deal of him in the country?

[2] Mrs. Elvsted here uses the formal pronoun *De,* whereupon Hedda rebukes her. In her next speech Mrs. Elvsted says *du.*

MRS. ELVSTED. Yes, he came to us every day. You see, he gave the children lessons; for in the long run I couldn't manage it all myself.

HEDDA. No, that's clear. And your husband——? I suppose he is often away from home?

MRS. ELVSTED. Yes. Being Sheriff, you know, he has to travel about a good deal in his district.

HEDDA (*leaning against the arm of the chair*). Thea—my poor, sweet Thea—now you must tell me everything—exactly as it stands.

MRS. ELVSTED. Well then, you must question me.

HEDDA. What sort of a man is your husband, Thea? I mean—you know —in everyday life. Is he kind to you?

MRS. ELVSTED (*evasively*). I am sure he means well in everything.

HEDDA. I should think he must be altogether too old for you. There is at least twenty years' difference between you, is there not?

MRS. ELVSTED (*irritably*). Yes, that is true, too. Everything about him is repellent to me! We have not a thought in common. We have no single point of sympathy—he and I.

HEDDA. But is he not fond of you all the same? In his own way?

MRS. ELVSTED. Oh, I really don't know. I think he regards me simply as a useful property. And then it doesn't cost much to keep me. I am not expensive.

HEDDA. That is stupid of you.

MRS. ELVSTED (*shakes her head*). It cannot be otherwise—not with him. I don't think he really cares for any one but himself—and perhaps a little for the children.

HEDDA. And for Eilert Lövborg, Thea.

MRS. ELVSTED (*looking at her*). For Eilert Lövborg? What puts that into your head?

HEDDA. Well, my dear—I should say,when he sends you after him all the way to town—— (*Smiling almost imperceptibly.*) And besides, you said so yourself, to Tesman.

MRS. ELVSTED (*with a little nervous twitch*). Did I? Yes, I suppose I did. (*Vehemently, but not loudly.*) No—I may just as well make a clean breast of it at once! For it must all come out in any case.

HEDDA. Why, my dear Thea——?

MRS. ELVSTED. Well, to make a long story short: My husband did not know that I was coming.

HEDDA. What! Your husband didn't know it!

MRS. ELVSTED. No, of course not. For that matter, he was away from home himself—he was traveling. Oh, I could bear it no longer, Hedda! I couldn't indeed—so utterly alone as I should have been in future.

HEDDA. Well? And then?

MRS. ELVSTED. So I put together some of my things—what I needed most—as quietly as possible. And then I left the house.

HEDDA. Without a word?

MRS. ELVSTED. Yes—and took the train straight to town.

HEDDA. Why, my dear, good Thea—to think of you daring to do it!

MRS. ELVSTED (*rises and moves about the room*). What else could I possibly do?

HEDDA. But what do you think your husband will say when you go home again?

MRS. ELVSTED (*at the table, looks at her*). Back to him.

HEDDA. Of course.

MRS. ELVSTED. I shall never go back to him again.

HEDDA (*rising and going towards her*). Then you have left your home —for good and all?

MRS. ELVSTED. Yes. There was nothing else to be done.

HEDDA. But then—to take flight so openly.

MRS. ELVSTED. Oh, it's impossible to keep things of that sort secret.

HEDDA. But what do you think people will say of you, Thea?

MRS. ELVSTED. They may say what they like for aught *I* care. (*Seats herself wearily and sadly on the sofa.*) I have done nothing but what I had to do.

HEDDA (*after a short silence*). And what are your plans now? What do you think of doing?

MRS. ELVSTED. I don't know yet. I only know this, that I must live here, where Eilert Lövborg is—if I am to live at all.

HEDDA (*takes a chair from the table, seats herself beside her, and strokes her hands*). My dear Thea—how did this—this friendship— between you and Eilert Lövborg come about?

MRS. ELVSTED. Oh, it grew up gradually. I gained a sort of influence over him.

HEDDA. Indeed?

MRS. ELVSTED. He gave up his old habits. Not because I asked him to, for I never dared do that. But of course he saw how repulsive they were to me; and so he dropped them.

HEDDA (*concealing an involuntary smile of scorn*). Then you have reclaimed him—as the saying goes—my little Thea.

MRS. ELVSTED. So he says himself, at any rate. And he, on his side, has made a real human being of me—taught me to think, and to understand so many things.

HEDDA. Did he give you lessons too, then?

MRS. ELVSTED. No, not exactly lessons. But he talked to me—talked about such an infinity of things. And then came the lovely, happy time when I began to share in his work—when he allowed me to help him!

HEDDA. Oh, he did, did he?

MRS. ELVSTED. Yes! He never wrote anything without my assistance.

HEDDA. You were two good comrades, in fact?

MRS. ELVSTED (*eagerly*). Comrades! Yes, fancy, Hedda—that is the

very word he used! Oh, I ought to feel perfectly happy; and yet I
cannot; for I don't know how long it will last.

HEDDA. Are you no surer of him than that?

MRS. ELVSTED (*gloomily*). A woman's shadow stands between Eilert
Lövborg and me.

HEDDA (*looks at her anxiously*). Who can that be?

MRS. ELVSTED. I don't know. Some one he knew in his—in his past.
Some one he has never been able wholly to forget.

HEDDA. What has he told you—about this?

MRS. ELVSTED. He has only once—quite vaguely—alluded to it.

HEDDA. Well! And what did he say?

MRS. ELVSTED. He said that when they parted, she threatened to shoot
him with a pistol.

HEDDA (*with cold composure*). Oh, nonsense! No one does that sort of
thing here.

MRS. ELVSTED. No. And that is why I think it must have been that red-
haired singing woman whom he once——

HEDDA. Yes, very likely.

MRS. ELVSTED. For I remember they used to say of her that she carried
loaded firearms.

HEDDA. Oh—then of course it must have been she.

MRS. ELVSTED (*wringing her hands*). And now just fancy, Hedda—I
hear that this singing woman—that she is in town again! Oh, I don't
know what to do——

HEDDA (*glancing towards the inner room*). Hush! Here comes Tesman.
(*Rises and whispers.*) Thea—all this must remain between you and
me.

MRS. ELVSTED (*springing up*). Oh, yes, yes! for heaven's sake——!

[GEORGE TESMAN, *with a letter in his hand, comes
from the right through the inner room.*]

TESMAN. There now—the epistle is finished.

HEDDA. That's right. And now Mrs. Elvsted is just going. Wait a
moment—I'll go with you to the garden gate.

TESMAN. Do you think Berta could post the letter, Hedda dear?

HEDDA (*takes it*). I will tell her to.

[BERTA *enters from the hall.*]

BERTA. Judge Brack wishes to know if Mrs. Tesman will receive him.

HEDDA. Yes, ask Judge Brack to come in. And look here—put this
letter in the post.

BERTA (*taking the letter*). Yes, ma'am.

[*She opens the door for* JUDGE BRACK *and goes out
herself.* BRACK *is a man of forty-five; thickset, but well
built and elastic in his movements. His face is roundish
with an aristocratic profile. His hair is short, still almost black, and carefully dressed. His eyes are lively
and sparkling. His eyebrows thick. His moustaches*

are also thick, with short-cut ends. He wears a well-
cut walking suit, a little too youthful for his age. He
uses an eyeglass, which he now and then lets drop.]

JUDGE BRACK (*with his hat in his hand, bowing*). May one venture to call so early in the day?

HEDDA. Of course one may.

TESMAN (*presses his hand*). You are welcome at any time. (*Introducing him.*) Judge Brack—Miss Rysing——

HEDDA. Oh——!

BRACK (*bowing*). Ah—delighted——

HEDDA (*looks at him and laughs*). It's nice to have a look at you by daylight, Judge!

BRACK. Do you find me—altered?

HEDDA. A little younger, I think.

BRACK. Thank you so much.

TESMAN. But what do you think of Hedda—eh? Doesn't she look flourishing? She has actually——

HEDDA. Oh, do leave me alone. You haven't thanked Judge Brack for all the trouble he has taken——

BRACK. Oh, nonsense—it was a pleasure to me——

HEDDA. Yes, you are a friend indeed. But here stands Thea all impatience to be off—so *au revoir,* Judge. I shall be back again presently. (*Mutual salutations.* MRS. ELVSTED *and* HEDDA *go out by the hall door.*)

BRACK. Well, is your wife tolerably satisfied——

TESMAN. Yes, we can't thank you sufficiently. Of course she talks of a little rearrangement here and there; and one or two things are still wanting. We shall have to buy some additional trifles.

BRACK. Indeed!

TESMAN. But we won't trouble you about these things. Hedda says she herself will look after what is wanting.—— Shan't we sit down? Eh?

BRACK. Thanks, for a moment. (*Seats himself beside the table.*) There is something I wanted to speak to you about, my dear Tesman.

TESMAN. Indeed? Ah, I understand! (*Seating himself.*) I suppose it's the serious part of the frolic that is coming now. Eh?

BRACK. Oh, the money question is not so very pressing; though, for that matter, I wish we had gone a little more economically to work.

TESMAN. But that would never have done, you know! Think of Hedda, my dear fellow! You, who know her so well—— I couldn't possibly ask her to put up with a shabby style of living!

BRACK. No, no—that is just the difficulty.

TESMAN. And then—fortunately—it can't be long before I receive my appointment.

BRACK. Well, you see—such things are often apt to hang fire for a time.

TESMAN. Have you heard anything definite? Eh?

BRACK. Nothing exactly definite—— (*Interrupting himself.*) But, by-the-bye—I have one piece of news for you.

TESMAN. Well?

BRACK. Your old friend, Eilert Lövborg, has returned to town.

TESMAN. I know that already.

BRACK. Indeed! How did you learn it?

TESMAN. From that lady who went out with Hedda.

BRACK. Really? What was her name? I didn't quite catch it.

TESMAN. Mrs. Elvsted.

BRACK. Aha—Sheriff Elvsted's wife? Of course—he has been living up in their regions.

TESMAN. And fancy—I'm delighted to hear that he is quite a reformed character!

BRACK. So they say.

TESMAN. And then he has published a new book—eh?

BRACK. Yes, indeed he has.

TESMAN. And I hear it has made some sensation!

BRACK. Quite an unusual sensation.

TESMAN. Fancy—isn't that good news! A man of such extraordinary talents—— I felt so grieved to think that he had gone irretrievably to ruin.

BRACK. That was what everybody thought.

TESMAN. But I cannot imagine what he will take to now! How in the world will he be able to make his living? Eh?

[*During the last words,* HEDDA *has entered by the hall door.*]

HEDDA (*to* BRACK, *laughing with a touch of scorn*). Tesman is forever worrying about how people are to make their living.

TESMAN. Well, you see, dear—we were talking about poor Eilert Lövborg.

HEDDA (*glancing at him rapidly*). Oh, indeed? (*Seats herself in the arm-chair beside the stove and asks indifferently.*) What is the matter with him?

TESMAN. Well—no doubt he has run through all his property long ago; and he can scarcely write a new book every year—eh? So I really can't see what is to become of him.

BRACK. Perhaps I can give you some information on that point.

TESMAN. Indeed!

BRACK. You must remember that his relations have a good deal of influence.

TESMAN. Oh, his relations, unfortunately, have entirely washed their hands of him.

BRACK. At one time they called him the hope of the family.

TESMAN. At one time, yes! But he has put an end to all that.

HEDDA. Who knows? (*With a slight smile.*) I hear they have reclaimed him up at Sheriff Elvsted's——

BRACK. And then this book that he has published——

TESMAN. Well, well, I hope to goodness they may find something for him to do. I have just written to him. I asked him to come and see us this evening, Hedda dear.

BRACK. But, my dear fellow, you are booked for my bachelors' party this evening. You promised on the pier last night.

HEDDA. Had you forgotten, Tesman?

TESMAN. Yes, I had utterly forgotten.

BRACK. But it doesn't matter, for you may be sure he won't come.

TESMAN. What makes you think that? Eh?

BRACK (*with a little hesitation, rising and resting his hands on the back of his chair*). My dear Tesman—and you too, Mrs. Tesman—I think I ought not to keep you in the dark about something that—that——

TESMAN. That concerns Eilert——?

BRACK. Both you and him.

TESMAN. Well, my dear Judge, out with it.

BRACK. You must be prepared to find your appointment deferred longer than you desired or expected.

TESMAN (*jumping up uneasily*). Is there some hitch about it? Eh?

BRACK. The nomination may perhaps be made conditional on the result of a competition——

TESMAN. Competition! Think of that, Hedda!

HEDDA (*leans farther back in the chair*). Aha—aha!

TESMAN. But who can my competitor be? Surely not——?

BRACK. Yes, precisely—Eilert Lövborg.

TESMAN (*clasping his hands*). No, no—it's quite inconceivable! Quite impossible! Eh?

BRACK. H'm—that is what it may come to, all the same.

TESMAN. Well but, Judge Brack—it would show the most incredible lack of consideration for me. (*Gesticulates with his arms.*) For— just think—I'm a married man. We have been married on the strength of these prospects, Hedda and I; and run deep into debt; and bor-rowed money from Aunt Julia too. Good heavens, they had as good as promised me the appointment. Eh?

BRACK. Well, well, well—no doubt you will get it in the end; only after a contest.

HEDDA (*immovable in her armchair*). Fancy, Tesman, there will be a sort of sporting interest in that.

TESMAN. Why, my dearest Hedda, how can you be so indifferent about it.

HEDDA (*as before*). I am not at all indifferent. I am most eager to see who wins.

BRACK. In any case, Mrs. Tesman, it is best that you should know how matters stand. I mean—before you set about the little purchases I hear you are threatening.

HEDDA. This can make no difference.

BRACK. Indeed! Then I have no more to say. Good-by! (*To* TESMAN.) I shall look in on my way back from my afternoon walk, and take you home with me.

TESMAN. Oh yes, yes—your news has quite upset me.

HEDDA (*reclining, holds out her hand*). Good-by, Judge; and be sure you call in the afternoon.

BRACK. Many thanks. Good-by, good-by!

TESMAN (*accompanying him to the door*). Good-by, my dear Judge! You must really excuse me—— (JUDGE BRACK *goes out by the hall door.*)

TESMAN (*crosses the room*). Oh, Hedda—one should never rush into adventures. Eh?

HEDDA (*looks at him, smiling*). Do you do that?

TESMAN. Yes, dear—there is no denying—it was adventurous to go and marry and set up house upon mere expectations.

HEDDA. Perhaps you are right there.

TESMAN. Well—at all events, we have our delightful home, Hedda! Fancy, the home we both dreamed of—the home we were in love with, I may almost say. Eh?

HEDDA (*rising slowly and wearily*). It was part of our compact that we were to go into society—to keep open house.

TESMAN. Yes, if you only knew how I had been looking forward to it! Fancy—to see you as hostess—in a select circle? Eh? Well, well, well—for the present we shall have to get on without society, Hedda —only to invite Aunt Julia now and then. Oh, I intended you to lead such an utterly different life, dear——!

HEDDA. Of course I cannot have my man in livery just yet.

TESMAN. Oh no, unfortunately. It would be out of the question for us to keep a footman, you know.

HEDDA. And the saddle horse I was to have had——

TESMAN (*aghast*). The saddle horse!

HEDDA. ——I suppose I must not think of that now.

TESMAN. Good heavens, no!—that's as clear as daylight.

HEDDA (*goes up the room*). Well, I shall have one thing at least to kill time with in the meanwhile.

TESMAN (*beaming*). Oh, thank heaven for that! What is it, Hedda? Eh?

HEDDA (*in the middle doorway, looks at him with covert scorn*). My pistols, George.

TESMAN (*in alarm*). Your pistols!

HEDDA (*with cold eyes*). General Gabler's pistols. (*She goes out through the inner room, to the left.*)

TESMAN (*rushes up to the middle doorway and calls after her*). No, for heaven's sake, Hedda darling—don't touch those dangerous things! For my sake, Hedda! Eh?

ACT II

꿍 Scene: *The room at the* TESMANS' *as in the first Act, except that the piano has been removed, and an elegant little writing table with bookshelves put in its place. A smaller table stands near the sofa at the left. Most of the bouquets have been taken away.* MRS. ELVSTED'S *bouquet is upon the large table in front. It is afternoon.*

HEDDA, *dressed to receive callers, is alone in the room. She stands by the open glass door, loading a revolver. The fellow to it lies in an open pistol case on the writing table.*

HEDDA (*looks down the garden, and calls*). So you are here again, Judge!
BRACK (*is heard calling from a distance*). As you see, Mrs. Tesman!
HEDDA (*raises the pistol and points*). Now I'll shoot you, Judge Brack!
BRACK (*calling unseen*). No, no, no! Don't stand aiming at me!
HEDDA. This is what comes of sneaking in by the back way.[1] (*She fires.*)
BRACK (*nearer*). Are you out of your senses——!
HEDDA. Dear me—did I happen to hit you?
BRACK (*still outside*). I wish you would let these pranks alone!
HEDDA. Come in then, Judge.
> [JUDGE BRACK, *dressed as though for a men's party, enters by the glass door. He carries a light overcoat over his arm.*]
BRACK. What the deuce—haven't you tired of that sport, yet? What are you shooting at?
HEDDA. Oh, I am only firing in the air.
BRACK (*gently takes the pistol out of her hand*). Allow me, madam! (*Looks at it.*) Ah—I know this pistol well! (*Looks around.*) Where is the case? Ah, here it is. (*Lays the pistol in it, and shuts it.*) Now we won't play at that game any more today.

[1] "Bagveje" means both "back ways" and "underhand courses."

HEDDA. Then what in heaven's name would you have me do with my-self?

BRACK. Have you had no visitors?

HEDDA (*closing the glass door*). Not one. I suppose all our set are still out of town.

BRACK. And is Tesman not at home either?

HEDDA (*at the writing table, putting the pistol case in a drawer which she shuts*). No. He rushed off to his aunt's directly after lunch; he didn't expect you so early.

BRACK. H'm—how stupid of me not to have thought of that!

HEDDA (*turning her head to look at him*). Why stupid?

BRACK. Because if I had thought of it I should have come a little— earlier.

HEDDA (*crossing the room*). Then you would have found no one to receive you; for I have been in my room changing my dress ever since lunch.

BRACK. And is there no sort of little chink that we could hold a parley through?

HEDDA. You have forgotten to arrange one.

BRACK. That was another piece of stupidity.

HEDDA. Well, we must just settle down here—and wait. Tesman is not likely to be back for some time yet.

BRACK. Never mind; I shall not be impatient.

> [HEDDA *seats herself in the corner of the sofa.* BRACK
> *lays his overcoat over the back of the nearest chair,
> and sits down, but keeps his hat in his hand. A short
> silence. They look at each other.*]

HEDDA. Well?

BRACK (*in the same tone*). Well?

HEDDA. I spoke first.

BRACK (*bending a little forward*). Come, let us have a cosy little chat, Mrs. Hedda.

HEDDA (*leaning further back in the sofa*). Does it not seem like a whole eternity since our last talk? Of course I don't count those few words yesterday evening and this morning.

BRACK. You mean since our last confidential talk? Our last tête-à-tête?

HEDDA. Well, yes—since you put it so.

BRACK. Not a day has passed but I have wished that you were home again.

HEDDA. And I have done nothing but wish the same thing.

BRACK. You? Really, Mrs. Hedda? And I thought you had been en-joying your tour so much!

HEDDA. Oh, yes, you may be sure of that!

BRACK. But Tesman's letters spoke of nothing but happiness.

HEDDA. Oh, Tesman! You see, he thinks nothing so delightful as grubbing in libraries and making copies of old parchments, or whatever you call them.

BRACK (*with a spice of malice*). Well, that is his vocation in life—or part of it at any rate.

HEDDA. Yes, of course; and no doubt when it's your vocation—— But *I!* Oh, my dear Mr. Brack, how mortally bored I have been.

BRACK (*sympathetically*). Do you really say so? In downright earnest?

HEDDA. Yes, you can surely understand it——! To go for six whole months without meeting a soul that knew anything of our circle, or could talk about the things we are interested in.

BRACK. Yes, yes—I too should feel that a deprivation.

HEDDA. And then, what I found most intolerable of all——

BRACK. Well?

HEDDA. ——was being everlastingly in the company of—one and the same person——

BRACK (*with a nod of assent*). Morning, noon, and night, yes—at all possible times and seasons.

HEDDA. I said "everlastingly."

BRACK. Just so. But I should have thought, with our excellent Tesman, one could——

HEDDA. Tesman is—a specialist, my dear Judge.

BRACK. Undeniably.

HEDDA. And specialists are not at all amusing to travel with. Not in the long run at any rate.

BRACK. Not even—the specialist one happens to love?

HEDDA. Faugh—don't use that sickening word!

BRACK (*taken aback*). What do you say, Mrs. Hedda?

HEDDA (*half laughing, half irritated*). You should just try it! To hear of nothing but the history of civilization, morning, noon, and night——

BRACK. Everlastingly.

HEDDA. Yes, yes, yes! And then all this about the domestic industry of the middle ages——! That's the most disgusting part of it!

BRACK (*looks searchingly at her*). But tell me—in that case, how am I to understand your——? H'm——

HEDDA. My accepting George Tesman, you mean?

BRACK. Well, let us put it so.

HEDDA. Good heavens, do you see anything so wonderful in that?

BRACK. Yes and no—Mrs. Hedda.

HEDDA. I had positively danced myself tired, my dear Judge. My day was done—— (*With a slight shudder.*) Oh no—I won't say that; nor think it either!

BRACK. You have assuredly no reason to.

HEDDA. Oh, reasons—— (*Watching him closely.*) George Tesman—after all, you must admit that he is correctness itself.

BRACK. His correctness and respectability are beyond all question.

HEDDA. And I don't see anything absolutely ridiculous about him. Do you?

BRACK. Ridiculous? N—no—I shouldn't exactly say so——

HEDDA. Well—and his powers of research, at all events, are untiring. I see no reason why he should not one day come to the front, after all.

BRACK (*looks at her hesitatingly*). I thought that you, like every one else, expected him to attain the highest distinction.

HEDDA (*with an expression of fatigue*). Yes, so I did.—And then, since he was bent, at all hazards, on being allowed to provide for me—I really don't know why I should not have accepted his offer?

BRACK. No—if you look at it in that light——

HEDDA. It was more than my other adorers were prepared to do for me, my dear Judge.

BRACK (*laughing*). Well, I can't answer for all the rest; but as for myself, you know quite well that I have always entertained a—a certain respect for the marriage tie—for marriage as an institution, Mrs. Hedda.

HEDDA (*jestingly*). Oh, I assure you I have never cherished any hopes with respect to you.

BRACK. All I require is a pleasant and intimate interior, where I can make myself useful in every way, and am free to come and go as—as a trusted friend——

HEDDA. Of the master of the house, do you mean?

BRACK (*bowing*). Frankly—of the mistress first of all; but of course of the master, too, in the second place. Such a triangular friendship—if I may call it so—is really a great convenience for all parties, let me tell you.

HEDDA. Yes, I have many a time longed for some one to make a third on our travels. Oh—those railway-carriage tête-à-têtes——!

BRACK. Fortunately your wedding journey is over now.

HEDDA (*shaking her head*). Not by a long—long way. I have only arrived at a station on the line.

BRACK. Well, then the passengers jump out and move about a little, Mrs. Hedda.

HEDDA. I never jump out.

BRACK. Really?

HEDDA. No—because there is always some one standing by to——

BRACK (*laughing*). To look at your ankles, do you mean?

HEDDA. Precisely.

BRACK. Well but, dear me——

HEDDA (*with a gesture of repulsion*). I won't have it. I would rather keep my seat where I happen to be—and continue the tête-à-tête.

BRACK. But suppose a third person were to jump in and join the couple.

HEDDA. Ah—that is quite another matter!

BRACK. A trusted, sympathetic friend——

HEDDA. ——with a fund of conversation on all sorts of lively topics——

BRACK. ——and not the least bit of a specialist!

HEDDA (*with an audible sigh*). Yes, that would be a relief indeed.

BRACK (*hears the front door open, and glances in that direction*). The triangle is completed.

HEDDA (*half aloud*). And on goes the train.

> [GEORGE TESMAN, *in a gray walking suit, with a soft felt hat, enters from the hall. He has a number of unbound books under his arm and in his pockets.*]

TESMAN (*goes up to the table beside the corner settee*). Ouf—what a load for a warm day—all these books. (*Lays them on the table.*) I'm positively perspiring, Hedda. Hallo—are you there already, my dear Judge? Eh? Berta didn't tell me.

BRACK (*rising*). I came in through the garden.

HEDDA. What books have you got there?

TESMAN (*stands looking them through*). Some new books on my special subjects—quite indispensable to me.

HEDDA. Your special subjects?

BRACK. Yes, books on his special subjects, Mrs. Tesman. (BRACK *and* HEDDA *exchange a confidential smile.*)

HEDDA. Do you need still more books on your special subjects?

TESMAN. Yes, my dear Hedda, one can never have too many of them. Of course one must keep up with all that is written and published.

HEDDA. Yes, I suppose one must.

TESMAN (*searching among his books*). And look here—I have got hold of Eilert Lövborg's new book too. (*Offering it to her.*) Perhaps you would like to glance through it, Hedda? Eh?

HEDDA. No, thank you. Or rather—afterwards perhaps.

TESMAN. I looked into it a little on the way home.

BRACK. Well, what do you think of it—as a specialist?

TESMAN. I think it shows quite remarkable soundness of judgment. He never wrote like that before. (*Putting the books together.*) Now I shall take all these into my study. I'm longing to cut the leaves——! And then I must change my clothes. (*To* BRACK.) I suppose we needn't start just yet? Eh?

BRACK. Oh, dear no—there is not the slightest hurry.

TESMAN. Well then, I will take my time. (*Is going with his books, but stops in the doorway and turns.*) By-the-bye, Hedda—Aunt Julia is not coming this evening.

HEDDA. Not coming? Is it that affair of the bonnet that keeps her away?

TESMAN. Oh, not at all. How could you think such a thing of Aunt Julia? Just fancy——! The fact is, Aunt Rina is very ill.

HEDDA. She always is.

TESMAN. Yes, but today she is much worse than usual, poor dear.

HEDDA. Oh, then it's only natural that her sister should remain with her. I must bear my disappointment.

TESMAN. And you can't imagine, dear, how delighted Aunt Julia seemed to be—because you had come home looking so flourishing!

HEDDA (*half aloud, rising*). Oh, those everlasting aunts!

TESMAN. What?

HEDDA (*going to the glass door*). Nothing.

TESMAN. Oh, all right. (*He goes through the inner room, out to the right.*)

BRACK. What bonnet were you talking about?

HEDDA. Oh, it was a little episode with Miss Tesman this morning. She had laid down her bonnet on the chair there—(*Looks at him and smiles.*)—and I pretended to think it was the servant's.

BRACK (*shaking his head*). Now my dear Mrs. Hedda, how could you do such a thing? To that excellent old lady, too!

HEDDA (*nervously crossing the room*). Well, you see—these impulses come over me all of a sudden; and I cannot resist them. (*Throws herself down in the easy chair by the stove.*) Oh, I don't know how to explain it.

BRACK (*behind the easy chair*). You are not really happy—that is at the bottom of it.

HEDDA (*looking straight before her*). I know of no reason why I should be—happy. Perhaps you can give me one?

BRACK. Well—amongst other things, because you have got exactly the home you had set your heart on.

HEDDA (*looks up at him and laughs*). Do you too believe in that legend?

BRACK. Is there nothing in it, then?

HEDDA. Oh, yes, there is something in it.

BRACK. Well?

HEDDA. There is this in it, that I made use of Tesman to see me home from evening parties last summer——

BRACK. I, unfortunately, had to go quite a different way.

HEDDA. That's true. I know you were going a different way last summer.

BRACK (*laughing*). Oh fie, Mrs. Hedda! Well, then—you and Tesman——?

HEDDA. Well, we happened to pass here one evening; Tesman, poor fellow, was writhing in the agony of having to find conversation; so I took pity on the learned man——

BRACK (*smiles doubtfully*). You took pity? H'm——

HEDDA. Yes, I really did. And so—to help him out of his torment—I happened to say, in pure thoughtlessness, that I should like to live in this villa.

BRACK. No more than that?

HEDDA. Not that evening.

BRACK. But afterwards?

HEDDA. Yes, my thoughtlessness had consequences, my dear Judge.

BRACK. Unfortunately that too often happens, Mrs. Hedda.

HEDDA. Thanks! So you see it was this enthusiasm for Secretary Falk's villa that first constituted a bond of sympathy between George Tesman and me. From that came our engagement and our marriage, and our wedding journey, and all the rest of it. Well, well, my dear Judge—as you make your bed so you must lie, I could almost say.

BRACK. This is exquisite! And you really cared not a rap about it all the time.

HEDDA. No, heaven knows I didn't.

BRACK. But now? Now that we have made it so homelike for you?

HEDDA. Uh—the rooms all seem to smell of lavender and dried rose leaves.—But perhaps it's Aunt Julia that has brought that scent with her.

BRACK (*laughing*). No, I think it must be a legacy from the late Mrs. Secretary Falk.

HEDDA. Yes, there is an odor of mortality about it. It reminds me of a bouquet—the day after the ball. (*Clasps her hands behind her head, leans back in her chair and looks at him.*) Oh, my dear Judge—you cannot imagine how horribly I shall bore myself here.

BRACK. Why should not you, too, find some sort of vocation in life, Mrs. Hedda?

HEDDA. A vocation—that should attract me?

BRACK. If possible, of course.

HEDDA. Heaven knows what sort of a vocation that could be. I often wonder whether—— (*Breaking off.*) But that would never do either.

BRACK. Who can tell? Let me hear what it is.

HEDDA. Whether I might not get Tesman to go into politics, I mean.

BRACK (*laughing*). Tesman? No, really now, political life is not the thing for him—not at all in his line.

HEDDA. No, I daresay not. But if I could get him into it all the same?

BRACK. Why—what satisfaction could you find in that? If he is not fitted for that sort of thing, why should you want to drive him into it?

HEDDA. Because I am bored, I tell you! (*After a pause.*) So you think it quite out of the question that Tesman should ever get into the ministry?

BRACK. H'm—you see, my dear Mrs. Hedda—to get into the ministry, he would have to be a tolerably rich man.

HEDDA (*rising impatiently*). Yes, there we have it! It is this genteel poverty I have managed to drop into——! (*Crosses the room.*) That is what makes life so pitiable! So utterly ludicrous! For that's what it is.

BRACK. Now *I* should say the fault lay elsewhere.

HEDDA. Where, then?

BRACK. You have never gone through any really stimulating experience.

HEDDA. Anything serious, you mean?

BRACK. Yes, you may call it so. But now you may perhaps have one in store.

HEDDA (*tossing her head*). Oh, you're thinking of the annoyances about this wretched professorship! But that must be Tesman's own affair. I assure you I shall not waste a thought upon it.

BRACK. No, no, I daresay not. But suppose now that what people call— in elegant language—a solemn responsibility were to come upon you? (*Smiling.*) A new responsibility, Mrs. Hedda?

HEDDA (*angrily*). Be quiet! Nothing of that sort will ever happen!

BRACK (*warily*). We will speak of this again a year hence—at the very outside.

HEDDA (*curtly*). I have no turn for anything of the sort, Judge Brack. No responsibilities for me!

BRACK. Are you so unlike the generality of women as to have no turn for duties which——?

HEDDA (*beside the glass door*). Oh, be quiet, I tell you! I often think there is only one thing in the world I have any turn for.

BRACK (*drawing near to her*). And what is that, if I may ask?

HEDDA (*stands looking out*). Boring myself to death. Now you know it. (*Turns, looks towards the inner room, and laughs.*) Yes, as I thought! Here comes the Professor.

BRACK (*softly, in a tone of warning*). Come, come, come, Mrs. Hedda!

[GEORGE TESMAN, *dressed for the party, with his gloves and hat in his hand, enters from the right through the inner room.*]

TESMAN. Hedda, has no message come from Eilert Lövborg? Eh?

HEDDA. No.

TESMAN. Then you'll see he'll be here presently.

BRACK. Do you really think he will come?

TESMAN. Yes, I am almost sure of it. For what you were telling us this morning must have been a mere floating rumor.

BRACK. You think so?

TESMAN. At any rate, Aunt Julia said she did not believe for a moment that he would ever stand in my way again. Fancy that!

BRACK. Well then, that's all right.

TESMAN (*placing his hat and gloves on a chair on the right*). Yes, but you must really let me wait for him as long as possible.

BRACK. We have plenty of time yet. None of my guests will arrive before seven or half-past.

TESMAN. Then meanwhile we can keep Hedda company, and see what happens. Eh?

HEDDA (*placing* BRACK'S *hat and overcoat upon the corner settee*). And at the worst Mr. Lövborg can remain here with me.

BRACK (*offering to take his things*). Oh, allow me, Mrs. Tesman! What do you mean by "At the worst"?

HEDDA. If he won't go with you and Tesman.

TESMAN (*looks dubiously at her*). But, Hedda dear—do you think it would quite do for him to remain with you? Eh? Remember, Aunt Julia can't come.

HEDDA. No, but Mrs. Elvsted is coming. We three can have a cup of tea together.

TESMAN. Oh, yes, that will be all right.

BRACK (*smiling*). And that would perhaps be the safest plan for him.

HEDDA. Why so?

BRACK. Well, you know, Mrs. Tesman, how you used to gird at my little bachelor parties. You declared they were adapted only for men of the strictest principles.

HEDDA. But no doubt Mr. Lövborg's principles are strict enough now. A converted sinner—— (BERTA *appears at the hall door.*)

BERTA. There's a gentleman asking if you are at home, ma'am——

HEDDA. Well, show him in.

TESMAN (*softly*). I'm sure it is he! Fancy that!

[EILERT LÖVBORG *enters from the hall. He is slim and lean; of the same age as* TESMAN, *but looks older and somewhat worn-out. His hair and beard are of a blackish brown, his face long and pale, but with patches of color on the cheekbones. He is dressed in a well-cut black visiting suit, quite new. He has dark gloves and a silk hat. He stops near the door, and makes a rapid bow, seeming somewhat embarrassed.*]

TESMAN (*goes up to him and shakes him warmly by the hand*). Well, my dear Eilert—so at last we meet again!

LÖVBORG (*speaks in a subdued voice*). Thanks for your letter, Tesman. (*Approaching* HEDDA.) Will you too shake hands with me, Mrs. Tesman?

HEDDA (*taking his hand*). I am glad to see you, Mr. Lövborg. (*With a motion of her hand.*) I don't know whether you two gentlemen——?

LÖVBORG (*bowing slightly*). Judge Brack, I think.

BRACK (*doing likewise*). Oh, yes, in the old days——

TESMAN (*to* LÖVBORG, *with his hands on his shoulders*). And now you must make yourself entirely at home, Eilert! Mustn't he, Hedda? For I hear you are going to settle in town again? Eh?

LÖVBORG. Yes, I am.

TESMAN. Quite right, quite right. Let me tell you, I have got hold of your new book; but I haven't had time to read it yet.

LÖVBORG. You may spare yourself the trouble.

TESMAN. Why so?

LÖVBORG. Because there is very little in it.

TESMAN. Just fancy—how can you say so?

BRACK. But it has been very much praised, I hear.

LÖVBORG. That was what I wanted; so I put nothing into the book but what every one would agree with.

BRACK. Very wise of you.

TESMAN. Well but, my dear Eilert——!

LÖVBORG. For now I mean to win myself a position again—to make a fresh start.

TESMAN (*a little embarrassed*). Ah, that is what you wish to do? Eh?

LÖVBORG (*smiling, lays down his hat, and draws a packet, wrapped in paper, from his coat pocket*). But when this one appears, George Tesman, you will have to read it. For this is the real book—the book I have put my true self into.

TESMAN. Indeed? And what is it?

LÖVBORG. It is the continuation.

TESMAN. The continuation? Of what?

LÖVBORG. Of the book.

TESMAN. Of the new book?

LÖVBORG. Of course.

TESMAN. Why, my dear Eilert—does it not come down to our own days?

LÖVBORG. Yes, it does; and this one deals with the future.

TESMAN. With the future! But, good heavens, we know nothing of the future!

LÖVBORG. No; but there is a thing or two to be said about it all the same. (*Opens the packet.*) Look here——

TESMAN. Why, that's not your handwriting.

LÖVBORG. I dictated it. (*Turning over the pages.*) It falls into two sections. The first deals with the civilizing forces of the future. And here is the second—(*running through the pages towards the end*)—forecasting the probable line of development.

TESMAN. How odd now! I should never have thought of writing anything of that sort.

HEDDA (*at the glass door, drumming on the pane*). H'm—I daresay not.

LÖVBORG (*replacing the manuscript in its paper and laying the packet on the table*). I brought it, thinking I might read you a little of it this evening.

TESMAN. That was very good of you, Eilert. But this evening——? (*Looking at* BRACK.) I don't quite see how we can manage it——

LÖVBORG. Well then, some other time. There is no hurry.

BRACK. I must tell you, Mr. Lövborg—there is a little gathering at my house this evening—mainly in honor of Tesman, you know——

LÖVBORG (*looking for his hat*). Oh—then I won't detain you——

BRACK. No, but listen—will you not do me the favor of joining us?

LÖVBORG (*curtly and decidedly*). No, I can't—thank you very much.

BRACK. Oh, nonsense—do! We shall be quite a select little circle. And I assure you we shall have a "lively time," as Mrs. Hed—as Mrs. Tesman says.

LÖVBORG. I have no doubt of it. But nevertheless——

BRACK. And then you might bring your manuscript with you, and read it to Tesman at my house. I could give you a room to yourselves.

TESMAN. Yes, think of that, Eilert,—why shouldn't you? Eh?

HEDDA (*interposing*). But, Tesman, if Mr. Lövborg would really rather not! I am sure Mr. Lövborg is much more inclined to remain here and have supper with me.

LÖVBORG (*looking at her*). With you, Mrs. Tesman?

HEDDA. And with Mrs. Elvsted.

LÖVBORG. Ah—— (*Lightly.*) I saw her for a moment this morning.

HEDDA. Did you? Well, she is coming this evening. So you see you are almost bound to remain, Mr. Lövborg, or she will have no one to see her home.

LÖVBORG. That's true. Many thanks, Mrs. Tesman—in that case I will remain.

HEDDA. Then I have one or two orders to give the servant——
[*She goes to the hall door and rings.* BERTA *enters.*
HEDDA *talks to her in a whisper, and points toward
the inner room.* BERTA *nods and goes out again.*]

TESMAN (*at the same time, to* LÖVBORG). Tell me, Eilert—is it this new subject—the future—that you are going to lecture about?

LÖVBORG. Yes.

TESMAN. They told me at the bookseller's, that you are going to deliver a course of lectures this autumn.

LÖVBORG. That is my intention. I hope you won't take it ill, Tesman.

TESMAN. Oh no, not in the least! But——?

LÖVBORG. I can quite understand that it must be disagreeable to you.

TESMAN (*cast down*). Oh, I can't expect you, out of consideration for me, to——

LÖVBORG. But I shall wait till you have received your appointment.

TESMAN. Will you wait? Yes, but—yes, but—are you not going to compete with me? Eh?

LÖVBORG. No; it is only the moral victory I care for.

TESMAN. Why, bless me—then Aunt Julia was right after all! Oh yes—I knew it! Hedda! Just fancy—Eilert Lövborg is not going to stand in our way!

HEDDA (*curtly*). Our way? Pray leave me out of the question.

[*She goes up towards the inner room, where* BERTA *is placing a tray with decanters and glasses on the table.* HEDDA *nods approval, and comes forward again.*
BERTA *goes out.*]

TESMAN (*at the same time*). And you, Judge Brack—what do you say to this? Eh?

BRACK. Well, I say that a moral victory—h'm—may be all very fine——

TESMAN. Yes, certainly. But all the same——

HEDDA (*looking at* TESMAN *with a cold smile*). You stand there looking as if you were thunderstruck——

TESMAN. Yes—so I am—I almost think——

BRACK. Don't you see, Mrs. Tesman, a thunderstorm has just passed over?

HEDDA (*pointing towards the inner room*). Will you not take a glass of cold punch, gentlemen?

BRACK (*looking at his watch*). A stirrup cup? Yes, it wouldn't come amiss.

TESMAN. A capital idea, Hedda! Just the thing? Now that the weight has been taken off my mind——

HEDDA. Will you not join them, Mr. Lövborg?

LÖVBORG (*with a gesture of refusal*). No, thank you. Nothing for me.

BRACK. Why, bless me—cold punch is surely not poison.

LÖVBORG. Perhaps not for every one.

HEDDA. I will keep Mr. Lövborg company in the meantime.

TESMAN. Yes, yes, Hedda dear, do.

[*He and* BRACK *go into the inner room, seat themselves, drink punch, smoke cigarettes, and carry on a lively conversation during what follows.* EILERT LÖVBORG *remains beside the stove.* HEDDA *goes to the writing table.*]

HEDDA (*raising her voice a little*). Do you care to look at some photographs, Mr. Lövborg? You know Tesman and I made a tour in the Tyrol on our way home?

[*She takes up an album, and places it on the table beside the sofa, in the further corner of which she seats herself.* EILERT LÖVBORG *approaches, stops, and looks at her. Then he takes a chair and seats himself at her left, with his back towards the inner room.*]

HEDDA (*opening the album*). Do you see this range of mountains, Mr. Lövborg? It's the Ortler group. Tesman has written the name underneath. Here it is: "The Ortler group near Meran."

LÖVBORG (*who has never taken his eyes off her, says softly and slowly*). Hedda—Gabler!

HEDDA (*glancing hastily at him*). Ah! Hush!

LÖVBORG (*repeats softly*). Hedda Gabler!

HEDDA (*looking at the album*). That was my name in the old days—when we two knew each other.

LÖVBORG. And I must teach myself never to say Hedda Gabler again—never, as long as I live.

HEDDA (*still turning over the pages*). Yes, you must. And I think you ought to practice in time. The sooner the better, I should say.

LÖVBORG (*in a tone of indignation*). Hedda Gabler married? And married to—George Tesman!

HEDDA. Yes—so the world goes.

LÖVBORG. Oh, Hedda, Hedda—how could you[2] throw yourself away!

HEDDA (*looks sharply at him*). What? I can't allow this!

LÖVBORG. What do you mean? (TESMAN *comes into the room and goes toward the sofa.*)

HEDDA (*hears him coming and says in an indifferent tone*). And this is a view from the Val d'Ampezzo, Mr. Lövborg. Just look at these peaks! (*Looks affectionately up at* TESMAN.) What's the name of these curious peaks, dear?

TESMAN. Let me see? Oh, those are the Dolomites.

HEDDA. Yes, that's it! Those are the Dolomites, Mr. Lövborg.

TESMAN. Hedda dear, I only wanted to ask whether I shouldn't bring you a little punch after all? For yourself at any rate—eh?

HEDDA. Yes, do, please; and perhaps a few biscuits.

TESMAN. No cigarettes?

HEDDA. No.

TESMAN. Very well.

> [*He goes into the inner room and out to the right.*
> BRACK *sits in the inner room, and keeps an eye from
> time to time on* HEDDA *and* LÖVBORG.]

LÖVBORG (*softly, as before*). Answer me, Hedda—how could you go and do this?

HEDDA (*apparently absorbed in the album*). If you continue to say *du* to me I won't talk to you.

LÖVBORG. May I say *du* when we are alone?

HEDDA. No. You may think it; but you mustn't say it.

LÖVBORG. Ah, I understand. It is an offense against George Tesman, whom you[3]—love.

HEDDA (*glances at him and smiles*). Love? What an idea!

LÖVBORG. You don't love him then!

HEDDA. But I won't hear of any sort of unfaithfulness! Remember that.

LÖVBORG. Hedda—answer me one thing——

---

[2] He uses the familiar *du*.

[3] From this point onward Lövborg uses the formal *De*.

HEDDA. Hush! (TESMAN *enters with a small tray from the inner room.*)
TESMAN. Here you are! Isn't this tempting? (*He puts the tray on the table.*)
HEDDA. Why do you bring it yourself?
TESMAN (*filling the glasses*). Because I think it's such fun to wait upon you, Hedda.
HEDDA. But you have poured out two glasses. Mr. Lövborg said he wouldn't have any——
TESMAN. No, but Mrs. Elvsted will soon be here, won't she?
HEDDA. Yes, by-the-bye—Mrs. Elvsted——
TESMAN. Had you forgotten her? Eh?
HEDDA. We were so absorbed in these photographs. (*Shows him a picture.*) Do you remember this little village?
TESMAN. Oh, it's that one just below the Brenner Pass. It was there we passed the night——
HEDDA. ——and met that lively party of tourists.
TESMAN. Yes, that was the place. Fancy—if we could only have had you with us, Eilert! Eh? (*He returns to the inner room and sits beside* BRACK.)
LÖVBORG. Answer me this one thing, Hedda——
HEDDA. Well?
LÖVBORG. Was there no love in your friendship for me either? Not a spark—not a tinge of love in it?
HEDDA. I wonder if there was? To me it seems as though we were two good comrades—two thoroughly intimate friends. (*Smilingly.*) You especially were frankness itself.
LÖVBORG. It was you that made me so.
HEDDA. As I look back upon it all, I think there was really something beautiful, something fascinating—something daring—in—in that secret intimacy—that comradeship which no living creature so much as dreamed of.
LÖVBORG. Yes, yes, Hedda! Was there not? When I used to come to your father's in the afternoon—and the General sat over at the window reading his papers—with his back towards us——
HEDDA. And we two on the corner sofa——
LÖVBORG. Always with the same illustrated paper before us——
HEDDA. For want of an album, yes.
LÖVBORG. Yes, Hedda, and when I made my confessions to you—told you about myself, things that at that time no one else knew! There I would sit and tell you of my escapades—my days and nights of devilment. Oh, Hedda—what was the power in you that forced me to confess these things?
HEDDA. Do you think it was any power in me?
LÖVBORG. How else can I explain it? And all those—those roundabout questions you used to put to me——

HEDDA. Which you understood so particularly well——

LÖVBORG. How could you sit and question me like that? Question me quite frankly——

HEDDA. In roundabout terms, please observe.

LÖVBORG. Yes, but frankly nevertheless. Cross-question me about—all that sort of thing?

HEDDA. And how could you answer, Mr. Lövborg?

LÖVBORG. Yes, that is just what I can't understand—in looking back upon it. But tell me now, Hedda—was there not love at the bottom of our friendship? On your side, did you not feel as though you might purge my stains away if I made you my confessor? Was it not so?

HEDDA. No, not quite.

LÖVBORG. What was your motive, then?

HEDDA. Do you think it quite incomprehensible that a young girl—when it can be done—without any one knowing——

LÖVBORG. Well?

HEDDA. ——should be glad to have a peep, now and then, into a world which——

LÖVBORG. Which——?

HEDDA. ——which she is forbidden to know anything about?

LÖVBORG. So that was it?

HEDDA. Partly. Partly—I almost think.

LÖVBORG. Comradeship in the thirst for life. But why should not that, at any rate, have continued?

HEDDA. The fault was yours.

LÖVBORG. It was you that broke with me.

HEDDA. Yes, when our friendship threatened to develop into something more serious. Shame upon you, Eilert Lövborg! How could you think of wronging your—your frank comrade?

LÖVBORG (clenching his hands). Oh, why did you not carry out your threat? Why did you not shoot me down?

HEDDA. Because I have such a dread of scandal.

LÖVBORG. Yes, Hedda, you are a coward at heart.

HEDDA. A terrible coward. (Changing her tone.) But it was a lucky thing for you. And now you have found ample consolation at the Elvsteds'.

LÖVBORG. I know what Thea has confided to you.

HEDDA. And perhaps you have confided to her something about us?

LÖVBORG. Not a word. She is too stupid to understand anything of that sort.

HEDDA. Stupid?

LÖVBORG. She is stupid about matters of that sort.

HEDDA. And I am cowardly. (Bends over towards him, without looking him in the face, and says more softly.) But now I will confide something to you.

LÖVBORG (*eagerly*). Well?

HEDDA. The fact that I dared not shoot you down——

LÖVBORG. Yes!

HEDDA. ——that was not my most arrant cowardice—that evening.

LÖVBORG (*looks at her a moment, understands, and whispers passionately*). Oh, Hedda! Hedda Gabler! Now I begin to see a hidden reason beneath our comradeship! You[4] and I——! After all, then, it was your craving for life——

HEDDA (*softly, with a sharp glance*). Take care! Believe nothing of the sort!

> [*Twilight has begun to fall. The hall door is opened
> from without by* BERTA.]

HEDDA (*closes the album with a bang and calls smilingly*). Ah, at last! My darling Thea, come along!

> [MRS. ELVSTED *enters from the hall. She is in evening
> dress. The door is closed behind her.*]

HEDDA (*on the sofa, stretches out her arms towards her*). My sweet Thea—you can't think how I have been longing for you!

> [MRS. ELVSTED, *in passing, exchanges slight salutations with the gentlemen in the inner room, then goes
> up to the table and gives* HEDDA *her hands.* EILERT
> LÖVBORG *has risen. He and* MRS. ELVSTED *greet each
> other with a silent nod.*]

MRS. ELVSTED. Ought I to go in and talk to your husband for a moment?

HEDDA. Oh, not at all. Leave those two alone. They will soon be going.

MRS. ELVSTED. Are they going out?

HEDDA. Yes, to a supper party.

MRS. ELVSTED (*quickly, to* LÖVBORG). Not you?

LÖVBORG. No.

HEDDA. Mr. Lövborg remains with us.

MRS. ELVSTED (*takes a chair and is about to seat herself at his side*) Oh, how nice it is here!

HEDDA. No, thank you, my little Thea! Not there! You'll be good enough to come over here to me. I will sit between you.

MRS. ELVSTED. Yes, just as you please.

> [*She goes round the table and seats herself on the
> sofa on* HEDDA'S *right.* LÖVBORG *reseats himself on his
> chair.*]

LÖVBORG (*after a short pause, to* HEDDA). Is not she lovely to look at?

HEDDA (*lightly stroking her hair*). Only to look at?

LÖVBORG. Yes. For we two—she and I—we are two real comrades. We have absolute faith in each other; so we can sit and talk with perfect frankness——

---

[4] In this speech he once more says *du*. Hedda addresses him throughout as *De*.

HEDDA. Not round about, Mr. Lövborg?

LÖVBORG. Well——

MRS. ELVSTED (*softly clinging close to* HEDDA). Oh, how happy I am, Hedda; for, only think, he says I have inspired him too.

HEDDA (*looks at her with a smile*). Ah! Does he say that, dear?

LÖVBORG. And then she is so brave, Mrs. Tesman!

MRS. ELVSTED. Good heavens—am I brave?

LÖVBORG. Exceedingly—where your comrade is concerned.

HEDDA. Ah, yes—courage! If one only had that!

LÖVBORG. What then? What do you mean?

HEDDA. Then life would perhaps be liveable, after all. (*With a sudden change of tone.*) But now, my dearest Thea, you really must have a glass of cold punch.

MRS. ELVSTED. No, thanks—I never take anything of that kind.

HEDDA. Well then, you, Mr. Lövborg.

LÖVBORG. Nor I, thank you.

MRS. ELVSTED. No, he doesn't either.

HEDDA (*looks fixedly at him*). But if I say you shall?

LÖVBORG. It would be no use.

HEDDA (*laughing*). Then I, poor creature, have no sort of power over you?

LÖVBORG. Not in that respect.

HEDDA. But seriously, I think you ought to—for your own sake.

MRS. ELVSTED. Why, Hedda——!

LÖVBORG. How so?

HEDDA. Or rather on account of other people.

LÖVBORG. Indeed?

HEDDA. Otherwise people might be apt to suspect that—in your heart of hearts—you did not feel quite secure—quite confident of yourself.

MRS. ELVSTED (*softly*). Oh please, Hedda——

LÖVBORG. People may suspect what they like—for the present.

MRS. ELVSTED (*joyfully*). Yes, let them!

HEDDA. I saw it plainly in Judge Brack's face a moment ago.

LÖVBORG. What did you see?

HEDDA. His contemptuous smile, when you dared not go with them into the inner room.

LÖVBORG. Dared not? Of course I preferred to stop here and talk to you.

MRS. ELVSTED. What could be more natural, Hedda?

HEDDA. But the Judge could not guess that. And I saw, too, the way he smiled and glanced at Tesman when you dared not accept his invitation to this wretched little supper party of his.

LÖVBORG. Dared not! Do you say I dared not?

HEDDA. *I* don't say so. But that was how Judge Brack understood it.

LÖVBORG. Well, let him.

HEDDA. Then you are not going with them?

LÖVBORG. I will stay here with you and Thea.

MRS. ELVSTED. Yes, Hedda—how can you doubt that?

HEDDA (*smiles and nods approvingly to* LÖVBORG). Firm as a rock!
Faithful to your principles, now and forever! Ah, that is how a man
should be! (*Turns to* MRS. ELVSTED *and caresses her.*) Well now,
what did I tell you, when you came to us this morning in such a
state of distraction——

LÖVBORG (*surprised*). Distraction!

MRS. ELVSTED (*terrified*). Hedda—oh Hedda——!

HEDDA. You can see for yourself; you haven't the slightest reason to be
in such mortal terror—— (*Interrupting herself.*) There! Now we
can all three enjoy ourselves!

LÖVBORG (*who has given a start*). Ah—what is all this, Mrs. Tesman?

MRS. ELVSTED. Oh my God, Hedda! What are you saying? What are
you doing?

HEDDA. Don't get excited! That horrid Judge Brack is sitting watching
you.

LÖVBORG. So she was in mortal terror! On my account!

MRS. ELVSTED (*softly and piteously*). Oh, Hedda—now you have
ruined everything!

LÖVBORG (*looks fixedly at her for a moment. His face is distorted*). So
that was my comrade's frank confidence in me?

MRS. ELVSTED (*imploringly*). Oh, my dearest friend—only let me tell
you——

LÖVBORG (*takes one of the glasses of punch, raises it to his lips, and
says in a low, husky voice*). Your health, Thea!

> [*He empties the glass, puts it down, and takes the
> second.*]

MRS. ELVSTED (*softly*). Oh, Hedda, Hedda—how could you do this?

HEDDA. *I* do it? *I*? Are you crazy?

LÖVBORG. Here's to your health too, Mrs. Tesman. Thanks for the
truth. Hurrah for the truth!

> [*He empties the glass and is about to refill it.*]

HEDDA (*lays her hand on his arm*). Come, come—no more for the
present. Remember you are going out to supper.

MRS. ELVSTED. No, no, no!

HEDDA. Hush! They are sitting watching you.

LÖVBORG (*putting down the glass*). Now, Thea—tell me the truth——

MRS. ELVSTED. Yes.

LÖVBORG. Did your husband know that you had come after me?

MRS. ELVSTED (*wringing her hands*). Oh, Hedda—do you hear what he
is asking?

LÖVBORG. Was it arranged between you and him that you were to come
to town and look after me? Perhaps it was the Sheriff himself that

urged you to come? Aha, my dear—no doubt he wanted my help in his office! Or was it at the card table that he missed me?

MRS. ELVSTED (*softly, in agony*). Oh, Lövborg, Lövborg——!

LÖVBORG (*seizes a glass and is on the point of filling it*). Here's a glass for the old Sheriff too!

HEDDA (*preventing him*). No more just now. Remember you have to read your manuscript to Tesman.

LÖVBORG (*calmly, putting down the glass*). It was stupid of me all this, Thea—to take it in this way, I mean. Don't be angry with me, my dear, dear comrade. You shall see—both you and the others— that if I was fallen once—now I have risen again! Thanks to you, Thea.

MRS. ELVSTED (*radiant with joy*). Oh, heaven be praised——!

[BRACK *has in the meantime looked at his watch. He and* TESMAN *rise and come into the drawing room.*]

BRACK (*takes his hat and overcoat*). Well, Mrs. Tesman, our time has come.

HEDDA. I suppose it has.

LÖVBORG (*rising*). Mine too, Judge Brack.

MRS. ELVSTED (*softly and imploringly*). Oh, Lövborg, don't do it!

HEDDA (*pinching her arm*). They can hear you!

MRS. ELVSTED (*with a suppressed shriek*). Ow!

LÖVBORG (*to* BRACK). You were good enough to invite me.

BRACK. Well, are you coming after all?

LÖVBORG. Yes, many thanks.

BRACK. I'm delighted——

LÖVBORG (*to* TESMAN, *putting the parcel of MS. in his pocket*). I should like to show you one or two things before I send it to the printer's.

TESMAN. Fancy—that will be delightful. But, Hedda dear, how is Mrs. Elvsted to get home? Eh?

HEDDA. Oh, that can be managed somehow.

LÖVBORG (*looking towards the ladies.*) Mrs. Elvsted? Of course, I'll come again and fetch her. (*Approaching.*) At ten or thereabouts, Mrs. Tesman? Will that do?

HEDDA. Certainly. That will do capitally.

TESMAN. Well, then, that's all right. But you must not expect me so early, Hedda.

HEDDA. Oh, you may stop as long—as long as ever you please.

MRS. ELVSTED (*trying to conceal her anxiety*). Well then, Mr. Lövborg—I shall remain here until you come.

LÖVBORG (*with his hat in his hand*). Pray do, Mrs. Elvsted.

BRACK. And now off goes the excursion train, gentlemen! I hope we shall have a lively time, as a certain fair lady puts it.

HEDDA. Ah, if only the fair lady could be present unseen——!

BRACK. Why unseen?

HEDDA. In order to hear a little of your liveliness at first hand, Judge Brack.

BRACK (*laughing*). I should not advise the fair lady to try it.

TESMAN (*also laughing*). Come, you're a nice one, Hedda! Fancy that!

BRACK. Well, good-by, good-by, ladies.

LÖVBORG (*bowing*). About ten o'clock, then.

> [BRACK, LÖVBORG, *and* TESMAN *go out by the hall door. At the same time* BERTA *enters from the inner room with a lighted lamp, which she places on the dining room table; she goes out by the way she came.*]

MRS. ELVSTED (*who has risen and is wandering restlessly about the room*). Hedda—Hedda—what will come of all this?

HEDDA. At ten o'clock—he will be here. I can see him already—with vine leaves in his hair—flushed and fearless——

MRS. ELVSTED. Oh, I hope he may.

HEDDA. And then, you see—then he will have regained control over himself. Then he will be a free man for all his days.

MRS. ELVSTED. Oh God!—if he would only come as you see him now!

HEDDA. He will come as I see him—so, and not otherwise! (*Rises and approaches* THEA). You may doubt him as long as you please; I believe in him. And now we will try——

MRS. ELVSTED. You have some hidden motive in this, Hedda!

HEDDA. Yes, I have. I want for once in my life to have power to mold a human destiny.

MRS. ELVSTED. Have you not the power?

HEDDA. I have not—and have never had it.

MRS. ELVSTED. Not your husband's?

HEDDA. Do you think that is worth the trouble? Oh, if you could only understand how poor I am. And fate has made you so rich! (*Clasps her passionately in her arms.*) I think I must burn your hair off, after all.

MRS. ELVSTED. Let me go! Let me go! I am afraid of you, Hedda!

BERTA (*in the middle doorway*). Tea is laid in the dining room, ma'am.

HEDDA. Very well. We are coming.

MRS. ELVSTED. No, no, no! I would rather go home alone! At once!

HEDDA. Nonsense! First you shall have a cup of tea, you little stupid. And then—at ten o'clock—Eilert Lövborg will be here—with vine leaves in his hair. (*She drags* MRS. ELVSTED *almost by force towards the middle doorway.*)

ACT III

‰§ Scene: *The room at the* TESMANS'. *The curtains are drawn over the middle doorway, and also over the glass door. The lamp, half turned down, and with a shade over it, is burning on the table. In the stove, the door of which stands open, there has been a fire, which is now nearly burnt out.*

MRS. ELVSTED, *wrapped in a large shawl, and with her feet upon a footrest, sits close to the stove, sunk back in the armchair.* HEDDA, *fully dressed, lies sleeping upon the sofa, with a sofa blanket over her.*

MRS. ELVSTED (*after a pause, suddenly sits up in her chair, and listens eagerly. Then she sinks back again wearily, moaning to herself*). Not yet!—Oh God—oh God—not yet!
　　　[BERTA *slips in by the hall door. She has a letter in her hand.*]
MRS. ELVSTED (*turns and whispers eagerly*). Well—has any one come?
BERTA (*softly*). Yes, a girl has brought this letter.
MRS. ELVSTED (*quickly, holding out her hand*). A letter! Give it to me!
BERTA. No, it's for Dr. Tesman, ma'am.
MRS. ELVSTED. Oh, indeed.
BERTA. It was Miss Tesman's servant that brought it. I'll lay it here on the table.
MRS. ELVSTED. Yes, do.
BERTA (*laying down the letter*). I think I had better put out the lamp. It's smoking.
MRS. ELVSTED. Yes, put it out. It must soon be daylight now.
BERTA (*putting out the lamp*). It is daylight already, ma'am.
MRS. ELVSTED. Yes, broad day! And no one come back yet——!
BERTA. Lord bless you, ma'am! I guessed how it would be.
MRS. ELVSTED. You guessed?
BERTA. Yes, when I saw that a certain person had come back to town —and that he went off with them. For we've heard enough about that gentleman before now.

MRS. ELVSTED. Don't speak so loud. You will waken Mrs. Tesman.

BERTA (*looks towards the sofa and sighs*). No, no—let her sleep, poor thing. Shan't I put some wood on the fire?

MRS. ELVSTED. Thanks, not for me.

BERTA. Oh, very well. (*She goes softly out by the hall door.*)

HEDDA (*is awakened by the shutting of the door, and looks up*). What's that——?

MRS. ELVSTED. It was only the servant——

HEDDA (*looking about her*). Oh, we're here——! Yes, now I remember. (*Sits erect upon the sofa, stretches herself, and rubs her eyes.*) What o'clock is it, Thea?

MRS. ELVSTED (*looks at her watch*). It's past seven.

HEDDA. When did Tesman come home?

MRS. ELVSTED. He has not come.

HEDDA. Not come home yet?

MRS. ELVSTED (*rising*). No one has come.

HEDDA. Think of our watching and waiting here till four in the morning——

MRS. ELVSTED (*wringing her hands*). And how I watched and waited for him!

HEDDA (*yawns, and says with her hand before her mouth*). Well, well—we might have spared ourselves the trouble.

MRS. ELVSTED. Did you get a little sleep?

HEDDA. Oh yes; I believe I have slept pretty well. Have you not?

MRS. ELVSTED. Not for a moment. I couldn't, Hedda—not to save my life.

HEDDA (*rises and goes towards her*). There, there, there! There's nothing to be so alarmed about. I understand quite well what has happened.

MRS. ELVSTED. Well, what do you think? Won't you tell me?

HEDDA. Why, of course it has been a very late affair at Judge Brack's——

MRS. ELVSTED. Yes, yes, that is clear enough. But all the same——

HEDDA. And then, you see, Tesman hasn't cared to come home and ring us up in the middle of the night. (*Laughing.*) Perhaps he wasn't inclined to show himself either—immediately after a jollification.

MRS. ELVSTED. But in that case—where can he have gone?

HEDDA. Of course he has gone to his aunts' and slept there. They have his old room ready for him.

MRS. ELVSTED. No, he can't be with them; for a letter has just come for him from Miss Tesman. There it lies.

HEDDA. Indeed? (*Looks at the address.*) Why yes, it's addressed in Aunt Julia's own hand. Well then, he has remained at Judge Brack's. And as for Eilert Lövborg—he is sitting, with vine leaves in his hair, reading his manuscript.

MRS. ELVSTED. Oh Hedda, you are just saying things you don't believe a bit.

HEDDA. You really are a little blockhead, Thea.

MRS. ELVSTED. Oh yes, I suppose I am.

HEDDA. And how mortally tired you look.

MRS. ELVSTED. Yes, I am mortally tired.

HEDDA. Well then, you must do as I tell you. You must go into my room and lie down for a little while.

MRS. ELVSTED. Oh no, no—I shouldn't be able to sleep.

HEDDA. I am sure you would.

MRS. ELVSTED. Well, but your husband is certain to come soon now; and then I want to know at once——

HEDDA. I shall take care to let you know when he comes.

MRS. ELVSTED. Do you promise me, Hedda?

HEDDA. Yes, rely upon me. Just you go in and have a sleep in the meantime.

MRS. ELVSTED. Thanks; then I'll try to. (*She goes off through the inner room.*)

> [*Hedda goes up to the glass door and draws back the curtains. The broad daylight streams into the room. Then she takes a little hand glass from the writing table, looks at herself in it, and arranges her hair. Next she goes to the hall door and presses the bell button.*]
>
> [BERTA *presently appears at the hall door.*]

BERTA. Did you want anything, ma'am?

HEDDA. Yes; you must put some more wood in the stove. I am shivering.

BERTA. Bless me—I'll make up the fire at once. (*She rakes the embers together and lays a piece of wood upon them; then stops and listens.*) That was a ring at the front door, ma'am.

HEDDA. Then go to the door. I will look after the fire.

BERTA. It'll soon burn up. (*She goes out by the hall door.*)

> [HEDDA *kneels on the footrest and lays some more pieces of wood in the stove.*]
>
> [*After a short pause,* GEORGE TESMAN *enters from the hall. He looks tired and rather serious. He steals on tiptoe towards the middle doorway and is about to slip through the curtains.*]

HEDDA (*at the stove, without looking up*). Good morning.

TESMAN (*turns*). Hedda! (*Approaching her.*) Good heavens—are you up so early? Eh?

HEDDA. Yes, I am up very early this morning.

TESMAN. And I never doubted you were still sound asleep! Fancy that, Hedda!

HEDDA. Don't speak so loud. Mrs. Elvsted is resting in my room.

TESMAN. Has Mrs. Elvsted been here all night?

HEDDA. Yes, since no one came to fetch her.

TESMAN. Ah, to be sure.

HEDDA (*closes the door of the stove and rises*). Well, did you enjoy yourself at Judge Brack's?

TESMAN. Have you been anxious about me? Eh?

HEDDA. No, I should never think of being anxious. But I asked if you had enjoyed yourself.

TESMAN. Oh yes—for once in a way. Especially the beginning of the evening; for then Eilert read me part of his book. We arrived more than an hour too early—fancy that! And Brack had all sorts of arrangements to make—so Eilert read to me.

HEDDA (*seating herself by the table on the right*). Well? Tell me, then——

TESMAN (*sitting on a footstool near the stove*). Oh Hedda, you can't conceive what a book that is going to be! I believe it is one of the most remarkable things that have ever been written. Fancy that!

HEDDA. Yes, yes; I don't care about that——

TESMAN. I must make a confession to you, Hedda. When he had finished reading—a horrid feeling came over me.

HEDDA. A horrid feeling?

TESMAN. I felt jealous of Eilert for having had it in him to write such a book. Only think, Hedda!

HEDDA. Yes, yes, I am thinking!

TESMAN. And then how pitiful to think that he—with all his gifts—should be irreclaimable after all.

HEDDA. I suppose you mean that he has more courage than the rest?

TESMAN. No, not at all—I mean that he is incapable of taking his pleasures in moderation.

HEDDA. And what came of it all—in the end?

TESMAN. Well, to tell the truth, I think it might best be described as an orgy, Hedda.

HEDDA. Had he vine leaves in his hair?

TESMAN. Vine leaves? No, I saw nothing of the sort. But he made a long, rambling speech in honor of the woman who had inspired him in his work—that was the phrase he used.

HEDDA. Did he name her?

TESMAN. No, he didn't; but I can't help thinking he meant Mrs. Elvsted. You may be sure he did.

HEDDA. Well—where did you part from him?

TESMAN. On the way to town. We broke up—the last of us at any rate

—all together; and Brack came with us to get a breath of fresh air. And then, you see, we agreed to take Eilert home; for he had had far more than was good for him.

HEDDA. I daresay.

TESMAN. But now comes the strange part of it, Hedda; or, I should rather say, the melancholy part of it. I declare I am almost ashamed —on Eilert's account—to tell you——

HEDDA. Oh, go on——

TESMAN. Well, as we were getting near town, you see, I happened to drop a little behind the others. Only for a minute or two—fancy that!

HEDDA. Yes, yes, yes, but——?

TESMAN. And then, as I hurried after them—what do you think I found by the wayside? Eh?

HEDDA. Oh, how should I know!

TESMAN. You mustn't speak of it to a soul, Hedda! Do you hear! Promise me, for Eilert's sake. (*Draws a parcel, wrapped in paper, from his coat pocket*). Fancy, dear—I found this.

HEDDA. Is not that the parcel he had with him yesterday?

TESMAN. Yes, it is the whole of his precious, irreplaceable manuscript! And he had gone and lost it, and knew nothing about it. Only fancy, Hedda! So deplorably——

HEDDA. But why did you not give him back the parcel at once?

TESMAN. I didn't dare to—in the state he was then in——

HEDDA. Did you not tell any of the others that you had found it?

TESMAN. Oh, far from it! You can surely understand that, for Eilert's sake, I wouldn't do that.

HEDDA. So no one knows that Eilert Lövborg's manuscript is in your possession?

TESMAN. No. And no one must know it.

HEDDA. Then what did you say to him afterwards?

TESMAN. I didn't talk to him again at all; for when we got in among the streets, he and two or three of the others gave us the slip and disappeared. Fancy that!

HEDDA. Indeed! They must have taken him home then.

TESMAN. Yes, so it would appear. And Brack, too, left us.

HEDDA. And what have you been doing with yourself since?

TESMAN. Well, I and some of the others went home with one of the party, a jolly fellow, and took our morning coffee with him; or perhaps I should rather call it our night coffee—eh? But now, when I have rested a little, and given Eilert, poor fellow, time to have his sleep out, I must take this back to him.

HEDDA (*holds out her hand for the packet*). No—don't give it to him! Not in such a hurry, I mean. Let me read it first.

TESMAN. No, my dearest Hedda, I mustn't, I really mustn't.

HEDDA. You must not?

TESMAN. No—for you can imagine what a state of despair he will be in when he awakens and misses the manuscript. He has no copy of it, you must know! He told me so.

HEDDA (*looking searchingly at him*). Can such a thing not be reproduced? Written over again?

TESMAN. No, I don't think that would be possible. For the inspiration, you see——

HEDDA. Yes, yes—I suppose it depends on that. (*Lightly.*) But, by-the-bye—here is a letter for you.

TESMAN. Fancy——!

HEDDA (*handing it to him.*) It came early this morning.

TESMAN. It's from Aunt Julia! What can it be? (*He lays the packet on the other footstool, opens the letter, runs his eye through it, and jumps up.*) Oh, Hedda—she says that poor Aunt Rina is dying!

HEDDA. Well, we were prepared for that.

TESMAN. And that if I want to see her again, I must make haste. I'll run in to them at once.

HEDDA (*suppressing a smile*). Will you run?

TESMAN. Oh, dearest Hedda—if you could only make up your mind to come with me! Just think!

HEDDA (*rises and says wearily, repelling the idea*). No, no, don't ask me. I will not look upon sickness and death. I loathe all sorts of ugliness.

TESMAN. Well, well, then——! (*Bustling around.*) My hat—my over-coat——? Oh, in the hall—I do hope I mayn't come too late, Hedda! Eh?

HEDDA. Oh, if you run——

[BERTA *appears at the hall door.*]

BERTA. Judge Brack is at the door, and wishes to know if he may come in.

TESMAN. At this time! No, I can't possibly see him.

HEDDA. But I can. (*To* BERTA.) Ask Judge Brack to come in. (BERTA *goes out.*)

HEDDA (*quickly whispering*). The parcel, Tesman! (*She snatches it up from the stool.*)

TESMAN. Yes, give it to me!

HEDDA. No, no, I will keep it till you come back.

[*She goes to the writing table and places it in the bookcase.* TESMAN *stands in a flurry of haste, and cannot get his gloves on.*]

[JUDGE BRACK *enters from the hall.*]

HEDDA (*nodding to him*). You are an early bird, I must say.

BRACK. Yes, don't you think so? (*To* TESMAN.) Are you on the move, too?

TESMAN. Yes, I must rush off to my aunts'. Fancy—the invalid one is lying at death's door, poor creature.

BRACK. Dear me, is she indeed? Then on no account let me detain you. At such a critical moment——

TESMAN. Yes, I must really rush——Good-by! Good-by! (*He hastens out by the hall door.*)

HEDDA (*approaching*). You seem to have made a particularly lively night of it at your rooms, Judge Brack.

BRACK. I assure you I have not had my clothes off, Mrs. Hedda.

HEDDA. Not you, either?

BRACK. No, as you may see. But what has Tesman been telling you of the night's adventures?

HEDDA. Oh, some tiresome story. Only that they went and had coffee somewhere or other.

BRACK. I have heard about that coffee-party already. Eilert Lövborg was not with them, I fancy?

HEDDA. No, they had taken him home before that.

BRACK. Tesman, too?

HEDDA. No, but some of the others, he said.

BRACK (*smiling*). George Tesman is really an ingenuous creature, Mrs. Hedda.

HEDDA. Yes, heaven knows he is. Then is there something behind all this?

BRACK. Yes, perhaps there may be.

HEDDA. Well then, sit down, my dear Judge, and tell your story in comfort.

[*She seats herself to the left of the table.* BRACK *sits near her, at the long side of the table.*]

HEDDA. Now then?

BRACK. I had special reasons for keeping track of my guests—or rather of some of my guests—last night.

HEDDA. Of Eilert Lövborg among the rest, perhaps?

BRACK. Frankly, yes.

HEDDA. Now you make me really curious——

BRACK. Do you know where he and one or two of the others finished the night, Mrs. Hedda?

HEDDA. If it is not quite unmentionable, tell me.

BRACK. Oh no, it's not at all unmentionable. Well, they put in an appearance at a particularly animated soirée.

HEDDA. Of the lively kind?

BRACK. Of the very liveliest——

HEDDA. Tell me more of this, Judge Brack——

BRACK. Lövborg, as well as the others, had been invited in advance. I knew all about it. But he had declined the invitation; for now, as you know, he has become a new man.

HEDDA. Up at the Elvsteds', yes. But he went after all, then?

BRACK. Well, you see, Mrs. Hedda—unhappily the spirit moved him at my rooms last evening——

HEDDA. Yes, I hear he found inspiration.

BRACK. Pretty violent inspiration. Well, I fancy that altered his purpose; for we men folk are unfortunately not always so firm in our principles as we ought to be.

HEDDA. Oh, I am sure you are an exception, Judge Brack. But as to Lövborg——?

BRACK. To make a long story short—he landed at last in Mademoiselle Diana's rooms.

HEDDA. Mademoiselle Diana's?

BRACK. It was Mademoiselle Diana that was giving the soirée, to a select circle of her admirers and her lady friends.

HEDDA. Is she a red-haired woman?

BRACK. Precisely.

HEDDA. A sort of a—singer?

BRACK. Oh yes—in her leisure moments. And moreover a mighty huntress—of men—Mrs. Hedda. You have no doubt heard of her. Eilert Lövborg was one of her most enthusiastic protectors—in the days of his glory.

HEDDA. And how did all this end?

BRACK. Far from amicably, it appears. After a most tender meeting, they seem to have come to blows——

HEDDA. Lövborg and she?

BRACK. Yes. He accused her or her friends of having robbed him. He declared that his pocketbook had disappeared—and other things as well. In short, he seems to have made a furious disturbance.

HEDDA. And what came of it all?

BRACK. It came to a general scrimmage, in which the ladies as well as the gentlemen took part. Fortunately the police at last appeared on the scene.

HEDDA. The police too?

BRACK. Yes. I fancy it will prove a costly frolic for Eilert Lövborg, crazy being that he is.

HEDDA. How so?

BRACK. He seems to have made a violent resistance—to have hit one of the constables on the head and torn the coat off his back. So they had to march him off to the police station with the rest.

HEDDA. How have you learnt all this?

BRACK. From the police themselves.

HEDDA (gazing straight before her). So that is what happened. Then he had no vine leaves in his hair.

BRACK. Vine leaves, Mrs. Hedda?

HEDDA (*changing her tone*). But tell me now, Judge—what is your real reason for tracking out Eilert Lövborg's movements so carefully?

BRACK. In the first place, it could not be entirely indifferent to me if it should appear in the police court that he came straight from my house.

HEDDA. Will the matter come into court, then?

BRACK. Of course. However, I should scarcely have troubled so much about that. But I thought that, as a friend of the family, it was my duty to supply you and Tesman with a full account of his nocturnal exploits.

HEDDA. Why so, Judge Brack?

BRACK. Why, because I have a shrewd suspicion that he intends to use you as a sort of blind.

HEDDA. Oh, how can you think such a thing!

BRACK. Good heavens, Mrs. Hedda—we have eyes in our head. Mark my words! This Mrs. Elvsted will be in no hurry to leave town again.

HEDDA. Well, even if there should be anything between them, I suppose there are plenty of other places where they could meet.

BRACK. Not a single home. Henceforth, as before, every respectable house will be closed against Eilert Lövborg.

HEDDA. And so ought mine to be, you mean?

BRACK. Yes. I confess it would be more than painful to me if this personage were to be made free of your house. How superfluous, how intrusive, he would be, if he were to force his way into——

HEDDA. ——into the triangle?

BRACK. Precisely. It would simply mean that I should find myself homeless.

HEDDA (*looks at him with a smile*). So you want to be the one cock in the basket—that is your aim.

BRACK (*nods slowly and lowers his voice*). Yes, that is my aim. And for that I will fight—with every weapon I can command.

HEDDA (*her smile vanishing*). I see you are a dangerous person—when it comes to the point.

BRACK. Do you think so?

HEDDA. I am beginning to think so. And I am exceedingly glad to think —that you have no sort of hold over me.

BRACK (*laughing equivocally*). Well, well, Mrs. Hedda—perhaps you are right there. If I had, who knows what I might be capable of?

HEDDA. Come, come now, Judge Brack. That sounds almost like a threat.

BRACK (*rising*). Oh, not at all! The triangle, you know, ought, if possible, to be spontaneously constructed.

HEDDA. There I agree with you.

BRACK. Well, now I have said all I had to say; and I had better be getting back to town. Good-by, Mrs. Hedda. (*He goes towards the glass door.*)

HEDDA (*rising*). Are you going through the garden?

BRACK. Yes, it's a short cut for me.

HEDDA. And then it is the back way, too.

BRACK. Quite so. I have no objection to back ways. They may be piquant enough at times.

HEDDA. When there is ball practice going on, you mean?

BRACK (*in the doorway, laughing to her*). Oh, people don't shoot their tame poultry, I fancy.

HEDDA (*also laughing*). Oh no, when there is only one cock in the basket——

> [*They exchange laughing nods of farewell. He goes. She closes the door behind him.*
>
> [HEDDA, *who has become quite serious, stands for a moment looking out. Presently she goes and peeps through the curtain over the middle doorway. Then she goes to the writing table, takes* LÖVBORG'S *packet out of the bookcase, and is on the point of looking through its contents.* BERTA *is heard speaking loudly in the hall.* HEDDA *turns and listens. Then she hastily locks up the packet in the drawer, and lays the key on the inkstand.*
>
> [EILERT LÖVBORG, *with his great coat on and his hat in his hand, tears open the hall door. He looks somewhat confused and irritated.*]

LÖVBORG (*looking towards the hall*). And I tell you I must and will come in! There!

> [*He closes the door, turns and sees* HEDDA, *at once regains his self-control, and bows.*]

HEDDA (*at the writing table*). Well, Mr. Lövborg, this is rather a late hour to call for Thea.

LÖVBORG. You mean rather an early hour to call on you. Pray pardon me.

HEDDA. How do you know that she is still here?

LÖVBORG. They told me at her lodgings that she had been out all night.

HEDDA (*going to the oval table*). Did you notice anything about the people of the house when they said that?

LÖVBORG (*looks inquiringly at her*). Notice anything about them?

HEDDA. I mean, did they seem to think it odd?

LÖVBORG (*suddenly understanding*). Oh yes, of course! I am dragging her down with me! However, I didn't notice anything.—I suppose Tesman is not up yet?

HEDDA. No—I think not——

LÖVBORG. When did he come home?

HEDDA. Very late.

LÖVBORG. Did he tell you anything?

HEDDA. Yes, I gathered that you had had an exceedingly jolly evening at Judge Brack's

LÖVBORG. Nothing more?

HEDDA. I don't think so. However, I was so dreadfully sleepy——

    [MRS. ELVSTED *enters through the curtains of the middle doorway.*]

MRS. ELVSTED (*going towards him*). Ah, Lövborg! At last——!

LÖVBORG. Yes, at last. And too late!

MRS. ELVSTED (*looks anxiously at him*). What is too late?

LÖVBORG. Everything is too late now. It is all over with me.

MRS. ELVSTED. Oh no, no—don't say that!

LÖVBORG. You will say the same when you hear——

MRS. ELVSTED. I won't hear anything!

HEDDA. Perhaps you would prefer to talk to her alone! If so, I will leave you.

LÖVBORG. No, stay—you too. I beg you to stay.

MRS. ELVSTED. Yes, but I won't hear anything, I tell you.

LÖVBORG. It is not last night's adventures that I want to talk about.

MRS. ELVSTED. What is it then——?

LÖVBORG. I want to say that now our ways must part.

MRS. ELVSTED. Part!

HEDDA (*involuntarily*). I knew it!

LÖVBORG. You can be of no more service to me, Thea.

MRS. ELVSTED. How can you stand there and say that! No more service to you! Am I not to help you now, as before? Are we not to go on working together?

LÖVBORG. Henceforward I shall do no work.

MRS. ELVSTED (*despairingly*). Then what am I to do with my life?

LÖVBORG. You must try to live your life as if you had never known me.

MRS. ELVSTED. But you know I cannot do that!

LÖVBORG. Try if you cannot, Thea. You must go home again——

MRS. ELVSTED (*in vehement protest*). Never in this world! Where you are, there will I be also! I will not let myself be driven away like this! I will remain here! I will be with you when the book appears.

HEDDA (*half aloud, in suspense*). Ah yes—the book!

LÖVBORG (*looks at her*). My book and Thea's; for that is what it is.

MRS. ELVSTED. Yes, I feel that it is. And that is why I have a right to be with you when it appears! I will see with my own eyes how respect and honor pour in upon you afresh. And the happiness—the happiness—oh, I must share it with you!

LÖVBORG. Thea—our book will never appear.

HEDDA. Ah!

MRS. ELVSTED. Never appear!

LÖVBORG. Can never appear.

MRS. ELVSTED (*in agonized foreboding*). Lövborg—what have you done with the manuscript?

HEDDA (*looks anxiously at him*). Yes, the manuscript——?

MRS. ELVSTED. Where is it?

LÖVBORG. Oh Thea—don't ask me about it!

MRS. ELVSTED. Yes, yes, I will know. I demand to be told at once.

LÖVBORG. The manuscript—Well then—I have torn the manuscript into a thousand pieces.

MRS. ELVSTED (*shrieks*). Oh no, no——!

HEDDA (*involuntarily*). But that's not——

LÖVBORG (*looks at her*). Not true, you think?

HEDDA (*collecting herself*). Oh well, of course—since you say so. But it sounded so improbable——

LÖVBORG. It is true, all the same.

MRS. ELVSTED (*wringing her hands*). Oh God—oh God, Hedda—torn his own work to pieces!

LÖVBORG. I have torn my own life to pieces. So why should I not tear my lifework too——?

MRS. ELVSTED. And you did this last night?

LÖVBORG. Yes, I tell you! Tore it into a thousand pieces and scattered them on the fiord—far out. There there is cool sea water at any rate—let them drift upon it—drift with the current and the wind. And then presently they will sink—deeper and deeper—as I shall, Thea.

MRS. ELVSTED. Do you know, Lövborg, that what you have done with the book—I shall think of it to my dying day as though you had killed a little child.

LÖVBORG. Yes, you are right. It is a sort of child murder.

MRS. ELVSTED. How could you, then——! Did not the child belong to me too?

HEDDA (*almost inaudibly*). Ah, the child——

MRS. ELVSTED (*breathing heavily*). It is all over then. Well, well, now I will go, Hedda.

HEDDA. But you are not going away from town?

MRS. ELVSTED. Oh, I don't know what I shall do. I see nothing but darkness before me. (*She goes out by the hall door.*)

HEDDA (*stands waiting for a moment*). So you are not going to see her home, Mr. Lövborg?

LÖVBORG. I? Through the streets? Would you have people see her walking with me?

HEDDA. Of course I don't know what else may have happened last night. But is it so utterly irretrievable?

LÖVBORG. It will not end with last night—I know that perfectly well.

And the thing is that now I have no taste for that sort of life either. I won't begin it anew. She has broken my courage and my power of braving life out.

HEDDA (*looking straight before her*). So that pretty little fool has had her fingers in a man's destiny. (*Looks at him.*) But all the same, how could you treat her so heartlessly?

LÖVBORG. Oh, don't say that it was heartless!

HEDDA. To go and destroy what has filled her whole soul for months and years! You do not call that heartless!

LÖVBORG. To you I can tell the truth, Hedda.

HEDDA. The truth?

LÖVBORG. First promise me—give me your word—that what I now confide to you Thea shall never know.

HEDDA. I give you my word.

LÖVBORG. Good. Then let me tell you that what I said just now was untrue.

HEDDA. About the manuscript?

LÖVBORG. Yes. I have not torn it to pieces—nor thrown it into the fiord.

HEDDA. No, n— But—where is it then!

LÖVBORG. I have destroyed it none the less—utterly destroyed it, Hedda!

HEDDA. I don't understand.

LÖVBORG. Thea said that what I had done seemed to her like a child murder.

HEDDA. Yes, so she said.

LÖVBORG. But to kill his child—that is not the worst thing a father can do to it.

HEDDA. Not the worst?

LÖVBORG. No. I wanted to spare Thea from hearing the worst.

HEDDA. Then what is the worst?

LÖVBORG. Suppose now, Hedda, that a man—in the small hours of the morning—came home to his child's mother after a night of riot and debauchery, and said: "Listen—I have been here and there—in this place and in that. And I have taken our child with me—to this place and to that. And I have lost the child—utterly lost it. The devil knows into what hands it may have fallen—who may have had their clutches on it."

HEDDA. Well—but when all is said and done, you know—that was only a book——

LÖVBORG. Thea's pure soul was in that book.

HEDDA. Yes, so I understand.

LÖVBORG. And you can understand, too, that for her and me together no future is possible.

HEDDA. What path do you mean to take then?

LÖVBORG. None. I will only try to make an end of it all—the sooner the better.

HEDDA (*a step nearer to him*). Eilert Lövborg—listen to me. Will you not try to—to do it beautifully?

LÖVBORG. Beautifully? (*Smiling.*) With vine leaves in my hair, as you used to dream in the old days——?

HEDDA. No, no. I have lost my faith in the vine leaves. But beautifully, nevertheless! For once in a way!—Good-by! You must go now—and do not come here any more.

LÖVBORG. Good-by, Mrs. Tesman. And give George Tesman my love. (*He is on the point of going.*)

HEDDA. No, wait! I must give you a memento to take with you.
    [*She goes to the writing table and opens the drawer
    and the pistol case; then returns to* LÖVBORG *with one
                    of the pistols.*]

LÖVBORG Good-by, Hedda Gabler. (*He goes out by the hall door.*)

HEDDA (*nodding slowly*). Do you recognize it? It was aimed at you once.

LÖVBORG. You should have used it then.

HEDDA. Take it—and do you use it now.

LÖVBORG (*puts the pistol in his breast pocket*). Thanks!

HEDDA. And beautifully, Eilert Lövborg. Promise me that!

LÖVBORG. Good-by, Hedda Gabler. (*He goes out by the hall door.*)
    [HEDDA *listens for a moment at the door. Then she
    goes up to the writing table, takes out the packet of
    manuscript, peeps under the cover, draws a few of the
    sheets half out, and looks at them. Next she goes over
    and seats herself in the armchair beside the stove,
    with the packet in her lap. Presently she opens the
                stove door, and then the packet.*]

HEDDA (*throws one of the quires into the fire and whispers to herself*). Now I am burning your child, Thea!—Burning it, curlylocks! (*Throwing one or two more quires into the stove.*) Your child and Eilert Lövborg's. (*Throws the rest in.*) I am burning—I am burning your child.

ACT IV

ઉ૭ Scene: *The same rooms at the* TESMANS'. *It is evening. The drawing room is in darkness. The back room is lighted by the hanging lamp over the table. The curtains over the glass door are drawn close.*

HEDDA, *dressed in black, walks to and fro in the dark room. Then she goes into the back room and disappears, for a moment to the left. She is heard to strike a few chords on the piano. Presently she comes in sight again, and returns to the drawing room.*

BERTA *enters from the right, through the inner room, with a lighted lamp, which she places on the table in front of the corner settee in the drawing room. Her eyes are red with weeping, and she has black ribbons in her cap. She goes quietly and circumspectly out to the right.*

HEDDA, *goes up to the glass door, lifts the curtain a little aside, and looks out into the darkness.*

Shortly afterwards, MISS TESMAN, *in mourning, with a bonnet and veil on, comes in from the hall.* HEDDA *goes towards her and holds out her hand.*

MISS TESMAN. Yes, Hedda, here I am, in mourning and forlorn; for now my poor sister has at last found peace.

HEDDA. I have heard the news already, as you see. Tesman sent me a card.

MISS TESMAN. Yes, he promised me he would. But nevertheless I thought that to Hedda—here in the house of life—I ought myself to bring the tidings of death.

HEDDA. That was very kind of you.

MISS TESMAN. Ah, Rina ought not to have left us just now. This is not the time for Hedda's house to be a house of mourning.

HEDDA (*changing the subject*). She died quite peacefully, did she not, Miss Tesman?

MISS TESMAN. Oh, her end was so calm, so beautiful. And then she had the unspeakable happiness of seeing George once more—and bidding him good-by. Has he come home yet?

HEDDA. No. He wrote that he might be detained. But won't you sit down?

MISS TESMAN. No thank you, my dear, dear Hedda. I should like to, but I have so much to do. I must prepare my dear one for her rest as well as I can. She shall go to her grave looking her best.

HEDDA. Can I not help you in any way?

MISS TESMAN. Oh, you must not think of it! Hedda Tesman must have no hand in such mournful work. Nor let her thoughts dwell on it either—not at this time.

HEDDA. One is not always mistress of one's thoughts——

MISS TESMAN (*continuing*). Ah yes, it is the way of the world. At home we shall be sewing a shroud; and here there will soon be sewing too, I suppose—but of another sort, thank God!

[GEORGE TESMAN *enters by the hall door.*]

HEDDA. Ah, you have come at last!

TESMAN. You here, Aunt Julia? With Hedda? Fancy that!

MISS TESMAN. I was just going, my dear boy. Well, have you done all you promised?

TESMAN. No; I'm really afraid I have forgotten half of it. I must come to you again tomorrow. Today my brain is all in a whirl. I can't keep my thoughts together.

MISS TESMAN. Why, my dear George, you mustn't take it in this way.

TESMAN. Mustn't——? How do you mean?

MISS TESMAN. Even in your sorrow you must rejoice, as I do—rejoice that she is at rest.

TESMAN. Oh yes, yes—you are thinking of Aunt Rina.

HEDDA. You will feel lonely now, Miss Tesman.

MISS TESMAN. Just at first, yes. But that will not last very long, I hope. I daresay I shall soon find an occupant for poor Rina's little room.

TESMAN. Indeed? Who do you think will take it? Eh?

MISS TESMAN. Oh, there's always some poor invalid or other in want of nursing, unfortunately.

HEDDA. Would you really take such a burden upon you again?

MISS TESMAN. A burden! Heaven forgive you, child—it has been no burden to me.

HEDDA. But suppose you had a total stranger on your hands——

MISS TESMAN. Oh, one soon makes friends with sick folk; and it's such an absolute necessity for me to have some one to live for. Well, heaven be praised, there may soon be something in this house, too, to keep an old aunt busy.

HEDDA. Oh, don't trouble about anything here.

TESMAN. Yes, just fancy what a nice time we three might have together, if——?

HEDDA. If——?

TESMAN (*uneasily*). Oh, nothing. It will all come right. Let us hope so—eh?

MISS TESMAN. Well, well, I daresay you two want to talk to each other. (*Smiling.*) And perhaps Hedda may have something to tell you too, George. Good-by! I must go home to Rina. (*Turning at the door.*) How strange it is to think that now Rina is with me and with my poor brother as well!

TESMAN. Yes, fancy that, Aunt Julia! Eh?

[MISS TESMAN *goes out by the hall door.*]

HEDDA (*follows* TESMAN *coldly and searchingly with her eyes*). I almost believe your Aunt Rina's death affects you more than it does your Aunt Julia.

TESMAN. Oh, it's not that alone. It's Eilert I am so terribly uneasy about.

HEDDA (*quickly*). Is there anything new about him?

TESMAN. I looked in at his rooms this afternoon, intending to tell him the manuscript was in safe keeping.

HEDDA. Well, did you not find him?

TESMAN. No. He wasn't at home. But afterwards I met Mrs. Elvsted, and she told me that he had been here early this morning.

HEDDA. Yes, directly after you had gone.

TESMAN. And he said that he had torn his manuscript to pieces—eh?

HEDDA. Yes, so he declared.

TESMAN. Why, good heavens, he must have been completely out of his mind! And I suppose you thought it best not to give it back to him, Hedda?

HEDDA. No, he did not get it.

TESMAN. But of course you told him that we had it?

HEDDA No. (*Quickly.*) Did you tell Mrs. Elvsted?

TESMAN. No, I thought I had better not. But you ought to have told him. Fancy, if, in desperation, he should go and do himself some injury! Let me have the manuscript, Hedda! I will take it to him at once. Where is it?

HEDDA (*cold and immovable, leaning on the armchair*). I have not got it.

TESMAN. Have not got it? What in the world do you mean?

HEDDA. I have burnt it—every line of it.

TESMAN (*with a violent movement of terror*). Burnt! Burnt Eilert's manuscript!

HEDDA. Don't scream so. The servant might hear you.

TESMAN. Burnt! Why, good God——! No, no, no! It's impossible!

HEDDA. It is so, nevertheless.

TESMAN. Do you know what you have done, Hedda? It's unlawful appropriation of lost property. Fancy that! Just ask Judge Brack, and he'll tell you what it is.

HEDDA. I advise you not to speak of it—either to Judge Brack, or to any one else.

TESMAN. But how could you do anything so unheard-of? What put it into your head? What possessed you? Answer me that—eh?

HEDDA (*suppressing an almost imperceptible smile*). I did it for your sake, George.

TESMAN. For my sake!

HEDDA. This morning, when you told me about what he had read to you——

TESMAN. Yes, yes—what then?

HEDDA. You acknowledged that you envied him his work.

TESMAN. Oh, of course I didn't mean that literally.

HEDDA. No matter—I could not bear the idea that any one should throw you into the shade.

TESMAN (*in an outburst of mingled doubt and joy*). Hedda! Oh, is this true? But—but—I never knew you to show your love like that before. Fancy that!

HEDDA. Well, I may as well tell you that—just at this time—— (*Impatiently, breaking off.*) No, no; you can ask Aunt Julia. She will tell you, fast enough.

TESMAN. Oh, I almost think I understand you, Hedda! (*Clasps his hands together.*) Great heavens! do you really mean it! Eh?

HEDDA. Don't shout so. The servant might hear.

TESMAN (*laughing in irrepressible glee*). The servant! Why, how absurd you are, Hedda. It's only my old Berta! Why, I'll tell Berta myself.

HEDDA (*clenching her hands together in desperation*). Oh, it is killing me—it is killing me, all this!

TESMAN. What is, Hedda? Eh?

HEDDA (*coldly, controlling herself*). All this—absurdity—George.

TESMAN. Absurdity! Do you see anything absurd in my being overjoyed at the news! But after all perhaps I had better not say anything to Berta.

HEDDA. Oh—why not that too?

TESMAN. No, no, not yet! But I must certainly tell Aunt Julia. And then that you have begun to call me George too! Fancy that! Oh, Aunt Julia will be so happy—so happy.

HEDDA. When she hears that I have burnt Eilert Lövborg's manuscript —for your sake?

TESMAN. No, by-the-bye—that affair of the manuscript—of course nobody must know about that. But that you love me so much, Hedda— Aunt Julia must really share my joy in that! I wonder, now, whether this sort of thing is usual in young wives? Eh?

HEDDA. I think you had better ask Aunt Julia that question too.

TESMAN. I will indeed, some time or other. (*Looks uneasy and downcast again.*) And yet the manuscript—the manuscript! Good God! It is terrible to think what will become of poor Eilert now.

[MRS. ELVSTED, *dressed as in the first Act, with hat
and cloak, enters by the hall door.*]

MRS. ELVSTED (*greets them hurriedly, and says in evident agitation*).
Oh, dear Hedda, forgive my coming again.

HEDDA. What is the matter with you, Thea?

TESMAN. Something about Eilert Lövborg again—eh?

MRS. ELVSTED. Yes! I am dreadfully afraid some misfortune has happened to him.

HEDDA (*seizes her arm*). Ah, do you think so?

TESMAN. Why, good Lord—what makes you think that, Mrs. Elvsted?

MRS. ELVSTED. I heard them talking of him at my boarding house—
just as I came in. Oh, the most incredible rumors are afloat about
him today.

TESMAN. Yes, fancy, so I heard too! And I can bear witness that he
went straight home to bed last night. Fancy that!

HEDDA. Well, what did they say at the boarding house?

MRS. ELVSTED. Oh, I couldn't make out anything clearly. Either they
knew nothing definite, or else—— They stopped talking when they
saw me; and I did not dare to ask.

TESMAN (*moving about uneasily*). We must hope—we must hope that
you misunderstood them, Mrs. Elvsted.

MRS. ELVSTED. No, no; I am sure it was of him they were talking. And
I heard something about the hospital or——

TESMAN. The hospital?

HEDDA. No—surely that cannot be!

MRS. ELVSTED. Oh, I was in such mortal terror! I went to his lodgings
and asked for him there.

HEDDA. You could make up your mind to that, Thea!

MRS. ELVSTED. What else could I do? I really could bear the suspense
no longer.

TESMAN. But you didn't find him either—eh?

MRS. ELVSTED. No. And the people knew nothing about him. He hadn't
been home since yesterday afternoon, they said.

TESMAN. Yesterday! Fancy, how could they say that?

MRS. ELVSTED. Oh, I am sure something terrible must have happened to
him.

TESMAN. Hedda dear—how would it be if I were to go and make in-
quiries——?

HEDDA. No, no—don't you mix yourself up in this affair.

[JUDGE BRACK, *with his hat in his hand, enters by the
hall door, which* BERTA *opens, and closes behind him.*
He looks grave and bows in silence.]

TESMAN. Oh, is that you, my dear Judge? Eh?

BRACK. Yes. It was imperative I should see you this evening.

TESMAN. I can see you have heard the news about Aunt Rina.

BRACK. Yes, that among other things.

TESMAN. Isn't it sad—eh?

BRACK. Well, my dear Tesman, that depends on how you look at it.

TESMAN (*looks doubtfully at him*). Has anything else happened?

BRACK. Yes.

HEDDA (*in suspense*). Anything sad, Judge Brack?

BRACK. That, too, depends on how you look at it, Mrs. Tesman.

MRS. ELVSTED (*unable to restrain her anxiety*). Oh! it is something about Eilert Lövborg!

BRACK (*with a glance at her*). What makes you think that, Madam? Perhaps you have already heard something——?

MRS. ELVSTED (*in confusion*). No, nothing at all, but——

TESMAN. Oh, for heaven's sake, tell us!

BRACK (*shrugging his shoulders*). Well, I regret to say Eilert Lövborg has been taken to the hospital. He is lying at the point of death.

MRS. ELVSTED (*shrieks*). Oh God! Oh God——

TESMAN. To the hospital! And at the point of death.

HEDDA (*involuntarily*). So soon then——

MRS. ELVSTED (*wailing*). And we parted in anger, Hedda!

HEDDA (*whispers*). Thea—Thea—be careful!

MRS. ELVSTED (*not heeding her*). I must go to him! I must see him alive!

BRACK. It is useless, Madam. No one will be admitted.

MRS. ELVSTED. Oh, at least tell me what has happened to him? What is it?

TESMAN. You don't mean to say that he has himself—— Eh?

HEDDA. Yes, I am sure he has.

TESMAN. Hedda, how can you——?

BRACK (*keeping his eyes fixed upon her*). Unfortunately you have guessed quite correctly, Mrs. Tesman.

MRS. ELVSTED. Oh, how horrible!

TESMAN. Himself, then! Fancy that!

HEDDA. Shot himself!

BRACK. Rightly guessed again, Mrs. Tesman.

MRS. ELVSTED (*with an effort at self-control*). When did it happen, Mr. Brack?

BRACK. This afternoon—between three and four.

TESMAN. But, good Lord, where did he do it? Eh?

BRACK (*with some hesitation*). Where? Well—I suppose at his lodgings.

MRS. ELVSTED. No, that cannot be; for I was there between six and seven.

BRACK. Well, then, somewhere else. I don't know exactly. I only know that he was found——. He had shot himself—in the breast.

MRS. ELVSTED. Oh, how terrible! That he should die like that!

HEDDA (*to* BRACK). Was it in the breast?

BRACK. Yes—as I told you.

HEDDA. Not in the temple?

BRACK. In the breast, Mrs. Tesman.

HEDDA. Well, well—the breast is a good place, too.

BRACK. How do you mean, Mrs. Tesman?

HEDDA (*evasively*). Oh, nothing—nothing.

TESMAN. And the wound is dangerous, you say—eh?

BRACK. Absolutely mortal. The end has probably come by this time.

MRS. ELVSTED. Yes, yes, I feel it. The end! The end! Oh, Hedda——!

TESMAN. But tell me, how have you learnt all this?

BRACK (*curtly*). Through one of the police. A man I had some business with.

HEDDA (*in a clear voice*). At last a deed worth doing!

TESMAN (*terrified*). Good heavens, Hedda! what are you saying?

HEDDA. I say there is beauty in this.

BRACK. H'm, Mrs. Tesman——

TESMAN. Beauty! Fancy that!

MRS. ELVSTED. Oh, Hedda, how can you talk of beauty in such an act!

HEDDA. Eilert Lövborg has himself made up his account with life. He has had the courage to do—the one right thing.

MRS. ELVSTED. No, you must never think that was how it happened! It must have been in delirium that he did it.

TESMAN. In despair!

HEDDA. That he did not. I am certain of that.

MRS. ELVSTED. Yes, yes! In delirium! Just as when he tore up our manuscript.

BRACK (*starting*). The manuscript? Has he torn that up?

MRS. ELVSTED. Yes, last night.

TESMAN (*whispers softly*). Oh, Hedda, we shall never get over this.

BRACK. H'm, very extraordinary.

TESMAN (*moving about the room*). To think of Eilert going out of the world in this way! And not leaving behind him the book that would have immortalized his name——

MRS. ELVSTED. Oh, if only it could be put together again!

TESMAN. Yes, if it only could! I don't know what I would not give——

MRS. ELVSTED. Perhaps it can, Mr. Tesman.

TESMAN. What do you mean?

MRS. ELVSTED (*searches in the pocket of her dress*). Look here. I have kept all the loose notes he used to dictate from.

HEDDA (*a step forward*). Ah——!

TESMAN. You have kept them, Mrs. Elvsted! Eh?

MRS. ELVSTED. Yes, I have them here. I put them in my pocket when I left home. Here they still are——

TESMAN. Oh, do let me see them!

MRS. ELVSTED (*hands him a bundle of papers*). But they are in such disorder—all mixed up.

TESMAN. Fancy, if we could make something out of them, after all! Perhaps if we two put our heads together——

MRS. ELVSTED. Oh, yes, at least let us try——

TESMAN. We will manage it! We must! I will dedicate my life to this task.

HEDDA. You, George? Your life?

TESMAN. Yes, or rather all the time I can spare. My own collections must wait in the meantime. Hedda—you understand, eh? I owe this to Eilert's memory.

HEDDA. Perhaps.

TESMAN. And so, my dear Mrs. Elvsted, we will give our whole minds to it. There is no use in brooding over what can't be undone—eh? We must try to control our grief as much as possible, and——

MRS. ELVSTED. Yes, yes, Mr. Tesman, I will do the best I can.

TESMAN. Well then, come here. I can't rest until we have looked through the notes. Where shall we sit? Here? No, in there, in the back room. Excuse me, my dear Judge. Come with me, Mrs. Elvsted.

MRS. ELVSTED. Oh, if only it were possible!

[TESMAN *and* MRS. ELVSTED *go into the back room.*
She takes off her hat and cloak. They both sit at the
table under the hanging lamp, and are soon deep in
an eager examination of the papers. HEDDA *crosses to*
the stove and sits in the armchair. Presently BRACK
goes up to her.]

HEDDA (*in a low voice*). Oh, what a sense of freedom it gives one, this act of Eilert Lövborg's.

BRACK. Freedom, Mrs. Hedda? Well, of course, it is a release for him——

HEDDA. I mean for me. It gives me a sense of freedom to know that a deed of deliberate courage is still possible in this world—a deed of spontaneous beauty.

BRACK (*smiling*). H'm—my dear Mrs. Hedda——

HEDDA. Oh, I know what you are going to say. For you are a kind of a specialist too, like—you know!

BRACK (*looking hard at her*). Eilert Lövborg was more to you than perhaps you are willing to admit to yourself. Am I wrong?

HEDDA. I don't answer such questions. I only know Eilert Lövborg has had the courage to live his life after his own fashion. And then— the last great act, with its beauty! Ah! that he should have the will and the strength to turn away from the banquet of life—so early.

BRACK. I am sorry, Mrs. Hedda—but I fear I must dispel an amiable illusion.

HEDDA. Illusion?

BRACK. Which could not have lasted long in any case.

HEDDA. What do you mean?

BRACK. Eilert Lövborg did not shoot himself voluntarily.

HEDDA. Not voluntarily?

BRACK. No. The thing did not happen exactly as I told it.

HEDDA (*in suspense*). Have you concealed something? What is it?

BRACK. For poor Mrs. Elvsted's sake I idealized the facts a little.

HEDDA. What are the facts?

BRACK. First, that he is already dead.

HEDDA. At the hospital?

BRACK. Yes—without regaining consciousness.

HEDDA. What more have you concealed?

BRACK. This—the event did not happen at his lodgings.

HEDDA. Oh, that can make no difference.

BRACK. Perhaps it may. For I must tell you—Eilert Lövborg was found shot in—in Mademoiselle Diana's boudoir.

HEDDA (*makes a motion as if to rise, but sinks back again*). That is impossible, Judge Brack! He cannot have been there again today.

BRACK. He was there this afternoon. He went there, he said, to demand the return of something which they had taken from him. Talked wildly about a lost child——

HEDDA. Ah—so that was why——

BRACK. I thought probably he meant his manuscript; but now I hear he destroyed that himself. So I suppose it must have been his pocket-book.

HEDDA. Yes, no doubt. And there—there he was found?

BRACK. Yes, there. With a pistol in his breast-pocket, discharged. The ball had lodged in a vital part.

HEDDA. In the breast—yes.

BRACK. No—in the bowels.

HEDDA (*looks up at him with an expression of loathing*). That too! Oh what curse is it that makes everything I touch turn ludicrous and mean?

BRACK. There is one point more, Mrs. Hedda—another disagreeable feature in the affair.

HEDDA. And what is that?

BRACK. The pistol he carried——

HEDDA (*breathless*). Well? What of it?

BRACK. He must have stolen it.

HEDDA (*leaps up*). Stolen it! That is not true! He did not steal it!

BRACK. No other explanation is possible. He must have stolen it—— Hush!

> [TESMAN *and* MRS. ELVSTED *have risen from the table
> in the back room, and come into the drawing room.*]

TESMAN (*with the papers in both his hands*). Hedda dear, it is almost impossible to see under that lamp. Think of that!

HEDDA. Yes, I am thinking.

TESMAN. Would you mind our sitting at your writing table—eh?

HEDDA. If you like. (*Quickly.*) No, wait! Let me clear it first!

TESMAN. Oh, you needn't trouble, Hedda. There is plenty of room.

HEDDA. No, no; let me clear it, I say! I will take these things in and put them on the piano. There! (*She has drawn out an object, covered with sheet music, from under the bookcase, places several other pieces of music upon it, and carries the whole into the inner room, to the left.* TESMAN *lays the scraps of paper on the writing table, and moves the lamp there from the corner table.* HEDDA *returns.*)

HEDDA (*behind* MRS. ELVSTED'S *chair, gently ruffling her hair*). Well, my sweet Thea, how goes it with Eilert Lövborg's monument?

MRS. ELVSTED (*looks dispiritedly up at her*). Oh, it will be terribly hard to put in order.

TESMAN. We must manage it. I am determined. And arranging other people's papers is just the work for me.

[HEDDA *goes over to the stove, and seats herself on one of the footstools.* BRACK *stands over her, leaning on the armchair.*]

HEDDA (*whispers*). What did you say about the pistol?

BRACK (*softly*). That he must have stolen it.

HEDDA. Why stolen it?

BRACK. Because every other explanation ought to be impossible, Mrs. Hedda.

HEDDA. Indeed?

BRACK (*glances at her*). Of course Eilert Lövborg was here this morning. Was he not?

HEDDA. Yes.

BRACK. Were you alone with him?

HEDDA. Part of the time.

BRACK. Did you not leave the room whilst he was here?

HEDDA. No.

BRACK. Try to recollect. Were you not out of the room a moment?

HEDDA. Yes, perhaps just a moment—out in the hall.

BRACK. And where was your pistol case during that time?

HEDDA. I had it locked up in——

BRACK. Well, Mrs. Hedda?

HEDDA. The case stood there on the writing table.

BRACK. Have you looked since, to see whether both the pistols are there?

HEDDA. No.

BRACK. Well, you need not. I saw the pistol found in Lövborg's pocket, and I knew it at once as the one I had seen yesterday—and before, too.

HEDDA. Have you it with you?

BRACK. No; the police have it.

HEDDA. What will the police do with it?

BRACK. Search till they find the owner.

HEDDA. Do you think they will succeed?

BRACK (*bends over her and whispers*). No, Hedda Gabler—not so long as I say nothing.

HEDDA (*looks frightened at him*). And if you do not say nothing—what then?

BRACK (*shrugs his shoulders*). There is always the possibility that the pistol was stolen.

HEDDA (*firmly*). Death rather than that.

BRACK (*smiling*). People say such things—but they don't do them.

HEDDA (*without replying*). And supposing the pistol was stolen, and the owner is discovered? What then?

BRACK. Well, Hedda—then comes the scandal.

HEDDA. The scandal!

BRACK. Yes, the scandal—of which you are mortally afraid. You will, of course, be brought before the court—both you and Mademoiselle Diana. She will have to explain how the thing happened—whether it was an accidental shot or murder. Did the pistol go off as he was trying to take it out of his pocket, to threaten her with? Or did she tear the pistol out of his hand, shoot him, and push it back into his pocket? That would be quite like her; for she is an able-bodied young person, this same Mademoiselle Diana.

HEDDA. But *I* have nothing to do with all this repulsive business.

BRACK. No. But you will have to answer the question: Why did you give Eilert Lövborg the pistol? And what conclusions will people draw from the fact that you did give it to him?

HEDDA (*lets her head sink*). That is true. I did not think of that.

BRACK. Well, fortunately, there is no danger, so long as I say nothing.

HEDDA (*looks up at him*). So I am in your power, Judge Brack. You have me at your beck and call, from this time forward.

BRACK (*whispers softly*). Dearest Hedda—believe me—I shall not abuse my advantage.

HEDDA. I am in your power none the less. Subject to your will and your demands. A slave, a slave then! (*Rises impetuously.*) No, I cannot endure the thought of that! Never!

BRACK (*looks half-mockingly at her*). People generally get used to the inevitable.

HEDDA (*returns his look*). Yes, perhaps. (*She crosses to the writing table. Suppressing an involuntary smile, she imitates* TESMAN'S *intonations.*) Well? Are you getting on, George? Eh?

TESMAN. Heaven knows, dear. In any case it will be the work of months.

HEDDA (*as before*). Fancy that! (*Passes her hands softly through* MRS. ELVSTED'S *hair.*) Doesn't it seem strange to you, Thea? Here are you sitting with Tesman—just as you used to sit with Eilert Lövborg?

MRS. ELVSTED. Ah, if I could only inspire your husband in the same way.

HEDDA. Oh, that will come too—in time.

TESMAN. Yes, do you know, Hedda—I really think I begin to feel something of the sort. But won't you go and sit with Brack again?

HEDDA. Is there nothing I can do to help you two?

TESMAN. No, nothing in the world. (*Turning his head.*) I trust to you to keep Hedda company, my dear Brack.

BRACK (*with a glance at* HEDDA). With the very greatest of pleasure.

HEDDA. Thanks. But I am tired this evening. I will go in and lie down a little on the sofa.

TESMAN. Yes, do dear—eh?

[HEDDA *goes into the back room and draws the curtains. A short pause. Suddenly she is heard playing
a wild dance on the piano.*]

MRS. ELVSTED (*starts from her chair*). Oh—what is that?

TESMAN (*runs to the doorway*). Why, my dearest Hedda—don't play dance music tonight! Just think of Aunt Rina! And of Eilert too!

HEDDA (*puts her head out between the curtains*). And of Aunt Julia. And of all the rest of them. After this, I will be quiet. (*Closes the curtains again.*)

TESMAN (*at the writing table*). It's not good for her to see us at this distressing work. I'll tell you what, Mrs. Elvsted, you shall take the empty room at Aunt Julia's, and then I will come over in the eve-nings, and we can sit and work there—eh?

HEDDA (*in the inner room*). I hear what you are saying, Tesman. But how am *I* to get through the evenings out here?

TESMAN (*turning over the papers*). Oh, I daresay Judge Brack will be so kind as to look in now and then, even though I am out.

BRACK (*in the armchair, calls out gaily*). Every blessed evening, with all the pleasure in life, Mrs. Tesman! We shall get on capitally to-gether, we two!

HEDDA (*speaking loud and clear*). Yes, don't you flatter yourself we will, Judge Brack? Now that you are the one cock in the basket——

[*A shot is heard within.* TESMAN, MRS. ELVSTED, *and*
BRACK *leap to their feet.*]

TESMAN. Oh, now she is playing with those pistols again.

[*He throws back the curtains and runs in, followed
by* MRS. ELVSTED. HEDDA *lies stretched on the sofa,
lifeless. Confusion and cries.* BERTA *enters in alarm
from the right.*]

TESMAN (*shrieks to* BRACK). Shot herself! Shot herself in the temple! Fancy that!

BRACK (*half-fainting in the armchair*). Good God!—people don't do such things.

QUESTIONS

ACT I

1. Miss Tesman's character is not very complex. She is the spokesman for one human value only. What is this value, and how is it estab-

lished? Does Miss Tesman's character help us understand Hedda
Gabler when she enters?

2. "Collecting and arranging," Miss Tesman says, is Tesman's strong
point. Is this a good description of his total character? What other
details—speech, dress, typical concerns—tie in with Tesman's character as a scholar?

3. Hedda has an interesting, though not unusual, way of speaking. The
surface of what she says is always polite, but there is often another
meaning lurking below the surface. Select several examples of this
manner, discuss them, and then show how her speech reveals her
character.

4. Look at the variety of subjects Hedda expresses herself on in Act I
(e.g., old slippers, sunshine, Miss Tessman's bonnet, a new piano,
pregnancy, etc.); see if you can find a basic attitude that appears in
each statement and opinion.

5. Forget for a moment the language in Act I and imagine it as a mime,
that is, as action without words. Do Hedda's actions taken by themselves suggest the same type of character that her way of speaking and
her opinions do?

6. Thea Elvsted's situation in life—her marriage to Elvsted, etc.—parallels Hedda Gabler's in some ways and contrasts with it in others.
What does this tell us about Hedda? Do the similarities help to "uni-
versalize" Hedda's situation as a woman?

ACT II

7 You will notice that Hedda goes certain places on the stage and does
certain things only when she is in a particular state of mind. Trace her
movements to the glass doors, to the stove, to the small private room
at the rear, and her return to her pistols; try to describe the way she
feels when she goes to each.

8. Why did Hedda marry Tesman? Is this characteristic of her?

9. What kind of "triangle" do both Judge Brack and Hedda want to
arrange? Why is this particular type of human relationship the kind
that both are apt to favor?

10. Tesman and Lövborg are both historians, but they are interested in
quite different kinds of history. What do their professional interests
tell us about them? Is Lövborg contrasted with Tesman in any other
ways?

11. When Hedda speaks to Lövborg of their past relationship, she remarks that he wanted to spoil their friendship, to allow it "to develop
into something more serious." Do you find this distaste for total com-
mitment in Hedda's other actions?

12. It becomes progressively clearer that Hedda is a complex character,
that there is a conflict within her between two basic values. Describe
these two conflicting values and show how they are manifested in her

speech, her movements, and her relations with the other characters.

13. What is the meaning of Hedda's determination to wrest control of Lövborg from Mrs. Elvsted? Why does she wish to send him back to drinking?

ACT III

14. Consider the details of the scene—the dying fire, the cold dawn—with which Act III opens. How does the scene reflect the situation of the characters?

15. In the notes he wrote while working on *Hedda Gabler*, Ibsen describes Thea Elvsted as "the conventional, sentimental, hysterical Philistine." Is this a fair description of the actual character created in the play?

16. By Act III it becomes fairly obvious that Lövborg's manuscript is a crucial object in the play. We might say, in fact, that the manuscript has in a curious way come to represent "meaningful life." Discuss the significance of the subject matter of the manuscript, and then describe the relationship of each of the major characters to the manuscript. What does their relationship to the manuscript tell us about their basic values, their fundamental characters?

17. Tesman says of Lövborg that he is "utterly incapable of . . . moderation." What actions of Lövborg's, past and present, bear this statement out?

18. What is the significance of the fact that Hedda gives Lövborg a pistol at the end of Act III? (In his notes for the play Ibsen planned to have Lövborg ask for a flower at parting.)

ACT IV

19. Judge Brack has a prominent part in the play, but his character lacks the complexity of Hedda's or Lövborg's. After collecting all the information provided about Brack—his clothes, what he knows about events in the town, his position, etc.—see if you can decide what value or quality is central to his character.

20. Hedda's desperate fear of scandal emerges in Act IV. Has there been evidence of this fear earlier in the play?

21. What is the significance of the terrible manner in which Lövborg dies? Why does the manner of his death upset Hedda?

22. In his notes Ibsen clearly planned to arrange the last scene to end with Tesman and Mrs. Elvsted puzzling over Lövborg's notes and able to make nothing of them because they both lack imagination. The play, however, ends quite differently. How does the present ending change the meaning?

23. Hedda's final act is suicide, which at first seems surprising, but on reflection seems peculiarly appropriate: the action finally expresses fully and unambiguously Hedda's nature. Go back through the play and see if you can relate any of Hedda's earlier actions and statements to her final self-defining act.

Character in

Expressionistic Drama

"People don't do such things" Judge Brack exclaims after Hedda Gabler commits suicide. But people, of course, *do* do such things, and there is nothing in *Hedda Gabler* that could not occur in the real world. Ibsen's play is a masterpiece of the dramatic mode known as *realism*. *Realism* and *realistic* are tricky terms, which are apt to shift meaning from age to age, or even from user to user, but for working purposes we may define *dramatic realism* as the maintenance of an appearance of life as it is ordinarily experienced. Realism is, of course, an illusion, because every dramatist, whether or not he preserves the appearance of reality, inevitably selects and shapes his material in order to construct not a photograph of the real world but a revealing image of it. Art and life are not, finally, the same thing.

In our earlier discussion of the ways in which a dramatist constructs a character, we considered only realistic techniques. In life as well as in a play, character is expressed indirectly by clothing, movement, thought, and style—though seldom as obviously, as precisely, as relentlessly, in short, as "dramatically," as in the theater. In life perhaps only the genius and the insane man achieve that concentration of being and that economy of gesture which we find in dramatic characters.

Many playwrights have wanted to present the deeper layers of characters more directly than realistic dramatic techniques will allow. To do this they have developed over time a number of devices for shifting the dramatic focus inward in order to portray motives as they take shape within the mind itself. Probably the simplest and most realistic device of this kind is the use of a *confidant,* a type of character whose sole function is to listen to the hero's frank explanation of his inmost thoughts. In the *soliloquy* there no longer is a confi-

dant present, and the hero, alone on stage, speaks as if he were thinking aloud. Another simple form of spoken thought is the *aside,* a few
words delivered by a character when several actors are present on the
stage but by convention heard only by the audience.

Masks have also been used as a way of presenting man's deepest
thoughts and feelings. They were used in the Greek and Roman
theaters where, in addition to serving several practical functions, they
probably revealed the tragic or comic sense of life, much as the de-
monic mask of the witch doctor expresses the nature of the forces
with which he is working. In our own century the American playwright Eugene O'Neill used masks in a number of plays in an attempt
to dramatize "those profound hidden conflicts of the mind which the
probings of psychology continue to disclose to us." The use of the
mask not only permitted O'Neill to present basic complexities of character, but it also allowed him to dramatize the fact that most men
make use of a public character, a mask that they show to the world,
which covers their inner reality.

Another device—which has been extremely popular in recent years
—for staging the relatively inaccessible parts of the mind is the
flashback. Its function is to make visible the memories stored in man's
mind, which are so crucial a part of his character. The flashback has
been used most frequently in the movies, a form well suited to handle it:
the camera comes in closer and closer on a face as the face begins
to dissolve into the remembered scene. The modern theater too has
made good use of the flashback, despite the fact that it is technically
somewhat more difficult to work on the stage than in the film. In
Arthur Miller's *Death of a Salesman,* Willy Loman's intense preoccupation with his past and his continuing search among his memories
for the point at which life began to go wrong is presented in a series
of scenes in which the lights dim as his mind begins to wander from
the present and come up again on a re-enactment of some event
twenty years past.

While such dramatic devices for revealing character as asides, flash-
backs, and masks are unrealistic—the general term for them is *expressionistic*—playwrights have frequently used them in plays that
otherwise maintain the pretense of showing life as we ordinarily experience it. Some of these devices are by now so commonplace that
they have become theatrical *conventions,* and audiences accept them
as realistic. When Hamlet steps out on stage and delivers a long
soliloquy in blank verse in a play that is otherwise quite realistic, no
one considers this any less lifelike than his speeches directed to other

characters. Realistic and expressionistic devices have usually been mixed, but some playwrights have been unwilling to accept this compromise. Instead they have wanted to open up the human mind and show directly what goes on inside the head. There are a number of terms for this kind of dramatic writing—*allegory, surrealism, morality play, expressionism,* etc.—but all refer to a type of play in which the pretense of realism has been largely or altogether abandoned in order to stage the mind.

In an allegorical play the conflicting forces at work within each man become the separate characters of the drama. The attributes of each character, such as clothing, movement, and speech, reveal the nature of that particular component of the human psyche; each character has a motive that presses "him" toward some goal. The arguments and struggles between these "characters" represent man's mental conflicts. *Everyman,* the best known English allegorical play, dramatizes the thoughts of man at the moment death seizes him. He at first refuses to believe what Death—a character in the play—tells him, but as the dreadful truth is borne home, he begins to cast about for someone to help him, to accompany him on the long journey he must now undertake. Each of the values he has based his life upon—friendship, material wealth, beauty, etc.—is *personified,* made into a character, and Everyman tests each in turn, only to be disappointed when each refuses to go into the grave with him. Finally he discovers that only Good Deeds will accompany him, and Good Deeds is terribly weak because Everyman, like most men, has never taken very good care of "him." Some of the characters of the allegory, such as Fellowship and Goods, may be thought of as having existence outside of Everyman's mind, but what is dramatized is his sense of their value to him. Probably, allegorical plays of this kind can only be written at times when there is some accepted theory about the constituent parts of the mind and the way it works. No allegorical play dramatizing Freudian psychology has yet been written, but it is possible to imagine a modern *Everyman* in which Ego, by pointing out practical reasons for a particular course of action, tries to mediate between a raging, selfish Id and a stern, puritanical Superego, while Pleasure Principle is locked in a grim combat with Death Wish.

In the modern *expressionistic* play, authors have not been certain enough of their theory of the mind to construct a complete dramatis personae out of mental characteristics. Instead, expressionistic dramatists have offered bizarre, unrealistic images of existence, not as it appears objectively to the senses and not as we ordinarily agree that it is, but as—so they maintain—we actually experience it subjectively. For example, in one scene of Georg Kaiser's *From Morn to Midnight* life is presented as a seven-day bicycle race in which a few active riders drive themselves to exhaustion to win fame and cash prizes, while the mass of people look on hoping that there will be a serious accident. This extended image is complicated in all of its details, but essentially it dramatizes in the round-and-round of the race the repetitive sameness of life and the sense of futility involved in going faster and faster to get to the same place, which is no place. What Kaiser has created is a dramatic equivalent for a feeling about life, living as it is sensed, not seen.

In *Waiting for Godot*, a play by Samuel Beckett that belongs to the special category of expressionism known as the *absurd*, two characters spend the entire play waiting on a stage empty of all objects but a stunted tree for the arrival of someone who never comes. In fact, they are not sure of the name of the person they expect, they don't know whether he plans to come, and they are not even certain that he exists. Whatever else *Godot* may mean, clearly it gives concrete form to that inner sense of life in which the material world is unreal, and living is only an anxious, uncertain wait for someone or something to save us from the bleakness of a meaningless existence.

Eugene Ionesco's *The Chairs* dramatizes man's frustrated desire to communicate with others. An old man and his wife, living alone on an island, prepare a large party and hire an orator to tell the guests what the old man has learned about life. The couple believes that a number of guests arrive, and they speak to them and provide a chair for each. But no guests actually appear, and the stage continues to fill with empty chairs. Later the orator really does arrive, but he proves to be a deaf mute. The old man and his wife commit suicide shortly after this, and the orator then tries to communicate his message by writing on a blackboard, but all he produces is a meaningless scribble.

Waiting for Godot and *The Chairs* are extreme examples of expressionism, but we should not think of an expressionistic play like *The Chairs* as fundamentally different from a realistic play like *Hedda Gabler* or a semi-realistic play like *Hamlet*. Each type of play presents characters who are images of man, and in each these characters are moved by one or two basic motives, which are expressed by their bodies, their clothes, their movements, and their words. In fact, while plays like *Waiting for Godot* and *The Chairs* may seem at first glance much more difficult than a play like *Hedda Gabler*, they are really much simpler and easier to understand. It takes a good deal of very careful reading to see that Hedda is torn between desire for and fear of freedom, but it requires very little effort to see that the motive of the characters in *Waiting for Godot* is to wait for salvation, and the motive of the old man in *The Chairs* is to communicate. In expressionistic drama everything is obvious once we adjust to the idiom, but in realistic drama gesture and language are muted so that we are in danger of missing the meaning. No matter how much the characters of an expressionistic play may seem like a fantastic dream or how much the characters of a realistic play may seem like real people, in both cases they are the playwright's images, definitions, of man.

In its presentation of character, however, expressionism in its various extreme forms arrives at a paradoxical situation. As an artistic form, expressionism is man-oriented, presenting the self and the world in the way men, with all their special values and human concerns, see and feel them. This emphasis on subjectivity should lead to a more complete and humane vision of man, but in practice its tendency has been to dehumanize its characters by reducing their individuality. Character in the more extreme forms of expressionism becomes universal rather than particular, and men appear as Everyman, as a robot in *R.U.R.*, as Zapo and Zépo in *Picnic on the Battlefield*, as a herd of galloping rhinoceros in *The Rhinoceros*, or, in general, as personifications of some single, abstracted human quality such as love, the desire to communicate, or the feeling of endless waiting.

EVERYMAN

The Moral Play of Everyman, to give the work its full title, is preserved in only two printed editions from the early sixteenth century. It was written, however, at some time during the fifteenth century, probably by a monk or clerk. Versions of Everyman exist in Dutch and German, as well as English, and in the past scholars have argued a good deal about the priority and relative literary merits of the different versions. Nowadays they are less concerned with comparisons and dates than they are with the fact that Everyman is the play of medieval Christendom. It reveals that society's understanding of life, its assumptions about the world, and its major questions in a manner comparable to the way in which Oedipus Rex, say, reveals the Greek mind and Hamlet expresses the mind of Renaissance England. Before beginning to read Everyman, it will be helpful to look briefly at some of the more obvious facts that the play assumes about the medieval Christian view of man and his world.

Everyman dramatizes the major crisis in the life of man, the moment of his death—when the world that had seemed so substantial slips away to the reality of God's judgment, to life or damnation eternal. True life, then, begins with death, and the crucial event of living is dying. Everyman has not committed any grave sins during his life, but neither has he done very much good; therefore, if justice were strictly rendered by God, Everyman would not fare very well. But God is merciful and has provided for such ordinary people who are neither saints nor devils. Besides a minimum of good works, repentance and humility before God are all that are necessary for salvation. Man is aided in achieving this condition of mind by the Church and its sacraments.

The most revealing insight into the medieval world view comes, however, not from the direct statements of doctrine in Everyman, but from the form of the play. While Oedipus Rex is set in the square of a Greek city, Thebes, and *Hamlet* is set in the castle of the King of Denmark, Elsinore, in *Everyman* the setting becomes *the mind of a man*. Reality, the play says, is not the physical world or the political and social scene in which man lives out his mortal life; it is, instead, his interior consciousness of himself as a soul created by God, owing certain duties to Him, and returning to Him for a final accounting. All else in the world is unreal and fleeting and therefore need not be represented on the stage. Strictly speaking, none of the personifications that make up the cast of characters in *Everyman* has any life of his own; their words and actions merely reflect the realization of Everyman as, dying, he turns his mind to each of the things that have meant so much to him and finds that each lacks essential realness, the ability to pass over from this false world to the real one beyond. This is not to say, however, that medieval man did not love the world of the here and now. Quite the reverse. Everyman endures his greatest agony in being torn away from the familiar and intensely valued world known to his senses.

Everyman is a fine companion piece for *Hedda Gabler* because between them they mark the full range of ways to present character in drama. In both plays the dramatists offer studies of the human mind and its operations. The anonymous author of *Everyman* presents this mind directly as the only reality. Ibsen, believing like most modern men that the workings of the mind are mysterious and that the material world in which the mind exists is very real indeed, presents that mind struggling to express itself in the present, through the muddle of daily life. Because Ibsen renders so perfectly the solid world of bodies and furniture, we become aware not only of Hedda Gabler's complex mind, but, perhaps even more powerfully, of her desperate attempts to find some satisfactory way of expressing her mind using the forms of the solid world. In *Hedda Gabler* the spirit of man is entangled, inextricably, with its immediate surroundings, whereas in *Everyman* mind, or consciousness, escapes the material world.

CHARACTERS

MESSENGER

GOD: *Adonai*

DEATH

EVERYMAN

FELLOWSHIP

COUSIN

KINDRED

GOODS

GOOD DEEDS

KNOWLEDGE

CONFESSION

BEAUTY

STRENGTH

DISCRETION

FIVE WITS

ANGEL

DOCTOR

EVERYMAN

Here beginneth a treatise how the High Father of Heaven sendeth Death to summon every creature to come and give account of their lives in this world, and is in manner of a moral play.

MESSENGER. I pray you all give your audience,
    And hear this matter with reverence,
    By figure° a moral play—
    The *Summoning of Everyman* called it is,
    That of our lives and ending shows   5
    How transitory we be all day.°
    This matter is wondrous precious,
    But the intent of it is more gracious,
    And sweet to bear away.
    The story saith: Man, in the beginning,   10
    Look well, and take good heed to the ending,
    Be you never so gay!
    Ye think sin in the beginning full sweet,
    Which in the end causeth the soul to weep,
    When the body lieth in clay.   15
    Here shall you see how Fellowship and Jollity,
    Both Strength, Pleasure, and Beauty,
    Will fade from thee as flower in May.
    For ye shall hear how our Heaven King
    Calleth Everyman to a general reckoning.   20

3. In the form of.   **6.** Always.

Give audience, and hear what he doth say.   *[Exit.]*
          [GOD *speaketh*.]

GOD. I perceive, here in my majesty,
    How that all creatures be to me unkind,°
    Living without dread in worldly prosperity.
    Of ghostly° sight the people be so blind,   25
    Drowned in sin, they know me not for their God.
    In worldly riches is all their mind,
    They fear not my rightwiseness, the sharp rod;
    My love that I showed when I for them died
    They forget clean, and shedding of my blood red;   30
    I hanged between two, it cannot be denied;
    To get them life I suffered to be dead;
    I healed their feet, with thorns hurt was my head.
    I could do no more than I did, truly;
    And now I see the people do clean forsake me.   35
    They use the seven deadly sins damnable,
    As pride, covetise, wrath, and lechery,
    Now in the world be made commendable;
    And thus they leave of angels the heavenly company.
    Every man liveth so after his own pleasure,   40
    And yet of their life they be nothing sure.
    I see the more that I them forbear
    The worse they be from year to year;
    All that liveth appaireth° fast.
    Therefore I will, in all the haste,   45
    Have a reckoning of every man's person;
    For, and I leave the people thus alone
    In their life and wicked tempests,
    Verily they will become much worse than beasts;
    For now one would by envy another up eat;   50
    Charity they all do clean forget.
    I hoped well that every man
    In my glory should make his mansion,
    And thereto I had them all elect;
    But now I see, like traitors deject,   55
    They thank me not for the pleasure that I to them meant,
    Nor yet for their being that I them have lent.
    I proffered the people great multitude of mercy,
    And few there be that asketh it heartily;
    They be so cumbered with worldly riches,   60
    That needs on them I must do justice,

---

23. Unnatural.   **25.** Spiritual.   **44.** Degenerates.

On every man living without fear.
Where art thou, Death, thou mighty messenger?
　　　　　　　[*Enter* DEATH.]
DEATH. Almighty God, I am here at your will,
　　　Your commandment to fulfil.　　　　　　　　　　65
GOD. Go thou to Everyman,
　　　And show him, in my name,
　　　A pilgrimage he must on him take,
　　　Which he in no wise° may escape;
　　　And that he bring with him a sure reckoning　　70
　　　Without delay or any tarrying. [*Exit* GOD.]
DEATH. Lord, I will in the world go run over all,
　　　And cruelly out search both great and small.
　　　Every man will I beset that liveth beastly
　　　Out of God's laws, and dreadeth not folly.　　　75
　　　He that loveth riches I will strike with my dart,
　　　His sight to blind, and from heaven to depart,°
　　　Except that alms° be his good friend,
　　　In hell for to dwell, world without end.　　[*Enter* EVERYMAN.]
　　　Lo, yonder I see Everyman walking;　　　　　　80
　　　Full little he thinketh on my coming.
　　　His mind is on fleshly lusts and his treasure,
　　　And great pain it shall cause him to endure
　　　Before the Lord, Heaven King.
　　　Everyman, stand still! Whither art thou going　85
　　　Thus gaily? Hast thou thy Maker forgot?
EVERYMAN. Why askest thou?
　　　Wouldst thou wete?°
DEATH. Yea, sir, I will show you:
　　　In great haste I am sent to thee　　　　　　　　90
　　　From God out of his Majesty.
EVERYMAN. What, sent to me?
DEATH. Yea, certainly.
　　　Though thou have forgot him here,
　　　He thinketh on thee in the heavenly sphere,　　95
　　　As, ere we depart, thou shalt know.
EVERYMAN. What desireth God of me?
DEATH. That shall I show thee:
　　　A reckoning he will needs have
　　　Without any longer respite.　　　　　　　　　　100
EVERYMAN. To give a reckoning, longer leisure I crave.
　　　This blind matter troubleth my wit.°

69. Manner, way. 77. Separate. 78. Almsgiving, charity. 88. Know.
102. "This dark problem confuses me."

DEATH. On thee thou must take a long journey;
    Therefore thy book of count° with thee thou bring;
    For turn again° thou can not by no way.   105
    And look thou be sure of thy reckoning,
    For before God thou shalt answer and show
    Thy many bad deeds, and good but a few,
    How thou hast spent thy life, and in what wise,
    Before the Chief Lord of paradise.   110
    Have ado that we were in that way,°
    For, wete thou well, thou shalt make none attorney.°
EVERYMAN. Full unready I am such reckoning to give.
    I know thee not. What messenger art thou?
DEATH. I am Death, that no man dreadeth.°   115
    For every man I 'rest,° and no man spareth;
    For it is God's commandment
    That all to me should be obedient.
EVERYMAN. O Death! thou comest when I had thee least in mind!
    In thy power it lieth me to save.   120
    Yet of my goods will I give thee, if thou will be kind;
    Yea, a thousand pound shalt thou have,
    If thou defer this matter till another day.
DEATH. Everyman, it may not be, by no way!
    I set not by° gold, silver, nor riches,   125
    Nor by pope, emperor, king, duke, nor princes.
    For, and I would receive gifts great,
    All the world I might get;
    But my custom is clean contrary.
    I give thee no respite. Come hence, and not tarry.   130
EVERYMAN. Alas! shall I have no longer respite?
    I may say Death giveth no warning.
    To think on thee, it maketh my heart sick,
    For all unready is my book of reckoning.
    But twelve year and I might have abiding,°   135
    My counting-book I would make so clear,
    That my reckoning I should not need to fear.
    Wherefore, Death, I pray thee, for God's mercy,
    Spare me till I be provided of remedy.°
DEATH. Thee availeth not to cry, weep, and pray;   140
    But haste thee lightly that thou were gone that journey,
    And prove thy friends if thou can.
    For wete thou well the tide abideth no man;

104. Accounts. 105. Return. 111. "Get ready to go." 112. Shall have
no lawyer. 115. "That fears no man." 116. Arrest. 125. Care not for.
135. "If I could remain for only twelve years." 139. With help.

           And in the world each living creature
           For Adam's sin must die of nature.   145
EVERYMAN. Death, if I should this pilgrimage take,
           And my reckoning surely make,
           Show me, for saint charity,
           Should I not come again shortly?
DEATH. No, Everyman; and thou be once there,   150
           Thou mayst never more come here,
           Trust me verily.
EVERYMAN. O gracious God, in the high seat celestial,
           Have mercy on me in this most need!
           Shall I have no company from this vale terrestrial   155
           Of mine acquaintance that way me to lead?
DEATH. Yea, if any be so hardy,
           That would go with thee and bear thee company.
           Hie thee that thou were gone° to God's magnificence,
           Thy reckoning to give before his presence.   160
           What! weenest° thou thy life is given thee,
           And thy worldly goods also?
EVERYMAN. I had weened so, verily.
DEATH. Nay, nay; it was but lent thee;
           For, as soon as thou art gone,   165
           Another a while shall have it, and then go therefrom
           Even as thou hast done.
           Everyman, thou art mad! Thou hast thy wits five,
           And here on earth will not amend thy life;
           For suddenly I do come.   170
EVERYMAN. O wretched caitiff! whither shall I flee,
           That I might 'scape endless sorrow?
           Now, gentle Death, spare me till tomorrow,
           That I may amend me
           With good advisement.°   175
DEATH. Nay, thereto I will not consent,
           Nor no man will I respite,
           But to the heart suddenly I shall smite
           Without any advisement.
           And now out of thy sight I will me hie;   180
           See thou make thee ready shortly,
           For thou mayst say this is the day
           That no man living may 'scape away.   [*Exit* DEATH.]
EVERYMAN. Alas! I may well weep with sighs deep.
           Now have I no manner of company   185
           To help me in my journey and me to keep;

159. "Hurry and go."   **161.** Judgest.   **175.** Warning.

And also my writing° is full unready.
How shall I do now for to excuse me?
I would to God I had never been get!°
To my soul a full great profit it had be,   190
For now I fear pains huge and great.
The time passeth; Lord, help, that all wrought.
For though I mourn it availeth naught.
The day passeth, and is almost a-go;
I wot° not well what for to do.   195
To whom were I best my complaint° to make?
What if I to Fellowship thereof spake,
And showed him of this sudden chance?
For in him is all mine affiance,°
We have in the world so many a day   200
Been good friends in sport and play.
I see him yonder, certainly;
I trust that he will bear me company;
Therefore to him will I speak to ease my sorrow.
Well met, good Fellowship, and good morrow!   205

[FELLOWSHIP *speaketh*.]

FELLOWSHIP. Everyman, good morrow, by this day!
  Sir, why lookest thou so piteously?
  If any thing be amiss, I pray thee me say,
  That I may help to remedy.
EVERYMAN. Yea, good Fellowship, yea,   210
  I am in great jeopardy.
FELLOWSHIP. My true friend, show to me your mind.
  I will not forsake thee to my life's end
  In the way of good company.
EVERYMAN. That was well spoken, and lovingly.   215
FELLOWSHIP. Sir, I must needs know your heaviness;
  I have pity to see you in any distress;
  If any have you wronged, ye shall revenged be,
  Though I on the ground be slain for thee,
  Though that I know before that I should die.   220
EVERYMAN. Verily, Fellowship, gramercy.
FELLOWSHIP. Tush! by thy thanks I set not a straw!
  Show me your grief, and say no more.
EVERYMAN. If I my heart should to you break,°
  And then you to° turn your mind from me,   225
  And would not me comfort when you hear me speak,
  Then should I ten times sorrier be.

187. Accounts. 189. Begotten. 195. Know. 196. Lament. 199. Trust
224. Reveal. 225. Were to.

FELLOWSHIP. Sir, I say as I will do, indeed.
EVERYMAN. Then be you a good friend at need;
    I have found you true here before.   230
FELLOWSHIP. And so ye shall evermore;
    For, in faith, and° thou go to hell,
    I will not forsake thee by the way!
EVERYMAN. Ye speak like a good friend. I believe you well;
    I shall deserve° it, and I may.°   235
FELLOWSHIP. I speak of no deserving, by this day!
    For he that will say and nothing do
    Is not worthy with good company to go;
    Therefore show me the grief of your mind,
    As to your friend most loving and kind.   240
EVERYMAN. I shall show you how it is:
    Commanded I am to go a journey,
    A long way, hard and dangerous,
    And give a strait count° without delay
    Before the high judge, Adonai.   245
    Wherefore, I pray you, bear me company,
    As ye have promised, in this journey.
FELLOWSHIP. That is matter indeed! Promise is duty;
    But, and I should take such a voyage on me,
    I know it well, it should be to my pain.   250
    Also it maketh me afeared, certain.
    But let us take counsel here as well as we can,
    For your words would fright a strong man.
EVERYMAN. Why, ye said if I had need,
    Ye would me never forsake, quick nor dead,   255
    Though it were to hell, truly.
FELLOWSHIP. So I said, certainly,
    But such pleasures be set aside, the sooth to say.°
    And also, if we took such a journey,
    When should we come again?   260
EVERYMAN. Nay, never again till the day of doom.
FELLOWSHIP. In faith, then will not I come there!
    Who hath you these tidings brought?
EVERYMAN. Indeed, Death was with me here.
FELLOWSHIP. Now, by God that all hath bought,°   265
    If Death were the messenger,
    For no man that is living today
    I will not go that loath journey—
    Not for the father that begat me!

---

232. If. **235.** Repay. If possible. **244.** Strict accounting. **258.** "Such pleasantries are, truly, only a way of speaking." **265.** Redeemed.

EVERYMAN. Ye promised otherwise, pardie.°   270
FELLOWSHIP. I wot well I said so, truly;
    And yet if thou wilt eat, and drink, and make good cheer,
    Or haunt to women the lusty company,°
    I would not forsake you while the day is clear,
    Trust me verily!   275
EVERYMAN. Yea, thereto ye would be ready.
    To go to mirth, solace, and play,
    Your mind will sooner apply
    Than to bear me company in my long journey.
FELLOWSHIP. Now, in good faith, I will not that way.   280
    But and thou wilt murder, or any man kill,
    In that I will help thee with a good will!
EVERYMAN. O, that is a simple advice indeed!
    Gentle fellow, help me in my necessity;
    We have loved long, and now I need,   285
    And now, gentle Fellowship, remember me!
FELLOWSHIP. Whether ye have loved me or no,
    By Saint John, I will not with thee go.
EVERYMAN. Yet, I pray thee, take° the labor, and do so much for
    me
    To bring me forward,° for saint charity,   290
    And comfort me till I come without the town.
FELLOWSHIP. Nay, and thou would give me a new gown,
    I will not a foot with thee go;
    But, and thou had tarried, I would not have left thee so.
    And as now God speed thee in thy journey,   295
    For from thee I will depart as fast as I may.
EVERYMAN. Whither away, Fellowship? Will you forsake me?
FELLOWSHIP. Yea, by my fay, to God I betake° thee.
EVERYMAN. Farewell, good Fellowship! For thee my heart is sore;
    Adieu for ever! I shall see thee no more.   300
FELLOWSHIP. In faith, Everyman, farewell now at the end!
    For° you I will remember that parting is mourning.
                              [*Exit* FELLOWSHIP.]
EVERYMAN. Alack! shall we thus depart indeed
    (Ah, Lady, help!) without any more comfort?
    Lo, Fellowship forsaketh me in my most need.   305
    For help in this world whither shall I resort?
    Fellowship here before with me would merry make,
    And now little sorrow for me doth he take.
    It is said, "In prosperity men friends may find,

270. *Par dieu,* by God.   **273.** Enjoy the companionship of joyful women.
289. Undertake.   **290.** Accompany me.   **298.** Commit.   **302.** Because of.

Which in adversity be full unkind."   310
Now whither for succor shall I flee,
Sith° that Fellowship hath forsaken me?
To my kinsmen I will,° truly,
Praying them to help me in my necessity;
I believe that they will do so,   315
For "kind will creep where it may not go." °
I will go say,° for yonder I see them go.
Where be ye now, my friends and kinsmen?

              [*Enter* KINDRED *and* COUSIN.]

KINDRED. Here be we now, at your commandment.
  Cousin,° I pray you show us your intent   320
  In any wise, and do not spare.
COUSIN. Yea, Everyman, and to us declare
  If ye be disposed to go any whither,
  For, wete you well, we will live and die together.
KINDRED. In wealth and woe we will with you hold,   325
  For over his kin a man may be bold.
EVERYMAN. Gramercy, my friends and kinsmen kind.
  Now shall I show you the grief of my mind.
  I was commanded by a messenger
  That is a high king's chief officer;   330
  He bade me go a pilgrimage, to my pain,
  And I know well I shall never come again;
  Also I must give a reckoning straight,°
  For I have a great enemy that hath me in wait,°
  Which intendeth me for to hinder.°   335
KINDRED. What account is that which ye must render?
  That would I know.
EVERYMAN. Of all my works I must show
  How I have lived, and my days spent;
  Also of ill deeds that I have used°   340
  In my time, sith life was me lent;
  And of all virtues that I have refused.
  Therefore I pray you go thither with me,
  To help to make mine account, for saint charity.
COUSIN. What, to go thither? Is that the matter?   345
  Nay, Everyman, I had liefer fast bread and water
  All this five year and more.
EVERYMAN. Alas, that ever I was bore!

312. Since. **313.** Will go. **316.** "Natural relationship will creep where
it may not walk," i.e. "blood is thicker than water." **317.** Test. **320.** A
term used at this time for any relative, except brother or sister. **333.** Both
"severe" and "immediately." **334.** In waiting, i.e. "controls me." **335.**
Harm. **340.** Practiced. **341.** Since.

For now shall I never be merry
If that you forsake me.   350
KINDRED. Ah, sir, what! Ye be a merry man!
Take good heart to you, and make no moan.
But one thing I warn you, by Saint Anne,
As for me, ye shall go alone.
EVERYMAN. My Cousin, will you not with me go?   355
COUSIN. No, by our Lady! I have the cramp in my toe.
Trust not to me, for, so God me speed,°
I will deceive you in your most need.
KINDRED. It availeth not us to tice.°
Ye shall have my maid with all my heart;   360
She loveth to go to feasts, there to be nice,°
And to dance, and abroad to start;°
I will give her leave to help you in that journey,
If that you and she may agree.
EVERYMAN. Now show me the very effect of your mind.   365
Will you go with me, or abide behind?
KINDRED. Abide behind? Yea, that will I, and I may!
Therefore, farewell till another day.   [Exit KINDRED.]
EVERYMAN. How should I be merry or glad?
For fair promises men to me make,   370
But when I have most need, they me forsake.
I am deceived; that maketh me sad.
COUSIN. Cousin Everyman, farewell now,
For verily I will not go with you;
Also of mine own life an unready reckoning   375
I have to account; therefore I make tarrying.°
Now, God keep thee, for now I go.   [Exit COUSIN.]
EVERYMAN. Ah, Jesus! is all come hereto?
Lo, fair words maketh fools fain;°
They promise and nothing will do, certain.   380
My kinsmen promised me faithfully
For to abide with me steadfastly,
And now fast away do they flee.
Even so Fellowship promised me.
What friend were best me of to provide?   385
I lose my time here longer to abide.
Yet in my mind a thing there is:
All my life I have loved riches;
If that my good now help me might,
He would make my heart full light.   390

357. Prosper. 359. Entice. 361. Wanton. 362. Travel about. 376. I
tarry. 379. Joyful.

I will speak to him in this distress.
Where art thou, my Goods and riches?
GOODS [*To one side.*] Who calleth me? Everyman? What, hast
    thou haste?
I lie here in corners, trussed and piled so high,
And in chests I am locked so fast,   395
Also sacked in bags—thou mayest see with thine eye—
I cannot stir; in packs low I lie.
What would ye have? Lightly° me say.
EVERYMAN. Come hither, Goods, in all the haste thou may.
For of counsel I must desire thee.   400
                       [*Enter* GOODS.]
GOODS. Sir, and ye in the world have sorrow or adversity,
That can I help you to remedy shortly.
EVERYMAN. It is another disease that grieveth me;
In this world it is not, I tell thee so.
I am sent for another way to go,   405
To give a strict count general
Before the highest Jupiter of all;
And all my life I have had joy and pleasure in thee,
Therefore I pray thee go with me,
For, peradventure, thou mayst before God Almighty   410
My reckoning help to clean and purify;
For it is said ever among,
That "money maketh all right that is wrong."
GOODS. Nay, Everyman; I sing another song,
I follow no man in such voyages;   415
For, and I went with thee,
Thou shouldst fare much the worse for me;
For because on me thou did set thy mind,
Thy reckoning I have made blotted and blind,°
That thine account thou cannot make truly;   420
And that hast thou for the love of me.
EVERYMAN. That would grieve me full sore,
When I should come to that fearful answer.
Up, let us go thither together.
GOODS. Nay, not so! I am too brittle, I may not endure;   425
I will follow no man one foot, be ye sure.
EVERYMAN. Alas! I have thee loved, and had great pleasure
All my life-days on goods and treasure.
GOODS. That is to thy damnation, without lesing!°
For my love is contrary to the love everlasting.   430
But if thou had me loved moderately during,°

398. Quickly.   419. Obscure.   429. Lying.   431. While living.

As to the poor to give part of me,
Then shouldst thou not in this dolor be,
Nor in this great sorrow and care.
EVERYMAN. Lo, now was I deceived ere I was ware,°   435
And all I may wyte my spending of time.°
GOODS. What, weenest thou that I am thine?
EVERYMAN. I had weened so.
GOODS. Nay, Everyman, I say no;
As for a while I was lent thee,   440
A season thou hast had me in prosperity.
My condition is man's soul to kill;
If I save one, a thousand I do spill;°
Weenest thou that I will follow thee
From this world? Nay, verily.   445
EVERYMAN. I had weened otherwise.
GOODS. Therefore to thy soul Goods is a thief;
For when thou art dead, this is my guise,°
Another to deceive in the same wise
As I have done thee, and all to his soul's reprief.°   450
EVERYMAN. O false Goods, curséd may thou be!
Thou traitor to God, that hast deceived me
And caught me in thy snare.
GOODS. Marry! thou brought thyself in care,
Whereof I am right glad.   455
I must needs laugh, I cannot be sad.
EVERYMAN. Ah, Goods, thou hast had long my heartly love;
I gave thee that which should be the Lord's above.
But wilt thou not go with me indeed?
I pray thee truth to say.   460
GOODS. No, so God me speed!
Therefore farewell, and have good day.   [*Exit* GOODS.]
EVERYMAN. O, to whom shall I make my moan
For to go with me in that heavy journey?
First Fellowship said he would with me gone;   465
His words were very pleasant and gay,
But afterward he left me alone.
Then spake I to my kinsmen, all in despair,
And also they gave me words fair,
They lacked no fair speaking,   470
But all forsook me in the ending.
Then went I to my Goods, that I loved best,
In hope to have comfort, but there had I least;

435. Aware.   436. "And I may blame all on the way I spent my time."
443. Kill, destroy.   448. Practice.   450. Reproof.

For my Goods sharply did me tell
That he bringeth many into hell.   475
Then of myself I was ashamed,
And so I am worthy to be blamed;
Thus may I well myself hate.
Of whom shall I now counsel take?
I think that I shall never speed°   480
Till that I go to my Good Deeds.
But alas! she is so weak
That she can neither go° nor speak.
Yet will I venture° on her now.
My Good Deeds, where be you?   485

        [GOOD DEEDS *speaks from below*.]

GOOD DEEDS. Here I lie, cold in the ground.
    Thy sins hath me sore bound,
    That I cannot stir.
EVERYMAN. O Good Deeds, I stand in fear!
    I must you pray of counsel,   490
    For help now should come right well.°
GOOD DEEDS. Everyman, I have understanding
    That ye be summoned account to make
    Before Messias, of Jerusalem King;
    And you do by me,° that journey with you will I take.   495
EVERYMAN. Therefore I come to you my moan to make;
    I pray you that ye will go with me.
GOOD DEEDS. I would full fain, but I cannot stand, verily.
EVERYMAN. Why, is there anything on you fall?
GOOD DEEDS. Yea, sir, I may thank you of all;°   500
    If ye had perfectly cheered° me,
    Your book of count full ready had be.
    Look, the books of your works and deeds eke.°
    Behold how they lie under the feet,
    To your soul's heaviness.   505
EVERYMAN. Our Lord Jesus help me!
    For one letter here I can not see.
GOOD DEEDS. There is a blind reckoning in time of distress!°
EVERYMAN. Good Deeds, I pray you, help me in this need,
    Or else I am for ever damned indeed.   510
    Therefore help me to make my reckoning
    Before the Redeemer of all thing,
    That King is, and was, and ever shall.

480. Prosper. **483.** Walk. **484.** Chance. **491.** Be welcome. **495.** "If
you follow my advice." **500.** For everything. **501.** Properly cared for.
503. Also. **508.** I.e., the sinner discovers that his account of good works is
hard to read when he is in trouble.

GOOD DEEDS. Everyman, I am sorry of your fall,
  And fain would I help you, and I were able.   515
EVERYMAN. Good Deeds, your counsel I pray you give me.
GOOD DEEDS. That shall I do verily;
  Though that on my feet I may not go,°
  I have a sister that shall with you also,
  Called Knowledge,° which shall with you abide,   520
  To help you to make that dreadful reckoning.
      [*Enter* KNOWLEDGE.]
KNOWLEDGE. Everyman, I will go with thee, and be thy guide,
  In thy most need to go by thy side.
EVERYMAN. In good condition I am now in every thing,
  And am wholly content with this good thing;   525
  Thanked be God my Creator.
GOOD DEEDS. And when he hath brought thee there,°
  Where thou shalt heal thee of thy smart,°
  Then go you with your reckoning and your Good Deeds to-
      gether
  For to make you joyful at heart   530
  Before the blesséd Trinity.
EVERYMAN. My Good Deeds, gramercy!
  I am well content, certainly,
  With your words sweet.
KNOWLEDGE. Now go we together lovingly   535
  To Confession, that cleansing river.
EVERYMAN. For joy I weep; I would we were there!
  But, I pray you, give me cognition°
  Where dwelleth that holy man, Confession.
KNOWLEDGE. In the house of salvation,   540
  We shall find him in that place,
  That shall us comfort, by God's grace.
      [KNOWLEDGE *leads* EVERYMAN *to* CONFESSION.]
  Lo, this is Confession. Kneel down and ask mercy,
  For he is in good conceit° with God almighty.
EVERYMAN. O glorious fountain, that all uncleanness doth clarify, 545
  Wash from me the spots of vice unclean,
  That on me no sin may be seen.
  I come, with Knowledge, for my redemption,
  Redempt with hearty and full contrition;°
  For I am commanded a pilgrimage to take,   550
  And great accounts before God to make.
  Now, I pray you, Shrift,° mother of salvation,

---

518. Walk. **520.** Knowledge here is knowledge of sin. **527.** To that
place. **528.** Pain. **538.** Understanding. **544.** Esteem. **549.** "Saved by
sincere and complete sorrow (for my sins)." **552.** Confession.

Help my Good Deeds for my piteous exclamation.
CONFESSION. I know your sorrow well, Everyman.
Because with Knowledge ye come to me,   555
I will you comfort as well as I can,
And a precious jewel I will give thee,
Called penance, voider of adversity.
Therewith shall your body chastised be
With abstinence and perseverance in God's service.   560
Here shall you receive that scourge of me
                    [*Gives* EVERYMAN *a scourge.*]
Which is penance strong that ye must endure
To remember thy Savior was scourged for thee
With sharp scourges and suffered it patiently.
So must thou ere thou 'scape° that painful pilgrimage.   565
Knowledge, keep him in this voyage,°
And by that time Good Deeds will be with thee.
But in any wise° be sure of mercy,
For your time draweth fast,° and ye will saved be;
Ask God mercy, and He will grant truly;   570
When with the scourge of penance man doth him bind,
The oil of forgiveness then shall he find.   [*Exit* CONFESSION.]
EVERYMAN. Thanked be God for his gracious work!
For now I will my penance begin;
This hath rejoiced and lighted my heart,   575
Though the knots be painful and hard within.
KNOWLEDGE. Everyman, look your penance that ye fulfil,
What pain that ever it to you be,
And Knowledge shall give you counsel at will°
How your account ye shall make clearly.   580
EVERYMAN. O eternal God! O heavenly figure!
O way of rightwiseness! O goodly vision!
Which descended down in a virgin pure
Because he would Everyman redeem,
Which Adam forfeited by his disobedience.   585
O blesséd Godhead! elect and high divine,
Forgive me my grievous offence;
Here I cry thee mercy in this presence.
O ghostly° treasure! O ransomer and redeemer!
Of all the world hope and conductor,   590
Mirror of joy, and founder of mercy,
Which illumineth heaven and earth thereby,
Hear my clamorous complaint, though it late be.

565. Finish. 566. "Moving in this direction." 568. Case. 569. To an end. 579. Whenever you desire it. 589. Spiritual.

    Receive my prayers; unworthy in this heavy life.
    Though I be a sinner most abominable,   595
    Yet let my name be written in Moses' table.°
    O Mary! pray to the Maker of all thing,
    Me for to help at my ending,
    And save me from the power of my enemy,
    For Death assaileth me strongly.   600
    And, Lady, that I may by means of thy prayer
    Of your Son's glory to be partner,
    By the means of his passion I it crave.
    I beseech you, help my soul to save.
    Knowledge, give me the scourge of penance.   605
    My flesh therewith shall give a quittance.°
    I will now begin, if God give me grace.
KNOWLEDGE. Everyman, God give you time and space.
    Thus I bequeath you in the hands of our Savior,
    Now may you make your reckoning sure.   610
EVERYMAN. In the name of the Holy Trinity,
    My body sore punished shall be.   *[Scourges himself.]*
    Take this, body, for the sin of the flesh.
    Also thou delightest to go gay and fresh,°
    And in the way of damnation thou did me bring;   615
    Therefore suffer now strokes of punishing.
    Now of penance I will wade the water clear,
    To save me from purgatory, that sharp fire.
               [GOOD DEEDS *rises from below*.]
GOOD DEEDS. I thank God, now I can walk and go,
    And am delivered of my sickness and woe.   620
    Therefore with Everyman I will go, and not spare;
    His good works I will help him to declare.
KNOWLEDGE. Now, Everyman, be merry and glad!
    Your Good Deeds cometh now, ye may not be sad.
    Now is your Good Deeds whole and sound,   625
    Going upright upon the ground.
EVERYMAN. My heart is light, and shall be evermore.
    Now will I smite faster than I did before.
GOOD DEEDS. Everyman, pilgrim, my special friend,
    Blessèd be thou without end.   630
    For thee is prepared the eternal glory.
    Ye have me made whole and sound,
    Therefore I will bide by thee in every stound.°
EVERYMAN. Welcome, my Good Deeds; now I hear thy voice,

596. Tablets, i.e., among the saved. **606.** Full payment (for sins). **614.**
Handsomely dressed. **633.** Trial.

I weep for very sweetness of love.   635
KNOWLEDGE. Be no more sad, but ever rejoice;
    God seeth thy living° in his throne above.
    Put on this garment to thy behoof,°
                    [*Handing* EVERYMAN *a cloak.*]
    Which is wet with your tears,
    Or else before God you may it miss,°   640
    When you to your journey's end come shall.
EVERYMAN. Gentle Knowledge, what do ye it call?
KNOWLEDGE. It is the garment of sorrow;
    From pain it will you borrow;°
    Contrition it is   645
    That getteth forgiveness;
    It pleaseth God passing well.
GOOD DEEDS. Everyman, will you wear it for your heal?
              [EVERYMAN *puts on the cloak.*]
EVERYMAN. Now blesséd be Jesu, Mary's Son,
    For now have I on true contrition.   650
    And let us go now without tarrying;
    Good Deeds, have we clear our reckoning?
GOOD DEEDS. Yea, indeed I have it here.
EVERYMAN. Then I trust we need not fear.
    Now, friends, let us not part in twain.°   655
KNOWLEDGE. Nay, Everyman, that will we not, certain.
GOOD DEEDS. Yet must thou lead with thee
    Three persons of great might.
EVERYMAN. Who should they be?
GOOD DEEDS. Discretion and Strength they hight,°   660
    And thy Beauty may not abide behind.
KNOWLEDGE. Also ye must call to mind
    Your Five Wits° as for your counselors.
GOOD DEEDS. You must have them ready at all hours.
EVERYMAN. How shall I get them hither?   665
KNOWLEDGE. You must call them all together,
    And they will hear you incontinent.°
EVERYMAN. My friends, come hither and be present,
    Discretion, Strength, my Five Wits, and Beauty.
    [*Enter* DISCRETION, STRENGTH, FIVE WITS, *and* BEAUTY.]
BEAUTY. Here at your will we be all ready.   670
    What will ye that we should do?
GOOD DEEDS. That ye would with Everyman go,
    And help him in his pilgrimage.

---

637. Way of living. **638.** Advantage. **640.** Lack (when you need it).
644. Release. **655.** Separate. **660.** Are called. **663.** Senses. **667.** At once.

Advise° you, will ye with him or not in that voyage?
STRENGTH. We will bring him all thither,   675
　　To his help and comfort, ye may believe me.
DISCRETION. So will we go with him all together.
EVERYMAN. Almighty God, lovéd may thou be!
　　I give thee laud° that I have hither brought
　　Strength, Discretion, Beauty, and Five Wits. Lack I naught.   680
　　And my Good Deeds, with Knowledge clear,
　　All be in company at my will here.
　　I desire no more to my business.
STRENGTH. And I, Strength, will by you stand in distress,
　　Though thou would in battle fight on the ground.   685
FIVE WITS. And though it were through the world round,
　　We will not depart for sweet nor sour.°
BEAUTY. No more will I, unto death's hour,
　　Whatsoever thereof befall.
DISCRETION. Everyman, advise you° first of all,   690
　　Go with a good advisement and deliberation.
　　We all give you virtuous monition°
　　That all shall be well.
EVERYMAN. My friends, hearken what I will tell:
　　I pray God reward you in his heavenly sphere.   695
　　Now hearken, all that be here,
　　For I will make my testament
　　Here before you all present:
　　In alms half my goods I will give with my hands twain
　　In the way of charity, with good intent,   700
　　And the other half still shall remain,
　　I it bequeath to be returned there° it ought to be.
　　This I do in despite of the fiend of hell,
　　To go quite out of his peril°
　　Ever after and this day.   705
KNOWLEDGE. Everyman, hearken what I say;
　　Go to Priesthood, I you advise,
　　And receive of him in any wise
　　The holy sacrament and ointment together;°
　　Then shortly see ye turn again hither;   710
　　We will all abide you here.
FIVE WITS. Yea, Everyman, hie you that ye ready were.
　　There is no emperor, king, duke, nor baron,
　　That of God hath commission

674. Say. 679. Praise. 687. I.e., no matter what. 690. Be assured.
692. Forewarning. 702. When. Everyman is probably disposing of his body.
704. "To escape his perilous power." 709. Communion and Extreme Unction.

As hath the least priest in the world being;   715
For of the blessèd sacraments pure and benign
He beareth the keys, and thereof hath the cure°
For man's redemption—it is ever sure—
Which God for our soul's medicine
Gave us out of his heart with great pain,   720
Here in this transitory life, for thee and me.
The blessèd sacraments seven there be:
Baptism, confirmation, with priesthood good,
And the sacrament of God's precious flesh and blood,
Marriage, the holy extreme unction, and penance.   725
These seven be good to have in remembrance,
Gracious sacraments of high divinity.

EVERYMAN. Fain would I receive that holy body
And meekly to my ghostly father I will go.

FIVE WITS. Everyman, that is the best that ye can do.   730
God will you to salvation bring,
For priesthood exceedeth all other thing;
To us Holy Scripture they do teach,
And converteth man from sin, heaven to reach;
God hath to them more power given,   735
Than to any angel that is in heaven.
With five words° he may consecrate
God's body in flesh and blood to make,
And handleth his Maker between his hands.
The priest bindeth and unbindeth all bands,°   740
Both in earth and in heaven.
Thou, ministers all the sacraments seven,
Though we kissed thy feet, thou wert worthy;
Thou art the surgeon that cureth sin deadly:
No remedy we find under God   745
But all only priesthood.
Everyman, God gave priests that dignity,
And setteth them in his stead° among us to be;
Thus be they above angels, in degree.   [Exit EVERYMAN.]

KNOWLEDGE. If priests be good, it is so, surely.   750
But when Jesus hanged on the cross with great smart,°
There he gave out of his blessèd heart
The same sacrament in great torment.
He sold them not to us, that Lord omnipotent.
Therefore Saint Peter the Apostle doth say   755
That Jesus' curse hath all they
Which God their Savior do buy or sell,

717. Charge.   737. I.e., *Hoc est enim corpus meum.*   740. Bonds, contracts.
748. Place, i.e., as his officers.   751. Pain.

    Or they for any money do take or tell.°
    Sinful priests giveth the sinners example bad;
    Their children sitteth by other men's fires, I have heard;   760
    And some haunteth women's company
    With unclean life, as lusts of lechery.
    These be with sin made blind.
FIVE WITS. I trust to God no such may we find.
    Therefore let us priesthood honor,   765
    And follow their doctrine for our souls' succour.
    We be their sheep, and they shepherds be
    By whom we all be kept in surety.
    Peace! for yonder I see Everyman come,
    Which hath made true satisfaction.   770
GOOD DEEDS. Methinketh it is he indeed.
               [Re-enter EVERYMAN.]
EVERYMAN. Now Jesu be your alder speed.°
    I have received the sacrament for my redemption,
    And then mine extreme unction.
    Blessèd be all they that counseled me to take it!   775
    And now, friends, let us go without longer respite.
    I thank God that ye have tarried so long.
    Now set each of you on this rood your hand,
    And shortly follow me.
    I go before, there I would be. God be our guide.   780
STRENGTH. Everyman, we will not from you go,
    Till ye have done this voyage long.
DISCRETION. I, Discretion, will bide by you also.
KNOWLEDGE. And though this pilgrimage be never so strong,
    I will never part you fro.   785
    Everyman, I will be as sure by thee
    As ever I did by Judas Maccabee.
               [They go to a grave.]
EVERYMAN. Alas! I am so faint I may not stand,
    My limbs under me do fold.
    Friends, let us not turn again to this land,   790
    Not for all the world's gold;
    For into this cave must I creep
    And turn to earth, and there to sleep.
BEAUTY. What, into this grave? Alas!
EVERYMAN. Yea, there shall you consume, more and less.°   795
BEAUTY. And what, should I smother here?
EVERYMAN. Yea, by my faith, and never more appear.
    In this world live no more we shall,
    But in heaven before the highest Lord of all.

758. Count.   **772.** "The help of all of you."   **778.** Cross.   **795.** Entirely.

BEAUTY. I cross out all this;° adieu, by Saint John!   800
    I take my cap in my lap° and am gone.
EVERYMAN. What, Beauty, whither will ye?
BEAUTY. Peace! I am deaf. I look not behind me,
    Not and thou would give me all the gold in thy chest.
                               [*Exit* BEAUTY.]
EVERYMAN. Alas, whereto may I trust?   805
    Beauty goeth fast away from me;
    She promised with me to live and die.
STRENGTH. Everyman, I will thee also forsake and deny.
    Thy game liketh me not at all.
EVERYMAN. Why, then ye will forsake me all?   810
    Sweet Strength, tarry a little space.
STRENGTH. Nay, sir, by the rood of grace,
    I will hie me from thee fast,
    Though thou weep till thy heart to-brast.°
EVERYMAN. Ye would ever bide by me, ye said.   815
STRENGTH. Yea, I have you far enough conveyed.
    Ye be old enough, I understand,
    Your pilgrimage to take on hand.
    I repent me that I hither came.
EVERYMAN. Strength, you to displease I am to blame;   820
    Yet promise is debt, this ye well wot.
STRENGTH. In faith, I care not!
    Thou art but a fool to complain.
    You spend your speech and waste your brain.
    Go, thrust thee into the ground.   [*Exit* STRENGTH.] 825
EVERYMAN. I had weened surer I should you have found.
    He that trusteth in his Strength
    She him deceiveth at the length.
    Both Strength and Beauty forsaketh me,
    Yet they promised me fair and lovingly.   830
DISCRETION. Everyman, I will after Strength be gone;
    As for me I will leave you alone.
EVERYMAN. Why, Discretion,° will ye forsake me?
DISCRETION. Yea, in faith, I will go from thee;
    For when Strength goeth before   835
    I follow after evermore.
EVERYMAN. Yet, I pray thee, for the love of the Trinity,
    Look in my grave once piteously.°
DISCRETION. Nay, so nigh will I not come.
    Farewell, every one!   [*Exit* DISCRETION.] 840
EVERYMAN. O all thing faileth, save God alone,

---

800. I.e., his former promises. 801. "Doff my cap low." 814. Break in
pieces. 833. Discretion here means judgment, or what we would now
call reason. 838. With pity.

Beauty, Strength, and Discretion;
For when Death bloweth his blast,
They all run from me full fast.
FIVE WITS. Everyman, my leave now of thee I take;   845
I will follow the other, for here I thee forsake.
EVERYTHING. Alas! then may I wail and weep,
For I took you for my best friend.
FIVE WITS. I will no longer thee keep;
Now farewell, and there an end.   [*Exit* FIVE WITS.]   850
EVERYMAN. O Jesu, help! All hath forsaken me!
GOOD DEEDS. Nay, Everyman; I will bide with thee,
I will not forsake thee indeed;
Thou shalt find me a good friend at need.
EVERYMAN. Gramercy, Good Deeds! Now may I true friends see.   855
They have forsaken me, every one;
I loved them better than my Good Deeds alone.
Knowledge, will ye forsake me also?
KNOWLEDGE. Yea, Everyman, when ye to death shall go;
But not yet, for no manner of danger.   860
EVERYMAN. Gramercy, Knowledge, with all my heart.
KNOWLEDGE. Nay, yet I will not from hence depart
Till I see where ye shall be come.
EVERYMAN. Methink, alas, that I must be gone
To make my reckoning and my debts pay,   865
For I see my time is nigh spent away.
Take example, all ye that this do hear or see,
How they that I loved best do forsake me,
Except my Good Deeds that bideth truly.
GOOD DEEDS. All earthly things is but vanity.   870
Beauty, Strength, and Discretion do man forsake,
Foolish friends and kinsmen, that fair spake,
All fleeth save Good Deeds, and that am I.
EVERYMAN. Have mercy on me, God most mighty;
And stand by me, thou Mother and Maid, holy Mary!   875
GOOD DEEDS. Fear not, I will speak for thee.
EVERYMAN. Here I cry God mercy!
GOOD DEEDS. Short our end, and 'minish our pain.°
Let us go and never come again.
EVERYMAN. Into thy hands, Lord, my soul I commend.   880
Receive it, Lord, that it be not lost.
As thou me boughtest, so me defend,
And save me from the fiend's boast,
That I may appear with that blessèd host
That shall be saved at the day of doom.   885
In manus tuas—of might's most

878. "Shorten our deaths and diminish our pains."

For ever—*commendo spiritum meum.*°

[EVERYMAN *and* GOOD DEEDS *go into the grave.*]

KNOWLEDGE. Now hath he suffered that we all shall endure;
The Good Deeds shall make all sure.
Now hath he made ending.   890
Methinketh that I hear angels sing
And make great joy and melody
Where Everyman's soul received shall be.

ANGEL. Come, excellent elect spouse to Jesu!
Here above thou shalt go   895
Because of thy singular virtue.
Now the soul is taken the body fro,
Thy reckoning is crystal clear.
Now shalt thou into the heavenly sphere,
Unto the which all ye shall come   900
That liveth well before the day of doom.

[*Exit* KNOWLEDGE. *Enter* DOCTOR.]

DOCTOR.° This moral men may have in mind;
Ye hearers, take it of worth,° old and young,
And forsake Pride, for he deceiveth you in the end,
And remember Beauty, Five Wits, Strength, and Discretion,   905
They all at the last do Everyman forsake,
Save his Good Deeds there doth he take.
But beware, and they be small
Before God he hath no help at all.
None excuse may be there for Everyman.   910
Alas, how shall he do then?
For, after death, amends may no man make,
For then mercy and pity doth him forsake.
If his reckoning be not clear when he doth come,
God will say, *"Ite, maledicti, in ignem aeternum."*   915
And he that hath his account whole and sound,
High in heaven he shall be crowned.
Unto which place God bring us all thither,
That we may live body and soul together.
Thereto help the Trinity!   920
Amen, say ye, for saint charity.

THUS ENDETH THIS MORAL PLAY OF EVERYMAN.

886–87. "Into thy hands, most mighty, I give my spirit forever." 902.
Teacher. 903. Value it. 915. "Hence, cursed one, into eternal fire."

QUESTIONS

1. For what reasons does God send Death to Everyman?
2. A character's manner of speaking tells us nearly as much about him

as the words he uses. Can you distinguish between God's manner and Death's? between Death's and Everyman's? What is the significance of the shift in Everyman's manner of speech after he realizes who Death is?

3. The characters of *Everyman* are personifications of such abstract ideas as death, man, and friendship; at the same time they are remarkably real and individual. How does the playwright make his characters seem so intensely alive and understandable?

4. Draw up a brief statement of the religious doctrine that the play teaches and then discuss the ways in which this doctrine is embodied in the characters and the action.

5. You will notice that there are no directions for costumes, no references to a setting, and no designation of physical characteristics for any of the characters. The original scribe or printer may simply have failed to include this material but its absence seems curiously right for *Everyman*. Do you agree, or would you costume all the characters and design scenery for the bare stage?

6. How would you describe Everyman's "motive"? Show how this motive appears in what he does.

7. Is Everyman a simple or a complex character? Do you find evidence of conflict within him? Does he change during the course of the action?

8. Are the characters Everyman visits in his attempt to find someone to accompany him into the grave sufficiently individualized so that it is possible to distingush among them? Are these characters complex or simple?

9. Do you see any dramatic value in the particular sequence of the visits: Fellowship, Kindred, and Goods? Could the playwright have rearranged the sequence without affecting the meaning of the play?

10. What is the significance of placing Good Deeds "in the ground"?

11. Consider yourself for the moment a realistic playwright who wants to make the same statements about human nature and human life that the anonymous *Everyman* playwright makes. You would be forced to work in the realistic rather than the allegorical mode; you would be unable to present personifications of Everyman's worldly posessions and his bodily and mental resources to dramatize his thoughts upon learning that death is at hand. Make an outline of a play that would permit you to make the same points as *Everyman* without destroying the illusion of reality. Would some points be impossible to make in the realistic mode?

12. Are the different attitudes taken toward the priesthood by Knowledge and Five Wits consistent with the nature of each character?

13. Why has the playwright placed the encounters with Beauty, Five Wits, and Discretion after the meetings with such figures as Goods and Kindred? What is the significance of the fact that Beauty, Five Wits, and the others first agree to go into the grave with Everyman and then refuse?

THE WORLD
OF THE PLAY

Every art form provides certain essential means of expression, which the artist may exploit or enlarge upon in whatever manner he chooses, but which he must continue to use so long as he wishes to work within the particular form he has chosen. The essentials of drama are only two: the actor and the stage. Abandon either and you are no longer writing drama. We already have seen what the playwright does with his actors—he uses them as characters, images of man in his many aspects. In this section we shall be concerned with what the playwright does with the space around his characters, how he uses it and enlarges it until it comes to represent the world in which his characters live.

In reading or seeing a play our attention usually centers on character and we sometimes pay little attention to the *setting*—the scenery and furnishings placed on stage. It is enough, we feel, that the scenery and properties provide the characters with the objects necessary for the action and a suitable background against which they can play out their parts. Ibsen in *Hedda Gabler,* for example, deals most immediately with life in Norway in the late nineteenth century, and appropriately enough sets his play in a middle-class drawing room of that period, complete with contemporary furniture—stove, carpets, and pictures. The set, looked at in this way, serves only to locate the play in time and perhaps to contribute something to the *mood:* a tragic set is usually heavy, confined, and somber; a comic set light, airy, open, and gaily colored.

But the care with which a dramatist like Ibsen sets his scene suggests that he makes use of it to supply more than the historical context or appropriate mood. Ibsen prescribes the general style and coloring of the furniture, draperies, and carpets; he is explicit about the pieces to be used in the set and where they are to be placed on the stage; and he provides a detailed plan of the room, locating doors and windows, marking the existence of another small room to the back of the main one, designating a veranda beyond the glass doors. Nor does he forget his room arrangement during the course of the play. Not only are changes carefully noted, such as the removal of the old piano to the back room and the addition of a small writing desk, but the characters are always specifically placed in the set: for example, "She forces Mrs. Elvsted to sit in the easy chair beside the stove, and seats herself on one of the footstools," or "She goes out through the inner room, to the left." (Directions are always given in relation to the stage; right is the right of an actor on stage facing the audience.)

A floor plan of the set for *Hedda Gabler* marked with the movements of the characters—in the theater this locating of characters on stage is known as *blocking*—makes it obvious that certain places or objects are associated with certain moods of the characters. It is clear enough that Hedda brings out the pistols whenever she is frustrated and in a "killing" mood. It is less obvious, perhaps, that she goes to the stove to warm herself—she is an unusually "cold" woman—only when she wants to hear the "warming" experiences of some other person; or that she goes to the glass doors and looks out only when she longs to escape the confinement of her life. Similarly, she moves into the small back room, which is peculiarly her own, and which is dominated, significantly, by a portrait of her father, General Gabler, only when she is retreating into herself, withdrawing from circumstances that do not suit her and that she can no longer control. In this way parts of the stage and the objects on it become associated with certain emotions and attitudes; a movement to one of these places or the handling of a certain prop gives a clue to what is occurring in the character's mind. Hedda's physical location often suggests her psychic or emotional location.

The use of a physical set to make visible a state of mind is a common dramatic technique, and we must always look carefully for the relation between place and character. Ibsen is unusual in the exactitude with which he plans his settings and the care with which he moves his characters about, but all good dramatists have used their stage in this way to some degree. In Shakespeare's *Julius Caesar,* for example, after the conspirators have murdered Caesar, Brutus goes to the Forum to explain to the citizens the necessity for the murder. His motives are lofty and his address appeals to such high-level abstractions as patriotism, duty, and reason. His idealism is apparent enough from what he says, but Shakespeare underlines it by presenting it in visual as well as verbal terms: while the mob remains below, Brutus ascends the rostrum and speaks from above. (In the Elizabethan theater for which the play was written he probably went to the upper stage, a balcony above and at the rear of the main platform stage.) After Brutus has finished, Mark Antony delivers a speech in which he fires the mob against the conspirators by appealing to their lower instincts—their greed, materialism, love of the sensational, and primitive delight in destruction. Antony begins on the rostrum above the crowd; as his appeals to baser emotions become cruder and more pronounced he descends from the rostrum and mingles with the crowd on stage. Language, action, and scene have combined to express the difference between Brutus and Antony.

In the Forum scene from *Julius Caesar* we would hesitate to assign any definite value to the places on stage unless the dramatist arranged matters in such a way as to suggest that a particular attitude was associated with a particular place. It is the high idealism of Brutus' speech which first suggests that the elevated stand he has taken above the crowd presents in visual terms his mental attitude and his relationship to the common people. The stove in *Hedda Gabler* seems to represent visually the warm energy of life that Hedda seeks since she goes to it when she wishes to extract from some other character the "warming" details of his life in the active, "fiery" world beyond the walls of her house. Brutus' position on the rostrum or Hedda's near the stove become perfect symbols for idealism and for warmth when fitted into a larger pattern, but they would never yield these meanings by themselves.

While the meaning of certain places or objects must often be sought out, dramatists frequently use scenes and objects that have immediately powerful *symbolic* values. To choose a few examples from Shakespeare: storm scenes, wild places such as the barren heaths in *Macbeth* and *Lear,* battle scenes composed of "alarums and excursions," and savage woods suggest destruction, waste, and disorder. The qualities of these scenes are often transferred to the characters placed in them: an unnatural and disordered place can imply that the characters are in unnatural and disordered states of mind. On the other hand, calm pastoral scenes, solemn social occasions (such as feasts, marriages, and coronations), fertile gardens, and ordered domestic scenes can reflect characters in a state of harmony, productive order, and social concord. Certain objects also have innate values: pistols, for example, or a cross, a marriage ring, a crown, even a loaf of bread.

But scenes and props do not always reflect character directly—a good man in a "good" setting—often they provide an illuminating contrast to the character by setting up an ironic perspective—a bad man in a "good" setting. The fresh, romantic love of Romeo and Juliet and their exclusive concern for one another is mirrored perfectly by the walled, isolated garden of the Capulets where they declare their love; but outside the walls of that enchanted, moonlit place are the sun-baked square, the countinghouses, and the graveyard of the city of Verona, where a deadly feud boils up. The realities of public life—feuds, money, politics, death—stated by these other scenes set off by contrast Romeo and Juliet's personal, private, and idealistic love. But whatever the manner in which a scene is related to a character, it usually provides some perspective on him, and the first question to be asked about any scene is how it helps to define the characters placed in it. Does it state their values in physical terms? Does it suggest contrasting values? Did they choose it or create it? Was it forced upon them?

While every effective dramatist uses his scene, at least in part, to tell us something about the characters he places in it, the scene performs other functions as well; the most important of these is to record in symbolic form the world that exists outside the individual. The scenes set in the pantry, the graveyard, the church, and the town square of Verona do not exist merely to provide an illuminating contrast to the ideal, impractical lovers, Romeo and Juliet. They represent the solid, objective world, where men have to eat, where they kill rather than love one another, and where in the end they die. We can say, then, that as a general rule the playwright uses his stage to represent the world in which his characters live. If the characters in a play are representations of human nature, of personality, the scene reflects the nature of the world, the environment of man.

Besides being fundamental terms of the drama, personality and environment are the basic terms used in most philosophies and in most theories of history. At different times and in different places men have believed that one or the other of these forces dominates human destiny. Christianity, for example, emphasizes "character" and assumes that man is free to achieve his own salvation, with the grace of God, no matter what the condition of the world around him. The theory of evolution, on the other hand, assumes environment to be the crucial factor of life: the nature of a living thing is the result of its successful adaptation to the changing world in which it lives. In the Marxist view of history man's personality is not determined by climatic conditions but by economic facts. Behaviorist psychology makes man little more than the product of external stimuli to which he responds in a mechanical fashion. Dramatists usually reflect some influential world view in their plays; the environmental determinists, for example, have had their exponents in the theater in the dramatic movement called *naturalism.* Naturalistic plays, as you might expect, show little interest in the complexities and depths of character; instead they emphasize the external world and the social conditions that are believed to shape human personality. Gerhart Hauptmann's *The Weavers* (1892) is a naturalistic play on the revolt of the Silesian workers in 1844 when the steam-powered loom eliminated the jobs of the old hand-weavers. The play lacks a hero (heroism is impossible when all actions are determined by environment); the characters introduced are extremely simple, almost rudimentary, versions of human beings—types rather than individuals. But the play details with elaborate care the economic facts of life, such as the rising cost of food, the operations of the new spinning mills, and the high tariffs, which force the manufacturers to turn to cheaper means of production.

If the world is everything in a naturalistic play and character merely one of its effects, the reverse is true of expressionistic drama. Here the world is shown not as it objectively is, but as man experiences it in his mind. In *Waiting for Godot,* for example, the real world of cities, factories, fields, and multitudes is dissolved into the subjective reality of a bare, nearly empty space and two men waiting. But naturalism and expressionism are extreme dramatic tendencies; the greater part of our drama has struck a balance somewhere between these two extremes by presenting both characters and the world.

Some brief explanation of how dramatists conceive of their theatrical worlds is necessary at this point. Just as stage characters are not total human beings but only dramatic representations of those motives the dramatist considers the essential part of man, so stage worlds are not reproductions of everything in the real world, but symbolic renderings of the essential qualities of our environment—human, social, or natural. Just as the dramatist presents man as a doer, as a power moving toward some fulfillment, so he presents the world not as a static object but as a force exerting pressure in some direction. What we must look for in the world of a play is that force, or those forces, expressed by the furniture, scenery, sounds, and words out of which a dramatist constructs his stage world.

Hedda Gabler illustrates one way in which a dramatist constructs his image of the world. The set is furnished in the formal, middle-class fashion of the late nineteenth century. The pieces are heavy, dark, ornate; the hangings and rugs rich and somber. Furthermore, if all the furniture Ibsen stipulates in his stage directions were used in a production, most stages would be difficult to move about on. The actors would be forced to thread their way between pieces of furniture to get from place to place. This room—typical of the houses of the Victorian well-to-do: formal, rich, crowded, and dark (which Hedda further darkens by insisting that the curtains be closed against the sunlight)—embodies nineteenth-century middle-class society with its emphasis on propriety, restraint, and material wealth, with its constriction of free, natural movement and its insistence that pretenses be maintained. The set makes visible the stodgy, deadening, constrictive society, the polite world, into which Hedda has married and which exerts a powerful influence on her and checks her free will.

All dramatists objectify their concept of the world in the immediate sets of their plays, and we must be careful to note stage descriptions and all other references to the arrangement of the stage. The information about the world of *Hedda Gabler* provided in the dialogue is almost as important as the explicit directions to the stage manager. Tesman's inability to afford the house that Hedda demands and that Judge Brack furnishes reminds us that this is a world in which appearances are more important than truth. The fact that the limited, unimaginative Tesman can pay for his house and furnishings only if he wins the professorship from the undisciplined but creative Lövborg, suggests that the kind of society represented by the set can survive only if vitality and imagination are suppressed.

Ibsen's single scene—an interior, realistically presented—is the usual way of setting the stage in the realistic theater, which simply means that most modern plays present man in a limited social context. But this is only one of many possible scenes, one of a nearly infinite number of worlds that can be created on the stage. If a play is set in a wild forest, on a battlefield, or in a crowded tenement, its world is one of primitive passions, rawness, and struggle. Set in a law court or place of government, it presents a man-made, orderly, traditional world. A stony wasteland suggests a hostile, ominous world; rich, fertile fields, a generous, burgeoning world. A consistently dark scene suggests a mysterious world filled with unknowns, while a brightly lighted scene suggests a reasonable, understandable world. Confining a play to a single scene creates a narrow, constricted world, while the presentation of a number of different scenes creates a varied, open world. An inside scene presents a man-made or social world, while an outdoor scene shows us a natural one. A bare stage implies a world in

which all seemingly solid objects—buildings, mountains, trees—are
no more than passing dreams; and if no attempt is made to disguise
the working parts of the theater with wings and scenery, the implication is that "all the world's a stage." It seems likely that even the
physical details and structure of the theaters of a given period constitute an image of the world. (The Glossary contains discussions of the
world views suggested by the theaters of various ages.)

Fortunately, playwrights are not limited to the use of the technical
resources of the theater—lumber, canvas, paint, furniture, lights—in
the construction of their dramatic worlds. "Characters" too can be
employed as expressions of the play's world. Characters used in this
way are really not personalities so much as they are parts of the scene,
personified expressions of the elemental forces of the world. The
witches in *Macbeth* are not individuals interesting in their own right,
but aspects of a world shot through with dark, disorderly powers. The
mob in *Julius Caesar,* and in other Shakespearean plays, is not properly understood as a collection of people so much as a representation
of a senseless, directionless power, which is a crucial part of the world
in which true characters like Brutus and Caesar have to live. Judge
Brack in *Hedda Gabler* is little more than a personification of the
social forces that constitute the immediate world in which the characters live. He is linked to the other expression of that world, the set,
for it was he who selected the furnishings and arranged for the house
—though Miss Tesman had to pay. Furthermore, Brack's title of
"Judge," his conventional way of looking at everything, his formal
dress on all occasions, and his intimate knowledge at all times of
"what people think," show that he, as much as the drawing-room set,
represents bourgeois values.

Once we have identified a character with the world, it follows that
all the components of his character—physical appearance, clothing,
movements, thought, and style—will express the nature of that world.
Characters of this type "act out" the world for us; they are not free
agents but simply manifestations of the scene. When Judge Brack, for
example, argues with Hedda that she must conceal the fact that
Lövborg was killed with her pistol, it becomes clear that this formal,
carefully mannered society for which he speaks is more concerned
with avoiding scandal than with being truthful. And when Hedda discovers that he is willing to suppress the facts in order to gain power
over her, we learn that in his world men may conceal the truth not
out of kindness but because the threat of scandal can be held over
the heads of those they wish to dominate. The Judge's unmarried,

childless state, his stag parties, his exceptional politeness and urbanity, his prosperity, and his concern for being properly dressed for all occasions—all these facts provide insights into the society for which he is the spokesman.

So far we have concentrated on the visible means used by the playwright—and enlarged upon by the scene designer—to create a world for the characters to move in. Considering the limited physical resources of the theater, particularly the Greek and Elizabethan theaters, which lacked artificial lights and had very little scenery, dramatists have still managed to present on the stage larger, more complex and mysterious worlds than would seem possible. The witches in *Macbeth,* for example, stirring their cauldron on a bare Elizabethan stage must have evoked then as now a vision of a universe filled with dark, primitive forces. The sentries in the opening scene of *Hamlet,* peering out from the upper balcony of the Elizabethan stage and straining their eyes to see the Ghost reenter from a realm beyond the visible, evoke a world of vast, mysterious spaces about which man, who knows only the limited area of his immediate surroundings, and that imperfectly, can only guess. While Yank dies below deck, in Eugene O'Neill's *Bound East for Cardiff,* the regular sounding of the ship's whistle as she moves through the fog creates an ominous world where man knows his direction only by instruments and where collision is an ever-present danger.

A playwright still would be severely limited if he were forced to rely entirely on sound effects, lights, scenery, and personifications to create his world. Since playing time is limited, and scene shifting takes a great deal of time, how can a very complex and enormously various world be set forth in the theater? The answer is, of course, through language. Every playwright brings his world into being largely, though not entirely, with words. In *Hedda Gabler* Ibsen confines his scene to a single set: the interior of the heavily furnished Tesman house. But the characters of the play speak of a much larger world just beyond our sight. This larger world is composed of such things as wild parties in Judge Brack's rooms and drunken brawls in Mademoiselle Diana's establishment. It extends from frozen and isolated villages in the north, where a widower marries to provide himself with a housekeeper and a nursemaid, to the Dolomites and the Brenner Pass, visited on the Tesmans' wedding trip. In this world beyond the walls of Hedda's drawing room an old lady is dying, and just beyond the closed doors the sun is shining in a garden where late fall flowers grow. The range of this world is even greater than these details suggest, for it reaches back in time to busy medieval households where cloth and other necessities of life were made (the subject of Tesman's book), and it goes onward into the future (the subject of Lövborg's book). No single detail of this larger world is very important by itself, but taken together they make up a world of pain and passion, growth and decay, vitality and movement. Within Hedda's house, however, we hear only the echoes of this large world of doing and suffering. Life stops at her doorway and its sounds are muted. In the immediate scenes of the play the curtains are closed against the sun, only "polite" subjects are discussed, the fire burns to provide artificial warmth, flowers with their sweet odors are not permitted, and Hedda regards her pregnancy as an unwelcome intrusion, too indelicate or too painful for discussion.

As vast as the world Ibsen calls into being with language is, it seems quite small compared with the world created by Shakespeare or the Greek dramatists. These playwrights present us with images of society and of the natural world, as does Ibsen, but they pass from houses and gardens to the realms of the cosmic and the supernatural. Disorders in the arrangement of the heavens, such as eclipses and meteors, the appearance of ghosts and witches, unusual changes in the pattern of nature—drought, plague, and flood—the voices of oracles, and references to the gods, all tell us that the characters in Greek and Elizabethan drama play out their lives in a much larger world than can usually be found in modern drama.

It is paradoxical that this should be so, for modern science has revealed an infinitely vaster cosmos and an infinitely more varied world than that known to the ancients or the men of the Renaissance. But the great reaches of galactic space and the incredible intricacy of the subatomic world, moving in absolute obedience to unchanging natural laws, do not answer back to man. Even as his scientific knowledge of the universe has expanded, man's sense of the purely human world has contracted. This sensed narrowness is manifested in the smaller and smaller dramatic worlds of modern drama, and the contraction has been intensified by the shift from poetry to prose as the medium for dramatic speech. The virtues of prose are explicitness and clarity, and it is no accident that the growth of scientific attitudes and the use of prose have been parallel, for both embody the same attitudes and values. But prose has its limitations as an artistic medium, and in drama, prose particularly limits the range of the dramatic world. Lacking the metaphorical profusion of poetry and its free methods of association, prose makes it necessary that every element of the world outside the range of vision be somehow introduced realistically into the dialogue or somehow suggested in the props or set. Thus in *Hedda Gabler* someone has to sit down with a collection of photographs and describe the pictures of the Brenner Pass and the Dolomites, and someone has to come in and say that Aunt Rina is dying in order to admit the power of nature and the fact of death into the world the playwright is constructing. Ibsen is marvelously economical in his management of such details; but even in the hands of so great a dramatist, prose severely limits the detail that a playwright can use to build the world of his play.

The use of poetry, and specifically the use of metaphor, a prominent feature of that way of using language which we call poetry, permits the dramatist to construct a vast and full world with the utmost economy. The famous line spoken by Macbeth as he feels the emptiness of his life coming over him at the end of his play, "I 'gin to be aweary of the sun," is a metaphorical way of saying, "I am tired of life." When Ibsen wishes to remind us of the sun shining bright and hot outside Hedda's dark room, he must arrange for her to see the sunlight pouring into the room, to register disapproval, and to have the curtains closed. In each case the playwright suggests that his hero has cut himself off from the source of life and growth in the natural world. Both techniques for bringing the sun in are effective, but Shakespeare's poetry gets the job done in a fraction of the time required by Ibsen. Because of this poetic economy, verse drama always makes the world of the play seem denser and more extensive, and therefore more actual, than does realistic prose drama. We can see the full value of poetry as a tool for constructing a dramatic world if we take such lines of poetry as the following and try to imagine what kind of dialogue or scenes the realistic prose dramatist would have to construct in order to build the same elements into his dramatic world. Here is Romeo speaking when he catches his first glimpse of Juliet on her balcony:

> But soft! What light through yonder window breaks?
> It is the east, and Juliet is the sun!

Othello, looking at the sleeping Desdemona before he kills her, reflects:

> But once put out thy light,
> Thou cunning'st pattern of excelling nature,
> I know not where is that Promethean heat
> That can thy light relume. When I have plucked the rose,
> I cannot give it vital growth again,
> It needs must wither.

Hamlet expresses his disgust with the world soon after Claudius has become king:

> How weary, stale, flat, and unprofitable
> Seem to me all the uses of this world!
> Fie on't, ah, fie! 'Tis an unweeded garden,
> That grows to seed; things rank and gross in nature
> Possess it merely.

Such passages demonstrate not only that poetry is more economical than prose, but that it permits associations between the human and the natural to be forged that would be impossible, or nearly so, in realistic prose drama.

So far we have concentrated on the ways a dramatist constructs single scenes to image his world, but now we must consider other techniques. Some plays offer a multiple world constructed from many different scenes. In *Julius Caesar,* for example, there is a scene at Caesar's house in which Calpurnia warns him of her dream that he will be assassinated; there is a night scene in the city where lions roam the streets and strange fires appear in the heavens; there is Brutus' garden where the cloaked conspirators meet to plan the assassination of Caesar; there is the senate chamber and its bloody murder; there is a short scene where the mob tears the poet Cinna to pieces because he bears the same name as one of the conspirators; and there is a battlefield where a series of accidents causes the defeat of Brutus and Cassius. On the surface these scenes are all quite different, yet a close examination reveals the presence in each of a mysterious, primal force flooding through the world and affecting the lives of men. Taken together these scenes, along with the others in the play, create a single world in which the irrational and inexplicable are manifested on many levels: in unnatural events in the cosmos, in the strange dreams and wild actions of men, and in the unforeseeable chances that shape history. Shakespeare has condensed the world of *Julius Caesar* to an essential force, and this force is shown to be not local and limited but pervasive and universal. In a play made up of many scenes, we should first try to determine whether or not these scenes present different aspects of the same world, that is, show the same force at work in different places, on different social levels, and on such different planes as nature, society, history, and man.

Often, however, the play presents not one world, but two or more, and to complicate matters even further, these worlds may be mutually exclusive, each denying the validity of the other as a true image of reality. When two worlds that deny or qualify one another are juxta-posed, we have another form of *dramatic irony*. In *Hedda Gabler* Ibsen achieves his ironic effect by using language to superimpose the large, active world outside the Tesman house on the small, still bour-geois world within. This common way of managing *scenic irony* is often supplemented or reinforced by the use of other methods. Two mutually exclusive worlds may be presented in physical terms on the same stage, as in Tennessee Williams' *Summer and Smoke,* in which one half of the stage is a bare doctor's office complete with micro-scope, skull, and anatomical chart, while the other side of the stage is a rectory with green plush sofa, a romantic landscape in a gilt frame, and a love seat. Between these two sets is the town square, which centers on a stone angel whose joined hands form a drinking basin for a fountain. Behind all this is the vast, intense blue sky of the cyclorama, a neutral background, as it were, for the scientific, materialistic world of the doctor, and the religious, moral world of the minister. Worlds that question one another in this way may also be presented in sequence rather than simultaneously. Shakespeare is the master of this technique, and the alternation of city scenes with coun-try scenes, indoor scenes with outdoor scenes, court scenes with tavern scenes, is one of his trademarks. A good example occurs in his *Henry V* where on the eve of the battle of Agincourt the English common soldiers, facing death the next day, gather in darkness around a small fire to talk of the plain realities of their world: the pain of dying, the wives and children left to starve, the sin of killing other men. The next scene shows the French nobles preparing for battle. Theirs is a splendid, chivalric world of glittering armor, brave ban-ners, colorful clothing, and they talk of honor, courage, glory—and ransom.

Scenic irony always raises the question of appearance and reality. If two or more opposing worlds exist in a play, which is the false image and which is the true? The only sure way of finding the answer is to look carefully at what happens in the play. In *Hedda Gabler* we need not look very long. The placidity of that small, polite world within Hedda's house is constantly being shattered by events such as Lövborg's messy death in the larger, more vital world outside; and the bourgeois vision of the world is finally revealed as an impossible sham by the crack of Hedda's pistol and Judge Brack's fatuous at-tempt to maintain the pretense, "People don't do such things." Simi-larly, in *Henry V* the scene of the battlefield of Agincourt, covered with the bodies of the French knights slain by the arrows of soldiers who took war more seriously, exposes the folly of French dreams of chivalry. One world drives out another, demonstrating its own validity by continuing to exist when the other has vanished. In *Summer and Smoke,* however, though the characters have undergone changes by the end of the play, the vast, neutral sky remains, and before it the two worlds of religion and science continue to stand. The play shows that both are valid and invalid ways of describing ultimate reality.

Where more than one world is presented as a possible image of man's environment, the progression of scenes, the unfolding of reality is often important. This unfolding usually shows the characters' growth in understanding or illustrates the results that past actions have on their lives. The scene in *Hedda Gabler* is restricted to one narrow space, which tells us that no matter what has happened Hedda continues to move within that stifling, restrictive society she and her age considered the proper setting for man. What a different play it would be if at some point in the third or fourth act Hedda were to rush out of the house into the streets of the town! In plays in which characters are forced to confront new experiences and come to new understandings of the world, this developing knowledge is expressed in the changes of scene. For example, the opening scene of *King Lear* is a rich, well-ordered palace. Lear's mistake of giving up his rule and banishing his truthful daughter, Cordelia, has fearful consequences. The changes of scene within the play dramatize these consequences. Never again does Lear regain his palace or his earlier certainty; he is forced out onto a bare heath in the middle of the night while the elements rage at him, and he can only conclude that man, far from being a king, is no more than a "poor, bare, forked animal." He runs wild like a hunted beast through the fields trying to elude his pursuers, he is cast into prison, and he ends his life on a desolate battlefield with all his daughters dead before him. His initial act forced him to move from a limited scene, which suggested that life was prosperous, orderly, and centered on man, to the bleak reality of a battlefield and the confrontation of a vast world extending through all time and space—a world in which man seems almost insignificant.

MOTHER COURAGE
AND HER
CHILDREN

BY

BERTOLT BRECHT

Bertolt Brecht (1898–1956) remarks in his *Short Organum for the Theater* (1948) on the suspicious, inquiring way in which Galileo looked at a swinging chandelier, as if he had not expected it to swing and could not at first understand why it should move. From this detached, surprised point of view Galileo was able to see the phenomenon of the chandelier afresh and ultimately discover the laws governing its movements. Brecht wanted a theater that would show our world in the same fresh, surprising way and thereby lead to a new understanding of life: "Here is the outlook, disconcerting but fruitful, which the theater must provoke with its representations of human social life. It must amaze its public, and it achieves this by a technique of making the familiar seem strange." The result achieved by present-

ing the familiar from a strange and revealing angle, thus forcing the
audience to think about rather than merely identify with the play,
Brecht called the *alienation effect.*

Brecht was born with an inquiring eye to which the familiar always
looked strange, and this faculty was intensified by the events of an age
in which, without the playwright's shaping hand, the familiar face of
the world began to assume grotesque, unexpected forms. Brecht was
a medical student in Munich during World War I and became an
orderly in a military hospital. The mutilations he saw there, as he
helped to patch up the wounded as quickly as possible in order to
send them back to be killed, shocked him profoundly and made a
pacifist of him for the remainder of his life. He began writing poems
and plays after the war and found his way to Berlin, where he saw
the poverty and hunger, the moral decadence, the futile political
squabbling, and the gross commercialism of the postwar world at its
worst. He showed this corrupt and crumbling society in a number of
plays and musical dramas—in which he collaborated with the composer Kurt Weill—in the 1920's and early 1930's. The most famous
of these works is the well-known *Threepenny Opera.* But then Hitler
came to power, and Brecht, by now one of the chief dramatists in
Germany, had to flee. The Nazis considered his work decadent, un-
patriotic, and defeatist. For years Brecht lived in exile, mostly in Denmark, where *Mother Courage* was written in 1939. In 1941 he escaped
through Finland to the United States and for several years made a
precarious living writing for the movies. In 1948 he returned to Europe
and went to East Berlin. The Communist government provided him
with a magnificent theater and acting company to produce his plays.
He had never, even in the days of fame in Germany, been free to
produce his plays the way he wanted; indeed for nearly fifteen years
he had had the greatest difficulty in getting a play of his staged in
any fashion. For the remaining eight years of his life he concentrated
on work in the theater, revising and bringing out a collected edition
of his works, and trying to stay out of trouble with the politicians.

It was this strange, distorted world in which he lived that Brecht
wanted to show in his plays; consequently he rejected the realistic
theater of Ibsen and his followers, where every effort is made to show
the familiar and the expected. Instead Brecht "invented" what he
called "the epic theater." Here the illusion of reality and the setting
of the middle-class drawing room are abandoned in favor of such
bizarre settings as a fantastic city in Florida in which the only crime

is to lack money. Scenery in the epic theater is openly theatrical: newsreels are projected on the backdrop, the price of bread is flashed on a sign, lights representing the moon are left undisguised. The epic style of acting emphasizes *acting;* that is, the actors do not pretend to *be* the person they play, but make it clear that they are *pretending.* The effect of all this is to create plays that are openly *images* of the world, not reproductions of it, in order to make the spectator think, to say, as Brecht describes it: "I should never have thought so.—That is not the way to do it.—This is most surprising, hardly credible.—This will have to stop. This human being's suffering moves me, because there would have been a way out for him. This is great art: nothing here seems inevitable—I am laughing about those who weep on the stage, weeping about those who laugh."

One other important distinction between Ibsen's realistic theater and Brecht's epic theater is the different emphasis placed on character. However much society may operate to control the actions of Hedda Gabler, it remains clear that she is free to choose her own fate. The focus of the play is on her character, what goes on inside of her head and what she does. But Brecht was a Marxist—whether he was ever a member of the Communist party remains doubtful—and for him character could be defined as "the totality of all social conditions." Man is at any given moment not an immutable entity but the product of his time and world. Brecht once put it this way, "Character should not be regarded like a stain of grease on a pair of trousers, which, however much you try to rub and wipe it away, will always come up again. In actual fact the question is always how a given person is going to act in a specified set of circumstances and conditions." This means that in his plays he was not so interested in probing deeply into character in order to get down to the permanent constituents of human nature as he was in showing the social and natural forces operating on man and moving him in certain directions. It means, in short, that his plays feature the "world."

While Brecht's critical pronouncements on drama provide interesting insights into his plays, they should never be taken as absolute descriptions of what you will find in them. Character is not very complicated in *Mother Courage,* but it is an important ingredient of the play; and, similarly, though Brecht thought that he was illustrating the Marxist theory of history—the inevitable class struggle for the control of the means of production in which the individual counts for very little—it is possible to read his plays as dramatization of man's attempt to establish his particular values in a hostile world, the eternal subject of tragedy.

CHARACTERS

RECRUITING OFFICER

SERGEANT

MOTHER COURAGE

EILIF

SWISS CHEESE

KATTRIN

COLONEL

SCRIVENER

OLDER SOLDIER

YOUNGER SOLDIER

FIRST SOLDIER

OLD PEASANT

SECOND SOLDIER

PEASANT WOMAN

COOK

COMMANDER

CHAPLAIN

ORDNANCE OFFICER

YVETTE POTTIER

ONE EYE

SOLDIER, *singing*

OLD WOMAN

VOICES, *two*

YOUNG MAN

VOICE, *girl singing*

LIEUTENANT

YOUNG PEASANT

(ONE SUPER)
(TWO EXTRAS)

The Time: *1624–1636.*
The Place: *Sweden, Poland, Germany.*

Scene I

Spring, 1624. In Dalarna, the Swedish Commander Oxenstierna is recruiting for the campaign in Poland. The canteen woman Anna Fierling, commonly known as Mother Courage, loses a son.

Highway outside a town. A SERGEANT *and a* RECRUITING OFFICER *stand shivering.*

RECRUITING OFFICER. How the hell can you line up a company in a place like this? You know what I keep thinking about, Sergeant? Suicide. I'm supposed to knock four platoons together by the twelfth —four platoons the Chief's asking for! And they're so friendly around here, I'm scared to go to sleep at night. Suppose I do get my hands on some character and squint at him so I don't notice he's pigeon-chested and has varicose veins. I get him drunk and relaxed, he signs on the dotted line. I pay for the drinks, he steps outside for a minute. I have a hunch I should follow him to the door, and am I right? Away he's gone like a louse from a scratch. You can't take a man's word any more, Sergeant. There's no loyalty left in the world, no trust, no faith, no sense of honour. I'm losing my confidence in mankind, Sergeant.

SERGEANT. What they could do with around here is a good war. What else can you expect with peace running wild all over the place? You know what the trouble with peace is? No organization. And when do you get organization? In a war. Peace is one big waste of equipment. Anything goes, no one gives a damn. See the way they eat? Cheese on pumpernickel, bacon on the cheese? Disgusting! How many horses have they got in this town? How many young men?

Nobody knows! They haven't bothered to count 'em! That's peace
for you! I've been in places where they haven't had a war for
seventy years and you know what? The people haven't even been
given names! They don't know who they are! It takes a war to fix
that. In a war, everyone registers, everyone's name's on a list. Their
shoes are stacked, their corn's in the bag, you count it all up—cattle,
men, *et cetera*—and you take it away! That's the story: no organization, no war!

RECRUITING OFFICER. It's God's truth, you know.

SERGEANT. Of course, a war's like any good deal: hard to get going.
But when it does get moving, it's a winner, and they're all scared of
peace, like a dice player who daren't stop—'cause when peace
comes they have to pay up. Of course, *until* it gets going, they're
just as scared of war, it's such a novelty!

RECRUITING OFFICER. Hey, look, here's a canteen wagon. Two women
and a couple of young lads. Stop the old lady, Sergeant. And if
there's nothing doing this time, you won't catch me freezing my arse
in the April wind a minute longer.

    [*A harmonica is heard. A canteen wagon rolls on,
    drawn by two young fellows.* MOTHER COURAGE *is
    sitting on it with her dumb daughter,* KATTRIN.]

MOTHER COURAGE. A good day to you, Sergeant!

SERGEANT (*barring the way*). Good day to *you*! Who d'you think you
are?

MOTHER COURAGE. Tradespeople.

               [*She sings.*]
Here's Mother Courage and her wagon!
    Hey, Captain, let them come and buy!
Beer by the keg! Wine by the flagon!
    Let your men drink before they die!
Sabres and swords are hard to swallow:
    First you must give them beer to drink.
Then they can face what is to follow—
    But let 'em swim before they sink!
            Christians, awake! The winter's gone!
            The snows depart, the dead sleep on.
            And though you may not long survive,
            Get out of bed and look alive!

Your men will march till they are dead, sir.
    But cannot fight unless they eat.
The blood they spill for you is red, sir,
    What fires that blood is my red meat.
For meat and soup and jam and jelly
    In this old cart of mine are found:

So fill the hole up in your belly
    Before you fill one underground.
        Christians, awake! The winter's gone!
        The snows depart, the dead sleep on.
        And though you may not long survive,
        Get out of bed and look alive!
            [*She prepares to go.*]

SERGEANT. Halt! Where are you from, riffraff?

EILIF. Second Finnish Regiment!

SERGEANT. Where are your papers?

MOTHER COURAGE. Papers?

SWISS CHEESE. But this is Mother Courage!

SERGEANT. Never heard of her. Where'd she get a name like that?

MOTHER COURAGE. They call me Mother Courage 'cause I was afraid I'd be ruined. So I drove through the bombardment of Riga like a madwoman, with fifty loaves of bread in my cart. They were going moldy, I couldn't please myself.

SERGEANT. No funny business! Where are your papers?

> [MOTHER COURAGE *rummages among papers in a tin box and clambers down from her wagon.*]

MOTHER COURAGE. Here, Sergeant! Here's a Bible—I got it in Altötting to wrap my cucumbers in. Here's a map of Moravia—God knows if I'll ever get there—the birds can have it. And here's a document saying my horse hasn't got foot and mouth disease—pity he died on us, he cost fifteen gilders, thank God I didn't pay it. Is that enough paper?

SERGEANT. Are you making a pass at me? Well, you've got another guess coming. You need a license and you know it.

MOTHER COURAGE. Show a little respect for a lady and don't go telling these half-grown children of mine I'm making a pass at you. What would I want with you? My license in the Second Protestant Regiment is an honest face. If *you* wouldn't know how to read it, that's not my fault, I want no rubber stamp on it anyhow.

RECRUITING OFFICER. Sergeant, we have a case of insubordination on our hands. Do you know what we need in the army? Discipline!

MOTHER COURAGE. I was going to say sausages.

SERGEANT. Name?

MOTHER COURAGE. Anna Fierling.

SERGEANT. So you're all Fierlings.

MOTHER COURAGE. I was talking about me.

SERGEANT. And I was talking about your children.

MOTHER COURAGE. Must they all have the same name?
            [*Pointing to the elder son.*]
    This fellow, for instance, I call him Eilif Noyocki—he got the name from his father who told me he was called Koyocki. Or was it

Moyocki? Anyhow, the lad remembers him to this day. Only the man he remembers is someone else, a Frenchman with a pointed beard. But he certainly has his father's brains—that man could whip the breeches off a farmer's backside before he could turn around. So we all have our own names.

SERGEANT. You're all called something different?

MOTHER COURAGE. Are you trying to make out you don't understand?

SERGEANT. (*Pointing at the younger son*). He's a Chinese, I suppose.

MOTHER COURAGE. Wrong again. A Swiss.

SERGEANT. After the Frenchman?

MOTHER COURAGE. Frenchman? What Frenchman? Don't confuse the issue, Sergeant, or we'll be here all day. He's a Swiss, but he happens to be called Feyos, a name that has nothing to do with his father, who was called something else—a military engineer, if you please, and a drunkard.

[SWISS CHEESE *nods, beaming; even* KATTRIN *smiles.*]

SERGEANT. Then how is it his name's Feyos?

MOTHER COURAGE. Oh, Sergeant, you have no imagination. *Of course* he's called Feyos: When he came, I was with a Hungarian. He didn't mind. He had a floating kidney, though he never touched a drop. He was a very *honest* man. The boy takes after him.

SERGEANT. But that wasn't his father!

MOTHER COURAGE. I said: he took after him. I call him Swiss Cheese. Why? Because he's good at pulling wagons.

[*Pointing to her daughter.*]

And that is Kattrin Haupt, she's half German.

SERGEANT. A nice family, I must say!

MOTHER COURAGE. And we've seen the whole wide world together— this wagonload and me.

SERGEANT. We'll need all that in writing.

[*He writes.*]

You're from Bamberg in Bavaria. What are you doing here?

MOTHER COURAGE. I can't wait till the war is good enough to come to Bamberg.

RECRUITING OFFICER. And you two oxen pull the cart. Jacob Ox and Esau Ox! D'you ever get out of harness?

EILIF. Mother! May I smack him in the kisser?

MOTHER COURAGE. You stay where you are. And now, gentlemen, what about a brace of pistols? Or a belt? Sergeant? Yours is worn clean through.

SERGEANT. It's something else *I'm* looking for. These lads of yours are straight as birch trees, strong limbs, massive chests . . . What are such fine specimens doing out of the army?

MOTHER COURAGE (*quickly*). A soldier's life is not for sons of mine.

RECRUITING OFFICER. Why not? It means money. It means fame. Peddling shoes is woman's work.

[*To* EILIF.]

Step this way and let's see if that's muscle or chicken fat.

MOTHER COURAGE. It's chicken fat. Give him a good hard look, and he'll fall right over.

RECRUITING OFFICER. Yes, and kill a calf in the falling!

[*He tries to hustle* EILIF *away.*]

MOTHER COURAGE. Let him alone! He's not for you!

RECRUITING OFFICER. He called my face a kisser. That is an insult. The two of us will now go and settle the affair on the field of honor.

EILIF. Don't worry, Mother, I can handle him.

MOTHER COURAGE. Stay here. You're never happy till you're in a fight. He has a knife in his boot and he knows how to use it.

RECRUITING OFFICER. I'll draw it out of him like a milk tooth. Come on, young fellow-me-lad!

MOTHER COURAGE. Officer, I'll report you to the Colonel, and he'll throw you in jail. His lieutenant is courting my daughter.

SERGEANT (*to* OFFICER). Go easy.

[*To* MOTHER COURAGE.]

What have you got against the service, wasn't his own father a soldier? Didn't you say he died a soldier's death?

MOTHER COURAGE. This one's just a baby. You'll lead him like a lamb to the slaughter. I know you. You'll get five gilders for him.

RECRUITING OFFICER (*to* EILIF). First thing you know, you'll have a lovely cap and high boots, how about it?

EILIF. Not from you.

MOTHER COURAGE. "Let's you and me go fishing," said the angler to the worm.

[*To* SWISS CHEESE.]

Run and tell everybody they're trying to steal your brother!

[*She draws a knife.*]

Yes, just you try, and I'll cut you down like dogs! We sell cloth, we sell ham, we are peaceful people!

SERGEANT. You're peaceful all right: your knife proves that. Why, you should be ashamed of yourself. Give me that knife, you hag! You admit you live off the war, what else *could* you live off? Now tell me, how can we have a war without soldiers?

MOTHER COURAGE. Do they have to be mine?

SERGEANT. So that's the trouble. The war should swallow the peach-stone and spit out the peach, hm? Your brood should get fat off the war, but the poor war must ask nothing in return, it can look after itself, can it? Call yourself Mother Courage and then get scared of the war, your breadwinner? Your sons aren't scared, I know that much.

EILIF. Takes more than a war to scare me.

SERGEANT. Correct! Take me. The soldier's life hasn't done *me* any harm, has it? I enlisted at seventeen.

MOTHER COURAGE. You haven't reached seventy.

SERGEANT. I will, though.

MOTHER COURAGE. Above ground?

SERGEANT. Are you trying to rile me, telling me I'll die?

MOTHER COURAGE. Suppose it's the truth? Suppose I see it's your fate? Suppose I *know* you're just a corpse on furlough?

SWISS CHEESE. She can look into the future. Everyone says so.

RECRUITING OFFICER. Then by all means look into the sergeant's future. It might amuse him.

SERGEANT. I don't believe in that stuff.

MOTHER COURAGE. Helmet!

[SERGEANT *gives her his helmet.*]

SERGEANT. It means less than a shit in the grass. Anything for a laugh.

[MOTHER COURAGE *takes a sheet of parchment and tears it in two.*]

MOTHER COURAGE. Eilif, Swiss Cheese, Kattrin! So shall we all be torn in two if we let ourselves get too deep into this war!

[*To the* SERGEANT.]

I'll give you the bargain rate, and do it free. Watch! Death is black, so I draw a black cross.

SWISS CHEESE. And the other she leaves blank, see?

MOTHER COURAGE. I fold them, put them in the helmet, and mix 'em up, the way all of us are mixed from our mother's womb on. Now draw!

[*The* SERGEANT *hesitates.*]

RECRUITING OFFICER (*to* EILIF). I don't take just anybody. I'm choosy. And you've got guts, I like that.

SERGEANT. It's silly. Means as much as blowing your nose.

SWISS CHEESE. The black cross! Oh, his number's up!

RECRUITING OFFICER. Don't let them get under your skin. There aren't enough bullets to go round.

SERGEANT (*hoarsely*). You cheated me!

MOTHER COURAGE. You cheated yourself the day you enlisted. And now we must drive on. There isn't a war every day in the week, we must get to work.

SERGEANT. Hell, you're not getting away with this! We're taking that bastard of yours with *us!*

EILIF. I'd like that, Mother.

MOTHER COURAGE. Quiet—you Finnish devil, you!

EILIF. And Swiss Cheese wants to be a soldier, too.

MOTHER COURAGE. That's news to me. I see I'll have to draw lots for all three of you.

*[She goes to the back to draw the crosses on bits of
paper.]*

RECRUITING OFFICER (*to* EILIF). People've been saying the Swedish
soldier is religious. That kind of loose talk has hurt us a lot. One
verse of a hymn every Sunday—and then only if you have a
voice . . .

*[MOTHER COURAGE returns with the slips and puts
them in the SERGEANT's helmet.]*

MOTHER COURAGE. So they'd desert their old mother, would they, the
rascals? They take to war like a cat to cream. But I'll consult these
slips, and they'll see the world's no promised land, with a "Join up,
son, you're officer material!" Sergeant, I'm afraid for them, very
afraid they won't get through this war. They have terrible qualities,
all three.

[She holds the helmet out to EILIF.]

There. Draw your lot.

*[EILIF fishes in the helmet, unfolds a slip. She snatches
it from him.]*

There you have it: a cross. Unhappy mother that I am, rich only
in a mother's sorrows! He dies. In the springtime of his life, he must
go. If he's a soldier, he must bite the dust, that's clear. He's too
brave, like his father. And if he doesn't use his head, he'll go the
way of all flesh, the slip proves it.

[Hectoring him.]

Will you use your head?

EILIF. Why not?

MOTHER COURAGE. It's using your head to stay with your mother. And
when they make fun of you and call you a chicken, just laugh.

RECRUITING OFFICER. If you're going to wet your pants, I'll try your
brother.

MOTHER COURAGE. I told you to laugh. Laugh! Now it's your turn,
Swiss Cheese. You should be a better bet, you're honest.

[He fishes in the helmet.]

Oh, dear, why are you giving that slip such a funny look? You've
drawn a blank for sure. It can't be there's a cross on it. It can't
be I'm going to lose *you*.

[She takes the slip.]

A cross? Him too! Could it be 'cause he's so simple-minded? Oh,
Swiss Cheese, you'll be a goner too, if you aren't honest, honest,
honest the whole time, the way I always brought you up to be, the
way you always bring me all the change when you buy me a loaf.
It's the only way you can save yourself. Look, Sergeant, if it isn't
a black cross!

SERGEANT. It's a cross! I don't understand how *I* got one. I always
stay well in the rear.

[*To the* OFFICER.]
But it can't be a trick: it gets *her* children too.

SWISS CHEESE. It gets me too. But I don't accept it!

MOTHER COURAGE (*to* KATTRIN). And now all I have left for certain is you, you're a cross in yourself, you have a good heart.

[*She holds the helmet up high toward the wagon
but takes the slip out herself.*]

Oh, I could give up in despair! There must be some mistake, I didn't mix them right. Don't be too kind, Kattrin, just don't, there's a cross in your path too. Always be very quiet, it can't be hard since you're dumb. Well, so now you know, all of you: be careful, you'll need to be. Now let's climb on the wagon and move on.

[*She returns the helmet to the* SERGEANT *and climbs
on the wagon.*]

RECRUITING OFFICER (*to the* SERGEANT). Do something!

SERGEANT. I don't feel very well.

RECRUITING OFFICER. Maybe you caught a chill when you handed over your helmet in all this wind. Get her involved in a business transaction!

[*Aloud.*]

That belt, Sergeant, you could at least take a look at it. These good people live by trade, don't they? Hey, all of you, the Sergeant wants to buy the belt!

MOTHER COURAGE. Half a gilder. A belt like that is worth two gilders.

[*She clambers down again from the wagon.*]

SERGEANT. It isn't new. But there's too much wind here. I'll go and look at it behind the wagon. (*He does so.*)

MOTHER COURAGE. I don't find it windy.

SERGEANT. Maybe it's worth half a gilder at that. There's silver on it.

MOTHER COURAGE (*following him behind the wagon*). A solid six ounces worth!

RECRUITING OFFICER (*to* EILIF). And we can have a drink, just us men. I'll advance you some money to cover it. Let's go.

[EILIF *stands undecided.*]

MOTHER COURAGE. Half a gilder, then.

SERGEANT. I don't understand it. I always stay in the rear. There's no safer spot for a sergeant to be. You can send the others on ahead in quest of fame. My appetite is ruined. I can tell you right now: I won't be able to get anything down.

MOTHER COURAGE. You shouldn't take on so, just because you can't eat. Just stay in the rear. Here, take a slug of brandy, man.

[*She gives him brandy.*]

RECRUITING OFFICER (*who has taken* EILIF *by the arm and is making off toward the back*). Ten gilders in advance and you're a soldier of the king and a stout fellow and the women will be mad about

you. And you can give me a smack in the kisser for insulting you.
(*Both leave.*)

[*Dumb* KATTRIN *jumps down from the wagon and
lets out harsh cries.*]

MOTHER COURAGE. Coming, Kattrin, coming! The sergeant's just paying
up.

[*She bites the half gilder.*]

I'm suspicious of all money, I've been badly burned, Sergeant. But
this money's good. And now we'll be going. Where's Eilif?

SWISS CHEESE. Gone with the recruiting officer.

MOTHER COURAGE (*stands quite still, then*). Oh, you simpleton!

[*To* KATTRIN.]

You *can't* speak, I know. You are innocent.

SERGEANT. That's life, Mother Courage. Take a slug yourself, Mother.
Being a soldier isn't the worst that could happen. You want to live
off war and keep you and yours out of it, do you?

MOTHER COURAGE. You must help your brother now, Kattrin.

[BROTHER *and* SISTER *get into harness together and
pull the wagon.* MOTHER COURAGE *walks at their side.
The wagon gets under way.*]

SERGEANT (*looking after them*).

When a war gives you all you earn
One day it may claim something in return!

Scene 2

In the years 1625 and 1626 Mother Courage journeys through Poland in the baggage train of the Swedish army. She meets her son again before Wallhof castle. Of the successful sale of a capon and great days for the brave son.

Tent of the Swedish Commander. Kitchen next to it. Thunder of cannon. The COOK *is quarreling with* MOTHER COURAGE *who is trying to sell him a capon.*

COOK. Sixty hellers for that paltry piece of poultry?

MOTHER COURAGE. Paltry poultry? Why, he's the fattest fowl you ever saw! I see no reason why I shouldn't get sixty hellers for him—this Commander can eat till the cows come home—and woe betide you when there's nothing in your pantry . . .

COOK. They're ten hellers a dozen on every street corner.

MOTHER COURAGE. A capon like this on every street corner! With a siege going on and people all skin and bones? Maybe you can get a field rat! I said maybe. Because we're all out of *them* too. Didn't you see the soldiers running five deep after one hungry little field rat? All right then, in a siege, my price for a giant capon is fifty hellers.

COOK. But we're not "in a siege," we're doing the besieging, it's the other side that's "in a siege," when will you get this into your head?

MOTHER COURAGE. A fat lot of difference that makes, *we* haven't got a thing to eat either. They took everything in the town with them before all this started, and now they've nothing to do but eat and drink, I hear. It's us I'm worried about. Look at the farmers round here, they haven't a thing.

COOK. Certainly they have. They hide it.

MOTHER COURAGE (*triumphant*). They have not! They're ruined, that's what. They're so hungry I've seen 'em digging up roots to eat. I could boil your leather belt and make their mouths water with it. That's how things are round here. And I'm expected to let a capon go for forty hellers!

COOK. Thirty. Not forty. I said thirty hellers.

MOTHER COURAGE. I say this is no ordinary capon. It was a talented animal, so I hear. It would only feed to music—one march in particular was its favorite. It was so intelligent it could count. Forty hellers is too much for all this? I know *your* problem: if you don't find something to eat and quick, the Chief will—cut—your—fat—head—off!

COOK. All right, just watch.

[*He takes a piece of beef and lays his knife on it.*]

Here's a piece of beef, I'm going to roast it. I give you one more chance.

MOTHER COURAGE. Roast it, go ahead, it's only one year old.

COOK. One *day* old! Yesterday it was a cow. I saw it running around.

MOTHER COURAGE. In that case it must have started stinking before it died.

COOK. I don't care if I have to cook it five hours: I *must* know if it'll still be hard.

[*He cuts into it.*]

MOTHER COURAGE. Put plenty of pepper in, so the Commander won't smell the smell.

[*The* SWEDISH COMMANDER: *a* CHAPLAIN *and* EILIF *enter the tent.*]

COMMANDER (*clapping* EILIF *on the shoulder*). In the Commander's tent with you, my son! Sit at my right hand, you happy warrior! You've played a hero's part, you've served the Lord in his own Holy War, *that's* the thing! And you'll get a gold bracelet out of it when we take the town if *I* have any say in the matter! We come to save their souls and what do they do, the filthy, irreligious sons of bitches? Drive their cattle away from us, while they stuff their priests with beef at both ends! But you showed 'em. So here's a can of red wine for you, we'll drink together!

[*They do so.*]

The chaplain gets the dregs, he's pious. Now what would you like for dinner, my hearty?

EILIF. How about a slice of meat?

COMMANDER. Cook, meat!

COOK. Nothing to eat, so he brings company to eat it!

[MOTHER COURAGE *makes him stop talking, she wants to listen.*]

EILIF. Tires you out, skinning peasants. Gives you an appetite.

MOTHER COURAGE. Dear God, it's my Eilif!

COOK. Who?

MOTHER COURAGE. My eldest. It's two years since I saw him, he was stolen from me right off the street. He must be in high favor if the Commander's invited him to dinner. And what do you have to eat? Nothing. You hear what the Commander's guest wants? Meat! Better take my advice, buy the capon. The price is one gilder.

COMMANDER (*who has sat down with* EILIF *and the* CHAPLAIN, *roaring*). Cook! Dinner, you pig, or I'll have your head!

COOK. This is blackmail. Give me the damn thing!

MOTHER COURAGE. Paltry poultry like this?

COOK. You were right. Give it here. It's highway robbery, fifty hellers.

MOTHER COURAGE. I said one gilder. Nothing's too high for my eldest, the Commander's guest of honor.

COOK (*giving her the money*). Well, you might at least pluck it till I have a fire going.

MOTHER COURAGE (*sitting down to pluck the capon*). I can't wait to see his face when he sees me. This is my brave and clever son. I also have a stupid one but he's honest. The daughter is nothing. At least, she doesn't talk: we must be thankful for small mercies.

COMMANDER. Have another glass, my son, it's my favorite Falernian. There's only one cask left—two at the most—but it's worth it to meet a soldier that still believes in God! The shepherd of our flock here just looks on, he only preaches, he hasn't a clue how anything gets done. So now, Eilif, my son, give us the details: tell us how you fixed the peasants and grabbed the twenty bullocks. And let's hope they'll soon be here.

EILIF. In one day's time. Two at most.

MOTHER COURAGE. Now that's considerate of Eilif—to bring the oxen tomorrow—otherwise my capon wouldn't have been so welcome today.

EILIF. Well, it was like this. I found out that the peasants had hidden their oxen and—on the sly and chiefly at night—had driven them into a certain wood. The people from the town were to pick them up there. I let them get their oxen in peace—they ought to know better than me where they are, I said to myself. Meanwhile I made my men crazy for meat. Their rations were short and I made sure they got shorter. Their mouths'd water at the sound of any word beginning with M, like mother.

COMMANDER. Smart fella.

EILIF. Not bad. The rest was a walkover. Only the peasants had clubs and outnumbered us three to one and made a murderous attack on us. Four of them drove me into a clump of trees, knocked my good sword from my hand, and yelled, "Surrender!" What now, I said to myself, they'll make mincemeat of me.

COMMANDER. What did you do?

EILIF. I laughed.

COMMANDER. You what?

EILIF. I laughed. And so we got to talking. I came right down to business and said: "Twenty gilders an ox is too much, I bid fifteen." Like I wanted to buy. That foxed 'em. So while they were scratching their heads, I reached for my good sword and cut 'em to pieces. Necessity knows no law, huh?

COMMANDER. What do *you* say, shepherd of the flock?

CHAPLAIN. Strictly speaking, that saying is not in the Bible. Our Lord made five hundred loaves out of five so that no such necessity would arise. When he told men to love their neighbors, their bellies were full. Nowadays things are different.

COMMANDER (*laughing*). Quite different. A swallow of wine for those wise words, you pharisee!

[*To* EILIF.]

You cut 'em to pieces in a good cause, our chaps were hungry and you gave 'em to eat. Doesn't it say in the Bible "Whatsoever thou doest to the least of these my children, thou doest unto me?" And what *did* you do to 'em? You got 'em the best steak dinner they ever tasted. Moldy bread is not what they're used to. They always ate white bread, and drank wine in their helmets, before going out to fight for God.

EILIF. I reached for my good sword and cut 'em to pieces.

COMMANDER. You have the makings of a Julius Caesar, why, you should be presented to the King!

EILIF. I've seen him—from a distance of course. He seemed to shed a light all around. I must try to be like him!

COMMANDER. I think you're succeeding, my boy! Oh, Eilif, you don't know how I value a brave soldier like you! I treat such a chap as my very own son.

[*He takes him to the map.*]

Take a look at our position, Eilif, it isn't all it might be, is it?

MOTHER COURAGE (*who has been listening and is now plucking angrily at her capon*). He must be a very bad commander.

COOK. Just a greedy one. Why bad?

MOTHER COURAGE. Because he needs *brave* soldiers, that's why. If his plan of campaign was any good, why would he need *brave* soldiers, wouldn't plain, ordinary soldiers do? Whenever there are great virtues, it's a sure sign something's wrong.

COOK. You mean, it's a sure sign something's right.

MOTHER COURAGE. I mean what I say. Listen. When a general or a king is stupid and leads his soldiers into a trap, they need this virtue of courage. When he's tightfisted and hasn't enough soldiers, the few he does have need the heroism of Hercules—another virtue. And if he's a sloven and doesn't give a damn about anything, they have to be wise as serpents or they're finished. Loyalty's another virtue and you need plenty of it if the king's always asking too much of you. All virtues which a well-regulated country with a good king or a good general wouldn't need. In a good country virtues wouldn't be necessary. Everybody could be quite ordinary, middling, and, for all I care, cowards.

COMMANDER. I bet your father was a soldier.

EILIF. I've heard he was a great soldier. My mother warned me. I know a song about that.

COMMANDER. Sing it to us.

                              [*Roaring.*]

Bring that meat!

EILIF. It's called "The Song of the Fishwife and the Soldier."

                    [*He sings and at the same time does a war dance
                                    with his sabre.*]

To a soldier lad comes an old fishwife
    And this old fishwife, says she:
A gun will shoot, a knife will knife,
    You will drown if you fall in the sea.
Keep away from the ice if you want my advice,
    Says the old fishwife, says she.
The soldier laughs and loads his gun
Then grabs his knife and starts to run:
    It's the life of a hero for me!
From the north to the south I shall march through the land
With a knife at my side and a gun in my hand!
    Says the soldier lad, says he.

When the lad defies the fishwife's cries
    The old fishwife, says she:
The young are young, the old are wise,
    You will drown if you fall in the sea.
Don't ignore what I say or you'll rue it one day!
    Says the old fishwife, says she.
But gun in hand and knife at side
The soldier steps into the tide:
    It's the life of a hero for me!
When the new moon is shining on shingle roofs white
We are all coming back, go and pray for that night!
    Says the soldier lad, says he.

                    [MOTHER COURAGE *continues the song from her
                        kitchen, beating on a pan with a spoon.*]

And the fishwife old does what she's told:
Down upon her knees drops she.
When the smoke is gone, the air is cold,
Your heroic deeds won't warm me!
See the smoke, how it goes! May God scatter his foes!
Down upon her knees drops she.

EILIF. What's that?

MOTHER COURAGE (*singing on*).
But gun in hand and knife at side
The lad is swept out by the tide:
He floats with the ice to the sea.
And the new moon is shining on shingle roofs white
But the lad and his laughter are lost in the night:
He floats with the ice to the sea.

COMMANDER. What a kitchen I've got! There's no end to the liberties they take!

EILIF (*has entered the kitchen and embraced his mother*). To see you again! Where are the others?

MOTHER COURAGE (*in his arms*). Happy as ducks in a pond. Swiss Cheese is paymaster with the Second Regiment, so at least he isn't in the fighting. I couldn't keep him out altogether.

EILIF. Are your feet holding up?

MOTHER COURAGE. I've a bit of trouble getting my shoes on in the morning.

COMMANDER (*who has come over*). So, you're his mother! I hope you have more sons for me like this chap.

EILIF. If I'm not the lucky one: you sit there in the kitchen and hear your son being feasted!

MOTHER COURAGE. Yes. I heard all right.

[*Gives him a box on the ear.*]

EILIF (*his hand to his cheek*). Because I took the oxen?

MOTHER COURAGE. No. Because you didn't surrender when the four peasants let fly at you and tried to make mincemeat of you! Didn't I teach you to take care of yourself? You Finnish devil, you!

[*The* COMMANDER *and the* CHAPLAIN *stand laughing in the doorway.*]

Scene 3

Three years pass and Mother Courage, with parts of a Finnish regiment, is taken prisoner. Her daughter is saved, her wagon likewise, but her honest son dies.

A camp. The regimental flag is flying from a pole. Afternoon. All sorts of wares hanging on the wagon. MOTHER COURAGE'*s clothes line is tied to the wagon at one end, to a cannon at the other. She and* KATTRIN *are folding the washing on the cannon. At the same time she is bargaining with an* ORDNANCE OFFICER *over a bag of bullets.* SWISS CHEESE, *in paymaster's uniform now, looks on.* YVETTE POTTER, *a very good-looking young person, is sewing at a colored hat, a glass of brandy before her. She is in stocking feet. Her red boots are near by.*

OFFICER. I'm letting you have the bullets for two gilders. Dirt cheap. 'Cause I need the money. The Colonel's been drinking with the officers for three days and we've run out of liquor.

MOTHER COURAGE. They're army property. If they find 'em on me, I'll be courtmartialed. You sell your bullets, you bastards, and send your men out to fight with nothing to shoot with.

OFFICER. Oh, come on, if you scratch my back, I'll scratch yours.

MOTHER COURAGE. I won't take army stuff. Not at *that* price.

OFFICER. You can resell 'em for five gilders, maybe eight, to the Ordnance Officer of the Fourth Regiment. All you have to do is give him a receipt for twelve. He hasn't a bullet left.

MOTHER COURAGE. Why don't you do it yourself?

OFFICER. I don't trust him. We're friends.

MOTHER COURAGE (*takes the bag*). Give it here.

[*To* KATTRIN.]

Take it round the back and pay him a gilder and a half.

[*As the* OFFICER *protests.*]

I said a gilder and a half!

[KATTRIN *drags the bag away. The* OFFICER *follows.*

MOTHER COURAGE *speaks to* SWISS CHEESE.]

Here's your underwear back, take care of it; it's October now, autumn may come at any time; I purposely don't say it must come, I've learnt from experience there's nothing that must come, not even the seasons. But your books *must* balance now you're the regimental paymaster. *Do* they balance?

SWISS CHEESE. Yes, Mother.

MOTHER COURAGE. Don't forget they made you paymaster because you're honest and so simple you'd never think of running off with the cash. Don't lose that underwear.

SWISS CHEESE. No, Mother. I'll put it under the mattress.

[*He starts to go.*]

OFFICER. I'll go with you, paymaster.

MOTHER COURAGE. Don't teach him any hanky-panky.

[*Without a good-bye the* OFFICER *leaves with* SWISS CHEESE.]

YVETTE (*waving to him*). You might at least say good-bye!

MOTHER COURAGE (*to* YVETTE). I don't like that. He's no sort of company for my Swiss Cheese. But the war's not making a bad start. Before all the different countries get into it, four or five years'll have gone by like nothing. If I look ahead and make no mistakes, business will be good. Don't you know you shouldn't drink in the morning with your illness?

YVETTE. Who says I'm ill? That's libel!

MOTHER COURAGE. They all say so.

YVETTE. They're all liars. I'm desperate, Mother Courage. They all avoid me like a stinking fish. Because of those lies. So what am I fixing my hat for?

[*She throws it down.*]

That's why I drink in the morning. I never used to, it gives you crow's feet. But now it's all one, every man in the regiment knows me. I should have stayed home when my first was unfaithful. But pride isn't for the likes of us, you eat dirt or down you go.

MOTHER COURAGE. Now don't you start again with your friend Peter and how it all happened—in front of my innocent daughter.

YVETTE. She's the one that should hear it. So she'll get hardened against love.

MOTHER COURAGE. That's something no one ever gets hardened against.

YVETTE. I'll tell you about it, and get it off my chest. I grew up in

Flanders' fields, that's where it starts, or I'd never even have caught
sight of him and I wouldn't be here in Poland today. He was an army
cook, blond, a Dutchman, but thin. Kattrin, beware of thin men! I
didn't. I didn't even know he'd had another girl before me and she
called him Peter Piper because he never took his pipe out of his
mouth the whole time, it meant so little to him.

[*She sings "The Fraternization Song."*]

Scarce seventeen was I when
 The foe came to our land
And laid aside his sabre
 And took me by the hand.
  And we performed by day
  The sacred rite of May
  And we performed by night
  Another sacred rite.
  The regiment, well exercised,
  Presented arms, then stood at ease,
  Then took us off behind the trees
  Where we fraternized.

Each of us had her foe and
 A cook fell to my lot.
I hated him by daylight
 But in the dark did not.
  So we perform by day
  The sacred rite of May
  And we perform by night
  That other sacred rite.
  The regiment, well exercised,
  Presents its arms, then stands at ease,
  Then takes us off behind the trees
  Where we fraternize.

Ecstasy filled my heart, O
 My love seemed heaven-born!
But why were people saying
 It was not love but scorn?
  The springtime's soft amour
  Through summer may endure
  But swiftly comes the fall
  And winter ends it all.
  December came. All of the men
  Filed past the trees where once we hid
  Then quickly marched away and did
  Not come back again.

I made the mistake of running after him, I never found him. It's ten years ago now.

[*With swaying gait she goes behind the wagon.*]

MOTHER COURAGE. You're leaving your hat.

YVETTE. For the birds.

MOTHER COURAGE. Let this be a lesson to you, Kattrin, never start anything with a soldier. Love does seem heaven-born, so watch out! Even with those who're not in the army life's no honey pot. He tells you he'd like to kiss the ground under your feet—did you wash 'em yesterday, while we're on the subject? And then if you don't look out, your number's up, you're his slave for life. Be glad you're dumb, Kattrin: you'll never contradict yourself, you'll never want to bite your tongue off because you spoke out of turn. Dumbness is a gift from God. Here comes the Commander's Cook, what's bothering *him?*

[*Enter the* COOK *and the* CHAPLAIN.]

CHAPLAIN. I bring a message from your son Eilif. The Cook came with me. You've made, ahem, an impression on him.

COOK. I thought I'd get a little whiff of the balmy breeze.

MOTHER COURAGE. You're always welcome to that if you behave yourself and, even if you don't, I think I can handle you. But what does Eilif want? I've no money to spare.

CHAPLAIN. Actually, I have something to tell his brother, the paymaster.

MOTHER COURAGE. He isn't here. And he isn't anywhere else either. He's not his brother's paymaster, and I won't have him led into temptation. Let Eilif try it on with someone else!

[*She takes money from the purse at her belt.*]

Give him this. It's a sin. He's speculating in mother love, he ought to be ashamed of himself.

COOK. Not for long. He has to go with his regiment now—to his death maybe. Send some more money, or you'll be sorry. You women are hard—and sorry afterwards. A glass of brandy wouldn't cost very much, but you refuse to provide it, and six feet under goes your man and you can't dig him up again.

CHAPLAIN. All very touching, my dear Cook, but to fall in this war is not a misfortune, it's a blessing. This is a war of religion. Not just any old war but a special one, a religious one, and therefore pleasing unto God.

COOK. Correct. In one sense it's a war because there's fleecing, bribing, plundering, not to mention a little raping, but it's different from all other wars because it's a war of religion. That's clear. All the same, it makes you thirsty.

CHAPLAIN (to MOTHER COURAGE, *pointing at the* COOK). I tried to hold him off but he said you'd bewitched him. He dreams about you.

COOK (*lighting a clay pipe*). Brandy from the fair hand of a lady, that's

for me. And don't embarrass me any more: the stories the chaplain
was telling on the way over still have me blushing.

MOTHER COURAGE. A man of his cloth! I must get you both something
to drink or you'll be making improper advances out of sheer boredom.

CHAPLAIN. That is indeed a temptation, said the Court Chaplain, and
gave way to it.

> [*Turning toward* KATTRIN *as he walks.*]

And who is this captivating young person?

MOTHER COURAGE. She's not a captivating young person, she's a respectable young person.

> [*The* CHAPLAIN *and the* COOK *go with* MOTHER COUR-
> AGE *behind the cart, and one hears them talk politics.*]

MOTHER COURAGE. The trouble here in Poland is that the Poles *would*
keep meddling. It's true our King moved in on them with man,
beast, and wagon, but instead of keeping the peace the Poles were
always meddling in their own affairs. They attacked the Swedish
King when he was in the act of peacefully withdrawing. So they
were guilty of a breach of the peace and their blood is on their own
heads.

CHAPLAIN. Anyway, our King was thinking of nothing but freedom.
The Kaiser enslaved them all, Poles and Germans alike, so our King
had to liberate them.

COOK. Just what *I* think. Your health! Your brandy is first rate, I'm
never mistaken in a face.

> [KATTRIN *looks after them, leaves the washing, and
> goes to the hat, picks it up, sits down, and takes up
> the red boots.*]

And the war is a war of religion.

> [*Singing while* KATTRIN *puts the boots on.*]

"A mighty fortress is our God . . ."

> [*He sings a verse or so of Luther's hymn.*]

And talking of King Gustavus, this freedom he tried to bring to
Germany cost him a pretty penny. Back in Sweden he had to levy
a salt tax, the poorer folks didn't like it a bit. Then, too, he had
to lock up the Germans and even cut their heads off, they clung
so to slavery and their Kaiser. Of course, if no one had *wanted* to
be free, the King wouldn't have had any fun. First it was just
Poland he tried to protect from bad men, specially the Kaiser, then
his appetite grew with eating, and he ended up protecting Germany
too. Now Germany put up a pretty decent fight. So the good King
had nothing but worries in return for his outlay and his goodness,
and of course he had to get his money back with taxes, which
made bad blood, but he didn't shrink even from that. For he had
one thing in his favor anyway, God's Holy Word, which was all to

the good, because otherwise they could have said he did it for himself or for profit. That's how he kept his conscience clear. He always
put conscience first.

MOTHER COURAGE. It's plain you're no Swede, or you'd speak differently of the Hero King.

CHAPLAIN. What's more, you eat his bread.

COOK. I don't eat his bread. I bake his bread.

MOTHER COURAGE. He can never be conquered, and I'll tell you why:
his men believe in him.

[*Earnestly.*]

To hear the big chaps talk, they wage the war from fear of God
and for all things bright and beautiful, but just look into it, and
you'll see they're not so silly: they want a good profit out of it, or
else the little chaps like you and me wouldn't back 'em up.

COOK. That's right.

CHAPLAIN. And as a Dutchman you'd do well to see which flag's flying
here before you express an opinion!

MOTHER COURAGE. All good Protestants for ever!

COOK. A health!

> [KATTRIN *has begun to strut around with* YVETTE'S
> *hat on, copying* YVETTE'S *sexy walk. Suddenly can-
> non and shots. Drums.* MOTHER COURAGE, *the* COOK,
> *and the* CHAPLAIN *rush round to the front of the cart,
> the two last with glasses in their hands. The* ORDNANCE
> OFFICER *and a* SOLDIER *come running to the cannon
> and try to push it along.*]

MOTHER COURAGE. What's the matter? Let me get my washing off that
gun, you slobs!

> [*She tries to do so.*]

OFFICER. The Catholics! Surprise attack! We don't know if we can get
away!

> [*To the* SOLDIER.]

Get that gun!

> [*Runs off.*]

COOK. For heaven's sake! I must go to the Commander. Mother Courage, I'll be back in a day or two—for a short conversation.

> [*Rushes off.*]

MOTHER COURAGE. Hey, you've left your pipe!

COOK (*off*). Keep it for me, I'll need it!

MOTHER COURAGE. This *would* happen when we were just making
money.

CHAPLAIN. Well, I must be going too. Yes, if the enemy's so close, it
can be dangerous. "Blessed are the peacemakers," a good slogan in
wartime! If only I had a cloak.

MOTHER COURAGE. I'm lending no cloaks. Not even to save a life I'm not. I've had experience in that line.

CHAPLAIN. But I'm in special danger. Because of my religion!

MOTHER COURAGE (*brings him a cloak*). It's against my better judgment. Now run!

CHAPLAIN. I thank you, you're very generous, but maybe I'd better stay and sit here. If I run, I might attract the enemy's attention. I might arouse suspicion.

MOTHER COURAGE (*to the* SOLDIER). Let it alone, you dolt, who's going to pay you for this? It'll cost you your life, let me hold it for you.

SOLDIER (*running away*). You're my witness: I tried!

MOTHER COURAGE. I'll swear to it!

[*Seeing* KATTRIN *with the hat.*]

What on earth are you up to—with a whore's hat! Take it off this minute! Are you crazy? With the enemy coming?

[*She tears the hat off her head.*]

Do you want them to find you and make a whore of you? And she has the boots on too, straight from Babylon. I'll soon fix that.

[*She tries to get them off.*]

Oh God, Chaplain, help me with these boots, I'll be back straightaway.

[*She runs to the wagon.*]

YVETTE (*entering and powdering her face*). What's that you say: the Catholics are coming? Where's my hat? Who's been trampling on it? I can't run around in that, what will they think of me? And I've no mirror either.

[*To the* CHAPLAIN.]

How do I look—too much powder?

CHAPLAIN. Just, er, right.

YVETTE. And where are my red boots?

[*She can't find them because* KATTRIN *is hiding her feet under her skirt.*]

I left them here! Now I've got to go barefoot to my tent, it's a scandal!   [*Exit.*]

[SWISS CHEESE *comes running in carrying a cashbox.*]

[MOTHER COURAGE *enters with her hands full of ashes.*]

[*To* KATTRIN.]

Ashes!

[*To* SWISS CHEESE.]

What have you got there?

SWISS CHEESE. The regimental cashbox.

MOTHER COURAGE. Throw it away! Your paymastering days are over!

SWISS CHEESE. It's a trust!

[He goes to the back.]

MOTHER COURAGE (*to the* CHAPLAIN). Off with your pastor's coat, Chaplain, or they'll recognize you, cloak or no cloak.

[She is rubbing ashes into KATTRIN's face.]

Keep still. A little dirt, and you're safe. A calamity! The sentries were drunk. Well, one must hide one's light under a bushel, as they say. When a soldier sees a clean face, there's one more whore in the world. Specially a Catholic soldier. For weeks on end, no grub. Then, when they get some by way of plunder, they jump on top of the womenfolk. That should do. Let me look at you. Not bad. Looks like you've been rolling in muck. Don't tremble. Nothing can happen to you now.

[To SWISS CHEESE.]*

Where've you left the cashbox?

SWISS CHEESE. I thought I'd just put it in the wagon.

MOTHER COURAGE (*horrified*). What!? In my wagon? God punish you for a prize idiot! If I just look away for a moment! They'll hang all three of us!

SWISS CHEESE. Then I'll put it somewhere else. Or escape with it.

MOTHER COURAGE. You'll stay where you are. It's too late.

CHAPLAIN (*still changing his clothes*). For Heaven's sake: the flag!

MOTHER COURAGE (*taking down the flag*). God in Heaven! I don't notice it any more. I've had it twenty-five years.

[The thunder of cannon grows.]

[Three days later. Morning. The cannon is gone.
MOTHER COURAGE, KATTRIN, *the* CHAPLAIN *and* SWISS
CHEESE *sit anxiously eating.*]

SWISS CHEESE. This is the third day I've been sitting here doing nothing, and the Sergeant, who's always been patient with me, may be slowly beginning to ask, "Where on earth is Swiss Cheese with that cashbox?"

MOTHER COURAGE. Be glad they're not on the scent.

CHAPLAIN. What about me? I can't hold service here or I'll be in hot water. It is written, "Out of the abundance of the heart, the tongue speaketh." But woe is me if *my* tongue speaketh!

MOTHER COURAGE. That's how it is. Here you sit—one with his religion, the other with his cashbox, I don't know which is more dangerous.

CHAPLAIN. We're in God's hands now!

MOTHER COURAGE. I hope we're not as desperate as *that,* but it *is* hard to sleep at night. 'Course it'd be easier if *you* weren't here, Swiss Cheese, all the same I've not done badly. I told them I was against the Antichrist, who's a Swede with horns on his head. I told them I noticed his left horn's a bit threadbare. When they cross-questioned me, I always asked where I could buy holy candles a bit cheaper.

I know these things because Swiss Cheese's father was a Catholic and made jokes about it. They didn't quite believe me but they needed a canteen, so they turned a blind eye. Maybe it's all for the best. We're prisoners. But so are lice in fur.

CHAPLAIN. The milk is good. As far as quantity goes, we may have to reduce our Swedish appetites somewhat. We are defeated.

MOTHER COURAGE. Who's defeated? The defeats and victories of the chaps at the top aren't always defeats and victories for the chaps at the bottom. Not at all. There've been cases where a defeat is a victory for the chaps at the bottom, it's only their honor that's lost, nothing serious. In Livonia once, our Chief took such a knock from the enemy, in the confusion I got a fine gray mare out of the baggage train, it pulled my wagon seven months—till we won and inventory was taken. But in general both defeat and victory are a costly business for us that haven't got much. The best thing is for politics to kind of get stuck in the mud.

[*To* SWISS CHEESE.]

Eat!

SWISS CHEESE. I don't like it. How will the Sergeant pay his men?

MOTHER COURAGE. Soldiers in flight don't get paid.

SWISS CHEESE. Well, they could claim to be. No pay, no flight. They can refuse to budge.

MOTHER COURAGE. Swiss Cheese, your sense of duty worries me. I've brought you up to be honest because you're not very bright. But don't go too far! And now I'm going with the Chaplain to buy a Catholic flag and some meat. There's no one can hunt out meat like him, sure as a sleepwalker. He can tell a good piece of meat from the way his mouth waters. A good thing they let me stay in the business. In business you ask what price, not what religion. And Protestant trousers keep you just as warm.

CHAPLAIN. As the mendicant monk said when there was talk of the Lutherans standing everything on its head in town and country: Beggars will *always* be needed.

[MOTHER COURAGE *disappears into the wagon.*]

She's worried about the cashbox. Up to now they've ignored us— as if we were part of the wagon—but can it last?

SWISS CHEESE. I can get rid of it.

CHAPLAIN. That's almost *more* dangerous. Suppose you're seen. They have spies. Yesterday morning one jumped out of the very hole I was relieving myself in. I was so off guard I almost broke out in prayer—*that* would have given me away all right! I believe their favorite way of finding a Protestant is smelling his, um, excrement. The spy was a little brute with a bandage over one eye.

MOTHER COURAGE (*clambering out of the wagon with a basket*). I've found you out, you shameless hussy!

[*She holds up* YVETTE's *red boots in triumph.*]

Yvette's red boots! She just swiped them—because you went and told her she was a captivating person.

[*She lays them in the basket.*]

Stealing Yvette's boots! But *she* disgraces herself for money, *you* do it for nothing—for pleasure! I told you, you must wait for the peace. No soldiers! Save your proud, peacock ways for peacetime!

CHAPLAIN. I don't find her proud.

MOTHER COURAGE. Prouder than she can afford to be. I like her when people say "I never noticed the poor thing." I like her when she's a stone in Dalarna where there's nothing but stones.

[*To* SWISS CHEESE.]

Leave the cashbox where it is, do you hear? And pay attention to your sister, she needs it. Between the two of you, you'll be the death of me yet. I'd rather take care of a bag of fleas.

[*She leaves with the* CHAPLAIN.]

[KATTRIN *clears the dishes away.*]

SWISS CHEESE. Not many days more when you can sit in the sun in your shirt sleeves.

[KATTRIN *points to a tree.*]

Yes, the leaves are yellow already.

[*With gestures,* KATTRIN *asks if he wants a drink.*]

I'm not drinking, I'm thinking.

[*Pause.*]

She says she can't sleep. So I *should* take the cashbox away. I've found a place for it. I'll keep it in the mole hole by the river till the time comes. I might get it tonight before sunrise and take it to the regiment. How far can they have fled in three days? The Sergeant's eyes'll pop out of his head. "You've disappointed me most pleasantly, Swiss Cheese," he'll say, "*I* trust you with the cashbox and *you* bring it back!" Yes, Kattrin, I *will* have a glass now!

[*When* KATTRIN *reappears behind the wagon two men confront her. One of them is a sergeant. The other doffs his hat and flourishes it in a showy greeting. He has a bandage over one eye.*]

THE MAN WITH THE BANDAGE. Good morning, young lady. Have you seen a man from the Second Protestant Regiment?

[*Terrified,* KATTRIN *runs away, spilling her brandy. The two men look at each other and then withdraw after seeing* SWISS CHEESE.]

SWISS CHEESE (*starting up from his reflection*). You're spilling it! What's the matter with you, can't you see where you're going? I don't understand you. Anyway, I must be off, I've decided it's the thing to do.

[*He stands up. She does all she can to make him
aware of the danger he is in. He only pushes her
away.*]

I'd like to know what you mean. I know you mean well, poor thing,
you just can't get it out. And don't trouble yourself about the
brandy, I'll live to drink so much of it, what's one glass?

[*He takes the cashbox out of the wagon and puts it
under his coat.*]

I'll be back straightaway. But don't hold me up or I'll have to scold
you. Yes, I know you mean well. If you could only speak!

[*When she tries to hold him back he kisses her and
pulls himself free. Exit. She is desperate and runs up
and down, emitting little sounds.* MOTHER COURAGE
and the CHAPLAIN *return.* KATTRIN *rushes at her
mother.*]

MOTHER COURAGE. What *is* it, what *is* it, Kattrin? Control yourself!
Has someone done something to you? Where is Swiss Cheese?

[*To the* CHAPLAIN.]

Don't stand around, get that Catholic flag up!

[*She takes a Catholic flag out of her basket and the*
CHAPLAIN *runs it up the pole.*]

CHAPLAIN (*bitterly*). All good Catholics forever!

MOTHER COURAGE. Now, Kattrin, calm down and tell all about it, your
mother understands. What, that little bastard of mine's taken the
cashbox away? I'll box his ears for him, the rascal! Now take your
time and don't try to talk, use your hands. I don't like it when you
howl like a dog, what'll the Chaplain think of you? See how shocked
he looks. A man with one eye was here?

CHAPLAIN. That fellow with one eye is an informer! Have they caught
Swiss Cheese?

[KATTRIN *shakes her head, shrugs her shoulders.*]

This is the end.

[*Voices off. The two men bring in* SWISS CHEESE.]

SWISS CHEESE. Let me go. I've nothing on me. You're breaking my
shoulder! I am innocent.

SERGEANT. This is where he comes from. These are his friends.

MOTHER COURAGE. Us? Since when?

SWISS CHEESE. I don't even know 'em. I was just getting my lunch
here. Ten hellers it cost me. Maybe you saw me sitting on that
bench. It was too salty.

SERGEANT. Who *are* you people, anyway?

MOTHER COURAGE. Law abiding citizens! It's true what he says. He
bought his lunch here. And it was too salty.

SERGEANT. Are you pretending you don't know him?

MOTHER COURAGE. I can't know all of them, can I? *I don't ask, "What's* your name and are you a heathen?" If they pay up, they're not heathens to me. Are you a heathen?

SWISS CHEESE. Oh, no!

CHAPLAIN. He sat there like a law-abiding chap and never once opened his mouth. Except to eat. Which is necessary.

SERGEANT. Who do you think *you* are?

MOTHER COURAGE. Oh, he's my barman. And you're thirsty, I'll bring you a glass of brandy. You must be footsore and weary!

SERGEANT. No brandy on duty.

[*To* SWISS CHEESE.]

You were carrying something. You must have hidden it by the river. We saw the bulge in your shirt.

MOTHER COURAGE. Sure it was him?

SWISS CHEESE. I think you mean another fellow. There *was* a fellow with something under his shirt, I saw him. I'm the wrong man.

MOTHER COURAGE. I think so too. It's a misunderstanding. Could happen to anyone. Oh, I know what people are like, I'm Mother Courage, you've heard of me, everyone knows about me, and I can tell you this: he looks honest.

SERGEANT. We're after the regimental cashbox. And we know what the man looks like who's been keeping it. We've been looking for him two days. It's you.

SWISS CHEESE. No, it's not!

SERGEANT. And if you don't shell out, you're dead, see? Where is it?

MOTHER COURAGE (*urgently*). 'Course he'd give it to you to save his life. He'd up and say, I do have it, here it is, you're stronger than me. He's not *that* stupid. Speak, little stupid, the Sergeant's giving you a chance!

SWISS CHEESE. What if I haven't got it?

SERGEANT. Come with us. We'll get it out of you.

[*They take him off.*]

MOTHER COURAGE (*shouting after them*). He'd tell you! He's not *that* stupid! And don't you break his shoulder blade! (*She runs after them.*)

[*The same evening. The* CHAPLAIN *and* KATTRIN *are rinsing glasses and polishing knives.*]

CHAPLAIN. Cases of people getting caught like this are by no means unknown in the history of religion. I am reminded of the Passion of Our Lord and Saviour. There's an old song about it.

[*He sings.*]

"The Song of the Hours"

In the first hour of the day
Simple Jesus Christ was

Presented as a murderer
To the heathen Pilate.

Pilate found no fault in him
No cause to condemn him
So he sent the Lord away.
Let King Herod see him!

Hour the third: the Son of God
Was with scourges beaten
And they set a crown of thorns
On the head of Jesus.

And they dressed him as a king
Joked and jested at him
And the cross to die upon
He himself must carry.

Six: they stripped Lord Jesus bare.
To the cross they nailed him.
When the blood came gushing, he
Prayed and loud lamented.

From their neighbour crosses, thieves
Mocked him like the others.
And the bright sun crept away
Not to see such doings.

Nine: Lord Jesus cried aloud
That he was forsaken!
In a sponge upon a pole
Vinegar was fed him.

Then the Lord gave up the ghost
And the earth did tremble.
Temple curtain split in twain.
Rocks fell in the ocean.

Evening: they broke the bones
Of the malefactors.
Then they took a spear and pierced
The side of gentle Jesus.

And the blood and water ran
And they laughed at Jesus.
Of this simple son of man
Such and more they tell us.

MOTHER COURAGE (*entering, excited*). It's life and death. But the
Sergeant will still listen to us. The only thing is, he mustn't know

it's our Swiss Cheese, or they'll say we helped him. It's only a matter
of money, but where can *we* get money? Wasn't Yvette here? I
met her on the way over. She's picked up a Colonel! Maybe he'll
buy her a canteen business!

CHAPLAIN. You'd sell the wagon, everything?

MOTHER COURAGE. Where else would I get the money for the Sergeant?

CHAPLAIN. What are you to live off?

MOTHER COURAGE. That's just it.

[*Enter* YVETTE POTTIER *with a hoary old* COLONEL.]

YVETTE (*embracing* MOTHER COURAGE). *Dear* Mistress Courage, we
meet again!

[*Whispering.*]

He didn't say no.

[*Aloud.*]

This is my friend, my, um, business adviser. I happened to hear
you might like to sell your wagon. Due to special circumstances, I'd
like to think about it.

MOTHER COURAGE. I want to pawn it, not sell it. And nothing hasty.
In war time you don't find another wagon like that so easy.

YVETTE (*disappointed*). Only pawn it? I thought you wanted to sell,
I don't know if I'm interested.

[*To the* COLONEL.]

What do *you* think, my dear?

COLONEL. I quite agree with you, ducky.

MOTHER COURAGE. It's only for pawn.

YVETTE. I thought you *had* to have the money.

MOTHER COURAGE (*firmly*). I do have to have it. But I'd rather wear
my feet off looking for an offer than just sell. We live off the wagon.
It's an opportunity for you, Yvette. Who knows when you'll have
another such? Who knows when you'll find another . . . business
adviser?

COLONEL. Take it, take it!

YVETTE. My friend thinks I should go ahead, but I'm not sure, if it's
only for pawn. You think we should buy it outright, don't you?

COLONEL. I do, ducky, I do!

MOTHER COURAGE. Then you must hunt up something that's for sale.
Maybe you'll find it—if you have the time, and your friend goes
with you, let's say in about a week, or two weeks, you may find
the right thing.

YVETTE. Yes, we can certainly look around for something. I love going
around looking, I love going around with you, Poldy . . .

COLONEL. Really? Do you?

YVETTE. Oh, it's lovely! I could take two weeks of it!

COLONEL. Really, could you?

YVETTE. If you get the money, when are you thinking of paying it back?

MOTHER COURAGE. In two weeks. Maybe one.

YVETTE. I can't make up my mind. Poldy, advise me, *chéri!*
        [*She takes the* COLONEL *to one side.*]
   She'll *have* to sell, don't worry. That lieutenant—the blond one—you know the one I mean—he'll lend me the money. He's *mad* about me, he says I remind him of someone. What do you advise?

COLONEL. Oh, I have to warn you against *him.* He's no good. He'll exploit the situation. I told you, ducky, I told you *I'd* buy you something, didn't I tell you that?

YVETTE. I simply can't let you!

COLONEL. Oh, please, please!

YVETTE. Well, if you think the lieutenant might exploit the situation I *will* let you!

COLONEL. I do think so.

YVETTE. So you advise me to?

COLONEL. I do, ducky, I do!

YVETTE (*returning to* MOTHER COURAGE). My friend says all right. Write me out a receipt saying the wagon's mine when the two weeks are up—with everything in it. I'll just run through it all now, the two hundred gilders can wait.
        [*To the* COLONEL.]
   You go on ahead to the camp, I'll follow, I must go over all this so nothing'll be missing later from *my* wagon!

COLONEL. Wait, I'll help you up!
        [*He does so.*]
   Come soon, ducky-wucky!
        [*Exit.*]

MOTHER COURAGE. Yvette, Yvette!

YVETTE. There aren't many boots left!

MOTHER COURAGE. Yvette, this is no time to go through the wagon, yours or not yours. You promised you'd talk to the Sergeant about Swiss Cheese. There isn't a minute to lose. He's up before the court martial one hour from now.

YVETTE. I just want to check through these shirts.

MOTHER COURAGE (*dragging her down the steps by the skirt*). You hyena, Swiss Cheese's life's at stake! And don't say who the money comes from. Pretend he's your sweetheart, for heaven's sake, or we'll all get it for helping him.

YVETTE. I've arranged to meet One Eye in the bushes. He must be there by now.

CHAPLAIN. And don't hand over all two hundred, a hundred and fifty's sure to be enough.

MOTHER COURAGE. Is it your money? I'll thank you to keep your nose out of this, I'm not doing *you* out of your porridge. Now run, and no haggling, remember his life's at stake.

[*She pushes* YVETTE *off.*]

CHAPLAIN. I didn't want to talk you into anything, but what are we going to live on? You have an unmarriageable daughter round your neck.

MOTHER COURAGE. I'm counting on that cashbox, smart alec. They'll pay his expenses out of it.

CHAPLAIN. You think she can work it?

MOTHER COURAGE. It's to her interest: I pay the two hundred and she gets the wagon. She knows what she's doing, she won't have her colonel on the string forever. Kattrin, go and clean the knives, use pumice stone. And don't *you* stand around like Jesus in Gethsemane. Get a move on, wash those glasses. There'll be over fifty cavalrymen here tonight, and you'll be saying you're not used to running around, "oh my poor feet, in church I never had to run around like this!" I think they'll let us have him. Thanks be to God they're corruptible. They're not wolves, they're human and after money. God is merciful, and men are bribable, that's how His will is done on earth as it is in Heaven. Corruption is our only hope. As long as there's corruption, there'll be merciful judges and even the innocent may get off.

YVETTE (*comes panting in*). They'll do it for two hundred if you make it snappy, these things change from one minute to the next. I'd better take One Eye to my colonel at once. He confessed he had the cashbox, they put the thumb screws on him. But he threw it in the river when he noticed them coming up behind him. So it's gone. Shall I run and get the money from my colonel?

MOTHER COURAGE. The cashbox gone? How'll I ever get my two hundred back?

YVETTE. So you thought you could get it from the cashbox? I *would* have been sunk. Not a hope, Mother Courage. If you want your Swiss Cheese, you'll have to pay. Or should I let the whole thing drop, so you can keep your wagon?

MOTHER COURAGE. I wasn't reckoning on this. But you needn't hound me, you'll get the wagon, it's yours already, and it's been mine seventeen years. I need a minute to think it over, it's all so sudden. What can I do? I *can't* pay two hundred. I *should* have haggled with them. I must hold on to something, or any passer-by can kick me in the ditch. Go and say I'll pay a hundred and twenty or the deal's off. Even then I lose the wagon.

YVETTE. I won't do it. And anyway, One Eye's in a hurry. He keeps looking over his shoulder all the time, he's so worked up. Hadn't I better give them the whole two hundred?

MOTHER COURAGE (*desperate*). I can't pay it! I've been working thirty years. She's twenty-five and still no husband. I have her to think of. So leave me alone, I know what I'm doing. A hundred and twenty or no deal.

YVETTE. You know best.   [*Runs off.*]

> [MOTHER COURAGE *turns away and slowly walks a few paces to the rear. Then she turns round, looks neither at the* CHAPLAIN *nor her daughter, and sits down to help* KATTRIN *polish the knives.*]

MOTHER COURAGE. Don't break the glasses, they're not ours. Watch what you're doing, you're cutting yourself. Swiss Cheese will be back, I'll give two hundred, if it's necessary. You'll get your brother back. With eighty gilders we could pack a hamper with goods and begin again. It wouldn't be the end of the world.

CHAPLAIN. The Bible says: the Lord will provide.

MOTHER COURAGE. You should rub them dry, I said!

> [*They clean the knives in silence. Suddenly* KATTRIN *runs sobbing behind the wagon.*]

YVETTE (*comes running in*). They won't do it. I warned you. One Eye was going to drop it then and there. There's no point, he said. He said the drums would roll any second now and that's the sign a verdict has been pronounced. I offered a hundred and fifty, he didn't even shrug his shoulders. I could hardly get him to stay there while I came to you.

MOTHER COURAGE. Tell him I'll pay two hundred. Run!

> [YVETTE *runs.* MOTHER COURAGE *sits, silent. The* CHAPLAIN *has stopped doing the glasses.*]

I believe—I've haggled too long.

> [*In the distance, a roll of drums. The* CHAPLAIN *stands up and walks toward the rear.* MOTHER COURAGE *remains seated. It grows dark. It gets light again.* MOTHER COURAGE *has not moved.*]

YVETTE (*appears, pale*). Now you've done it—with your haggling. You can keep the wagon now. He got eleven bullets, that's what. I don't know why I still bother about you, you don't deserve it, but I just happened to learn they don't think the cashbox is really in the river. They suspect it's here, they think you have something to do with him. I think they mean to bring him here to see if you'll give yourself away when you see him. You'd better not know him or we're in for it. And I'd better tell you straight, they're just behind me. Shall I keep Kattrin away?

> [MOTHER COURAGE *shakes her head.*]

Does she know? Maybe she never heard the drums or didn't understand.

MOTHER COURAGE. She knows. Bring her.

> [YVETTE *brings* KATTRIN, *who walks over to her mother and stands by her.* MOTHER COURAGE *takes her hand. Two men come on with a stretcher; there is a sheet on it and something underneath. Beside them, the* SERGEANT. *They put the stretcher down.*]

SERGEANT. Here's a man we don't know the name of. But he has to be registered to keep the records straight. He bought a meal from you. Look at him, see if you know him.

> [*He pulls back the sheet.*]

Do you know him?

> [MOTHER COURAGE *shakes her head.*]

What? You never saw him before he took that meal?

> [MOTHER COURAGE *shakes her head.*]

Lift him up. Throw him on the junk heap. He has no one that knows him.　　　　　　　　　　　　　　　　[*They carry him off.*]

Scene 4

Mother Courage sings "The Song of the Great Capitulation."

[*Outside an officer's tent,* MOTHER COURAGE *waits. A*
SCRIVENER *looks out of the tent.*]

SCRIVENER. I know you. You had a Protestant paymaster with you,
he was hiding with you. Better make no complaint.

MOTHER COURAGE. I will too! I'm innocent and if I give up it'll look
like I have a bad conscience. They cut everything in my wagon to
ribbons with their sabres and then claimed a fine of five thalers for
nothing and less than nothing.

SCRIVENER. For your own good, keep your trap shut. We haven't
many canteens, so we let you stay in business, especially if you've
a bad conscience and have to pay a fine now and then.

MOTHER COURAGE. I'm going to lodge a complaint.

SCRIVENER. As you wish. Wait here till the captain has time.
[*Withdraws into the tent.*]

YOUNG SOLDIER (*comes storming in*). Bugger the captain! Where *is*
the son of a bitch? Swiping my reward, spending it on brandy for
his whores, I'll rip his belly open!

OLDER SOLDIER (*coming after him*). Shut your hole, you'll wind up in
the stocks.

YOUNG SOLDIER. Come out, you thief, I'll make lamb chops out of you!
I was the only one in the squad who swam the river and *he* grabs
my money, I can't even buy myself a beer. Come on out! And let
me slice you up!

OLDER SOLDIER. Holy Christ, he'll destroy himself!

YOUNG SOLDIER. Let me go or I'll run *you* down too. This thing has got to be settled!

OLDER SOLDIER. Saved the colonel's horse and didn't get the reward. He's young, he hasn't been at it long.

MOTHER COURAGE. Let him go. He doesn't have to be chained, he's not a dog. Very reasonable to want a reward. Why else should he want to shine?

YOUNG SOLDIER. He's in there pouring it down! You're all chickens. I've done something special, I want the reward!

MOTHER COURAGE. Young man, don't scream at *me*, I have my own troubles. And go easy on your voice, you may need it when the Captain comes. The Captain'll come and you'll be hoarse and can't make a sound, so he'll have to deny himself the pleasure of sticking you in the stocks till you pass out. The screamers don't scream long, only half an hour, after which they have to be sung to sleep, they're all in.

YOUNG SOLDIER. I'm not all in, and sleep's out of the question. I'm hungry. They're making their bread out of acorns and hemp-seed, and not even much of that. He's whoring on my money, and I'm hungry. I'll murder him!

MOTHER COURAGE. I understand: you're hungry. Last year your Commander ordered you people out of the streets and into the fields. So the crops got trampled down. I could have got ten gilders for boots, if anyone'd had ten gilders, and if I'd had any boots. He didn't expect to be around this year, but he is, and there's famine. I understand: you're angry.

YOUNG SOLDIER. It's no use you talking. I won't stand for injustice!

MOTHER COURAGE. You're quite right. But how long? How long won't you stand for injustice? One hour? Or two? You haven't asked yourself that, have you? And yet it's the main thing. It's pure misery to sit in the stocks. Especially if you leave it till then to decide you do stand for injustice.

YOUNG SOLDIER. I don't know why I listen to you. Bugger that captain! Where is he?

MOTHER COURAGE. You listen because you know I'm right. Your rage has calmed down already. It was a short one and you'd need a long one. But where would you find it?

YOUNG SOLDIER. Are you trying to say it's not right to ask for the money?

MOTHER COURAGE. Just the opposite. I only say, your rage won't last. You'll get nowhere with it, it's a pity. If your rage was a long one, I'd urge you on. Slice him up, I'd advise you. But what's the use if you *don't* slice him up because you can feel your tail between your legs? You stand there and the captain lets you have it.

OLDER SOLDIER. You're quite right, he's mad.

YOUNG SOLDIER. All right, we'll see whether I slice him up or not.
                    [*Draws his sword.*]
    When he comes out, I slice him up!
SCRIVENER (*looking out*). The captain will be out in a minute.
                    [*In the tone of military command.*]
    Be seated!
                    [*The* YOUNG SOLDIER *sits.*]
MOTHER COURAGE. And he *is* seated. What did I tell you? You are
    seated. They know us through and through. They know how they
    must work it. Be seated! And we sit. And in sitting there's no revolt.
    Better not stand up again—not the way you did before—don't stand
    up again. And don't be embarrassed in front of me, I'm no better,
    not a scrap. We don't stick our necks out, do we, and why not? It
    wouldn't be good for business. Let me tell you about the great
    capitulation.

    [*She sings* "The Song of the Great Capitulation."]

    Long, long ago, a green beginner
        I thought myself a special case.
    (None of your ordinary, run of the mill girls, with my looks and
        my talent and my love of the higher things!)
    I picked a hair out of my dinner
        And put the waiter in his place.
    (All or nothing. Anyway, never the second best. I am the master
        of my fate. I'll take no orders from no one.)
    Then a little bird whispers!
        The bird says: "Wait a year or so
        And marching with the band you'll go
        Keeping in step, now fast, now slow,
        And piping out your little spiel.
        Then one day the battalions wheel
        And you go down upon your knees
        To God Almighty if you please!"

    My friend, before that year was over
        I'd learned to drink their cup of tea.
    (Two children round your neck and the price of bread and what
        all!)
    When they were through with me, moreover,
        They had me where they wanted me.
    (You must get well in with people. If you scratch my back, I'll
        scratch yours. Never stick your neck out!)
    Then a little bird whispered!
        The bird says: "Scarce a year or so

And marching with the band she'd go
Keeping in step, now fast, now slow,
And piping out her little spiel.
Then one day the battalions wheel
And she goes down upon her knees
To God Almighty if you please!"

Our plans are big, our hopes colossal.
    We hitch our wagon to a star.
(Where there's a will, there's a way. You can't hold a good man
    down.)
"We can lift mountains," says the apostle.
    And yet: how heavy one cigar!
(You must cut your coat according to your cloth.)
That little bird whispers!
    The bird says: "Wait a year or so
    And marching with the band we go
    Keeping in step, now fast, now slow,
    And piping out our little spiel.
    Then one day the battalions wheel
    And we go down upon our knees
    To God Almighty if you please!"

MOTHER COURAGE. And so I think you should stay here with your
    sword drawn if you're set on it and your anger is big enough. You
    have good cause, I admit. But if your anger is a short one, you'd
    better go.
YOUNG SOLDIER. Oh, shove it up!
        [*He stumbles off, the other soldier following him.*]
SCRIVENER (*sticks his head out*). The captain is here. You can lodge
    your complaint.
MOTHER COURAGE. I've thought better of it. I'm not complaining.
        [*Exit. The* SCRIVENER *looks after her, shaking his head.*]

Scene 5

Two years have passed. The war covers wider and wider territory. Forever on the move the little wagon crosses Poland, Moravia, Bavaria, Italy, and again Bavaria. 1631. Tilly's victory at Magdeburg costs Mother Courage four officer shirts.

[*The wagon stands in a war-ruined village. Faint military music from the distance. Two soldiers are being served at a counter by* KATTRIN *and* MOTHER COURAGE. *One of them has a woman's fur coat about his shoulders.*]

MOTHER COURAGE. What, you can't pay? No money, no brandy! They can play victory marches, they should pay their men.

FIRST SOLDIER. I want my brandy! I arrived too late for plunder. The Chief allowed one hour to plunder the town, it's a swindle. He's not inhuman, he says. So I suppose they bought him off.

CHAPLAIN (*staggering in*). There are more in the farmhouse. A family of peasants. Help me someone. I need linen!

[*The* SECOND SOLDIER *goes with him.* KATTRIN *is getting very excited. She tries to get her mother to bring linen out.*]

MOTHER COURAGE. I have none. I sold all my bandages to the regiment. I'm not tearing up my officer's shirts for these people.

CHAPLAIN (*calling over his shoulder*). I said I need linen!

MOTHER COURAGE (*stopping* KATTRIN *from entering the wagon*). Not a thing! They have nothing and they pay nothing!

CHAPLAIN (*to a woman he is carrying in*). Why did you stay out there in the line of fire?

WOMAN. Our farm—

MOTHER COURAGE. Think they'd ever let go of *anything*? And now I'm supposed to pay. Well, I won't!

FIRST SOLDIER. They're Protestants, why should they be Protestants?

MOTHER COURAGE. Protestant, Catholic, what do *they* care? Their farm's gone, that's what.

SECOND SOLDIER. They're not Protestants anyway, they're Catholics.

FIRST SOLDIER. In a bombardment we can't pick and choose.

PEASANT (*brought on by* CHAPLAIN). My arm's gone.

CHAPLAIN. Where's that linen?

[*All look at Mother Courage who doesn't budge.*]

MOTHER COURAGE. I can't give you any. With all I have to pay out— taxes, duties, bribes . . .

[KATTRIN *takes up a board and threatens her mother with it, emitting gurgling sounds.*]

Are you out of your mind? Put that board down or I'll fetch you one, you lunatic! I'm giving nothing, I daren't, I have myself to think of.

[*The* CHAPLAIN *lifts her bodily off the steps of the wagon and sets her down on the ground. He takes out shirts from the wagon and tears them in strips.*]

My shirts, my officer's shirts!

[*From the house comes the cry of a child in pain.*]

PEASANT. The child's still in there!

[KATTRIN *runs in.*]

CHAPLAIN (*to the woman*). Stay where you are. She's getting it for you.

MOTHER COURAGE. Hold her back, the roof may fall in!

CHAPLAIN. I'm not going back in there!

MOTHER COURAGE (*pulled in both directions at once*). Go easy on my expensive linen.

[*The* SECOND SOLDIER *holds her back.*]

[KATTRIN *brings a baby out of the ruins.*]

MOTHER COURAGE. Another baby to drag around, you must be pleased with yourself. Give it to its mother this minute! Or do I have to fight you again for hours till I get it from you? Are you deaf?

[*To the* SECOND SOLDIER.]

Don't stand around gawking, go back there and tell 'em to stop that music, I can see their victory without it. I have nothing but losses from your victory!

CHAPLAIN (*bandaging*). The blood's coming through.

[KATTRIN *is rocking the child and half-humming a lullaby.*]

MOTHER COURAGE. There she sits, happy as a lark in all this misery. Give the baby back, the mother is coming to!

[*She sees the* FIRST SOLDIER. *He had been handling
the drinks, and is now trying to make off with the
bottle.*]

God's blood! You beast! You want another victory, do you? Then
pay for it!

FIRST SOLDIER. I have nothing.

MOTHER COURAGE (*snatching the fur coat back*). Then leave this coat,
it's stolen goods anyhow.

CHAPLAIN. There's still someone in there.

Scene 6

Before the City of Ingolstadt in Bavaria Mother Courage is present at the funeral of the fallen commander, Tilly. Conversations take place about war heroes and the duration of the war. The chaplain complains that his talents are lying fallow and Kattrin gets the red boots. The year is 1632.

[*The inside of a canteen tent. The inner side of a counter at the rear. Rain. In the distance, drums and funeral music. The* CHAPLAIN *and the* REGIMENTAL CLERK *are playing checkers.* MOTHER COURAGE *and her* DAUGHTER *are taking inventory.*]

CHAPLAIN. The funeral procession is just starting out.

MOTHER COURAGE. Pity about the Chief—twenty-two pairs of socks—getting killed that way. They say it was an accident. There was a fog over the fields that morning, and the fog was to blame. The Chief called up another regiment, told 'em to fight to the death, rode back again, missed his way in the fog, went forward instead of back, and ran smack into a bullet in the thick of the battle—only four lanterns left.

[*A whistle from the rear. She goes to the counter. To a soldier.*]

It's a disgrace the way you're all skipping your Commander's funeral!

[*She pours a drink.*]

SCRIVENER. They shouldn't have handed the money out before the funeral. Now the men are all getting drunk instead of going to it.

CHAPLAIN (*to the* SCRIVENER). Don't you have to be there?

SCRIVENER. I stayed away because of the rain.

MOTHER COURAGE. It's different for you, the rain might spoil your uniform. I hear they wanted to ring the bells for his funeral, which is natural, but it came out that the churches had been shot up by his orders, so the poor Commander won't be hearing any bells when they lower him in his grave. Instead, they will fire off three shots so the occasion won't be *too* sober—sixteen leather belts.

VOICE FROM THE COUNTER. Service! One brandy!

MOTHER COURAGE. Your money first. No, you *can't* come inside the tent, not with those boots on. You can drink outside, rain or no rain. I only let officers in here.

[*To* SCRIVENER.]

The Chief had his troubles lately, I hear. There was unrest in the Second Regiment because he didn't pay 'em but said it was a war of religion and they must fight it free of charge.

[*Funeral March. All look towards the rear.*]

CHAPLAIN. Now they're filing past the body.

MOTHER COURAGE. I feel sorry for a commander or an emperor like that—when he might have had something special in mind, something they'd talk about in times to come, something they'd raise a statue to him for. The conquest of the world now, *that's* a goal for a commander, he couldn't do better than *that*, could he? . . . Lord, worms have got into the biscuits. . . . In short he works his hands to the bone and then it's all spoiled by the common riffraff that only wants a jug of beer or a bit of company, not the higher things in life. The finest plans have always been spoiled by the littleness of them that should carry them out. Even emperors can't do it all by themselves. They count on support from their soldiers and the people round about. Am I right?

CHAPLAIN (*laughing*). You're right, Mother Courage, till you come to the soldiers. They do what they can. Those chaps outside, for example, drinking their brandy in the rain, I'd trust 'em to fight a hundred years, one war after another, two at a time if necessary. And I wasn't trained as a Commander.

MOTHER COURAGE. . . . Seventeen leather belts . . . Then you don't think the war might end?

CHAPLAIN. Because a Commander's dead? Don't be childish, they're sixpence a dozen. There are always heroes.

MOTHER COURAGE. Well, I wasn't asking just for the sake of argument. I was wondering if I should buy up a lot of supplies. They happen to be cheap just now. But if the war ended, I might just as well throw them away.

CHAPLAIN. I realize you are serious, Mother Courage. Well, there's always been people going around saying someday the war will end. I

say, you can't be sure the war will *ever* end. Of course it may have
to pause occasionally—for breath, as it were—it can even meet
with an accident—nothing on this earth is perfect—a war of which
we could say it left nothing to be desired will probably never exist. A
war can come to a sudden halt—from unforeseen causes—you can't
think of everything—a little oversight, and the war's in the hole, and
someone's got to pull it out again! The someone is the Emperor or
the King or the Pope. They're such friends in need, the war has
really nothing to worry about, it can look forward to a prosperous
future.

        [*A* SOLDIER *sings at the counter.*]

    One schnapps, mine host, be quick, make haste!
    A soldier's got no time to waste:
    He must be shooting, shooting, shooting,
    His Kaiser's enemies unrooting!
    Make it a double. This is a holiday.

MOTHER COURAGE. If I was sure you're right . . .

CHAPLAIN. Think it out for yourself: how *could* the war end?

SOLDIER.

    Two breasts, my girl, be quick, make haste!
    A soldier's got no time to waste:
    He must be hating, hating, hating,
    He cannot keep his Kaiser waiting!

SCRIVENER (*suddenly*). What about peace? Yes, peace. I'm from
Bohemia. I'd like to get home once in a while.

CHAPLAIN. Oh, you would, would you? Dear old peace! What happens
to the hole when the cheese is gone?

SOLDIER (*off stage*).

    Your blessing, priest, be quick, make haste!
    A soldier's got no time to waste:
    He must be dying, dying, dying,
    His Kaiser's greatness glorifying!

SCRIVENER. In the long run you can't live without peace!

CHAPLAIN. Well, I'd say there's peace even in war, war has its islands of
peace. For war satisfies *all* needs, even those of peace, yes, they're
provided for, or the war couldn't keep going. In war—as in the very
thick of peace—you can empty your bowels, and between one battle
and the next there's always a beer, and even on the march you can
take a nap—on your elbow maybe, in a gutter—something can always be managed. Of course you can't play cards during an attack,
but neither can you while plowing the fields in peacetime; it's when
the victory's won that there are possibilities. You have your leg shot
off, and at first you raise quite an outcry as if it *was* something, but
soon you calm down or take a swig of brandy, and you end up
hopping around, and the war is none the worse for your little mis-

adventure. And can't you be fruitful and multiply in the thick of slaughter—behind a barn or somewhere? Nothing can keep you from it very long in any event. And so the war has your offspring and can carry on. War is like love, it always finds a way. Why *should* it end?

> [KATTRIN *has stopped working. She stares at the*
> CHAPLAIN.]

MOTHER COURAGE. Then I *will* buy those supplies, I'll rely on you.

> [KATTRIN *suddenly bangs a basket of glasses down on*
> *the ground and runs out.* MOTHER COURAGE *laughs.*]

Kattrin! Lord, Kattrin's still going to wait for peace. I promised her she'll get a husband—when it's peace.

> [*Runs after her.*]

SCRIVENER (*standing up*). I win. You were talking. You pay.

MOTHER COURAGE (*returning with* KATTRIN). Be sensible, the war'll go on a bit longer, and we'll make a bit more money, then peace'll be all the nicer. Now you go into the town, it's not ten minutes' walk, and bring the things from the Golden Lion, just the dearer ones, we can get the rest later in the wagon. It's all arranged, the clerk will go with you, most of the soldiers are at the Commander's funeral, nothing can happen to you. Do a good job, don't lose anything, Kattrin, think of your trousseau!

> [KATTRIN *ties a cloth round her head and leaves with*
> *the* SCRIVENER.]

CHAPLAIN. You don't mind her going with Scrivener?

MOTHER COURAGE. She's not so pretty anyone would want to ruin her.

CHAPLAIN. The way you run your business and always come through is highly commendable, Mother Courage—I see how you got your name.

MOTHER COURAGE. The poor need courage. They're lost, that's why. That they even get up in the morning is something—in *their* plight. Or that they plow a field—in war time. Even their bringing children into the world shows they have courage, for they have no prospects. They have to hang each other one by one and slaughter each other in the lump, so if they want to look each other in the face once in a while, well, it takes courage. That they put up with an Emperor and a Pope, that takes an unnatural amount of courage, for *they* cost you your life.

> [*She sits, takes a small pipe from her pocket and*
> *smokes it.*]

You might chop me a bit of firewood.

CHAPLAIN (*reluctantly taking his coat off and preparing to chop wood*). Properly speaking, I'm a pastor of souls, not a woodcutter.

MOTHER COURAGE. But I don't have a soul. And I do need wood.

CHAPLAIN. What's that little pipe you've got there?

MOTHER COURAGE. Just a pipe.

CHAPLAIN. I think it's a very particular pipe.

MOTHER COURAGE. Oh?

CHAPLAIN. The cook's pipe in fact. The cook from the Oxenstiern Regiment.

MOTHER COURAGE. If you know, why beat about the bush?

CHAPLAIN. Because I don't know if you've been *aware* that's what you've been smoking. It was possible you just rummaged among your belongings and your fingers just lit on a pipe and you just took it. In pure absentmindedness.

MOTHER COURAGE. How do you know that's not it?

CHAPLAIN. It isn't. You *are* aware of it.

[*He brings the ax down on the block with a crash.*]

MOTHER COURAGE. What if I was?

CHAPLAIN. I must give you a warning, Mother Courage, it's my duty. You are unlikely ever again to see the gentleman but that's no pity, you're in luck. Mother Courage, he did not impress me as trustworthy. On the contrary.

MOTHER COURAGE. Really? He was such a nice man.

CHAPLAIN. Well! So that's what you call a nice man. I do not.

[*The ax falls again.*]

Far be it from me to wish him ill, but I cannot—cannot—describe him as nice. No, no, he's a Don Juan, a cunning Don Juan. Just look at that pipe if you don't believe me. You must admit it tells all.

MOTHER COURAGE. I see nothing special in it. It's been, um, used.

CHAPLAIN. It's bitten half-way through! He's a man of great violence! It is the pipe of a man of great violence, you can see *that* if you've any judgment left!

[*He deals the block a tremendous blow.*]

MOTHER COURAGE. Don't bite my chopping block halfway through!

CHAPLAIN. I told you I had no training as a woodcutter. The care of souls was my field. Around here my gifts and capabilities are grossly misused. In physical labor my god-given talents find no—um—adequate expression—which is a sin. You haven't heard me preach. Why, I can put such spirit into a regiment with a single sermon that the enemy's a mere flock of sheep to them and their own lives no more than smelly old shoes to be thrown away at the thought of final victory! God has given me the gift of tongues. I can preach you out of your senses!

MOTHER COURAGE. I need my senses, what would I do without them?

CHAPLAIN. Mother Courage, I have often thought that—under a veil of plain speech—you conceal a heart. You are human, you need warmth.

MOTHER COURAGE. The best way of warming this tent is to chop plenty of firewood.

CHAPLAIN. You're changing the subject. Seriously, my dear Courage, I sometimes ask myself how it would be if our relationship should be somewhat more firmly cemented. I mean, now the wind of war has whirled us so strangely together.

MOTHER COURAGE. The cement's pretty firm already. I cook your meals. And you lend a hand—at chopping firewood, for instance.

CHAPLAIN (*going over to her, gesturing with the ax*). You know what I mean by a close relationship. It has nothing to do with eating and woodcutting and such base necessities. Let your heart speak!

MOTHER COURAGE. Don't come at me like that with your ax, that'd be *too* close a relationship!

CHAPLAIN. This is no laughing matter, I am in earnest. I've thought it all over.

MOTHER COURAGE. Dear Chaplain, be a sensible fellow. I like you, and I don't want to heap coals of fire on your head. All I'm after is to bring me and my children through in that wagon. It isn't just mine, the wagon, and anyway I've no mind to start having a private life. At the moment I'm taking quite a risk buying these things when the Commander's fallen and there's all this talk of peace. Where would you go, if I was ruined? See? You don't even know. Now chop some firewood and it'll be warm of an evening, which is quite a lot in times like these. What was that?

> [*She stands up.* KATTRIN *enters, breathless, with a wound across the eye and forehead. She is dragging all sorts of articles, parcels, leather goods, a drum, etc.*]

MOTHER COURAGE. What is it, were you attacked? On the way back? She was attacked on the way back! I'll bet it was that soldier who got drunk on my liquor. I should never have let you go. Dump all that stuff! It's not bad, the wound is only a flesh wound. I'll bandage it for you, it'll be all healed up in a week. They're worse than animals.

> [*She bandages the wound.*]

CHAPLAIN. I reproach them with nothing. At home they never did these shameful things. The men who start the wars are responsible, they bring out the worst in people.

MOTHER COURAGE. Didn't the Scrivener walk you back home? That's because you're a respectable girl, he thought they'd leave you alone. The wound's not at all deep, it will never show. There: all bandaged up. Now, I've got something for you, rest easy. I secret. I've been holding it, you'll see.

> [*She digs Yvette's red boots out of a bag.*]

Well, what do you see? You always wanted them. Now you have them. Put them on quick, before I'm sorry I let you have them. (*She helps her to put the boots on.*) It will never show, though it wouldn't bother *me* if it did. The fate of the ones they like is the worst. They drag them around with them till they're through. A girl they don't care for they leave alone. I've seen so many girls, pretty as they come in the beginning, then all of a sudden they looked a fright—enough to scare a wolf. They can't even go behind a tree on the street without having something to fear from it. They lead a frightful life. Like with trees: the tall, straight ones are cut down for roof timber, and the crooked ones can enjoy life. So this wound here is really a piece of luck. The boots have kept well, I cleaned them good before I put them away.

[KATTRIN *leaves the boots and creeps into the wagon.*]

CHAPLAIN (*when she's gone*). I hope she won't be disfigured?

MOTHER COURAGE. There'll be a scar. She needn't wait for peace now.

CHAPLAIN. She didn't let them get any of the stuff away from her.

MOTHER COURAGE. Maybe I shouldn't have made such a point of it. If only I ever knew what went on inside her head. One time she stayed out all night, once in all the years. I could never get out of her what happened, I racked my brains for quite a while.

[*She picks up the things* KATTRIN *spilled and sorts them angrily.*]

This is war. A nice source of income, I must say!

[*Cannon shots.*]

CHAPLAIN. Now they're lowering the Commander in his grave! A historic moment.

MOTHER COURAGE. It's a historic moment to me when they hit my daughter over the eye. She's all but finished now, she'll never get a husband, and she's so mad about children! Even her dumbness comes from the war. A soldier stuck something in her mouth when she was little. I'll not see Swiss Cheese again, and where my Eilif is the Good Lord knows. Curse the war!

Scene 7

Mother Courage at the height of her business career.

[*A highway. The* CHAPLAIN, MOTHER COURAGE, *and her daughter* KATTRIN *pull the wagon, and new wares are hanging from it.* MOTHER COURAGE *wears a necklace: a chain of silver coins.*]

MOTHER COURAGE. I won't let you spoil my war for me. Destroys the weak, does it? Well, what does peace do for 'em, huh? War feeds its people better.

[*She sings*]

If war don't suit your disposition
When victory comes you will be dead.
War is a business proposition:
Not with cream-cheese but steel and lead.

And staying in one place won't help either. Those who stay home are the first to go.

[*She sings.*]

Too many seek a bed to sleep in:
Each ditch is taken, and each cave,
And he who digs a hole to creep in
Finds he has dug an early grave.
And many a man spends many a minute
In hurrying toward some resting place.
You wonder, when at last he's in it,
Just why the fellow forced the pace.

[*The wagon proceeds.*]

Scene 8

1632. In this same year Gustavus Adolphus fell in the battle of Lützen. The peace threatens Mother Courage with ruin. Her brave son performs one heroic deed too many and comes to a shameful end.

[*A camp. A summer morning. In front of the wagon, an old woman and her son. The son is dragging a large bag of bedding.*]

MOTHER COURAGE (*from inside the wagon*). Must you come at the crack of dawn?

YOUNG MAN. We've been walking all night, twenty miles it was, we have to be back today.

MOTHER COURAGE (*still inside*). What do I want with bed feathers? People don't even have houses.

YOUNG MAN. At least wait till you see 'em.

OLD WOMAN. Nothing doing here either, let's go.

YOUNG MAN. And let 'em sign away the roof over our heads for taxes? Maybe she'll pay three gilders if you throw in that bracelet.
[*Bells start ringing.*]
You hear, mother?

VOICES (*from the rear*). It's peace! The King of Sweden's been killed!

MOTHER COURAGE (*sticking her head out of the wagon. She hasn't done her hair yet*). Bells! What are the bells for, middle of the week?

CHAPLAIN (*crawling out from under the wagon*). What's that they're shouting?

YOUNG MAN. It's peace.

CHAPLAIN. Peace?

MOTHER COURAGE. Don't tell me peace has broken out—when I've just gone and bought all these supplies!

CHAPLAIN (*calling, toward the rear*). Is it peace?

VOICE (*from a distance*). They say the war stopped three weeks ago, I've only just heard.

CHAPLAIN (*to* MOTHER COURAGE). Or why would they ring the bells?

VOICE. A great crowd of Lutherans have just arrived with wagons— they brought the news.

YOUNG MAN. It's peace, mother.

[*The* OLD WOMAN *collapses.*]

What's the matter?

MOTHER COURAGE (*back in the wagon*). Kattrin, it's peace! Put on your black dress, we're going to church, we owe it to Swiss Cheese! Can it be true?

YOUNG MAN. The people here say so too, the war's over. Can you stand up?

[*The* OLD WOMAN *stands up, dazed.*]

I'll get the harness shop going again now, I promise you. Everything'll be all right, father will get his bed back. . . . Can you walk?

[*To the* CHAPLAIN.]

She felt sick, it was the news. She didn't believe there'd ever be peace again. Father always said there would. We're going home.

[*They leave.*]

MOTHER COURAGE (*off*). Give her some brandy.

CHAPLAIN. They've left already.

MOTHER COURAGE (*still off*). What's going on in the camp over there?

CHAPLAIN. They're all getting together, I think I'll go over. Shall I put my pastor's clothes on again?

MOTHER COURAGE. Better get the exact news first, and not risk being taken for the Antichrist. I'm glad about the peace even though I'm ruined. At least I've got two of my children through the war. Now I'll see my Eilif again.

CHAPLAIN. And who may this be coming down from the camp? Well, if it isn't our Swedish Commander's cook!

COOK (*somewhat bedraggled, carrying a bundle*). Who's here? The Chaplain!

CHAPLAIN. Mother Courage, a visitor!

[MOTHER COURAGE *clambers out.*]

COOK. Well, I promised I'd come over for a brief conversation as soon as I had time. I didn't forget your brandy, Mrs. Fierling.

MOTHER COURAGE. Jesus, the Commander's cook! After all these years! Where is Eilif, my eldest?

COOK. Isn't he here yet? He went on ahead yesterday, he was on his way over.

CHAPLAIN. I *will* put my pastor's clothes on. I'll be back.

[*He goes behind the wagon.*]

MOTHER COURAGE. He may be here any minute then.

[*Calls toward the wagon.*]

Kattrin, Eilif's coming! Bring a glass of brandy for the cook, Kattrin!

[KATTRIN *doesn't come.*]

Pull your hair over it and have done. Mr. Lamb is no stranger.

[*She gets the brandy herself.*]

She won't come out. Peace is nothing to her, it was too long coming. They hit her right over the eye. You can hardly see it now. But she thinks people stare at her.

COOK. Ah yes, war!

[*He and* MOTHER COURAGE *sit.*]

MOTHER COURAGE. Cook, you come at a bad time: I'm ruined.

COOK. What? That's terrible!

MOTHER COURAGE. The peace has broken my neck. On the Chaplain's advice I've gone and bought a lot of supplies. Now everybody's leaving and I'm holding the baby.

COOK. How could you listen to the Chaplain? If I'd had time—but the Catholics were too quick for me—I'd have warned you against him. He's a windbag. Well, so now he's the big man round here!

MOTHER COURAGE. He's been doing the dishes for me and helping with the wagon.

COOK. With the wagon—him! And I'll bet he's told you a few of his jokes. He has a most unhealthy attitude to women. I tried to influence him but it was no good. He isn't sound.

MOTHER COURAGE. Are you sound?

COOK. If I'm nothing else, I'm sound. Your health!

MOTHER COURAGE. Sound! Only one person around here was ever sound, and I never had to slave as I did then. He sold the blankets off the children's beds in the spring, and he found my harmonica unchristian. You aren't recommending yourself if you *admit* you're sound.

COOK. You fight tooth and nail, don't you? I like that.

MOTHER COURAGE. Don't tell me you've been dreaming of my teeth and nails.

COOK. Well, here we sit, while the bells of peace do ring, and you pouring your famous brandy as only you know how!

MOTHER COURAGE. I don't think much of the bells of peace at the moment. I don't see how they can hand out all this pay that's in arrears. And then where shall I be with my famous brandy? Have you all been paid?

COOK (*hesitating*). Not exactly. That's why we disbanded. In the circumstances, I thought, why stay? For the time being, I'll look up a couple of friends. So here I sit—with you.

MOTHER COURAGE. In other words, you're broke.

COOK (*annoyed by the bells*). It's about time they stopped that racket! I'd like to set myself up in some business. I'm fed up with being their cook. I'm supposed to make do with tree roots and shoe leather, and then they throw the hot soup in my face. Being a cook nowadays is a dog's life. I'd sooner do war service, but of course it's peace now.

[*As the* CHAPLAIN *turns up, wearing his old costume.*]

We'll talk it over later.

CHAPLAIN. The coat's pretty good. Just a few moth holes.

COOK. I don't know why you take the trouble. You won't find another job. Who could you incite now to earn an honorable wage or risk his life for a cause? Besides I have a bone to pick with you.

CHAPLAIN. Have you?

COOK. I have. You advised a lady to buy superfluous goods on the pretext that the war would never end.

CHAPLAIN (*hotly*). I'd like to know what business it is of yours?

COOK. It's unprincipled behavior! How can you give unwanted advice? And interfere with the conduct of other people's businesses?

CHAPLAIN. Who's interfering now, I'd like to know?

[*To* MOTHER COURAGE.]

I had no idea you were such a close friend of this gentleman and had to account to him for everything.

MOTHER COURAGE. Now don't get excited. The Cook's giving his personal opinion. You can't deny your war was a frost.

CHAPLAIN. You mustn't take the name of peace in vain, Courage. Remember, you're a hyena of the battlefield!

MOTHER COURAGE. A what?

COOK. If you insult my girl friend, you'll have to reckon with me!

CHAPLAIN. I am *not* speaking to you, your intentions are only too transparent!

[*To* MOTHER COURAGE.]

But when I see *you* take peace between finger and thumb like a snotty old hanky, my humanity rebels! It shows that you want war, not peace, for what you get out of it. But don't forget the proverb: he who sups with the devil must use a long spoon!

MOTHER COURAGE. Remember what one fox said to another that was caught in a trap? "If you stay there, you're just asking for trouble!" There isn't much love lost between me and the war. And when it comes to calling me a hyena, you and I part company.

CHAPLAIN. Then why all this grumbling about the peace just as everyone's heaving a sigh of relief? Is it just for the junk in your wagon?

MOTHER COURAGE. My goods are not junk. I live off them. *You've* been living off them.

CHAPLAIN. You live off war. Exactly.

COOK (*to the* CHAPLAIN). As a grown man, you should know better than to go around advising people.

[*To* MOTHER COURAGE.]

Now, in your situation you'd be wise to get rid of certain goods at once—before the prices sink to nothing. Get ready and get going, there isn't a moment to lose!

MOTHER COURAGE. That's sensible advice, I think I'll take it.

CHAPLAIN. Because the Cook says so.

MOTHER COURAGE. Why didn't *you* say so? He's right, I must get to the market.

[*She climbs into the wagon.*]

COOK. One up for me, Chaplain. You have no presence of mind. You should have said, "*I* gave you advice? Why, I was just talking politics!" And you shouldn't take me on as a rival. Cockfights are not becoming to your cloth.

CHAPLAIN. If you don't shut your trap, I'll murder you, cloth or no cloth!

COOK (*taking his boots off and unwinding the wrappings on his feet*). If you hadn't degenerated into a godless tramp, you could easily get yourself a parsonage, now it's peace. Cooks won't be needed, there's nothing to cook, but there's still plenty to believe, and people are prepared to go right on believing it.

CHAPLAIN. Mr. Lamb, please don't drive me out! Since I became a tramp, I'm a somewhat better man. I couldn't preach to 'em any more.

[YVETTE POTTIER *enters, decked out in black, with a stick. She is much older, fatter, and heavily powdered. Behind her, a servant.*]

YVETTE. Hullo, everybody! Is this Mother Courage's establishment?

CHAPLAIN. Quite right. And with whom have we the pleasure?

YVETTE. I am Madame Colonel Starhemberg, good people. Where's Mother Courage?

CHAPLAIN (*calling to the wagon*). Madame Colonel Starhemberg wants to speak with you!

MOTHER COURAGE (*from inside*). Coming!

YVETTE (*calling*). It's Yvette!

MOTHER COURAGE (*inside*). Yvette!

YVETTE. Just to see how you're getting on!

[*As the* COOK *turns round in horror.*]

Peter!

COOK. Yvette!

YVETTE. Of all things! How did *you* get here?

COOK. On a cart.

CHAPLAIN. Well! You know each other? Intimately?

YVETTE. Not half.

[*Scrutinizing the* COOK.]

You're fat.

COOK. For that matter, *you're* no beanpole.

YVETTE. Anyway, nice meeting you, tramp. Now I can tell you what I think of you.

CHAPLAIN. Do so, tell him all, but wait till Mother Courage comes out.

COOK. Now don't make a scene . . .

MOTHER COURAGE (*comes out, laden with goods*). Yvette!

[*They embrace.*]

But why are you in mourning?

YVETTE. Doesn't it suit me? My husband, the colonel, died several years ago.

MOTHER COURAGE. The old fellow that nearly bought my wagon?

YVETTE. His older brother.

MOTHER COURAGE. So you're not doing badly. Good to see one person who got somewhere in the war.

YVETTE. I've had my ups and downs.

MOTHER COURAGE. Don't let's speak ill of Colonels. They make money like hay.

CHAPLAIN (*to the* COOK). If I were you, I'd put my shoes on again.

[*To* YVETTE.]

You promised to give us your opinion of this gentleman.

COOK. Now, Yvette, don't make a stink!

MOTHER COURAGE. He's a friend of mine, Yvette.

YVETTE. He's—Peter Piper, that's who.

MOTHER COURAGE. What!?

COOK. Cut the nicknames. My name's Lamb.

MOTHER COURAGE (*laughing*). Peter Piper? Who turned the women's heads? And I've been keeping your pipe for you.

CHAPLAIN. And smoking it.

YVETTE. Lucky I can warn you against him. He's a bad lot. You won't find a worse on the whole coast of Flanders. He got more girls in trouble than . . .

COOK. That's a long time ago, it isn't true any more.

YVETTE. Stand up when you talk to a lady! Oh, how I loved that man! And all the time he was having a little bowlegged brunette. He got *her* in trouble too, of course.

COOK. I seem to have brought *you* luck!

YVETTE. Shut your trap, you hoary ruin! And you take care, Mother Courage, this type is still dangerous even in decay!

MOTHER COURAGE (*to* YVETTE). Come with me, I must get rid of this stuff before the prices fall.

YVETTE (*concentrating on* COOK). Miserable cur!

MOTHER COURAGE. Maybe you can help me at army headquarters, you have contacts.

YVETTE. Damnable whore hunter!

MOTHER COURAGE (*shouting into the wagon*). Kattrin, church is all off, I'm going to market!

YVETTE. Inveterate seducer!

MOTHER COURAGE (*still to* KATTRIN). When Eilif comes, give him something to drink!

YVETTE. That a man of *his* ilk should have been able to turn me from the straight and narrow! I have only my own star to thank that I rose nonetheless to the heights! But I've put an end to your tricks, Peter Piper, and one day—in a better life than this—the Lord God will reward me! Come, Mother Courage!

[*Leaves with* MOTHER COURAGE.]

CHAPLAIN. As our text this morning let us take the saying, the mills of God grind slowly. And you complain of my jokes!

COOK. I never have any luck. I'll be frank, I was hoping for a good hot dinner, I'm starving. And now they'll be talking about me, and she'll get a completely wrong picture. I think I should go before she comes back.

CHAPLAIN. I think so too.

COOK. Chaplain, peace makes me sick. Mankind must perish by fire and sword, we're born and bred in sin! Oh, how I wish I was roasting a great fat capon for the Commander—God knows where *he's* got to—with mustard sauce and those little yellow carrots . . .

CHAPLAIN. Red cabbage—with capon, red cabbage.

COOK. You're right. But he always wanted yellow carrots.

CHAPLAIN. He never understood a thing.

COOK. You always put plenty away.

CHAPLAIN. Under protest.

COOK. Anyway, you must admit, those were the days.

CHAPLAIN. Yes, that I might admit.

COOK. Now you've called her a hyena, there's not much future for you here either. What are you staring at?

CHAPLAIN. It's Eilif!

[*Followed by two soldiers with halberds,* EILIF *enters. His hands are fettered. He is white as chalk.*] What's happened to you?

EILIF. Where's mother?

CHAPLAIN. Gone to town.

EILIF. They said she was here. I was allowed a last visit.

COOK (*to the soldiers*). Where are you taking him?

SOLDIER. For a ride.

[*The other soldier makes the gesture of throat cutting.*]

CHAPLAIN. What has he done?

SOLDIER. He broke in on a peasant. The wife is dead.

CHAPLAIN. Eilif, how could you?

EILIF. It's no different. It's what I did before.
COOK. That was in wartime.
EILIF. Shut your hole. Can I sit down till she comes?
SOLDIER. No.
CHAPLAIN. It's true. In war time they honored him for it. He sat at
the Commander's right hand. It was bravery. Couldn't we speak
with the provost?
SOLDIER. What's the use? Stealing cattle from a peasant, what's brave
about that?
COOK. It was just stupid.
EILIF. If I'd been stupid, I'd have starved, clever dick.
COOK. So you were bright and paid for it.
CHAPLAIN. At least we must bring Kattrin out.
EILIF. Let her alone. Just give me some brandy.
SOLDIER. No.
CHAPLAIN. What shall we tell your mother?
EILIF. Tell her it was no different. Tell her it was the same. Oh, tell her
nothing. [*The soldiers take him away.*]
CHAPLAIN. I'll come with you, I'll . . .
EILIF. I don't need a priest!
CHAPLAIN. You don't know—yet.
                          [*Follows him.*]
COOK (*calling after him*). I'll have to tell her, she'll want to see him!
CHAPLAIN. Better tell her nothing. Or maybe just that he was here, and
he'll return, maybe tomorrow. Meantime I'll be back and can break
the news.
        [*Leaves quickly. The* COOK *looks after him, shakes
        his head, then walks uneasily around. Finally, he ap-
        proaches the wagon.*]
COOK. Hi! Won't you come out? You want to sneak away from the
peace, don't you? Well, so do I! I'm the Swedish Commander's
cook, remember me? I was wondering if you've got anything to eat
in there—while we're waiting for your mother. I wouldn't mind a
bit of bacon—or even bread—just to pass the time.
                       [*He looks in.*]
She's got a blanket over her head.
                  [*The thunder of cannon.*]
MOTHER COURAGE (*running, out of breath, still carrying the goods*).
Cook, the peace is over, the war's on again, has been for three days!
I didn't get rid of this stuff after all, thank God! There's a shooting
match in the town already—with the Lutherans. We must get away
with the wagon. Pack, Kattrin! What's on *your* mind? Something
the matter?
COOK. Nothing.
MOTHER COURAGE. But there is. I see it in your face.

COOK. Because the war's on again, most likely. May it last till tomorrow evening, so I can get something in my belly!

MOTHER COURAGE. You're not telling me.

COOK. Eilif was here. Only he had to go away again.

MOTHER COURAGE. He was here? Then we'll see him on the march. I'll be with our side this time. How'd he look?

COOK. The same.

MOTHER COURAGE. He'll *never* change. And the war couldn't get *him*, he's bright. Help me with the packing.

[*She starts it.*]

Did he tell you anything? Is he well in with the captain? Did he tell you about his heroic deeds?

COOK (*darkly*). He's done one of them again.

MOTHER COURAGE. Tell me about it later.

[KATTRIN *appears.*]

Kattrin, the peace is all through, we're on the move again.

[*To the* COOK.]

What *is* biting you?

COOK. I'll enlist.

MOTHER COURAGE. A good idea. Where's the Chaplain?

COOK. In the town. With Eilif.

MOTHER COURAGE. Stay with us a while, Lamb, I need a bit of help.

COOK. This matter of Yvette . . .

MOTHER COURAGE. Hasn't done you any harm at all in my eyes. Just the opposite. Where there's smoke, there's fire, they say. You'll come?

COOK. I may as well.

MOTHER COURAGE. The twelfth regiment's under way. Into harness with you! Maybe I'll see Eilif before the day is out, just think! That's what I like best. Well, it wasn't such a long peace, we can't grumble. Let's go!

[*The* COOK *and* KATTRIN *are in harness.*]

[MOTHER COURAGE *sings.*]

Up hill, down dale, past dome and steeple,
  My wagon always moves ahead.
The war can care for all its people
  So long as there is steel and lead.
Though steel and lead are stout supporters
  A war needs human beings too.
Report today to your headquarters!
  If it's to last, this war needs you!
    Christians, awake! The winter's gone!
    The snows depart, the dead sleep on.
    And though you may not long survive
    Get out of bed and look alive!

Scene 9

The great war of religion has lasted sixteen years and Germany
has lost half its inhabitants. Those who are spared in battle
die by plague. Over once blooming countryside hunger rages.
Towns are burned down. Wolves prowl the empty streets. In
the autumn of 1634 we find Mother Courage in the Fichtelge-
birge not far from the road the Swedish army is taking. Winter
has come early and is hard. Business is bad. Only begging
remains. The cook receives a letter from Utrecht and is sent
packing.

[*In front of a half-ruined parsonage. Early winter.
A grey morning. Gusts of wind.* MOTHER COURAGE
and the COOK *at the wagon in shabby clothes.*]

COOK. There are no lights on. No one's up.

MOTHER COURAGE. But it's a parsonage. The parson'll have to leave
his feather bed and ring the bells. Then he'll have some hot soup.

COOK. Where'll he get it from? The whole village is starving.

MOTHER COURAGE. The house is lived in. There was a dog barking.

COOK. If the parson has anything, he'll stick to it.

MOTHER COURAGE. Maybe if we sang him something . . .

COOK. I've had enough.

[*Suddenly.*]

I didn't tell you, a letter came from Utrecht. My mother's died of
cholera, the inn is mine. There's the letter, if you don't believe me.
I'll show it to you, though my aunt's railing about me and my ups
and downs is none of your business.

MOTHER COURAGE (*reading*). Lamb, I'm tired of wandering, too. I feel like a butcher's dog taking meat to my customers and getting none myself. I've nothing more to sell and people have nothing to pay with. In Saxony someone tried to saddle me with a chestful of books in return for two eggs. And in Württemberg they would have let me have their plough for a bag of salt. Nothing grows any more, only thorn bushes. I hear that in Pomerania the villagers have been eating their younger children. Nuns have been caught committing robbery.

COOK. The world's dying out.

MOTHER COURAGE. Sometimes I see myself driving through hell with this wagon and selling brimstone. And sometimes I'm driving through heaven handing out provisions to wandering souls! If only we could find a place where there's no shooting, me and my children—what's left of 'em—we might rest a while.

COOK. We could open this inn together. Think about it, Courage. *My* mind's made up. With or without you, I'm leaving for Utrecht. And today too.

MOTHER COURAGE. I must talk to Kattrin, it's a little bit sudden, and I don't like to make my decisions in the cold on an empty stomach.

[KATTRIN *emerges from the wagon.*]

Kattrin, I've something to tell you. The cook and I want to go to Utrecht, he's been left an inn. You'd be able to stay put and get to know some people. Many a man'd be prepared to take on a girl with a position. Looks aren't everything. I wouldn't mind it. I get on well with the Cook. I'll say this for him: he has a head for business. We'd be sure of our dinner, that would be all right, wouldn't it? You'd have your own bed, what do you think of *that?* In the long run, this is no life, on the road. You might be killed any time. You're already lousy. And we must decide now, because otherwise we go north with the Swedes. They must be over there somewhere.

[*She points to the left.*]

I think we'll decide to go, Kattrin.

COOK. Anna, I must have a word with you alone.

MOTHER COURAGE. Go back inside, Kattrin.

[KATTRIN *does so.*]

COOK. I'm interrupting because there's a misunderstanding, Anna. I thought I wouldn't have to say it right out, but I see I must. If you're bringing *her,* it's all off. Do we understand each other?

[KATTRIN *has her head out of the back of the wagon*
and is listening.]

MOTHER COURAGE. You mean I leave Kattrin behind?

COOK. What do you think? There's no room in the inn, it isn't one of those places with three counters. If the two of us look lively we can earn a living, but three's too many. Let Kattrin keep your wagon.

MOTHER COURAGE. I was thinking we might find her a husband in Utrecht.

COOK. Don't make me laugh. With that scar? And old as she is? And dumb?

MOTHER COURAGE. Not so loud!

COOK. Loud or soft, what is, is. That's another reason I can't have her in the inn. Customers don't like having something like that always before their eyes. You can't blame them.

MOTHER COURAGE. Shut up. I told you not to talk so loud.

COOK. There's a light in the parsonage, we can sing now!

MOTHER COURAGE. Cook, how could she pull the wagon by herself? The war frightens her. She can't bear it. She has terrible dreams. I hear her groan at night, especially after battles. What she sees in her dreams I don't know. She suffers from pity. The other day I found a hedgehog with her that we'd run over.

COOK. The inn's too small.

[*Calling.*]

Worthy Sir, menials, and all within! We now present the song of Solomon, Julius Caesar, and other great souls who came to no good, so you can see we're law-abiding folk too, and have a hard time getting by, especially in winter.

[*He sings:* "The Song of the Great Souls of This Earth."]

    You've heard of wise old Solomon
        You know his history.
    He thought so little of this earth
    He cursed the hour of his birth
        Declaring: all is vanity.
    How very wise was Solomon!
        But ere night came and day did go
    This fact was clear to everyone:
        It was his wisdom that had brought him low.
    Better for you if you have none.

For the virtues are dangerous in this world, as our fine song tells. You're better off without, you have a nice life, breakfast included— some good hot soup maybe . . . I'm an example of a man who's not had any, and I'd like some, I'm a soldier, but what good did my bravery do me in all those battles? None at all. I might just as well have wet my pants like a poltroon and stayed home. For why?

    And Julius Caesar, who was brave,
        You saw what came of him.
    He sat like God on an altar-piece
        And yet they tore him limb from limb
    While his prestige did still increase!
    "Et tu, Brute, I am undone!"
        And ere night came and day did go

This fact was clear to everyone:
  It was his bravery that brought him low
Better for you if you have none.
                    [*Under his breath.*]
They don't even look out.

                    [*Aloud.*]
Worthy Sir, menials, and all within! You should say, no, courage isn't the thing to fill a man's belly, try honesty, that should be worth a dinner, at any rate it must have *some* effect. Let's see.
  You all know honest Socrates
    Who always spoke the truth.
  They owed him thanks for that, you'd think,
  Yet they put hemlock in his drink
    And swore that he was bad for youth.
  How honest was the people's son!
    But ere night came and day did go
  This fact was clear to everyone:
    It was his honesty that brought him low.
Better for you if you have none.

Yes, we're told to be unselfish and share what we have, but what if we have nothing? And those who do share it don't have an easy time either, for what's left when you've finished sharing? Unselfishness is a very rare virtue—it doesn't pay.
  Unselfish Martin could not bear
    His fellow creature's woes.
  He met a beggar in the snows
  And gave him half his cloak to wear:
    So both of them fell down and froze.
  What an unselfish paragon!
    But ere night came and day did go
  This fact was clear to everyone:
    It was unselfishness that brought him low.
Better for you if you have none.

That's how it is with us. We're law-abiding folk, we keep to ourselves, don't steal, don't kill, don't burn the place down. And in this way we sink lower and lower and the song proves true and there's no soup going. And if we were different, if we were thieves and killers, maybe we could eat our fill! For virtues bring no reward, only vices. Such is the world, need it be so?
  God's Ten Commandments we have kept
    And acted as we should.
    It has not done us any good.
  O you who sit beside a fire
  Please help us now: our need is dire!
  Strict godliness we've always shown
    But ere night came and day did go

This fact was clear to everyone:
It was our godliness that brought us low.
Better for you if you have none!

VOICES (*from above*). You there! Come up! There's some soup here
for you!

MOTHER COURAGE. Lamb, I couldn't swallow a thing. I don't say what
you said is unreasonable, but was it your last word? We've always
understood each other.

COOK. Yes, Anna. Think it over.

MOTHER COURAGE. There's nothing to think over. I'm not leaving her
here.

COOK. You're going to be silly, but what can I do? I'm not inhuman,
it's just that the inn's a small one. And now we must go up, or it'll
be nothing doing here too, and we've been singing in the cold to no
avail.

MOTHER COURAGE. I'll fetch Kattrin.

COOK. Better stick something in your pocket for her. If there are three
of us, they'll get a shock.

[*Exeunt.*]

[KATTRIN *clambers out of the wagon with a bundle.
She makes sure they're both gone. Then, on a wagon
wheel, she lays out a skirt of her mother's and a pair
of the* COOK's *trousers side by side and easy to see.
She has just finished, and has picked up her bundle,
when* MOTHER COURAGE *returns.*]

MOTHER COURAGE (*with a plate of soup*). Kattrin! Stay where you
are, Kattrin! Where do you think you're going with that bundle?

[*She examines the bundle.*]

She's packed her things. Were you listening? I told him there was
nothing doing, he can *have* Utrecht and his lousy inn, what would
we want with a lousy inn?

[*She sees the skirt and trousers.*]

Oh, you're a stupid girl, Kattrin, what if I'd seen that and you gone?

[*She takes hold of* KATTRIN, *who's trying to leave.*]

And don't think I've sent him packing on your account. It was the
wagon. You can't part us, I'm too used to it, *you* didn't come into
it, it was the wagon. Now we're leaving, and we'll put the cook's
things here where he'll find 'em, the stupid man.

[*She clambers up and throws a couple of things down
to go with the trousers.*]

There! He's sacked! The last man I'll take into *this* business! Now
let's be going, you and me. Get into harness. This winter'll pass—
like all the others.

[*They harness themselves to the wagon, turn it
around, and start out. A gust of wind. Enter the*
COOK, *still chewing. He sees his things.*]

Scene 10

*During the whole of 1635 Mother Courage and Kattrin pull
the wagon along the roads of central Germany in the wake of
the ever more ragged armies.*

> [*On the highway,* MOTHER COURAGE *and* KATTRIN
> *are pulling the wagon. They come to a prosperous
> farmhouse. Someone inside is singing.*]
> "The Song of Shelter"

THE VOICE.

In March a tree we planted
    To make the garden gay.
In June we were enchanted:
A lovely rose was blooming
The balmy air perfuming!
    Blest of the gods are they
    Who have a garden gay!
In June we were enchanted.

When snow falls helter-skelter
    And loudly blows the storm
Our farmhouse gives us shelter.
The winter's in a hurry
But we've no cause to worry.
    Cosy are we and warm
    Though loudly blows the storm
Our farmhouse gives us shelter.

> [MOTHER COURAGE *and* KATTRIN *have stopped to
> listen. Then they start out again.*]

Scene 11

January, 1636. Catholic troops threaten the Protestant town of Halle. The stone begins to speak. Mother Courage loses her daughter and journeys onwards alone. The war is not yet near its end.

[*The wagon, very far gone now, stands near a farmhouse with a straw roof. It is night. Out of the wood come a* LIEUTENANT *and* THREE SOLDIERS *in full armor.*]

LIEUTENANT. And there mustn't be a sound. If anyone yells, cut him down.

FIRST SOLDIER. But we'll have to knock—if we want a guide.

LIEUTENANT. Knocking's a natural noise, it's all right, could be a cow hitting the wall of the cowshed.

[*The* SOLDIERS *knock at the farmhouse door. An old peasant woman opens. A hand is clapped over her mouth. Two soldiers enter.*]

MAN'S VOICE. What is it?

[*The* SOLDIERS *bring out an old peasant and his son.*]

LIEUTENANT (*pointing to the wagon on which* KATTRIN *has appeared*). There's one.

[*A soldier pulls her out.*]

Is this everybody that lives here?

PEASANTS (*alternating*). That's our son. And that's a girl that can't talk. Her mother's in town buying up stocks because the shopkeepers are running away and selling cheap. They're canteen people.

LIEUTENANT. I'm warning you. Keep quiet. One sound and we'll crack you one with a pike. And I need someone to show us the path to the town.

[*Points to the* YOUNG PEASANT.]

You! Come here!

YOUNG PEASANT. I don't know any path!

SECOND SOLDIER (*grinning*). He don't know any path!

YOUNG PEASANT. I don't help Catholics.

LIEUTENANT (*to* SECOND SOLDIER). Let him feel your pike in his side.

YOUNG PEASANT (*forced to his knees, the pike at his throat*). I'd rather die!

SECOND SOLDIER (*again mimicking*). He'd rather die!

FIRST SOLDIER. I know how to change his mind.

[*Walks over to the cowshed.*]

Two cows and a bull. Listen, you. If you aren't going to be reasonable, I'll sabre your cattle.

YOUNG PEASANT. Not the cattle!

PEASANT WOMAN (*weeping*). Spare the cattle, captain, or we'll starve!

LIEUTENANT. If he must be pigheaded!

FIRST SOLDIER. I think I'll start with the bull.

YOUNG PEASANT (*to the old one*). Do I have to?

[*The* OLDER ONE *nods.*]

I'll do it.

PEASANT WOMAN. Thank you, thank you, captain, for sparing us, for ever and ever. Amen.

[*The old man stops her going on thanking him.*]

FIRST SOLDIER. I knew the bull came first all right!

[*Led by the* YOUNG PEASANT, *the* LIEUTENANT *and the* SOLDIERS *go on their way.*]

OLD PEASANT. I wish we knew what it was. Nothing good, I suppose.

PEASANT WOMAN. Maybe they're just scouts. What are you doing?

OLD PEASANT (*setting a ladder against the roof and climbing up*). I'm seeing if they're alone.

[*On the roof.*]

Things are moving—all over. I can see armor. And a cannon. There must be more than a regiment. God have mercy on the town and all within!

PEASANT WOMAN. Are there lights in the town?

OLD PEASANT. No, they're all asleep.

[*He climbs down.*]

There'll be an attack, and they'll all be slaughtered in their beds.

PEASANT WOMAN. The watchman'll give warning.

OLD PEASANT. They must have killed the watchman in the tower on the hill or he'd have sounded his horn before this.

PEASANT WOMAN. If there were more of us . . .

OLD PEASANT. But being that we're alone with that cripple . . .

PEASANT WOMAN. There's nothing we can do, is there?

OLD PEASANT. Nothing.

PEASANT WOMAN. We can't get down there. In the dark.

OLD PEASANT. The whole hillside's swarming with 'em.

PEASANT WOMAN. We could give a sign?

OLD PEASANT. And be cut down for it?

PEASANT WOMAN. No, there's nothing we can do.

[*To* KATTRIN.]

Pray, poor thing, pray! There's nothing we can do to stop this blood-shed, so even if you can't talk, at least pray! He hears, if no one else does. I'll help you.

[*All kneel,* KATTRIN *behind.*]

Our Father, which art in Heaven, hear our prayer, let not the town perish with all that lie therein asleep and fearing nothing. Wake them, that they rise and go to the walls and see the foe that comes with fire and sword in the night down the hill and across the fields. [*Back to* KATTRIN.] God protect our mother and make the watchman not sleep but wake ere it's too late. And save our son-in-law too, O God, he's there with his four children, let them not perish, they're innocent, they know nothing [*to* KATTRIN, *who groans*], one of them's not two years old, the eldest is seven.

[KATTRIN *rises, troubled.*]

Heavenly Father, hear us, only Thou canst help us or we die, for we are weak and have no sword nor nothing; we cannot thrust our own strength but only Thine, O Lord; we are in Thy hands, our cattle, our farm, and the town too, we're all in Thy hands, and the foe is nigh unto the walls with all his power.

[KATTRIN *unperceived, has crept off to the wagon, has taken something out of it, put it under her apron, and has climbed up the ladder to the roof.*]

Be mindful of the children in danger, especially the little ones, be mindful of the old folk who cannot move, and of all Christian souls, O Lord.

OLD PEASANT. And forgive us our trespasses as we forgive them that trespass against us. Amen.

[*Sitting on the roof,* KATTRIN *takes a drum from under her apron, and starts to beat it.*]

PEASANT WOMAN. Heavens, what's she doing?

OLD PEASANT. She's out of her mind!

PEASANT WOMAN. Bring her down, quick!

[*The* OLD PEASANT *runs to the ladder but* KATTRIN *pulls it up on the roof.*]

She'll get us in trouble.

OLD PEASANT. Stop it this minute, you silly cripple!

PEASANT WOMAN. The soldiers'll come!

OLD PEASANT (*looking for stones*). I'll stone you!

PEASANT WOMAN. Have you no pity, have you no heart? We have relations there too, four grandchildren, but there's nothing we can do. If they find us now, it's the end, they'll stab us to death!

[KATTRIN *is staring into the far distance, toward the town. She goes on drumming*.]

PEASANT WOMAN (*to the* PEASANT). I told you not to let that riffraff in your farm. What do *they* care if we lose our cattle?

LIEUTENANT (*running back with* SOLDIERS *and* YOUNG PEASANT). I'll cut you all to bits!

PEASANT WOMAN. We're innocent, sir, there's nothing we can do. She did it, a stranger!

LIEUTENANT. Where's the ladder?

OLD PEASANT. On the roof.

LIEUTENANT (*calling*). Throw down the drum. I order you!

[KATTRIN *goes on drumming*.]

You're all in this, but you won't live to tell the tale.

OLD PEASANT. They've been cutting down fir trees around here. If we bring a tall enough trunk we can knock her off the roof . . .

FIRST SOLDIER (*to the* LIEUTENANT). I beg leave to make a suggestion.

[*He whispers something to the* LIEUTENANT, *who nods*.]

Listen, you! We have an idea—for your own good. Come down and go with us to the town. Show us your mother and we'll spare her.

[KATTRIN *replies and goes on drumming*.]

LIEUTENANT (*pushing him away*). She doesn't trust you, no wonder with your face.

[*He calls up to* KATTRIN.]

Hey, you! Suppose I give you my word? I'm an officer, my word's my bond!

[KATTRIN *drums louder*.]

Nothing is sacred to her.

YOUNG PEASANT. Sir, it's not just because of her mother!

FIRST SOLDIER. This can't go on, they'll hear it in the town as sure as hell.

LIEUTENANT. We must make another noise with something. Louder than that drum. What can we make a noise with?

FIRST SOLDIER. But we mustn't make a noise!

LIEUTENANT. A harmless noise, fool, a peacetime noise!

OLD PEASANT. I could start chopping wood.

LIEUTENANT. That's it!

[*The* PEASANT *brings his ax and chops away*.]

Chop! Chop harder! Chop for your life! [KATTRIN *has been listening, beating her drum less hard. Very upset, and peering around, She now goes on drumming*.] It's not enough.

[*To* FIRST SOLDIER.]

You chop too!

OLD PEASANT. I've only one ax. [*He stops chopping.*]

LIEUTENANT. We must set fire to the farm. Smoke her out.

OLD PEASANT. That's no good, Captain, when they see fire from the town, they'll know everything.

> [*During the drumming* KATTRIN *has been listening again. Now she laughs.*]

LIEUTENANT. She's laughing at us, that's too much, I'll have her guts if it's the last thing I do. Bring a musket!

> [*Two* SOLDIERS *off.* KATTRIN *goes on drumming.*]

PEASANT WOMAN. I have it, Captain. That's their wagon over there, Captain. If we smash that, she'll stop. It's all they have, Captain.

LIEUTENANT (*to the* YOUNG PEASANT). Smash it!

> [*Calling.*]

If you don't stop that noise, we'll smash your wagon!

> [*The* YOUNG PEASANT *deals the wagon a couple of feeble blows with a board.*]

PEASANT WOMAN (*to* KATTRIN). Stop, you little beast!

> [KATTRIN *stares at the wagon and pauses. Noises of distress come out of her. But she goes on drumming.*]

LIEUTENANT. Where are those sons of bitches with that gun?

FIRST SOLDIER. They can't have heard anything in the town or we'd hear their cannon.

LIEUTENANT (*calling*). They don't hear you. And now we're going to shoot you. I'll give you one more chance: throw down that drum!

YOUNG PEASANT (*dropping the board, screaming to* KATTRIN). Don't stop now! Or they're all done for. Go on, go on, go on . . .

> [*The* SOLDIER *knocks him down and beats him with his pike.* KATTRIN *starts crying but goes on drumming.*]

PEASANT WOMAN. Not in the back, you're killing him!

> [*The* SOLDIERS *arrive with the musket.*]

SECOND SOLDIER. The Colonel's foaming at the mouth. We'll be court-martialed.

LIEUTENANT. Set it up! Set it up!

> [*Calling while the musket is set up on forks.*]

Once for all: stop that drumming!

> [*Still crying,* KATTRIN *is drumming as hard as she can.*]

> [*The* SOLDIERS *fire.* KATTRIN *is hit. She gives the drum another feeble beat or two, then slowly collapses.*]

LIEUTENANT. That's an end to the noise.

> [*But the last beats of the drum are lost in the din of cannon from the town. Mingled with the thunder of cannon, alarm bells are heard in the distance.*]

FIRST SOLDIER. She did it.

Scene 12

[*Toward morning. The drums and pipes of troops on the march, receding. In front of the wagon* MOTHER COURAGE *sits by* KATTRIN'S *body. The peasants of the last scene are standing near.*]

PEASANTS. You must leave, ma'am. There's only one regiment to go. You can never get away by yourself.

MOTHER COURAGE. Maybe she's fallen asleep.

[*She sings.*]

    Lullay, lullay, what's that in the hay?
    The neighbor's babes cry but mine are gay.
    The neighbor's babes are dressed in dirt:
    Your silks were cut from an angel's skirt.
    They are all starving: you have a cake;
    If it's too stale, you need but speak.
    Lullay, lullay, what's rustling there?
    One lad fell in Poland. The other is where?

You shouldn't have told her about the children.

PEASANTS. If you hadn't gone off to the town to get your cut, maybe it wouldn't have happened.

MOTHER COURAGE. She's asleep now.

PEASANTS. She's not asleep, it's time you realized. She's through. You must get away. There are wolves in these parts. And the bandits are worse.

MOTHER COURAGE. That's right.

[*She goes and fetches a piece of cloth from the wagon to cover the body.*]

PEASANTS. Have you no one now? Someone you can go to?

MOTHER COURAGE. There's one. My Eilif.

PEASANTS (*while* COURAGE *covers the body*). Leave *her* to us. We'll give her a proper burial. You needn't worry.

MOTHER COURAGE. Here's money for the expenses.

[*She pays the peasant. The* PEASANT *and his son shake
her hand and carry* KATTRIN *away.*]

PEASANT WOMAN (*also taking her hand, and bowing, as she goes away*).
Hurry!

MOTHER COURAGE (*harnessing herself to the wagon*). I hope I can
pull the wagon by myself. Yes, I'll manage, there's not much in it
now. I must start up again in business.

[*Another regiment passes at the rear with pipe and
drum.*]

MOTHER COURAGE. Hey! Take me with you!

[*She starts pulling the wagon. Soldiers are heard
singing.*]

Dangers, surprises, devastations—
The war takes hold and will not quit.
But though it last three generations
We shall get nothing out of it.
Starvation, filth, and cold enslave us.
The army robs us of our pay.
Only a miracle can save us
And miracles have had their day.
Christians, awake! The winter's gone!
The snows depart. The dead sleep on.
And though you may not long survive
Get out of bed and look alive!

TRANSLATOR'S NOTES TO MOTHER COURAGE

When I first translated *Mother Courage,* I worked from a copy of the play
as printed in the *Versuche* series. It was marked up by a member of the
staff of the Berlin Ensemble: I made the cuts indicated and put in the
penciled additions. The translation appeared in *The Modern Theatre,* Volume 2, 1955, Doubleday Anchor Books.

Next I made a somewhat shorter stage version with new lyrics, which
Darius Milhaud set to music. This version was published in *Seven Plays* by
Bertolt Brecht, 1961.

The present text, commissioned by Methuen & Co. for their collected
Brecht, is the only one of my three versions which is complete. The basis
of this version is, in general, the text in the *Versuche,* but I have frequently
consulted the text in the *Stücke* too.

The few words in my translation for which no equivalent will be found
in either the *Versuche* or the *Stücke* I took from the Berlin Ensemble copy

mentioned above; and Brecht has recorded them permanently in the Notes to the special Modell edition published by Henschel in East Berlin, 1958.

To the list of helpers acknowledged in former editions of the English *Mother Courage*, I should like to add the names of two who helped with this new effort: Miss Jill Booty and Dr. Hugo Schmidt.

The music for the lyrics here printed, which is by Darius Milhaud, has not yet (early 1962) been made available to producers. A score by Paul Dessau has been used in all authorized English-language productions. A piano reduction of Dessau's songs will be found in the Doubleday Anchor edition of *Mother Courage* with English words to fit. Some of these songs are to be found, sung by Germaine Montero, on a 12-inch disc (VKS-9022) distributed in the United States by Vanguard Records. The East-German records of some of the *Mother Courage* songs, performed by the original Berlin Ensemble cast, have usually been available from Deutsche Schallplatten, Deutscher Buch Export, Leninstrasse 16, Leipzig C.1, Germany. There is an East-German movie of the play which has not yet been generally released, and there is a British TV-film of the Bentley version which has not been shown outside Britain.

Mother Courage was first produced in 1941 in Zurich and since the Berlin Ensemble production (1949) has been performed in many countries. The Bentley version alone has been professionally produced in Dublin, London (TV only), Cleveland, and San Francisco. Pictures of each scene in the Berlin Ensemble production are provided in *Courage-Modell 1949*, published by the Henschel Verlag in East Berlin, along with Brecht's own scene-by-scene analysis of the play.

Eric Bentley

QUESTIONS

SCENE 1

1. The play opens with two recruiters discussing the advantages of war over peace. What is the major advantage? Does the attribution of this value to war link war with certain other social and political philosophies?

2. In the course of Scene 1 a number of traditional moral values, such as courage and patriotism, are brought under discussion indirectly. Do the Fierlings and the recruiters fulfill our usual moral expectations? Is "morality" perhaps redefined in this scene?

3. What is the meaning of everyone's drawing a black cross from the helmet? Is death brought into the first scene in other ways?

4. Do you see any significance in the manner in which the recruiter gets Eilif? Consider Eilif's actions as well as Mother Courage's.

SCENE 2

5. How does Brecht introduce religion into the play? How do men in general use religion?

6. What effect is achieved by having Eilif sing the first two stanzas of "The Fishwife and the Soldier," and Mother Courage sing the third?

7. How would you describe the "world" of the play? Out of what components has Brecht constructed it?

8. While the commander and Eilif discuss the "glories of war" in the front of the tent, Mother Courage and the cook bargain over a capon in the back. Two ways of life are thus juxtaposed. Find other places and other ways in which Brecht manages this same kind of juxtaposition.

SCENE 3

9. Consider carefully the things Mother Courage does and says and describe her basic "motive."

10. Why does this motive bring her into conflict with her world? How is the conflict realized dramatically?

11. Mother Courage's wagon is the one prop continually on stage. What does it represent? In answering this question take into account not only what the wagon looks like but the changes it undergoes and the observations that are made about it.

12. The third scene centers on a few props: a cashbox, a pair of red boots, a fancy hat, and a flag. What do these objects have in common, and why are they all dangerous to their possessors?

13. On several occasions Kattrin's muteness has serious consequences. What point do you think Brecht is making?

14. How does Brecht make us sympathize with Mother Courage even when her haggling over price costs the life of Swiss Cheese and when she denies that she recognizes his corpse? Is the word "courage" taking on a new meaning?

SCENE 4

15. What understanding of justice is dramatized by the incident of the young soldier?

16. Who are the "they" of Mother Courage's song, "The Great Capitulation"? Are there any characters in the play who can be identified as "they"?

SCENE 5

17. Sound effects are as much a part of the scene as objects. What function does the victory march played in the background serve?

18. Do you see any progression in the first five episodes of the play? Any regression?

SCENE 6

19. Are the Chaplain's statement that the war "can look forward to a prosperous future" and his view that war is the natural state of man successfully dramatized? That is, is the Chaplain's *idea* translated into theatrical terms?

20. *Mother Courage* was written in 1939 when Brecht was an exile from Hitler's Germany. Can you see any reason for setting the play in the religious wars of the seventeenth century? Why not dramatize the same ideas in contemporary terms?

21. What is the meaning of Kattrin's longing for children? What does the attack on her tell us about the nature of war?

22. What comment does the attack on Kattrin make on the "jolly" picture of war the Chaplain has presented at the beginning of this episode?

SCENE 7

23. Mother Courage's song faces directly and states succinctly the frightening facts of life as the play presents them. What response to the facts does Mother Courage suggest in her song?

SCENE 8

24. What point is Brecht making by having Eilif executed in peacetime for the same kind of act that won him great praise during wartime? Is Brecht defending Eilif? Is he presenting him in a favorable light?

25. How is the relationship between war and the business of earning a living established in this scene? Has Brecht drawn this parallel in other ways in the play?

SCENE 9

26. Brecht argued that he was interested in presenting in his plays human character as it is shaped by the conditions of the time, by the society and the world. How has Mother Courage been shaped by her time? Is she, however, entirely a product of social conditions, conforming entirely to the necessities the times force on her?

27. Is the effect of this scene with its "Song of the Wise and the Good" to persuade us that all conventional virtue is a disaster for its possessor?

SCENE 10

28. Does "The Song of Shelter" offer any genuine alternative for man, any escape from pulling the wagon from battlefield to battlefield?

SCENE 11

29. What three virtues or human qualities do Mother Courage's three children represent? Does Mother Courage share in these virtues or does she lack them?

30. Are we meant to despise the peasants who will destroy a town to save their cattle?

SCENE 12

31. Is Mother Courage able to live without illusions?

32. *Mother Courage* has been played most successfully on a revolving stage. At the end Mother Courage moves off pulling her wagon in one direction while the stage revolves in the opposite direction. In what ways is this an appropriate statement in visual terms of the play as a whole? If you were the director, would you have the wagon and stage move at the same speed, have the wagon move faster, or have the stage move faster? Why?

33. Should the song end as Mother Courage and her wagon exit from the stage, or should it continue after all movement on stage has ceased and the lights have darkened?

The World in Expressionistic Drama

A realistic playwright like Ibsen tries to construct plays in which the surface contains nothing surprising, nothing we would not expect to encounter in day-to-day existence. Shakespeare, like most playwrights, shows less concern for reproducing the familiar and unremarkable, and his scenes, his images of the world, tend to slip away from the strictly realistic toward the expressionistic; he is less concerned with making his stage world resemble everyday reality and more concerned with creating visual and verbal images that fully reveal the nature of the world. For example, in *Timon of Athens* he sets the first half of the play in the house of the wealthy Timon, who loves all mankind and overwhelms his friends and acquaintances with gifts and feasting. When Timon discovers that his friends are false and that his own wealth is exhausted, he turns into as great an enemy of mankind as he was once its friend, and he departs from the city into a desert where nature is grudging and brutal. There is nothing unrealistic about a great house or a desert—they can be seen every day—but it is quite clear from the way in which Shakespeare has juxtaposed these two places that he is not so concerned with presenting realistic scenes as he is with finding appropriate images for two types of worlds existing side by side—the rich and prosperous social setting, which man creates, and the harsh, isolated world of barren, hostile nature.

Brecht's methods for creating the world in *Mother Courage* are closer to Shakespeare's than to Ibsen's. While it is true that wagons, cannons, soldiers, battlefields, cookshacks, and cashboxes are all drawn from the real world, it is nonetheless startling to find our world represented as a continuous battlefield on which man earns his living by pulling a wagon from place to place. Brecht's scenes are realistic enough in one sense—they do show aspects of what can be seen in reality—but they are unrealistic or expressionistic ultimately, since they portray the world as a never-ending war, which is not the *literal* truth.

A number of modern dramatists have carried this technique a step further and have created scenes that bear little resemblance to what can be seen on earth. Nevertheless, they register forcefully the nature of our environment as man apprehends it with his feelings. In Arthur Miller's *Death of a Salesman* realism and expressionism are mixed; the salesman, Willy Loman, is crushed down by the weight of the world in which he lives. The set of the play represents this expressionistically: his house stands between two towering apartment buildings, which lean menacingly—in a structurally impossible manner—over it and block the sunlight. The flimsiness of Willy's hope is made visible by the construction of his house. While the walls of the apartment houses seem to be solid, the walls of the Loman house consist of flimsy, open framework; the furnishings—like the salesman's achievements—are few: a brass bed, a refrigerator, a silver trophy, and a few sticks of furniture. Other modern dramatists have made good use of similar sets to suggest the insubstantiality, the dreamlike quality, of the material goods that man believes so solid and permanent. For example, in Thornton Wilder's *The Skin of Our Teeth,* a play celebrating man's indomitable will to survive, the play centers in a house made of simple painted flats, which are knocked down the moment disaster strikes and restored the moment things improve. Our worldly goods, the play seems to say, are no more substantial than these light frames out of which this stage house is constructed. Human qualities alone are real and lasting.

The use of expressionistic devices to portray the world is as old as the theater. In one of the earliest tragedies, Aeschylus' *Prometheus Bound,* produced in Athens about 460 B.C., the hero Prometheus is chained to a rock in the center of the stage throughout the play. He has been placed there by Zeus because he defied him and brought fire to man, who, Zeus fears, may now challenge the rule of the gods. If one believes literally in the Greek gods, this is a "realistic" enough explanation of events, but the rock and the chains are principally a dramatic device for showing a "hard" world that resists and punishes any attempt to control and utilize for human purposes the gigantic powers—"gods" in Aeschylus' terms—of the universe. Medieval drama was even more openly expressionistic. In medieval plays the entire Christian world was often laid out schematically on the "stage" —often a town square—with no concern for the fact that this scene violated normal understanding of time and space. On one side was the mouth of Hell, on the other the mountain of Paradise and the Garden of Eden. In between was the field where Cain strikes Abel, Mount Ararat where the ark of Noah grounds, and Calvary where Christ dies, all represented symbolically and all in front of the still visible buildings of the town where, Christians believed, the sins and sufferings, the just acts and rewards dramatized in the Bible were daily re-enacted in contemporary costumes and accents.

This distortion of the familiar surface of reality to reveal "true reality," this telescoping of time and space to present the world in which man "actually" lives, this concentration of the endless variety of life into a single essential image, is the primary technique of all art, including drama.

THE SKIN
OF OUR TEETH
BY
THORNTON WILDER

When *The Skin of Our Teeth* opened in New Haven in 1942 the taxi
drivers, who usually waited until the final curtain, appeared outside the
theater at the first intermission to pick up the playgoers, who streamed
out, baffled, confused, and agreeing with Miss Somerset, the actress
playing the part of Sabina: "Oh—why can't we have plays like we
used to have—*Peg o' My Heart,* and *Smilin' Thru,* and *The Bat*—
good entertainment with a message you can take home with you?" Instead of this accustomed fare, Thornton Wilder (b. 1897) had given
them a play in which the ice age and the affairs of suburban New
Jersey were frantically mixed together, in which it was impossible
to tell whether the George Antrobus family was a typical modern
middle-class family or the family in Genesis. Newsreels flashed on a
screen announcing the rising of the sun that morning, Noah's flood
overwhelmed a convention at Atlantic City, the scenery flew up and
down wildly, there was no beginning and no end, and at times the play
simply stopped while the stage manager and the cast talked over the
almost insuperable difficulties of putting on this crazy play with its
weird cast of actors and actresses.

Wilder's expressionistic style—which owed much to James Joyce's
Finnegan's Wake—was not, of course, really very new, even in 1942;
it was only unfamiliar to American theater audiences. Since that time
the theater has become increasingly less realistic, less likely to provide neat little entertainments complete with a message to take home.
The Skin of Our Teeth and its poetic, expressionistic style no longer
seem very strange at all in a theater where throughout the play two
tramps simply wait on stage for someone named Godot to arrive, or
where an old couple gradually fill the stage with empty chairs. As a

result of this pronounced shift in theatrical style, it is now much easier to perceive beneath the jumble of words and events in *The Skin of Our Teeth* a very ordinary *situation comedy,* in which a very ordinary American family weathers a series of very ordinary domestic difficulties: a daughter who wears lipstick at too early an age, a son who throws stones at the neighbor children, an infatuation at Atlantic City, a threatened divorce, a pregnancy, and a violent quarrel between father and son. The basic situations are all staples of the theater— even a grumbling maid always threatening to quit—and the playwright frequently laughs at the hackneyed events and speeches of his own play.

But even as he laughs, he praises. For he sees in this unheroic stock story a low-key statement of the great comedy of human life. Working in the city, sending singing telegrams, and raising difficult children are, the play insists, the twentieth-century enactments of the marvel of life, of that remarkable, ongoing struggle of man against death, which began ages ago in the primeval ooze and has continued through the long process of human evolution and history. Meeting crisis after crisis, we somehow escape each time into the future by the skin of our teeth. In *The Skin of Our Teeth* modern man's rather dreary struggle to raise his family and earn his living becomes one, by means of Wilder's style, with man's past trials— geologic catastrophe, expulsion from Eden, and apocalyptic wars. To this struggle the urban breadwinner brings the same powers of mind that conceived the wheel, the alphabet, the concept of number, the Ten Commandments, and the *Iliad*; the same will to begin again that survived ice, flood, and fire.

Wilder's democratic humanism sees the heroic in the ordinary and the noble past in the limited present, and his dramatic method for presenting this vision is bold and direct. Instead of limiting his perception to verbal metaphor—instead of having his characters say, "The barbarism of Nazi Germany is like a new ice age," or "Father's infatuation with that tramp in Atlantic City is just another manifestation of human sexuality which has allowed man to outbreed the saber-toothed tiger"—Wilder abandons the pretense of realism and stages directly what is usually concealed in metaphor. Just outside the windows of the house in Excelsior, New Jersey, *is* the glacier; the other animals whom man has surpassed through evolution watch George Antrobus seduce Lily Fairweather; and the out-of-luck depression friends whom Antrobus brings home unexpectedly for dinner *are* Moses, Socrates, Homer, and the Muses. Instead of having his characters remark how much life is like a bad play or how their lives seem only the endless playing out of ridiculous parts, Wilder discards the play's pretense at being real and reveals, from time to time, the workings of the playhouse and the difficulties of this particular company in staging this play.

Not only in *The Skin of Our Teeth*, but in *Our Town* (1938), *The Matchmaker* (1954), and in a long succession of short plays, novels, and stories, Wilder has been the celebrant of a particularly gentle and peculiarly American comic view of life. His comedy is not the kind that laughs uproariously and unmercifully at the grotesque pretensions of the human animal; rather, while it never loses sight of the fact that man is a bit funny, it continues to sympathize with humanity. It never loses hope that this strange and bumbling creature will continue to stagger on into history, thinking his odd thoughts, raising his children, burying his dead, and somehow finding the absurd courage and hope to confront the next crisis that the working of the world and of his own complex nature makes inevitable.

CHARACTERS (*in the order of their appearance*)

ANNOUNCER	MISS E. MUSE
SABINA	MISS T. MUSE
MR. FITZPATRICK	MISS M. MUSE
MRS. ANTROBUS	TWO USHERS
DINOSAUR	TWO DRUM MAJORETTES
MAMMOTH	FORTUNE TELLER
TELEGRAPH BOY	TWO CHAIR PUSHERS
GLADYS	SIX CONVEENERS
HENRY	BROADCAST OFFICIAL
MR. ANTROBUS	DEFEATED CANDIDATE
DOCTOR	MR. TREMAYNE
PROFESSOR	HESTER
JUDGE	IVY
HOMER	FRED BAILEY

Act I. *Home, Excelsior, New Jersey.*
Act II. *Atlantic City Boardwalk.*
Act III. *Home, Excelsior, New Jersey.*

ACT I

A projection screen in the middle of the curtain. The first lantern slide: the name of the theatre, and the words: NEWS EVENTS OF THE WORLD. An ANNOUNCER'S *voice is heard.*

ANNOUNCER. The management takes pleasure in bringing to you—The News Events of the World:
> [*Slide of the sun appearing above the horizon.*]

Freeport, Long Island:
The sun rose this morning at 6:32 a.m. This gratifying event was first reported by Mrs. Dorothy Stetson of Freeport, Long Island, who promptly telephoned the Mayor.
The Society for Affirming the End of the World at once went into a special session and postponed the arrival of that event for TWENTY-FOUR HOURS.
All honor to Mrs. Stetson for her public spirit.

New York City:
> [*Slide of the front doors of the theatre in which this*
> *play is playing; three cleaning women with mops and*
> *pails.*]

The X Theatre. During the daily cleaning of this theatre a number of lost objects were collected as usual by Mesdames Simpson, Pateslewski, and Moriarty.
Among these objects found today was a wedding ring, inscribed: To Eva from Adam. Genesis II:18.
The ring will be restored to the owner or owners, if their credentials are satisfactory.

Tippehatchee, Vermont:
>   [*Slide representing a glacier.*]

The unprecedented cold weather of this summer has produced a condition that has not yet been satisfactorily explained. There is a report that a wall of ice is moving southward across these counties. The disruption of communications by the cold wave now crossing the country has rendered exact information difficult, but little credence is given to the rumor that the ice had pushed the Cathedral of Montreal as far as St. Albans, Vermont.

For further information see your daily papers.

Excelsior, New Jersey:
>   [*Slide of a modest suburban home.*]

The home of Mr. George Antrobus, the inventor of the wheel. The discovery of the wheel, following so closely on the discovery of the lever, has centered the attention of the country on Mr. Antrobus of this attractive suburban residence district. This is his home, a commodious seven-room house, conveniently situated near a public school, a Methodist church, and a firehouse; it is right handy to an A and P.

>   [*Slide of* MR. ANTROBUS *on his front steps, smiling and lifting his straw hat. He holds a wheel.*]

Mr. Antrobus, himself. He comes of very old stock and has made his way up from next to nothing.

It is reported that he was once a gardener, but left that situation under circumstances that have been variously reported.

Mr. Antrobus is a veteran of foreign wars, and bears a number of scars, front and back.

>   [*Slide of* MRS. ANTROBUS, *holding some roses.*]

This is Mrs. Antrobus, the charming and gracious president of the Excelsior Mothers' Club.

Mrs. Antrobus is an excellent needlewoman; it is she who invented the apron on which so many interesting changes have been rung since.

>   [*Slide of the* FAMILY *and* SABINA.]

Here we see the Antrobuses with their two children, Henry and Gladys, and friend. The friend in the rear is Lily Sabina, the maid.

I know we all want to congratulate this typical American family on its enterprise. We all wish Mr. Antrobus a successful future. Now the management takes you to the interior of this home for a brief visit.

>   [*Curtain rises. Living room of a commuter's home.*
>   SABINA—*straw-blonde, over-rouged—is standing by the window back center, a feather duster under her elbow.*]

SABINA. Oh, oh, oh! Six o'clock and the master not home yet.

Pray God nothing serious has happened to him crossing the Hudson River. If anything happened to him, we would certainly be inconsolable and have to move into a less desirable residence district.

The fact is I don't know what'll become of us. Here it is the middle of August and the coldest day of the year. It's simply freezing; the dogs are sticking to the sidewalks; can anybody explain that? No.

But I'm not surprised. The whole world's at sixes and sevens, and why the house hasn't fallen down about our ears long ago is a miracle to me.

[*A fragment of the right wall leans precariously over the stage.* SABINA *looks at it nervously and it slowly rights itself.*]

Every night this same anxiety as to whether the master will get home safely: whether he'll bring home anything to eat. In the midst of life we are in the midst of death, a truer word was never said.

[*The fragment of scenery flies up into the lofts.* SABINA *is struck dumb with surprise, shrugs her shoulders and starts dusting* MR. ANTROBUS' *chair, including the under side.*]

Of course, Mr. Antrobus is a very fine man, an excellent husband and father, a pillar of the church, and has all the best interests of the community at heart. Of course, every muscle goes tight every time he passes a policeman; but what I think is that there are certain charges that ought not to be made, and I think I may add, ought not to be allowed to be made; we're all human; who isn't? (*She dusts* MRS. ANTROBUS' *rocking chair.*)

Mrs. Antrobus is as fine a woman as you could hope to see. She lives only for her children; and if it would be any benefit to her children she'd see the rest of us stretched out dead at her feet without turning a hair,—that's the truth. If you want to know anything more about Mrs. Antrobus, just go and look at a tigress, and look hard.

As to the children—

Well, Henry Antrobus is a real, clean-cut American boy. He'll graduate from High School one of these days, if they make the alphabet any easier.—Henry, when he has a stone in his hand, has a perfect aim; he can hit anything from a bird to an older brother—Oh! I didn't mean to say that!—but it certainly was an unfortunate accident, and it was very hard getting the police out of the house.

Mr. and Mrs. Antrobus' daughter is named Gladys. She'll make some good man a good wife some day, if he'll just come down off the movie screen and ask her.

So here we are!

We've managed to survive for some time now, catch as catch can, the fat and the lean, and if the dinosaurs don't trample us to death, and if the grasshoppers don't eat up our garden, we'll all live to see better days, knock on wood.

Each new child that's born to the Antrobuses seems to them to be sufficient reason for the whole universe's being set in motion; and each new child that dies seems to them to have been spared a whole world of sorrow, and what the end of it will be is still very much an open question.

We've rattled along, hot and cold, for some time now—(*A portion of the wall above the door, right, flies up into the air and disappears.*)—and my advice to you is not to inquire into why or whither, but just enjoy your ice cream while it's on your plate— that's my philosophy.

Don't forget that a few years ago we came through the depression by the skin of our teeth! One more tight squeeze like that and where will we be?" (*This is a cue line.* SABINA *looks angrily at the kitchen door and repeats.*) . . . we came through the depression by the skin of our teeth; one more tight squeeze like that and where will we be? (*Flustered, she looks through the opening in the right wall; then goes to the window and reopens the Act.*)

Oh, oh, oh! Six o'clock and the master not home yet. Pray God nothing has happened to him crossing the Hudson. Here it is the middle of August and the coldest day of the year. It's simply freezing; the dogs are sticking. One more tight squeeze like that and where will we be?

VOICE (*off stage*). Make up something! Invent something!

SABINA. Well . . . uh . . . this certainly is a fine American home . . . and—uh . . . everybody's very happy . . . and—uh . . . (*Suddenly flings pretense to the winds and coming downstage says with indignation:*) I can't invent any words for this play, and I'm glad I can't. I hate this play and every word in it.

As for me, I don't understand a single word of it, anyway,— all about the troubles the human race has gone through, there's a subject for you.

Besides, the author hasn't made up his silly mind as to whether we're all living back in caves or in New Jersey today, and that's the way it is all the way through.

Oh—why can't we have plays like we used to have—*Peg o' My Heart,* and *Smilin' Thru,* and *The Bat*—good entertainment with a message you can take home with you?

I took this hateful job because I had to. For two years I've sat up in my room living on a sandwich and a cup of tea a day, waiting for better times in the theatre. And look at me now: I—I who've played *Rain* and *The Barretts of Wimpole Street* and *First Lady*— God in Heaven!

[*The* STAGE MANAGER *puts his head out from the hole in the scenery.*]

MR. FITZPATRICK. Miss Somerset! Miss Somerset!

SABINA. Oh! Anyway!—nothing matters! It'll all be the same in a hundred years. (*Loudly.*) We came through the depression by the skin of our teeth,—that's true!—one more tight squeeze like that and where will we be?

[*Enter* MRS. ANTROBUS, *a mother.*]

MRS. ANTROBUS. Sabina, you've let the fire go out.

SABINA (*in a lather*). One-thing-and-another; don't-know-whether-my-wits-are-upside-or-down; might-as-well-be-dead-as-alive-in-a-house-all sixes-and-sevens. . . .

MRS. ANTROBUS. You've let the fire go out. Here it is the coldest day of the year right in the middle of August, and you've let the fire go out.

SABINA. Mrs. Antrobus, I'd like to give my two weeks' notice, Mrs. Antrobus. A girl like I can get a situation in a home where they're rich enough to have a fire in every room, Mrs. Antrobus, and a girl don't have to carry the responsibility of the whole house on her two shoulders. And a home without children, Mrs. Antrobus, because children are a thing only a parent can stand, and a truer word was never said; and a home, Mrs. Antrobus, where the master of the house don't pinch decent, self-respecting girls when he meets them in a dark corridor. I mention no names and make no charges. So you have my notice, Mrs. Antrobus. I hope that's perfectly clear.

MRS. ANTROBUS. You've let the fire go out!—Have you milked the mammoth?

SABINA. I don't understand a word of this play.—Yes, I've milked the mammoth.

MRS. ANTROBUS. Until Mr. Antrobus comes home we have no food and we have no fire. You'd better go over to the neighbors and borrow some fire.

SABINA. Mrs. Antrobus! I can't! I'd die on the way, you know I would. It's worse than January. The dogs are sticking to the sidewalks. I'd die.

MRS. ANTROBUS. Very well, I'll go.

SABINA (*even more distraught, coming forward and sinking on her knees*). You'd never come back alive; we'd all perish; if you weren't here, we'd just perish. How do we know Mr. Antrobus'll be back? We don't know. If you go out, I'll just kill myself.

MRS. ANTROBUS. Get up, Sabina.

SABINA. Every night it's the same thing. Will he come back safe, or won't he? Will we starve to death, or freeze to death, or boil to death or will we be killed by burglars? I don't know why we go on living. I don't know why we go on living at all. It's easier being dead. (*She flings her arms on the table and buries her head in them. In each of the succeeding speeches she flings her head up—and sometimes her hands—then quickly buries her head again.*)

MRS. ANTROBUS. The same thing! Always throwing up the sponge, Sabina. Always announcing your own death. But give you a new hat—or a plate of ice cream—or a ticket to the movies, and you want to live forever.

SABINA. You don't care whether we live or die; all you care about is those children. If it would be any benefit to them you'd be glad to see us all stretched out dead.

MRS. ANTROBUS. Well, maybe I would.

SABINA. And what do they care about? Themselves—that's all they care about. (*Shrilly.*) They make fun of you behind your back. Don't tell me: they're ashamed of you. Half the time, they pretend they're someone else's children. Little thanks you get from them.

MRS. ANTROBUS. I'm not asking for any thanks.

SABINA. And Mr. Antrobus—you don't understand *him*. All that work he does—trying to discover the alphabet and the multiplication table. Whenever he tries to learn anything you fight against it.

MRS. ANTROBUS. Oh, Sabina, I know you.

When Mr. Antrobus raped you home from your Sabine hills, he did it to insult me.

He did it for your pretty face, and to insult me.

You were the new wife, weren't you?

For a year or two you lay on your bed all day and polished the nails on your hands and feet:

You made puff-balls of the combings of your hair and you blew them up to the ceiling.

And I washed your underclothes and I made you chicken broths.

I bore children and between my very groans I stirred the cream that you'd put on your face.

But I knew you wouldn't last.

You didn't last.

SABINA. But it was I who encouraged Mr. Antrobus to make the alphabet. I'm sorry to say it, Mrs. Antrobus, but you're not a beautiful woman, and you can never know what a man could do if he tried. It's girls like I who inspire the multiplication table.

I'm sorry to say it, but you're not a beautiful woman, Mrs. Antrobus, and that's the God's truth.

MRS. ANTROBUS. And you didn't last—you sank to the kitchen. And what do you do there? *You let the fire go out!*

No wonder to you it seems easier being dead.

Reading and writing and counting on your fingers is all very well in their way,—but I keep the home going.

MRS. ANTROBUS. —There's that dinosaur on the front lawn again.—
Shoo! Go away. Go away.

[*The baby* DINOSAUR *puts his head in the window.*]

DINOSAUR. It's cold.

MRS. ANTROBUS. You go around to the back of the house where you
belong.

DINOSAUR. It's cold.

[*The* DINOSAUR *disappears.* MRS. ANTROBUS *goes
calmly out.* SABINA *slowly raises her head and speaks
to the audience. The central portion of the center wall
rises, pauses, and disappears into the loft.*]

SABINA. Now that you audience are listening to this, too, I understand
it a little better.

I wish eleven o'clock were here; I don't want to be dragged
through this whole play again.

[*The* TELEGRAPH BOY *is seen entering along the back
wall of the stage from the right. She catches sight of
him and calls.*]

Mrs. Antrobus! Mrs. Antrobus! Help! There's a strange man coming to the house. He's coming up the walk, help!

[*Enter* MRS. ANTROBUS *in alarm, but efficient.*]

MRS. ANTROBUS. Help me quick! (*They barricade the door by piling
the furniture against it.*) Who is it? What do you want?

TELEGRAPH BOY. A telegram for Mrs. Antrobus from Mr. Antrobus in
the city.

SABINA. Are you sure, are you sure? Maybe it's just a trap!

MRS. ANTROBUS. I know his voice, Sabina. We can open the door.

[*Enter the* TELEGRAPH BOY, *twelve years old, in uniform. The* DINOSAUR *and* MAMMOTH *slip by him into
the room and settle down front right.*]

I'm sorry we kept you waiting. We have to be careful, you know.
(*To the* ANIMALS.) Hm! . . . Will you be quiet? (*They nod.*) Have
you had your supper? (*They nod.*) Are you ready to come in?
(*They nod.*) Young man, have you any fire with you? Then light
the grate, will you? (*He nods, produces something like a briquet;
and kneels by the imagined fireplace, footlights center. Pause.*) What
are people saying about this cold weather? (*He makes a doubtful
shrug with his shoulders.*) Sabina, take this stick and go and light
the stove.

SABINA. Like I told you, Mrs. Antrobus; two weeks. That's the law.
I hope that's perfectly clear. (*Exit.*)

MRS. ANTROBUS. What about this cold weather?

TELEGRAPH BOY (*lowered eyes*). Of course, I don't know anything
. . . but they say there's a wall of ice moving down from the North,
that's what they say. We can't get Boston by telegraph, and they're
burning pianos in Hartford.

. . . It moves everything in front of it, churches and post offices and city halls.

I live in Brooklyn myself.

MRS. ANTROBUS. What are people doing about it?

TELEGRAPH BOY. Well . . . uh . . . Talking, mostly.

Or just what you'd do a day in February.

There are some that are trying to go South and the roads are crowded; but you can't take old people and children very far in a cold like this.

MRS. ANTROBUS.—What's this telegram you have for me?

TELEGRAPH BOY (*fingertips to his forehead*). If you wait just a minute; I've got to remember it.

> [*The* ANIMALS *have left their corner and are nosing
> him. Presently they take places on either side of him,
> leaning against his hips, like heraldic beasts.*]

This telegram was flashed from Murray Hill to University Heights! And then by puffs of smoke from University Heights to Staten Island.

And then by lantern from Staten Island to Plainfield, New Jersey. What hath God wrought! (*He clears his throat.*)

"To Mrs. Antrobus, Excelsior, New Jersey:

"My dear wife, will be an hour late. Busy day at the office.

"Don't worry the children about the cold just keep them warm burn everything except Shakespeare." (*Pause.*)

MRS. ANTROBUS. Men!—He knows I'd burn ten Shakespeares to prevent a child of mine from having one cold in the head. What does it say next?

> [*Enter* SABINA.]

TELEGRAPH BOY. "Have made great discoveries today have separated em from en."

SABINA. I know what that is, that's the alphabet, yes it is. Mr. Antrobus is just the cleverest man. Why, when the alphabet's finished, we'll be able to tell the future and everything.

TELEGRAPH BOY. Then listen to this: "Ten tens make a hundred semicolon consequences far-reaching." (*Watches for effect.*)

MRS. ANTROBUS. The earth's turning to ice, and all he can do is to make up new numbers.

TELEGRAPH BOY. Well, Mrs. Antrobus, like the head man at our office said: a few more discoveries like that and we'll be worth freezing.

MRS. ANTROBUS. What does he say next?

TELEGRAPH BOY. I . . . I can't do this last part very well. (*He clears his throat and sings.*) "Happy w'dding ann'vers'ry to you, Happy ann'vers'ry to you—"

> [*The* ANIMALS *begin to howl soulfully;* SABINA *screams
> with pleasure.*]

MRS. ANTROBUS. Dolly! Frederick! Be quiet.

TELEGRAPH BOY (*above the din*). "Happy w'dding ann'vers'ry, dear Eva; happy w'dding ann'vers'ry to you."

MRS. ANTROBUS. Is that in the telegram? Are they singing telegrams now? (*He nods.*) The earth's getting so silly no wonder the sun turns cold.

SABINA. Mrs. Antrobus, I want to take back the notice I gave you. Mrs. Antrobus, I don't want to leave a house that gets such interesting telegrams and I'm sorry for anything I said. I really am.

MRS. ANTROBUS. Young man, I'd like to give you something for all this trouble; Mr. Antrobus isn't home yet and I have no money and no food in the house—

TELEGRAPH BOY. Mrs. Antrobus . . . I don't like to . . . appear to . . . ask for anything, but . . .

MRS. ANTROBUS. What is it you'd like?

TELEGRAPH BOY. Do you happen to have an old needle you could spare? My wife just sits home all day thinking about needles.

SABINA (*shrilly*). We only got two in the house. Mrs. Antrobus, you know we only got two in the house.

MRS. ANTROBUS (*after a look at* SABINA *taking a needle from her collar*). Why yes, I can spare this.

TELEGRAPH BOY (*lowered eyes*). Thank you, Mrs. Antrobus. Mrs. Antrobus, can I ask you something else? I have two sons of my own; if the cold gets worse, what should I do?

SABINA. I think we'll all perish, that's what I think. Cold like this in August is just the end of the whole world. (*Silence.*)

MRS. ANTROBUS. I don't know. After all, what does one do about anything? Just keep as warm as you can. And don't let your wife and children see that you're worried.

TELEGRAPH BOY. Yes . . . Thank you, Mrs. Antrobus. Well, I'd better be going.—Oh, I forgot! There's one more sentence in the telegram. "Three cheers have invented the wheel."

MRS. ANTROBUS. A wheel? What's a wheel?

TELEGRAPH BOY. I don't know. That's what it said. The sign for it is like this. Well, goodbye.

[*The* WOMEN *see him to the door, with goodbyes and injunctions to keep warm.*]

SABINA (*apron to her eyes, wailing*). Mrs. Antrobus, it looks to me like all the nice men in the world are already married; I don't know why that is. (*Exit.*)

MRS. ANTROBUS (*thoughtful; to the* ANIMALS). Do you ever remember hearing tell of any cold like this in August? (*The* ANIMALS *shake their heads.*) From your grandmothers or anyone? (*They shake their heads.*) Have you any suggestions? (*They shake their heads. She pulls her shawl around, goes to the front door and opening it an inch calls:*) HENRY. GLADYS. CHILDREN. Come right in and get warm. No, no, when mama says a thing she means it.

Henry! HENRY. Put down that stone. You know what happened last time. (*Shriek.*) HENRY! Put down that stone! Gladys! Put down your dress!! Try and be a lady."

[*The* CHILDREN *bound in and dash to the fire. They take off their winter things and leave them in heaps on the floor.*]

GLADYS. Mama, I'm hungry. Mama, why is it so cold?

HENRY (*at the same time*). Mama, why doesn't it snow? Mama, when's supper ready? Maybe, it'll snow and we can make snowballs.

GLADYS. Mama, it's so cold that in one more minute I just couldn't of stood it.

MRS. ANTROBUS. Settle down, both of you, I want to talk to you.

[*She draws up a hassock and sits front center over the orchestra pit before the imaginary fire. The* CHILDREN *stretch out on the floor, leaning against her lap. Tableau by Raphael. The* ANIMALS *edge up and complete the triangle.*]

It's just a cold spell of some kind. Now listen to what I'm saying: When your father comes home I want you to be extra quiet. He's had a hard day at the office and I don't know but what he may have one of his moods.

I just got a telegram from him very happy and excited, and you know what that means. Your father's temper's uneven; I guess you know that. (*Shriek.*)

Henry! Henry!

Why—why can't you remember to keep your hair down over your forehead? You must keep that scar covered up. Don't you know that when your father sees it he loses all control over himself? He goes crazy. He wants to die. (*After a moment's despair she collects herself decisively, wets the hem of her apron in her mouth and starts polishing his forehead vigorously.*)

Lift your head up. Stop squirming. Blessed me, sometimes I think that it's going away—and then there it is; just as red as ever.

HENRY. Mama, today at school two teachers forgot and called me by my old name. They forgot, Mama. You'd better write another letter to the principal, so that he'll tell them I've changed my name. Right out in class they called me: Cain.

MRS. ANTROBUS (*putting her hand on his mouth, too late; hoarsely*). Don't say it. (*Polishing feverishly.*) If you're good they'll forget it. Henry, you didn't hit anyone . . . today, did you?

HENRY. Oh . . . no-o-o!

MRS. ANTROBUS (*still working, not looking at Gladys*). And, Gladys, I want you to be especially nice to your father tonight. You know what he calls you when you're good—his little angel, his little star. Keep your dress down like a little lady. And keep your voice nice and low. Gladys Antrobus!! What's that red stuff you have on your face? (*Slaps her.*) You're a filthy detestable child! (*Rises in real, though temporary, repudiation and despair.*) Get away from me, both of you! I wish I'd never seen sight or sound of you. Let the cold come! I can't stand it. I don't want to go on. (*She walks away.*)

GLADYS (*weeping*). All the girls at school do, Mama.

MRS. ANTROBUS (*shrieking*). I'm through with you, that's all!—Sabina! Sabina!—Don't you know your father'd go crazy if he saw that paint on your face? Don't you know your father thinks you're perfect? Don't you know he couldn't live if he didn't think you were perfect? —Sabina!

[*Enter* SABINA.]

SABINA. Yes, Mrs. Antrobus!

MRS. ANTROBUS. Take this girl out into the kitchen and wash her face with the scrubbing brush.

MR. ANTROBUS (*outside, roaring*). "I've been working on the railroad, all the livelong day . . . etc."

[*The* ANIMALS *start running around in circles, bellowing.* SABINA *rushes to the window.*]

MRS. ANTROBUS. Sabina, what's that noise outside?

SABINA. Oh, it's a drunken tramp. It's a giant, Mrs. Antrobus. We'll all be killed in our beds, I know it!

MRS. ANTROBUS. Help me quick. Quick. Everybody. (*Again they stack all the furniture against the door.* MR. ANTROBUS *pounds and bellows.*) Who is it? What do you want?—Sabina, have you any boiling water ready?—Who is it?

MR. ANTROBUS. Broken-down camel of a pig's snout, open this door.

MRS. ANTROBUS. God be praised! It's your father.—Just a minute, George!—Sabina, clear the door, quick. Gladys, come here while I clean your nasty face!

MR. ANTROBUS. She-bitch of a goat's gizzard, I'll break every bone in your body. Let me in or I'll tear the whole house down.

MRS. ANTROBUS. Just a minute, George, something's the matter with the lock.

MR. ANTROBUS. Open the door or I'll tear your livers out. I'll smash your brains on the ceiling, and Devil take the hindmost.

MRS. ANTROBUS. Now, you can open the door, Sabina, I'm ready.

[*The door is flung open. Silence.* MR. ANTROBUS—*face of a Keystone Comedy Cop—stands there in fur cap and blanket. His arms are full of parcels, including a large stone wheel with a center in it. One hand carries a railroad man's lantern. Suddenly he bursts into joyous roar.*]

MR. ANTROBUS. Well, how's the whole crooked family?

[*Relief. Laughter. Tears. Jumping up and down.* ANIMALS *cavorting.* ANTROBUS *throws the parcels on the*

*ground. Hurls his cap and blanket after them. Heroic
embraces. Melee of* HUMANS *and* ANIMALS, SABINA *included.*]

I'll be scalded and tarred if a man can't get a little welcome when
he comes home. Well, Maggie, you old gunny-sack, how's the
broken down old weather hen?—Sabina, old fishbait, old skunkpot.
—And the children,—how've the little smellers been?

GLADYS. Papa, Papa, Papa, Papa, Papa.

MR. ANTROBUS. How've they been, Maggie?

MRS. ANTROBUS. Well, I must say, they've been as good as gold. I
haven't had to raise my voice once. I don't know what's the matter
with them.

ANTROBUS (*kneeling before* GLADYS). Papa's little weasel, eh?—Sabina,
there's some food for you.—Papa's little gopher?

GLADYS (*her arm around his neck*). Papa, you're always teasing me.

ANTROBUS. And Henry? Nothing rash today, I hope. Nothing rash?

HENRY. No, Papa.

ANTROBUS (*roaring*). Well that's good, that's good—I'll bet Sabina let
the fire go out.

SABINA. Mr. Antrobus, I've given my notice. I'm leaving two weeks
from today. I'm sorry, but I'm leaving.

ANTROBUS (*roar*). Well, if you leave now you'll freeze to death, so go
and cook the dinner.

SABINA. Two weeks, that's the law. (*Exit.*)

ANTROBUS. Did you get my telegram?

MRS. ANTROBUS. Yes.—What's a wheel?

[*He indicates the wheel with a glance.* HENRY *is rolling
it around the floor.*]

[*Rapid, hoarse interchange.*]

MRS. ANTROBUS. What does this cold weather mean? It's below freezing.

ANTROBUS. Not before the children!

MRS. ANTROBUS. Shouldn't we do something about it?—start off, move?

ANTROBUS. Not before the children!!! (*He gives* HENRY *a sharp slap.*)

HENRY. Papa, you hit me!

ANTROBUS. Well, remember it. That's to make you remember today.
Today. The day the alphabet's finished; and the day that we *saw* the
hundred—the hundred, the hundred, the hundred, the hundred, the
hundred—there's no end to 'em.

I've had a day at the office!

Take a look at that wheel, Maggie—when I've got that to rights:
you'll see a sight.

There's a reward there for all the walking you've done.

MRS. ANTROBUS. How do you mean?

ANTROBUS (*on the hassock looking into the fire; with awe*). Maggie,
we've reached the top of the wave. There's not much more to be
done. We're there!

MRS. ANTROBUS (*cutting across his mood sharply*). And the ice?

ANTROBUS. The ice!

HENRY (*playing with the wheel*). Papa, you could put a chair on this.

ANTROBUS (*broodingly*). Ye-e-s, any booby can fool with it now,—but I thought of it first.

MRS. ANTROBUS. Children, go out in the kitchen. I want to talk to your father alone.

> [*The* CHILDREN *go out.* ANTROBUS *has moved to his chair up left. He takes the goldfish bowl on his lap; pulls the canary cage down to the level of his face. Both the* ANIMALS *put their paws up on the arm of his chair.* MRS. ANTROBUS *faces him across the room, like a judge.*]

MRS. ANTROBUS. Well?

ANTROBUS (*shortly*). It's cold.—How things been, eh? Keck, keck, keck.—And you, Millicent?

MRS. ANTROBUS. I know it's cold.

ANTROBUS (*to the canary*). No spilling of sunflower seed, eh? No singing after lights-out, y'know what I mean?

MRS. ANTROBUS. You can try and prevent us freezing to death, can't you? You can do something? We can start moving. Or we can go on the animals' backs?

ANTROBUS. The best thing about animals is that they don't talk much.

MAMMOTH. It's cold.

ANTROBUS. Eh, eh, eh! Watch that!—

—By midnight we'd turn to ice. The roads are full of people now who can scarcely lift a foot from the ground. The grass out in front is like iron,—which reminds me, I have another needle for you.— The people up north—where are they? Frozen . . . crushed. . . .

MRS. ANTROBUS. Is that what's going to happen to us?—Will you answer me?

ANTROBUS. I don't know. I don't know anything. Some say that the ice is going slower. Some say that it's stopped. The sun's growing cold. What can I do about that? Nothing we can do but burn everything in the house, and the fenceposts and the barn. Keep the fire going. When we have no more fire, we die.

MRS. ANTROBUS. Well, why didn't you say so in the first place?

> [MRS. ANTROBUS *is about to march off when she catches sight of two* REFUGEES, *men, who have appeared against the back wall of the theatre and who are soon joined by others.*]

REFUGEES. Mr. Antrobus! Mr. Antrobus! Mr. An-nn-tro-bus!

MRS. ANTROBUS. Who's that? Who's that calling you?

ANTROBUS (*clearing his throat guiltily*). Hm—let me see.

> [*Two* REFUGEES *come up to the window.*]

REFUGEE. Could we warm our hands for a moment, Mr. Antrobus. It's very cold, Mr. Antrobus.

ANOTHER REFUGEE. Mr. Antrobus, I wonder if you have a piece of bread or something that you could spare.

> [*Silence. They wait humbly.* MRS. ANTROBUS *stands rooted to the spot. Suddenly a knock at the door, then another hand knocking in short rapid blows.*]

MRS. ANTROBUS. Who are these people? Why, they're all over the front yard. What have they come *here* for?

> [*Enter* SABINA.]

SABINA. Mrs. Antrobus! There are some tramps knocking at the back door.

MRS. ANTROBUS. George, tell these people to go away. Tell them to move right along. I'll go and send them away from the back door. Sabina, come with me. (*She goes out energetically.*)

ANTROBUS. Sabina! Stay here! I have something to say to you. (*He goes to the door and opens it a crack and talks through it.*) Ladies and gentlemen! I'll have to ask you to wait a few minutes longer. It'll be all right . . . while you're waiting you might each one pull up a stake of the fence. We'll need them all for the fireplace. There'll be coffee and sandwiches in a moment.

> [SABINA *looks out door over his shoulder and suddenly extends her arm pointing, with a scream.*]

SABINA. Mr. Antrobus, what's that??—that big white thing? Mr. Antrobus, it's ICE. It's ICE!!

ANTROBUS. Sabina, I want you to go in the kitchen and make a lot of coffee. Make a whole pail full.

SABINA. Pail full!!

ANTROBUS (*with gesture*). And sandwiches . . . piles of them . . . like this.

SABINA. Mr. An . . . !! (*Suddenly she drops the play, and says in her own person as* MISS SOMERSET, *with surprise.*) Oh, *I* see what this part of the play means now! This means refugees. (*She starts to cross to the proscenium.*) Oh, I don't like it. I don't like it. (*She leans against the proscenium and bursts into tears.*)

ANTROBUS. Miss Somerset!

Voice of the STAGE MANAGER. Miss Somerset!

SABINA (*energetically, to the audience*). Ladies and gentlemen! Don't take this play serious. The world's not coming to an end. You know it's not. People exaggerate! Most people really have enough to eat and a roof over their heads. Nobody actually starves—you can always eat grass or something. That ice-business—why, it was a long, long time ago. Besides they were only savages. Savages don't love their families—not like we do.

ANTROBUS *and* STAGE MANAGER. Miss Somerset!!

> [*There is renewed knocking at the door.*]

SABINA. All right. I'll say the lines, but I won't think about the play.
[*Enter* MRS. ANTROBUS.]
SABINA (*parting thrust at the audience*). And I advise *you* not to think about the play, either. (*Exit* SABINA.)
MRS. ANTROBUS. George, these tramps say that you asked them to come to the house. What does this mean?
[*Knocking at the door.*]
ANTROBUS. Just . . . uh . . . There are a few friends, Maggie, I met on the road. Real nice, real useful people. . . .
MRS. ANTROBUS (*back to the door*). Now, don't you ask them in!
George Antrobus, not another soul comes in here over my dead body.
ANTROBUS. Maggie, there's a doctor there. Never hurts to have a good doctor in the house. We've lost a peck of children, one way and another. You can never tell when a child's throat will get stopped up. What you and I have seen—!!! (*He puts his fingers on his throat, and imitates diphtheria.*)
MRS. ANTROBUS. Well, just one person then, the Doctor. The others can go right along the road.
ANTROBUS. Maggie, there's an old man, particular friend of mine—
MRS. ANTROBUS. I won't listen to you—
ANTROBUS. It was he that really started off the A.B.C.'s.
MRS. ANTROBUS. I don't care if he perishes. We can do without reading or writing. We can't do without food.
ANTROBUS. Then let the ice come!! Drink your coffee!! I don't want any coffee if I can't drink it with some good people.
MRS. ANTROBUS. Stop shouting. Who else is there trying to push us off the cliff?
ANTROBUS. Well, there's the man . . . who makes all the laws. Judge Moses!
MRS. ANTROBUS. Judges can't help us now.
ANTROBUS. And if the ice melts? . . . and if we pull through? Have you and I been able to bring up Henry? What have we done?
MRS. ANTROBUS. Who are those old women?
ANTROBUS (*coughs*). Up in town there are nine sisters. There are three or four of them here. They're sort of music teachers . . . and one of them recites and one of them—
MRS. ANTROBUS. That's the end. A singing troupe! Well, take your choice, live or die. Starve your own children before your face.
ANTROBUS (*gently*). These people don't take much. They're used to starving. They'll sleep on the floor.
Besides, Maggie, listen: no, listen:
Who've we got in the house, but Sabina? Sabina's always afraid the worst will happen. Whose spirits can she keep up? Maggie, these people never give up. They think they'll live and work forever.
MRS. ANTROBUS (*walks slowly to the middle of the room*). All right,

let them in. Let them in. You're master here. (*Softly.*) —But these
animals must go. Enough's enough. They'll soon be big enough to
push the walls down, anyway. Take them away.

ANTROBUS (*sadly*). All right. The dinosaur and mammoth—! Come on,
baby, come on Frederick. Come for a walk. That's a good little
fellow.

DINOSAUR. It's cold.

ANTROBUS. Yes, nice cold fresh air. Bracing.

> [*He holds the door open and the* ANIMALS *go out. He
> beckons to his friends. The* REFUGEES *are typical eld-
> erly out-of-works from the streets of New York to-
> day.* JUDGE MOSES *wears a skull cap.* HOMER *is a
> blind beggar with a guitar. The seedy crowd shuffles
> in and waits humbly and expectantly.* ANTROBUS *in-
> troduces them to his wife who bows to each with a
> stately bend of her head.*]

Make yourself at home, Maggie, this is the doctor . . . m . . . Cof-
fee'll be here in a minute. . . . Professor, this is my wife. . . .
And: . . . Judge . . . Maggie, you know the Judge. (*An old blind
man with a guitar.*) Maggie, you know . . . you know Homer?—
Come right in, Judge.—Miss Muse—are some of your sisters here?
Come right in. . . . Miss E. Muse; Miss T. Muse, Miss M. Muse.

MRS. ANTROBUS. Pleased to meet you.

Just . . . make yourself comfortable. Supper'll be ready in a
minute. (*She goes out, abruptly.*)

ANTROBUS. Make yourself at home, friends. I'll be right back. (*He
goes out.*)

> [*The* REFUGEES *stare about them in awe. Presently
> several voices start whispering "Homer! Homer!" All
> take it up.* HOMER *strikes a chord or two on his
> guitar, then starts to speak.*]

HOMER.

> Μῆνιν ἄειδε, θεά, Πηληϊάδεω 'Αχιλῆος,
> οὐλομένην, ἣ μυρί' 'Αχαιοῖς ἄλγε' ἔθηκεν,
> πολλὰς, δ' ἰφθίμους ψυχὰς—[1]

> [HOMER'S *face shows he is lost in thought and
> memory and the words die away on his lips. The*
> REFUGEES *likewise nod in dreamy recollection. Soon
> the whisper "Moses, Moses!" goes around. An aged
> Jew parts his beard and recites dramatically.*]

[1] "Sing, goddess, the wrath of Peleus' son Achilleus, the baneful wrath,
which made countless pains for the Achaians, and [hurled to Hades] many
mighty souls [of heroes]" (*Iliad*, I. 1–3).

MOSES.

בְּרֵאשִׁית בָּרָא אֱלֹהִים אֵת הַשָּׁמַיִם וְאֵת הָאָרֶץ: וְהָאָרֶץ הָיְתָה תֹהוּ

וָבֹהוּ וְחֹשֶׁךְ עַל־פְּנֵי תְהוֹם וְרוּחַ אֱלֹהִים מְרַחֶפֶת עַל־פְּנֵי הַמָּיִם:[2]

[*The same dying away of the words takes place, and on the part of the* REFUGEES *the same retreat into recollection. Some of them murmur, "Yes, yes." The mood is broken by the abrupt entrance of* MR. *and* MRS. ANTROBUS *and* SABINA *bearing platters of sandwiches and a pail of coffee.* SABINA *stops and stares at the guests.*]

MR. ANTROBUS. Sabina, pass the sandwiches.

SABINA. I thought I was working in a respectable house that had respectable guests. I'm giving my notice, Mr. Antrobus: two weeks, that's the law.

MR. ANTROBUS. Sabina! Pass the sandwiches.

SABINA. Two weeks, that's the law.

MR. ANTROBUS. There's the law. That's Moses.

SABINA (*stares*). The Ten Commandments—FAUGH!!—(*To Audience.*) That's the worst line I've ever had to say on any stage.

ANTROBUS. I think the best thing to do is just not to stand on ceremony, but pass the sandwiches around from left to right.—Judge, help yourself to one of these.

MRS. ANTROBUS. The roads are crowded, I hear?

THE GUESTS (*all talking at once*). Oh, ma'am, you can't imagine. . . . You can hardly put one foot before you . . . people are trampling one another. (*Sudden silence.*)

MRS. ANTROBUS. Well, you know what I think it is,—I think it's sunspots!

THE GUESTS (*discreet hubbub*). Oh, you're right, Mrs. Antrobus . . . that's what it is. . . . That's what I was saying the other day. (*Sudden silence.*)

ANTROBUS. Well, I don't believe the whole world's going to turn to ice. (*All eyes are fixed on him, waiting.*) I can't believe it. Judge! Have we worked for nothing? Professor! Have we just failed in the whole thing?

MRS. ANTROBUS. It is certainly very strange—well fortunately on both sides of the family we come of very hearty stock.—Doctor, I want you to meet my children. They're eating their supper now. And of course I want them to meet you.

[2] "In the beginning God created the heaven and the earth. And the earth was without form, and void; and darkness was upon the face of the deep. And the spirit of God moved upon the face of the waters" (Genesis 1: 1–2, King James Version).

MISS M. MUSE. How many children have you, Mrs. Antrobus?

MRS. ANTROBUS. I have two—a boy and a girl.

MOSES (*softly*). I understand you had two sons, Mrs. Antrobus.

[MRS. ANTROBUS *in blind suffering; she walks toward the footlights.*]

MRS. ANTROBUS (*in a low voice*). Abel, Abel, my son, my son, Abel, my son, Abel, Abel, my son.

[*The* REFUGEES *move with few steps toward her as though in comfort murmuring words in Greek, Hebrew, German, et cetera. A piercing shriek from the kitchen,—*SABINA'S *voice. All heads turn.*]

ANTROBUS. What's that?

[SABINA *enters, bursting with indignation, pulling on her gloves.*]

SABINA. Mr. Antrobus—that son of yours, that boy Henry Antrobus—I don't stay in this house another moment!—He's not fit to live among respectable folks and that's a fact.

MRS. ANTROBUS. Don't say another word, Sabina. I'll be right back. (*Without waiting for an answer she goes past her into the kitchen.*)

SABINA. Mr. Antrobus, Henry has thrown a stone again and if he hasn't killed the boy that lives next door, I'm very much mistaken. He finished his supper and went out to play; and I heard such a fight; and then I saw it. I saw it with my own eyes. And it looked to me like stark murder.

[MRS. ANTROBUS *appears at the kitchen door, shielding* HENRY *who follows her. When she steps aside, we see on* HENRY'S *forehead a large ochre and scarlet scar in the shape of a C.* MR. ANTROBUS *starts toward him. A pause.* HENRY *is heard saying under his breath:*]

HENRY. He was going to take the wheel away from me. He started to throw a stone at me first.

MRS. ANTROBUS. George, it was just a boyish impulse. Remember how young he is. (*Louder, in an urgent wail.*) George, he's only four thousand years old.

SABINA. And everything was going along so nicely!

[*Silence.* ANTROBUS *goes back to the fireplace.*]

ANTROBUS. Put out the fire! Put out all the fires. (*Violently.*) No wonder the sun grows cold. (*He starts stamping on the fireplace.*)

MRS. ANTROBUS. Doctor! Judge! Help me!—George, have you lost your mind?

ANTROBUS. There is no mind. We'll not try to live. (*To the guests.*) Give it up. Give up trying.

[MRS. ANTROBUS *seizes him.*]

SABINA. Mr. Antrobus! I'm downright ashamed of you.

MRS. ANTROBUS. George, have some more coffee.—Gladys! Where's
    Gladys gone?

[GLADYS *steps in, frightened.*]

GLADYS. Here I am, Mama.

MRS. ANTROBUS. Go upstairs and bring your father's slippers. How
    could you forget a thing like that, when you know how tired he is?
    (ANTROBUS *sits in his chair. He covers his face with his hands.* MRS.
    ANTROBUS *turns to the* REFUGEES.) Can't some of you sing? It's your
    business in life to sing, isn't it? Sabina!

[*Several of the women clear their throats tentatively,
and with frightened faces gather around* HOMER'S *guitar. He establishes a few chords. Almost inaudibly
they start singing, led by* SABINA: *"Jingle Bells."* MRS.
ANTROBUS *continues to* ANTROBUS *in a low voice, while
taking off his shoes.*]

George, remember all the other times. When the volcanoes came
right up in the front yard.

And the time the grasshoppers ate every single leaf and blade of
grass, and all the grain and spinach you'd grown with your own
hands. And the summer there were earthquakes every night.

ANTROBUS. Henry! Henry! (*Puts his hand on his forehead.*) Myself.
All of us, we're covered with blood.

MRS. ANTROBUS. Then remember all the times you were pleased with
him and when you were proud of yourself.—Henry! Henry! Come
here and recite to your father the multiplication table that you do
so nicely.

[HENRY *kneels on one knee beside his father and
starts whispering the multiplication table.*]

HENRY (*finally*). Two times six is twelve; three times six is eighteen—
I don't think I know the sixes.

[*Enter* GLADYS *with the slippers.* MRS. ANTROBUS
*makes stern gestures to her: Go in there and do your
best. The* GUESTS *are now singing "Tenting Tonight."*]

GLADYS (*putting slippers on his feet*). Papa . . . papa . . . I was
very good in school today. Miss Conover said right out in class that
if all the girls had as good manners as Gladys Antrobus, that the
world would be a very different place to live in.

MRS. ANTROBUS. You recited a piece at assembly, didn't you? Recite it
to your father.

GLADYS. Papa, do you want to hear what I recited in class? (*Fierce
directorial glance from her mother.*) "THE STAR" by Henry
Wadsworth LONGFELLOW.

MRS. ANTROBUS. Wait!!! The fire's going out. There isn't enough wood!
Henry, go upstairs and bring down the chairs and start breaking
up the beds.

[*Exit* HENRY. *The singers return to "Jingle Bells," still
very softly.*]

GLADYS. Look, Papa, here's my report card. Lookit. Conduct A! Look,
Papa. Papa, do you want to hear the Star, by Henry Wadsworth
Longfellow? Papa, you're not mad at me, are you?—I know it'll get
warmer. Soon it'll be just like spring, and we can go to a picnic at
the Hibernian Picnic Grounds like you always like to do, don't you
remember? Papa, just look at me once.

[*Enter* HENRY *with some chairs.*]

ANTROBUS. You recited in assembly, did you? (*She nods eagerly.*) You
didn't forget it?

GLADYS. No!!! I was perfect.

[*Pause. Then* ANTROBUS *rises, goes to the front door
and opens it. The* REFUGEES *draw back timidly; the
song stops; he peers out of the door, then closes it.*]

ANTROBUS (*with decision, suddenly*). Build up the fire. It's cold. Build
up the fire. We'll do what we can. Sabina, get some more wood.
Come around the fire, everybody. At least the young ones may pull
through. Henry, have you eaten something?

HENRY. Yes, Papa.

ANTROBUS. Gladys, have you had some supper?

GLADYS. I ate in the kitchen, papa.

ANTROBUS. If you do come through this—what'll you be able to do?
What do you know? Henry, did you take a good look at that wheel?

HENRY. Yes, papa.

ANTROBUS (*sitting down in his chair*). Six times two are—

HENRY. —twelve; six times three are eighteen; six times four are—Papa,
it's hot and cold. It makes my head all funny. It makes me sleepy.

ANTROBUS (*gives him a cuff*). Wake up. I don't care if your head is
sleepy. Six times four are twenty-four. Six times five are—

HENRY. Thirty. Papa!

ANTROBUS. Maggie, put something into Gladys' head on the chance
she can use it.

MRS. ANTROBUS. What do you mean, George?

ANTROBUS. Six times six are thirty-six.

Teach her the beginnings of the Bible.

GLADYS. But, Mama, it's so cold and close.

[HENRY *has all but drowsed off. His father slaps him
sharply and the lesson goes on.*]

MRS. ANTROBUS. "In the beginning God created the heavens and the
earth; and the earth was waste and void; and the darkness was upon
the face of the deep—"

[*The singing starts up again louder.* SABINA *has returned with wood.*]

SABINA (*after placing wood on the fireplace comes down to the foot-*

lights and addresses the audience). "Will you please start handing up your chairs? We'll need everything for this fire. Save the human race.—Ushers, will you pass the chairs up here? Thank you.

HENRY. Six times nine are fifty-four; six times ten are sixty.

> [*In the back of the auditorium the sound of chairs be-*
> *ing ripped up can be heard. Ushers rush down the*
> *aisles with chairs and hand them over.*]

GLADYS. "And God called the light Day and the darkness he called Night."

SABINA. Pass up your chairs, everybody. Save the human race.

ACT II

◄੶ *Toward the end of the intermission, though with the house-lights still up, lantern slide projections begin to appear on the curtain. Time-tables for trains leaving Pennsylvania Station for Atlantic City. Advertisements of Atlantic City hotels, drugstores, churches, rug merchants; fortune tellers, Bingo parlors.*
When the house-lights go down, the voice of an ANNOUNCER *is heard.*

ANNOUNCER. The Management now brings you the News Events of the
World. Atlantic City, New Jersey:
    [*Projection of a chrome postcard of the waterfront,*
    trimmed in mica with the legend: FUN AT THE
                            BEACH.]
This great convention city is playing host this week to the anni-
versary convocation of that great fraternal order,—the Ancient and
Honorable Order of Mammals, Subdivision Humans. This great fra-
ternal, militant and burial society is celebrating on the Boardwalk,
ladies and gentlemen, its six hundred thousandth Annual Convention.
    It has just elected its president for the ensuing term,—
    [*Projection of* MR. *and* MRS. ANTROBUS *posed as they*
                will be shown a few moments later.]
Mr. George Antrobus of Excelsior, New Jersey. We show you
President Antrobus and his gracious and charming wife, every inch
a mammal. Mr. Antrobus has had a long and chequered career.
Credit has been paid to him for many useful enterprises including
the introduction of the lever, of the wheel and the brewing of beer.
Credit has also been extended to President Antrobus's gracious and
charming wife for many practical suggestions, including the hem,
the gore, and the gusset; and the novelty of the year,—frying in oil.
Before we show you Mr. Antrobus accepting the nomination, we
have an important announcement to make. As many of you know,

this great celebration of the Order of the Mammals has received delegations from the other rival Orders,—or shall we say: esteemed concurrent Orders: the WINGS, the FINS, the SHELLS, and so on. These Orders are holding their conventions also, in various parts of the world, and have sent representatives to our own, two of a kind.

Later in the day we will show you President Antrobus broadcasting his words of greeting and congratulation to the collected assemblies of the whole natural world.

Ladies and Gentlemen! We give you President Antrobus!

[*The screen becomes a transparency.* MR. ANTROBUS *stands beside a pedestal;* MRS. ANTROBUS *is seated wearing a corsage of orchids.* ANTROBUS *wears an untidy Prince Albert; spats; from a red rosette in his buttonhole hangs a fine long purple ribbon of honor. He wears a gay lodge hat,—something between a fez and a legionnaire's cap.*]

ANTROBUS. Fellow-mammals, fellow-vertebrates, fellow-humans, I thank you. Little did my dear parents think,—when they told me to stand on my own two feet,—that I'd arrive at this place.

My friends, we have come a long way.

During this week of happy celebration it is perhaps not fitting that we dwell on some of the difficult times we have been through. The dinosaur is extinct—(*Applause.*)—the ice has retreated; and the common cold is being pursued by every means within our power.

[MRS. ANTROBUS *sneezes, laughs prettily, and murmurs: "I beg your pardon."*]

In our memorial service yesterday we did honor to all our friends and relatives who are no longer with us, by reason of cold, earthquakes, plagues and . . . and . . . (*Coughs.*) differences of opinion.

As our Bishop so ably said . . . uh . . . so ably said. . . .

MRS. ANTROBUS (*closed lips*). Gone, but not forgotten.

ANTROBUS. "They are gone, but not forgotten."

I think I can say, I think I can prophesy with complete . . . uh . . . with complete . . . .

MRS. ANTROBUS. Confidence.

ANTROBUS. Thank you, my dear,—With complete lack of confidence, that a new day of security is about to dawn.

The watchword of the closing year was: Work. I give you the watchword for the future: Enjoy Yourselves.

MRS. ANTROBUS. George, sit down!

ANTROBUS. Before I close, however, I wish to answer one of those unjust and malicious accusations that were brought against me during this last electoral campaign.

Ladies and gentlemen, the charge was made that at various points in my career I leaned toward joining some of the rival orders,—that's a lie.

As I told reporters of the *Atlantic City Herald,* I do not deny that a few months before my birth I hesitated between . . . uh . . . between pinfeathers and gill-breathing,—and so did many of us here,—but for the last million years I have been viviparous, hairy and diaphragmatic.

[*Applause. Cries of "Good old Antrobus," "The Prince chap!" "Georgie," etc.*]

ANNOUNCER. Thank you. Thank you very much, Mr. Antrobus.

Now I know that our visitors will wish to hear a word from that gracious and charming mammal, Mrs. Antrobus, wife and mother,—Mrs. Antrobus!

[MRS. ANTROBUS *rises, lays her program on her chair, bows and says:*]

MRS. ANTROBUS. Dear friends, I don't really think I should say anything. After all, it was my husband who was elected and not I.

Perhaps, as president of the Women's Auxiliary Bed and Board Society,—I had some notes here, oh, yes, here they are:—I should give a short report from some of our committees that have been meeting in this beautiful city.

Perhaps it may interest you to know that it has at last been decided that the tomato is edible. Can you all hear me? The tomato *is* edible.

A delegate from across the sea reports that the thread woven by the silkworm gives a cloth . . . I have a sample of it here . . . can you see it? smooth, elastic. I should say that it's rather attractive, —though personally I prefer less shiny surfaces. Should the windows of a sleeping apartment be open or shut? I know all mothers will follow our debates on this matter with close interest. I am sorry to say that the most expert authorities have not yet decided. It does seem to me that the night air would be bound to be unhealthy for our children, but there are many distinguished authorities on both sides. Well, I could go on talking forever,—as Shakespeare says: a woman's work is seldom done; but I think I'd better join my husband in saying thank you, and sit down. Thank you. (*She sits down.*)

ANNOUNCER. Oh, Mrs. Antrobus!

MRS. ANTROBUS. Yes?

ANNOUNCER. We understand that you are about to celebrate a wedding anniversary. I know our listeners would like to extend their felicitations and hear a few words from you on that subject.

MRS. ANTROBUS. I have been asked by this kind gentleman . . . yes, my friends, this Spring Mr. Antrobus and I will be celebrating our five thousandth wedding anniversary.

I don't know if I speak for my husband, but I can say that, as for me, I regret every moment of it. (*Laughter of confusion.*) I beg your pardon. What I *mean* to say is that I do not regret one moment of it. I hope none of you catch my cold. We have two children. We've always had two children, though it hasn't always been the same two. But as I say, we have two fine children, and we're very grateful for that. Yes, Mr. Antrobus and I have been married five thousand years. Each wedding anniversary reminds me of the times when there were no weddings. We had to crusade for marriage. Perhaps there are some women within the sound of my voice who remember that crusade and those struggles; we fought for it, didn't we? We chained ourselves to lampposts and we made disturbances in the Senate,—anyway, at last we women got the ring.

A few men helped us, but I must say that most men blocked our way at every step: they said we were unfeminine.

I only bring up these unpleasant memories, because I see some signs of backsliding from that great victory.

Oh, my fellow mammals, keep hold of that.

My husband says that the watchword for the year is Enjoy Yourselves. I think that's very open to misunderstanding. My watchword for the year is: Save the Family. It's held together for over five thousand years: Save it! Thank you.

ANNOUNCER. Thank you, Mrs. Antrobus. (*The transparency disappears.*) We had hoped to show you the Beauty Contest that took place here today.

President Antrobus, an experienced judge of pretty girls, gave the title of Miss Atlantic City 1942, to Miss Lily-Sabina Fairweather, charming hostess of our Boardwalk Bingo Parlor.

Unfortunately, however, our time is up, and I must take you to some views of the Convention City and conveeners,—enjoying themselves.

[*A burst of music; the curtain rises.*

[*The Boardwalk. The audience is sitting in the ocean. A hand rail of scarlet cord stretches across the front of the stage. A ramp—also with scarlet hand rail—descends to the right corner of the orchestra pit where a great scarlet beach umbrella or a cabana stands. Front and right stage left are benches facing the sea; attached to each bench is a street-lamp.*

[*The only scenery is two cardboard cut-outs six feet high, representing shops at the back of the stage Reading from left to right they are: SALT WATER TAFFY; FORTUNE TELLER; then the blank space; BINGO PARLOR; TURKISH BATH. They have practical doors, that of the Fortune Teller's being hung with bright gypsy curtains.*

[*By the left proscenium and rising from the orchestra pit is the weather signal; it is like the mast of a ship with cross bars. From time to time black discs are hung on it to indicate the storm and hurricane warnings. Three roller chairs, pushed by melancholy Negroes, file by empty. Throughout the act they traverse the stage in both directions.*

[*From time to time,* CONVEENERS, *dressed like* MR. ANTROBUS, *cross the stage. Some walk sedately by; others engage in inane horseplay. The old gypsy* FORTUNE TELLER *is seated at the door of her shop, smoking a corncob pipe.*

[*From the Bingo Parlor comes the voice of the* CALLER.]

BINGO CALLER. A-Nine; A-Nine. C-Twenty-six; C-Twenty-six. A-Four; A-Four. B-Twelve.

CHORUS (*back-stage*). Bingo!!! (*The front of the Bingo Parlor shudders, rises a few feet in the air and returns to the ground trembling.*)

FORTUNE TELLER (*mechanically, to the unconscious back of a passerby, pointing with her pipe*). Bright's disease! Your partner's deceiving you in that Kansas City deal. You'll have six grandchildren. Avoid high places. (*She rises and shouts after another.*) Cirrhosis of the liver!

[SABINA *appears at the door of the Bingo Parlor. She hugs about her a blue raincoat that almost conceals her red bathing suit. She tries to catch the* FORTUNE TELLER'S *attention.*]

SABINA. Sssssst! Esmeralda! Sssssst!

FORTUNE TELLER. Keck!

SABINA. Has President Antrobus come along yet?

FORTUNE TELLER. No, no, no. Get back there. Hide yourself.

SABINA. I'm afraid I'll miss him. Oh, Esmeralda, if I fail in this, I'll die; I know I'll die. President Antrobus!!! And I'll be his wife! If it's the last thing I'll do, I'll be Mrs. George Antrobus.—Esmeralda, tell me my future.

FORTUNE TELLER. Keck!

SABINA. All right, I'll tell *you* my future. (*Laughing dreamily and tracing it out with one finger on the palm of her hand.*) I've won the Beauty Contest in Atlantic City,—well, I'll win the Beauty Contest of the whole world. I'll take President Antrobus away from that wife of his. Then I'll take every man away from his wife. I'll turn the whole earth upside down.

FORTUNE TELLER. Keck!

SABINA. When all those husbands just think about me they'll get dizzy. They'll faint in the streets. They'll have to lean against lampposts.— Esmeralda, who was Helen of Troy?

FORTUNE TELLER (*furiously*). Shut your foolish mouth. When Mr. Antrobus comes along you can see what you can do. Until then,— go away.

> [SABINA *laughs. As she returns to the door of her Bingo Parlor a group of* CONVEENERS *rush over and smother her with attention:* "Oh, Miss Lily, you know me. You've known me for years."]

SABINA. Go away, boys, go away. I'm after bigger fry than you are.— Why, Mr. Simpson!! How *dare* you!! I expect that even you nobodies must have girls to amuse you; but where you find them and what you do with them, is of absolutely no interest to me. (*Exit. The* CONVEENERS *squeal with pleasure and stumble in after her.*)

> [*The* FORTUNE TELLER *rises, puts her pipe down on the stool, unfurls her voluminous skirts, gives a sharp wrench to her bodice and strolls towards the audience, swinging her hips like a young woman.*]

FORTUNE TELLER. I tell the future. Keck. Nothing easier. Everybody's future is in their face. Nothing easier.

But who can tell your past,—eh? Nobody!

Your youth,—where did it go? It slipped away while you weren't looking. While you were asleep. While you were drunk? Puh! You're like our friends, Mr. and Mrs. Antrobus; you lie awake nights trying to know your past. What did it mean? What was it trying to say to you?

Think! Think! Split your heads. I can't tell the past and neither can you. If anybody tries to tell you the past, take my word for it, they're charlatans! Charlatans! But I can tell you the future. (*She suddenly barks at a passing chair-pusher.*) Apoplexy! (*She returns to the audience.*) Nobody listens.—Keck! I see a face among you now—I won't embarrass him by pointing him out, but, listen, it may be you: Next year the watchsprings inside you will crumple up. Death by regret,—Type Y. It's in the corners of your mouth. You'll decide that you should have lived for pleasure, but that you missed it. Death by regret,—Type Y. . . . Avoid mirrors. You'll try to be angry,—but no!—no anger. (*Far forward, confidentially.*) And now what's the immediate future of our friends, the Antrobuses? Oh, you've seen it as well as I have, keck,—that dizziness of the head; that Great Man dizziness? The inventor of beer and gunpowder? The sudden fits of temper and then the long stretches of inertia? "I'm a sultan; let my slave-girls fan me?"

You know as well as I do what's coming. Rain. Rain. Rain in floods. The deluge. But first you'll see shameful things—shameful things. Some of you will be saying: "Let him drown. He's not worth saving. Give the whole thing up." I can see it in your faces. But you're wrong. Keep your doubts and despairs to yourselves.

Again there'll be the narrow escape. The survival of a handful.

From destruction,—total destruction. (*She points sweeping with her hand to the stage.*) Even of the animals, a few will be saved: two of a kind, male and female, two of a kind. (*The heads of* CONVEENERS *appear about the stage and in the orchestra pit, jeering at her.*)

CONVEENERS. Charlatan! Madame Kill-joy! Mrs. Jeremiah! Charlatan!

FORTUNE TELLER. And *you!* Mark my words before it's too late. Where'll *you* be?

CONVEENERS. The croaking raven. Old dust and ashes. Rags, bottles, sacks.

FORTUNE TELLER. Yes, stick out your tongues. You can't stick your tongues out far enough to lick the death-sweat from your foreheads. It's too late to work now—bail out the flood with your soup spoons. You've had your chance and you've lost.

CONVEENERS. Enjoy yourselves!!! (*They disappear.*)

[*The* FORTUNE TELLER *looks off left and puts her finger on her lip.*]

FORTUNE TELLER. They're coming—the Antrobuses. Keck. Your hope. Your despair. Your selves.

[*Enter from the left,* MR. *and* MRS. ANTROBUS *and* GLADYS.]

MRS. ANTROBUS. Gladys Antrobus, stick your stummick in.

GLADYS. But it's easier this way.

MRS. ANTROBUS. Well, it's too bad the new president has such a clumsy daughter, that's all I can say. Try and be a lady.

FORTUNE TELLER. Aijah! That's been said a hundred billion times.

MRS. ANTROBUS. Goodness! Where's Henry? He was here just a minute ago. Henry!

[*Sudden violent stir. A roller-chair appears from the left. About it are dancing in great excitement* HENRY *and a* NEGRO CHAIR-PUSHER.]

HENRY (*slingshot in hand*). I'll put your eye out. I'll make you yell, like you never yelled before.

NEGRO (*at the same time*). Now, I warns you. I warns you. If you make me mad, you'll get hurt.

ANTROBUS. Henry! What is this? Put down that slingshot.

MRS. ANTROBUS (*at the same time*). "Henry! HENRY! Behave yourself.

FORTUNE TELLER. That's right, young man. There are too many people in the world as it is. Everybody's in the way, except one's self.

HENRY. All I wanted to do was—have some fun.

NEGRO. Nobody can't touch my chair, nobody, without I allow 'em to. You get clean away from me and you get away fast. (*He pushes his chair off, muttering.*)

ANTROBUS. What were you doing, Henry?

HENRY. Everybody's always getting mad. Everybody's always trying to push you around. I'll make him sorry for this; I'll make him sorry.

ANTROBUS. Give me that slingshot.

HENRY. I won't. I'm sorry I came to this place. I wish I weren't here. I wish I weren't anywhere.

MRS. ANTROBUS. Now, Henry, don't get so excited about nothing. I declare I don't know what we're going to do with you. Put your slingshot in your pocket, and don't try to take hold of things that don't belong to you.

ANTROBUS. After this you can stay home. I wash my hands of you.

MRS. ANTROBUS. Come now, let's forget all about it. Everybody take a good breath of that sea air and calm down. (*A passing* CONVEENER *bows to* ANTROBUS *who nods to him.*) Who was that you spoke to, George?

ANTROBUS. Nobody, Maggie. Just the candidate who ran against me in the election.

MRS. ANTROBUS. The man who ran against you in the election!! (*She turns and waves her umbrella after the disappearing* CONVEENER.) My husband didn't speak to you and he never will speak to you.

ANTROBUS. Now, Maggie.

MRS. ANTROBUS. After those lies you told about him in your speeches! Lies, that's what they were.

GLADYS *and* HENRY. Mama, everybody's looking at you. Everybody's laughing at you.

MRS. ANTROBUS. If you must know, my husband's a SAINT, a downright SAINT, and you're not fit to speak to him on the street.

ANTROBUS. Now, Maggie, now, Maggie, that's enough of that.

MRS. ANTROBUS. George Antrobus, you're a perfect worm. If you won't stand up for yourself, I will.

GLADYS. Mama, you just act awful in public.

MRS. ANTROBUS (*laughing*). Well, I must say I enjoyed it. I feel better. Wish his wife had been there to hear it. Children, what do you want to do?

GLADYS. Papa, can we ride in one of those chairs? Mama, I want to ride in one of those chairs.

MRS. ANTROBUS. No, sir. If you're tired you just sit where you are. We have no money to spend on foolishness.

ANTROBUS. I guess we have enough for a thing like that. It's one of the things you do at Atlantic City.

MRS. ANTROBUS. Oh, we have? I tell you it's a miracle my children have shoes to stand up in. I didn't think I'd ever live to see them pushed around in chairs.

ANTROBUS. We're on a vacation, aren't we? We have a right to some treats, I guess. Maggie, some day you're going to drive me crazy.

MRS. ANTROBUS. All right, go. I'll just sit here and laugh at you. And you can give me my dollar right in my hand. Mark my words, a rainy day is coming. There's a rainy day ahead of us. I feel it in my bones. Go on, throw your money around. I can starve. I've starved before. I know how.

[*A* CONVEENER *puts his head through Turkish Bath window, and says with raised eyebrows:*]

CONVEENER. Hello, George. How are ya? I see where you brought the WHOLE family along.

MRS. ANTROBUS. And what do you mean by that?

[CONVEENER *withdraws head and closes window.*]

ANTROBUS. Maggie, I tell you there's a limit to what I can stand. God's Heaven, haven't I worked *enough?* Don't I get *any* vacation? Can't I even give my children so much as a ride in a roller-chair?

MRS. ANTROBUS (*putting her hand out for raindrops*). Anyway, it's going to rain very soon and you have your broadcast to make.

ANTROBUS. Now, Maggie, I warn you. A man can stand a family only just so long. I'm warning you.

[*Enter* SABINA *from the Bingo Parlor. She wears a flounced red silk bathing suit, 1905. Red stockings, shoes, parasol. She bows demurely to* ANTROBUS *and starts down the ramp.* ANTROBUS *and the* CHILDREN *stare at her.* ANTROBUS *bows gallantly.*]

MRS. ANTROBUS. Why, George Antrobus, how can you say such a thing! You have the best family in the world.

ANTROBUS. Good morning, Miss Fairweather.

[SABINA *finally disappears behind the beach umbrella or in a cabana in the orchestra pit.*]

MRS. ANTROBUS. Who on earth was that you spoke to, George?

ANTROBUS (*complacent; mock-modest*). Hm . . . m . . . just a . . . solambaka keray.

MRS. ANTROBUS. What? I can't understand you.

GLADYS. Mama, wasn't she beautiful?

HENRY. Papa, introduce her to me.

MRS. ANTROBUS. Children, will you be quiet while I ask your father a simple question?—Who did you say it was, George?

ANTROBUS. Why-uh . . . a friend of mine. Very nice refined girl.

MRS. ANTROBUS. I'm waiting.

ANTROBUS. Maggie, that's the girl I gave the prize to in the beauty contest,—that's Miss Atlantic City 1942.

MRS. ANTROBUS. Hm! She looked like Sabina to me.

HENRY (*at the railing*). Mama, the life-guard knows her, too. Mama, he knows her well.

ANTROBUS. Henry, come here.—She's a very nice girl in every way and the sole support of her aged mother.

MRS. ANTROBUS. So was Sabina, so was Sabina; and it took a wall of ice to open your eyes about Sabina.—Henry, come over and sit down on this bench.

ANTROBUS. She's a very different matter from Sabina. Miss Fairweather is a college graduate, Phi Beta Kappa.

MRS. ANTROBUS. Henry, you sit here by mama. Gladys—

ANTROBUS (*sitting*). Reduced circumstances have required her taking a position as hostess in a Bingo Parlor; but there isn't a girl with higher principles in the country.

MRS. ANTROBUS. Well, let's not talk about it.—Henry, I haven't seen a whale yet.

ANTROBUS. She speaks seven languages and has more culture in her little finger than you've acquired in a lifetime.

MRS. ANTROBUS (*assuming amiability*). All right, all right, George. I'm glad to know there are such superior girls in the Bingo Parlors.— Henry, what's that? (*Pointing at the storm signal, which has one black disk.*)

HENRY. What is it, Papa?

ANTROBUS. What? Oh, that's the storm signal. One of those black disks means bad weather; two means storm; three means hurricane; and four means the end of the world.

[*As they watch it a second black disk rolls
into place.*]

MRS. ANTROBUS. Goodness! I'm going this very minute to buy you all some raincoats.

GLADYS (*putting her cheek against her father's shoulder*). Mama, don't go yet. I like sitting this way. And the ocean coming in and coming in. Papa, don't you like it?

MRS. ANTROBUS. Well, there's only one thing I lack to make me a perfectly happy woman: I'd like to see a whale.

HENRY. Mama, we saw two. Right out there. They're delegates to the convention. I'll find you one.

GLADYS. Papa, ask me something. Ask me a question.

ANTROBUS. Well . . . how big's the ocean?

GLADYS. Papa, you're teasing me. It's—three-hundred and sixty million square-miles—and—it—covers—three-fourths—of—the—earth's—surface—and—its—deepest-place—is—five—and—a—half—miles—deep—and—its—average—depth—is—twelve-thousand—feet. No, Papa, ask me something hard, real hard.

MRS. ANTROBUS (*rising*). Now I'm going off to buy those raincoats. I think that bad weather's going to get worse and worse. I hope it doesn't come before your broadcast. I should think we have about an hour or so.

HENRY. I hope it comes and zzzzzz everything before it. I hope it—

MRS. ANTROBUS. Henry!—George, I think . . . maybe, it's one of those storms that are just as bad on land as on the sea. When you're just as safe and safer in a good stout boat.

HENRY. There's a boat out at the end of the pier.

MRS. ANTROBUS. Well, keep your eye on it. George, you shut your eyes and get a good rest before the broadcast.

ANTROBUS. Thundering Judas, do I have to be told when to open and shut my eyes? Go and buy your raincoats.

MRS. ANTROBUS. Now, children, you have ten minutes to walk around. Ten minutes. And, Henry: control yourself. Gladys, stick by your brother and don't get lost. (*They run off.*)

MRS. ANTROBUS. Will you be all right, George?

> [CONVEENERS *suddenly stick their heads out of the Bingo Parlor and Salt Water Taffy store, and voices rise from the orchestra pit.*]

CONVEENERS. George. Geo-r-r-rge! George! Leave the old hen-coop at home, George. Do-mes-ticated Georgie!

MRS. ANTROBUS (*shaking her umbrella*). Low common oafs! That's what they are. Guess a man has a right to bring his wife to a convention, if he wants to. (*She starts off.*) What's the matter with a family, I'd like to know. What else have they got to offer? (*Exit.*)

> [ANTROBUS *has closed his eyes. The* FORTUNE TELLER *comes out of her shop and goes over to the left proscenium. She leans against it watching* SABINA *quizzically.*]

FORTUNE TELLER. Heh! Here she comes!

SABINA (*loud whisper*). What's he doing?

FORTUNE TELLER. Oh, he's ready for you. Bite your lips, dear, take a long breath and come on up.

SABINA. I'm nervous. My whole future depends on this. I'm nervous.

FORTUNE TELLER. Don't be a fool. What more could you want? He's forty-five. His head's a little dizzy. He's just been elected president. He's never known any other woman than his wife. Whenever he looks at her he realizes that she knows every foolish thing he's ever done.

SABINA (*still whispering*). I don't know why it is, but every time I start one of these I'm nervous.

> [*The* FORTUNE TELLER *stands in the center of the stage watching the following:*]

FORTUNE TELLER. You make me tired.

SABINA. First tell me my fortune. (*The* FORTUNE TELLER *laughs drily and makes the gesture of brushing away a nonsensical question.* SABINA *coughs and says:*) Oh, Mr. Antrobus,—dare I speak to you for a moment?

ANTROBUS. What?—Oh, certainly, certainly, Miss Fairweather.

SABINA. Mr. Antrobus . . . I've been so unhappy. I've wanted . . . I've wanted to make sure that you don't think that I'm the kind of girl who goes out for beauty contests.

FORTUNE TELLER. That's the way!

ANTROBUS. Oh, I understand. I understand perfectly.

FORTUNE TELLER. Give it a little more. Lean on it.

SABINA. I knew you would. My mother said to me this morning: Lily, she said, that fine Mr. Antrobus gave you the prize because he saw at once that you weren't the kind of girl who'd go in for a thing

like that. But, honestly, Mr. Antrobus, in this world, honestly, a
good girl doesn't know where to turn.

FORTUNE TELLER. Now you've gone too far.

ANTROBUS. My dear Miss Fairweather!

SABINA. You wouldn't know how hard it is. With that lovely wife and
daughter you have. Oh, I think Mrs. Antrobus is the finest woman
I ever saw. I wish I were like her.

ANTROBUS. There, there. There's . . . uh . . . room for all kinds of
people in the world, Miss Fairweather.

SABINA. How wonderful of you to say that. How generous!—Mr.
Antrobus, have you a moment free? . . . I'm afraid I may be a
little conspicuous here . . . could you come down, for just a moment, to my beach cabana . . . ?

ANTROBUS. Why-uh . . . yes, certainly . . . for a moment . . . just
for a moment.

SABINA. There's a deck chair there. Because: you know you *do* look
tired. Just this morning my mother said to me: Lily, she said, I hope
Mr. Antrobus is getting a good rest. His fine strong face has deep
deep lines in it. Now isn't it true, Mr. Antrobus: you work too hard?

FORTUNE TELLER. Bingo! (*She goes into her shop.*)

SABINA. Now you will just stretch out. No, I shan't say a word, not
a word. I shall just sit there,—privileged. That's what I am.

ANTROBUS (*taking her hand*). Miss Fairweather . . . you'll . . .
spoil me.

SABINA. Just a moment. I have something I wish to say to the audience.—Ladies and gentlemen. I'm not going to play this particular
scene tonight. It's just a short scene and we're going to skip it. But
I'll tell you what takes place and then we can continue the play
from there on. Now in this scene—

ANTROBUS (*between his teeth*). But, Miss Somerset!

SABINA. I'm sorry. I'm sorry. But I have to skip it. In this scene, I talk
to Mr. Antrobus, and at the end of it he decides to leave his wife,
get a divorce at Reno and marry me. That's all.

ANTROBUS. Fitz!—Fitz!

SABINA. So that now I've told you we can jump to the end of it,—
where you say:

[*Enter in fury* MR. FITZPATRICK, *the stage manager.*]

MR. FITZPATRICK. Miss Somerset, we insist on your playing this scene.

SABINA. I'm sorry, Mr. Fitzpatrick, but I can't and I won't. I've told
the audience all they need to know and now we can go on.

[*Other* ACTORS *begin to appear on the stage, listening.*]

MR. FITZPATRICK. And *why* can't you play it?

SABINA. Because there are some lines in that scene that would hurt
some people's feelings and I don't think the theatre is a place where
people's feelings ought to be hurt.

MR. FITZPATRICK. Miss Somerset, you can pack up your things and go home. I shall call the understudy and I shall report you to Equity.

SABINA. I sent the understudy up to the corner for a cup of coffee and if Equity tries to penalize me I'll drag the case right up to the Supreme Court. Now listen, everybody, there's no need to get excited.

MR. FITZPATRICK *and* ANTROBUS. Why can't you play it . . . what's the matter with the scene?

SABINA. Well, if you must know, I have a personal guest in the audience tonight. Her life hasn't been exactly a happy one. I wouldn't have my friend hear some of these lines for the whole world. I don't suppose it occurred to the author that some other women might have gone through the experience of losing their husbands like this. Wild horses wouldn't drag from me the details of my friend's life . . . well, they'd been married twenty years, and before he got rich, why, she'd done the washing and everything.

MR. FITZPATRICK. Miss Somerset, your friend will forgive you. We must play this scene.

SABINA. Nothing, nothing will make me say some of those lines . . . about "a man outgrows a wife every seven years" and . . . and that one about "the Mohammedans being the only people who looked the subject square in the face." Nothing.

MR. FITZPATRICK. Miss Somerset! Go to your dressing room. I'll *read* your lines.

SABINA. Now everybody's nerves are on edge.

MR. ANTROBUS. Skip the scene.

[MR. FITZPATRICK *and the other* ACTORS *go off*.]

SABINA. Thank you. I knew you'd understand. We'll do just what I said. So Mr. Antrobus is going to divorce his wife and marry me. Mr. Antrobus, you say: "It won't be easy to lay all this before my wife."

[*The* ACTORS *withdraw*. ANTROBUS *walks out, his hand to his forehead, muttering:*]

ANTROBUS. Wait a minute. I can't get back into it as easily as all that. "My wife is a very obstinate woman." Hm . . . then you say . . . hm . . . Miss Fairweather, I mean Lily, it won't be easy to lay all this before my wife. It'll hurt her feelings a little.

SABINA. Listen, George: *other* people haven't got feelings. Not in the same way that we have,—we who are presidents like you and prizewinners like me. Listen, other people haven't got feelings; they just imagine they have. Within two weeks they go back to playing bridge and going to the movies.

Listen, dear: everybody in the world except a few people like you and me are just people of straw. Most people have no insides at all. Now that you're president you'll see that. Listen, darling, there's a kind of secret society at the top of the world,—like you and me,— that know this. The world was made for us. What's life anyway? Except for two things, pleasure and power, what is life? Boredom! Foolishness. You know it is. Except for those two things, life's nause-at-ing. So,—come here! (*She moves close. They kiss.*) So.

Now when your wife comes, it's really very simple; just tell her.

ANTROBUS. Lily, Lily: you're a wonderful woman.

SABINA. Of course I am. (*They enter the cabana and it hides them from view.*)

> [*Distant roll of thunder. A third black disk appears on the weather signal. Distant thunder is heard.* MRS. ANTROBUS *appears carrying parcels. She looks about, seats herself on the bench left, and fans herself with her handkerchief. Enter* GLADYS *right, followed by two* CONVEENERS. *She is wearing red stockings.*]

MRS. ANTROBUS. Gladys!

GLADYS. Mama, here I am.

MRS. ANTROBUS. Gladys Antrobus!!! Where did you get those dreadful things?

GLADYS. Wh-a-t? Papa liked the color.

MRS. ANTROBUS. You go back to the hotel this minute!

GLADYS. I won't. I won't. Papa liked the color.

MRS. ANTROBUS. All right. All right. You stay here. I've a good mind to let your father see you that way. You stay right here.

GLADYS. I . . . I don't want to stay . . . if you don't think he'd like it.

MRS. ANTROBUS. Oh . . . it's all one to me. I don't care what happens. I don't care if the biggest storm in the whole world comes. Let it come. (*She folds her hands.*) Where's your brother?

GLADYS (*in a small voice*). He'll be here.

MRS. ANTROBUS. Will he? Well, let him get into trouble. I don't care. I don't know where your father is, I'm sure.

> [*Laughter from the cabana.*]

GLADYS (*leaning over the rail*). I think he's . . . Mama, he's talking to the lady in the red dress.

MRS. ANTROBUS. Is that so? (*Pause.*) We'll wait till he's through. Sit down here beside me and stop fidgeting . . . what are you crying about? (*Distant thunder. She covers* GLADYS' *stocking with a raincoat.*)

GLADYS. You don't like my stockings.

> [*Two* CONVEENERS *rush in with a microphone on a standard and various paraphernalia. The* FORTUNE TELLER *appears at the door of her shop. Other characters gradually gather.*]

BROADCAST OFFICIAL. Mrs. Antrobus! Thank God we've found you at last. Where's Mr. Antrobus? We've been hunting everywhere for him. It's about time for the broadcast to the conventions of the world.

MRS. ANTROBUS (*calm*). I expect he'll be here in a minute.

BROADCAST OFFICIAL. Mrs. Antrobus, if he doesn't show up in time, I hope you will consent to broadcast in his place. It's the most important broadcast of the year.

> [SABINA *enters from the cabana followed by* ANTROBUS.]

MRS. ANTROBUS. No, I shan't. I haven't one single thing to say.

BROADCAST OFFICIAL. Then won't you help us find him, Mrs. Antrobus? A storm's coming up. A hurricane. A deluge!

SECOND CONVEENER (*who has sighted* ANTROBUS *over the rail*). Joe! Joe! Here he is.

BROADCAST OFFICIAL. In the name of God, Mr. Antrobus, you're on the air in five minutes. Will you kindly please come and test the instrument? That's all we ask. If you just please begin the alphabet slowly.

> [ANTROBUS, *with set face, comes ponderously up the ramp. He stops at the point where his waist is level with the stage and speaks authoritatively to the* OFFICIALS.]

ANTROBUS. I'll be ready when the time comes. Until then, move away. Go away. I have something I wish to say to my wife.

BROADCAST OFFICIAL (*whimpering*). Mr. Antrobus! This is the most important broadcast of the year. (*The* OFFICIALS *withdraw to the edge of the stage.*)

> [SABINA *glides up the ramp behind* ANTROBUS.]

SABINA (*whispering*). Don't let her argue. Remember arguments have nothing to do with it.

ANTROBUS. Maggie, I'm moving out of the hotel. In fact, I'm moving out of everything. For good. I'm going to marry Miss Fairweather. I shall provide generously for you and the children. In a few years you'll be able to see that it's all for the best. That's all I have to say.

BROADCAST OFFICIAL. Mr. Antrobus! I hope you'll be ready. This is the most important broadcast of the year.

GLADYS. What did Papa say, Mama? I didn't hear what Papa said.

BROADCAST OFFICIAL. Mr. Antrobus. All we want to do is test your voice with the alphabet.

BINGO ANNOUNCER. A—nine; A—nine. D—forty-two; D—forty-two. C—thirty; C—thirty. B—seventeen; B—seventeen. C—forty; C—forty.

CHORUS. Bingo!!

ANTROBUS. Go away. Clear out.

MRS. ANTROBUS (*composedly with lowered eyes*). George, I can't talk to you until you wipe those silly red marks off your face.

ANTROBUS. I think there's nothing to talk about. I've said what I have to say.

SABINA. Splendid!!

ANTROBUS. You're a fine woman, Maggie, but . . . but a man has his own life to lead in the world.

MRS. ANTROBUS. Well, after living with you for five thousand years I guess I have a right to a word or two, haven't I?

ANTROBUS (*to* SABINA). What can I answer to that?

SABINA. Tell her that conversation would only hurt her feelings. It's-kinder-in-the-long-run-to-do-it-short-and-quick.

ANTROBUS. I want to spare your feelings in every way I can, Maggie.

BROADCAST OFFICIAL. Mr. Antrobus, the hurricane signal's gone up. We could begin right now.

MRS. ANTROBUS (*calmly, almost dreamily*). I didn't marry you because you were perfect. I didn't even marry you because I loved you. I married you because you gave me a promise. (*She takes off her ring and looks at it.*) That promise made up for your faults. And the promise I gave you made up for mine. Two imperfect people got married and it was the promise that made the marriage.

ANTROBUS. Maggie, . . . I was only nineteen.

MRS. ANTROBUS (*she puts her ring back on her finger*). And when our children were growing up, it wasn't a house that protected them; and it wasn't our love, that protected them—it was that promise.

And when that promise is broken—this can happen! (*With a sweep of the hand she removes the raincoat from* GLADYS' *stockings.*)

ANTROBUS (*stretches out his arm, apoplectic*). Gladys!! Have you gone crazy? Has everyone gone crazy? (*Turning on* SABINA.) You did this. You gave them to her.

SABINA. I never said a word to her.

ANTROBUS (*to* GLADYS). You go back to the hotel and take those horrible things off.

GLADYS (*pert*). Before I go, I've got something to tell you,—it's about Henry.

MRS. ANTROBUS (*claps her hands peremptorily*). Stop your noise,— I'm taking her back to the hotel, George. Before I go I have a letter. . . . I have a message to throw into the ocean. (*Fumbling in her handbag.*) Where is the plagued thing? Here it is. (*She flings something—invisible to us—far over the heads of the audience to the back of the auditorium.*) It's a bottle. And in the bottle's a letter. And in the letter is written all the things that a woman knows.

It's never been told to any man and it's never been told to any woman, and if it finds its destination, a new time will come. We're not what books and plays say we are. We're not what advertisements say we are. We're not in the movies and we're not on the radio.

We're not what you're all told and what you think we are: We're ourselves. And if any man can find one of us he'll learn why the whole universe was set in motion. And if any man harm any one of us, his soul—the only soul he's got—had better be at the bottom of that ocean,—and that's the only way to put it. Gladys, come here. We're going back to the hotel. (*She drags* GLADYS *firmly off by the hand, but* GLADYS *breaks away and comes down to speak to her father.*)

SABINA. Such goings-on. Don't give it a minute's thought.

GLADYS. Anyway, I think you ought to know that Henry hit a man with a stone. He hit one of those colored men that push the chairs and the man's very sick. Henry ran away and hid and some policemen are looking for him very hard. And I don't care a bit if you don't want to have anything to do with mama and me, because I'll never like you again and I hope nobody ever likes you again,— so there! (*She runs off.* ANTROBUS *starts after her.*)

ANTROBUS. I . . . I have to go and see what I can do about this.

SABINA. You stay right here. Don't go now while you're excited. Gracious sakes, all these things will be forgotten in a hundred years. Come, now, you're on the air. Just say anything,—it doesn't matter what. Just a lot of birds and fishes and things.

BROADCAST OFFICIAL. Thank you, Miss Fairweather. Thank you very much. Ready, Mr. Antrobus.

ANTROBUS (*touching the microphone*). What is it, what is it? Who am I talking to?

BROADCAST OFFICIAL. Why, Mr. Antrobus! To our order and to all the other orders.

ANTROBUS (*raising his head*). What are all those birds doing?

BROADCAST OFFICIAL. Those are just a few of the birds. Those are the delegates to our convention,—two of a kind.

ANTROBUS (*pointing into the audience*). Look at the water. Look at them all. Those fishes jumping. The children should see this!— There's Maggie's whales!! Here are your whales, Maggie!!

BROADCAST OFFICIAL. I hope you're ready, Mr. Antrobus.

ANTROBUS. And look on the beach! You didn't tell me these would be here!

SABINA. Yes, George. Those are the animals.

BROADCAST OFFICIAL (*busy with the apparatus*). Yes, Mr. Antrobus, those are the vertebrates. We hope the lion will have a word to say when you're through. Step right up, Mr. Antrobus, we're ready. We'll just have time before the storm. (*Pause. In a hoarse whisper.*) They're wait-ing.

> [*It has grown dark. Soon after he speaks a high whistling noise begins. Strange veering lights start whirling about the stage. The other characters disappear from the stage.*]

ANTROBUS. Friends. Cousins. Four score and ten billion years ago our forefather brought forth upon this planet the spark of life,—(*He is drowned out by thunder. When the thunder stops the* FORTUNE TELLER *is seen standing beside him.*)

FORTUNE TELLER. Antrobus, there's not a minute to be lost. Don't you see the four disks on the weather signal? Take your family into that boat at the end of the pier.

ANTROBUS. My family? I have no family. Maggie! Maggie! They won't come.

FORTUNE TELLER. They'll come.—Antrobus! Take these animals into that boat with you. All of them,—two of each kind.

SABINA. George, what's the matter with you? This is just a storm like any other storm.

ANTROBUS. Maggie!

SABINA. Stay with me, we'll go. . . . (*Losing conviction.*) This is just another thunderstorm,—isn't it? Isn't it?

ANTROBUS. Maggie!!! (MRS. ANTROBUS *appears beside him with* GLADYS.)

MRS. ANTROBUS (*matter-of-fact*). Here I am and here's Gladys.

ANTROBUS. Where've you been? Where have you been? Quick, we're going into that boat out there.

MRS. ANTROBUS. I know we are. But I haven't found Henry. (*She wanders off into the darkness calling "Henry!"*)

SABINA (*low urgent babbling, only occasionally raising her voice*). I don't believe it. I don't believe it's anything at all. I've seen hundreds of storms like this.

FORTUNE TELLER. There's no time to lose. Go. Push the animals along before you. Start a new world. Begin again.

SABINA. Esmeralda! George! Tell me,—is it really serious?

ANTROBUS (*suddenly very busy*). Elephants first. Gently, gently.— Look where you're going.

GLADYS (*leaning over the ramp and striking an animal on the back*). Stop it or you'll be left behind!

ANTROBUS. Is the Kangaroo there? *There* you are! Take those turtles in your pouch, will you? (*To some other animals, pointing to his shoulder.*) Here! You jump up here. You'll be trampled on.

GLADYS (*to her father, pointing below*). Papa, look,—the snakes!

MRS. ANTROBUS. I can't find Henry. Hen-ry!

ANTROBUS. Go along. Go along. Climb on their backs.—Wolves! Jackals,—whatever you are,—tend to your own business!

GLADYS (*pointing, tenderly*). Papa,—look.

SABINA. Mr. Antrobus—take me with you. Don't leave me here. I'll work. I'll help. I'll do anything.

[THREE CONVEENERS *cross the stage, marching with
a banner.*]

CONVEENERS. George! What are you scared of?—George! Fellas, it looks like rain.—"Maggie, where's my umbrella?"—George, setting up for Barnum and Bailey.

ANTROBUS (*again catching his wife's hand*). Come on now, Maggie,— the pier's going to break any minute.

MRS. ANTROBUS. I'm not going a step without Henry. Henry!

GLADYS (*on the ramp*). Mama! Papa! Hurry. The pier's cracking, Mama. It's going to break.

MRS. ANTROBUS. Henry! Cain! CAIN!

[HENRY *dashes into the stage and joins his mother.*]

HENRY. Here I am, Mama.

MRS. ANTROBUS. Thank God!—now come quick.

HENRY. I didn't think you wanted me.

MRS. ANTROBUS. Quick! (*She pushes him down before her into the aisle.*)

SABINA (*all the* ANTROBUSES *are now in the theatre aisle;* SABINA *stands at the top of the ramp*). Mrs. Antrobus, take me. Don't you remember me? I'll work. I'll help. Don't leave me here!

MRS. ANTROBUS. (*impatiently, but as though it were of no importance*). Yes, yes. There's a lot of work to be done. Only hurry.

FORTUNE TELLER (*now dominating the stage. To* SABINA *with a grim smile*). Yes, go—back to the kitchen with you.

SABINA (*half-down the ramp, to* FORTUNE TELLER). I don't know why my life's always being interrupted—just when everything's going fine!! (*She dashes up the aisle. Now the* CONVEENERS *emerge doing a serpentine dance on the stage. They jeer at the* FORTUNE TELLER.)

CONVEENERS. Get a canoe—there's not a minute to be lost! Tell me my future, Mrs. Croaker.

FORTUNE TELLER. Paddle in the water, boys—enjoy yourselves.

VOICE (*from the Bingo Parlor*). A-nine; A-nine. C-twenty-four. C-twenty-four.

CONVEENERS. Rags, bottles, and sacks.

FORTUNE TELLER. Go back and climb on your roofs. Put rags in the cracks under your doors.—Nothing will keep out the flood. You've had your chance. You've had your day. You've failed. You've lost.

VOICE (*from the Bingo Parlor*). B-fifteen. B-fifteen.

FORTUNE TELLER (*shading her eyes and looking out to sea*). They're safe. George Antrobus! Think it over! A new world to make.—think it over!

ACT III

▂◿ *Just before the curtain rises, two sounds are heard from the stage: a cracked bugle call.*

The curtain rises on almost total darkness. Almost all the flats composing the walls of MR. ANTROBUS'S *house, as of Act I, are up, but they lean helter-skelter against one another, leaving irregular gaps. Among the flats missing are two in the back wall, leaving the frames of the window and door crazily out of line. Off stage, back right, some red Roman fire is burning. The bugle call is repeated. Enter* SABINA *through the tilted door. She is dressed as a Napoleonic camp follower, "la fille du regiment," in begrimed reds and blues.*

SABINA. Mrs. Antrobus! Gladys! Where are you?

    The war's over. The war's over. You can come out. The peace treaty's been signed.

    Where are they?—Hmpf! Are they dead, too? Mrs. Annnntrobus! Glaaaadus! Mr. Antrobus'll be here this afternoon. I just saw him downtown. Huuuurry and put things in order. He says that now that the war's over we'll all have to settle down and be perfect.

    [*Enter* MR. FITZPATRICK, *the stage manager, followed by the whole company, who stand waiting at the edges of the stage.* MR. FITZPATRICK *tries to interrupt* SA-
BINA.]

MR. FITZPATRICK. Miss Somerset, we have to stop a moment.

SABINA. They may be hiding out in the back—

MR. FITZPATRICK. Miss Somerset! We have to stop a moment.

SABINA. What's the matter?

MR. FITZPATRICK. There's an explanation we have to make to the audience.—Lights, please. (*To the actor who plays* MR. ANTROBUS.) Will you explain the matter to the audience?

[*The lights go up. We now see that a balcony or ele-vated runway has been erected at the back of the stage, back of the wall of the Antrobus house. From its extreme right and left ends ladder-like steps de-scend to the floor of the stage.*]

ANTROBUS. Ladies and gentlemen, an unfortunate accident has taken place back stage. Perhaps I should say *another* unfortunate accident.

SABINA. I'm sorry. I'm sorry.

ANTROBUS. The management feels, in fact, we all feel that you are due an apology. And now we have to ask your indulgence for the most serious mishap of all. Seven of our actors have . . . have been taken ill. Apparently, it was something they ate. I'm not exactly clear what happened. (*All the* ACTORS *start to talk at once.* AN-TROBUS *raises his hand.*) Now, now—not all at once. Fitz, do you know what it was?

MR. FITZPATRICK. Why, it's perfectly clear. These seven actors had dinner together, and they ate something that disagreed with them.

SABINA. Disagreed with them!!! They have ptomaine poisoning. They're in Bellevue Hospital this very minute in agony. They're having their stomachs pumped out this very minute, in perfect agony.

ANTROBUS. Fortunately, we've just heard they'll all recover.

SABINA. It'll be a miracle if they do, a downright miracle. It was the lemon meringue pie.

ACTORS. It was the fish . . . it was the canned tomatoes . . . it was the fish.

SABINA. It was the lemon meringue pie. I saw it with my own eyes; it had blue mould all over the bottom of it.

ANTROBUS. Whatever it was, they're in no condition to take part in this performance. Naturally, we haven't enough understudies to fill all those roles; but we do have a number of splendid volunteers who have kindly consented to help us out. These friends have watched our rehearsals, and they assure me that they know the lines and the business very well. Let me introduce them to you—my dresser, Mr. Tremayne,—himself a distinguished Shakespearean actor for many years; our wardrobe mistress, Hester; Miss Somerset's maid, Ivy; and Fred Bailey, captain of the ushers in this theatre. (*These per-sons bow modestly.* IVY *and* HESTER *are colored girls.*) Now this scene takes place near the end of the act. And I'm sorry to say we'll need a short rehearsal, just a short run-through. And as some of it takes place in the auditorium, we'll have to keep the curtain up. Those of you who wish can go out in the lobby and smoke some more. The rest of you can listen to us, or . . . or just talk quietly among yourselves, as you choose. Thank you. Now will you take it over, Mr. Fitzpatrick?

MR. FITZPATRICK. Thank you.—Now for those of you who are listen-ing perhaps I should explain that at the end of this act, the men have come back from the War and the family's settled down in the house. And the author wants to show the hours of the night passing by over their heads, and the planets crossing the sky . . . uh . . . over their heads. And he says—this is hard to explain—that each of the hours of the night is a philosopher, or a great thinker. Eleven o'clock, for instance, is Aristotle. And nine o'clock is Spinoza. Like that. I don't suppose it means anything. It's just a kind of poetic effect.

SABINA. Not mean anything! Why, it certainly does. Twelve o'clock goes by saying those wonderful things. I think it means that when people are asleep they have all those lovely thoughts, much better than when they're awake.

IVY. Excuse me, I think it means,—excuse me, Mr. Fitzpatrick—

SABINA. What were you going to say, Ivy?

IVY. Mr. Fitzpatrick, you let my father come to a rehearsal; and my father's a Baptist minister, and he said that the author meant that —just like the hours and stars go by over our heads at night, in the same way the ideas and thoughts of the great men are in the air around us all the time and they're working on us, even when we don't know it.

MR. FITZPATRICK. Well, well, maybe that's it. Thank you, Ivy. Any-way,—the hours of the night are philosophers. My friends, are you ready? Ivy, can you be eleven o'clock? "This good estate of the mind possessing its object in energy we call divine." Aristotle.

IVY. Yes, sir. I know that and I know twelve o'clock and I know nine o'clock.

MR. FITZPATRICK. Twelve o'clock? Mr. Tremayne, the Bible.

TREMAYNE. Yes.

MR. FITZPATRICK. Ten o'clock? Hester,—Plato? (*She nods eagerly.*) Nine o'clock, Spinoza,—Fred?

BAILEY. Yes, *sir.* (FRED BAILEY *picks up a great gilded cardboard numeral IX and starts up the steps to the platform.* MR. FITZPATRICK *strikes his forehead.*)

MR. FITZPATRICK. The planets!! We forgot all about the planets.

SABINA. O my God! The planets! Are they sick too? (ACTORS *nod.*)

MR. FITZPATRICK. Ladies and gentlemen, the planets are singers. Of course, we can't replace them, so you'll have to imagine them sing-ing in this scene. Saturn sings from the orchestra pit down here. The Moon is way up there. And Mars with a red lantern in his hand, stands in the aisle over there—Tz-tz-tz. It's too bad; it all makes a very fine effect. However! Ready—nine o'clock: Spinoza.

BAILEY (*walking slowly across the balcony, left to right*). "After ex-perience had taught me that the common occurrences of daily life are vain and futile—"

FITZPATRICK. Louder, Fred. "And I saw that all the objects of my de-sire and fear—"

BAILEY. "And I saw that all the objects of my desire and fear were in themselves nothing good nor bad save insofar as the mind was affected by them—"

FITZPATRICK. Do you know the rest? All right. Ten o'clock. Hester. Plato.

HESTER. "Then tell me, O Critias, how will a man choose the ruler that shall rule over him? Will he not—"

FITZPATRICK. Thank you. Skip to the end, Hester.

HESTER. ". . . can be multiplied a thousand fold in its effects among the citizens."

FITZPATRICK. Thank you.—Aristotle, Ivy?

IVY. "This good estate of the mind possessing its object in energy we call divine. This we mortals have occasionally and it is this energy which is pleasantest and best. But God has it always. It is wonderful in us; but in Him how much more wonderful."

FITZPATRICK. Midnight. Midnight, Mr. Tremayne. That's right,— you've done it before.—All right, everybody. You know what you have to do.—Lower the curtain. House lights up. Act Three of THE SKIN OF OUR TEETH. (*As the curtain descends he is heard saying: "You volunteers, just wear what you have on. Don't try to put on the costumes today." House lights go down. The Act begins again. The Bugle call. Curtain rises. Enter* SABINA.)

SABINA. Mrs. Antrobus! Gladys! Where are you? The war's over.— You've heard all this— (*She gabbles the main points.*) Where—are —they? Are—they—dead, too, et cetera. I—just—saw—Mr.—An- trobus—down town, et cetera. (*Slowing up.*) He says that now that the war's over we'll all have to settle down and be perfect. They may be hiding out in the back somewhere. Mrs. An-tro-bus. (*She wanders off.*)

> [*It has grown lighter. A trapdoor is cautiously raised
> and* MRS. ANTROBUS *emerges waist-high and listens.
> She is disheveled and worn; she wears a tattered dress
> and a shawl half covers her head. She talks down
> through the trapdoor.*]

MRS. ANTROBUS. It's getting light. There's still something burning over there—Newark, or Jersey City. What? Yes, I could swear I heard someone moving about up here. But I can't see anybody. I say: I can't see anybody. (*She starts to move about the stage.* GLADYS' *head appears at the trapdoor. She is holding a baby.*)

GLADYS. Oh, Mama. Be careful.

MRS. ANTROBUS. Now, Gladys, you stay out of sight.

GLADYS. Well, let me stay here just a minute. I want the baby to get some of this fresh air.

MRS. ANTROBUS. All right, but keep your eyes open. I'll see what I can find. I'll have a good hot plate of soup for you before you can say Jack Robinson. Gladys Antrobus! Do you know what I think I see?

There's old Mr. Hawkins sweeping the sidewalk in front of his A and P store. Sweeping it with a broom. Why, he must have gone crazy, like the others! I see some other people moving about, too.

GLADYS. Mama, come back, come back.

[MRS. ANTROBUS *returns to the trapdoor and listens.*]

MRS. ANTROBUS. Gladys, there's something in the air. Everybody's movement's sort of different. I see some women walking right out in the middle of the street.

SABINA'S VOICE. Mrs. An-tro-bus!

MRS. ANTROBUS *and* GLADYS. What's that?!!

SABINA'S VOICE. Glaaaadys! Mrs. An-tro-bus! (*Enter* SABINA.)

MRS. ANTROBUS. Gladys, that's Sabina's voice as sure as I live.— Sabina! Sabina!—Are you alive?!!

SABINA. Of course, I'm alive. How've you girls been?—Don't try and kiss me. I never want to kiss another human being as long as I live. Sh'sh, there's nothing to get emotional about. Pull yourself together, the war's over. Take a deep breath,—the war's over.

MRS. ANTROBUS. The war's over!! I don't believe you. I don't believe you. I can't believe you.

GLADYS. Mama!

SABINA. Who's that?

MRS. ANTROBUS. That's Gladys and her baby. I don't believe you. Gladys, Sabina says the war's over. Oh, Sabina.

SABINA (*leaning over the baby*). Goodness! Are there any babies left in the world! Can it *see?* And can it cry and everything?

GLADYS. Yes, he can. He notices everything very well.

SABINA. Where on earth did you get it? Oh, I won't ask.—Lord, I've lived all these seven years around camp and I've forgotten how to behave.—Now we've got to think about the men coming home.— Mrs. Antrobus, go and wash your face, I'm ashamed of you. Put your best clothes on. Mr. Antrobus'll be here this afternoon. I just saw him downtown.

MRS. ANTROBUS *and* GLADYS. He's alive!! He'll be here!! Sabina, you're not joking?

MRS. ANTROBUS. And Henry?

SABINA (*dryly*). Yes, Henry's alive, too, that's what they say. Now don't stop to talk. Get yourselves fixed up. Gladys, you look terrible. Have you any decent clothes? (SABINA *has pushed them toward the trapdoor.*)

MRS. ANTROBUS (*half down*). Yes, I've something to wear just for this very day. But, Sabina,—who won the war?

SABINA. Don't stop now,—just wash your face. (*A whistle sounds in the distance.*) Oh, my God, what's that silly little noise?

MRS. ANTROBUS. Why, it sounds like . . . it sounds like what used to be the noon whistle at the shoe-polish factory. (*Exit.*)

SABINA. That's what it is. Seems to me like peacetime's coming along pretty fast—shoe polish!

GLADYS (*half down*). Sabina, how soon after peacetime begins does the milkman start coming to the door?

SABINA. As soon as he catches a cow. Give him time to catch a cow, dear. (*Exit* GLADYS. SABINA *walks about a moment, thinking.*) Shoe polish! My, I'd forgotten what peacetime was like. (*She shakes her head, then sits down by the trapdoor and starts talking down the hole.*) Mrs. Antrobus, guess what I saw Mr. Antrobus doing this morning at dawn. He was tacking up a piece of paper on the door of the Town Hall. You'll die when you hear: it was a recipe for grass soup, for a grass soup that doesn't give you the diarrhea. Mr. Antrobus is still thinking up new things.—He told me to give you his love. He's got all sorts of ideas for peacetime, he says. No more laziness and idiocy, he says. And oh, yes! Where are his books? What? Well, pass them up. The first thing he wants to see are his books. He says if you've burnt those books, or if the rats have eaten them, he says it isn't worthwhile starting over again. Everybody's going to be beautiful, he says, and diligent, and very intelligent. (*A hand reaches up with two volumes.*) What language is that? Pu-u-gh, mold! And he's got such plans for you, Mrs. Antrobus. You're going to study history and algebra—and so are Gladys and I—and philosophy. You should hear him talk. (*Taking two more volumes.*) Well, these are in English, anyway.—To hear him talk, seems like he expects you to be a combination, Mrs. Antrobus, of a saint and a college professor, and a dancehall hostess, if you know what I mean. (*Two more volumes.*) Ugh. German! (*She is lying on the floor; one elbow bent, her cheek on her hand, meditatively.*) Yes, peace will be here before we know it. In a week or two we'll be asking the Perkinses in for a quiet evening of bridge. We'll turn on the radio and hear how to be big successes with a new toothpaste. We'll trot down to the movies and see how girls with wax faces live—all that will begin again. Oh, Mrs. Antrobus, God forgive me but I enjoyed the war. Everybody's at their best in wartime. I'm sorry it's over. And, oh, I forgot! Mr. Antrobus sent you another message—can you hear me?—

[*Enter* HENRY, *blackened and sullen. He is wearing torn overalls, but has one gaudy admiral's epaulette hanging by a thread from his right shoulder, and there are vestiges of gold and scarlet braid running down his left trouser leg. He stands listening.*]

Listen! Henry's never to put foot in this house again, he says. He'll kill Henry on sight, if he sees him.

You don't know about Henry??? Well, where have you been? What? Well, Henry rose right to the top. Top of *what?* Listen, I'm telling you. Henry rose from corporal to captain, to major, to general.—I don't know how to say it, but the enemy is *Henry;* Henry *is* the enemy. Everybody knows that.

HENRY. He'll kill me, will he?

SABINA. Who are *you?* I'm not afraid of you. The war's over.

HENRY. I'll kill him so fast. I've spent seven years trying to find him; the others I killed were just substitutes.

SABINA. Goodness! It's Henry!—(*He makes an angry gesture.*) Oh, I'm not afraid of you. The war's over, Henry Antrobus, and you're not any more important than any other unemployed. You go away and hide yourself, until we calm your father down.

HENRY. The first thing to do is to burn up those old books; it's the ideas he gets out of those old books that . . . that makes the whole world so you can't live in it. (*He reels forward and starts kicking the books about, but suddenly falls down in a sitting position.*)

SABINA. You leave those books alone!! Mr. Antrobus is looking forward to them a-special.—Gracious sakes, Henry, you're so tired you can't stand up. Your mother and sister'll be here in a minute and we'll think what to do about you.

HENRY. What did they ever care about me?

SABINA. There's that old whine again. All you people think you're not loved enough, nobody loves you. Well, you start being lovable and we'll love you.

HENRY (*outraged*). I don't want anybody to love me.

SABINA. Then stop talking about it all the time.

HENRY. I *never* talk about it. The last thing I want is anybody to pay any attention to me.

SABINA. I can hear it behind every word you say.

HENRY. I want everybody to hate me.

SABINA. Yes, you've decided that's second best, but it's still the same thing.—Mrs. Antrobus! Henry's here! He's so tired he can't stand up.

[MRS. ANTROBUS *and* GLADYS, *with her baby emerge. They are dressed as in Act I.* MRS. ANTROBUS *carries some objects in her apron, and* GLADYS *has a blanket over her shoulder.*]

MRS. ANTROBUS *and* GLADYS. Henry! Henry! Henry!

HENRY (*glaring at them*). Have you anything to eat?

MRS. ANTROBUS. Yes, I have, Henry. I've been saving it for this very day,—two good baked potatoes. No! Henry! one of them's for your father. Henry!! Give me that other potato back this minute.

[SABINA *sidles up behind him and snatches the other potato away.*]

SABINA. He's so dog-tired he doesn't know what he's doing.

MRS. ANTROBUS. Now you just rest there, Henry, until I can get your room ready. Eat that potato good and slow, so you can get all the nourishment out of it.

HENRY. You all might as well know right now that I haven't come back here to live.

MRS. ANTROBUS. Sh. . . . I'll put this coat over you. Your room's hardly damaged at all. Your football trophies are a little tarnished, but Sabina and I will polish them up tomorrow.

HENRY. Did you hear me? I don't live here. I don't belong to anybody.

MRS. ANTROBUS. Why, how can you say a thing like that! You certainly do belong right here. Where else would you want to go? Your forehead's feverish, Henry, seems to me. You'd better give me that gun, Henry. You won't need that any more.

GLADYS (*whispering*). Look, he's fallen asleep already, with his potato half-chewed.

SABINA. Puh! The terror of the world.

MRS. ANTROBUS. Sabina, you mind your own business, and start putting the room to rights.

> [HENRY *has turned his face to the back of the sofa.*
> MRS. ANTROBUS *gingerly puts the revolver in her apron pocket, then helps* SABINA. SABINA *has found a rope hanging from the ceiling. Grunting, she hangs all her weight on it, and as she pulls the walls begin to move into their right places.* MRS. ANTROBUS *brings the overturned tables, chairs and hassock into the positions of Act I.*]

SABINA. That's all we do—always beginning again! Over and over again. Always beginning again. (*She pulls on the rope and a part of the wall moves into place. She stops. Meditatively.*) How do we know that it'll be any better than before? Why do we go on pretending? Some day the whole earth's going to have to turn cold anyway, and until that time all these other things'll be happening again: it will be more wars and more walls of ice and floods and earthquakes.

MRS. ANTROBUS. Sabina!! Stop arguing and go on with your work.

SABINA. All right. I'll go on just out of *habit*, but I won't believe in it.

MRS. ANTROBUS (*aroused*). Now, Sabina. I've let you talk long enough. I don't want to hear any more of it. Do I have to explain to you what everybody knows,—everybody who keeps a home going? Do I have to say to you what nobody should ever *have* to say, because they can read it in each other's eyes?

Now listen to me. (MRS. ANTROBUS *takes hold of the rope.*)

I could live for seventy years in a cellar and make soup out of grass and bark, without ever doubting that this world has a work to do and will do it.

Do you hear me?

SABINA (*frightened*). Yes, Mrs. Antrobus.

MRS. ANTROBUS. Sabina, do you see this house,—216 Cedar Street,—do you see it?

SABINA. Yes, Mrs. Antrobus.

MRS. ANTROBUS. Well, just to have known this house is to have seen the idea of what we can do someday if we keep our wits about us.

Too many people have suffered and died for my children for us to start reneging now. So we'll start putting this house to rights. Now, Sabina, go and see what you can do in the kitchen.

SABINA. Kitchen! Why is it that however far I go away, I always find myself back in the kitchen? (*Exit.*)

MRS. ANTROBUS (*still thinking over her last speech, relaxes and says with a reminiscent smile:*) Goodness gracious, wouldn't you know that my father was a parson? It was just like I heard his own voice speaking and he's been dead five thousand years. There! I've gone and almost waked Henry up.

HENRY (*talking in his sleep, indistinctly*). Fellows . . . what have they done for us? . . . Blocked our way at every step. Kept everything in their own hands. And you've stood it. When are you going to wake up?

MRS. ANTROBUS. Sh, Henry. Go to sleep. Go to sleep. Go to sleep.— Well, that looks better. Now let's go and help Sabina.

GLADYS. Mama, I'm going out into the backyard and hold the baby right up in the air. And show him that we don't have to be afraid any more. (*Exit GLADYS to the kitchen.*)

> [MRS. ANTROBUS *glances at* HENRY, *exits into kitchen.* HENRY *thrashes about in his sleep. Enter* ANTROBUS, *his arms full of bundles, chewing the end of a carrot. He has a slight limp. Over the suit of Act I he is wearing an overcoat too long for him, its skirts trailing on the ground. He lets his bundles fall and stands looking about. Presently his attention is fixed on* HENRY, *whose words grow clearer.*]

HENRY. All right! What have you to lose? What have they done for us? That's right—nothing. Tear everything down. I don't care what you smash. We'll begin again and we'll show 'em. (ANTROBUS *takes out his revolver and holds it pointing downwards. With his back towards the audience he moves toward the footlights.* HENRY'S *voice grows louder and he wakes with a start. They stare at one another. Then* HENRY *sits up quickly. Throughout the following scene* HENRY *is played, not as a misunderstood or misguided young man, but as a representation of strong unreconciled evil.*) All right! Do something. (*Pause.*) Don't think I'm afraid of you, either. All right, do what you were going to do. Do it. (*Furiously.*) Shoot me, I tell you. You don't have to think I'm any relation of yours. I haven't got any father or any mother, or brothers or sisters. And I don't want any. And what's more I haven't got anybody over me; and I never will have. I'm alone, and that's all I want to be: alone. So you can shoot me.

ANTROBUS. You're the last person I wanted to see. The sight of you dries up all my plans and hopes. I wish I were back at war still, because it's easier to fight you than to live with you. War's a pleasure—do you hear me?—War's a pleasure compared to what faces us now: trying to build up a peacetime with you in the middle of it. (ANTROBUS *walks up to the window.*)

HENRY. I'm not going to be a part of any peacetime of yours. I'm going a long way from here and make my own world that's fit for a man to live in. Where a man can be free, and have a chance, and do what he wants to do in his own way.

ANTROBUS (*his attention arrested; thoughtfully. He throws the gun out of the window and turns with hope*). . . . Henry, let's try again.

HENRY. Try what? Living *here?*—Speaking polite downtown to all the old men like you? Standing like a sheep at the street corner until the red light turns to green? Being a good boy and a good sheep, like all the stinking ideas you get out of your books? Oh, no. I'll make a world, and I'll show you.

ANTROBUS (*hard*). How can you make a world for people to live in, unless you've first put order in yourself? Mark my words: I shall continue fighting you until my last breath as long as you mix up your idea of liberty with your idea of hogging everything for yourself. I shall have no pity on you. I shall pursue you to the far corners of the earth. You and I want the same thing; but until you think of it as something that everyone has a right to, you are my deadly enemy and I will destroy you.—I hear your mother's voice in the kitchen. Have you seen her?

HENRY. I have no mother. Get it into your head. I don't belong here. I have nothing to do here. I have no home.

ANTROBUS. Then why did you come here? With the whole world to choose from, why did you come to this one place: 216 Cedar Street, Excelsior, New Jersey. . . . Well?

HENRY. What if I did? What if I wanted to look at it once more, to see if—

ANTROBUS. Oh, you're related, all right—When your mother comes in you must behave yourself. Do you hear me?

HENRY (*wildly*). What is this?—*must behave* yourself. Don't you say *must* to me.

ANTROBUS. Quiet!

[*Enter* MRS. ANTROBUS *and* SABINA.]

HENRY. Nobody can say *must* to me. All my life everybody's been crossing me,—everybody, everything, all of you. I'm going to be free, even if I have to kill half the world for it. Right now, too. Let me get my hands on his throat. I'll show him.

[*He advances toward* ANTROBUS. *Suddenly,* SABINA *jumps between them and calls out in her own person.*]

SABINA. Stop! Stop! Don't play this scene. You know what happened last night. Stop the play. (*The men fall back, panting.* HENRY *covers his face with his hands.*) Last night you almost strangled him. You became a regular savage. Stop it!

HENRY. It's true. I'm sorry. I don't know what comes over me. I have nothing against him personally. I respect him very much . . . I . . . I admire him. But something comes over me. It's like I become fifteen years old again. I . . . I . . . listen: my own father used to whip me and lock me up every Saturday night. I never had enough to eat. He never let me have enough money to buy decent clothes. I was ashamed to go downtown. I never could go to the dances. My father and my uncle put rules in the way of everything I wanted to do. They tried to prevent my living at all.—I'm sorry. I'm sorry.

MRS. ANTROBUS (*quickly*). No, go on. Finish what you were saying. Say it all.

HENRY. In this scene it's as though I were back in High School again. It's like I had some big emptiness inside me.—the emptiness of being hated and blocked at every turn. And the emptiness fills up with the one thought that you have to strike and fight and kill. Listen, it's as though you have to kill somebody else so as not to end up killing yourself.

SABINA. That's not true. I knew your father and your uncle and your mother. You imagined all that. Why, they did everything they could for you. How can you say things like that? They didn't lock you up.

HENRY. They did. They did. They wished I hadn't been born.

SABINA. That's not true.

ANTROBUS (*in his own person, with self-condemnation, but cold and proud*). Wait a minute. I have something to say, too. It's not wholly his fault that he wants to strangle me in this scene. It's my fault, too. He wouldn't feel that way unless there were something in me that reminded him of all that. He talks about an emptiness. Well, there's an emptiness in me, too. Yes,—work, work, work,—that's all I do. I've ceased to *live*. No wonder he feels that anger coming over him.

MRS. ANTROBUS. There! At least you've said it.

SABINA. We're all just as wicked as we can be, and that's the God's truth.

MRS. ANTROBUS (*nods a moment, then comes forward; quietly*). Come. Come and put your head under some cold water.

SABINA (*in a whisper*). I'll go with him. I've known him a long while. You have to go on with the play. Come with me.

[HENRY *starts out with* SABINA, *but turns at the exit and says to* ANTROBUS:]

HENRY. Thanks. Thanks for what you said. I'll be all right tomorrow. I won't lose control in that place. I promise.

[*Exeunt* HENRY *and* SABINA. ANTROBUS *starts toward the front door, fastens it.* MRS. ANTROBUS *goes up stage and places the chair close to table.*]

MRS. ANTROBUS. George, do I see you limping?

ANTROBUS. Yes, a little. My old wound from the other war started smarting again. I can manage.

MRS. ANTROBUS (*looking out of the window*). Some lights are coming on,—the first in seven years. People are walking up and down looking at them. Over in Hawkins' open lot they've built a bonfire to celebrate the peace. They're dancing around it like scarecrows.

ANTROBUS. A bonfire! As though they hadn't seen enough things burning.—Maggie,—the dog died?

MRS. ANTROBUS. Oh, yes. Long ago. There are no dogs left in Excelsior.—You're back again! All these years. I gave up counting on letters. The few that arrived were anywhere from six months to a year late.

ANTROBUS. Yes, the ocean's full of letters, along with the other things.

MRS. ANTROBUS. George, sit down, you're tired.

ANTROBUS. No, you sit down. I'm tired but I'm restless. (*Suddenly, as she comes forward.*) Maggie! I've lost it. I've lost it.

MRS. ANTROBUS. What, George? What have you lost?

ANTROBUS. The most important thing of all: The desire to begin again, to start building.

MRS. ANTROBUS (*sitting in the chair right of the table*). Well, it will come back.

ANTROBUS (*at the window*). I've lost it. This minute I feel like all those people dancing around the bonfire—just relief. Just the desire to settle down; to slip into the old grooves and keep the neighbors from walking over my lawn.—Hm. But during the war,—in the middle of all that blood and dirt and hot and cold—every day and night, I'd have moments, Maggie, when I *saw* the things that we could do when it was over. When you're at war you think about a better life; when you're at peace you think about a more comfortable one. I've lost it. I feel sick and tired.

MRS. ANTROBUS. Listen! The baby's crying.

I hear Gladys talking. Probably she's quieting Henry again. George, while Gladys and I were living here—like moles, like rats, and when we were at our wits' end to save the baby's life—the only thought we clung to was that you were going to bring something good out of this suffering. In the night, in the dark, we'd whisper about it, starving and sick.—Oh, George, you'll have to get it back again. Think! What else kept us alive all these years? Even now, it's not comfort we want. We can suffer whatever's necessary; only give us back that promise.

[*Enter* SABINA *with a lighted lamp. She is dressed as in Act I.*]

SABINA. Mrs. Antrobus . . .

MRS. ANTROBUS. Yes, Sabina?

SABINA. Will you need me?

MRS. ANTROBUS. No, Sabina, you can go to bed.

SABINA. Mrs. Antrobus, if it's all right with you, I'd like to go to the bonfire and celebrate seeing the war's over. And, Mrs. Antrobus, they've opened the Gem Movie Theatre and they're giving away a hand-painted soup tureen to every lady, and I thought one of us ought to go.

ANTROBUS. Well, Sabina, I haven't any money. I haven't seen any money for quite a while.

SABINA. Oh, you don't need money. They're taking anything you can give them. And I have some . . . some . . . Mrs. Antrobus, promise you won't tell anyone. It's a little against the law. But I'll give you some, too.

ANTROBUS. What is it?

SABINA. I'll give you some, too. Yesterday I picked up a lot of . . . of beef-cubes!

[MRS. ANTROBUS *turns and says calmly:*]

MRS. ANTROBUS. But, Sabina, you know you ought to give that in to the Center downtown. They know who needs them most.

SABINA (*outburst*). Mrs. Antrobus, I didn't make this war. I didn't ask for it. And, in my opinion, after anybody's gone through what we've gone through, they have a right to grab what they can find. You're a very nice man, Mr. Antrobus, but you'd have got on better in the world if you'd realized that dog-eat-dog was the rule in the beginning and always will be. And most of all now. (*In tears.*) Oh, the world's an awful place, and you know it is. I used to think something could be done about it; but I know better now. I hate it. I hate it. (*She comes forward slowly and brings six cubes from the bag.*) All right. All right. You can have them.

ANTROBUS. Thank you, Sabina.

SABINA. Can I have . . . can I have one to go to the movies? (ANTROBUS *in silence gives her one.*) Thank you.

ANTROBUS. Good night, Sabina.

SABINA. Mr. Antrobus, don't mind what I say. I'm just an ordinary girl, you know what I mean, I'm just an ordinary girl. But you're a bright man, you're a very bright man, and of course you invented the alphabet and the wheel, and, my God, a lot of things . . . and if you've got any other plans, my God, don't let me upset them. Only every now and then I've got to go to the movies. I mean my nerves can't stand it. But if you have any ideas about improving the crazy old world, I'm really with you. I really am. Because it's . . . it's . . . Good night. (*She goes out.* ANTROBUS *starts laughing softly with exhilaration.*)

ANTROBUS. Now I remember what three things always went together when I was able to see things most clearly: three things. Three things. (*He points to where* SABINA *has gone out.*) The voice of the people in their confusion and their need. And the thought of you and the children and this house . . . And . . . Maggie! I didn't dare ask you: my books! They haven't been lost, have they?

MRS. ANTROBUS. No. There are some of them right here. Kind of tattered.

ANTROBUS. Yes.—Remember, Maggie, we almost lost them once before? And when we finally did collect a few torn copies out of old cellars they ran in everyone's head like a fever. They as good as re-built the world. (*Pauses, book in hand, and looks up.*) Oh, I've never forgotten for long at a time that living is struggle. I know that every good and excellent thing in the world stands moment by moment on the razor-edge of danger and must be fought for—whether it's a field, or a home, or a country. All I ask is the chance to build new worlds and God has always given us that. And has given us (*opening the book*) voices to guide us; and the memory of our mistakes to warn us. Maggie, you and I will remember in peacetime all the resolves that were so clear to us in the days of war. We've come a long ways. We've learned. We're learning. And the steps of our journey are marked for us here. (*He stands by the table turning the leaves of a book.*) Sometimes out there in the war,—standing all night on a hill—I'd try and remember some of the words in these books. Parts of them and phrases would come back to me. And after a while I used to give names to the hours of the night. (*He sits, hunting for a passage in the book.*) Nine o'clock I used to call Spinoza. Where is it: "After experience had taught me—"

> [*The back wall has disappeared, revealing the platform.* FRED BAILEY *carrying his numeral has started from left to right.* MRS. ANTROBUS *sits by the table sewing.*]

BAILEY. "After experience had taught me that the common occurrences of daily life are vain and futile; and I saw that all the objects of my desire and fear were in themselves nothing good nor bad save insofar as the mind was affected by them; I at length determined to search out whether there was something truly good and communicable to man."

> [*Almost without break* HESTER, *carrying a large Roman numeral ten, starts crossing the platform.* GLADYS *appears at the kitchen door and moves towards her mother's chair.*]

HESTER. "Then tell me, O Critias, how will a man choose the ruler that shall rule over him? Will he not choose a man who has first established order in himself, knowing that any decision that has its spring from anger or pride or vanity can be multiplied a thousand fold in its effects upon the citizens?"

> [HESTER *disappears and* IVY, *as eleven o'clock, starts speaking.*]

IVY. "This good estate of the mind possessing its object in energy we call divine. This we mortals have occasionally and it is this energy which is pleasantest and best. But God has it always. It is wonderful in us; but in Him how much more wonderful."

> [*As* MR. TREMAYNE *starts to speak,* HENRY *appears at the edge of the scene, brooding and unreconciled, but present.*]

TREMAYNE. "In the beginning, God created the Heavens and the Earth; and the Earth was waste and void; And the darkness was upon the face of the deep. And the Lord said let there be light and there was light."

> [*Sudden black-out and silence, except for the last strokes of the midnight bell. Then just as suddenly the lights go up, and* SABINA *is standing at the window, as at the opening of the play.*]

SABINA. Oh, oh, oh. Six o'clock and the master not home yet. Pray God nothing serious has happened to him crossing the Hudson River. But I wouldn't be surprised. The whole world's at sixes and sevens, and why the house hasn't fallen down about our ears long ago is a miracle to me. (*She comes down to the footlights.*) This is where you came in. We have to go on for ages and ages yet.

You go home.

The end of this play isn't written yet.

Mr. and Mrs. Antrobus! Their heads are full of plans and they're as confident as the first day they began,—and they told me to tell you: good night.

QUESTIONS

ACT I

1. Does presenting the everyday occurrence of the sunrise as an item in a newsreel force us to see this familiar event from a new perspective? Consider other devices Wilder uses to achieve Brecht's "alienation effect," the sight of the familiar from a new and revealing angle.

2. "The author hasn't made up his silly mind as to whether we're all living back in caves or in New Jersey today," says Sabina, but the chronology is even more mixed than Sabina seems to know. Looking at the various events, the names of the characters, and the references to different historical periods, make a list of the different periods conflated in the world of this play. What point is being made about the nature of history and time?

3. The characters are all types rather than individuals, almost personifications of certain basic human traits that appear under different names at different times. Try to define the leading trait or motive of each of the characters and trace its variety of manifestations.

4. When Antrobus returns home, he appears with the face of a Keystone Comedy Cop. Is this appropriate for the inventor of the wheel and the progenitor of the human race? Is this comic perspective maintained through the play?

5. The face of reality keeps flickering back and forth. The refugees from Hitler become at once the victims of the depression, men fleeing before the oncoming glacier, the Nine Muses, and the great literary and historical figures of the past who suffered for their visions. Look carefully at this scene and observe the various methods by which Wilder manages to focus so many diverse forms of persecuted life in a single scene.

6. The threats to life are both external to man and internal. What seeds of man's destruction are within him?

7. What are the internal and external qualities that save life and urge it onward?

ACT II

8. In each act the chief threat to human life comes from a different source and the challenges are of a different kind. Discuss the differences in these destructive powers and see if you can work out the structural scheme on which the progression of the play is built.

9. Is Mrs. Antrobus' "invention" and defense of marriage consistent with her other attitudes and virtues?

10. Despite its apparent simplicity, the play's presentation of overall human character is quite complicated. As in *Everyman,* each character represents only one of many human powers, but their interaction with one another and their effect upon events is complex. Is there evidence that the forces that threaten the continuation of the race in one set of circumstances further and protect life at other times? Does the energy of one character, his particular virtue, conflict with other equally important virtues? How is this antagonism, seemingly inherent in human beings, resolved?

11. What part does racism play in an act centering on man's extended biological struggle?

12. To what unexpected uses are Antrobus' inventions of Act I put in II?

13. What is the function of the Fortune Teller? Does she appear in other forms elsewhere in the play?

14. Do you think that Mrs. Antrobus' view of the sacredness of womankind, expressed in her letter, should be taken seriously, or is it typical overstatement? Is your answer an expression of your own values or can you support it with evidence from the play?

ACT III

15. The method by which mankind escapes from catastrophe and oblivion in each act is never specified. Somehow, the characters simply
turn up again, already involved in a new crisis. Is this absence of information a flaw in the play's construction, or does it contribute to,
even create, its particular meaning? Does this plot device relate to
the title of the play?

16. Explaining that each of the hours of the night will be presented as a
philosopher or "culture hero," the stage manager says, "I don't suppose it means anything. It's just a kind of poetic effect." Do you agree?

17. Several other characters then try their hands at explaining the *meaning* of this somewhat bizarre theatrical device. Which of the explanations seems correct and why? What theory of the way in which a play
achieves meaning is implicit in these explanations?

18. Looking back can you find other places where the play examines its
own meaning or questions itself and its own devices?

19. Throughout, the play's pretense of reality is continually breaking down
to reveal the mechanism of the theater behind it. Actors forget or
refuse to play their parts, players get sick, the audience is asked to
join in the play, props and scenery escape control and reveal their
"staginess." In short, the play is always revealing itself as play, as
artifice. Look at all instances where the theater breaks through the
play and see if you can explain the effects of breaking the illusion.
Consider whether the difficulty of staging this play relates in any
functional way to the central plot, the adventures of the Antrobus
family in history.

20. In the manner typical of comedy, *The Skin of Our Teeth* refuses to
exclude any human quality, no matter how destructive, from the feast
of life, from the family of man. Nor can any of the characters themselves ever quite leave that family, though they threaten to do so.
In the end even Henry-Cain and Sabina have their value in the scheme
of disaster and narrow escape. How does Wilder show the unbreak-
able ties of these characters to the family and their necessary contri-
butions to the continuation of life?

21. Is there finally any sense of progress, or even change, built into the
play? Consider the last lines of the play and their relationship to the
beginning.

22. *The Skin of Our Teeth* was written in 1942, during World War II.
If Wilder were to rewrite his play, would he be forced to change it
in any important respects? Sketch out a plot for Act IV dealing with
the post-atomic world.

PLOT

"FOR FAITH AND PHILOSOPHY ARE AIR, BUT EVENTS ARE BRASS. AMIDST
HIS GRAY PHILOSOPHIZINGS, LIFE BREAKS UPON A MAN LIKE A MORNING."
(Herman Melville, *Pierre*.)

In these lines Melville expresses the sense of life fundamental to the
drama: that actions have consequences, that life is always in movement, and that the meaning of being only becomes apparent in events.
Ophelia's plaintive cry in *Hamlet*, "Lord, we know what we are, but
know not what we may be," expresses poignantly the painful knowledge that only in events can we truly discover ourselves. This view is
not, of course, peculiar to the drama; most forms of history, the theory
of evolution, and philosophical dialectic assume that life can be defined
not by fine analysis of the single static object, but only by observation
of the changes through which creation moves. The primacy of movement in the drama is reflected in all basic dramatic terms. The verbs "to
act" and "to perform" mean not only "to pretend" but also "to do
something." "Drama" derives from a Greek root, the verb *dran*, meaning "to do" or "to act." "Play" comes from the Old English *plegan*,
which means in one of its senses "to strive." "Protagonist" and "antagonist," the technical names for the chief character and his opponent, mean literally "the first struggler" (i.e., the principal character)
and "the struggler against." The over-all term for the movement in a
play is, of course, the *plot*, and, though the word originally had no
connection with the concept of action, in modern English it may be
used as a verb meaning "to plan to achieve something." With this
sense of the word we can begin our discussion of the nature of *plot*.

First we must look for the origins of the forces that set the play in
motion. The prime mover is usually some tendency inherent in one
or both of the two constituents of drama already discussed: in the

world of the play or in the characters. When the world of the play—the environment—has an important role, it will show a definite direction, a tendency to complete a pattern. In Shakespeare's *Antony and Cleopatra,* Octavius Caesar conceives of the world as a constant ebbing and flowing movement, a ceaseless process of recurring change in which all life is caught up. The world has a tendency "to rot itself with motion." This tendency is at work in everything in the play: men, love, friendship, marriage, empire, and reputation all move, change, dissolve, and ultimately become as "indistinct as water is in water." The pressure of the world here is like the action of the sea upon the beach, consistent only in the destruction of existing shapes and the replacement of them with new shapes, which in their turn are washed away. The world of *Mother Courage* has a similar direction, though its changes are more brutal. Here the nature of the world leads toward an extinction of life, a slowing down of all moving things—the beat of a heart or the wheels of Mother Courage's wagon.

It requires some care to discern the direction in which the world of a play is moving, for the actions in which its nature becomes manifest are not always conspicuous, and we often "sense" its presence before we recognize it. In *Mother Courage* the efforts necessary to move the wagon suggest—for we do not actually see it—the enormous resistance of the world to all movement. And in *Hedda Gabler* the clutter of furniture on stage, which makes free movement difficult, suggests that the social world the furniture represents is crowding in on life, channeling it into restrained movements. These single effects are not, fortunately, isolated expressions of the world's pressure; they join with other effects to form a larger, more definite pattern, which we must seek out. But the first step is to look closely at individual movements, which express the nature of the world. We can expect to find the world's motive expressed in such events as a storm at sea and the swing of a clock's pendulum, in the shape taken by a battle, and in the activities of those characters who do not move of their own volition. Whenever movement is not directed by the human will—in the splashing of rain on a window or in the gradual decay of a body—the world has traced its passage in matter.

John Synge's *Riders to the Sea* is set inside a fisherman's hut on an Atlantic island; throughout the play the roar of the nearby sea can be heard as it smashes against the rocks of the coast and eats away at the land. During the play, news is brought to the hut of a succession of broken boats and drowned men; eventually the smashed body of the last man in the family is carried in wrapped in a sail, dripping with

water from the sea in which he has just drowned. The sea, which represents the world, during the play comes to have a monstrous, malevo-
lent life of its own and a will to smash and engulf all that is human
and has shape.

In *Riders to the Sea* the principal motive force is the world, but in
most plays it is the characters that are the obvious prime movers. No
matter how complex a dramatic character may be, all his nature is
usually condensed into one or two fundamental desires toward which
he moves. Mother Courage strives to protect her family and her life;
this basic motive is visible in her shabby wagon stocked, somehow,
with shoddy goods, which she doggedly keeps moving across the stage
by putting her children and herself between the shafts. Her feeling
for life and her tough courage, which endure despite many defeats,
also ring in her song:

> Christians, awake! The winter's gone!
> The snows depart, the dead sleep on.
> And though you may not long survive,
> Get out of bed and look alive!

A character seems always to reach out, trying to realize in his actions
and in his speeches the effect that it is his nature to want and to strive
for. We become aware of Hedda's desire to be free from involvement,
to remain her own possessor, by even such trivial events as her pulling
herself out of Miss Tesman's embrace in Act I, saying at the same
time, "Oh! Let me go." The same determination appears in her refusal
to admit that she is pregnant and in her denial that her husband has
any "opportunities" to see her unclothed. Later on her attempts to defy
restraint become more obvious and wilder as she urges Lövborg to
debauchery and suicide in an effort to realize her own longing for an
absolute, nihilistic freedom, and as she kills herself to escape Judge
Brack.

By definition a motive is the force that moves a person to seek the
satisfaction of some need. (Hunger is the motive forcing us to seek
food.) A dramatic motive forces the character into the world in his
effort to realize the goal his motive directs him toward. Hedda Gabler
tries to control and destroy Eilert Lövborg; Mother Courage tries to
keep her family together and her wagon moving. But as soon as this
movement toward realization begins it encounters an opposing force,
and *conflict* results. The law that every body moving in one direction
is opposed by a force exerted in another direction is as fundamental
to the drama as it is to physics. That is to say, all drama turns on a

conflict of some kind. If the character is complex, the opposing forces may be internal. Hedda Gabler is torn by her conflicting fear of scandal and desire to live without restraint. Or the force opposing a character's realization of his motive may come from another character, whose own motive causes him to move in a contrary direction. Hedda's desire to control Lövborg meets the counter desire of Mrs. Elvsted, who wishes to protect him. Or the conflict may be between a character and the world, as Mother Courage's desire to protect herself and her children sets her in opposition to a world whose tendency is to bring life to a stop.

This is only an outline of the many possibilities for conflict that the dramatist can exploit in order to generate the forward movement of his play. In the greatest drama, conflicts usually occur on several levels and each conflict mirrors the others. In *Hedda Gabler,* for example, we are first aware of a conflict within the character of Hedda herself, between her excessive desire for respectability and her equally fierce desire for freedom. This same struggle is projected in Hedda's efforts to control and use Eilert Lövborg. By listening to his tales about his wild life, by engaging in a carefully controlled flirtation with him, and by sending him out to commit violent acts, she achieves her freedom by proxy. Hedda is actually engaged in conflict with nearly every character in the play—with her husband, his aunt, and Judge Brack; they represent some repression of the free play of instinct, while she struggles for freedom from restraint. The same conflict appears in her struggle with society, represented by her house, by Judge Brack, and by the family into which she has married. She is also at odds with the long historical process—her husband's special subject, which bores her profoundly—which has resulted in the civilization now represented by Tesman and Judge Brack. The play then is not one but a series of internal and external conflicts between two basic principles of life: freedom vs. suppression, anarchy vs. order, self vs. society.

To recapitulate: the basic forces at work within a play seek fulfillment, and as they do they come into conflict. Out of this conflict, or, more accurately, out of a series of conflicts, the plot emerges. Although the actions of the characters and the events of the world are the elements which compose plot, it is still possible in a general way to distinguish plot from the motives of the characters and the pressure of the dramatic world in which they move. A character strives in one direction to achieve some particular goal, but his movements are deflected by some other force or forces, such as another character, or society, or the nature of reality, or some countering motive within himself. The plot grows out of these *conflicts,* and we can think of it as a linear progression produced by, but differing in direction from, two or more forces that have come together:

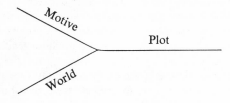

In some plays, of course, the character's motive and the plot are the same, or nearly the same. Everyman sets out to find someone who will accompany him into the grave, and after several disappointments he finds Good Works, who goes with him to the place of judgment. What Everyman tries to do is in fact accomplished; the character's motive and the plot are nearly identical.

In other types of plays, the plot is made by the world, and man is merely the helpless victim of events over which he has no control. In *Tiger at the Gates,* the principal characters are determined that the Trojan War will not take place, but fate decrees otherwise, and each attempt to prevent the war ironically brings it closer. There is something in human nature and in history—the "tiger" of the play—that moves slowly and inevitably toward its own fulfillment in war, brushing aside, even using for its purposes, man's longing for peace and his desire for a world ruled by obvious good sense.

The majority of plays, however, show man's destiny as more dependent on human action. In plays where man helps determine his own fate, the plot is likely to be the result of complex interacting factors, and it will be difficult to separate plot from what the characters are trying to do. The point to remember is that *plot is what actually happens.* The distinction is easy to make in some types of comedy: the fool tries to show that he is a learned man, but succeeds only in showing again and again that he is a fool. But let us take a more complicated case. Hedda Gabler is in conflict with a restraining social world. She reaches out for freedom from all bonds and seems to be successful in her attempts: she refuses to have anything to do with

Tesman's family or his career; she controls Mrs. Elvsted; she sends Lövborg out to a drunken party; and she persuades him to commit suicide in what seems to her a truly glorious manner. When she appears to be trapped by Judge Brack, she escapes his control by killing herself. But this is really a description of the way things *seem* to be going, the way Hedda herself understands the progression of events. At the end of the play Lövborg does not die gloriously like an ancient Viking hero or the Greek celebrant in Bacchic rites with vine leaves in his hair, as Hedda had planned, but in a sordid accident in the local bawdyhouse, shot not cleanly through the heart but through the bowels. This brutal, ugly business is the real end to which Hedda's acts have led. It reveals what she has really been building all the time and forces us to see that her every act has not been the noble, romantic movement toward freedom and joy that she thought, but a step toward confusion and death. Foreseeing the inevitable fall of Troy despite all its heroism and suffering, Hector in Shakespeare's *Troilus and Cressida* understands the plot of the play in which he is an actor and sums it up in words that define perfectly the way in which plot functions in drama: "The end crowns all,/and the old common arbitrator, Time,/ Will one day end it." Aristotle called the point at which a character discovers that the effect of his actions has been the opposite of what he intended the *reversal,* and near the end of her play Hedda Gabler encounters and phrases her reversal: "Oh what curse is it that makes everything I touch turn ludicrous and mean?"

An even more frightful irony awaits Hedda than Lövborg's shabby death. She hoped to gain vicariously through him that freedom she longs for—escape from the boring, restrictive middle-class society of Tesman—which, because of her nearly pathological fear of scandal, she dared not seize for herself. Actually, the opposite results. Judge Brack recognizes her pistol and uses his knowledge to blackmail her. She is, she says, now "subject" to his "will" and "demands. A slave, a slave then!" Her actions have led not to the freedom she sought, but to slavery. She kills herself to remain free. But still the irony rings through her act, for the course of actions she undertakes to grasp "life"—true life as opposed to the slow stagnation of the Tesman household—leads in fact to death.

Irony based on this kind of exact reversal of intent is not uncommon in great tragedy. Oedipus leaves Corinth to free himself from the prediction of the oracle that he will kill his father and marry his mother, but each step he takes toward escape leads him nearer to the fulfillment of the oracle. Othello sets out to kill Desdemona in the manner of a judge executing justice on a criminal, but he ends by discovering that he is a criminal guilty of a ghastly crime, and is forced to judge and execute himself.

Having distinguished the general nature of the plot as the *actual events of a play*, we can now discuss the constituent parts of a plot and the ways in which these are related. Ordinarily, a description of the events that make up a plot will include only the major occurrences. Hedda Gabler returns from her wedding trip, is visited by Mrs. Elvsted who tells her what has happened to Eilert Lövborg. Hedda then meets Lövborg and persuades him to go to Judge Brack's party. Lövborg loses the manuscript of his new book, Tesman finds it, and Hedda burns it. She then persuades Lövborg to kill himself, but he dies in an unpleasant accident, and Judge Brack, knowing of Hedda's implication, tries to control her by threatening scandal. She shoots herself in order to escape. Describing the plot in this way amounts to no more than telling the *story* of the play and provides little or no insight into its meaning. We only recount the obvious.

If plot is to be a useful tool for dramatic analysis, we must refine our definition. We can begin by sharpening the meaning of the word "events." When we recount the *story*, the only events dealt with are the largest, the grossest of happenings. But is not Hedda's reaction to Miss Tesman's bonnet just as much an "event" as her suicide? A plot is actually constructed of a great many events, some ordinary and apparently trivial, others more unusual and obviously critical; if the play is artistically made, every event has meaning. We must accustom ourselves to thinking of the plot as the totality of events, not as a few crucial occurrences surrounded by a number of unimportant, expository details, if we are to understand plot in its most significant sense: a *continuous movement* in a certain direction. This movement in a great play is as much present, though muted, in the drawing of a shade, the theft of a pair of red boots, as it is in more spectacular events, such as the burning of a manuscript or the destruction of a town. The larger events, the kind we select when telling the story, are the culmination of the smaller events that have preceded them. Firing the pistol at Judge Brack and burning Lövborg's manuscript are crucial events in *Hedda Gabler*—anyone telling the story will probably include them—but these spectacularly destructive acts gain full meaning only when we realize that they serve to focus a number of Hedda's less obviously destructive acts, such as refusing to admit that she is pregnant, treating her husband and his aunt cruelly, rejecting the flowers, and insisting that Tesman's precarious financial and professional affairs are none of her concern.

Plot properly understood, then, includes not only the major events, but *all* the actions and occurrences of the play. Ordinarily, a dramatist plots his play so that a number of these minor events *build up* to an explosive scene in which an obviously crucial event occurs. Ibsen is predictably regular in his use of this plot pattern. The movement in each of the four acts of *Hedda Gabler* builds from quiet, ordinary events at the beginning to some spectacular decision or violent action at the end. Just as each act moves from calm to *crisis,* so the crises of the four acts, taken together, form an ascending scale in which the crisis of each new act is more violent than that of the last, with the *climax* of the play, Hedda's suicide, coming at the very end. One school of dramatic criticism explains this pattern, which is a fairly common one, as the release and tightening of tension necessary to keep the spectator interested without exhausting him emotionally. It may do this, but its most important function is to give concrete form to the playwright's sense of the characteristic movement of the affairs of men: long, slow periods in which apparently nothing happens suddenly culminate in a burst of action, which releases the energy built up previously, just as lightning releases in a flash a slowly accumulated electrical charge.

We must always pay close attention to the particular manner in which scenes of comparative rest and scenes of direct action are spaced, for this is one of the playwright's principal devices for giving form to his sense of the rhythm of life. In some plays—Chekhov's, for example—the body of the work consists of what appear to be trivial happenings. Nothing important seems to happen until the end of the play, when all the powers that have been collecting underneath the surface explode in one violent act. Some modern dramatists have attempted to recreate *only* the dull sameness of lives that *never* reach a climax. In Samuel Beckett's *Waiting for Godot,* for example, the two characters who are waiting for someone to appear when the play begins are still waiting at the end. In *Mother Courage,* however, the brief intervals of comparative peace simply emphasize the fact that life is one crisis after another. Clearly, the plots that Ibsen, Chekhov, Beckett, and Brecht constructed have quite different "rhythms," and these rhythms are a fundamental part of the meaning of the plays. No one rhythm is inherently superior to the others—though Ibsen's is the most traditional. Each reproduces the playwright's estimate of the basic rhythm of life. We can judge its effectiveness only by observing how well it is realized and how well it supports the vision of life created by the other details of the play.

Now that we have extended our definition of plot to cover *all* of the events of the play and have taken into account plot rhythm, we must examine the causal relationship between the events that comprise plot. To describe a plot accurately, it is not enough to recount the events *chronologically;* it is necessary to explain how the events are related. E. M. Forster in his *Aspects of the Novel* says that "the King died and then the Queen died" is a story, but that "the King died and then the Queen died of grief" is a plot. In other words, according to Forster, plot requires a cause-and-effect relationship between events. This common view goes back to the *Poetics,* in which Aristotle wrote that a well-constructed tragic plot "must neither begin nor end at haphazard" but must be a whole.

A whole is that which has a beginning, a middle, and an end. A beginning is that which does not itself follow anything by causal necessity, but after which something naturally is or comes to be. An end, on the contrary, is that which itself naturally follows some other thing, either by necessity, or as a rule, but has nothing following it. A middle is that which follows something, as some other thing follows it.

Most tragic drama has this cause-and-effect progression. Among the plays in this volume, *Hedda Gabler* provides us with a perfect example. Because Hedda wants to send Lövborg out as her agent to live for her, to "be a free man," she says, "for all his days," she must first break up his relationship with Mrs. Elvsted, who acts as a restraining, civilizing force on the wild Lövborg. Once Hedda has set her plan in motion, she follows it relentlessly, and each succeeding step—Lövborg's drunkenness, the loss of his manuscript, Hedda's giving him the pistol, his death, and hers—follows inevitably from what has gone before; not one of the steps could have occurred without the event that preceded it. We may speak therefore of a chain of cause and effect.

The use of such Aristotelian terms as "probable" and "necessary" to describe the relationship of the events that form plot is in some ways misleading. To say that one event must necessarily follow another in a play is to suggest that this particular sequence is as inevitable as is that which follows the introduction of two parts of hydrogen to one part of oxygen at a particular temperature and pressure. In the latter case only one result is possible, but in a play any event may have a variety of possible consequences. *Hedda Gabler* could end in a number of ways. Instead of shooting herself, Hedda might be killed by Tesman; Lövborg might return to kill her before killing himself; or she might kill Judge Brack and be executed for the crime. Speculations of this kind are idle, of course, but they serve to make the point that the *exact* outcome of an event is not as predictable in the drama, or in human life, as it would be in science. However, no ending is really possible for *Hedda Gabler* that does not involve the death of the protagonist, and Ibsen's choice, suicide, is the most proper form for her death to take because Hedda has been "killing herself" piece by piece throughout the play. Her ultimate death by suicide may then be said to be a "probable or necessary" consequence of her previous actions because it grows inevitably from her consistent refusal to participate in life. In any probable or necessary sequence, the dramatist is free to create any particular event he chooses, but no event can reverse or negate the trend established by preceding events.

No matter what variations are made in this plot pattern, it remains essentially a cause-and-effect progression in which every event in the play results from the initial act; given *that* act, the cause-and-effect type of plot requires that *this* event must follow. But it would be a mistake to assume, as Forster and most critics have, that the cause-and-effect relationship is the only true plot pattern. It is the most suitable plot for tragedy. Tragedy assumes a world in which man makes a choice and abides by the inevitable consequences of that choice. Hedda Gabler puts the matter more simply: "They say, as you make your bed, so you must lie." Tragic life is an iron chain of causation in which the characters can never escape the consequences of their acts, which are usually performed in ignorance of what the results will be.

Comedy shows life from a different perspective and therefore makes use of a different type of plot. In comedy, character is neither so constant nor so important that it can determine the course of events. Men make foolish mistakes in comedy, and for a time it looks as if these mistakes will be fatal, but at the opportune moment some stroke of good luck occurs and all is well. A will is discovered revealing that the poor young man who loves the wealthy girl is really well-born and incredibly rich; a wealthy uncle, hitherto not heard from, returns to the country at the right moment to reward the virtuous nephew and punish the wicked one; or the wife and child, whom the tyrant thought he had killed in his jealousy twenty years before, miraculously turn out to have been saved. The world of comedy is filled with good fortune and unexpected surprise; therefore the comic plot shows sudden changes and effects that have no causes, at least no cause in what has gone before in the play. The introduction of some person from outside the play or the use of some fortuitous happening to resolve the plot is known as a *deus ex machina,* literally "the god from the machine," referring to the occasional practice in the Greek theater of lowering a god onto the stage from a machine to settle the issues of the play.

The point to be made is that there is no one "right" kind of plot, no type of relationship between events that is inherently superior to all other types. The dramatist connects the events that make up the play in the manner that will best reflect the relationship between events in the world as he understands it. Brecht's *Mother Courage*, for example, has an *episodic plot*, which is usually said, following Aristotle, to be an inferior type of plot arrangement. The more traditional plot arrangement is one in which X causes Y and Y leads inevitably to Z. The plot of *Mother Courage* might be described as X, X, X, since no necessary relationship exists between events. The play consists of a series of scenes, each of which displays the same forces in conflict, the brutal world and the sharp-witted Mother Courage trying to preserve life and family. The scenes are related *thematically*, each one presenting a variation on the central theme of the play, but it cannot be said that the situation in Scene 10 is the result of what Mother Courage did in Scene 1. It might be argued that the plot develops, that it moves toward a climax, for the world grinds Mother Courage down—though it never defeats her—robbing her of one child after another until all are gone. But there is no climax in the ordinary sense, for there is no real change: at the end of the play as at the beginning the two ancient antagonists, destruction and creation, the world and Mother Courage, are left locked in a battle that will never cease. In this play the episodic plot is not a failure but a great success, for it shows consistently and perfectly Brecht's view of a world where there is no longer any necessary connection between events, only the certainty that the war in Sweden will occur again in Germany, in Poland, in Bohemia, that the army will always want the young men, that the rapist will always be waiting for the daughter, and that the wagon will always be hard to pull.

Having examined the nature of the plot, we must now consider the question of the number of plots possible in a play. Aristotle laid down the rule (and the classicists have maintained it until this day) that the action of a tragedy must be unified, that it cannot consist of episodes or parts "which follow one another without any probable or necessary connection." This has traditionally been interpreted to mean that all the events in a play must contribute to one central plot, that the dramatist must present one story, and one story only. But during the Renaissance the English playwrights frequently built their plays around two or more plots, which crossed one another only rarely or not at all. In Robert Greene's *Friar Bacon and Friar Bungay*, for example, there are two quite distinct plots, one involving the romantic loves of Margaret, "the fair maid of Fressingham," and the other dealing with the magical exploits of Roger Bacon and his apprentice, Friar Bungay. Margaret and Bacon never meet and do not affect one another's destiny. It would at first appear that Greene wanted to provide a mixed fare of love and magic to satisfy the varied interests of his audience, but a closer look at the play reveals that Greene is suggesting that both beauty and magic—or the learning that magic represents—are related, god-given powers, which must be used with care and for proper purposes.

Shakespeare's double plots are never so separated. For example, the plot involving Gloucester and his two sons is a distinct plot in *King Lear,* running parallel to the plot of Lear and his three daughters. But Gloucester is one of Lear's nobles; he encounters the King at several points on their respective journeys, and at one point he risks his life to save him. The multiple plot is managed in the same way in *I Henry IV.* Here three plots are distinguishable: the first dealing with Falstaff and the Boarshead Tavern, a second centering on King Henry and the palace at Westminster, and a third involving Hotspur in his northern castle. The characters in each plot are intensely aware of what is going on in the other plots, and at the conclusion of the play the characters from the three plots join at the great battle of Shrewsbury where Hotspur is killed. By strict classical standards *I Henry IV* is not a well-constructed play, for the three plot lines are distinguishable throughout the play, and this means that the action is not one and unified. But does it mean this? When we look closely at these three plots we discover that Shakespeare has paralleled them in a remarkable fashion. A plot to rob some travelers, planned in the Boarshead Tavern, is paralleled by a plot to steal a kingdom, planned in the palace. A stately council scene at Westminster is followed by a mock council in the alehouse. The preparations for a battle, in which chivalric knights anticipate winning great honor, is followed by a cynical preparation for the same battle, in which an officer commissioned to draft a company of soldiers takes bribes to release the well-to-do and able, enlisting only the dregs of the population with the cynical comment that they will fill a ditch as well as their betters.

What Shakespeare and other Elizabethan playwrights discovered was a new kind of plot unity, not the Aristotelian unity of a single chain of "probable or necessary" events, but a unity based on the principle of *parallelism.* Different kinds of people do the same things—plot a theft, prepare for war, hold a council. The single plot is duplicated and distributed to all levels of society.

The values derived from this type of plot construction will depend on the skill and the interests of the particular playwright, but it will be useful to outline a few of the major possibilities. First of all, the multiple plot has a potential for making universal the image of life presented in the play. The duplication of the same problems and the same patterns of events on two or more social levels suggests that these particular problems and patterns are common to all humanity rather than peculiar to one person at one time. The multiple plot also allows the playwright to provide a perspective on his plots or to suggest a complicated attitude toward them. To juxtapose a plot to overthrow a king with a plot to hold up travelers on the highway is to suggest that the difference between usurpation and armed robbery is not so great as we might think, that the difference is one of degree, not of kind. But comments of this nature always work in both directions. If Falstaff's cynically realistic comments about the nature of war mock Hotspur's romanticism, then Hotspur's idealism, courage, and energy force us to question Falstaff's military "prudence," his reduction of all life to a whole skin and a full belly.

The most obvious form of the multiple plot disappeared from the stage about the middle of the seventeenth century, but in one way or another the multiple plot has always been and still is a standard dramatic technique, although the different strands may no longer stand out so clearly as the three plot lines of *1 Henry IV. Hedda Gabler* appears to be a play plotted according to the Aristotelian formula: one plot line only, and that consisting of a necessary or probable series of events. But though they intertwine, it is still possible to discern several plots moving through the play. Mrs. Elvsted is trapped, as Hedda is, in a marriage of convenience. She married Sheriff Elvsted because he needed a housekeeper and she had no other place to go; Hedda, getting too old to play the belle any longer and with no other offers, marries Tesman, who also was moved not by love but by her beauty and the opportunity to marry someone from a family that was socially superior to his own. Both women hate the domestic cages in which they are placed, but both face scandal if they leave. Both see in Lövborg a man who transcends their dreary circumstances. But here, because of their differing natures, their paths (plots) divide. Mrs. Elvsted first nourishes the creative instincts in Lövborg, restores him to normal life, and, finally, courageously leaves her home to follow and protect him. Hedda, motivated by her conflicting fear of scandal and her fascination with absolute freedom, first encourages Lövborg and then refuses to take him as a lover; after he leaves and ruins himself, she recaptures him and sends him out to drunkenness and death. It might appear that Hedda has triumphed and

Mrs. Elvsted has lost; actually, the endings of the two plots force a different judgment. Mrs. Elvsted, though she has lost Lövborg, remains creative, for she still has his manuscript, which will permit her, with Tesman's aid, to reconstruct "the future of civilization." Hedda loses Lövborg, her freedom, her husband, and finally her life. Since her way has been the way of death, it leads to death. Mrs. Elvsted's way has been the way of creation and it leads to creation. Dissimilar natures faced with similar circumstances have achieved different results, and the plot of Mrs. Elvsted provides a perspective on the plot of Hedda.

Since both characters are involved in one central plot turning on the struggle for Eilert Lövborg, it may be technically correct to consider the play as having a single plot. But it is often useful for critical purposes to think of each major character as having a separate plot and to investigate the similarities and differences of these plots. Mother Courage and her three children face the same problems and, acting on different values, come to different conclusions. Her three children die—Eilif through valor, Swiss Cheese through honesty, and Kattrin through idealism—while resourcefulness, cunning, and pertinacity keep their mother alive. But can we conclude from these facts that the plot unambiguously demonstrates the superiority of Mother Courage's values and actions? Brecht would disagree violently. Does not Kattrin's dying to save the people of a town, and particularly its children, suggest that there are values more important than survival? The play really leaves us with an unanswerable question: Who has met this brutal world of war and struggle most successfully, the dead girl or the old woman, staggering on, pulling her wagon to another battlefield?

It may be a simple enough matter to see *what really happens* in *Hedda Gabler*—a woman balanced on the razor edge of a desire for freedom and a fear of it destroys herself—but in plays like *Mother Courage* the plots often lead not to a flat definition of the meaning of a particular course of action, but to a sharply etched image of an abiding human problem that defies any easy solution. Are the bodies of Romeo and Juliet lying together in the gloomy tomb of the Capulets an image of triumph or defeat? Have they won a battle with life and made their love eternal? Or are they merely the pitiful victims of their own impetuousness and of the hatred that surrounds them? The play poses the question rather than answers it, suggesting that life, at least tragic life, is always double in nature, always a mystery, and that what we gain in one way we must pay for in another.

In summary: a plot is composed of a series of related events. These events are initiated by the characters trying to realize their motives, or by the world pressing in the direction which it is its nature to move in, or by some interaction of these forces. What happens in the play happens to the characters and to the world, and is manifested in their changed conditions and situations. But the dramatic focus is not finally on the characters or the world; it is on "what happens," on the plot, on the fundamental pattern of movement and change, which is given substantial form by the events of the play. What the dramatist imitates, as Aristotle pointed out, is "action," and the plot is his primary mode of imitation. Everything in a play exists to give form to the plot, and the plot in turn represents, or imitates, what a dramatist conceives as the recurring movement of human life in time.

ANTIGONE

BY

SOPHOCLES

At different times during his life, Sophocles (496–406 B.C.) wrote dramatic versions of all the major events in the tragic history of the ruling house of Thebes. *Oedipus the King* tells the grim story of the infant son of Jocasta and Laius, the king and queen of Thebes. When the child Oedipus is born, the oracle foretells that he will grow up to kill his father and marry his mother. Frightened by the prophecy, the rulers of Thebes pierce the ankles of the child—thus the name Oedipus, or "swollen foot"—and expose him on the mountain to die, but he is found and saved by an old shepherd who carries the child to Corinth, where he is adopted by the king of that city. Grown to manhood, Oedipus consults the oracle about his future and is told that he will kill his father and marry his mother. Thinking to escape his fate, Oedipus flees from his supposed parents and comes to a cross-roads where he meets Laius and kills him in a violent argument over the right of way. He then passes on toward Thebes and encounters the Sphinx—a half-woman, half-beast who is terrifying the country-side—and vanquishes her. He enters Thebes in triumph, and is rewarded for his feat by marriage to Jocasta. Several children are born to them before Oedipus learns that even as he sought to escape the fate predicted by the oracle, he fulfilled it. Overwhelmed by shame, plunged from being the greatest of men to the most miserable, he blinds himself and goes out, an exile from his city and the human community, to wander the land, led by his young daughter Antigone. After many years and much suffering they come at last to the grove at Colonus, outside Athens, where Sophocles picks up the story again in his last play, *Oedipus at Colonus*. Here this aged man who has tasted all sufferings possible is at last accepted by the gods, who have seemingly hated him so long, and becomes, like Hercules, who also endured long and painful trials, a god himself.

But the sufferings of his family are still not at an end. The two sons of the incestuous marriage, Eteocles and Polyneices, are destined to kill one another, and the daughter Antigone to die by her own hand. Polyneices attacks Thebes, now ruled by Creon, the brother of Jocasta, who serves as Eteocles' regent, and is killed on the walls by his brother, who then dies himself. Creon, as defender of the state and the public virtues, gives Eteocles a hero's funeral but leaves the body of the traitor Polyneices to rot in the sun on the plain outside the city. Antigone believes that the laws of the gods, which demand that a kinsman bury his relatives and thus release the spirit from the body, take precedence over the laws of the state, and she therefore risks her life to sprinkle some dust on the decaying corpse, an act that brings her into conflict with Creon and the state and leads, ultimately, to her own death.

In discussions of *Antigone* critics have tended to choose sides. Some have argued that Antigone is right and that sacred matters, the laws of the gods, always take precedence over the laws of the state. Others have argued with equal strength that Creon is right and that the good of the city must come before any "higher laws," for it is in the city that man must live. The question is complicated by the unattractive natures of Antigone and Creon; but it now seems clear that Sophocles was not writing a *thesis play* proving that man should obey the state or the gods, but rather a tragedy in which one good in human life is somehow always opposed to another good. The history of the royal Theban family was for Sophocles not an object lesson in morality but an image of tragic man, capable of reaching the heights of greatness and yet at the same time doomed in his very greatness to degradation and destruction.

In *Antigone* plot stands out as a distinct element of construction, quite separate from the characters and the world of the play. The major characters, Antigone and Creon, are surely and definitely, if not elaborately, drawn, and their motives are sharply defined. The play also has a vivid setting: the center of the city of Thebes, which has just been attacked by Polyneices' fierce and determined army. During the course of the action the body of Polyneices lies unburied in the sun just outside the gates, a fact that no one in the play can forget. But despite the clarity and economy with which the characters and the world are constructed, and the ways in which they help to shape events, the dramatic focus is not on them.

It used to be common for critics to argue that *Antigone* is a poorly constructed play because the heroine disappears halfway through the action, and we hear of her only by report after that time. Such an argument makes sense only if one believes the play to be a study of the character of Antigone. If one argues that it is a character study of Creon, then one is faced with the difficulty that he emerges as the central figure only after Antigone has been sent to her death. Had Sophocles been interested in providing a dramatic study of a particular character, he would have focused his play on that character from beginning to end, as Ibsen concentrated his play on Hedda Gabler. A careful reading of *Antigone* shows that neither Antigone nor Creon singly is the true subject, but that the play is designed to show a pattern of events, a pattern that emerges in the life of Antigone *and* in the life of Creon, as well as in the lives of the brothers Eteocles and Polyneices and a number of other figures mentioned, chiefly by the Chorus, during the course of the action. Choose one good to the exclusion of another—and it seems to be the nature of great men to do so—the play shows, and *this* will inevitably happen. *This* is the plot of the play, and the play is shaped in all its parts to reveal and define this plot.

Sophocles lived in the great age of Athens. He grew up in the brightness of the day that dawned with the Athenian defeat of the Persians at Marathon and Salamis, and he died before his city was finally defeated by Sparta and her allies. During his lifetime the Athenians brought to perfection not only a political and artistic ideal, but an ideal of character, an *ethos*. The key term in the Greeks' new definition of man was *harmony,* a balance and adjustment of thought and action that led to proportionate expression of man's many faculties and abilities. The ideal man was philosopher, artist, soldier, and politician because all of these activities expressed him, and because in each he could shape himself and his world to that harmonious balanced form which eliminated all violent exaggeration and disordered enthusiasm. It is against this ideal of completeness, of proportion, and of control—in short, of wisdom—that the characters of Antigone and Creon and their ultimate fate must be seen.

But *Antigone* is not a "problem play." That is, it does not merely show us wrong conduct and provide a forceful object lesson in what happens when men become "unbalanced" and pursue one value to the exclusion of other equally necessary values. Instead, it suggests that it is in the very nature of men—at least of heroes—to choose this course, even though they know better; and, furthermore, that political and

social situations regularly occur that require a choice of one value because other values directly conflict with it.

Antigone was presented at the annual festival of Dionysus (March–
April) around the year 442 B.C. A description of the Greek theater
and of the occasion of Greek dramatic production appears in the
glossary.

PERSONS REPRESENTED

ANTIGONE   HAIMON
ISMENE   TEIRESIAS
EURYDICE   A SENTRY
CREON   A MESSENGER
                          CHORUS

᪐ Scene: *Before the palace of Creon, King of Thebes. A central double door, and two lateral doors. A platform extends the length of the façade, and from this platform three steps lead down into the "orchestra," or chorus-ground.* Time: *dawn of the day after the repulse of the Argive army from the assault on Thebes.*

The Antigone of Sophocles: An English Version by Dudley Fitts and Robert Fitzgerald, copyright 1939 by Harcourt, Brace & World, Inc. and reprinted with their permission.

Prologue

[ANTIGONE *and* ISMENE *enter from the central door of
the Palace.*]

ANTIGONE. Ismene, dear sister,
   You would think that we had already suffered enough
   For the curse on Oedipus:
   I cannot imagine any grief
   That you and I have not gone through. And now—
   Have they told you of the new decree of our King Creon?
ISMENE. I have heard nothing: I know
   That two sisters lost two brothers, a double death
   In a single hour; and I know that the Argive army
   Fled in the night; but beyond this, nothing.
ANTIGONE. I thought so. And that is why I wanted you
   To come out here with me. There is something we must do.
ISMENE. Why do you speak so strangely?
ANTIGONE. Listen, Ismene:
   Creon buried our brother Eteocles
   With military honors, gave him a soldier's funeral,
   And it was right that he should; but Polyneices,
   Who fought as bravely and died as miserably,—
   They say that Creon has sworn
   No one shall bury him, no one mourn for him,
   But his body must lie in the fields, a sweet treasure
   For carrion birds to find as they search for food.
   That is what they say, and our good Creon is coming here
   To announce it publicly; and the penalty—
   Stoning to death in the public square!
                                      There it is,
   And now you can prove what you are:
   A true sister, or a traitor to your family.

ISMENE. Antigone, you are mad! What could I possibly do?
ANTIGONE. You must decide whether you will help me or not.
ISMENE. I do not understand you. Help you in what?
ANTIGONE. Ismene, I am going to bury him. Will you come?
ISMENE. Bury him! You have just said the new law forbids it.
ANTIGONE. He is my brother. And he is your brother, too.
ISMENE. But think of the danger! Think what Creon will do!
ANTIGONE. Creon is not strong enough to stand in my way.
ISMENE. Ah sister!
     Oedipus died, everyone hating him
     For what his own search brought to light, his eyes
     Ripped out by his own hand; and Iocaste died,
     His mother and wife at once: she twisted the cords
     That strangled her life; and our two brothers died,
     Each killed by the other's sword. And we are left:
     But oh, Antigone,
     Think how much more terrible than these
     Our own death would be if we should go against Creon
     And do what he has forbidden! We are only women,
     We cannot fight with men, Antigone!
     The law is strong, we must give in to the law
     In this thing, and in worse. I beg the Dead
     To forgive me, but I am helpless: I must yield
     To those in authority. And I think it is dangerous business
     To be always meddling.
ANTIGONE.   If that is what you think,
     I should not want you, even if you asked to come.
     You have made your choice, you can be what you want to be.
     But I will bury him; and if I must die,
     I say that this crime is holy: I shall lie down
     With him in death, and I shall be as dear
     To him as he to me.
               It is the dead,
     Not the living, who make the longest demands:
     We die for ever . . .
               You may do as you like,
     Since apparently the laws of the gods mean nothing to you.
ISMENE. They mean a great deal to me; but I have no strength
     To break laws that were made for the public good.
ANTIGONE. That must be your excuse, I suppose. But as for me,
     I will bury the brother I love.
ISMENE.   Antigone,
     I am so afraid for you!
ANTIGONE.   You need not be:
     You have yourself to consider, after all.

ISMENE. But no one must hear of this, you must tell no one!

    I will keep it a secret, I promise!

ANTIGONE.   Oh tell it! Tell everyone!

    Think how they'll hate you when it all comes out

    If they learn that you knew about it all the time!

ISMENE. So fiery! You should be cold with fear.

ANTIGONE. Perhaps. But I am doing only what I must.

ISMENE. But can you do it? I say that you cannot.

ANTIGONE. Very well: when my strength gives out, I shall do no more.

ISMENE. Impossible things should not be tried at all.

ANTIGONE. Go away, Ismene:

    I shall be hating you soon, and the dead will too,

    For your words are hateful. Leave me my foolish plan:

    I am not afraid of the danger; if it means death,

    It will not be the worst of deaths—death without honor.

ISMENE. Go then, if you feel that you must.

    You are unwise,

    But a loyal friend indeed to those who love you.

                       [*Exit into the Palace.* ANTIGONE *goes off, L.*]

                       [*Enter the* CHORUS.]

Párodos

STROPHE 1

CHORUS. Now the long blade of the sun, lying
    Level east to west, touches with glory
    Thebes of the Seven Gates. Open, unlidded
    Eye of golden day! O marching light
    Across the eddy and rush of Dirce's stream,
    Striking the white shields of the enemy
    Thrown headlong backward from the blaze of morning!
CHORAGOS. Polyneices their commander
    Roused them with windy phrases,
    He the wild eagle screaming
    Insults above our land,
    His wings their shields of snow,
    His crest their marshalled helms.

ANTISTROPHE 1

CHORUS. Against our seven gates in a yawning ring
    The famished spears came onward in the night;
    But before his jaws were sated with our blood,
    Or pinefire took the garland of our towers,
    He was thrown back; and as he turned, great Thebes—
    No tender victim for his noisy power—
    Rose like a dragon behind him, shouting war.
CHORAGOS. For God hates utterly
    The bray of bragging tongues;
    And when he beheld their smiling,
    Their swagger of golden helms,
    The frown of his thunder blasted
    Their first man from our walls.

STROPHE 2

CHORUS. We heard his shout of triumph high in the air
          Turn to a scream; far out in a flaming arc
          He fell with his windy torch, and the earth struck him.
          And others storming in fury no less than his
          Found shock of death in the dusty joy of battle.
CHORAGOS. Seven captains at seven gates
          Yielded their clanging arms to the god
          That bends the battle-line and breaks it.
          These two only, brothers in blood,
          Face to face in matchless rage,
          Mirroring each the other's death,
          Clashed in long combat.

ANTISTROPHE 2

CHORUS. But now in the beautiful morning of victory
          Let Thebes of the many chariots sing for joy!
          With hearts for dancing we'll take leave of war:
          Our temples shall be sweet with hymns of praise,
          And the long night shall echo with our chorus.

Scene I

CHORAGOS. But now at last our new King is coming:
Creon of Thebes, Menoikeus' son.
In this auspicious dawn of his reign
What are the new complexities
That shifting Fate has woven for him?
What is his counsel? Why has he summoned
The old men to hear him?

[*Enter* CREON *from the Palace, C. He addresses the*
CHORUS *from the top step.*]

CREON. Gentlemen: I have the honor to inform you that our Ship
of State, which recent storms have threatened to destroy, has
come safely to harbor at last, guided by the merciful wisdom
of Heaven. I have summoned you here this morning because I
know that I can depend upon you: your devotion to King
Laïos was absolute; you never hesitated in your duty to our
late ruler Oedipus; and when Oedipus died, your loyalty was
transferred to his children. Unfortunately, as you know, his
two sons, the princes Eteocles and Polyneices, have killed each
other in battle; and I, as the next in blood, have succeeded to
the full power of the throne.

I am aware, of course, that no Ruler can expect complete loyalty
from his subjects until he has been tested in office. Nevertheless, I say to you at the very outset that I have nothing but
contempt for the kind of Governor who is afraid, for whatever reason, to follow the course that he knows is best for the
State; and as for the man who sets private friendship above
the public welfare,—I have no use for him, either. I call God
to witness that if I saw my country headed for ruin, I should
not be afraid to speak out plainly; and I need hardly remind
you that I would never have any dealings with an enemy of

the people. No one values friendship more highly than I; but we must remember that friends made at the risk of wrecking our Ship are not real friends at all.

These are my principles, at any rate, and that is why I have made the following decision concerning the sons of Oedipus: Eteocles, who died as a man should die, fighting for his country, is to be buried with full military honors, with all the ceremony that is usual when the greatest heroes die; but his brother Polyneices, who broke his exile to come back with fire and sword against his native city and the shrines of his fathers' gods, whose one idea was to spill the blood of his blood and sell his own people into slavery—Polyneices, I say, is to have no burial: no man is to touch him or say the least prayer for him; he shall lie on the plain, unburied; and the birds and the scavenging dogs can do with him whatever they like.

This is my command, and you can see the wisdom behind it. As long as I am King, no traitor is going to be honored with the loyal man. But whoever shows by word and deed that he is on the side of the State,—he shall have my respect while he is living, and my reverence when he is dead.

CHORAGOS. If that is your will, Creon son of Menoikeus,
You have the right to enforce it: we are yours.

CREON. That is my will. Take care that you do your part.

CHORAGOS. We are old men: let the younger ones carry it out.

CREON. I do not mean that: the sentries have been appointed.

CHORAGOS. Then what is it that you would have us do?

CREON. You will give no support to whoever breaks this law.

CHORAGOS. Only a crazy man is in love with death!

CREON. And death it is; yet money talks, and the wisest
Have sometimes been known to count a few coins too many.

[*Enter* SENTRY *from L.*]

SENTRY. I'll not say that I'm out of breath from running, King, because every time I stopped to think about what I have to tell you, I felt like going back. And all the time a voice kept saying, "You fool, don't you know you're walking straight into trouble?"; and then another voice: "Yes, but if you let somebody else get the news to Creon first, it will be even worse than that for you!" But good sense won out, at least I hope it was good sense, and here I am with a story that makes no sense at all; but I'll tell it anyhow, because, as they say, what's going to happen's going to happen, and—

CREON. Come to the point. What have you to say?

SENTRY. I did not do it. I did not see who did it. You must not punish me for what someone else has done.

CREON. A comprehensive defense! More effective, perhaps,
      If I knew its purpose. Come: what is it?
SENTRY. A dreadful thing . . . I don't know how to put it—
CREON. Out with it!
SENTRY.   Well, then;
      The dead man—
                        Polyneices—
      [*Pause. The* SENTRY *is overcome, fumbles for words.*
            CREON *waits impassively.*]
                        out there—
                              someone,—
New dust on the slimy flesh!
                  [*Pause. No sign from* CREON.]
Someone has given it burial that way, and
Gone . . .
      [*Long pause.* CREON *finally speaks with deadly con-
                  trol:*]
CREON. And the man who dared do this?
SENTRY.   I swear I
      Do not know! You must believe me!
                              Listen:
      The ground was dry, not a sign of digging, no,
      Not a wheeltrack in the dust, no trace of anyone.
      It was when they relieved us this morning: and one of them,
      The corporal, pointed to it.
                              There it was,
      The strangest—
                  Look:
      The body, just mounded over with light dust: you see?
      Not buried really, but as if they'd covered it
      Just enough for the ghost's peace. And no sign
      Of dogs or any wild animal that had been there.

      And then what a scene there was! Every man of us
      Accusing the other: we all proved the other man did it,
      We all had proof that we could not have done it.
      We were ready to take hot iron in our hands,
      Walk through fire, swear by all the gods,
      It was not I!
      I do not know who it was, but it was not I!
            [CREON'S *rage has been mounting steadily, but the*
                  SENTRY *is too intent upon his story to notice it.*]
      And then, when this came to nothing, someone said
      A thing that silenced us and made us stare

Down at the ground: you had to be told the news,
And one of us had to do it! We threw the dice,
And the bad luck fell to me. So here I am,
No happier to be here than you are to have me:
Nobody likes the man who brings bad news.

CHORAGOS. I have been wondering, King: can it be that the gods have
   done this?

[Furiously]

CREON. Stop!
Must you doddering wrecks
Go out of your heads entirely? "The gods!"
Intolerable!
The gods favor this corpse? Why? How had he served them?
Tried to loot their temples, burn their images,
Yes, and the whole State, and its laws with it!
Is it your senile opinion that the gods love to honor bad men?
A pious thought!—
                    No, from the very beginning
There have been those who have whispered together,
Stiff-necked anarchists, putting their heads together,
Scheming against me in alleys. These are the men,
And they have bribed my own guard to do this thing.

[Sententiously]

Money!
There's nothing in the world so demoralizing as money.
Down go your cities,
Homes gone, men gone, honest hearts corrupted,
Crookedness of all kinds, and all for money!

[To SENTRY]

                                        But you—!
I swear by God and by the throne of God,
The man who has done this thing shall pay for it!
Find that man, bring him here to me, or your death
Will be the least of your problems: I'll string you up
Alive, and there will be certain ways to make you
Discover your employer before you die;
And the process may teach you a lesson you seem to have missed:
The dearest profit is sometimes all too dear:
That depends on the source. Do you understand me?
A fortune won is often misfortune.

SENTRY. King, may I speak?
CREON.   Your very voice distresses me.
SENTRY. Are you sure that it is my voice, and not your conscience?
CREON. By God, he wants to analyze me now!

SENTRY. It is not what I say, but what has been done, that hurts you.
CREON. You talk too much.
SENTRY.   Maybe; but I've done nothing.
CREON. Sold your soul for some silver: that's all you've done.
SENTRY. How dreadful it is when the right judge judges wrong!
CREON. Your figures of speech
     May entertain you now; but unless you bring me the man,
     You will get little profit from them in the end.

                                   [*Exit* CREON *into the Palace.*]
SENTRY. "Bring me the man"—!
     I'd like nothing better than bringing him the man!
     But bring him or not, you have seen the last of me here.
     At any rate, I am safe!   [*Exit* SENTRY.]

Ode I

CHORUS. Numberless are the world's wonders, but none
        More wonderful than man; the stormgray sea
        Yields to his prows, the huge crests bear him high;
        Earth, holy and inexhaustible, is graven
        With shining furrows where his plows have gone
        Year after year, the timeless labor of stallions.

ANTISTROPHE 1

The lightboned birds and beasts that cling to cover,
The lithe fish lighting their reaches of dim water,
All are taken, tamed in the net of his mind;
The lion on the hill, the wild horse windy-maned,
Resign to him; and his blunt yoke has broken
The sultry shoulders of the mountain bull.

STROPHE 2

Words also, and thought as rapid as air,
He fashions to his good use; statecraft is his,
And his the skill that deflects the arrows of snow,
The spears of winter rain: from every wind
He has made himself secure—from all but one:
In the late wind of death he cannot stand.

ANTISTROPHE 2

O clear intelligence, force beyond all measure!
O fate of man, working both good and evil!
When the laws are kept, how proudly his city stands!
When the laws are broken, what of his city then?
Never may the anárchic man find rest at my hearth,
Never be it said that my thoughts are his thoughts.

Scene 2

[*Re-enter* SENTRY *leading* ANTIGONE.]

CHORAGOS. What does this mean? Surely this captive woman
  Is the Princess, Antigone. Why should she be taken?
SENTRY. Here is the one who did it! We caught her
  In the very act of burying him.—Where is Creon?
CHORAGOS. Just coming from the house.

[*Enter* CREON, *C.*]

CREON.   What has happened?
  Why have you come back so soon?

[*Expansively*]

SENTRY.   O King,
  A man should never be too sure of anything: I would have sworn
  That you'd not see me here again: your anger
  Frightened me so, and the things you threatened me with;
  But how could I tell then
  That I'd be able to solve the case so soon?

  No dice-throwing this time: I was only too glad to come!

  Here is this woman. She is the guilty one:
  We found her trying to bury him.
  Take her, then; question her; judge her as you will.
  I am through with the whole thing now, and glád óf it.
CREON. But this is Antigone! Why have you brought her here?
SENTRY. She was burying him, I tell you!

[*Severely*]

CREON.   Is this the truth?
SENTRY. I saw her with my own eyes. Can I say more?
CREON. The details: come, tell me quickly!
SENTRY.   It was like this:
  After those terrible threats of yours, King,

We went back and brushed the dust away from the body.
The flesh was soft by now, and stinking,
So we sat on a hill to windward and kept guard.
No napping this time! We kept each other awake.
But nothing happened until the white round sun
Whirled in the center of the round sky over us:
Then, suddenly,
A storm of dust roared up from the earth, and the sky
Went out, the plain vanished with all its trees
In the stinging dark. We closed our eyes and endured it.
The whirlwind lasted a long time, but it passed;
And then we looked, and there was Antigone!
I have seen
A mother bird come back to a stripped nest, heard
Her crying bitterly a broken note or two
For the young ones stolen. Just so, when this girl
Found the bare corpse, and all her love's work wasted,
She wept, and cried on heaven to damn the hands
That had done this thing.

                And then she brought more dust
And sprinkled wine three times for her brother's ghost.

We ran and took her at once. She was not afraid,
Not even when we charged her with what she had done.
She denied nothing.

                And this was a comfort to me,
And some uneasiness: for it is a good thing
To escape from death, but it is no great pleasure
To bring death to a friend.

                Yet I always say
There is nothing so comfortable as your own safe skin!
                [*Slowly, dangerously*]

CREON. And you, Antigone,
    You with your head hanging,—do you confess this thing?
ANTIGONE. I do. I deny nothing.
                [*To* SENTRY:]
CREON.   You may go.   [*Exit* SENTRY.]
                [*To* ANTIGONE:]
    Tell me, tell me briefly:
    Had you heard my proclamation touching this matter?
ANTIGONE. It was public. Could I help hearing it?
CREON. And yet you dared defy the law.
ANTGIONE.   I dared.
    It was not God's proclamation. That final Justice
    That rules the world below makes no such laws.

Your edict, King, was strong,
But all your strength is weakness itself against
The immortal unrecorded laws of God.
They are not merely now: they were, and shall be,
Operative for ever, beyond man utterly.

I knew I must die, even without your decree:
I am only mortal. And if I must die
Now, before it is my time to die,
Surely this is no hardship: can anyone
Living, as I live, with evil all about me,
Think Death less than a friend? This death of mine
Is of no importance; but if I had left my brother
Lying in death unburied, I should have suffered.
Now I do not.
                    You smile at me. Ah Creon,
Think me a fool, if you like; but it may well be
That a fool convicts me of folly.

CHORAGOS. Like father, like daughter: both headstrong, deaf to reason!
    She has never learned to yield.
CREON.   She has much to learn.
    The inflexible heart breaks first, the toughest iron
    Cracks first, and the wildest horses bend their necks
    At the pull of the smallest curb.
                                Pride? In a slave?
    This girl is guilty of a double insolence,
    Breaking the given laws and boasting of it.
    Who is the man here,
    She or I, if this crime goes unpunished?
    Sister's child, or more than sister's child,
    Or closer yet in blood—she and her sister
    Win bitter death for this!
                    [*To servants:*]
                        Go, some of you,
    Arrest Ismene. I accuse her equally.
    Bring her: you will find her sniffling in the house there.

    Her mind's a traitor: crimes kept in the dark
    Cry for light, and the guardian brain shudders;
    But how much worse than this
    Is brazen boasting of barefaced anarchy!
ANTIGONE. Creon, what more do you want than my death?
CREON.   Nothing.
    That gives me everything.
ANTIGONE.   Then I beg you: kill me.

This talking is a great weariness: your words
Are distasteful to me, and I am sure that mine
Seem so to you. And yet they should not seem so:
I should have praise and honor for what I have done.
All these men here would praise me
Were their lips not frozen shut with fear of you.

                    [*Bitterly*]
Ah the good fortune of kings,
Licensed to say and do whatever they please!

CREON. You are alone here in that opinion.

ANTIGONE. No, they are with me. But they keep their tongues in leash.

CREON. Maybe. But you are guilty, and they are not.

ANTIGONE. There is no guilt in reverence for the dead.

CREON. But Eteocles—was he not your brother too?

ANTIGONE. My brother too.

CREON.   And you insult his memory?

                    [*Softly*]

ANTIGONE. The dead man would not say that I insult it.

CREON. He would: for you honor a traitor as much as him.

ANTIGONE. His own brother, traitor or not, and equal in blood.

CREON. He made war on his country. Eteocles defended it.

ANTIGONE. Nevertheless, there are honors due all the dead.

CREON. But not the same for the wicked as for the just.

ANTIGONE. Ah Creon, Creon,

Which of us can say what the gods hold wicked?

CREON. An enemy is an enemy, even dead.

ANTIGONE. It is my nature to join in love, not hate.

                    [*Finally losing patience*]

CREON. Go join them, then; if you must have your love,
    Find it in hell!

CHORAGOS. But see, Ismene comes:

                    [*Enter* ISMENE, *guarded.*]

Those tears are sisterly, the cloud
That shadows her eyes rains down gentle sorrow.

CREON. You too, Ismene,

Snake in my ordered house, sucking my blood
Stealthily—and all the time I never knew
That these two sisters were aiming at my throne!

                                        Ismene,
Do you confess your share in this crime, or deny it?
Answer me.

ISMENE. Yes, if she will let me say so. I am guilty.

                    [*Coldly*]

ANTIGONE. No, Ismene. You have no right to say so.
    You would not help me, and I will not have you help me.

ISMENE. But now I know what you meant; and I am here
      To join you, to take my share of punishment.
ANTIGONE. The dead man and the gods who rule the dead
      Know whose act this was. Words are not friends.
ISMENE. Do you refuse me, Antigone? I want to die with you:
      I too have a duty that I must discharge to the dead.
ANTIGONE. You shall not lessen my death by sharing it.
ISMENE. What do I care for life when you are dead?
ANTIGONE. Ask Creon. You're always hanging on his opinions.
ISMENE. You are laughing at me. Why, Antigone?
ANTIGONE. It's a joyless laughter, Ismene.
ISMENE.   But can I do nothing?
ANTIGONE. Yes. Save yourself. I shall not envy you.
      There are those who will praise you; I shall have honor, too.
ISMENE. But we are equally guilty!
ANTIGONE.   No more, Ismene.
      You are alive, but I belong to Death.
                    [*To the* CHORUS:]
CREON. Gentlemen, I beg you to observe these girls:
      One has just now lost her mind; the other,
      It seems, has never had a mind at all.
ISMENE. Grief teaches the steadiest minds to waver, King.
CREON. Yours certainly did, when you assumed guilt with the guilty!
ISMENE. But how could I go on living without her?
CREON.   You are.
      She is already dead.
ISMENE.   But your own son's bride!
CREON. There are places enough for him to push his plow.
      I want no wicked women for my sons!
ISMENE. O dearest Haimon, how your father wrongs you!
CREON. I've had enough of your childish talk of marriage!
CHORAGOS. Do you really intend to steal this girl from your son?
CREON. No; Death will do that for me.
CHORAGOS.   Then she must die?
                    [*Ironically*]
CREON. You dazzle me.
                    —But enough of this talk!
                    [*To* GUARDS:]
      You, there, take them away and guard them well:
      For they are but women, and even brave men run
      When they see Death coming.
                    [*Exeunt* ISMENE, ANTIGONE, *and* GUARDS.]

Ode 2

CHORUS. Fortunate is the man who has never tasted God's vengeance!
Where once the anger of heaven has struck, that house is shaken
For ever: damnation rises behind each child
Like a wave cresting out of the black northeast,
When the long darkness under sea roars up
And bursts drumming death upon the windwhipped sand.

ANTISTROPHE 1

I have seen this gathering sorrow from time long past
Loom upon Oedipus' children: generation from generation
Takes the compulsive rage of the enemy god.
So lately this last flower of Oedipus' line
Drank the sunlight! but now a passionate word
And a handful of dust have closed up all its beauty.

STROPHE 2

What mortal arrogance
Transcends the wrath of Zeus?
Sleep cannot lull him, nor the effortless long months
Of the timeless gods: but he is young for ever,
And his house is the shining day of high Olympos.
All that is and shall be,
And all the past, is his.
No pride on earth is free of the curse of heaven.

ANTISTROPHE 2

The straying dreams of men
May bring them ghosts of joy:

But as they drowse, the waking embers burn them;
Or they walk with fíxed éyes, as blind men walk.
But the ancient wisdom speaks for our own time:

      Fate works most for woe
      With Folly's fairest show.

Man's little pleasure is the spring of sorrow.

Scene 3

CHORAGOS. But here is Haimon, King, the last of all your sons.
   Is it grief for Antigone that brings him here,
   And bitterness at being robbed of his bride?
                    [*Enter* HAIMON.]
CREON. We shall soon see, and no need of diviners.
                                                   —Son,
      You have heard my final judgment on that girl:
      Have you come here hating me, or have you come
      With deference and with love, whatever I do?
HAIMON. I am your son, father. You are my guide.
      You make things clear for me, and I obey you.
      No marriage means more to me than your continuing wisdom.
CREON. Good. That is the way to behave: subordinate
      Everything else, my son, to your father's will.
      This is what a man prays for, that he may get
      Sons attentive and dutiful in his house,
      Each one hating his father's enemies,
      Honoring his father's friends. But if his sons
      Fail him, if they turn out unprofitably,
      What has he fathered but trouble for himself
      And amusement for the malicious?
                                       So you are right
      Not to lose your head over this woman.
      Your pleasure with her would soon grow cold, Haimon,
      And then you'd have a hellcat in bed and elsewhere.
      Let her find her husband in Hell!
      Of all the people in this city, only she
      Has had contempt for my law and broken it.

Do you want me to show myself weak before the people?
Or to break my sworn word? No, and I will not.
The woman dies.
I suppose she'll plead "family ties." Well, let her.
If I permit my own family to rebel,
How shall I earn the world's obedience?
Show me the man who keeps his house in hand,
He's fit for public authority.

                         I'll have no dealings
With law-breakers, critics of the government:
Whoever is chosen to govern should be obeyed—
Must be obeyed, in all things, great and small,
Just and unjust! O Haimon,
The man who knows how to obey, and that man only,
Knows how to give commands when the time comes.
You can depend on him, no matter how fast
The spears come: he's a good soldier, he'll stick it out.

Anarchy, anarchy! Show me a greater evil!
This is why cities tumble and the great houses rain down,
This is what scatters armies!

No, no: good lives are made so by discipline.
We keep the laws then, and the lawmakers,
And no woman shall seduce us. If we must lose,
Let's lose to a man, at least! Is a woman stronger than we?
CHORAGOS. Unless time has rusted my wits,
    What you say, King, is said with point and dignity.
                    [*Boyishly earnest*]
HAIMON. Father:
    Reason is God's crowning gift to man, and you are right
    To warn me against losing mine. I cannot say—
    I hope that I shall never want to say!—that you
    Have reasoned badly. Yet there are other men
    Who can reason, too; and their opinions might be helpful.
    You are not in a position to know everything
    That people say or do, or what they feel:
    Your temper terrifies them—everyone
    Will tell you only what you like to hear.
    But I, at any rate, can listen; and I have heard them
    Muttering and whispering in the dark about this girl.
    They say no woman has ever, so unreasonably,
    Died so shameful a death for a generous act:
    "She covered her brother's body. Is this indecent?

She kept him from dogs and vultures. Is this a crime?
Death?—She should have all the honor that we can give her!"

This is the way they talk out there in the city.

You must believe me:
Nothing is closer to me than your happiness.
What could be closer? Must not any son
Value his father's fortune as his father does his?
I beg you, do not be unchangeable:
Do not believe that you alone can be right.
The man who thinks that,
The man who maintains that only he has the power
To reason correctly, the gift to speak, the soul—
A man like that, when you know him, turns out empty.

It is not reason never to yield to reason!

In flood time you can see how some trees bend,
And because they bend, even their twigs are safe,
While stubborn trees are torn up, roots and all.
And the same thing happens in sailing:
Make your sheet fast, never slacken,—and over you go,
Head over heels and under: and there's your voyage.
Forget you are angry! Let yourself be moved!
I know I am young; but please let me say this:
The ideal condition
Would be, I admit, that men should be right by instinct;
But since we are all too likely to go astray,
The reasonable thing is to learn from those who can teach.
CHORAGOS. You will do well to listen to him, King,
If what he says is sensible. And you, Haimon,
Must listen to your father.—Both speak well.
CREON. You consider it right for a man of my years and experience
To go to school to a boy?
HAIMON.   It is not right
If I am wrong. But if I am young, and right,
What does my age matter?
CREON. You think it right to stand up for an anarchist?
HAIMON. Not at all. I pay no respect to criminals.
CREON. Then she is not a criminal?
HAIMON. The City would deny it, to a man.
CREON. And the City proposes to teach me how to rule?
HAIMON. Ah. Who is it that's talking like a boy now?
CREON. My voice is the one voice giving orders in this City!

HAIMON. It is no City if it takes orders from one voice.
CREON. The State is the King!
HAIMON.   Yes, if the State is a desert.
                  [*Pause*]
CREON. This boy, it seems, has sold out to a woman.
HAIMON. If you are a woman: my concern is only for you.
CREON. So? Your "concern"! In a public brawl with your father!
HAIMON. How about you, in a public brawl with justice?
CREON. With justice, when all that I do is within my rights?
HAIMON. You have no right to trample on God's right.
                  [*Completely out of control*]
CREON. Fool, adolescent fool! Taken in by a woman!
HAIMON. You'll never see me taken in by anything vile.
CREON. Every word you say is for her!
                  [*Quietly, darkly*]
HAIMON.   And for you.
      And for me. And for the gods under the earth.
CREON. You'll never marry her while she lives.
HAIMON. Then she must die.—But her death will cause another.
CREON. Another?
      Have you lost your senses? Is this an open threat?
HAIMON. There is no threat in speaking to emptiness.
CREON. I swear you'll regret this superior tone of yours!
      You are the empty one!
HAIMON.   If you were not my father,
      I'd say you were perverse.
CREON. You girlstruck fool, don't play at words with me!
HAIMON. I am sorry. You prefer silence.
CREON.   Now, by God—!
      I swear, by all the gods in heaven above us,
      You'll watch it, I swear you shall!
                  [*To the* SERVANTS:]
                         Bring her out!
      Bring the woman out! Let her die before his eyes!
      Here, this instant, with her bridegroom beside her!
HAIMON. Not here, no; she will not die here, King.
      And you will never see my face again.
      Go on raving as long as you've a friend to endure you.
                              [*Exit* HAIMON.]

CHORAGOS. Gone, gone.
      Creon, a young man in a rage is dangerous!
CREON. Let him do, or dream to do, more than a man can.
      He shall not save these girls from death.
CHORAGOS.   These girls?
      You have sentenced them both?

CREON.   No, you are right.
    I will not kill the one whose hands are clean.
CHORAGOS. But Antigone?
                [*Somberly*]
CREON.   I will carry her far away
    Out there in the wilderness, and lock her
    Living in a vault of stone. She shall have food,
    As the custom is, to absolve the State of her death.
    And there let her pray to the gods of hell:
    They are her only gods:
    Perhaps they will show her an escape from death,
    Or she may learn,
              though late,
    That piety shown the dead is pity in vain.   [*Exit* CREON.]

Ode 3

CHORUS. Love, unconquerable
　　　Waster of rich men, keeper
　　　Of warm lights and all-night vigil
　　　In the soft face of a girl:
　　　Sea-wanderer, forest-visitor!
　　　Even the pure Immortals cannot escape you,
　　　And mortal man, in his one day's dusk,
　　　Trembles before your glory.

　　　Surely you swerve upon ruin
　　　The just man's consenting heart,
　　　As here you have made bright anger
　　　Strike between father and son—
　　　And none has conquered but Love!
　　　A girl's glánce wórking the will of heaven:
　　　Pleasure to her alone who mocks us,
　　　Merciless Aphrodite.

Scene 4

[*As* ANTIGONE *enters guarded.*]
CHORAGOS. But I can no longer stand in awe of this,
   Nor, seeing what I see, keep back my tears.
   Here is Antigone, passing to that chamber
   Where all find sleep at last.

ANTIGONE. Look upon me, friends, and pity me
   Turning back at the night's edge to say
   Good-by to the sun that shines for me no longer;
   Now sleepy Death
   Summons me down to Acheron, that cold shore:
   There is no bridesong there, nor any music.
CHORUS. Yet not unpraised, not without a kind of honor,
   You walk at last into the underworld;
   Untouched by sickness, broken by no sword.
   What woman has ever found your way to death?

ANTIGONE. How often I have heard the story of Niobe,
   Tantalos' wretched daughter, how the stone
   Clung fast about her, ivy-close: and they say
   The rain falls endlessly
   And sifting soft snow; her tears are never done.
   I feel the loneliness of her death in mine.
CHORUS. But she was born of heaven, and you
   Are woman, woman-born. If her death is yours,
   A mortal woman's, is this not for you
   Glory in our world and in the world beyond?

STROPHE 2

ANTIGONE. You laugh at me. Ah, friends, friends,
    Can you not wait until I am dead? O Thebes,
    O men many-charioted, in love with Fortune,
    Dear springs of Dirce, sacred Theban grove,
    Be witnesses for me, denied all pity,
    Unjustly judged! and think a word of love
    For her whose path turns
    Under dark earth, where there are no more tears.
CHORUS. You have passed beyond human daring and come at last
    Into a place of stone where Justice sits.
    I cannot tell
    What shape of your father's guilt appears in this.

ANTISTROPHE 2

ANTIGONE. You have touched it at last: that bridal bed
    Unspeakable, horror of son and mother mingling:
    Their crime, infection of all our family!
    O Oedipus, father and brother!
    Your marriage strikes from the grave to murder mine.
    I have been a stranger here in my own land:
    All my life
    The blasphemy of my birth has followed me.
CHORUS. Reverence is a virtue, but strength
    Lives in established law: that must prevail.
    You have made your choice,
    Your death is the doing of your conscious hand.

EPODE

ANTIGONE. Then let me go, since all your words are bitter,
    And the very light of the sun is cold to me.
    Lead me to my vigil, where I must have
    Neither love nor lamentation; no song, but silence.
              [CREON interrupts impatiently.]
CREON. If dirges and planned lamentations could put off death,
    Men would be singing for ever.
              [To the SERVANTS:]
                    Take her, go!
    You know your orders: take her to the vault
    And leave her alone there. And if she lives or dies,
    That's her affair, not ours: our hands are clean.
ANTIGONE. O tomb, vaulted bride-bed in eternal rock,
    Soon I shall be with my own again
    Where Persephone welcomes the thin ghosts underground.

And I shall see my father again, and you, mother,
And dearest Polyneices—
                              dearest indeed
To me, since it was my hand
That washed him clean and poured the ritual wine:
And my reward is death before my time!

And yet, as men's hearts know, I have done no wrong,
I have not sinned before God. Or if I have,
I shall know the truth in death. But if the guilt
Lies upon Creon who judged me, then, I pray,
May his punishment equal my own.
CHORAGOS.   O passionate heart,
Unyielding, tormented still by the same winds!
CREON. Her guards shall have good cause to regret their delaying.
ANTIGONE. Ah! That voice is like the voice of death!
CREON. I can give you no reason to think you are mistaken.
ANTIGONE. Thebes, and you my fathers' gods,
And rulers of Thebes, you see me now, the last
Unhappy daughter of a line of kings,
Your kings, led away to death. You will remember
What things I suffer, and at what men's hands,
Because I would not transgress the laws of heaven.
                    [*To the* GUARDS, *simply*:]
Come: let us wait no longer.

                              [*Exit* ANTIGONE, *L., guarded.*]

Ode 4

CHORUS. All Danae's beauty was locked away
   In a brazen cell where the sunlight could not come:
   A small room, still as any grave, enclosed her.
   Yet she was a princess too,
   And Zeus in a rain of gold poured love upon her.
   O child, child,
   No power in wealth or war
   Or tough sea-blackened ships
   Can prevail against untiring Destiny!

ANTISTROPHE 1

   And Dryas' son also, that furious king,
   Bore the god's prisoning anger for his pride:
   Sealed up by Dionysos in deaf stone,
   His madness died among echoes.
   So at the last he learned what dreadful power
   His tongue had mocked:
   For he had profaned the revels,
   And fired the wrath of the nine
   Implacable Sisters that love the sound of the flute.

STROPHE 2

   And old men tell a half-remembered tale
   Of horror done where a dark ledge splits the sea
   And a double surf beats on the gráy shóres:
   How a king's new woman, sick
   With hatred for the queen he had imprisoned,
   Ripped out his two sons' eyes with her bloody hands

While grinning Ares watched the shuttle plunge
Four times: four blind wounds crying for revenge,

ANTISTROPHE 2

Crying, tears and blood mingled.—Piteously born,
Those sons whose mother was of heavenly birth!
Her father was the god of the North Wind
And she was cradled by gales,
She raced with young colts on the glittering hills
And walked untrammeled in the open light:
But in her marriage deathless Fate found means
To build a tomb like yours for all her joy.

Scene 5

[*Enter blind* TEIRESIAS, *led by a boy. The opening speeches of* TEIRESIAS *should be in singsong contrast to the realistic lines of* CREON.]

TEIRESIAS. This is the way the blind man comes, Princes, Princes,
Lock-step, two heads lit by the eyes of one.

CREON. What new thing have you to tell us, old Teiresias?

TEIRESIAS. I have much to tell you: listen to the prophet, Creon.

CREON. I am not aware that I have ever failed to listen.

TEIRESIAS. Then you have done wisely, King, and ruled well.

CREON. I admit my debt to you. But what have you to say?

TEIRESIAS. This, Creon: you stand once more on the edge of fate.

CREON. What do you mean? Your words are a kind of dread.

TEIRESIAS. Listen, Creon:
I was sitting in my chair of augury, at the place
Where the birds gather about me. They were all a-chatter,
As is their habit, when suddenly I heard
A strange note in their jangling, a scream, a
Whirring fury; I knew that they were fighting,
Tearing each other, dying
In a whirlwind of wings clashing. And I was afraid.
I began the rites of burnt-offering at the altar,
But Hephaistos failed me: instead of bright flame,
There was only the sputtering slime of the fat thigh-flesh
Melting: the entrails dissolved in gray smoke,
The bare bone burst from the welter. And no blaze!

This was a sign from heaven. My boy described it,
Seeing for me as I see for others.

I tell you, Creon, you yourself have brought
This new calamity upon us. Our hearths and altars

Are stained with the corruption of dogs and carrion birds
That glut themselves on the corpse of Oedipus' son.
The gods are deaf when we pray to them, their fire
Recoils from our offering, their birds of omen
Have no cry of comfort, for they are gorged
With the thick blood of the dead.

                O my son,
These are no trifles! Think: all men make mistakes,
But a good man yields when he knows his course is wrong,
And repairs the evil. The only crime is pride.

Give in to the dead man, then: do not fight with a corpse—
What glory is it to kill a man who is dead?
Think, I beg you:
It is for your own good that I speak as I do.
You should be able to yield for your own good.

CREON. It seems that prophets have made me their especial province.
    All my life long
    I have been a kind of butt for the dull arrows
    Of doddering fortune-tellers!
                No, Teiresias:
    If your birds—if the great eagles of God himself
    Should carry him stinking bit by bit to heaven,
    I would not yield. I am not afraid of pollution:
    No man can defile the gods.
              Do what you will,
    Go into business, make money, speculate
    In India gold or that synthetic gold from Sardis,
    Get rich otherwise than by my consent to bury him.
    Teiresias, it is a sorry thing when a wise man
    Sells his wisdom, lets out his words for hire!
TEIRESIAS. Ah Creon! Is there no man left in the world—
CREON. To do what?—Come, let's have the aphorism!
TEIRESIAS. No man who knows that wisdom outweighs any wealth?
CREON. As surely as bribes are baser than any baseness.
TEIRESIAS. You are sick, Creon! You are deathly sick!
CREON. As you say: it is not my place to challenge a prophet.
TEIRESIAS. Yet you have said my prophecy is for sale.
CREON. The generation of prophets has always loved gold.
TEIRESIAS. The generation of kings has always loved brass.
CREON. You forget yourself! You are speaking to your King.
TEIRESIAS. I know it. You are a king because of me.
CREON. You have a certain skill; but you have sold out.
TEIRESIAS. King, you will drive me to words that—

CREON.   Say them, say them!
    Only remember: I will not pay you for them.
TEIRESIAS. No, you will find them too costly.
CREON.   No doubt. Speak:
    Whatever you say, you will not change my will.
TEIRESIAS. Then take this, and take it to heart!
    The time is not far off when you shall pay back
    Corpse for corpse, flesh of your own flesh.
    You have thrust the child of this world into living night,
    You have kept from the gods below the child that is theirs:
    The one in a grave before her death, the other,
    Dead, denied the grave. This is your crime:
    And the Furies and the dark gods of Hell
    Are swift with terrible punishment for you.

    Do you want to buy me now, Creon?
                                Not many days,
    And your house will be full of men and women weeping,
    And curses will be hurled at you from far
    Cities grieving for sons unburied, left to rot
    Before the walls of Thebes.

    These are my arrows, Creon: they are all for you.

                           [*To* BOY:]
    But come, child: lead me home.
    Let him waste his fine anger upon younger men.
    Maybe he will learn at last
    To control a wiser tongue in a better head.   [*Exit* TEIRESIAS.]
CHORAGOS. The old man has gone, King, but his words
    Remain to plague us. I am old, too,
    But I cannot remember that he was ever false.
CREON. That is true. . . . It troubles me.
    Oh it is hard to give in! but it is worse
    To risk everything for stubborn pride.
CHORAGOS. Creon: take my advice.
CREON.   What shall I do?
CHORAGOS. Go quickly: free Antigone from her vault
    And build a tomb for the body of Polyneices.
CREON. You would have me do this?
CHORAGOS.   Creon, yes!
    And it must be done at once: God moves
    Swiftly to cancel the folly of stubborn men.
CREON. It is hard to deny the heart! But I
    Will do it: I will not fight with destiny.

CHORAGOS. You must go yourself, you cannot leave it to others.
CREON. I will go.
　　　　　　—Bring axes, servants:
Come with me to the tomb. I buried her, I
Will set her free.
　　　　　　Oh quickly!
My mind misgives—
The laws of the gods are mighty, and a man must serve them
To the last day of his life!　　　　　　*[Exit* CREON.]

Paean

CHORAGOS. God of many names
CHORUS.   O Iacchos
                                                   son
   of Kadmeian Sémele
                        O born of the Thunder!
   Guardian of the West
                        Regent
   of Eleusis' plain
                        O Prince of maenad Thebes
   and the Dragon Field by rippling Ismenos:

CHORAGOS. God of many names
CHORUS.   the flame of torches
   flares on our hills
                        the nymphs of Iacchos
   dance at the spring of Castalia:

   from the vine-close mountain
                                 come ah come in ivy:
   Evohé evohé! sings through the streets of Thebes

CHORAGOS. God of many names
CHORUS.   Iacchos of Thebes
   heavenly Child
                        of Sémele bride of the Thunderer!
   The shadow of plague is upon us:
                                 come

with clement feet
oh come from Parnasos
down the long slopes
across the lamenting water

CHORAGOS. Io Fire! Chorister of the throbbing stars!
O purest among the voices of the night!
Thou son of God, blaze for us!
CHORUS. Come with choric rapture of circling Maenads
Who cry *Io Iacche!*
God of many names!

Éxodos

[*Enter* MESSENGER, *L.*]

MESSENGER. Men of the line of Kadmos, you who live
  Near Amphion's citadel:
                    I cannot say
  Of any condition of human life "This is fixed,
  This is clearly good, or bad." Fate raises up,
  And Fate casts down the happy and unhappy alike:
  No man can foretell his Fate.
                    Take the case of Creon:
  Creon was happy once, as I count happiness:
  Victorious in battle, sole governor of the land,
  Fortunate father of children nobly born.
  And now it has all gone from him! Who can say
  That a man is still alive when his life's joy fails?
  He is a walking dead man. Grant him rich,
  Let him live like a king in his great house:
  If his pleasure is gone, I would not give
  So much as the shadow of smoke for all he owns.

CHORAGOS. Your words hint at sorrow: what is your news for us?

MESSENGER. They are dead. The living are guilty of their death.

CHORAGOS. Who is guilty? Who is dead? Speak!

MESSENGER.   Haimon.
  Haimon is dead; and the hand that killed him
  Is his own hand.

CHORAGOS.   His father's? or his own?

MESSENGER. His own, driven mad by the murder his father had done.

CHORAGOS. Teiresias, Teiresias, how clearly you saw it all!

MESSENGER. This is my news: you must draw what conclusions you can
  from it.

CHORAGOS. But look: Eurydice, our Queen:
    Has she overheard us?

                [Enter EURYDICE *from the Palace, C.]*

EURYDICE. I have heard something, friends:
    As I was unlocking the gate of Pallas' shrine,
    For I needed her help today, I heard a voice
    Telling of some new sorrow. And I fainted
    There at the temple with all my maidens about me.
    But speak again: whatever it is, I can bear it:
    Grief and I are no strangers.

MESSENGER.   Dearest Lady,
    I will tell you plainly all that I have seen.
    I shall not try to comfort you: what is the use,
    Since comfort could lie only in what is not true?
    The truth is always best.

                   I went with Creon
    To the outer plain where Polyneices was lying,
    No friend to pity him, his body shredded by dogs.
    We made our prayers in that place to Hecate
    And Pluto, that they would be merciful. And we bathed
    The corpse with holy water, and we brought
    Fresh-broken branches to burn what was left of it,
    And upon the urn we heaped up a towering barrow
    Of the earth of his own land.

                   When we were done, we ran
    To the vault where Antigone lay on her couch of stone.
    One of the servants had gone ahead,
    And while he was yet far off he heard a voice
    Grieving within the chamber, and he came back
    And told Creon. And as the King went closer,
    The air was full of wailing, the words lost,
    And he begged us to make all haste. "Am I a prophet?"
    He said, weeping, "And must I walk this road,
    The saddest of all that I have gone before?
    My son's voice calls me on. Oh quickly, quickly!
    Look through the crevice there, and tell me
    If it is Haimon, or some deception of the gods!"
    We obeyed; and in the cavern's farthest corner
    We saw her lying:
    She had made a noose of her fine linen veil
    And hanged herself. Haimon lay beside her,
    His arms about her waist, lamenting her,
    His love lost under ground, crying out
    That his father had stolen her away from him.
    When Creon saw him the tears rushed to his eyes

And he called to him: "What have you done, child? Speak to me.
What are you thinking that makes your eyes so strange?
O my son, my son, I come to you on my knees!"
But Haimon spat in his face. He said not a word,
Staring—
                    And suddenly drew his sword
And lunged. Creon shrank back, the blade missed; and the boy,
Desperate against himself, drove it half its length
Into his own side, and fell. And as he died
He gathered Antigone close in his arms again,
Choking, his blood bright red on her white cheek.
And now he lies dead with the dead, and she is his
At last, his bride in the houses of the dead.
                              [*Exit* EURYDICE *into the Palace.*]
CHORAGOS. She has left us without a word. What can this mean?
MESSENGER. It troubles me, too; yet she knows what is best,
    Her grief is too great for public lamentation,
    And doubtless she has gone to her chamber to weep
    For her dead son, leading her maidens in his dirge.
CHORAGOS. It may be so: but I fear this deep silence
                              [*Pause*]
MESSENGER. I will see what she is doing. I will go in.
                              [*Exit* MESSENGER *into the Palace.*]
            [*Enter* CREON *with attendants, bearing* HAIMON'S
                          body.]
CHORAGOS. But here is the King himself: oh look at him,
    Bearing his own damnation in his arms.
CREON. Nothing you say can touch me any more.
    My own blind heart has brought me
    From darkness to final darkness. Here you see
    The father murdering, the murdered son—
    And all my civic wisdom!

    Haimon my son, so young, so young to die,
    I was the fool, not you; and you died for me.
CHORAGOS. That is the truth; but you were late in learning it.
CREON. This truth is hard to bear. Surely a god
    Has crushed me beneath the hugest weight of heaven.
    And driven me headlong a barbaric way
    To trample out the thing I held most dear.

    The pains that men will take to come to pain!
                              [*Enter* MESSENGER *from the Palace.*]
MESSENGER. The burden you carry in your hands is heavy,
    But it is not all: you will find more in your house.

CREON. What burden worse than this shall I find there?
MESSENGER. The Queen is dead.
CREON. O port of death, deaf world,
    Is there no pity for me? And you, Angel of evil,
    I was dead, and your words are death again.
    Is it true, boy? Can it be true?
    Is my wife dead? Has death bred death?
MESSENGER. You can see for yourself.
       [*The doors are opened, and the body of* EURYDICE *is*
                  disclosed within.]
CREON. Oh pity!
    All true, all true, and more than I can bear!
    O my wife, my son!
MESSENGER. She stood before the altar, and her heart
    Welcomed the knife her own hand guided,
    And a great cry burst from her lips for Megareus dead,
    And for Haimon dead, her sons; and her last breath
    Was a curse for their father, the murderer of her sons.
    And she fell, and the dark flowed in through her closing eyes
CREON. O God, I am sick with fear.
    Are there no swords here? Has no one a blow for me?
MESSENGER. Her curse is upon you for the deaths of both.
CREON. It is right that it should be. I alone am guilty.
    I know it, and I say it. Lead me in,
    Quickly, friends.
    I have neither life nor substance. Lead me in.
CHORAGOS. You are right, if there can be right in so much wrong.
    The briefest way is best in a world of sorrow.
CREON. Let it come,
    Let death come quickly, and be kind to me.
    I would not ever see the sun again.
CHORAGOS. All that will come when it will; but we, meanwhile,
    Have much to do. Leave the future to itself.
CREON. All my heart was in that prayer!
CHORAGOS. Then do not pray any more: the sky is deaf.
CREON. Lead me away. I have been rash and foolish.
    I have killed my son and my wife.
    I look for comfort; my comfort lies here dead.
    Whatever my hands have touched has come to nothing.
    Fate has brought all my pride to a thought of dust.
      [*As* CREON *is being led into the house, the* CHORAGOS
        advances and speaks directly to the audience.]
CHORAGOS. There is no happiness where there is no wisdom;
    No wisdom but in submission to the gods.
    Big words are always punished,
    And proud men in old age learn to be wise.

TRANSLATOR'S COMMENTARY

*Et quod propriè dicitur in idiomate Picardorum horrescit
apud Burgundos, immò apud Gallicos viciniores; quanto
igitur magis accidet hoc apud linguas diversas! Qua-
propter quod bene factum est in unâ linguâ non est pos-
sibile ut transferatur in aliam secundum ejus proprietatem
quam habuerit in priori.*

ROGER BACON

I. In the Commentary appended to our version of Euripides' *Alcestis*
we wrote: "Our object was to make the *Alcestis* clear and credible
in English. Since it is a poem, it had to be made clear as a poem; and
since it is a play, it had to be made credible as a play. We set for ourselves no fixed rules of translation or of dramatic verse: often we found
the best English equivalent in a literalness which extended to the texture
and rhythm of the Greek phrasing; at other times we were forced to a
more or less free paraphrase in order to achieve effects which the
Greek conveyed in ways impossible to English. Consequently, this
version of the *Alcestis* is not a 'translation' in the classroom sense of
the word. The careful reader, comparing our text with the original, will
discover alterations, suppressions, expansions—a word, perhaps, drawn
out into a phrase, or a phrase condensed to a word: a way of saying
things that is admittedly not Euripidean, if by Euripidean one means a
translation *ad verbum expressa* of Euripides' poem. In defense we can
say only that our purpose was to reach—and, if possible, to render
precisely—the emotional and sensible meaning in every speech in the
play; we could not follow the Greek word for word, where to do so
would have been weak and therefore false." We have been guided by
the same principles in making this version of the *Antigone*.

II. We have made cuts only when it seemed absolutely necessary. The
most notable excision is that of a passage of sixteen lines beginning
with 904 (Antigone's long speech near the end of Scene 4), which has
been bracketed as spurious, either in whole or in part, by the best
critics. Aristotle quotes two verses from it, which proves, as Professor
Jebb points out, that if it is an interpolation it must have been made
soon after Sophocles' death, possibly by his son Iophon. However that
may be, it is dismal stuff. Antigone is made to interrupt her lamentation by a series of limping verses whose sense is as discordant as their

sound. We quote the Oxford Translation, the style of which is for once wholly adequate to the occasion:

And yet, in the opinion of those who have just sentiments, I honoured you [Polyneices] aright. For neither, though I had been the mother of children, nor though my husband dying, had mouldered away, would I have undertaken this toil against the will of the citizens. On account of what law do I say this? There would have been another husband for me if the first died, and if I lost my child there would have been another from another man! but my father and my mother being laid in the grave, it is impossible a brother should ever be born to me. On the principle of such a law, having preferred you, my brother, to all other considerations, I seemed to Creon to commit a sin, and to dare what was dreadful. And now, seizing me by force, he thus leads me away, having never enjoyed the nuptial bed, nor heard the nuptial lay, nor having gained the lot of marriage, nor of rearing my children; but thus I, an unhappy woman, deserted by my friends, go, while alive, to the cavern of the dead.

There are other excisions of less importance. Perhaps the discussion of one of them will serve to explain them all. Near the end of the *Éxodos,* Creon is told of his wife's suicide. The Messenger has five very graphic lines describing Eurydice's suicide, to which Creon responds with an outburst of dread and grief; yet two lines later, as if he had not heard the first time, he is asking the Messenger how Eurydice died. The Messenger replies that she stabbed herself to the heart. There is no evidence that the question and reply are interpolations: on the contrary, they serve the definite purpose of filling out the iambic interlude between two lyric strophes; but in a modern version which does not attempt to reproduce the strophic structure of this *Kommós* they merely clog the dialogue. Therefore we have skipped them; and the occasional suppression of short passages throughout the play is based upon similar considerations.

III. In a like manner, we have not hesitated to use free paraphrase when a literal rendering of the Greek would result in obscurity. Again, the discussion of a specific instance may illuminate the whole question.

After Antigone has been led away to death, the Chorus, taking a hint from her having compared her own fate to that of Niobe, proceeds to elaborate the stories of mythological persons who have suffered similar punishment. The Fourth Ode cites Danaë, Lycurgos, the son of Dryas, and Cleopatra, the daughter of Boreas and wife of the Thracian king Phineus. Only Danaë is mentioned by name; the others are allusively identified. The difficulty arises from the allusive method. Sophocles' audience would be certain to recognize the allusions, but that is not true of ours. To what extent can we depend upon the audience's recognition in a day when, to quote Mr. I. A. Richards, "we can no longer refer with any confidence to any episode in the Bible, or to any nursery tale or any piece of mythology"? We can assume that the story of Danaë is still current; but Lycurgos is forgotten now, and the sordid Phineus-Cleopatra-Eidothea affair no longer stirs so much as an echo. Nevertheless, Sophocles devotes two of his four strophes to this Cleopatra, and he does it in so oblique a manner that 'translation' is out of the question. We have therefore rendered these strophes with such slight additions to the Greek sense as might convey an equivalent suggestion of fable to a modern audience.

IV. The Chorus is composed, says the Scholiast, of "certain old men of Thebes": leading citizens ("O men many-charioted, in love with Fortune") to whom Creon addresses his fatal decree, and from whom he later takes advice. Sophocles' Chorus numbered fifteen, including the Choragos, or Leader; its function was to chant the Odes and, in the person of the Choragos, to participate in the action. In a version designed for the modern stage certain changes are inevitable. It cannot be urged too strongly that the words of the Odes must be intelligible to the audience; and they are almost certain not to be intelligible if they are chanted in unison by so large a group, with or without musical accompaniment. It is suggested, then, that in producing this play no attempt be made to follow the ancient choric method. There should be no dancing. The *Párodos,* for example, should be a solemn but almost unnoticeable evolution of moving or still patterns accompanied by a drum-beat whose rhythm may be derived from the cadence of the Ode itself. The lines given to the Chorus in the Odes should probably be spoken by single voices. The only accompaniment should be percussion: we follow Allan Sly's score of the *Alcestis* in suggesting a large side drum from which the snares have been removed, to be struck with two felt-headed tympani sticks, one hard, one soft.

V. A careful production might make successful use of masks. They should be of the Benda type used in the production of O'Neill's *The Great God Brown:* lifelike, closely fitting the contours of the face, and valuable only as they give the effect of immobility to character. On no account should there be any attempt to reproduce the Greek mask, which was larger than life size and served a function non-existent on the modern stage—the amplification of voice and mood for projection to the distant seats of the outdoor theater.

If masks are used at all, they might well be allotted only to those characters who are somewhat depersonalized by official position or discipline: Creon, Teiresias, the Chorus and Choragos, possibly the Messenger. By this rule, Antigone has no mask; neither has Ismene, Haimon, nor Eurydice. If Creon is masked, we see no objection, in art or feeling, to the symbolic removal of his mask before he returns with the dead body of his son.

QUESTIONS

PROLOGUE

1. What is Antigone's expressed purpose in the Prologue? How does Sophocles use a contrasting character here to emphasize her determination to achieve her end?

2. Usually the expressed purpose of a dramatic character is only the objective form of a more basic motive. Is it possible to discover from Antigone's lines a more basic motive here?

PÁRODOS

3. The relationship of the Chorus to the action in Greek tragedy is complicated, but the first step in understanding this relationship is to ask how the subject they discuss and their attitude toward it bear on the characters and actions of the preceding scene. What is the connection here between the exultant description of the destruction of Polyneices and his army and the scene between Antigone and Ismene?

4. What does Antigone's "family tree" tell us about her nature and her prospects?

SCENE 1

5. How would you describe Creon's speech? Do his values accord with his manner of speaking?

6. A character reveals a good deal of himself in the motives he consistently attributes to others. What is Creon's repeated explanation of the actions of others? How does this fit in with the other details of his characters?

7. What function, other than to bring the news of Polyneices' burial, does the messenger serve? Consider the meaning of the manner in which he was chosen to carry the message to Creon.

8. By the end of Scene 1 the conflict of Antigone and Creon has occurred and the initial action has been taken. Re-examine Antigone and Creon and try to state what general principles, or values, are represented by the two characters, and why a conflict between them is inevitable. What enduring human problem is presented in this conflict?

ODE 1

9. What attitude toward Man is expressed in the ode? Is Man simple or complex?

10. In this ode the prime mover seems to be the human will alone. Does the "world" have any effect on the course of events in the play?

SCENE 2

11. When Antigone returns to bury Polyneices, her movements are for a time covered by a whirlwind. Is this merely a realistic detail that makes plausible Antigone's ability to reach the body undetected, or is there some relationship between her and the whirlwind?

12. Both Antigone and Creon present themselves as the selfless defenders of "the law." What evidence in this scene suggests that they both have additional motives?

ODE 2

13. The Chorus is made up of the elderly men of Thebes who move and speak as a group, except when the Chorus Leader speaks for all of them. Can you see any relationship between these facts and the explanation they give in this ode for the disaster that has struck Antigone?

SCENE 3

14. In one sense the word "necessary" in Aristotle's prescription for the tragic plot as a chain of "necessary or probable" events means the inevitable unfolding of the full significance of taking a particular stand or committing a particular act. Can the disruption of the marriage plans be seen as such an elaboration of Antigone's original decision to bury the body of Polyneices and Creon's determination to leave it unburied?

15. What is Creon's view of women? Is there any significance in the sex of the two major characters? Would it do just as well to make Antigone a man?

ODE 3

16. Can you trace in the first three odes a progression in the attitude of the Chorus toward the events to which they are spectators?

SCENE 4

17. Why does Antigone say "You laugh at me" to the Chorus after they have tried to console her by describing the glory of her death? Has her attitude changed in the interval between this scene and her last appearance?

18. Is the Chorus right when they tell Antigone, "Your death is the doing

of your conscious hand"? Pay particular attention to the word "conscious."

19. Do the arrangements Creon makes for Antigone's death tell us anything about her nature? That is, does the *scene* of her death suit her nature as Hedda Gabler's does?

ODE 4

20. In what way do the tragic tales referred to by the Chorus in this ode constitute abbreviated *double* plots? Do all these stories parallel Antigone's situation, or do some of them serve as contrasts? (For identification of the persons referred to here see Section III of the Translator's Commentary.)

SCENE 5

21. What course of action does Teiresias recommend and why does Creon refuse to accept it at first? What causes him to change his mind?

22. What does the fact that the seer is blind contribute to the meaning of what he says? Look back at the people Creon has encountered and see if they have anything in common.

PAEAN

23. Why should the Chorus invoke the god at this moment when Creon has gone to free Antigone and all should be well?

ÉXODOS

24. The messenger reporting the disasters in Creon's house says, "Fate raises up, and Fate casts down the happy and unhappy alike . . . ." For him, then, the plot of *Antigone* reveals the movements of Fortune's wheel: whoever rises and becomes great must expect to fall as the wheel turns. Does the play, however, allow us to accept such an interpretation? Is Fate the prime mover in the plot or does the action grow from other causes? Could these causes be called "Fate" also?

25. At the end of the play Creon says, "I alone am guilty," and accepts full responsibility for all the deaths. Is he correct in his self-accusation, or is the matter more complicated?

26. Throughout the play the Chorus and Teiresias have recommended that Antigone and Creon abandon their extreme positions and follow a middle course. Such action would have prevented disaster, but does anything in the play suggest that it was ever a genuine possibility?

27. Antigone's major effort was "to cover the body of Polyneices," and Creon's major effort was "to keep the body uncovered." Taking these two contrary actions as metaphors, can you see how the motives expressed in each action are present in all that is said and done in the play?

Plot on the Psychological Level

Maurice Maeterlinck, in *The Tragedy of Daily Life,* says:

I have come to believe that an old man seated in his armchair, waiting quietly under the lamplight, listening without knowing it to all the eternal laws which reign about his house, interpreting without understanding it all that there is in the silence of doors and windows . . . I have come to believe that this motionless old man lived really a more profound, human, and universal life than the lover who strangles his mistress, the captain who gains a victory, or the husband who "avenges his honor."

In this passage, and in his plays, the Belgian dramatist turns away from objective, physical action—strangling a mistress, winning a victory—and focuses attention on subjective, psychological action—listening, interpreting. For Maeterlinck and for a great many modern dramatists, the most meaningful action occurs in the mind of man, not out in the visible, audible world of bodies, objects, and voices. W. B. Yeats puts the same idea into specifically dramatic terms: "After all, is not the greatest play not the play that gives the sensation of an external reality but the play in which there is the greatest abundance of life itself, of the reality that is in our minds?"

But even if Maeterlinck and Yeats are right in claiming that true life is located within the mind, how can the movement of this life, its plot, be represented in the play, a form which by its very nature requires that everything be objectified in a physical set, in audible words, in visible movements, in clothing, and in bodies? A novelist would have no difficulty at all in presenting the thoughts of "an old man seated in his armchair, waiting quietly under the lamplight," but a play that consisted of only a man sitting motionless in a chair would convey next to nothing. The ways in which mental conditions can be objectified are discussed in the section on character; but there character is largely treated as if it were unchanging, as if a character continued throughout a play with exactly the same motives and exactly the same attitudes. In some plays this is nearly the case. Hedda Gabler has the same values and is trying to do the same thing at the beginning and at the end of the play. Nevertheless it is impossible to think of her mind as static; her motives remain the same, but she passes through a series of moods and mental states. On the other hand, Antigone and Creon, though they cannot escape the consequences of the train of action they set in motion with their initial acts, undergo radical changes of character during the course of the play. Since some dramatists try to show a psychological as well as an objective reality, and since the minds of their characters move from one condition to another, we can speak of *psychological plots* and try to describe their dynamics.

Most major playwrights have been concerned, though not as exclusively as Maeterlinck and Yeats were, to find a way to present on the stage the mental life of at least their major characters, and to record the changes in their minds. *Macbeth,* for example, has a striking objective plot composed of great battles, the murder of a king, the disruption of a kingdom, and the violent deaths of the usurper and his queen. Below this objective plot, and parallel to it, runs the psychological plot, the chain of mental "events" or conditions in Macbeth's mind. In the depths of his being he is first courageous, simple, and loyal; he passes on to nervous indecision as ambition leads him to kill the king and loyalty and reverence for human life cause him to recoil from the act; he nearly turns into a maniac as fear breaks his "single state of man" and he begins to see visions; he hardens as he becomes accustomed to the business of killing all who threaten his rule; and, finally, just before he dies fighting like an enraged animal, he changes to a walking ghost, a man for whom life has lost all meaning and has become no more than "sound and fury, signifying nothing." The plot of Macbeth's mind as he changes from a loyal and straightforward subject to an empty husk is as important to the play as what happens in the kingdom of Scotland. However, the subjective and objective plots of *Macbeth* are not unrelated; they mirror one another in such a way that the events of one reflect the events of the other. As the first, half-formed thoughts of ambition take shape in Macbeth's mind, they take shape physically in the form of witches, who suddenly appear on the heath. As he destroys the ruling principles of loyalty and reverence for life in himself, so he kills his king. The hand and the heart go together. As his mind progresses from disorder to joylessness and hopelessness, so the country he rules is thrown into turmoil and becomes finally a wasteland. But the events of the physical plot do not exist here, as they would in an expressionistic play, merely to give objective form to Macbeth's mental processes. Scotland and the mind of Macbeth are equally real, and they parallel one another because the same principles are at work with the same effects in both. The forces that destroy a kingdom also destroy the little kingdom, man, in Shakespeare's coherent view of existence.

Few playwrights have coordinated their physical and psychological plots so perfectly as Shakespeare did, but as a rule the objective plot does double duty. It records the changes that take place in the objective world and in the material condition of man, and it provides a rough parallel to what is taking place in the minds of the central characters. Once the fact is established that the objective plot reflects the subjective plot, we can begin to examine the way the subjective, or psychological, plot functions. It is composed and structured in the same manner as the external plot. Just as conflict results in the external, objective world from the collision of opposing forces, so certain forces within a person can cause internal, or mental conflict. Hedda Gabler is both fascinated by freedom and afraid of it. Hamlet is torn by a longing to retire from the world to escape the struggle with evil and an equally powerful longing to be active and to bring about the needed changes in Denmark. Macbeth is torn between his ambition and his loyalty. The conflict causing psychological changes need not, however, be entirely internal. A change of mind may be brought about by a character's realization of what he has done, or not done, in the objective world. Creon's major change of mind occurs, for example, when he realizes that his course of action has destroyed his son and his wife. Once the conflict has begun, the psychological plot, made up of a series of mental events, is under way. We must watch for the way these mental events are related, just as we would in an objective plot, and we must look for the way in which changes come about.

For example, there is a considerable difference in the way changes occur in the psychological plots of *Macbeth* and *Antigone*. Macbeth's progress from one mental state to another is a gradual and continuous movement toward a climax: the absolute emptiness expressed in the speech beginning, "Tomorrow, and tomorrow . . ." Antigone shifts abruptly. She appears, during the first part of the play, to be absolute for death and completely without fear; suddenly, when she is condemned to be buried alive, the full significance of what she has done comes home to her. She prevents herself from becoming a hysterical girl at this point, but she is nonetheless radically changed. Sharp intrusions of truth, prepared for but coming suddenly, are called *recognitions*. If a character recognizes that the truth is quite the opposite of what he has previously believed to be the case, we have a *reversal*. Oedipus, for example, discovers that by his intelligence and skill he has fulfilled rather than evaded the oracular prophecy that he would kill his father and marry his mother. The reversal occurs when he learns these facts and is forced to see that he is not the greatest of men, but the weakest and most pitiable.

Psychological plots can be arranged in as many ways as physical plots. The events of Macbeth's mind are connected in a cause-and-effect pattern: because his ambition overcomes his care for human life, his own life becomes meaningless to him. Mother Courage does not undergo any development or change, except that her hope is perhaps dimmer by the end of the play. Her toughness, her common sense, her wit, and her courage are permanent parts of her mental makeup and can only be qualified or destroyed by death. Probably no psychological plot has so distressed the critics as the familiar comic plot in which a character who has been consistently single-minded suddenly and without warning changes. This psychological version of the *deus ex machina* is frequent in love comedy: a man and a woman (Beatrice and Benedick in Shakespeare's *Much Ado About Nothing*, for example) who have previously hated one another discover in a flash that they love one another. Shakespeare presents an elaborate form of this same change of mind in *A Midsummer Night's Dream*: the four lovers in the forest get completely mixed up as Puck's magic potion causes them to love where once they hated. Such changes are often explained as mere devices used by the author to tie up his play, without regard for credibility; but surely these psychological shifts, particularly when they involve love, are just as credible, as lifelike, as the relentless pattern along which Macbeth's mind moves. We all know that love is close to hate, and we can accept also what Shakespeare tells us in *A Midsummer Night's Dream*, that sudden love is a magical quality in man which transforms what was once hated into something desirable and lovely. We must try to approach psychological plots as well as physical plots without preconceptions about how the playwright ought to portray the workings of human nature. In his depiction of the process of mental change he offers an image of the dynamics of the human mind, and we are likely to miss his point completely if we fail to take his plot seriously.

THE STRONGER

BY

AUGUST STRINDBERG

August Strindberg (1849–1912), the foremost Swedish dramatist, was one of the originators of the modern theater. While the other great Scandinavian dramatist of the nineteenth century, Henrik Ibsen, developed and perfected the beautifully machined realistic play to present the interaction of man and society, Strindberg constantly experimented with dramatic forms ranging from the extreme naturalism of *The Father* to the equally extreme surrealism of *The Ghost Sonata*. He moved restlessly from one dramatic style to another in search of a theatrical idiom that could convey the subject which most interested him—man's intense, explosive passions and his strange, unexplored inner life. *The Stronger* (1889), though extremely short, is one of his most successful attempts at finding a way to dramatize in the realistic mode the workings of the mind.

CHARACTERS

MRS. X., *actress, married*
MISS Y., *actress, unmarried*
A WAITRESS

*⊰§ Scene: *A corner of a ladies' café (in Stockholm in the 1880's).
Two small wrought-iron tables, a red plush settee and a few chairs.*

MISS Y. *is sitting with a half-empty bottle of beer on the table before
her, reading an illustrated weekly which from time to time she ex-
changes for another.*

MRS. X. *enters, wearing a winter hat and coat and carrying a decorative Japanese basket.*

MRS. X. Why, Millie, my dear, how are you? Sitting here all alone on
Christmas Eve like some poor bachelor.
  [MISS Y. *looks up from her magazine, nods, and con-*
                tinues to read.]
MRS. X. You know it makes me feel really sad to see you. Alone.
Alone in a café and on Christmas Eve of all times. It makes me
feel as sad as when once in Paris I saw a wedding party at a restaurant. The bride was reading a comic paper and the bridegroom
playing billiards with the witnesses. Ah me, I said to myself, with
such a beginning how will it go, and how will it end? He was playing
billiards on his wedding day! And she, you were going to say, was
reading a comic paper on hers. But that's not quite the same.
  [*A* WAITRESS *brings a cup of chocolate to* MRS. X.
                and goes out.]
MRS. X. Do you know, Amelia, I really believe now you would have
done better to stick to him. Don't forget I was the first who told you
to forgive him. Do you remember? Then you would be married now

and have a home. Think how happy you were that Christmas when you stayed with your fiancé's people in the country. How warmly you spoke of domestic happiness! You really quite longed to be out of the theatre. Yes, Amelia dear, home is best—next best to the stage, and as for children—but you couldn't know anything about that.

[MISS Y.'s *expression is disdainful.* MRS. X. *sips a few spoonfuls of chocolate, then opens her basket and displays some Christmas presents.*]

MRS. X. Now you must see what I have bought for my little chicks. (*Takes out a doll.*) Look at this. That's for Liza. Do you see how she can roll her eyes and turn her head. Isn't she lovely? And here's a toy pistol for Maja. (*She loads the pistol and shoots it at* MISS Y. *who appears frightened.*)

MRS. X. Were you scared? Did you think I was going to shoot you? Really, I didn't think you'd believe that of me. Now if *you* were to shoot *me* it wouldn't be so surprising, for after all I did get in your way, and I know you never forget it—although I was entirely innocent. You still think I intrigued to get you out of the Grand Theatre, but I didn't. I didn't, however much you think I did. Well, it's no good talking, you will believe it was me . . . (*Takes out a pair of embroidered slippers.*) And these are for my old man, with tulips on them that I embroidered myself. As a matter of fact I hate tulips, but he has to have tulips on everything.

[MISS Y. *looks up, irony and curiosity in her face.*]

MRS. X. (*putting one hand in each slipper*). Look what small feet Bob has, hasn't he? And you ought to see the charming way he walks—you've never seen him in slippers, have you?

[MISS Y. *laughs.*]

MRS. X. Look, I'll show you. (*She makes the slippers walk across the table, and* MISS Y. *laughs again.*)

MRS. X. But when he gets angry, look, he stamps his foot like this. "Those damn girls who can never learn how to make coffee! Blast! That silly idiot hasn't trimmed the lamp properly!" Then there's a draught under the door and his feet get cold. "Hell, it's freezing, and the damn fools can't even keep the stove going!" (*She rubs the sole of one slipper against the instep of the other.* MISS Y. *roars with laughter.*)

MRS. X. And then he comes home and has to hunt for his slippers, which Mary has pushed under the bureau . . . Well, perhaps it's not right to make fun of one's husband like this. He's sweet anyhow, and a good, dear husband. You ought to have had a husband

like him, Amelia. What are you laughing at? What is it? Eh? And,
you see, I know he is faithful to me. Yes, I know it. He told me
himself—what *are* you giggling at?—that while I was on tour in
Norway that horrible Frederica came and tried to seduce him. Can
you imagine anything more abominable? (*Pause.*) I'd have scratched
her eyes out if she had come around while I was at home. (*Pause.*)
I'm glad Bob told me about it himself, so I didn't just hear it from
gossip. (*Pause.*) And as a matter of fact, Frederica wasn't the only
one. I can't think why, but all the women in the Company seem
to be crazy about my husband. They must think his position gives
him some say in who is engaged at the Theatre. Perhaps you have
run after him yourself? I don't trust you very far, but I know he
has never been attracted by you, and you always seemed to have
some sort of grudge against him, or so I felt. (*Pause. They look at
one another guardedly.*)

MRS. X. Do come and spend Christmas Eve with us tonight, Amelia—
just to show that you're not offended with us, or anyhow not with
me. I don't know why, but it seems specially unpleasant not to be
friends with you. Perhaps it's because I did get in your way that
time . . . (*slowly*) or—I don't know—really, I don't know at all
why it is.

[*Pause.* MISS Y. *gazes curiously at* MRS. X.]

MRS. X. (*thoughtfully*). It was so strange when we were getting to
know one another. Do you know, when we first met, I was frightened of you, so frightened I didn't dare let you out of my sight. I
arranged all my goings and comings to be near you. I dared not be
your enemy, so I became your friend. But when you came to our
home, I always had an uneasy feeling, because I saw my husband
didn't like you, and that irritated me—like when a dress doesn't fit.
I did all I could to make him be nice to you, but it was no good—
until you went and got engaged. Then you became such tremendous
friends that at first it looked as if you only dared show your real
feelings then—when you were safe. And then, let me see, how was
it after that? I wasn't jealous—that's queer. And I remember at the
christening, when you were the godmother, I told him to kiss you.
He did, and you were so upset . . . As a matter of fact I didn't
notice that then . . . I didn't think about it afterwards either
. . . I've never thought about it—until *now!* (*Rises abruptly.*)
Why don't you say something? You haven't said a word all this time.
You've just let me go on talking. You have sat there with your eyes
drawing all these thoughts out of me—they were there in me like
silk in a cocoon—thoughts . . . Mistaken thoughts? Let me think.

Why did you break off your engagement? Why did you never come
to our house after that? Why don't you want to come to us tonight?

[MISS Y. *makes a motion, as if about to speak.*]

MRS. X. No. You don't need to say anything, for now I see it all. That
was why—and why—and why. Yes. Yes, that's why it was. Yes,
yes, all the pieces fit together now. That's it. I won't sit at the same
table as you. (*Moves her things to the other table.*) That's why I
have to embroider tulips, which I loathe, on his slippers—because
you liked tulips. (*Throws the slippers on the floor.*) That's why we
have to spend the summer on the lake—because you couldn't bear
the seaside. That's why my son had to be called Eskil—because it
was your father's name. That's why I had to wear your colours,
read your books, eat the dishes you liked, drink your drinks—your
chocolate, for instance. That's why—oh my God, it's terrible to
think of, terrible! Everything, everything came to me from you—
even your passions. Your soul bored into mine like a worm into an
apple, and ate and ate and burrowed and burrowed, till nothing
was left but the skin and a little black mould. I wanted to fly from
you, but I couldn't. You were there like a snake, your black eyes
fascinating me. When I spread my wings, they only dragged me
down. I lay in the water with my feet tied together, and the harder
I worked my arms, the deeper I sank—down, down, till I reached
the bottom, where you lay in waiting like a giant crab to catch me
in your claws—and now here I am. Oh how I hate you! I hate you,
I hate you! And you just go on sitting there, silent, calm, indifferent,
not caring whether the moon is new or full, if it's Christmas or New
Year, if other people are happy or unhappy. You don't know how
to hate or to love. You just sit there without moving—like a cat
at a mouse hole. You can't drag your prey out, you can't chase it,
but you can outstay it. Here you sit in your corner—you know they
call it the rattrap after you—reading the papers to see if anyone's
ruined or wretched or been thrown out of the Company. Here you
sit sizing up your victims and weighing your chances—like a pilot
his shipwrecks for the salvage. (*Pause.*) Poor Amelia! Do you know,
I couldn't be more sorry for you. I know you are miserable, miserable like some wounded creature, and vicious because you are
wounded. I can't be angry with you. I should like to be, but after
all you are the small one—and as for your affair with Bob, that
doesn't worry me in the least. Why should it matter to me? And
if you, or somebody else taught me to drink chocolate, what's the
difference? (*Drinks a spoonful. Smugly.*) Chocolate is very wholesome anyhow. And if I learnt from you how to dress, *tant mieux!*—-

that only gave me a stronger hold over my husband, and you have lost what I gained. Yes, to judge from various signs, I think you have now lost him. Of course, you meant me to walk out, as you once did, and which you're now regretting. But I won't do that, you may be sure. One shouldn't be narrow-minded, you know. And why should nobody else want what I have? (*Pause.*) Perhaps, my dear, taking everything into consideration, at this moment it is I who am the stronger. You never got anything from me, you just gave away—from yourself. And now, like the thief in the night, when you woke up I had what you had lost. Why was it then that everything you touched became worthless and sterile? You couldn't keep a man's love—for all your tulips and your passions—but I could. You couldn't learn the art of living from your books—but I learnt it. You bore no little Eskil, although that was your father's name. (*Pause.*) And why is it you are silent—everywhere always silent? Yes, I used to think this was strength, but perhaps it was because you hadn't anything to say, because you couldn't think of anything. (*Rises and picks up the slippers.*) Now I am going home, taking the tulips with me—*your* tulips. You couldn't learn from others, you couldn't bend, and so you broke like a dry stick. I did not. Thank you, Amelia, for all your good lessons. Thank you for teaching my husband how to love. Now I am going home—to love him. (*Exit.*)

QUESTIONS

1. To whom does the title refer? Your answer will depend on how you define the word "stronger." Does the play itself suggest a definition?
2. Though physical action is kept to a minimum, can it be said that the play lacks a plot?
3. What is the effect of using "X" and "Y" for the characters' names? Is "Z" suggested?
4. Miss Y's wordless gestures focus the attention of Mrs. X, but do they also express Miss Y's own nature? Do these wordless gestures act out any of the things Mrs. X tells us about Miss Y at the end of the play, or any of the descriptions she provides of her?
5. What effect does the device of never having Miss Y speak have on the meaning of the play? Where does it locate the action?
6. How does the setting of Christmas Eve add dimension to the discoveries and decisions of Mrs. X?
7. Describe the states of mind through which Mrs. X passes. What causes

the progression from one state to another? What physical actions accompany and underscore these changes?

8. Does the conflict in Mrs. X's mind parallel the external conflict between her and Miss Y? In other words, is there a Miss Y *in* Mrs. X? Can you find a passage where Mrs. X describes attitudes and feelings within her that resemble those shown by Miss Y?

9. Does Miss Y also have a plot? If so, describe it and compare it with Mrs. X's plot.

10. Mrs. X begins by rationalizing a good many unpleasant facts. Find several of these rationalizations. Can it be argued that her last words are still a rationalization?

11. Although Mr. X never appears, we learn a great deal about him. What kind of man is he?

THE NATURE
OF DRAMA

The play is a technique, or medium, that makes use of actors and a stage for a great many quite different purposes: to sell soap and deodorant, as short television advertising skits do; to persuade children to brush their teeth and show them the best way to do it; to entertain by presenting sights we all enjoy, such as dancing bears, pretty girls, elaborate costumes, and spectacles; to act out our fears of murder and rape, our desires for unflinching courage and self-sacrifice; to teach a doctrine, as the medieval mystery plays taught the tenets of the Christian faith; to persuade us to adopt a course of action, as Brecht's plays, by showing the desperate results of continuing old ways of thinking and action, seek to make us change the social structure. Instruction, persuasion, explanation, entertainment, exhortation to action are all possible uses of the play, and even the greatest drama continues to perform these functions, though they are not central to its purpose. *Antigone,* for example, is a thrilling play by any standards, containing a great deal of excitement and entertainment: pitiful farewells of separated lovers, suspenseful conflicts between a young girl and a proud older ruler, cruel deaths and unusual punishments. At the same time the play analyzes social problems in fifth-century B.C. Athens, and by showing the gap between practical politics and morality, it at least implies the value of careful and balanced approaches to matters of state and of moderation in taking moral stands.

But *Antigone,* of course, goes far beyond providing entertainment and hints of moral instruction to focus on an unchanging fundamental condition of being: the inescapable conflict in the mind and life of man between one good and another equal good. What is true of *Antigone* is equally true of other great plays. While they necessarily entertain, analyze local social conditions and particular moral problems, and stage our human fears and desires, they ultimately cut through the temporal and the passing to expose some enduring aspect of the human condition. Hamlet defines this ultimate function with precision:

The purpose of playing . . . was and is to hold as 'twere the mirror up to Nature—to show Virtue her own feature, Scorn her own image, and the very age and body of the time his form and pressure.

In making its universal statements about the human condition, the drama, like the other arts, uses not the abstract languages of science and philosophy but the concrete, immediate terms of experience—specific characters, definite settings, solid events, and powerful feelings. Much of the pleasure and the meaning of a great play comes from the vividness of specific characters moving and speaking on stage and taking part in realized events. That mankind is infinitely durable and quick-witted is a truism not likely to arouse much enthusiasm, but Mother Courage, providing for her children by pulling her wagon across Europe to sell her wares, is extremely moving. A tract about our need for involvement with life is not nearly so compelling, so "true," as seeing a particular woman, Hedda Gabler, refusing to acknowledge that she is pregnant, handling her pistols, shutting out the sunlight, and pacing back and forth in a dark, encumbered room.

Here is one way in which a play achieves meaning. It creates existence on the most immediate, personal level, presenting the basic facts of life as we live it: the turbulence of love and hate, the terror of death, the stubbornness of pride, the persistence of living things. It shows the world not only as it is perceived and ordered by the mind but also as it is felt and sensed in the fullness of being. Romeo's love and Hamlet's despair are true and meaningful precisely because they are so fully and powerfully realized in words and acts. Philosophy, science, theology, and statistics all make statements about reality in abstract terms—the good, the one, the true, or the norm; but the arts, drama included, use images of life to make their statements—Hamlet, Claudius, Elsinore, the Ghost, Polonius.

In great drama, intensely specific images take on universal meaning. Great drama creates a living "here and now" and then extends it to "everywhere and always." If the play creates a convincing image of some primary human situation or attitude—love, the difficulty of communication, loneliness, fear of death, the relationship of man and woman, the conflict of fate and will—then its bearing on all life becomes apparent. The audience recognizes itself because it has shared in the passions, hopes, and struggles to which the actors give voice and body. It was once believed that only an action of magnitude, such as the struggle for a kingdom, involving heroes such as kings and queens, could serve as the subject of great drama. We now know that it is not the apparent grandeur of the play's subject that bestows importance on it, but the fact that it depicts powerfully and truthfully some eternal aspect of the human condition. A salesman can face the same overwhelming questions and the same terrors that the Prince of Denmark can—though the fact that he is a salesman, not a prince, suggests that he will have less success in answering his questions and that his failure or his achievement will have less impact on the world at large. The action of a woman trying to give a successful garden party may be very important because it embodies a characteristic human attempt to create, by means of tact, graciousness, and planning, an ordered and mutually satisfying relationship between human beings, while a play about the fall of kingdoms, in which such subjects as free will, honor, and death are openly and frequently discussed, may be no more than philosophical "horse opera."

In earlier discussions of character, world, and plot, another answer to the question of how a play acquires universal meaning was stated implicitly a number of times. A dramatic character, we said, is made up of numerous distinct details: his way of dressing, physical characteristics, traits of speech, recurrent use of certain images, way of acting. But in trying to understand the whole character we examined each detail to see what it had in common with the other details. We tried to locate the center of the character, the essential being. The term that best describes that essence in the drama is *motive*, the basic act that the character is trying to perform, which is expressed in each of the details. The critical term used to describe this relation of one detail to another is *structure*, and the presence of structure is one of the distinguishing marks of the play that is also literature. As we read a play of the first rank, we gradually become aware of emerging patterns; we begin to sense the relationship between apparently diverse events. Characters come into focus as we see that each is not a collection of disparate traits, but a unity. The furniture on the stage, the arrangement of the props, the decor, the references to a world just beyond the stage, coalesce to suggest some one force or recurring conflict. We discover a central power moving through the plays as we observe that events have a characteristic direction and that again and again the same order of consequences results from the same kind of cause. Ultimately, if we read the play well, it becomes apparent that all the components—characters, world, and plot—are not only unified within themselves but comprise a total unity: a coherent image of man and his world in movement.

As we become aware that the parts of a play are closely related, we begin to understand its universal implications. Everything Hedda Gabler does manifests what we have called a drive toward freedom, an attempt to escape all restraints. This drive always encounters an opposing power in some form, which seeks to enclose her and limit her actions. Thus it becomes obvious that this particular woman in this particular setting is but one instance (a late nineteenth-century version) of a universal struggle between man's desire to be absolutely, anarchically free and the bonds imposed on him by his own nature, by other people, and by social arrangements.

The dramatist may stress the universal implications of his image of life in several ways. All of these may be regarded as aspects of structure, but it will be helpful to examine a few of them separately. In the discussion of plot, we noticed that the device of the multiple plot tends to expand the meaning of the play. If we observe the same events, the same problems, the same human actions, occurring in more than one life, in more than one place, the implication is that this is not a unique but a common pattern of life. W. B. Yeats referred to this effect as the "emotion of multitude" and illustrated it in this way:

The Shakespearean drama gets the emotion of multitude out of the subplot which copies the main plot, much as a shadow upon the wall copies one's body in the firelight. We think of *King Lear* less as the history of one man and his sorrows than as the history of a whole evil time. Lear's shadow is in Gloster, who also has ungrateful children, and the mind goes on imagining other shadows, shadow beyond shadow till it has pictured the world.

Except for the Elizabethans, few dramatists have felt free to construct two or three distinct plots in a single play; but modified multiple plots have been a fairly constant feature of Western drama. In the modern theater the dramatist often weaves two or more plots into one, as Wilder does in *The Skin of Our Teeth.* Any historical drama collapses two plots, though we are scarcely aware that the process is taking place. Bernard Shaw's *Saint Joan,* for example, dramatizes the career of Joan of Arc. But the Joan of the play speaks in the accents of twentieth-century England. She discusses such matters as nationalism, religion, and feminine rights in the sprightly manner of a good Fabian Socialist like Bernard Shaw. The play is not, then, just the story of the historical Joan, nor that of a twentieth-century liberal:

it is both, and by implication a continuing pattern in life. Any stage production of a play that uses costumes of another age than that specified—*Julius Caesar* done in black shirts with all the trappings of Mussolini's Italy, for example—provides a variety of the double plot. In such cases, of course, the additional plot is the director's, not the playwright's, and its effectiveness will depend on how well it suits the original meaning of the play.

There are other techniques for widening the range of meaning by placing the immediate dramatic event in an expanded context. A mere touch is often enough to suggest that the action before us is not "separated . . . from all but itself." In *Antigone* the name of Antigone's father, Oedipus, is mentioned naturally enough on several occasions, and at one point the Chorus draws an analogy between present and past difficulties in the Theban royal family. This is all, but it is enough to tell us that Antigone is motivated in somewhat the same way her father was and that she is following the same tragic path. In *Mother Courage* a song on the wisdom of Solomon, the bravery of Caesar, the honesty of Socrates, and the charity of St. Martin tells us that great virtue is a misfortune, which has in every case led to disaster. Exalted as these men are compared with the homely characters in *Mother Courage*, their lives serve as grim parallels to the fates of the heroic Eilif, the honest Swiss Cheese, and the charitable Kattrin. The universality of a particular experience is frequently underlined within a play by duplication: Hamlet loses his father and must revenge his death, and Fortinbras and Laertes go through the same experience.

So far we have discussed how playwrights enrich the meaning of their plays by expanding the human context. But dramatists, and particularly poetic dramatists, frequently extend the meaning of their action beyond the range of the human. For instance, in Shakespeare's *The Winter's Tale*, the literal action of the play consists of a sequence of events in which a king, because of unwarranted jealousy, destroys his growing family, breaks off an old friendship, and disrupts the order of his kingdom. When he learns of his mistake and repents, his children and his wife are dead, or so he believes. But sixteen years later his daughter and her mother are miraculously returned to him, and the ancient friendship is renewed by the marriage of his daughter to the son of his old friend. At several points in the plot, the characters and their activities are compared to the changes of the seasons, to domestic animals such as sheep, and to fruits and flowers. This sustained development of one theme of imagery is known as an *imagery pattern,* and in this play it is arranged in such a way that the seasons of the year and the changes in nature parallel the human events of the primary plot. The King's destruction of his family, his kingdom, and his peace of mind is linked by imagery with winter; the rescue of his daughter and her growth to womanhood are compared to the events of spring; and the restoration of the King and the marriage of his daughter become the fruition of summer. The round of the seasons with their attendant growth and death of natural things forms in this way a second plot, and through its imagery the play suggests that all creation passes through the same cycle.

Shakespeare's plays regularly show this type of secondary plot constructed by means of imagery patterns that interweave the human and natural worlds. When Macbeth enters on his course of murder and tyranny, the imagery tells us that he leaves the light behind and passes into darker and darker night. His acts are like the extinction of sunlight and the coming of darkness, confusion, and terror over the earth. The pattern of light and darkness is established chiefly by the language, as in Lady Macbeth's invocation to night when she plans the murder of Duncan:

> Come, thick night,
> And pall thee in the dunnest smoke of Hell,
> That my keen knife see not the wound it makes,
> Nor Heaven peep through the blanket of the dark
> To cry "Hold, hold!"

But the darkness pattern emerges or expands into the scene of the play as well. Day fades and darkness falls as Duncan arrives at the castle of Macbeth. The murder is done in the deepest hour of the night and is discovered as the night moves toward day again. Banquo is murdered in darkness; Lady Macbeth sleepwalks in the night, unable to forget her crime; day comes again to the world as Macbeth is killed.

In realistic prose drama, where the playwright attempts to make his dialogue approximate daily speech, metaphor is not used as freely as in poetic drama—though traces of it always remain—and *scenic metaphor,* a form of *symbolism,* is used to expand the meanings of particular events to their universal implications. For example, in Ibsen's *The Wild Duck,* a family that has failed to meet life successfully retreats to a make-believe world where each member can escape the intrusions of reality and pretend that everything is as he would like it to be. Instead of using verbal imagery to extend the "withdrawal" to other areas of life, Ibsen constructs a series of symbolic parallels. In the attic of their house, these lost people create an imaginary wild forest in which they can pretend to be mighty hunters. This mock forest is populated with small, harmless animals, as ineffective as the people who put them there. The prize is a wild duck, which, when wounded by a hunter, dived to the bottom of a lake and locked itself in the weeds until it was brought up by the hunter's dog. The family earns its living by taking photographic portraits, but these portraits have to be touched up carefully to conceal blemishes and create illusions of beauty before they are acceptable to the customers. Symbolism may be used to form a continuing pattern, as in *The Wild Duck,* or to create one brief, sharp effect. Tennessee Williams regularly makes use of symbolism in this second way. At the opening of *A Streetcar Named Desire,* Stanley Kowalski, returning home from work, throws a package of dripping, red meat to his wife waiting on the steps. The symbol, which suggests that Stanley is a cave man returning with the meat killed on the day's hunt, provides an illuminating parallel to the brutal, direct, primitive manner in which Stanley lives in twentieth-century New Orleans.

These are a few of the dramatist's major techniques for expanding the meaning of his image of life and making it universal. Multiple plot, analogue, duplication of situations and characters, imagery pattern, and symbol are all different aspects of what we generally term *imagery.* This word is ordinarily used in a limited sense to refer to comparisons in which one thing is said to be *like* another thing—"The Chair she sat in, *like* a burnished throne,/Glowed on the marble"— or in which one thing is said *to be* another thing—"I have measured out my life with coffee spoons." In these examples of simile and metaphor (two varieties of imagery) meaning is achieved by yoking one thing with some other thing that it resembles or with which, according to the poetic statement, it is identical. The dramatist uses this same process more elaborately when he establishes meaning by paralleling his main action with imagery patterns, extended symbols, and multiple plots. Ultimately, the artifice of the entire play may itself profitably be considered a single complex image; every serious dramatist is saying in effect, "Life is like this play."

In some ways the play seems to have no special subject matter or techniques. The dramatist seems free, using the devices of actor and stage, to present any subject that interests him, and he shares such techniques as character, language, imagery, and plot with the lyric poet and the novelist. The dramatist can, as he chooses, use his medium to sell soap or revolution, to provide entertainment or present the most profound truths. And yet, despite this apparent freedom, the greatest dramatists have perceived that, to use the terms of Marshall McLuhan, "the medium is the message"; in other words, the meaning of any play is somehow inherent in the theater and in the way a play must be written and presented. The content of drama is, in this view, not so much the specific subject of the play—the quarrel of Creon and Antigone or Mother Courage's struggle to make a living in a world of war—as it is the peculiar perspective from which man and his world are seen when presented as actors placed on a stage in a theater. The rather surprising idea that the dramatic medium is itself the message—what every playwright finally has to say—is implicit in the familiar comparisons of life to a play, man to an actor, and the world to a stage. At certain times, particularly in the Renaissance and in the twentieth century, dramatists have grown self-conscious about their medium and have made the similarity of life and play their explicit subject, thus developing a theory of the nature and meaning of drama. In this volume, *Mother Courage* and *The Skin of Our Teeth* reflect this attitude. Both Brecht, by his refusal to disguise his stage and pretend that it is reality rather than theater, and Wilder, with his frank exposure of the theater and acting company behind the adventures of the Antrobus family, keep before us the concept that for all its seeming reality life is finally a play. But the most thorough exploration of the relation of life and acting, the most complete investigation of the meaning of seeing the world as theater, comes in Shakespeare's *Hamlet*. Let us therefore trace with some care its development of the playing metaphor and its contribution to an understanding of drama.

As the word itself implies, literature is art that is written down, stabilized in a text printed by hand or machine. But each of the three great literary modes—dramatic, lyric, and narrative—had its origin in some nonliterary activity. Drama, before it was written down, was acting and showing; lyric was singing; and narrative was telling. The older arts of acting, singing, and telling remain fundamental human gestures, and literature, though it may seem to be far removed from these basic modes of expression, is still based on them. In a novel or narrative poem, someone (the "speaker," as he is sometimes styled) still relates events that happened in the past. In a lyric poem, someone (we usually say "the poet") still breaks into song, with the rhythm of the poem for music, expressing an immediate and personal sorrow or joy so intense that it cannot be kept inside the self. In a printed play, the characters are still actors pretending to be people they are not, and their world is still only the make-believe one of the stage.

Each of these ways of presenting life is at the same time a mode of vision, a perspective, a way of seeing and understanding. To present the world in the narrative mode is, inescapably, to view life as consisting of past events being filtered through the consciousness of a man who somehow knows of those events and chooses to remember and tell them. The narrative mode can be and has been endlessly complicated by writers, but the blind bard who accompanied himself on the harp and told an audience about the ancient wars before the walls of Troy, the omniscient Victorian author who knew every detail of the moral lives of his characters and judged them with the absoluteness of a god, and the modern, troubled, self-conscious narrator, such as Quentin Compson in William Faulkner's *Absalom! Absalom!*, who struggles to reconcile in his own mind his contradictory and incomplete information about the past, all view life from the same angle, and all share, no matter how different their immediate styles and subjects, the fundamental style *and* subject matter of the narrative mode: the present consciousness trying to deal with and transmit that which is past.

We are likely to think of the artist, in good Romantic fashion, as a man whose vision and ideas go beyond the traditional media—language, stone, paint—and styles in which he is expected to express his dreams. His art thus becomes the invention of new languages and new forms that are capable of realizing his vision. But there is another way of understanding the artist: not as a revolutionary destroying the old and the outworn, but as a craftsman who by practice slowly learns and exploits the meaning inherent in his chosen medium, as Michelangelo said he released form from marble. Each great work of art is, in this view, not a triumph over recalcitrant materials but a discovery of what those materials really mean, a discovery of what the instrument tradition has passed on is really capable of saying. Just as the great painter discovers what line, color, and two-dimensional space are really all about, what they reveal about reality, so the great dramatist discovers and reveals in his plays what it truly means to see men as actors and the world as a stage. In this way, artists become critics who draw out and reveal the meaning of the modes in which they work. This is most easily demonstrable in extremely self-conscious works, such as *Hamlet*, where the subject of the play is largely an exploration of the meaning of plays and the art of playing. This kind of dramatic self-consciousness was encouraged by the theatrical conventions of the Elizabethan public theater, where the stage, undisguised by scenery or lights, remained always visible behind the action, constantly questioning the play's pretense of being "real." Unlike the realistic dramatist, the Renaissance dramatist did not try to hide the fact that his setting was a theater and his play a play; rather, he frequently drew attention to this fact by the use of a great many self-conscious references to the theater: plays within plays, scenes in which actors discuss their roles and the play they are about to perform, direct addresses to the audience by the players, and imagery that compares men to actors and their world to theaters. Nowhere in Elizabethan drama are the references to theaters and playing more concentrated and more complex in meaning than in *Hamlet*.

To help us understand the extremely complicated game that Shakespeare is playing, we might put the matter this way: the characters of *Hamlet*, moving about the corridors of Elsinore, engaged in the deadly business of revenge for a father and struggle for a kingdom, are so completely absorbed in the realities of their immediate existence that they are totally unaware of the theater in which they act. Claudius is preoccupied with his lust for power and for Gertrude, Hamlet is fascinated with his interior struggle between the need for action and the passive desire for rest, Ophelia is trapped within her bewildered suffering over the loss of a lover and a father, Polonius is serenely happy with his smug, pedantic certainty that he knows all there is to know. Each character has not the slightest awareness that he is but an actor in a play and that his world of Elsinore is no more than a fiction in a theater, which has been and will again be many other equally unreal places.

Yet in the midst of their certainty and absorption in what they take for reality, the surface of that reality is constantly parting to reveal the theater inherent in it. This is obvious enough at the end of Act II when the players from the city arrive at Elsinore, and the Player King, at the prompting of Hamlet, delivers a long speech from an older play, *The Murder of Priam*, which deals with events similar to those that have taken place in Elsinore, the murder of a revered king and the sorrow of his bereaved queen. The playlike qualities of the Danish court become even more obvious in the following act when Hamlet instructs the players in the art of playing and they proceed to perform *The Murder of Gonzago*, which re-enacts some of the recent events in Elsinore. These overt plays within the play alert us to the existence of others that are less obvious. When Hamlet enters his mother's room and holds up, side by side, the pictures of the two kings, old Hamlet and Claudius, and then proceeds to show his mother the true nature of the choice she has made, he is presenting truth by means of a show, or a play. Similarly, he leaps into the open grave at Ophelia's funeral, ranting and swearing in high heroic terms, showing or acting out, for a

Laertes still unaccustomed to the pain of death, the ridiculousness of excessive, melodramatic expressions of grief. In the concluding scene of the play, the duel scene between Laertes and Hamlet, there is another elaborately staged play within the play. The duel is a play in the sense of an exercise or game of skill; it is also a play in the sense that each of the persons on stage is an actor playing a role. The King is pretending to be a beneficent ruler and a concerned but loyal stepfather, who is sponsoring the exercise of warlike and manly skills within his court; Hamlet is pretending to be simply a duelist, with no misgivings whatsoever about the dangers lurking in the situation; and Laertes is playing the part of the honest sportsman out for a little exercise and pleased with an opportunity to display his skill with the rapier. The Queen and the courtiers, gathered around watching the duel, form an audience, and are specifically identified as such by Hamlet: "You . . . that are but mutes or audience to this act."

Once we begin looking at *Hamlet* in this fashion, it immediately becomes apparent that there are few moments that are not a play within the play. When Rosencrantz and Guildenstern go to greet Hamlet after their arrival in Elsinore, they pretend that they are merely old friends concerned about his moodiness and melancholy, when in fact they are spies sent by Claudius to find out what is troubling Hamlet and whether he is dangerous. When Polonius sends a messenger to his son in Paris, he advises the man to pretend that he does not know Laertes while asking questions about Laertes' morals. When Claudius and Polonius wish to find out whether Hamlet's madness results from disappointed love, they characteristically stage a little play in which Ophelia pretends to pray in order to draw Hamlet out, while Claudius and Polonius stand like directors behind the arras. Whenever Claudius appears, in fact, he is playing a part. The reality of the man is that he is a murderer, a regicide, and an adulterer; but the part that he continually plays is that of a wise and efficient king, acting always for the good of his kingdom and urging the members of his family and his court to follow sensible courses of action. Hamlet too is never very far removed from the theatrical situation: he is forced for his own protection to assume and maintain an "antic disposition," a pretense of madness, which he wears with great ingenuity and uses to counter the attempts of his antagonists to "play" upon him. Playing is the way of life in Elsinore, where even death does not remove one from the stage: "Let four captains," says Fortinbras giving burial directions for the Danish prince, "bear Hamlet like a soldier to the stage."

The theatrical quality of the *Hamlet* world is obvious. In Act II,

Scene 2, the comparison is made explicit when Hamlet refers to the
earth as "this goodly frame" (frame was the technical term for the
outer walls of the auditorium). And Shakespeare floods the play with
language that suggests playing and theaters. We are never at any point
very far from such words as *act, shape, play, perform, stage, counterfeit, paint, shadow, mirror, plot, show, part, put on, trappings, motive,
cue, prologue, audience,* and *scene.* When Hamlet in the midst of the
duel scene refuses a drink from the poisoned cup saying, "I'll play this
bout first," or when he tells Rosencrantz and Guildenstern that they
cannot "play" upon him like a pipe and sound his mystery, the references to the theater are clear. They are not so clear, though still present, when Polonius instructs his son Laertes on the proper way to live,
as if he were an actor learning a part: "And these few precepts in
thy memory/Look thou character." They are even less clear, but still
present, when Hamlet orders his mother not to go to his uncle's bed
but to "assume a virtue, if you have it not."

Despite the insistent presence of plays within the play and language
which suggests constantly that all human activities are a form of playing, the hero of *Hamlet* is an idealistic young prince who intensely
dislikes all forms of playing and pretense. When we first encounter
Hamlet in the throne room of Elsinore, his mother the queen is asking
him why, since the death of fathers is "common," he is so unrelenting
in his mourning. "Why seems it so particular with thee?" she demands.
Hamlet replies,

> Seems, madam! Nay, it *is.* I know not "seems."
> 'Tis not alone my inky cloak, good Mother,
> Nor customary suits of solemn black,
> Nor windy suspiration of forced breath—
> No, nor the fruitful river in the eye,
> Nor the dejected havior of the visage,
> Together with all forms, moods, shapes of grief—
> That can denote me truly. These indeed seem,
> For they are actions that a man might play.
> But I have that within which passeth show,
> These but the trappings and the suits of woe.

Though forced to express his mourning for his father by means of
customary actions—sighs and tears—and the prescribed costume of
black clothing, Hamlet is impatient with "the trappings and the suits of
woe," which cannot truly and fully express his intense and particular
loss and which may be used by others to suggest a grief they in fact do
not feel.

For Hamlet, outward forms cannot convey inner truth, and his natural, idealistic dislike for all forms of playing and pretending is heightened to disgust when he encounters among those at court a base type of playing that is contrary to nature. His mother, who had once seemed to him so excellent a woman, so model a wife and queen, is now revealed as an adulteress and a woman of the most undiscriminating sexual appetite. In the light of her actions, Hamlet can only assume that her earlier appearance of virtue was a sham, an "act." As the play proceeds, he discovers that as it is with his mother, so is it with all else that he values. A murderer pretends to be a kind king, and a fool pretends to be a wise councilor. Ophelia, whom he had thought of as another Juliet, a beloved faithful to death, now has changed and seems to him only a timid daughter tamely obeying her father's commands not to speak to Hamlet. Rosencrantz and Guildenstern, who had seemed from childhood his most faithful and trusted friends, are now revealed as mere instruments of the King, a pair of toadies thinking in terms of their own interests without regard for former friendship. He who had once been a most hopeful prince, a student at Wittenberg, heir to the throne of Denmark, "the glass of fashion, and the mold of form," the very embodiment of Renaissance optimism about the nature of man and the beauty of his world, has now become an object of mockery in his own palace, a disappointed cynic, and a man who has lost all belief in himself and his own ability to act effectively. Faced with the evidence of the Danish court, Hamlet can only conclude that man is truly "beastly" and that any appearance of being otherwise is only an act, a pretense, which hides the truth.

Despite this deeply ingrained dislike for all forms of playing, Hamlet is gradually forced to realize first the necessity for playing and then, more slowly and imperfectly, the value and meaning of playing. His first attempt at acting comes when he puts on his "antic disposition," pretending to be mad for safety's sake. But this guise of madness, as Hamlet becomes more accustomed to it, serves more functions than merely providing him with a cover. It enables him to reveal the truth about such fools as Rosencrantz and Guildenstern and Polonius. Acting like a madman, Hamlet contrives scenes that reveal Rosencrantz and Guildenstern as the hapless idiots they actually are and arranges situations that strip away from Polonius the appearance of gravity and wisdom to expose him as a conventional, bumbling fool. Unbeknown to Hamlet, this same madness reveals a truth about him: his excessive agony over "the thousand natural shocks that flesh is heir to" and his consequent hatred of the world and the flesh—the attitudes expressed in his madness—are views of life akin to insanity.

As the playing intensifies, the usefulness of the players' art is further demonstrated. When the traveling company of players arrives in Elsinore, the leading tragedian performs at Hamlet's request a scene from an old play about the death of Priam, King of Troy. In Troy, as in Elsinore, a great king was killed by a foul and brutal murderer, and in Troy, but not in Elsinore, a great queen nobly lamented. Ironically enough, the player who delivers the speech, knowing of and caring nothing for Hecuba, expresses fully and powerfully the appropriate feelings of anger and sorrow, whereas Hamlet, who has actually had a father murdered, and a mother stained as well, cannot find suitable heroic words and gestures for his feelings. Playing can distort the truth but can also be a means of realizing it; it is, in fact, the only method by which truth can be revealed. Only a play, *The Murder of Gonzago,* can "catch the conscience of the king": by re-enacting the murder of old Hamlet before his murderer, it forces Claudius to see himself as in a mirror and allows others to know and understand who he is and what he has done. After he has found that a play can catch the King's conscience, Hamlet goes on to catch the conscience of the Queen by holding before her the pictures of her two husbands; using words like daggers, he turns her eyes into her very soul to reveal "such black and grainèd spots/As will not leave their tinct."

Further revelation of the meaning and value of playing comes in the scene in which Hamlet watches the army of Fortinbras move across the stage on its way to fight in Poland for a plot of ground not large enough to bury all the men who will be slain in the struggle for it. Hamlet's remarks on the spectacle of this great army reveal that he fully understands that the struggle—"even for an eggshell"—has neither sufficient causes nor sufficient rewards to justify it in any practical sense. Instead, it is a brave and desperate search for honor;

> Rightly to be great
> Is not to stir without great argument,
> But greatly to find quarrel in a straw
> When honor's at the stake.

In this world, the Fortinbras incident seems to say, all that man desires most—his honor and his values—cannot be manifested by purely realistic means. Reality will not support man's dreams, and man must therefore contrive situations, such as the Polish adventure, to realize and play out his dream of honor.

The paradox, which becomes increasingly obvious to both Hamlet and the audience as the play proceeds, is that playing is the only method for expressing the deepest truths. Man pretends in order to be real. In terms of the great central paradox of *Hamlet,* this truth takes the form: to act (in the sense of doing) is necessarily to act (in the sense of playing or pretending).

Shakespeare's exploration of the inevitability and the nature of playing goes, however, even deeper than the perception that acting is the only means man has for revealing human truth and expressing human values. We noticed earlier that all of life in *Hamlet* is somehow involved in acting; the play is made up of a continuing series of plays within the play, which suggests that playing is the inescapable human condition and that man plays whether he wills it or not. This sense of "life as play" is focused on and explored in depth at the beginning of Act V, where Hamlet, returned from his sea voyage, stands in the graveyard looking at the skull of Yorick and expounding on the meaning of death. All mankind, he realizes, must come to this state. The lady with her fine clothes and her cosmetics, the lawyer with all his skills and learning, the landowner with his deeds and charters, the conquerors of the world like Caesar and Alexander must end, Hamlet now knows, as a heap of bones and a handful of dust. If this is the way life ends, the reality from which we come and to which we return, then how can man regard that portion of existence we call life as any more than a part, be it that of a king or beggar, played by an actor on the stage of the world? Because the individual life is transient, because the flesh does not endure, and because all that we take as real dissolves into the ultimate reality of dust, life *is* a play and the world *is* a stage.

We can turn for a moment to the plot of *Hamlet* to see the manner in which this identification of life as theater is actively depicted. In the beginning, Hamlet is buried under his own grief and is incapable of action. At the same time, he totally rejects playing as a way of life. As the play progresses and as the necessity for acting in order to revenge his father's murder becomes more intense, Hamlet finds himself drawn more and more into the art of playing. He puts on the "antic disposition," instructs a group of players in the art of playing, and stages several plays in order to achieve his ends. But to the end of Act IV, Hamlet regards playing as an instrument that he controls and can use to implement his goals; up to this point he resembles Claudius and Polonius, who always find out and do things by means of staging some kind of a pretense. When Hamlet returns from his sea voyage at the beginning of Act V, he is a greatly changed man, much calmer, much more serene, much more willing to accept the world in all its complexity. He has, by the merest chance and not by his own will or cunning, barely escaped Claudius' plot to have him executed in England. Upon his return he can face and accept the fact of death—now recognizing that all of life is a play and that every man, including himself, is a player in the great scheme of things that lie outside his control. There is, he now accepts, "a divinity that shapes our ends,/Rough-hew them how we will." There is a plot to life written not by the players but by some unknown author outside and beyond the play:

Not a whit, we defy augury. There's special providence in the fall of a sparrow. If it be now, 'tis not to come; if it be not to come, it will be now; if it be not now, yet it will come. The readiness is all. Since no man has aught of what he leaves, what is't to leave betimes? Let be.

Accepting his own part in a play he did not write, Hamlet discovers, ironically, that the revenge and the execution of Claudius, which he has long futilely sought, is now achieved in a moment. But the play is still larger than the one Hamlet would have written, for the death of Claudius requires also the death of Hamlet, of Laertes, and of Gertrude.

What *Hamlet* reveals is that the form of the play, the dramatic mode, far from being some kind of unnatural artistic contrivance, some intricate human invention "from the purpose of nature," is in fact a most realistic representation of the human condition, a true way of imaging life. In pretending is our reality. What man seems to be at one moment, he is not at the next; and the human condition may therefore be correctly defined as that of an actor playing a part. Man's life is never entirely within his own control, and he is thus properly figured as an actor who thinks that he is creating the plot, while in fact he is only the product of the mind of some distant author who does not appear in the play but has laid down the inevitable, inescapable order of events. It is not the contents of a play (the subject matter) but the dramatic mode itself that finally serves "to hold the mirror up to Nature—to show Virtue her own feature, Scorn her own image, and the very age and body of the time his form and pressure."

Hamlet explores by means of the theatrical metaphor something fundamental about the nature of drama. Inherent in the very form of a play, there is always a conflict between the characters and the play itself. Every great character resolutely refuses to admit that his reality is only that of an actor, that his control over events is only illusory, and that his world is only a stage. Great dramatic characters are determined realists. From the point of view of the audience, theirs is thus always an ironic position: Oedipus and Hamlet see themselves shaping the world according to their desires, but we know them as actors playing Oedipus and Hamlet in plots written by Sophocles and Shakespeare.

What Shakespeare works out explicitly in terms of the theater, other great dramatists have worked out in more indirect ways. The validity of Shakespeare's constant comparison of life to theater rests on the fact that the conditions of life—its transiency, its mutability, and its resistance to our control—all resemble very closely the conditions of the dramatic mode. But a great dramatist need not be so self-conscious as Shakespeare. He can grasp and present the implications of showing man as an actor in a play in more familiar terms. Sophocles, for example, in *Oedipus the King* dramatizes the events in the life of a great man who refuses to believe that the world is not his to control and that his life is not his own creation. When Oedipus learns from the oracle that he will kill his father and marry his mother, he immediately leaves Corinth to avoid his fate, and by doing so ensures that he will fulfill it. His very determination not to play in a plot written by someone else directs him inevitably toward the crossroads where he kills his father, and on to Thebes, where he vanquishes the Sphinx and marries Jocasta. The man who began as the embodiment of all that is great and free in human nature ends as a blind outcast and an incestuous parricide. Without use of the theater as a metaphor for life, Sophocles, using the concepts of fate and chance rather than actor and play, exploits as surely as Shakespeare the meanings inherent in the form of the play.

Using different concepts—fate, history, determinism, theater, mutability, actor—all great dramatists have found their way inevitably to that conflict lying at the center of the dramatic mode: the conflict between the great character and the play in which he performs. Nowhere is this conflict presented in more essential form with its meanings more precisely and thoroughly worked out than in *Hamlet*. In one play within the play, *The Murder of Gonzago,* there are only two characters, the Player Queen and the Player King. Their status as actors is doubly ensured by the fact that they are not only players in *Hamlet* but also players in another play contained in *Hamlet*. The Player Queen speaks for all great dramatic characters when she speaks of the eternal resoluteness of her love:

Oh, confound the rest!
Such love must needs be treason in my breast.

> In second husband let me be accurst!
> None wed the second but who killed the first.
>
>   .   .   .
>
> The instances that second marriage move
> Are base respects of thrift, but none of love.
> A second time I kill my husband dead
> When second husband kisses me in bed.

Without perhaps realizing how deeply his life is involved in the theater, the Player King still knows that life is a play, and his voice speaks the eternal truth of the theater:

> I do believe you think what now you speak,
> But what we do determine oft we break.
> Purpose is but the slave to memory,
> Of violent birth but poor validity,
> Which now, like fruit unripe, sticks on the tree
> But fall unshaken when they mellow be.
> Most necessary 'tis that we forget
> To pay ourselves what to ourselves is debt.
> What to ourselves in passion we propose,
> The passion ending, doth the purpose lose.
> The violence of either grief or joy
> Their own enactures with themselves destroy.
> Where joy most revels, grief doth most lament,
> Grief joys, joy grieves, on slender accident.
> This world is not for aye, nor 'tis not strange
> That even our loves should with our fortunes change,
> For 'tis a question left us yet to prove
> Whether love lead fortune or else fortune love.
>
>   .   .   .
>
> But, orderly to end where I begun,
> Our wills and fates do so contrary run
> That our devices still are overthrown,
> Our thoughts are ours, their ends none of our own.

THE TRAGEDY OF
HAMLET
PRINCE OF DENMARK

BY

WILLIAM SHAKESPEARE

Hamlet does not require the kind of introduction given the other plays in this volume. It is the most famous and the most prized of all English plays. Nearly everyone can quote several passages from it. Many of its phrases have become a permanent part of the English language because they catch so perfectly some of the crucial facts of existence: "To be or not to be," "hoist by his own petard," "we know what we are but not what we may be," "readiness is all." Yet in another way it remains the least known of plays, for it seems both bottomless in its presentation of human nature and infinitely complex in its depiction of life.

What is most necessary, but most difficult to achieve, for an understanding of *Hamlet* is some sense of it as a whole, some grasp of the sweep of events, leading from a bleak, cold battlement on the edge of an impenetrable darkness to the "stage" on which the body of Hamlet is placed, which also opens onto the impenetrable darkness. Between these two darknesses the full life of man is played out with all of its hopes, its losses, its searchings, its pride and hatred of self, its love and agony. Before us in the lighted space of Elsinore we see for an instant the full range of humanity: the sensual, crafty, politically effective Claudius; the unreflective, optimistic Gertrude; the foolish-wise councilor Polonius; the innocent, trusting, obedient daughter Ophelia; the fiery young man of fashion Laertes; his grotesque parody, the courtier

Osric; the affable, self-seeking, but vaguely uneasy opportunists Rosen-crantz and Guildenstern; the cracker-barrel philosopher, the insensitive gravedigger; the heroic voice of the past, old Hamlet; the silent, trustworthy Horatio, unmoved by his grim world; and, finally, that mixture of all qualities, Hamlet himself.

Such a play as this serves well as a capstone for the plays that have gone before it because all of the dramatic techniques discussed earlier and illustrated in the other plays are brought to their fulfillment here. Here every resource of the theater is used to create character and bring into being the world in which the characters move. Here the plot is not only the shape the dramatist gives to events, but it is also the very subject of the play. And here the magnificent use of the theater coupled with an unparalleled command of language lays down level after level of meaning until the central action of the play gathers into itself all of human life.

DRAMATIS PERSONAE

CLAUDIUS, *King of Denmark*
HAMLET, *son to the late, and nephew to the present King*
POLONIUS, *Lord Chamberlain*
HORATIO, *friend to Hamlet*
LAERTES, *son to Polonius*

VOLTIMAND
CORNELIUS
ROSENCRANTZ ⎫
GUILDENSTERN ⎬ *courtiers*
OSRIC
A GENTLEMAN ⎭

A PRIEST

MARCELLUS ⎫
BERNARDO ⎬ *officers*
FRANCISCO, *a soldier*
REYNALDO, *servant to Polonius*
PLAYERS
TWO CLOWNS, *gravediggers*
FORTINBRAS, *Prince of Norway*
A CAPTAIN
ENGLISH AMBASSADORS
GERTRUDE, *Queen of Denmark, and mother to Hamlet*
OPHELIA, *daughter to Polonius*
LORDS, LADIES, OFFICERS, SOLDIERS, SAILORS,
MESSENGERS, *and other* ATTENDANTS
GHOST *of Hamlet's father*

SCENE —— *Denmark.*

From Shakespeare: The Complete Works edited by G. B. Harrison, copyright 1948, 1952 by Harcourt, Brace & World, Inc. and reprinted with their permission. Line numbers do not represent the actual lineation of this edition but are keyed to the Globe Shakespeare to provide for easy cross reference to other editions of the play.

ACT I

Scene 1 ⌇ *Elsinore. A platform° before the castle.*

[FRANCISCO *at his post. Enter to him* BERNARDO.]

BERNARDO. Who's there?

FRANCISCO. Nay, answer me. Stand, and unfold yourself.°

BERNARDO. Long live the King!°

FRANCISCO. Bernardo?

BERNARDO. He.   5

FRANCISCO. You come most carefully upon your hour.

BERNARDO. 'Tis now struck twelve. Get thee to bed, Francisco.

FRANCISCO. For this relief much thanks. 'Tis bitter cold,
    And I am sick at heart.

BERNARDO. Have you had quiet guard?

FRANCISCO.   Not a mouse stirring.   10

BERNARDO. Well, good night.
    If you do meet Horatio and Marcellus,
    The rivals° of my watch, bid them make haste.

FRANCISCO. I think I hear them. Stand, ho! Who is there?

[*Enter* HORATIO *and* MARCELLUS.]

HORATIO. Friends to this ground.

MARCELLUS.   And liegemen° to the Dane.   15

FRANCISCO. Give you good night.

MARCELLUS.   Oh, farewell, honest soldier.
    Who hath relieved you?

FRANCISCO.   Bernardo hath my place.
    Give you good night.   [*Exit.*]

MARCELLUS.   Holloa! Bernardo!

BERNARDO.   Say,
    What, is Horatio there?

Act I, Sc. 1: s.d., platform: the level place on the ramparts where the cannon were mounted. 2. unfold yourself: reveal who you are. 3. Long . . .
King: probably the password for the night. 13. rivals: partners. 15. liege-
men: loyal subjects.

HORATIO.   A piece of him.
BERNARDO. Welcome, Horatio. Welcome, good Marcellus.   20
MARCELLUS. What, has this thing appeared again tonight?
BERNARDO. I have seen nothing.
MARCELLUS. Horatio says 'tis but our fantasy,°
    And will not let belief take hold of him
    Touching this dreaded sight twice seen of us,   25
    Therefore I have entreated him along
    With us to watch the minutes of this night,
    That if again this apparition come,
    He may approve our eyes° and speak to it.
HORATIO. Tush, tush, 'twill not appear.
BERNARDO.   Sit down awhile,   30
    And let us once again assail your ears,
    That are so fortified against our story,
    What we have two nights seen.
HORATIO.   Well, sit we down,
    And let us hear Bernardo speak of this.
BERNARDO. Last night of all,   35
    When yond same star that's westward from the pole°
    Had made his course to illume° that part of heaven
    Where now it burns, Marcellus and myself,
    The bell then beating one——
                    [*Enter* GHOST.]
MARCELLUS. Peace, break thee off. Look where it comes again!   40
BERNARDO. In the same figure, like the King that's dead.
MARCELLUS. Thou art a scholar.° Speak to it, Horatio.
BERNARDO. Looks it not like the King? Mark it, Horatio.
HORATIO. Most like. It harrows° me with fear and wonder.
BERNARDO. It would be spoke to.
MARCELLUS.   Question it, Horatio.   45
HORATIO. What art thou that usurp'st this time of night,
    Together with° that fair and warlike form
    In which the majesty of buried Denmark°
    Did sometimes march? By Heaven I charge thee, speak!
MARCELLUS. It is offended.
BERNARDO.   See, it stalks away!   50
HORATIO. Stay! Speak, speak! I charge thee, speak!
                    [*Exit* GHOST.]

---

23. fantasy: imagination.   29. approve our eyes: verify what we have seen.
36. pole: Polestar.   37. illume: light.   42. scholar: As Latin was the proper
language in which to address and exorcise evil spirits, a scholar was necessary.
44. harrows: distresses; lit., plows up.   47. Together with: i.e., appearing in.
48. majesty . . . Denmark: the dead King.

MARCELLUS. 'Tis gone, and will not answer.
BERNARDO. How now, Horatio! You tremble and look pale.
    Is not this something more than fantasy?
    What think you on 't? 55
HORATIO. Before my God, I might not this believe
    Without the sensible and true avouch
    Of mine own eyes.°
MARCELLUS.   Is it not like the King?
HORATIO. As thou art to thyself.
    Such was the very armor he had on 60
    When he the ambitious Norway combated.
    So frowned he once when, in an angry parle,°
    He smote the sledded Polacks° on the ice.
    'Tis strange.
MARCELLUS. Thus twice before, and jump at this dead hour,° 65
    With martial stalk hath he gone by our watch.
HORATIO. In what particular thought to work I know not,
    But in the gross and scope° of my opinion
    This bodes some strange eruption° to our state.
MARCELLUS. Good now, sit down and tell me, he that knows, 70
    Why this same strict and most observant watch
    So nightly toils° the subject° of the land;
    And why such daily cast of brazen cannon
    And foreign mart° for implements of war;
    Why° such impress° of shipwrights, whose sore task 75
    Does not divide the Sunday from the week;
    What might be toward,° that this sweaty haste
    Doth make the night joint laborer with the day.
    Who is 't that can inform me?
HORATIO.   That can I,
    At least the whisper goes so. Our last King, 80
    Whose image even but now appeared to us,
    Was, as you know, by Fortinbras of Norway,
    Thereto pricked° on by a most emulate° pride,

57–58. Without . . . eyes: unless my own eye had vouched for it. **sensible:**
perceived by my senses. **62. parle:** parley. **63. sledded Polacks:** There has
been much controversy about this phrase. Q1 and Q2 read "sleaded Pollax,"
F1 reads "sledded Pollax." Either the late King smote his heavy (leaded)
poleax on the ice, or else he attacked the Poles in their sledges. There is no
further reference to this incident. **65. jump . . . hour:** just at deep midnight. **68. gross . . . scope:** general conclusion. **69. eruption:** violent disturbance. **72. toils:** wearies. **subject:** subjects. **74. foreign mart:** purchase
abroad. **75–78. Why . . . day:** i.e., workers in shipyards and munition factories are working night shifts and Sundays. **impress:** conscription. **toward:**
in preparation. **83. pricked:** spurred. **emulate:** jealous.

Dared to the combat, in which our valiant Hamlet—
For so this side of our known world esteemed him—   85
Did slay this Fortinbras. Who° by a sealed compact,°
Well ratified by law and heraldry,°
Did forfeit, with his life, all those his lands
Which he stood seized of° to the conqueror.
Against the which, a moiety competent°   90
Was gagèd° by our King, which had returned
To the inheritance of Fortinbras
Had he been vanquisher, as by the same covenant
And carriage of the article designed°
His fell to Hamlet. Now, sir, your Fortinbras,   95
Of unimprovèd° mettle° hot and full,
Hath in the skirts° of Norway here and there
Sharked° up a list of lawless resolutes,°
For food and diet,° to some enterprise
That hath a stomach° in 't. Which is no other—   100
As it doth well appear unto our state—
But to recover of us, by strong hand
And terms compulsatory,° those foresaid lands
So by his father lost. And this, I take it,
Is the main motive of our preparations,   105
The source of this our watch and the chief head°
Of this posthaste and romage° in the land.
BERNARDO. I think it be no other but e'en so.
    Well may it sort° that this portentous figure
Comes armèd through our watch, so like the King   110
That was and is the question of these wars.
HORATIO. A mote° it is to trouble the mind's eye.
    In the most high and palmy° state of Rome,
A little ere the mightiest Julius fell,
The graves stood tenantless, and the sheeted° dead   115

86–95. Who . . . Hamlet: i.e., before the combat it was agreed that the vic-
tor should win the lands of the vanquished.   86. sealed compact: formal
agreement.   87. heraldry: The heralds were responsible for arranging formal
combats.   89. seized of: possessed of, a legal term.   90. moiety competent:
adequate portion.   91. gaged: pledged.   94. carriage . . . designed: fulfillment of the clause in the agreement.   96. unimproved mettle: untutored, wild
material, nature.   97. skirts: outlying parts.   98. Sharked: collected indiscriminately, as a shark bolts its prey. lawless resolutes: gangsters.   99. diet:
maintenance.   100. stomach: resolution.   103. terms compulsatory: force.
106. chief head: main purpose.   107. posthaste . . . romage: urgency and
bustle.   109. Well . . . sort: it would be a natural reason.   112. mote: speck
of dust.   113. palmy: flourishing.   115. sheeted: in their shrouds.

Did squeak and gibber° in the Roman streets.
As stars° with trains of fire and dews of blood,
Disasters° in the sun, and the moist star°
Upon whose influence Neptune's empire stands
Was sick almost to doomsday with eclipse.   120
And even the like precurse° of fierce events,
As harbingers° preceding still the fates
And prologue to the omen° coming on,
Have Heaven and earth together demonstrated
Unto our climatures° and countrymen.   125
[*Re-enter* GHOST.] But soft, behold! Lo where it comes again!
I'll cross it,° though it blast me. Stay, illusion!
If thou hast any sound, or use of voice,
Speak to me.
If° there be any good thing to be done   130
That may to thee do ease and grace to me,°
Speak to me.
If thou art privy to° thy country's fate,
Which, happily,° foreknowing may avoid,
Oh, speak!   135
Or if thou hast uphoarded in thy life
Extorted° treasure in the womb of earth,
For which, they say, you spirits oft walk in death,
Speak of it. Stay, and speak! [*The cock crows.*°] Stop it,
     Marcellus.
MARCELLUS. Shall I strike at it with my partisan?°   140
HORATIO. Do, if it will not stand.
BERNARDO.   'Tis here!
HORATIO.   'Tis here!
MARCELLUS. 'Tis gone!   [*Exit* GHOST.]
     We do it wrong, being so majestical,

---

116. gibber: utter strange sounds.   117. As stars: The sense of the passage is
here broken; possibly a line has been omitted after l. 116.   118. Disasters:
unlucky signs. moist star: the moon, which influences the tides.   121. pre-
curse: forewarning.   122. harbingers: forerunners. The harbinger was an officer of the Court who was sent ahead to make the arrangements when the
Court went on progress.   123. omen: disaster.   125. climatures: regions.
127. cross it: stand in its way.   130–39. If . . . speak: In popular belief
there were four reasons why the spirit of a dead man should *walk:* (a) to reveal a secret, (b) to utter a warning, (c) to reveal concealed treasure, (d)
to reveal the manner of its death. Horatio thus adjures the ghost by three potent reasons, but before he can utter the fourth the cock crows.   131. grace
to me: bring me into a state of spiritual grace.   133. Extorted: evilly acquired.
139. s.d., cock crows: i.e., a sign that dawn is at hand. See ll. 147–64.   140.
partisan: a spear with a long blade.

To offer it the show of violence,
For it is as the air invulnerable,   145
And our vain blows malicious mockery.
BERNARDO. It was about to speak when the cock crew.
HORATIO. And then it started like a guilty thing
  Upon a fearful° summons. I have heard
  The cock, that is the trumpet to the morn,   150
  Doth with his lofty and shrill-sounding throat
  Awake the god of day, and at his warning,
  Whether in sea or fire, in earth or air,
  The extravagant and erring° spirit hies
  To his confine.° And of the truth herein   155
  This present object made probation.°
MARCELLUS. It faded on the crowing of the cock.
  Some say that ever 'gainst° that season comes
  Wherein Our Saviour's birth is celebrated,
  The bird of dawning singeth all night long.   160
  And then, they say, no spirit dare stir abroad,
  The nights are wholesome, then no planets° strike,
  No fairy takes° nor witch hath power to charm,
  So hallowed and so gracious is the time.
HORATIO. So have I heard and do in part believe it.   165
  But look, the morn, in russet mantle clad,
  Walks o'er the dew of yon high eastward hill.
  Break we our watch up, and by my advice
  Let us impart what we have seen tonight
  Unto young Hamlet, for upon my life,   170
  This spirit, dumb to us, will speak to him.
  Do you consent we shall acquaint him with it,
  As needful in our loves, fitting our duty?
MARCELLUS. Let's do 't, I pray. And I this morning know
  Where we shall find him most conveniently.   [Exeunt.] 175

---

149. fearful: causing fear.   **154. extravagant . . . erring:** both words mean "wandering."   **155. confine:** place of confinement.   **156. probation:** proof.   **158. 'gainst:** in anticipation of.   **162. planets:** Planets were supposed to bring disaster.   **163. takes:** bewitches.

Scene 2 ⨳ *A room of state in the castle.*

[*Flourish.*° *Enter the* KING, QUEEN, HAMLET, POLONIUS,
LAERTES, VOLTIMAND, CORNELIUS, LORDS, *and* ATTENDANTS.]
KING. Though yet of Hamlet our dear brother's death
    The memory be green,° and that it us befitted
    To bear our hearts in grief and our whole kingdom
    To be contracted in one brow of woe,°
    Yet so far hath discretion° fought with nature°   5
    That we with wisest sorrow think on him,
    Together with remembrance of ourselves.
    Therefore our sometime sister,° now our Queen,
    The imperial jointress° to this warlike state,
    Have we, as 'twere with a defeated joy—   10
    With an auspicious and a dropping eye,°
    With mirth in funeral and with dirge in marriage,
    In equal scale weighing delight and dole°—
    Taken to wife. Nor have we herein barred
    Your better wisdoms,° which have freely gone   15
    With this affair along. For all, our thanks.
    Now follows that you know. Young Fortinbras,
    Holding a weak supposal° of our worth,
    Or thinking by our late dear brother's death
    Our state to be disjoint and out of frame,   20

Sc. 2: s.d., Flourish: fanfare of trumpets. **2. green:** fresh. **4. contracted
. . . woe:** i.e., every subject's forehead should be puckered with grief. **5.
discretion:** common sense. **nature:** natural sorrow. **8. sister:** i.e., my
brother's wife. **9. jointress:** partner by marriage. **11. auspicious . . . eye:**
an eye at the same time full of joy and of tears. **13. dole:** grief. **14–15.
barred . . . wisdoms:** i.e., in taking this step we have not shut out your advice. As is obvious throughout the play, the Danes chose their King by election and not by right of birth. See V.2.65, 366. **18. weak supposal:** poor
opinion.

Colleagued with the dream of his advantage,°
He hath not failed to pester us with message
Importing the surrender of those lands
Lost by his father, with all bonds of law,°
To our most valiant brother. So much for him.   25
Now for ourself, and for this time of meeting.
Thus much the business is: We have here writ
To Norway, uncle of young Fortinbras—
Who, impotent and bedrid, scarcely hears
Of this his nephew's purpose—to suppress   30
His further gait° herein, in that the levies,
The lists° and full proportions,° are all made
Out of his subject.° And we here dispatch
You, good Cornelius, and you, Voltimand,
For bearers of this greeting to old Norway,   35
Giving to you no further personal power
To business with the King more than the scope°
Of these delated articles° allow.
Farewell, and let your haste commend° your duty.
CORNELIUS & VOLTIMAND. In that and all things will we show our
duty.   40
KING. We doubt it nothing. Heartily farewell.
                              [*Exeunt* VOLTIMAND *and* CORNELIUS.]
And now, Laertes, what's the news with you?
You told us of some suit°—what is 't, Laertes?
You cannot speak of reason to the Dane
And lose your voice. What wouldst thou beg, Laertes,   45
That shall not be my offer, not thy asking?
The head is not more native° to the heart,
The hand more instrumental° to the mouth,
Than is the throne of Denmark to thy father.
What wouldst thou have, Laertes?
LAERTES.   My dread° lord,   50
Your leave and favor to return to France,
From whence though willingly I came to Denmark

21. **Colleagued . . . advantage:** uniting himself with this dream that here
was a good opportunity.   24. **with . . . law:** legally binding, as already explained in I.1.80–95.   31. **gait:** progress.   32. **lists:** rosters. **proportions:** military establishments.   33. **subject:** subjects.   37. **scope:** limit.   38. **delated articles:** detailed instructions. Claudius is following usual diplomatic procedure.
Ambassadors sent on a special mission carried with them a letter of introduction and greeting to the King of the foreign Court and detailed instructions
to guide them in the negotiations.   39. **commend:** display; lit., recommend.
43. **suit:** petition.   47. **native:** closely related.   48. **instrumental:** serviceable.
50. **dread:** dreaded, much respected.

To show my duty in your coronation,
Yet now, I must confess, that duty done,
My thoughts and wishes bend again toward France   55
And bow them to your gracious leave and pardon.
KING. Have you your father's leave? What says Polonius?
POLONIUS. He hath, my lord, wrung from me my slow leave
    By laborsome petition, and at last
    Upon his will° I sealed my hard consent.°   60
    I do beseech you give him leave to go.
KING. Take thy fair hour, Laertes, time be thine,
    And thy best graces spend° it at thy will!
    But now, my cousin° Hamlet, and my son——
HAMLET. [Aside] A little more than kin and less than kind.°   65
KING. How is it that the clouds still hang on you?
HAMLET. Not so, my lord. I am too much i' the sun.
QUEEN. Good Hamlet, cast thy nighted color° off,
    And let thine eye look like a friend on Denmark.
    Do not forever with thy vailèd lids°   70
    Seek for thy noble father in the dust.
    Thou know'st 'tis common—all that lives must die,
    Passing through nature to eternity.
HAMLET. Aye, madam, it is common.
QUEEN.   If it be,
    Why seems it so particular with thee?   75
HAMLET. Seems, madam! Nay, it is. I know not "seems."
    'Tis not alone my inky cloak, good Mother,
    Nor customary suits of solemn black,
    Nor windy suspiration of forced breath—
    No, nor the fruitful river° in the eye,   80
    Nor the dejected havior of the visage,°
    Together with all forms, moods, shapes of grief—
    That can denote me truly. These indeed seem,
    For they are actions that a man might play.°
    But I have that within which passeth show,   85
    These but the trappings° and the suits of woe.
KING. 'Tis sweet and commendable in your nature, Hamlet,
    To give these mourning duties to your father.

---

60. will: desire. sealed . . . consent: agreed to, but with great reluctance.
63. best . . . spend: i.e., use your time well. 64. cousin: kinsman. The word
was used for any near relation. 65. A . . . kind: too near a relation (uncle-
father) and too little natural affection. kind: affectionate. 68. nighted color:
black. Hamlet alone is in deep mourning; the rest of the Court wear gay
clothes. 70. vailed lids: lowered eyelids. 80. fruitful river: stream of tears.
81. dejected . . . visage: downcast countenance. 84. play: act, as in a play.
86. trappings: ornaments.

But you must know your father lost a father,
That father lost, lost his, and the survivor bound   90
In filial obligation for some term
To do obsequious sorrow.° But to perséver
In obstinate condolement° is a course
Of impious stubbornness, 'tis unmanly grief.
It shows a will most incorrect to Heaven,   95
A heart unfortified,° a mind impatient,
An understanding simple and unschooled.
For what we know must be and is as common
As any the most vulgar° thing to sense,
Why should we in our peevish opposition   100
Take it to heart? Fie! 'Tis a fault to Heaven,
A fault against the dead, a fault to nature,
To reason most absurd, whose common theme
Is death of fathers, and who still hath cried,
From the first corse° till he that died today,   105
"This must be so." We pray you throw to earth
This unprevailing° woe, and think of us
As of a father. For let the world take note,
You are the most immediate° to our throne,
And with no less nobility of love   110
Than that which dearest father bears his son
Do I impart toward you. For your intent
In going back to school° in Wittenberg,
It is most retrograde° to our desire.
And we beseech you bend you° to remain   115
Here in the cheer and comfort of our eye,
Our chiefest courtier, cousin, and our son.
QUEEN. Let not thy mother lose her prayers, Hamlet.
     I pray thee, stay with us, go not to Wittenberg.
HAMLET. I shall in all my best obey you, madam.   120
KING. Why, 'tis a loving and a fair reply.
     Be as ourself in Denmark. Madam, come,
     This gentle and unforced accord of Hamlet
     Sits smiling to my heart. In grace whereof,
     No jocund health that Denmark drinks today   125

---

92. obsequious sorrow: the sorrow usual at funerals.   93. obstinate condole-
ment: lamentation disregarding the will of God.   96. unfortified: not strength-
ened with the consolation of religion.   99. vulgar: common.   105. corse:
corpse. There is unconscious irony in this remark, for the first corpse was that
of Abel, also slain by his brother.   107. unprevailing: futile.   109. most immediate: next heir.   113. school: university.   114. retrograde: contrary.
115. bend you: incline.

But the great cannon° to the clouds shall tell,
And the King's rouse° the Heaven shall bruit° again,
Respeaking earthly thunder. Come away.

             [Flourish. Exeunt all but HAMLET.]

HAMLET. Oh, that this too too solid flesh would melt,
Thaw, and resolve itself into a dew!   130
Or that the Everlasting had not fixed
His canon° 'gainst self-slaughter! Oh, God! God!
How weary, stale, flat, and unprofitable
Seem to me all the uses° of this world!
Fie on 't, ah, fie! 'Tis an unweeded garden,   135
That grows to seed, things rank° and gross in nature
Possess it merely.° That it should come to this!
But two months dead! Nay, not so much, not two.
So excellent a King, that was, to this,
Hyperion° to a satyr.° So loving to my mother   140
That he might not beteem° the winds of heaven
Visit her face too roughly. Heaven and earth!
Must I remember? Why, she would hang on him
As if increase of appetite had grown
By what it fed on. And yet within a month——   145
Let me not think on 't.—Frailty, thy name is woman!—
A little month, or ere those shoes were old
With which she followed my poor father's body,
Like Niobe° all tears.—Why she, even she—
Oh, God! A beast that wants discourse of reason°   150
Would have mourned longer—married with my uncle,
My father's brother, but no more like my father
Than I to Hercules. Within a month,
Ere yet the salt of most unrighteous tears
Had left the flushing in her gallèd° eyes,   155
She married. Oh, most wicked speed, to post°
With such dexterity° to incestuous sheets!
It is not, nor it cannot, come to good.
But break, my heart, for I must hold my tongue!

---

126. great cannon: This Danish custom of discharging cannon when the King proposed a toast was much noted by Englishmen. **127. rouse:** deep drink. **bruit:** sound loudly, echo. **132. canon:** rule, law. **134. uses:** ways. **136. rank:** coarse. **137. merely:** entirely. **140. Hyperion:** the sun god. **satyr:** a creature half man, half goat—ugly and lecherous. **141. beteem:** allow. **149. Niobe:** She boasted of her children, to the annoyance of the goddess Artemis, who slew them all. Thereafter Niobe became so sorrowful that she changed into a rock everlastingly dripping water. **150. wants . . . reason:** is without ability to reason. **155. galled:** sore. **156. post:** hasten. **157. dexterity:** nimbleness.

[*Enter* HORATIO, MARCELLUS, *and* BERNARDO.]

HORATIO. Hail to your lordship!

HAMLET.   I am glad to see you well.   160
Horatio—or I do forget myself.

HORATIO. The same, my lord, and your poor servant ever.

HAMLET. Sir, my good friend—I'll change that name° with you.
And what make you from Wittenberg, Horatio?
Marcellus?   165

MARCELLUS. My good lord?

HAMLET. I am very glad to see you. [*To* BERNARDO] Good even,
sir.
But what, in faith, make you from Wittenberg?

HORATIO. A truant disposition, good my lord.

HAMLET. I would not hear your enemy say so,   170
Nor shall you do my ear that violence
To make it truster of your own report
Against yourself. I know you are no truant.
But what is your affair in Elsinore?
We'll teach you to drink deep° ere you depart.   175

HORATIO. My lord, I came to see your father's funeral.

HAMLET. I pray thee do not mock me, fellow student.
I think it was to see my mother's wedding.

HORATIO. Indeed, my lord, it followed hard upon.

HAMLET. Thrift, thrift, Horatio! The funeral baked meats   180
Did coldly furnish forth the marriage tables.°
Would I had met my dearest° foe in Heaven
Or ever I had seen that day, Horatio!
My father!—Methinks I see my father.

HORATIO. Oh, where, my lord?

HAMLET.   In my mind's eye, Horatio.   185

HORATIO. I saw him once. He was a goodly King.

HAMLET. He was a man, take him for all in all.
I shall not look upon his like again.

HORATIO. My lord, I think I saw him yesternight.

HAMLET. Saw? Who?   190

HORATIO. My lord, the King your father.

HAMLET.   The King my father!

HORATIO. Season your admiration° for a while
With an attent° ear till I may deliver,

164. that name: i.e., friend.   175. drink deep: For more on the drunken habits
of the Danes, see I.4.8–38.   180–81. Thrift . . . tables: they hurried on the
wedding for economy's sake, so that the remains of food served at the funeral
might be used cold for the wedding. baked meats: feast.   182. dearest: best-
hated.   192. Season . . . admiration: moderate your wonder.   193. attent:
attentive.

Upon the witness of these gentlemen,
This marvel to you.
HAMLET.   For God's love, let me hear.   195
HORATIO. Two nights together had these gentlemen,
    Marcellus and Bernardo, on their watch
    In the dead vast and middle of the night,°
    Been thus encountered. A figure like your father,
    Armèd at point exactly, cap-a-pie,°
    Appears before them and with solemn march
    Goes slow and stately by them. Thrice he walked
    By their oppressed and fear-surprisèd eyes
    Within his truncheon's° length, whilst they, distilled°
    Almost to jelly with the act of fear,   205
    Stand dumb, and speak not to him. This to me
    In dreadful secrecy impart they did,
    And I with them the third night kept the watch.
    Where, as they had delivered, both in time,
    Form of the thing, each word made true and good,   210
    The apparition comes. I knew your father.
    These hands are not more like.
HAMLET.   But where was this?
MARCELLUS. My lord, upon the platform where we watched.
HAMLET. Did you not speak to it?
HORATIO.   My lord, I did,
    But answer made it none. Yet once methought   215
    It lifted up it° head and did address
    Itself to motion, like as it would speak.
    But even then the morning cock crew loud,
    And at the sound it shrunk in haste away
    And vanished from our sight.
HAMLET.   'Tis very strange.   220
HORATIO. As I do live, my honored lord, 'tis true,
    And we did think it writ down in our duty
    To let you know of it.
HAMLET. Indeed, indeed, sirs, but this troubles me.
    Hold you the watch tonight?
MARCELLUS & BERNARDO.   We do, my lord.   225
HAMLET. Armed, say you?
MARCELLUS & BERNARDO. Armed, my lord.
HAMLET.   From top to toe?
MARCELLUS & BERNARDO. My lord, from head to foot.

---

198. dead . . . night: deep, silent midnight. 200. at . . . cap-a-pie: complete in every detail, head to foot. 204. truncheon: a general's staff. dis-
tilled: melted. 216. it: its.

HAMLET. Then saw you not his face?
HORATIO. Oh yes, my lord, he wore his beaver° up.
HAMLET. What, looked he frowningly?   230
HORATIO. A countenance more in sorrow than in anger.
HAMLET. Pale, or red?
HORATIO. Nay, very pale.
HAMLET.   And fixed his eyes upon you?
HORATIO. Most constantly.
HAMLET.   I would I had been there.   235
HORATIO. It would have much amazed you.
HAMLET. Very like, very like. Stayed it long?
HORATIO. While one with moderate haste might tell° a hundred.
MARCELLUS & BERNARDO. Longer, longer.
HORATIO. Not when I saw 't.
HAMLET.   His beard was grizzled?° No?   240
HORATIO. It was as I have seen it in his life,
    A sable silvered.°
HAMLET.   I will watch tonight.
    Perchance 'twill walk again.
HORATIO.   I warrant it will.
HAMLET. If it assume my noble father's person,
    I'll speak to it though Hell itself should gape   245
    And bid me hold my peace. I pray you all,
    If you have hitherto concealed this sight,
    Let it be tenable° in your silence still,
    And whatsoever else shall hap tonight,
    Give it an understanding, but no tongue.   250
    I will requite° your loves. So fare you well.
    Upon the platform, 'twixt eleven and twelve,
    I'll visit you.
ALL.   Our duty to your Honor.
HAMLET. Your loves, as mine to you. Farewell.
                            [*Exeunt all but* HAMLET.]
    My father's spirit in arms! All is not well.   255
    I doubt° some foul play. Would the night were come!
    Till then sit still, my soul. Foul deeds will rise,
    Though all the earth o'erwhelm them, to men's eyes.
                                        [*Exit.*]

229. beaver: front part of the helmet, which could be raised. 238. tell: count. 240. grizzled: gray. 242. sable silvered: black mingled with white. 248. tenable: held fast. 251. requite: repay. 256. doubt: suspect.

Scene 3 ᴈᱤ *A room in* POLONIUS'S *house.*

[*Enter* LAERTES *and* OPHELIA.]
LAERTES. My necessaries° are embarked. Farewell.
And, Sister, as the winds give benefit
And convoy is assistant,° do not sleep,
But let me hear from you.
OPHELIA.   Do you doubt that?
LAERTES. For Hamlet, and the trifling of his favor,°   5
Hold it a fashion and a toy in blood,°
A violet in the youth of primy° nature,
Forward, not permanent, sweet, not lasting,
The perfume and suppliance of a minute°—
No more.
OPHELIA. No more but so?
LAERTES.   Think it no more.   10
For Nature crescent does not grow alone
In thews and bulk,° but as this temple° waxes
The inward service of the mind and soul
Grows wide withal. Perhaps he loves you now,
And now no soil nor cautel° doth besmirch   15
The virtue of his will.° But you must fear,
His greatness weighed,° his will is not his own,
For he himself is subject to his birth.
He may not, as unvalued persons do,
Carve° for himself, for on his choice depends   20
The safety and health of this whole state,

Scn. 3: 1. necessaries: baggage. 3. convoy . . . assistant: means of conveyance is available. 5. favor: i.e., toward you. 6. toy in blood: trifling impulse. 7. primy: springtime; i.e., youthful. 8. perfume . . . minute: perfume which lasts only for a minute. 11–12. For . . . bulk: for natural growth is not only in bodily bulk. 12. temple: i.e., the body. 15. cautel: deceit. 16. will: desire. 17. His . . . weighed: when you consider his high position. 20. Carve: choose.

And therefore must his choice be circumscribed°
Unto the voice and yielding of that body
Whereof he is the head. Then if he says he loves you,
It fits your wisdom so far to believe it   25
As he in his particular act and place
May give his saying deed, which is no further
Than the main voice of Denmark goes withal.
Then weigh what loss your honor may sustain
If with too credent° ear you list his songs,   30
Or lose your heart, or your chaste treasure° open
To his unmastered importunity.
Fear it, Ophelia, fear it, my dear sister,
And keep you in the rear° of your affection,
Out of the shot and danger of desire.   35
The chariest maid is prodigal enough
If she unmask her beauty to the moon.
Virtue itself 'scapes not calumnious strokes.
The canker galls the infants° of the spring
Too oft before their buttons° be disclosed,   40
And in the morn and liquid dew of youth
Contagious blastments° are most imminent.
Be wary, then, best safety lies in fear.
Youth to itself rebels, though none else near.°
OPHELIA. I shall the effect of this good lesson keep   45
As watchman to my heart. But, good my brother,
Do not, as some ungracious pastors do,
Show me the steep and thorny way to Heaven
Whilst, like a puffed° and reckless libertine,
Himself the primrose path of dalliance° treads   50
And recks not his own rede.°
LAERTES.   Oh, fear me not.
I stay too long. But here my father comes.
[*Enter* POLONIUS.] A double blessing is a double grace,
Occasion smiles° upon a second leave.
POLONIUS. Yet here, Laertes! Aboard, aboard, for shame!   55
The wind sits in the shoulder of your sail
And you are stayed° for. There, my blessing with thee!

22. **circumscribed:** restricted.   30. **credent:** credulous.   31. **chaste treasure:**
the treasure of your chasity.   34. **in . . . rear:** i.e., farthest from danger.
39. **canker . . . infants:** maggot harms the unopened buds.   40. **buttons:**
buds.   42. **Contagious blastments:** infectious blasts.   44. **though . . . near:**
without anyone else to encourage it.   49. **puffed:** panting.   50. **primrose
. . . dalliance:** i.e., the pleasant way of love-making.   51. **recks . . . rede:**
takes no heed of his own advice.   54. **Occasion smiles:** i.e., here is a happy
chance.   57. **stayed:** waited.

And these few precepts in thy memory
Look thou chárácter.° Give thy thoughts no tongue,
Nor any unproportioned° thought his act.   60
Be thou familiar, but by no means vulgar.
Those friends thou hast, and their adoption tried,°
Grapple them to thy soul with hoops of steel,
But do not dull thy palm with entertainment°
Of each newhatched unfledged° comrade. Beware   65
Of entrance to a quarrel, but being in,
Bear 't that the opposèd may beware of thee.
Give every man thy ear, but few thy voice.°
Take each man's censure,° but reserve thy judgment.
Costly thy habit° as thy purse can buy,   70
But not expressed in fancy°—rich, not gaudy.
For the apparel oft proclaims the man,
And they in France of the best rank and station
Are of a most select and generous chief in that.°
Neither a borrower nor a lender be,   75
For loan oft loses both itself and friend
And borrowing dulls the edge of husbandry.°
This above all: To thine own self be true,
And it must follow, as the night the day,
Thou canst not then be false to any man.   80
Farewell. My blessing season° this in thee!
LAERTES. Most humbly do I take my leave, my lord.
POLONIUS. The time invites you. Go, your servants tend.°
LAERTES. Farewell, Ophelia, and remember well
    What I have said to you.
OPHELIA.   'Tis in my memory locked,   85
And you yourself shall keep the key of it.
LAERTES. Farewell.   [Exit.]
POLONIUS. What is 't, Ophelia, he hath said to you?
OPHELIA. So please you, something touching the Lord Hamlet.
POLONIUS. Marry,° well bethought.°   90

---

59. character: inscribe.   **60. unproportioned:** unsuitable.   **62. adoption tried:**
friendship tested by experience.   **64. dull . . . entertainment:** let your hand
grow callous with welcome.   **65. unfledged:** lit., newly out of the egg, immature.   **68. Give . . . voice:** listen to everyone but commit yourself to few.
69. censure: opinion.   **70. habit:** dress.   **71. expressed in fancy:** fantastic.
74. Are . . . that: A disputed line; this is the F1 reading. Q2 reads "Or of
the most select and generous, chief in that"; i.e., the best noble and gentle
families are very particular in their dress. **generous:** of gentle birth.   **77.**
husbandry: economy.   **81. season:** bring to fruit.   **83. tend:** attend.   **90.**
Marry: Mary, by the Virgin Mary. **well bethought:** well remembered.

'Tis told me he hath very oft of late
Given private time to you, and you yourself
Have of your audience been most free and bounteous.
If it be so—as so 'tis put on me,
And that in way of caution—I must tell you   95
You do not understand yourself so clearly
As it behooves° my daughter and your honor.
What is between you? Give me up the truth.

OPHELIA. He hath, my lord, of late made many tenders°
Of his affection to me.   100

POLONIUS. Affection! Pooh! You speak like a green girl,
Unsifted° in such perilous circumstance.
Do you believe his tenders, as you call them?

OPHELIA. I do not know, my lord, what I should think.

POLONIUS. Marry, I'll teach you. Think yourself a baby   105
That you have ta'en these tenders° for true pay,
Which are not sterling.° Tender yourself more dearly,
Or—not to crack the wind of° the poor phrase,
Running it thus—you'll tender me a fool.

OPHELIA. My lord, he hath importuned me with love   110
In honorable fashion.

POLONIUS. Aye, fashion° you may call it. Go to, go to.

OPHELIA. And hath given countenance to his speech,° my lord,
With almost all the holy vows of Heaven.

POLONIUS. Aye, springes° to catch woodcocks.° I do know,   115
When the blood burns, how prodigal° the soul
Lends the tongue vows. These blazes,° daughter,
Giving more light than heat, extinct in both,
Even in their promise as it is a-making,
You must not take for fire. From this time   120
Be something scanter of your maiden presence,
Set your entreatments at a higher rate
Than a command to parley.° For Lord Hamlet,
Believe so much in him, that he is young,
And with a larger tether° may he walk   125
Than may be given you. In few,° Ophelia,

97. behooves: is the duty of.   99. tenders: offers.   102. Unsifted: untried.
106–109. tenders . . . tender: Polonius puns on "tenders," counters (used
for money in games); "tender," value; "tender," show.   107. sterling: true
currency.   108. crack . . . of: i.e., ride to death.   112. fashion: mere
show.   113. given . . . speech: confirmed his words.   115. springes: snares.
woodcocks: foolish birds.   116. prodigal: extravagantly.   117. blazes: flashes,
quickly extinguished (*extinct.*)   122–23. Set . . . parley: when you are asked
to see him do not regard it as a command to negotiate. parley: meeting to
discuss terms.   125. tether: rope by which a grazing animal is fastened to
its peg.   126. In few: in short.

Do not believe his vows, for they are brokers,°
Not of that dye which their investments° show,
But mere implorators° of unholy suits,
Breathing like sanctified and pious bawds°   130
The better to beguile. This is for all.
I would not, in plain terms, from this time forth
Have you so slander any moment leisure°
As to give words or talk with the Lord Hamlet.
Look to 't, I charge you. Come your ways.   135
OPHELIA. I shall obey, my lord.   [*Exeunt.*]

Scene 4 ⚜ *The platform.*

[*Enter* HAMLET, HORATIO, *and* MARCELLUS.]
HAMLET. The air bites shrewdly.° It is very cold.
HORATIO. It is a nipping and an eager° air.
HAMLET. What hour now?
HORATIO.   I think it lacks of twelve.
MARCELLUS. No, it is struck.
HORATIO. Indeed? I heard it not. It then draws near the season   5
    Wherein the spirit held his wont to walk.
        [*A flourish of trumpets, and ordnance shot off within.*°]
    What doth this mean, my lord?
HAMLET. The King doth wake° tonight and takes his rouse,°
    Keeps wassail,° and the swaggering upspring reels.°
    And as he drains his draughts of Rhenish° down,   10
    The kettledrum and trumpet thus bray out
    The triumph of his pledge.
HORATIO.   Is it a custom?

---

127. brokers: traveling salesmen. 128. investments: garments. 129. im-
plorators: men who solicit. 130. bawds: keepers of brothels. F1 and Q2 read
"bond," an easy misprint for "baud"—the Elizabethan spelling of "bawd."
133. slander . . . leisure: misuse any moment of leisure.
    Sc. 4: 1. shrewdly: bitterly. 2. eager: sharp. 6. s.d., within: off stage.
8. wake: "makes a night of it." rouse: See I.2.127, n. 9. wassail. revelry.
swaggering . . . reels: reel in a riotous dance. 10. Rhenish: Rhine wine.

HAMLET. Aye, marry, is 't.
  But to my mind, though I am native here
  And to the manner born, it is a custom   15
  More honored in the breach than the observance.
  This heavy-headed revel° east and west
  Makes us traduced and taxed of° other nations.
  They clepe° us drunkards, and with swinish phrase
  Soil our addition,° and indeed it takes   20
  From our achievements, though performed at height,°
  The pith and marrow of our attribute.°
  So oft it chances in particular men,
  That for some vicious mole° of nature in them,
  As in their birth—wherein they are not guilty,   25
  Since nature cannot choose his origin—
  By the o'ergrowth of some complexion,°
  Oft breaking down the pales° and forts of reason,
  Or by some habit that too much o'erleavens°
  The form of plausive° manners, that these men—   30
  Carrying, I say, the stamp of one defect,
  Being Nature's livery,° or Fortune's star°—
  Their virtues else—be they as pure as grace,
  As infinite as man may undergo—
  Shall in the general censure take corruption   35
  From that particular fault. The dram of eale
  Doth all the noble substance of a doubt
  To his own scandal.°
                    [*Enter* GHOST.]
HORATIO.   Look, my lord, it comes!

17. **heavy-headed revel**: drinking which produces a thick head.   18. **traduced . . . of**: disgraced and censured by.   19. **clepe**: call.   20. **soil . . . addition**: smirch our honor.   **addition**: lit., title of honor added to a man's name.   21. **though . . . height**: though of the highest merit.   22: **pith . . . attribute**: essential part of our honor due to our achievements because of our reputation for drunkenness.   24. **mole**: blemish.   27. **o'ergrowth . . . complexion**: some quality allowed to overbalance the rest.   28. **pales**: defenses.   29. **o'erleavens**: mixes with.   30. **plausive**: agreeable.   32. **Nature's livery**: i. e., inborn. **Fortune's star**: the result of ill luck.   36–38. **The . . . scandal**: This is the most famous of all disputed passages in Shakespeare's plays. The general meaning is clear: "a small portion of evil brings scandal on the whole substance, however noble." "Eale" is an Elizabethan spelling and pronunciation of "evil," as later in Q2 (II.2.628); "deale" is the spelling and pronunciation of "Devil." The difficulty lies in "of a doubt," which is obviously a misprint of some such word as "corrupt"; but to be satisfactory it must fit the meter and be a plausible misprint. So far, although many guesses have been made, none is wholly convincing. The best is perhaps "often dout"—often put out.

HAMLET. Angels and ministers of grace defend us!
  Be thou a spirit of health or goblin damned.°   40
  Bring with thee airs from Heaven or blasts from Hell,
  Be thy intents wicked or charitable,
  Thou comest in such a questionable° shape
  That I will speak to thee. I'll call thee Hamlet,
  King, Father, royal Dane. Oh, answer me!   45
  Let me not burst in ignorance, but tell
  Why thy canónized° bones, hearsèd° in death,
  Have burst their cerements,° why the sepulcher
  Wherein we saw thee quietly inurned°
  Hath oped his ponderous and marble jaws   50
  To cast thee up again. What may this mean,
  That thou, dead corse, again, in complete steel,°
  Revisit'st thus the glimpses of the moon,
  Making night hideous, and we fools° of nature
  So horridly to shake our disposition°   55
  With thoughts beyond the reaches of our souls?
  Say, why is this? Wherefore? What should we do?
                [GHOST *beckons* HAMLET.]
HORATIO. It beckons you to go away with it,
  As if it some impartment° did desire
  To you alone.
MARCELLUS.   Look with what courteous action   60
  It waves you to a more removèd ground.
  But do not go with it.
HORATIO.   No, by no means.
HAMLET. It will not speak. Then I will follow it.
HORATIO. Do not, my lord.
HAMLET.   Why, what should be the fear?
  I do not set my life at a pin's fee,°   65
  And for my soul, what can it do to that,
  Being a thing immortal as itself?
  It waves me forth again. I'll follow it.
HORATIO. What if it tempt you toward the flood, my lord,
  Or to the dreadful summit of the cliff   70

40. spirit . . . damned: a holy spirit or damned fiend. Hamlet, until convinced at the end of the play scene (III.2.298), is perpetually in doubt
whether the ghost which he sees is a good spirit sent to warn him, a devil
sent to tempt him into some damnable action, or a hallucination created by
his own diseased imagination. See II.2.627–32. 43. questionable: inviting
question. 47. canonized: buried with full rites according to the canon of the
Church. hearsed: buried. 48. cerements: waxen shroud, used to wrap the
bodies of the illustrious dead. 49. inurned: buried. 52. complete steel: full
armor. 54. fools: dupes. 55. disposition: nature. 59. impartment: communication. 65. fee: value.

That beetles o'er° his base into the sea,
And there assume some other horrible form
Which might deprive your sovereignty of reason°
And draw you into madness? Think of it.
The very place puts toys of desperation,°   75
Without more motive, into every brain
That looks so many fathoms to the sea
_And hears it roar beneath.

HAMLET.   It waves me still.
    Go on. I'll follow thee.
MARCELLUS. You shall not go, my lord.
HAMLET.   Hold off your hands.   80
HORATIO. Be ruled. You shall not go.
HAMLET.   My fate cries out,
And makes each petty artery in this body
As hardy as the Nemean lion's nerve.°
Still am I called. Unhand me, gentlemen.
By Heaven, I'll make a ghost of him that lets° me!   85
I say, away! Go on. I'll follow thee.
                              [*Exeunt* GHOST *and* HAMLET.]
HORATIO. He waxes desperate with imagination.
MARCELLUS. Let's follow. 'Tis not fit thus to obey him.
HORATIO. Have after. To what issue will this come?
MARCELLUS. Something is rotten in the state of Denmark.   90
HORATIO. Heaven will direct it.
MARCELLUS.   Nay, let's follow him. [*Exeunt.*]

Scene 5 ⚜ *Another part of the platform.*

                    [*Enter* GHOST *and* HAMLET.]
HAMLET. Whither wilt thou lead me? Speak. I'll go no further.
GHOST. Mark me.
HAMLET.   I will.
GHOST.   My hour is almost come

71. **beetles o'er:** juts out over.   73. **sovereignty of reason:** control of your reason over your actions.   75. **toys of desperation:** desperate fancies.   83.
Nemean . . . nerve: sinew of a fierce beast slain by Hercules.   85. **lets:**
hinders.

When I to sulphurous and tormenting flames
Must render up myself.
HAMLET.   Alas, poor ghost!
GHOST. Pity me not, but lend thy serious hearing   5
To what I shall unfold.
HAMLET.   Speak. I am bound to hear.
GHOST. So art thou to revenge, when thou shalt hear.
HAMLET. What?
GHOST. I am thy father's spirit,
Doomed for a certain term to walk the night   10
And for the day confined to fast in fires
Till the foul crimes done in my days of nature
Are burnt and purged away. But that I am forbid
To tell the secrets of my prison house,
I could a tale unfold whose lightest word   15
Would harrow up thy soul, freeze thy young blood,
Make thy two eyes, like stars,° start from their spheres,°
Thy knotted and combinèd° locks to part
And each particular° hair to stand an° end
Like quills upon the fretful porpentine.°   20
But this eternal blazon° must not be
To ears of flesh and blood. List, list, oh, list!
If thou didst ever thy dear father love——
HAMLET. Oh, God!
GHOST. Revenge his foul and most unnatural murder.   25
HAMLET. Murder!
GHOST. Murder most foul, as in the best° it is,
But this most foul, strange, and unnatural.
HAMLET. Haste me to know 't, that I, with wings as swift
As meditation or the thoughts of love,   30
May sweep to my revenge.
GHOST.   I find thee apt,
And duller shouldst thou be than the fat° weed
That roots itself in ease° on Lethe wharf°
Wouldst thou not stir in this. Now, Hamlet, hear.
'Tis given out that, sleeping in my orchard,   35
A serpent stung me—so the whole ear of Denmark
Is by a forgèd process° of my death

Sc. 5: 17. **stars:** planets. **spheres:** the courses of planets in the heavens.   18.
knotted . . . combined: the hair that lies together in a mass.   19. **particular:**
individual. **an:** on.   20. **porpentine:** porcupine.   21. **eternal blazon:** description of eternity.   27. **in . . . best:** i.e., murder is foul even when there is a
good excuse.   32. **fat:** thick, slimy, motionless.   33. **in ease:** undisturbed.
Lethe wharf: the bank of Lethe, the river of forgetfulness in the underworld.
37. **forged process:** false account.

Rankly abused. But know, thou noble youth,
The serpent that did sting thy father's life
Now wears his crown.
HAMLET.   Oh, my prophetic soul!   40
My uncle!
GHOST. Aye, that incestuous, that adulterate beast,
With witchcraft of his wit, with traitorous gifts—
O wicked wit and gifts, that have the power
So to seduce!—won to his shameful lust   45
The will of my most seeming-virtuous Queen.
O Hamlet, what a falling-off was there!
From me, whose love was of that dignity
That it went hand in hand even with the vow
I made to her in marriage, and to decline   50
Upon a wretch whose natural gifts were poor
To those of mine!
But virtue, as it never will be moved
Though lewdness court it in a shape of Heaven,°
So Lust, though to a radiant angel linked,   55
Will sate itself° in a celestial bed
And prey on garbage.
But soft! Methinks I scent the morning air.
Brief let me be. Sleeping within my orchard,
My custom always of the afternoon,   60
Upon my secure hour° thy uncle stole
With juice of cursèd hebenon° in a vial,
And in the porches° of my ears did pour
The leperous distillment,° whose effect
Holds such an enmity with blood of man   65
That swift as quicksilver it courses through
The natural gates and alleys of the body,
And with a sudden vigor it doth posset°
And curd, like eager° droppings into milk,
The thin and wholesome blood. So did it mine,   70
And a most instant tetter barked° about,
Most lazarlike,° with vile and loathsome crust,
All my smooth body.
Thus was I, sleeping, by a brother's hand
Of life, of crown, of Queen, at once dispatched—   75

---

54. lewdness . . . Heaven: though wooed by Lust disguised as an angel.
56. sate itself: gorge. 61. secure hour: time of relaxation. 62. hebenon:
probably henbane, a poisonous plant. 63. porches: entrances. 64. leperous
distillment: distillation causing leprosy. 68. posset: curdle. 69. eager: acid.
71. tetter barked: eruption formed a bark. 72. lazarlike: like leprosy.

Cut off even in the blossoms of my sin,°
Unhouseled, disappointed, unaneled,°
No reckoning made, but sent to my account
With all my imperfections on my head.
Oh, horrible! Oh, horrible, most horrible!   80
If thou hast nature° in thee, bear it not.
Let not the royal bed of Denmark be
A couch for luxury° and damned incest.
But, howsoever thou pursuest this act,
Taint not thy mind, nor let thy soul contrive   85
Against thy mother aught. Leave her to Heaven
And to those thorns that in her bosom lodge
To prick and sting her. Fare thee well at once!
The glowworm shows the matin° to be near,
And 'gins to pale his uneffectual° fire.   90
Adieu, adieu, adieu! Remember me.   [*Exit.*]

HAMLET. O all you host of Heaven! O earth! What else?
And shall I couple Hell? Oh, fie! Hold, hold, my heart,
And you, my sinews, grow not instant old
But bear me stiffly up. Remember thee!   95
Aye, thou poor ghost, while memory holds a seat
In this distracted globe.° Remember thee!
Yea, from the table° of my memory
I'll wipe away all trivial fond° recórds,
All saws° of books, all forms,° all pressures° past,   100
That youth and observation copied there,
And thy commandment all alone shall live
Within the book and volume of my brain,
Unmixed with baser matter. Yes, by Heaven!
O most pernicious woman!   105
O villain, villain, smiling, damnèd villain!
My tables—meet it is I set it down
[*Writing*] That one may smile, and smile, and be a villain.
At least I'm sure it may be so in Denmark.
So, Uncle, there you are. Now to my word.°   110
It is "Adieu, adieu! Remember me."
I have sworn 't.

76. **Cut . . . sin**: cut off in a state of sin and so in danger of damnation. See
III.3.80–86.   77. **Unhouseled . . . unaneled**: without receiving the sacrament of penance, not properly prepared, unanointed—without extreme unction.   81. **nature**: natural feelings.   83. **luxury**: lust.   89. **matin**: morning.
90. **uneffectual**: made ineffectual by daylight.   97. **globe**: i.e., head.   98.
table: notebook. Intellectual young men carried notebooks in which they
recorded good sayings and notable observations. See III.2.42, n.   99. **fond**:
trifling.   100. **saws**: wise sayings. **forms**: images in the mind. **pressures**: im-
pressions.   110. **word**: cue.

HORATIO & MARCELLUS. [*Within*] My lord, my lord!
        [*Enter* HORATIO *and* MARCELLUS.]
MARCELLUS.   Lord Hamlet!
HORATIO.   Heaven secure him!
HAMLET. So be it!
MARCELLUS. Illo, ho, ho,° my lord!   115
HAMLET. Hillo, ho, ho, boy! Come, bird, come.
MARCELLUS. How is 't, my noble lord?
HORATIO.   What news, my lord?
HAMLET. Oh, wonderful!
HORATIO. Good my lord, tell it.
HAMLET.   No, you will reveal it.
HORATIO. Not I, my lord, by Heaven.
MARCELLUS.   Nor I, my lord.   120
HAMLET. How say you, then, would heart of man once think it?
    But you'll be secret?
HORATIO & MARCELLUS.   Aye, by Heaven, my lord.
HAMLET. There's ne'er a villain dwelling in all Denmark
    But he's an arrant° knave.
HORATIO. There needs no ghost, my lord, come from the grave   125
    To tell us this.
HAMLET.   Why, right, you are i' the right.
    And so, without more circumstance° at all,
    I hold it fit that we shake hands and part—
    You as your business and desire shall point you,
    For every man hath business and desire,   130
    Such as it is. And for my own poor part,
    Look you, I'll go pray.
HORATIO. These are but wild and whirling° words, my lord.
HAMLET. I'm sorry they offend you, heartily,
    Yes, faith, heartily.
HORATIO.   There's no offense, my lord.   135
HAMLET. Yes, by Saint Patrick, but there is, Horatio,
    And much offense too. Touching this vision here,
    It is an honest° ghost, that let me tell you.
    For your desire to know what is between us,
    O'ermaster 't as you may. And now, good friends,   140
    As you are friends, scholars, and soldiers,
    Give me one poor request.
HORATIO. What is 't, my lord? We will.
HAMLET. Never make known what you have seen tonight.
HORATIO & MARCELLUS. My lord, we will not.

115. **Illo . . . ho:** the falconer's cry to recall the hawk. 124. **arrant:** out-and-out. 127. **circumstance:** ceremony. 133. **whirling:** violent. 138. **honest:** true. See I.4.40, n.

HAMLET.   Nay, but swear 't.
HORATIO.

                             In faith,   145
My lord, not I.
MARCELLUS.   Nor I, my lord, in faith.
HAMLET. Upon my sword.
MARCELLUS.   We have sworn, my lord, already.
HAMLET. Indeed, upon my sword,° indeed.
GHOST. [*Beneath*] Swear.
HAMLET. Ah, ha, boy! Say'st thou so? Art thou there, true-
    penny?°   150
    Come on. You hear this fellow in the cellarage.
    Consent to swear.
HORATIO.   Propose the oath, my lord.
HAMLET. Never to speak of this that you have seen,
    Swear by my sword.
GHOST. [*Beneath*] Swear.   155
HAMLET. *Hic et ubique?*° Then we'll shift our ground.
    Come hither, gentlemen,
    And lay your hands again upon my sword.
    Never to speak of this that you have heard,
    Swear by my sword.   160
GHOST. [*Beneath*] Swear.
HAMLET. Well said, old mole! Canst work i' the earth so fast?
    A worthy pioner!° Once more remove,° good friends.
HORATIO. Oh, day and night, but this is wondrous strange!
HAMLET. And therefore as a stranger give it welcome.   165
    There are more things in Heaven and earth, Horatio,
    Than are dreamt of in your philosophy.
    But come,
    Here, as before, never, so help you mercy,
    How strange or odd soe'er I bear myself,   170
    As I perchance hereafter shall think meet
    To put an antic disposition° on,
    That you, at such times seeing me, never shall,
    With arms encumbered° thus, or this headshake,
    Or by pronouncing of some doubtful phrase,   175
    As "Well, well, we know," or "We could an if we would,"
    Or "If we list to speak," or "There be, an if they might,"
    Or such ambiguous giving out, to note
    That you know aught of me. This not to do,

---

148. upon . . . sword: on the cross made by the hilt of the sword; but for
soldiers the sword itself was a sacred object.   150. truepenny: old boy.   156.
Hic et ubique: here and everywhere.   163. pioner: miner. remove: move.
172. antic disposition: mad behavior.   174. encumbered: folded.

So grace and mercy at your most need help you,   180
Swear.

GHOST. [*Beneath*] Swear.

HAMLET. Rest, rest, perturbèd spirit! [*They swear.*] So, gentle-
    men,
    With all my love I do commend me to you.
    And what so poor a man as Hamlet is   185
    May do to express his love and friending° to you,
    God willing, shall not lack. Let us go in together.
    And still your fingers on your lips, I pray.
    The time is out of joint. Oh, cursèd spite
    That ever I was born to set it right!   190
    Nay, come, let's go together.   [*Exeunt.*]

186. friending: friendship.

ACT II

Scene 1 🪶 *A room in* POLONIUS'S *house.*

[*Enter* POLONIUS *and* REYNALDO.]

POLONIUS. Give him this money and these notes, Reynaldo.

REYNALDO. I will, my lord.

POLONIUS. You shall do marvelous wisely, good Reynaldo,
Before you visit him, to make inquire
Of his behavior.

REYNALDO.   My lord, I did intend it.   5

POLONIUS. Marry, well said, very well said. Look you, sir,
Inquire me first what Danskers° are in Paris,
And how, and who, what means,° and where they keep,°
What company, at what expense, and finding
By this encompassment and drift of question°   10
That they do know my son, come you more nearer
Than your particular demands will touch it.°
Take you, as 'twere, some distant knowledge of him,
As thus, "I know his father and his friends,
And in part him." Do you mark this, Reynaldo?   15

REYNALDO. Aye, very well, my lord.

POLONIUS. "And in part him, but," you may say, "not well.
But if 't be he I mean, he's very wild,
Addicted so and so"—and there put on him
What forgeries° you please. Marry, none so rank°   20
As may dishonor him, take heed of that,
But, sir, such wanton, wild, and usual slips
As are companions noted and most known
To youth and liberty.

Act II, Sc. 1: **7. Danskers:** Danes.   **8. what means:** what their income is.
keep: live.   **10. encompassment . . . question:** roundabout method of questioning.   **12. your . . . it:** i.e., you won't get at the truth by straight questions.   **20. forgeries:** inventions. **rank:** gross.

REYNALDO.   As gaming, my lord.

POLONIUS. Aye, or drinking, fencing,° swearing, quarreling,   25
    Drabbing.° You may go so far.

REYNALDO. My lord, that would dishonor him.

POLONIUS. Faith, no, as you may season° it in the charge.
    You must not put another scandal on him,
    That he is open to incontinency.°   30
    That's not my meaning. But breathe his faults so quaintly°
    That they may seem the taints of liberty,
    The flash and outbreak of a fiery mind,
    A savageness in unreclaimèd° blood,
    Of general assault.°

REYNALDO.   But, my good lord——   35

POLONIUS. Wherefore should you do this?

REYNALDO.   Aye, my lord,
    I would know that.

POLONIUS.   Marry, sir, here's my drift,°
    And I believe it is a fetch of warrant.°
    You laying these slight sullies° on my son,
    As 'twere a thing a little soiled i' the working,   40
    Mark you,
    Your party in converse, him you would sound,
    Having ever seen° in the prenominate° crimes
    The youth you breathe of guilty, be assured
    He closes with you in this consequence°—   45
    "Good sir," or so, or "friend," or "gentleman,"
    According to the phrase or the addition°
    Of man and country.

REYNALDO.   Very good, my lord.

POLONIUS. And then, sir, does he this—he does—   50
    What was I about to say? By the mass, I was about
    to say something. Where did I leave?

REYNALDO. At "closes in the consequence," at "friend or so," and
    "gentleman."

POLONIUS. At "closes in the consequence," aye, marry,
    He closes with you thus: "I know the gentleman.   55

---

25. fencing: A young man who haunted fencing schools would be regarded as quarrelsome and likely to belong to the sporting set. **26. Drabbing:** whoring. **28. season:** qualify. **30. open . . . incontinency:** So long as Laertes does his drabbing inconspicuously Polonius would not be disturbed. **31. quaintly:** skillfully. **34. unreclaimed:** naturally wild. **35. Of . . . assault:** common to all men. **37. drift:** intention. **38. fetch . . . warrant:** trick warranted to work. **39. sullies:** blemishes. **43. Having . . . seen:** if ever he has seen. **prenominate:** aforementioned. **45. closes . . . consequence:** follows up with this reply. **47. addition:** title. See I.4.20.

I saw him yesterday, or t'other day,
Or then, or then, with such, or such, and, as you say,
There was a' gaming, there o'ertook in 's rouse,
There falling out at tennis."° Or perchance,
"I saw him enter such a house of sale,"   60
Videlicet,° a brothel, or so forth.
See you now,
Your bait of falsehood takes this carp of truth.
And thus do we of wisdom and of reach,°
With windlasses° and with assays of bias,°   65
By indirections find directions out.°
So, by my former lecture and advice,
Shall you my son. You have me, have you not?
REYNALDO. My lord, I have.
POLONIUS.   God be wi' ye, fare ye well.
REYNALDO. Good my lord!   70
POLONIUS. Observe his inclination in° yourself.
REYNALDO. I shall, my lord.
POLONIUS. And let him ply his music.
REYNALDO.   Well, my lord.
POLONIUS. Farewell!   [*Exit* REYNALDO.]
     [*Enter* OPHELIA.] How now, Ophelia! What's the matter?
OPHELIA. Oh, my lord, my lord, I have been so affrighted!   75
POLONIUS. With what, i' the name of God?
OPHELIA. My lord, as I was sewing in my closet,°
     Lord Hamlet, with his doublet° all unbraced,
     No hat upon his head, his stockings fouled,
     Ungartered and down-gyved° to his ankle,   80
     Pale as his shirt, his knees knocking each other,
     And with a look so piteous in purport
     As if he had been loosèd out of Hell
     To speak of horrors, he comes before me.
POLONIUS. Mad for thy love?
OPHELIA.   My lord, I do not know,   85
     But truly I do fear it.
POLONIUS.   What said he?

---

59. tennis: Visitors to France were much impressed by the enthusiasm of all
classes of Frenchmen for tennis, which in England was mainly a courtier's
game.   61. Videlicet: namely, "viz."   64. wisdom . . . reach: of far-reaching wisdom.   65. windlasses: roundabout methods. assays of bias: making
our bowl take a curved course.   66. indirections . . . out: by indirect means
come at the direct truth.   71. in: for.   77. closet: private room.   78. doublet:
the short close-fitting coat which was braced to the hose by laces. When a
man was relaxing or careless of appearance, he *unbraced,* as a modern man
takes off his coat.   80. down-gyved: hanging around his ankles like fetters.

OPHELIA. He took me by the wrist and held me hard.
　　　Then goes he to the length of all his arm,
　　　And with his other hand thus o'er his brow,
　　　He falls to such perusal of my face   90
　　　As he would draw it. Long stayed he so.
　　　At last, a little shaking of mine arm,
　　　And thrice his head thus waving up and down,
　　　He raised a sigh so piteous and profound
　　　As it did seem to shatter all his bulk   95
　　　And end his being. That done, he lets me go.
　　　And with his head over his shoulder turned,
　　　He seemed to find his way without his eyes;
　　　For out o' doors he went without their helps,
　　　And to the last bended their light on me.   100
POLONIUS. Come, go with me. I will go seek the King.
　　　This is the very ecstasy° of love,
　　　Whose violent property fordoes° itself
　　　And leads the will to desperate undertakings
　　　As oft as any passion under heaven   105
　　　That does afflict our natures. I am sorry.
　　　What, have you given him any hard words of late?
OPHELIA. No, my good lord, but, as you did command,
　　　I did repel his letters and denied
　　　His access to me.
POLONIUS.　　　　　　That hath made him mad.   110
　　　I am sorry that with better heed and judgment
　　　I had not quoted° him. I feared he did but trifle
　　　And meant to wreck thee, but beshrew° my jealousy!
　　　By Heaven, it is as proper° to our age
　　　To cast beyond ourselves° in our opinions   115
　　　As it is common for the younger sort
　　　To lack discretion. Come, go we to the King.
　　　This must be known, which, being kept close, might move
　　　More grief to hide than hate to utter love.°
　　　Come.   [Exeunt.]   120

102. ecstasy: frenzy.　103. property fordoes: natural quality destroys.　112. quoted: observed carefully.　113. beshrew: a plague on.　114. proper: natural.　115. cast . . . ourselves: be too clever.　118–19. which . . . love: by being kept secret it may cause more sorrow than it will cause anger by being revealed; i.e., the King and Queen may be angry at the thought of the Prince's marrying beneath his proper rank.

Scene 2 ⚜ *A room in the castle.*

[*Flourish. Enter* KING, QUEEN, ROSENCRANTZ,
GUILDENSTERN, *and* ATTENDANTS.]

KING. Welcome, dear Rosencrantz and Guildenstern!
Moreover° that we much did long to see you,
The need we have to use you did provoke
Our hasty sending. Something have you heard
Of Hamlet's transformation—so call it,   5
Sith° nor the exterior nor the inward man
Resembles that it was. What it should be,
More than his father's death, that thus hath put him
So much from the understanding of himself
I cannot dream of. I entreat you both   10
That, being of so young days brought up with him
And sith so neighbored to his youth and havior°
That you vouchsafe your rest° here in our Court
Some little time, so by your companies
To draw him on to pleasures, and to gather   15
So much as from occasion you may glean,
Whether aught to us unknown afflicts him thus
That opened lies within our remedy.°
QUEEN. Good gentlemen, he hath much talked of you,
And sure I am two men there art not living   20
To whom he more adheres.° If it will please you
To show us so much gentry° and good will
As to expend your time with us a while
For the supply and profit of our hope,°

Sc. 2: 2. **Moreover:** in addition to the fact that. 6. **Sith:** since. 12.
neighbored . . . havior: so near to his youthful manner of living. 13. **vouchsafe . . . rest:** consent to stay. 18. **opened . . . remedy:** if revealed, might
be put right by us. 21. **To . . . adheres:** whom he regards more highly.
22. **gentry:** courtesy. 24. **supply . . . hope:** to bring a profitable conclusion
to our hope.

Your visitation shall receive such thanks   25
    As fits a king's remembrance.
ROSENCRANTZ.   Both your Majesties
    Might, by the sovereign power you have of us,
    Put your dread pleasures more into command
    Than to entreaty.
GUILDENSTERN.   But we both obey,
    And here give up ourselves, in the full bent°   30
    To lay our service freely at your feet,
    To be commanded.
KING. Thanks, Rosencrantz and gentle Guildenstern.
QUEEN. Thanks, Guildenstern and gentle Rosencrantz.
    And I beseech you instantly to visit   35
    My too-much-changèd son. Go, some of you,
    And bring these gentlemen where Hamlet is.
GUILDENSTERN. Heavens make our presence and our practices
    Pleasant and helpful to him!
QUEEN.   Aye, amen!
                [*Exeunt* ROSENCRANTZ, GUILDENSTERN,
                              and some ATTENDANTS.]
                    [*Enter* POLONIUS.]
POLONIUS. The ambassadors from Norway, my good lord,   40
    Are joyfully returned.
KING. Thou still° hast been the father of good news.
POLONIUS. Have I, my lord? I assure my good liege
    I hold my duty as I hold my soul,
    Both to my God and to my gracious King.   45
    And I do think, or else this brain of mine
    Hunts not the trail of policy so sure
    As it hath used to do,° that I have found
    The very cause of Hamlet's lunacy.
KING. Oh, speak of that. That do I long to hear.   50
POLONIUS. Give first admittance to the ambassadors.
    My news shall be the fruit° to that great feast.
KING. Thyself do grace° to them and bring them in.
                              [*Exit* POLONIUS.]
    He tells me, my dear Gertrude, he hath found
    The head and source of all your son's distemper.°   55
QUEEN. I doubt it is no other but the main,°

---

30. in . . . bent: stretched to our uttermost.   42. still: always.   47–48.
Hunts . . . do: is not so good at following the scent of political events as
it used to be.   52. fruit: the dessert, which comes at the end of the feast.
53. do grace: honor; i.e., by escorting them into the royal presence.   55. distemper: mental disturbance.   56. main: principal cause.

His father's death and our o'erhasty marriage.
KING. Well, we shall sift him.
          [*Re-enter* POLONIUS, *with* VOLTIMAND *and* CORNELIUS.]
                              Welcome, my good friends!
          Say, Voltimand, what from our brother Norway?
VOLTIMAND. Most fair return of greetings and desires.   60
          Upon our first,° he sent out to suppress
          His nephew's levies, which to him appeared
          To be a preparation 'gainst the Polack,
          But better looked into, he truly found
          It was against your Highness, whereat, grieved   65
          That so his sickness, age, and impotence
          Was falsely borne in hand,° sends out arrests
          On Fortinbras; which he, in brief, obeys,
          Receives rebuke from Norway, and in fine°
          Makes vow before his uncle never more   70
          To give the assay of arms° against your Majesty.
          Whereon old Norway, overcome with joy,
          Gives him three thousand crowns in annual fee
          And his commission to employ those soldiers,
          So levied as before, against the Polack.   75
          With an entreaty, herein further shown, [*Giving a paper*]
          That it might please you to give quiet pass°
          Through your dominions for this enterprise,
          On such regards of safety and allowance°
          As therein are set down.
KING.   It likes° us well,   80
          And at our more considered time we'll read,
          Answer, and think upon this business.
          Meantime we thank you for your well-took labor.
          Go to your rest. At night we'll feast together.
          Most welcome home!
                              [*Exeunt* VOLTIMAND *and* CORNELIUS.]
POLONIUS.   This business is well ended.   85
          My liege, and madam, to expostulate°
          What majesty should be, what duty is,
          Why day is day, night night, and time is time,
          Were nothing but to waste night, day, and time.
          Therefore, since brevity is the soul of wit   90
          And tediousness the limbs and outward flourishes,°

61. **first:** i.e., audience. 67. **borne in hand:** imposed upon. 69. **in fine:** in the end. 71. **give . . . arms:** make an attack. 77. **quiet pass:** unmolested passage. 79. **regards . . . allowance:** safeguard and conditions. 80. **likes:** pleases. 86. **expostulate:** indulge in an academic discussion. 91. **flourishes:** ornaments.

I will be brief. Your noble son is mad.
Mad call I it, for to define true madness,
What is 't but to be nothing else but mad?
But let that go.
QUEEN.   More matter, with less art.°   95
POLONIUS. Madam, I swear I use no art at all.
That he is mad, 'tis true. 'Tis true 'tis pity,
And pity 'tis 'tis true—a foolish figure,°
But farewell it, for I will use no art.
Mad let us grant him, then. And now remains   100
That we find out the cause of this effect,
Or rather say the cause of this defect,
For this effect defective comes by cause.
Thus it remains and the remainder thus.
Perpend.°   105
I have a daughter—have while she is mine—
Who in her duty and obedience, mark,
Hath given me this. Now gather and surmise.°
[Reads.]
"To the celestial, and my soul's idol, the most beautified°
          Ophelia—"   110
That's an ill phrase, a vile phrase, "beautified" is a vile
phrase. But you shall hear. Thus: [Reads.]
"In her excellent white bosom, these," and so forth.
QUEEN. Came this from Hamlet to her?
POLONIUS. Good madam, stay awhile, I will be faithful.   115
[Reads.] "Doubt thou the stars are fire,
          Doubt that the sun doth move,
          Doubt truth to be a liar,
          But never doubt I love.
"Oh dear Ophelia, I am ill at these numbers,° I have not   120
art to reckon my groans, but that I love thee best, believe it.
Adieu.
          "Thine evermore, most dear lady, whilst this
                    machine° is to him, HAMLET."
This is obedience hath my daughter shown me,   125
And more above, hath his solicitings,
As they fell out by time, by means and place,
All given to mine ear.
KING.   But how hath she
Received his love?

95. art: ornament.   98. figure: i.e., a figure of speech.   105. Perpend: note
carefully.   108. surmise: guess the meaning.   110. beautified: beautiful.
120. numbers: verses.   124. machine: i.e., body, an affected phrase.

POLONIUS.   What do you think of me?
KING. As of a man faithful and honorable.   130
POLONIUS. I would fain prove so. But what might you think,
 When I had seen this hot love on the wing—
 As I perceived it, I must tell you that,
 Before my daughter told me—what might you
 Or my dear Majesty your Queen here think   135
 If I had played the desk or table book,°
 Or given my heart awinking, mute and dumb,
 Or looked upon this love with idle sight—
 What might you think? No, I went round° to work,
 And my young mistress thus I did bespeak:°   140
 "Lord Hamlet is a Prince, out of thy star.°
 This must not be." And then I prescripts° gave her
 That she should lock herself from his resort,
 Admit no messengers, receive no tokens.
 Which done, she took the fruits of my advice.   145
 And he, repulsèd, a short tale to make,
 Fell into a sadness, then into a fast,
 Thence to a watch, thence into a weakness,
 Thence to a lightness,° and by this declension°
 Into the madness wherein now he raves   150
 And all we mourn for.
KING. Do you think this?
QUEEN.   It may be, very like.
POLONIUS. Hath there been such a time, I'd fain know that,
 That I have positively said " 'Tis so"
 When it proved otherwise?
KING.   Not that I know.   155
POLONIUS. [*Pointing to his head and shoulder.*] Take this from
 this, if this be otherwise.
 If circumstances lead me, I will find
 Where truth is hid, though it were hid indeed
 Within the center.°
KING.   How may we try it further?

---

136. desk . . . book: i.e., acted as silent go-between (desks and books being natural post offices for a love letter), or been a recipient of secrets but took no action (as desks and notebooks are the natural but inanimate places for keeping secrets). **139. round:** straight. **140. bespeak:** address. **141. out . . . star:** above your destiny. **142. prescripts:** instructions. **147–49. Fell . . . lightness:** Hamlet's case history, according to Polonius, develops by stages—melancholy, loss of appetite, sleeplessness, physical weakness, mental instability, and finally madness. **149. declension:** decline. **159. center:** the very center of the earth, regarded before Copernicus as the center of the Universe.

POLONIUS. You know sometimes he walks four hours together   160
  Here in the lobby.
QUEEN.   So he does indeed.
POLONIUS. At such a time I'll loose° my daughter to him.
  Be you and I behind an arras° then.
  Mark the encounter. If he love her not,
  And be not from his reason fall'n thereon,   165
  Let me be no assistant for a state,
  But keep a farm and carters.°
KING.   We will try it.
QUEEN. But look where sadly the poor wretch comes reading.
POLONIUS. Away, I do beseech you, both away.
  I'll board° him presently.   [Exeunt KING, QUEEN,   170
                                        and ATTENDANTS.]
    [Enter HAMLET, reading.] Oh, give me leave. How does my
      good Lord Hamlet?
HAMLET. Well, God-a-mercy.
POLONIUS. Do you know me, my lord?
HAMLET. Excellent well. You are a fishmonger.°
POLONIUS. Not I, my lord.   175
HAMLET. Then I would you were so honest a man.
POLONIUS. Honest, my lord!
HAMLET. Aye, sir, to be honest, as this world goes, is to be one
  man picked out of ten thousand.
POLONIUS. That's very true, my lord.   180
HAMLET. For if the sun breed maggots° in a dead dog, being a
  god° kissing carrion°——Have you a daughter?
POLONIUS. I have, my lord.   184
HAMLET. Let her not walk i' the sun. Conception is a blessing,
  but not as your daughter may conceive—friend, look to 't.
POLONIUS. [Aside] How say you by that? Still harping on my
  daughter. Yet he knew me not at first, he said I was a fish-
  monger. He is far gone, far gone. And truly in my youth I
  suffered much extremity for love, very near this. I'll speak to
  him again.—What do you read, my lord?   193
HAMLET. Words, words, words.
POLONIUS. What is the matter, my lord?
HAMLET. Between who?   196
POLONIUS. I mean the matter that you read, my lord.

---

162. loose: turn loose.   163. arras: tapestry hanging.   167. keep . . . carters:
i.e., turn country squire—like Justice Shallow. See II Hen IV.   170. board:
accost.   174. fishmonger: Hamlet is now in his "antic disposition," enjoying
himself by fooling Polonius.   181. sun . . . maggots: a general belief. Cf.
Ant & Cleo, II.7.29–31.   182. god: Q2 and F1 read "good." carrion: flesh.

HAMLET. Slanders, sir. For the satirical rogue says here that old
  men have gray beards, that their faces are wrinkled, their
  eyes purging thick amber and plum-tree gum, and that they
  have a plentiful lack of wit, together with most weak hams.°
  All which, sir, though I most powerfully and potently believe, yet I hold it not honesty to have it thus set down;
  for yourself, sir, should be old as I am if like a crab you
  could go backward.   206
POLONIUS. [Aside] Though this be madness, yet there is method°
  in 't.—Will you walk out of the air, my lord?
HAMLET. Into my grave.
POLONIUS. Indeed, that's out of the air. [Aside] How pregnant°   212
  sometimes his replies are! A happiness° that often madness hits on, which reason and sanity could not so pros-
  perously be delivered of. I will leave him, and suddenly contrive the means of meeting between him and my daughter.
  —My honorable lord, I will most humbly take my leave
  of you.   218
HAMLET. You cannot, sir, take from me anything that I will more
  willingly part withal—except my life, except my life, except
  my life.   215
POLONIUS. Fare you well, my lord.
HAMLET. These tedious old fools!
        [Enter ROSENCRANTZ and GUILDENSTERN.]
POLONIUS. You go to seek the Lord Hamlet. There he is.
ROSENCRANTZ. [To POLONIUS] God save you, sir!   225
                                    [Exit POLONIUS.]
GUILDENSTERN. My honored lord!
ROSENCRANTZ. My most dear lord!
HAMLET. My excellent good friends!° How dost thou, Guilden-   228
  stern? Ah, Rosencrantz! Good lads, how do you both?
ROSENCRANTZ. As the indifferent° children of the earth.
GUILDENSTERN. Happy in that we are not overhappy.
  On Fortune's cap we are not the very button.°
HAMLET. Nor the soles of her shoe?
ROSENCRANTZ. Neither, my lord.   235
HAMLET. Then you live about her waist, or in the middle of her
  favors?
GUILDENSTERN. Faith, her privates° we.

202. hams: knee joints. 208. method: order, sense. 212. pregnant: apt,
meaningful. 212. happiness: good turn of phrase. 228. My . . . friends:
As soon as Polonius has gone, Hamlet drops his assumed madness and greets
Rosencrantz and Guildenstern naturally. 231. indifferent: neither too great
nor too little. 233. button: i.e., at the top. 238. privates: with a pun on
"private parts" and "private," not concerned with politics.

HAMLET. In the secret parts of Fortune? Oh, most true, she is a
strumpet. What's the news?   240

ROSENCRANTZ. None, my lord, but that the world's grown honest.

HAMLET. Then is Doomsday near. But your news is not true. Let
me question more in particular. What have you, my good
friends, deserved at the hands of Fortune, that she sends you
to prison hither?   247

GUILDENSTERN. Prison, my lord!

HAMLET. Denmark's a prison.

ROSENCRANTZ. Then is the world one.

HAMLET. A goodly one, in which there are many confines,°
wards,° and dungeons, Denmark being one o' the worst.

ROSENCRANTZ. We think not so, my lord.   254

HAMLET. Why, then 'tis none to you, for there is nothing either
good or bad but thinking makes it so. To me it is a prison.

ROSENCRANTZ. Why, then your ambition° makes it one. 'Tis too
narrow for your mind.   259

HAMLET. Oh, God, I could be bounded in a nutshell and count
myself a king of infinite space were it not that I have bad
dreams.

GUILDENSTERN. Which dreams indeed are ambition, for the very
substance of the ambitious° is merely the shadow of a dream.

HAMLET. A dream itself is but a shadow.   265

ROSENCRANTZ. Truly, and I hold ambition of so airy and light a
quality that it is but a shadow's shadow.

HAMLET. Then are our beggars bodies, and our monarchs and
outstretched heroes the beggars' shadows.° Shall we to the
Court? For, by my fay,° I cannot reason.°   271

ROSENCRANTZ & GUILDENSTERN. We'll wait upon you.°

HAMLET. No such matter. I will not sort° you with the rest of my
servants, for, to speak to you like an honest man, I am most
dreadfully attended.° But in the beaten way of friendship,
what make you at Elsinore?   278

ROSENCRANTZ. To visit you, my lord, no other occasion.

HAMLET. Beggar that I am, I am even poor in thanks, but I thank
you. And sure, dear friends, my thanks are too dear a half-

252. confines: places of confinement. wards: cells. 258. your ambition:
Rosencrantz is feeling after one possible cause of Hamlet's melancholy—
thwarted ambition. 264. substance . . . ambitious: that on which an ambitious man feeds his fancies. 269-71. Then . . . shadows: i.e., by your
reasoning beggars are the only men of substance, for kings and heroes are
by nature ambitious and therefore "the shadows of a dream." outstretched:
of exaggerated reputation. 271. fay: faith. 272. reason: argue. 273. wait
. . . you: be your servants. 274. sort: class. 276. dreadfully attended: my
attendants are a poor crowd.

penny.° Were you not sent for? Is it your own inclining?
Is it a free visitation?° Come, deal justly with me. Come,
come. Nay, speak.   285

GUILDENSTERN. What should we say, my lord?

HAMLET. Why, anything, but to the purpose.° You were sent for,
and there is a kind of confession in your looks which your
modesties have not craft enough to color.° I know the good
King and Queen have sent for you.

ROSENCRANTZ. To what end, my lord?   292

HAMLET. That you must teach me. But let me conjure° you, by
the rights of our fellowship,° by the consonancy° of our
youth, by the obligation of our ever preserved love, and by
what more dear a better proposer could charge you withal,
be even° and direct with me, whether you were sent for,
or no.   299

ROSENCRANTZ. [Aside to GUILDENSTERN] What say you?

HAMLET. [Aside] Nay, then, I have an eye of you.—If you love
me, hold not off.

GUILDENSTERN. My lord, we were sent for.   303

HAMLET. I will tell you why. So shall my anticipation prevent
your discovery, and your secrecy to the King and Queen
molt no feather.° I have of late—but wherefore I know not
—lost all my mirth, forgone all custom of exercises, and
indeed it goes so heavily with my disposition that this goodly
frame the earth seems to me a sterile promontory. This   310
most excellent canopy,° the air, look you, this brave o'erhanging firmament,° this majestical roof fretted° with
golden fire—why, it appears no other thing to me than a
foul and pestilent congregation of vapors. What a piece of
work is a man! How noble in reason! How infinite in fac-   315
ulty!° In form and moving° how express° and admirable!
In action how like an angel! In apprehension how like a god!
The beauty of the world! The paragon of animals! And yet,
to me, what is this quintessence° of dust? Man delights not
me—no, nor woman neither, though by your smiling you   320

282–83. too . . . halfpenny: not worth a halfpenny.   283. free visitation:
voluntary visit.   287. anything . . . purpose: anything so long as it is not
true.   290. color: conceal.   294. conjure: make solemn appeal to.   fellowship: comradeship.   295. consonancy: concord.   298. even: straight.   304–
06. So . . . feather: i.e., so by my telling you first you will not be obliged
to betray the secrets of the King. prevent: forestall. molt no feather: be
undisturbed.   311. canopy: covering.   312. firmament: sky.   313. fretted:
ornamented.   316. faculty: power of the mind.   317. moving: movement.
express: exact.   319. quintessence: perfection; the fifth essence, which
would be left if the four elements were taken away.

seem to say so.

ROSENCRANTZ. My lord, there was no such stuff in my thoughts.

HAMLET. Why did you laugh, then, when I said "Man delights
not me"?

ROSENCRANTZ. To think, my lord, if you delight not in man, what
lenten entertainment° the players shall receive from you. We
coted° them on the way, and hither are they coming to
offer you service.   331

HAMLET. He that plays the King shall be welcome, His Majesty
shall have tribute of me. The adventurous knight shall use
his foil and target,° the lover shall not sigh gratis, the humorous man° shall end his part in peace, the clown shall
make those laugh whose lungs are tickle o' the sere,° and
the lady shall say her mind freely or the blank verse shall
halt° for 't. What players are they?   340

ROSENCRANTZ. Even those you were wont to take such delight in,
the tragedians of the city.

HAMLET. How chances it they travel? Their residence, both in
reputation and profit, was better both ways.°   345

ROSENCRANTZ. I° think their inhibition° comes by the means of
the late innovation.°

HAMLET. Do they hold the same estimation they did when I was
in the city? Are they so followed?

ROSENCRANTZ. No, indeed are they not.   350

HAMLET. How comes it? Do they grow rusty?

ROSENCRANTZ. Nay, their endeavor keeps in the wonted pace.°
But there is, sir, an eyrie° of children, little eyases,° that cry
out on the top of question° and are most tyrannically°
clapped for 't. These are now the fashion, and so berattle°   356
the common stages°—so they call them—that many wear-
ing rapiers are afraid of goose quills° and dare scarce come

---

329. lenten entertainment: mager welcome.   **330. coted:** overtook.   **334. foil
. . . target:** rapier and small shield.   **335. humorous man:** the man who spe-
cializes in character parts; e.g., Jaques in *AYLI.*   **338. are . . . sere:** explode
at a touch. The *sere* is part of the trigger mechanism of a gun which if "tick-
lish" will go off at a touch.   **340. halt:** limp.   **343–45. Their . . . way:** i.e.,
if they stayed in the city, it would bring them more profit and fame.   **346–79.
I . . . too:** This is one of the several topical references in *Hamlet.* In 1600
and 1601 there was fierce competition between the professional players and
the two companies of boy actors, formed from the choir boys of the royal
chapels and St. Paul's.   **346. inhibition:** formal prohibition.   **347. innovation:**
riot.   **352–53. endeavor . . . pace:** they try as hard as ever.   **353. eyrie:**
nest.   **354. eyases:** young hawks.   **354. cry . . . question:** either "cry in a
shrill voice" or perhaps "cry out the latest detail of the dispute."   **355. ty-
rannically:** outrageously.   **356. berattle:** abuse.   **357. common stages:** the
professional players. The boys acted in "private" playhouses.   **359. goose
quills:** pens; i.e., of such as Ben Jonson.

thither.   360

HAMLET. What, are they children? Who maintains 'em? How
are they escoted?° Will they pursue the quality° no longer
than they can sing? Will they not say afterward, if they
should grow themselves to common players—as it is most
like if their means are no better—their writers do them
wrong to make them exclaim against their own succession?°   368

ROSENCRANTZ. Faith, there has been much to-do on both sides,
and the nation holds it no sin to tarre° them to controversy. There was for a while no money bid for argu-
ment° unless the poet and the player went to cuffs° in the
question.

HAMLET. Is 't possible?   373

GUILDENSTERN. Oh, there has been much throwing-about of
brains.

HAMLET. Do the boys carry it away?

ROSENCRANTZ. Aye, that they do, my lord, Hercules and his
load° too.   379

HAMLET. It is not very strange, for my uncle is King of Denmark, and those that would make mows° at him while my
father lived give twenty, forty, fifty, a hundred ducats apiece
for his picture in little. 'Sblood,° there is something in this
more than natural, if philosophy could find it out.   385

[*Flourish of trumpets within.*]

GUILDENSTERN. There are the players.

HAMLET. Gentlemen, you are welcome to Elsinore. Your hands.
Come then. The appurtenance of welcome is fashion and
ceremony.° Let me comply° with you in this garb,° lest my
extent° to the players—which, I tell you, must show fairly   390
outward—should more appear like entertainment° than
yours. You are welcome. But my uncle-father and aunt-
mother are deceived.

GUILDENSTERN. In what, my dear lord?   395

HAMLET. I am but mad north-northwest.° When the wind is

362. escoted: paid.   363. quality: acting profession.   368. exclaim . . . succession: abuse the profession to which they will afterward belong.   370. tarre:
urge on to fight; generally used of encouraging a dog.   372. argument: plot
of a play. See III.2.242.   372–73. went to cuffs: boxed each other's ears.
378–79. Hercules . . . load: Hercules carrying the globe on his shoulders
was the sign of the Globe Playhouse.   381. mows: grimaces.   384. 'Sblood:
by God's blood.   388–89. appurtenance . . . ceremony: that which pertains
to welcome is formal ceremony.   389. comply: use the formality of welcome;
i.e., shake hands with you.   390. garb: fashion.   extent: outward behavior.
392. entertainment: welcome.   396. north-northwest: i.e., 327° (out of 360°)
of the compass.

southerly,° I know a hawk from a handsaw.°

[*Re-enter* POLONIUS.]

POLONIUS. Well be with you, gentlemen!

HAMLET. Hark you, Guildenstern, and you too—at each ear a
hearer. That great baby you see there is not yet out of his
swaddling clouts.°   401

ROSENCRANTZ. Happily he's the second time come to them, for
they say an old man is twice a child.

HAMLET. I will prophesy he comes to tell me of the players, mark
it. You say right, sir. O' Monday morning, 'twas so in-
deed.   407

POLONIUS. My lord, I have news to tell you.

HAMLET. My lord, I have news to tell you. When Roscius° was
an actor in Rome——

POLONIUS. The actors are come hither, my lord.

HAMLET. Buzz, buzz!°

POLONIUS. Upon my honor——   413

HAMLET. Then came each actor on his ass——

POLONIUS. The° best actors in the world, either for tragedy,
comedy, history, pastoral, pastoral-comical, historical-pasto-
ral, tragical-historical, tragical-comical-historical-pastoral,
scene individable° or poem unlimited.° Seneca cannot be
too heavy, nor Plautus° too light. For the law of writ° and   420
the liberty,° these are the only men.

HAMLET. O Jephthah,° judge of Israel, what a treasure hadst
thou!

POLONIUS. What a treasure had he, my lord?

HAMLET. Why,   425

     "One° fair daughter, and no more,
     The which he lovèd passing well."

---

397. **wind is southerly:** The south wind was considered unhealthy.   **396–97.**
hawk . . . handsaw: Either "handsaw" is a corruption of "heronshaw," heron,
or a hawk is a tool like a pickax. The phrase means "I'm not so mad as you
think."   **401. clouts:** clothes.   **410. Roscius:** the most famous of Roman actors.   **412. Buzz, buzz:** slang for "stale news."   **415–21. The . . . men:**
Polonius reads out the accomplishments of the actors from the license which
they have presented him.   **418. scene individable:** i.e., a play preserving the
unities.   **418–19. poem unlimited:** i.e., a play which disregards the rules.
419–20. Seneca . . . Plautus: the Roman writers of tragedy and comedy
with whose plays every educated man was familiar.   **420. law of writ:** the
critical rules; i.e., classical plays. **liberty:** plays freely written; i.e., "modern"
drama.   **422. Jephthah:** The story of Jephthah is told in Judges, Chapter 11.
He vowed that if successful against the Ammonites he would sacrifice the
first creature to meet him on his return, which was his daughter.   **426–37.**
One . . . was: Quotations from a ballad of Jephthah.

POLONIUS. [*Aside*] Still° on my daughter.

HAMLET. Am I not i' the right, old Jephthah?

POLONIUS. If you call me Jephthah, my lord, I have a daughter
    that I love passing well.   431

HAMLET. Nay, that follows not.

POLONIUS. What follows, then, my lord?

HAMLET. Why,

               "As by lot, God wot,"°   435
and then you know,
         "It came to pass, as most like it was—"
the first row° of the pious chanson° will show you more, for
look where my abridgement° comes. [*Enter four or five*   439
PLAYERS.] You are welcome, masters, welcome all. I am glad
to see thee well. Welcome, good friends. Oh, my old friend!°
Why, thy face is valanced° since I saw thee last. Comest thou
to beard° me in Denmark? What, my young lady° and mistress! By 'r Lady, your ladyship is nearer to Heaven than
when I saw you last, by the altitude of a chopine.° Pray God   446
your voice, like a piece of uncurrent gold, be not cracked
within the ring.° Masters, you are all welcome. We'll e'en to
't like French falconers,° fly at anything we see. We'll have
a speech straight. Come, give us a taste of your quality°—
come, a passionate speech.   453

FIRST PLAYER. What speech, my good lord?

HAMLET. I heard thee speak me a speech once, but it was never
acted, or if it was, not above once; for the play, I remember, pleased not the million, 'twas caviar° to the general.°
But it was—as I received it, and others, whose judgments
in such matters cried in the top of mine°—an excellent play,
well digested° in the scenes, set down with as much mod-   460
esty° as cunning. I remember one said there were no sallets°

---

428. Still: always.   435. wot: knows.   438. row: line.   pious chanson: godly
poem.   439. abridgement: entertainment.   441. old friend: i.e., the leading
player.   442. valanced: bearded. A valance is a fringe hung round the sides
and bottom of a bed.   443. beard: dare, with a pun on "valanced." young
lady: i.e., the boy who takes the woman's parts.   446. chopine: lady's shoe
with thick cork sole.   447. cracked . . . ring: Before coins were milled on
the rim they were liable to crack. When the crack reached the ring surrounding the device, the coin was no longer valid.   450. French falconers: They
were famous for their skill in hawking.   452. quality: skill as an actor.   457.
caviar: sturgeon's roe, a Russian delicacy not then appreciated (or known)
by any but gourmets. general: common herd.   459. cried . . . mine: surpassed mine.   460. digested: composed.   461. modesty: moderation.   462.
sallets: tasty bits.

in the lines to make the matter savory, nor no matter in the
phrase that might indict the author of affection,° but called
it an honest method, as wholesome as sweet, and by very   465
much more handsome than fine.° One speech in it I chiefly
loved. 'Twas Aeneas' tale to Dido,° and thereabout of it es-
pecially where he speaks of Priam's° slaughter. If it live in
your memory, begin at this line—let me see, let me see—   471
    "The rugged Pyrrhus,° like th' Hyrcanian beast,°—"
It is not so. It begins with "Pyrrhus."
"The° rugged Pyrrhus, he whose sable° arms,
  Black as his purpose, did the night resemble   475
  When he lay couchèd in the ominous° horse,°
  Hath now this dread and black complexion smeared
  With heraldry° more dismal. Head to foot
  Now is he total gules, horridly tricked
  With blood of fathers, mothers, daughters, sons,   480
  Baked and impasted° with the parching streets
  That lend a tyrannous and a damnèd light
  To their lord's murder. Roasted in wrath and fire,
  And thus o'ersized with coagulate gore,°
  With eyes like carbuncles, the hellish Pyrrhus   485
  Old grandsire Priam seeks."
So, proceed you.
POLONIUS. 'Fore God, my lord, well spoken, with good accent and
    good discretion.
FIRST PLAYER.   "Anon he finds him   490
    Striking too short at Greeks. His antique sword,
    Rebellious to his arm, lies where it falls,

463–64. phrase . . . affection: nothing in the language which could charge
the author with affectation.   466. fine: subtle.   467. Aeneas' . . . Dido: the
story of the sack of Troy as told by Aeneas to Dido, Queen of Carthage. The
original is in Virgil's *Aeneid*. A similar speech occurs in Marlowe's play *Dido,
Queen of Carthage*.   469. Priam: the old King of Troy.   472. Pyrrhus: the
son of Achilles, one of the Greeks concealed in the Wooden Horse.   472.
Hyrcanian beast: the tiger.   474–541. The . . . gods: The speech may be
from some lost play of *Dido and Aeneas,* but more likely it is Shakespeare's
own invention. It is written in the heavy elaborate style still popular in the
dramas of the Admiral's Men. The first player delivers it with excessive gesture
and emotion.   474. sable: black.   476. ominous: fateful. horse: the Wooden
Horse by which a small Greek force was enabled to make a secret entry into
Troy.   478. heraldry: painting. The image of heraldic painting is kept up in
gules (the heraldic term for red) and *tricked* (painted).   481. impasted:
turned into a crust by the heat of the burning city.   484. o'ersized . . . gore:
covered over with congealed blood.

Repugnant to command.° Unequal matched,
Pyrrhus at Priam drives, in rage strikes wide,
But with the whiff and wind of his fell sword   495
The unnerved father falls. Then senseless Ilium,°
Seeming to feel this blow, with flaming top
Stoops to his base,° and with a hideous crash
Takes prisoner Pyrrhus' ear. For, lo! his sword,
Which was declining° on the milky° head   500
Of reverend Priam, seemed i' the air to stick.
So as a painted tyrant° Pyrrhus stood,
And like a neutral to his will and matter,°
Did nothing.
But as we often see, against° some storm   505
A silence in the heavens, the rack° stand still,
The bold winds speechless and the orb° below
As hush as death, anon the dreadful thunder
Doth rend the region°—so after Pyrrhus' pause
Aroused vengeance sets him new awork.   510
And never did the Cyclops'° hammers fall
On Mars's armor, forged for proof eterne,°
With less remorse° than Pyrrhus' bleeding sword
Now falls on Priam.
Out, out, thou strumpet, Fortune! All you gods,   515
In general synod° take away her power,
Break all the spokes and fellies° from her wheel,
And bowl the round nave° down the hill of Heaven
As low as to the fiends!"
POLONIUS. This is too long.   520
HAMLET. It shall to the barber's, with your beard. Prithee, say on.
    He's for a jig° or a tale of bawdry, or he sleeps. Say on.
    Come to Hecuba.
FIRST PLAYER. "But who, oh, who had seen the mobled°
    Queen—"   525
HAMLET. "The mobled Queen"?

---

493. Repugnant to command: refusing to be used.   496. Ilium: the citadel
of Troy.   498. stoops . . . base: collapses.   500. declining: bending toward.
milky: milk-white.   502. painted tyrant: as in the painting of a tyrant.   503.
neutral . . . matter: one midway (neutral) between his desire (will) and
action (matter).   505. against: just before.   506. rack: the clouds in the
upper air.   507. orb: world.   509. region: the country round.   511. Cyclops':
of Titans, giants who aided Vulcan, the blacksmith god, to make armor for
Mars, the war god.   512. proof eterne: everlasting protection.   513. re-
morse: pity.   516. synod: council.   517. fellies: the pieces forming the cir-
cumference of a wooden wheel.   518. nave: center of the wheel.   522. jig:
bawdy dance.   525. mobled: muffled.

POLONIUS. That's good, "mobled Queen" is good.

FIRST PLAYER. "Run barefoot up and down, threatening the flames
    With bisson rheum,° a clout° upon that head
    Where late the diadem stood, and for a robe,   530
    About her lank and all o'erteemèd° loins
    A blanket, in the alarm of fear caught up.
    Who this had seen, with tongue in venom steeped
    'Gainst Fortune's state would treason have pronounced.°
    But if the gods themselves did see her then,   535
    When she saw Pyrrhus make malicious sport
    In mincing with his sword her husband's limbs,
    The instant burst of clamor that she made,
    Unless things mortal move them not at all,
    Would have made milch° the burning eyes of Heaven   540
    And passion in the gods."

POLONIUS. Look whether he has not turned his color and has tears
    in 's eyes. Prithee, no more.

HAMLET. 'Tis well; I'll have thee speak out the rest of this soon.
    Good my lord, will you see the players well bestowed?° Do
    you hear, let them be well used, for they are the abstract
    and brief chronicles of the time.° After your death you   550
    were better have a bad epitaph than their ill report while
    you live.

POLONIUS. My lord, I will use them according to their desert.°

HAMLET. God's bodykins,° man, much better. Use every man
    after his desert and who shall 'scape whipping? Use them
    after your own honor and dignity. The less they deserve,
    the more merit is in your bounty. Take them in.

POLONIUS. Come, sirs.   559

HAMLET. Follow him, friends. We'll hear a play tomorrow. [*Exit*
    POLONIUS *with all the* PLAYERS *but the* FIRST.] Dost thou
    hear me, old friend? Can you play *The Murder of Gonzago*?

FIRST PLAYER. Aye, my lord.   564

HAMLET. We'll ha 't tomorrow night. You could, for a need, study
    a speech of some dozen or sixteen lines which I would set
    down and insert in 't, could you not?

529. bisson rheum: blinding moisture. clout: rag.   531. o'erteemed: exhausted by bearing children; she had borne fifty-two.   533–34. Who . . .
pronounced: anyone who had seen this sight would with bitter words have
uttered treason against the tyranny of Fortune.   540. milch: milky, i.e., dripping moisture.   548. bestowed: housed.   549–50. abstract . . . time: they
summarize and record the events of our time. Elizabethan players were often
in trouble for too saucily commenting on their betters in plays dealing with
history or contemporary events and persons.   552. desert: rank.   553. God's
bodykins: by God's little body.

FIRST PLAYER. Aye, my lord.   569
HAMLET. Very well. Follow that lord, and look you mock him
    not. [*Exit* FIRST PLAYER.] My good friends, I'll leave you till
    night. You are welcome to Elsinore.
ROSENCRANTZ. Good my lord!   574
HAMLET. Aye, so, God be wi' ye! [*Exeunt* RESENCRANTZ *and*
    GUILDENSTERN.] Now I am alone.
    Oh, what a rogue and peasant slave am I!
    Is it not monstrous that this player here,
    But in a fiction, in a dream of passion,°
    Could force his soul so to his own conceit°
    That from her working° all his visage wanned,°   580
    Tears in his eyes, distraction° in 's aspect,°
    A broken voice, and his whole function° suiting
    With forms to his conceit? And all for nothing!
    For Hecuba!
    What's Hecuba to him or he to Hecuba,   585
    That he should weep for her? What would he do
    Had he the motive and the cue for passion
    That I have? He would drown the stage with tears
    And cleave the general ear° with horrid speech,
    Make mad the guilty and appal the free,°   590
    Confound the ignorant, and amaze indeed
    The very faculties of eyes and ears.
    Yet I,
    A dull and muddy-mettled° rascal, peak,°
    Like John-a-dreams,° unpregnant of my cause,°   595
    And can say nothing—no, not for a King
    Upon whose property° and most dear life
    A damned defeat° was made. Am I a coward?
    Who° calls me villain? Breaks my pate across?
    Plucks off my beard and blows it in my face?   600
    Tweaks me by the nose? Gives me the lie i' the throat
    As deep as to the lungs? Who does me this?
    Ha!

---

578. dream of passion: imaginary emotion.   579. conceit: imagination.   580.
her working: i.e., the effect of imagination. wanned: went pale.   581. distraction: frenzy. aspect: countenance.   582. function: behavior.   589. general
ear: ears of the audience.   590. free: innocent.   594. muddy-mettled: made
of mud, not iron. peak: mope.   595. John-a-dreams: "Sleepy Sam." unpreg-
nant . . . cause: barren of plans for vengeance.   597. property: personality,
life.   598. defeat: ruin.   599–602. Who . . . this: Hamlet runs through all
the insults which provoked a resolute man to mortal combat. pate: head. lie
. . . throat: the bitterest of insults.

'Swounds,° I should take it. For it cannot be
But I am pigeon-livered° and lack gall°   605
To make oppression bitter, or ere this
I should have fatted all the region kites
With this slave's offal.° Bloody, bawdy villain!
Remorseless, treacherous, lecherous, kindless° villain!
Oh, vengeance!   610
Why, what an ass am I! This is most brave,
That I, the son of a dear father murdered,
Prompted to my revenge by Heaven and Hell,
Must, like a whore, unpack my heart with words
And fall a-cursing like a very drab,°   615
A scullion!°
Fie upon 't! Foh! About, my brain! Hum, I have heard
That guilty creatures sitting at a play
Have by the very cunning of the scene
Been struck so to the soul that presently°   620
They have proclaimed their malefactions;°
For murder, though it have no tongue, will speak
With most miraculous organ. I'll have these players
Play something like the murder of my father
Before mine uncle. I'll observe his looks,   625
I'll tent° him to the quick. If he but blench,°
I know my course. The° spirit that I have seen
May be the Devil, and the Devil hath power
To assume a pleasing shape. Yea, and perhaps
Out of my weakness and my melancholy,   630
As he is very potent with such spirits,
Abuses me to damn me.° I'll have grounds°
More relative than this.° The play's the thing
Wherein I'll catch the conscience of the King.

                                        [*Exit.*]

---

604. 'Swounds: by God's wounds.   **605. pigeon-livered:** "as gentle as a dove."
gall: spirit.   **606–08. I . . . offal:** before this I would have fed this slave's
(i.e., the King's) guts to the kites. **fatted:** made fat.   **609. kindless:** unnatural.
615. drab: "moll."   **616. scullion:** the lowest of the kitchen servants.   **620.
presently:** immediately.   **621. proclaimed . . . malefactions:** shouted out
their crimes.   **626. tent:** probe. **blench:** flinch.   **627–32. The . . . me:** an
illusion sent by the Devil, or caused by acute melancholy.   **632. Abuses . . .
me:** i.e., deceives me so that I may commit the sin of murder which will
bring me to damnation. **grounds:** reasons for action.   **633. relative . . .
this:** i.e., more convincing than the appearance of a ghost.

ACT III

Scene 1 ⌇ *A room in the castle.*

[*Enter* KING, QUEEN, POLONIUS, OPHELIA, ROSENCRANTZ,
and GUILDENSTERN.]

KING. And can you, by no drift of circumstance,°
    Get from him why he puts on this confusion,
    Grating° so harshly all his days of quiet
    With turbulent and dangerous lunacy?
ROSENCRANTZ. He does confess he feels himself distracted,   5
    But from what cause he will by no means speak.
GUILDENSTERN. Nor do we find him forward to be sounded,°
    But, with a crafty madness, keeps aloof
    When we would bring him on to some confession
    Of his true state.
QUEEN.   Did he receive you well?   10
ROSENCRANTZ. Most like a gentleman.
GUILDENSTERN. But with much forcing of his disposition.°
ROSENCRANTZ. Niggard of question,° but of our demands
    Most free in his reply.
QUEEN.   Did you assay him
    To any pastime?°   15
ROSENCRANTZ. Madam, it so fell out that certain players
    We o'erraught° on the way. Of these we told him,
    And there did seem in him a kind of joy
    To hear of it. They are about the Court,
    And, as I think, they have already order   20
    This night to play before him.

    Act III, Sc. 1: 1. drift of circumstance: circumstantial evidence, hint. **3. grating:** disturbing. **7. forward . . . sounded:** eager to be questioned. **12. much . . . disposition:** making a great effort to be civil to us. **13. Niggard of question:** not asking many questions. **14–15. Did . . . pastime:** Did you try to interest him in any amusement. **17. o'erraught:** overtook.

POLONIUS.   'Tis most true.
    And he beseeched me to entreat your Majesties
    To hear and see the matter.
KING. With all my heart, and it doth much content me
    To hear him so inclined.   25
    Good gentlemen, give him a further edge,°
    And drive his purpose on to these delights.
ROSENCRANTZ. We shall, my lord.
                [*Exeunt* ROSENCRANTZ *and* GUILDENSTERN.]
KING.   Sweet Gertrude, leave us too,
    For we have closely° sent for Hamlet hither,
    That he, as 'twere by accident, may here   30
    Affront° Ophelia.
    Her father and myself, lawful espials,°
    Will so bestow ourselves that, seeing unseen,
    We may of their encounter frankly judge
    And gather by him, as he is behaved,°   35
    If 't be the affliction of his love or no
    That thus he suffers for.
QUEEN.   I shall obey you.
    And for your part, Ophelia, I do wish
    That your good beauties be the happy cause
    Of Hamlet's wildness. So shall I hope your virtues   40
    Will bring him to his wonted way° again,
    To both your honors.
OPHELIA. Madam, I wish it may.   [*Exit* QUEEN.]
POLONIUS. Ophelia, walk you here. Gracious,° so please you,
    We will bestow ourselves. [*To* OPHELIA] Read on this book,°
    That show of such an exercise may color   45
    Your loneliness. We are oft to blame in this—
    'Tis too much proved—that with devotion's visage°
    And pious action we do sugar o'er
    The Devil himself.
KING. [*Aside*] Oh, 'tis too true!
    How smart a lash that speech doth give my conscience!   50
    The harlot's cheek, beautied with plastering art,
    Is not more ugly to the thing that helps it°

---

26. edge: encouragement. **29. closely:** secretly. **31. Affront:** encounter.
32. lawful espials: who are justified in spying on him. **35. by . . . behaved:**
from him, from his behavior. **41. wonted way:** normal state. **43. Gracious:**
your Majesty—addressed to the King. **44. book:** i.e., of devotions. **47. devotion's visage:** an outward appearance of religion. **52. ugly . . . it:** i.e.,
lust, which is the cause of its artificial beauty.

Than is my deed to my most painted° word.
Oh, heavy burden!
POLONIUS. I hear him coming. Let's withdraw, my lord.   55
            [*Exeunt* KING *and* POLONIUS.]
            [*Enter* HAMLET.°]
HAMLET. To be, or not to be—that is the question.
      Whether 'tis nobler in the mind to suffer
      The slings and arrows of outrageous° fortune,
      Or to take arms against a sea° of troubles
      And by opposing end them. To die, to sleep—   60
      No more, and by a sleep to say we end
      The heartache and the thousand natural shocks
      That flesh is heir to. 'Tis a consummation°
      Devoutly to be wished. To die, to sleep,
      To sleep—perchance to dream. Aye, there's the rub,°   65
      For in that sleep of death what dreams may come
      When we have shuffled off this mortal coil°
      Must give us pause. There's the respect°
      That makes calamity of so long life.°
      For who would bear the whips and scorns of time,   70
      The oppressor's wrong, the proud man's contumely°
      The pangs of déspised love, the law's delay,
      The insolence of office° and the spurns
      That patient merit of the unworthy takes,°
      When he himself might his quietus° make   75
      With a bare bodkin?° Who would fardels° bear,
      To grunt and sweat under a weary life,
      But that the dread of something after death,
      The undiscovered country from whose bourn°
      No traveler returns, puzzles the will,°   80
      And makes us rather bear those ills we have
      Than fly to others that we know not of?

53. painted: i.e., false.   55. s.d., Enter Hamlet: In Q1 the King draws attention to Hamlet's approach with the words "See where he comes poring upon a
book." Hamlet is again reading, and is too much absorbed to notice Ophelia.
58. outrageous: cruel.   59. sea: i.e., an endless turmoil.   63. consummation:
completion.   65. rub: impediment.   67. shuffled . . . coil: cast off this fuss
of life.   68. respect: reason.   69. makes . . . life: makes it a calamity to
have to live so long.   71. contumely: insulting behavior.   73. insolence of
office: insolent behavior of government officials.   73–74. spurns . . . takes:
insults which men of merit have patiently to endure from the unworthy.
75. quietus: discharge.   76. bodkin: dagger. fardels: burdens, the coolie's
pack.   79. bourn: boundary.   80. will: resolution, ability to act.

Thus° conscience does make cowards of us all,
And thus the native hue° of resolution
Is sicklied o'er with the pale cast° of thought,   85
And enterprises of great pitch° and moment
With this regard their currents turn awry
And lose the name of action.°—Soft you now!
The fair Ophelia! Nymph, in thy orisons°
Be all my sins remembered.

OPHELIA.   Good my lord,   90
How does your Honor for this many a day?

HAMLET. I humbly thank you—well, well, well.

OPHELIA. My lord, I have remembrances of yours
That I have longed long to redeliver.
I pray you now receive them.

HAMLET.   No, not I.   95
I never gave you aught.

OPHELIA. My honored lord, you know right well you did,
And with them words of so sweet breath composed
As made the things more rich. Their perfume lost,
Take these again, for to the noble mind   100
Rich gifts wax poor when givers prove unkind.
There, my lord.

HAMLET. Ha, ha! Are you honest?°

OPHELIA. My lord?

HAMLET. Are you fair?   105

OPHELIA. What means your lordship?

HAMLET. That if you be honest and fair, your honesty should
admit no discourse to your beauty.°

OPHELIA. Could beauty, my lord, have better commerce than with
honesty?   110

HAMLET. Aye, truly, for the power of beauty will sooner trans-
form honesty from what it is to a bawd° than the force of
honesty can translate beauty into his likeness. This was
sometime a paradox,° but now the time gives it proof. I did
love you once.   116

OPHELIA. Indeed, my lord, you made me believe so.

HAMLET. You should not have believed me, for virtue cannot so

---

83–88. Thus . . . action: the religious fear that death may not be the end
makes men shrink from heroic actions.   84. native hue: natural color.   85.
cast: color.   86. pitch: height; used of the soaring flight of a hawk.   87–88.
With . . . action: by brooding on this thought great enterprises are diverted
from their course and fade away.   89. orisons: prayers.   103. honest: chaste.
107–08. That . . . beauty: if you are chaste and beautiful your chasity should
have nothing to do with your beauty—because (so Hamlet thinks in his bitterness) beautiful women are seldom chaste.   112. bawd: brothel-keeper.
115. paradox: statement contrary to accepted opinion.

inoculate our old stock but we shall relish° of it. I loved
you not.   120

OPHELIA. I was the more deceived.

HAMLET. Get thee to a nunnery. Why wouldst thou be a breeder
of sinners? I am myself indifferent honest,° but yet I could   124
accuse me of such things that it were better my mother had
not borne me. I am very proud, revengeful, ambitious, with
more offenses at my beck° than I have thoughts to put them
in, imagination to give them shape, or time to act them in.
What should such fellows as I do crawling between heaven
and earth? We are arrant knaves all. Believe none of us. Go
thy ways to a nunnery.° Where's your father?   132

OPHELIA. At home, my lord.

HAMLET. Let the doors be shut upon him, that he may play the
fool nowhere but in 's own house. Farewell.   137

OPHELIA. Oh, help him, you sweet Heavens!

HAMLET. If thou dost marry, I'll give thee this plague for thy
dowry: Be thou as chaste as ice, as pure as snow—thou
shalt not escape calumny.° Get thee to a nunnery, go. Fare-   141
well. Or if thou wilt needs marry, marry a fool, for wise
men know well enough what monsters° you make of them.
To a nunnery, go, and quickly too. Farewell.

OPHELIA. O heavenly powers, restore him!   147

HAMLET. I have heard of your paintings° too, well enough. God
hath given you one face and you make yourselves another.
You jig,° you amble,° and you lisp,° and nickname God's
creatures, and make your wantonness your ignorance.° Go
to, I'll no more on 't—it hath made me mad. I say we will
have no more marriages. Those that are married already, all
but one, shall live; the rest shall keep as they are. To a nun-   156
nery, go.   [Exit.]

OPHELIA. Oh, what a noble mind is here o'erthrown!
The courtier's, soldier's, scholar's, eye, tongue, sword—
The expectancy and rose° of the fair state,   160
The glass° of fashion and the mold of form,°

---

120. **relish:** have some trace.   123–24. **indifferent honest:** moderately honorable.   127. **at . . . beck:** waiting to come when I beckon.   132. **nunnery:**
i.e., a place where she will be removed from temptation.   141. **calumny:**
slander.   145. **monsters:** horned beasts, cuckolds—husbands, deceived by
their wives, who were supposed to wear invisible horns.   148. **paintings:**
using make-up.   150. **jig:** dance lecherously. **amble:** walk artificially.   151.
lisp: talk affectedly.   152–53. **nickname . . . ignorance:** give things indecent
names and pretend to be too simple to understand their meanings.   160. **expectancy . . . rose:** bright hope. The rose is used as a symbol for beauty and
perfection. Cf. *I Hen IV*, I.3.175.   161. **glass:** mirror. **mold of form:** perfect
pattern of manly beauty.

The observed of all observers—quite, quite down!
And I, of ladies most deject and wretched,
That sucked the honey of his music vows,
Now see that noble and most sovereign reason,   165
Like sweet bells jangled, out of tune and harsh,
That unmatched° form and feature of blown° youth
Blasted with ecstasy.° Oh, woe is me,
To have seen what I have seen, see what I see!
        [*Re-enter* KING *and* POLONIUS.]
KING. Love! His affections° do not that way tend,   170
    Nor what he spake, though it lacked form a little,
    Was not like madness. There's something in his soul
    O'er which his melancholy sits on brood,°
    And I do doubt the hatch and the disclose°
    Will be some danger. Which for to prevent,   175
    I have in quick determination
    Thus set it down: He shall with speed to England,
    For the demand of our neglected tribute.
    Haply° the seas and countries different
    With variable objects° shall expel   180
    This something-settled° matter in his heart
    Whereon his brains still beating puts him thus
    From fashion of himself.° What think you on 't?
POLONIUS. It shall do well. But yet do I believe
    The origin and commencement of his grief   185
    Sprung from neglected love. How now, Ophelia!
    You need not tell us what Lord Hamlet said,
    We heard it all. My lord, do as you please,
    But, if you hold it fit, after the play
    Let his Queen mother all alone entreat him   190
    To show his grief. Let her be round° with him,
    And I'll be placed, so please you, in the ear
    Of all their conference. If she find him not,
    To England send him, or confine him where
    Your wisdom best shall think.
KING.   It shall be so.   195
    Madness in great ones must not unwatched go.   [*Exeunt.*]

---

167. unmatched: unmatchable. **blown:** perfect, like an open flower at its best. **168. Blasted . . . ecstasy:** ruined by madness. **170. affections:** state of mind. **173. sits . . . brood:** sits hatching. **174. doubt . . . disclose:** suspect the brood which will result. **179. Haply:** perhaps. **180. variable objects:** novel sights. **181. something-settled:** somewhat settled; i.e., not yet incurable. **182–83. puts . . . himself:** i.e., separates him from his normal self. **191. round:** direct.

Scene 2 ⚜ A hall in the castle.

[*Enter* HAMLET *and* PLAYERS.]

HAMLET. Speak the speech,° I pray you, as I pronounced it to
you, trippingly° on the tongue. But if you mouth° it, as
many of your players do, I had as lief° the town crier spoke
my lines. Nor do not saw the air too much with your hand,
thus, but use all gently. For in the very torrent, tempest,   5
and, as I may say, whirlwind of passion, you must acquire
and beget a temperance that may give it smoothness. Oh, it
offends me to the soul to hear a robustious° periwig-pated°
fellow tear a passion to tatters, to very rags, to split the ears   10
of the groundlings,° who for the most part are capable of
nothing but inexplicable dumb shows° and noise. I would
have such a fellow whipped for o'erdoing Termagant°—   15
it out-Herods Herod. Pray you, avoid it.

FIRST PLAYER. I warrant your Honor.

HAMLET. Be not too tame neither, but let your own discretion be
your tutor. Suit the action to the word, the word to the action, with this special observance, that you o'erstep not the   20
modesty of nature. For anything so overdone is from° the
purpose of playing, whose end, both at the first and now,
was and is to hold as 'twere the mirror up to Nature—to
show Virtue her own feature, scorn her own image, and   25

Sc. 2: 1. the speech: which he has written. See ll. 266–67. The whole passage which follows is Shakespeare's own comment on the actor's art and states
the creed and practice of his company as contrasted with the more violent
methods of Edward Alleyn and his fellows of the Admiral's company.   2.
trippingly: smoothly, easily.   3. mouth: "ham" it.   4. lief: soon.   9. robus-
tious: ranting.   10. periwig-pated: wearing a wig.   11. groundlings: the
poorer spectators, who stood in the yard of the playhouse.   14. dumb shows:
an old-fashioned dramatic device, still being used by the Admiral's Men:
before a tragedy, and sometimes before each act, the characters mimed the
action which was to follow. See later, l. 145.   15. Termagant: God of the
Saracens, who, like Herod, was presented in early stage plays as a roaring
tyrant.   22. from: contrary to.

the very age and body of the time his form and pressure.°
Now this overdone or come tardy off, though it make the
unskillful laugh, cannot but make the judicious grieve, the
censure of the which one° must in your allowance o'erweigh   30
a whole theater of others. Oh, there be players° that I have
seen play, and heard others praise—and that highly, not to
speak it profanely—that neither having the accent of Christians nor the gait of Christian, pagan, nor man, have so
strutted and bellowed that I have thought some of Nature's   35
journeymen° had made men, and not made them well, they
imitated humanity so abominably.

FIRST PLAYER. I hope we have reformed that indifferently° with   41
us, sir.

HAMLET. Oh, reform it altogether. And let those that play your
clowns° speak no more than is set down for them. For there
be of them that will themselves laugh, to set on some quantity of barren spectators to laugh too, though in the mean-   45
time some necessary question of the play be then to be considered. That's villainous, and shows a most pitiful° ambition
in the fool that uses it. Go, make you ready. [*Exeunt*   50
PLAYERS. *Enter* POLONIUS, ROSENCRANTZ, *and* GUILDEN-
STERN.] How now, my lord! Will the King hear this piece of
work?

POLONIUS. And the Queen too, and that presently.

HAMLET. Bid the players make haste. [*Exit* POLONIUS.] Will you
two help to hasten them?   55

ROSENCRANTZ & GUILDENSTERN. We will, my lord.

[*Exeunt* ROSENCRANTZ *and* GUILDENSTERN.]

HAMLET. What ho! Horatio!

[*Enter* HORATIO.]

HORATIO. Here, sweet lord, at your service.

HAMLET. Horatio, thou art e'en as just a man

26–27. very . . . pressure: an exact reproduction of the age. **form:** shape.
pressure: imprint (of a seal). **30. the . . . one:** i.e., the judicious spectator.
31. there . . . players: An obvious attack on Alleyn. **36. journeymen:** hired
workmen, not masters of the trade. **41. indifferently:** moderately. **42–43.
those . . . clowns:** a hit at Will Kempe, the former clown of Shakespeare's
company, now with a rival company. Q1 adds the passage "And then you
have some again that keep one suit of jests, as a man is known by one suit of
apparel, and gentlemen quote his jests down in their tables before they come
to the play, as thus: 'Cannot you stay till I eat my porridge?' and 'You owe
me a quarter's wages,' and 'My coat wants a cullison,' and 'Your beer is sour,'
and blabbering with his lips, and thus keeping in his cinquepace of jests,
when God knows the warm clown cannot make a jest unless by chance, as the
blind man catcheth a hare. Masters tell him of it." **49. pitiful:** contemptible.

As e'er my conversation coped° withal.   60
HORATIO. Oh, my dear lord——
HAMLET.   Nay, do not think I flatter,
    For what advancement° may I hope from thee,
    That no revénue hast but thy good spirits
    To feed and clothe thee? Why should the poor be flattered?
    No, let the candied° tongue lick absurd pomp   65
    And crook the pregnant hinges of the knee
    Where thrift may follow fawning.° Dost thou hear?
    Since my dear soul was mistress of her choice
    And could of men distinguish, her election
    Hath sealed° thee for herself. For thou hast been   70
    As one in suffering all that suffers nothing,
    A man that fortune's buffets and rewards
    Hast ta'en with equal thanks. And blest are those
    Whose blood and judgment are so well commingled
    That they are not a pipe° for fortune's finger   75
    To sound what stop she please. Give me that man
    That is not passion's slave, and I will wear him
    In my heart's core—aye, in my heart of heart,
    As I do thee. Something too much of this.
    There is a play tonight before the King.   80
    One scene of it comes near the circumstance
    Which I have told thee of my father's death.
    I prithee when thou seest that act afoot,
    Even with the very comment° of thy soul
    Observe my uncle. If his occulted° guilt   85
    Do not itself unkennel° in one speech
    It is a damnèd ghost° that we have seen
    And my imaginations are as foul
    As Vulcan's° stithy.° Give him heedful note,°
    For I mine eyes will rivet to his face,   90
    And after we will both our judgments join
    In censure of his seeming.°
HORATIO.   Well, my lord.
    If he steal aught the whilst this play is playing,
    And 'scape detecting, I will pay the theft.
HAMLET. They are coming to the play. I must be idle.°   95

60. coped: met.   62. advancement: promotion.   65. candied: sugared over
with hypocrisy.   66–67. crook . . . fawning: bend the ready knees whenever gain will follow flattery.   70. sealed: set a mark on.   75. pipe: an instrument that varies its notes.   84. comment: close observation.   85. occulted:
concealed.   86. unkennel: come to light; lit., force a fox from his hole.   87.
damned ghost: See II.2.627.   89. Vulcan: the blacksmith god. stithy: smithy.
heedful note: careful observation.   92. censure . . . seeming: judgment on
his looks.   95. be idle: seem crazy.

Get you a place.

> [*Danish march. A flourish. Enter* KING, QUEEN,
> POLONIUS, OPHELIA, ROSENCRANTZ, GUILDENSTERN,
> *and other* LORDS *attendant, with the* GUARD
> *carrying torches.*]

KING. How fares our cousin Hamlet?

HAMLET. Excellent, i' faith, of the chameleon's dish. I eat the air, promise-crammed. You cannot feed capons so.° 100

KING. I have nothing with this answer,° Hamlet. These words are not mine.

HAMLET. No, nor mine now. [*To* POLONIUS] My lord, you played once i' the university, you say?

POLONIUS. That did I, my lord, and was accounted a good actor. 106

HAMLET. What did you enact?

POLONIUS. I did enact Julius Caesar. I was killed i' the Capitol. Brutus killed me.

HAMLET. It was a brute part of him to kill so capital a calf there. Be the players ready? 111

ROSENCRANTZ. Aye, my lord, they stay upon your patience.°

QUEEN. Come hither, my dear Hamlet, sit by me.

HAMLET. No, good Mother, here's metal more attractive. 117

POLONIUS. [*To the* KING] Oh ho! Do you mark that?

HAMLET. Lady, shall I lie in your lap?

> [*Lying down at* OPHELIA'*s feet*]

OPHELIA. No, my lord. 120

HAMLET. I mean, my head upon your lap?

OPHELIA. Aye, my lord.

HAMLET. Do you think I meant country matters?°

OPHELIA. I think nothing, my lord.

HAMLET. That's a fair thought to lie between maids' legs. 126

OPHELIA. What is, my lord?

HAMLET. Nothing.

OPHELIA. You are merry, my lord.

HAMLET. Who, I?

OPHELIA. Aye, my lord.

HAMLET. Oh God, your only jig-maker.° What should a man do 132

98–100. **Excellent . . . so:** Hamlet takes "fare" literally as "what food are you eating." The chameleon was supposed to feed on air. **promise-crammed:** stuffed, like a fattened chicken (*capon*)—but with empty promises. 101. **I . . . answer:** I cannot make any sense of your answer. 103. **nor . . . now:** i.e., once words have left the lips they cease to belong to the speaker. 112. **stay . . . patience:** wait for you to be ready. 123. **country matters:** something indecent. 132. **jig-maker:** composer of jigs.

but be merry? For look you how cheerfully my mother
looks, and my father died within 's two hours.

OPHELIA. Nay, 'tis twice two months, my lord.

HAMLET. So long? Nay, then, let the Devil wear black, for I'll
have a suit of sables.° Oh heavens! Die two months ago,   138
and not forgotten yet? Then there's hope a great man's
memory may outlive his life half a year. But, by 'r Lady,
he must build churches then, or else shall he suffer not
thinking on, with the hobbyhorse,° whose epitaph is "For,
oh, for oh, the hobbyhorse is forgot."°   145

[*Hautboys° play. The dumb show enters.° Enter a* KING *and
a* QUEEN *very lovingly, the* QUEEN *embracing him and he
her. She kneels, and makes show of protestation unto him.
He takes her up, and declines his head upon her neck, lays
him down upon a bank of flowers. She, seeing him asleep,
leaves him. Anon comes in a fellow, takes off his crown,
kisses it, and pours poison in the* KING's *ears, and exit. The*
QUEEN *returns, finds the* KING *dead, and makes passionate
action. The Poisoner, with some two or three Mutes, comes
in again, seeming to lament with her. The dead body is carried away. The Poisoner woos the* QUEEN *with gifts. She
seems loath and unwilling awhile, but in the end accepts his
love.*   Exeunt.]

OPHELIA. What means this, my lord?

HAMLET. Marry, this is miching mallecho.° It means mischief.

OPHELIA. Belike this show imports the argument° of the play.   149

[*Enter* PROLOGUE.]

HAMLET. We shall know by this fellow. The players cannot keep
counsel, they'll tell all.

OPHELIA. Will he tell us what this show meant?

HAMLET. Aye, or any show that you'll show him. Be not you
ashamed to show, he'll not shame to tell you what it
means.

---

138. suit of sables: a quibble on "sable," black, and "sable," gown trimmed
with sable fur, worn by wealthy old gentlemen.   **144. hobbyhorse:** imitation
horse worn by performers in a morris dance, an amusement much disapproved
of by the godly.   **145. s.d., Hautboys:** oboes. **The dumb show enters:** Critics
have been disturbed because this dumb show cannot be exactly paralleled in
any other Elizabethan play, and because the King is apparently not disturbed
by it. Shakespeare's intention, however, in presenting a play within a play is
to produce something stagy and artificial compared with the play proper.
Moreover, as Hamlet has already complained, dumb shows were often inexplicable.   **147. miching mallecho:** slinking mischief.   **149. argument:** plot.
She too is puzzled by the dumb show.

OPHELIA. You are naught,° you are naught. I'll mark the play.   157
PROLOGUE.   For us, and for our tragedy,
                          Here stooping to your clemency,
                          We beg your hearing patiently.
HAMLET. Is this a prologue, or the posy of a ring?°   162
OPHELIA. 'Tis brief, my lord.
HAMLET. As woman's love.
                 [*Enter two* PLAYERS, KING *and* QUEEN.]
PLAYER KING. Full° thirty times hath Phoebus' cart° gone round   165
          Neptune's° salt wash and Tellus'° orbèd ground,
          And thirty dozen moons with borrowed sheen°
          About the world have times twelve thirties been,
          Since love our hearts and Hymen° did our hands
          Unite commutual° in most sacred bands.   170
PLAYER QUEEN. So many journeys may the sun and moon
          Make us again count o'er ere love be done!
          But, woe is me, you are so sick of late,
          So far from cheer and from your former state,
          That I distrust° you. Yet, though I distrust,   175
          Discomfort you, my lord, it nothing must.
          For women's fear and love holds quantity°
          In neither aught or in extremity.°
          Now what my love is, proof hath made you know,
          And as my love is sized, my fear is so.   180
          Where love is great, the littlest doubts are fear,
          Where little fears grow great, great love grows there.
PLAYER KING. Faith, I must leave thee,° love, and shortly too,
          My operant powers° their functions leave to do.
          And thou shalt live in this fair world behind,   185
          Honored, beloved, and haply one as kind
          For husband shalt thou——
PLAYER . QUEEN.   Oh, confound the rest!
          Such love must needs be treason in my breast.
          In second husband let me be accurst!
          None wed the second but who killed the first.   190
HAMLET. [*Aside*] Wormwood,° wormwood.

157. naught: i.e., disgusting.   162. posy . . . ring: It was a pretty custom to inscribe rings with little mottoes or messages, which were necessarily brief. 165–238. Full . . . twain: The play is deliberately written in crude rhyming verse, full of ridiculous and bombastic phrases.   165. Phoebus' cart: the chariot of the sun.   166. Neptune: the sea god. Tellus: the earth goddess.   167. borrowed sheen: light borrowed from the sun.   169. Hymen: god of marriage.   170. commutual: mutually.   175. distrust: am anxious about.   177. quantity: proportion.   178. In . . . extremity: either nothing or too much. 183. leave thee: i.e., die.   184. operant powers: bodily strength.   191. Wormwood: bitterness.

PLAYER QUEEN. The instances° that second marriage move
    Are base respects of thrift,° but none of love.
    A second time I kill my husband dead
    When second husband kisses me in bed.   195
PLAYER KING. I do believe you think what now you speak,
    But what we do determine oft we break.
    Purpose is but the slave to memory,
    Of violent birth but poor validity,
    Which now, like fruit unripe, sticks on the tree   200
    But fall unshaken when they mellow be.
    Most necessary 'tis that we forget
    To pay ourselves what to ourselves is debt.
    What to ourselves in passion we propose,
    The passion ending, doth the purpose lose.   205
    The violence of either grief or joy
    Their own enactures° with themselves destroy.
    Where joy most revels, grief doth most lament,
    Grief joys, joy grieves, on slender accident.
    This world is not for aye,° nor 'tis not strange   210
    That even our loves should with our fortunes change,
    For 'tis a question left us yet to prove
    Whether love lead fortune or else fortune love.
    The great man down, you mark his favorite flies.
    The poor advanced makes friends of enemies.   215
    And hitherto doth love on fortune tend,
    For who not needs shall never lack a friend,
    And who in want a hollow friend doth try
    Directly seasons° him his enemy.
    But, orderly to end where I begun,   220
    Our wills and fates do so contráry run
    That our devices still are overthrown,
    Out thoughts are ours, their ends none of our own.
    So think thou wilt no second husband wed,
    But die thy thoughts when thy first lord is dead.   225
PLAYER QUEEN. Nor earth to me give food nor Heaven light!
    Sport and repose lock from me day and night!
    To desperation turn my trust and hope!
    An anchor's° cheer in prison be my scope!
    Each opposite that blanks° the face of joy   230
    Meet what I would have well and it destroy!
    Both here and hence pursue me lasting strife
    If, once a widow, ever I be wife!

192. instances: arguments.   193. respects of thrift: considerations of gain.
207. enactures: performances.   210. aye: ever.   219. seasons: ripens into.
229. anchor: anchorite, hermit.   230. blanks: makes pale.

HAMLET. If she should break it now!

PLAYER KING. 'Tis deeply sworn. Sweet, leave me here a while.   235
My spirits grow dull, and fain I would beguile
The tedious day with sleep.   [*Sleeps.*]

PLAYER QUEEN.   Sleep rock thy brain,
And never come mischance between us twain!   [*Exit.*]

HAMLET. Madam, how like you this play?

QUEEN. The lady doth protest too much, methinks.   240

HAMLET. Oh, but she'll keep her word.

KING. Have you heard the argument?° Is there no offense in 't?

HAMLET. No, no, they do but jest, poison in jest—no offense i'
the world.   245

KING. What do you call the play?

HAMLET. *The Mousetrap.*° Marry, how? Tropically.° This play is
the image of a murder done in Vienna. Gonzago is the
Duke's name, his wife, Baptista. You shall see anon. 'Tis a
knavish piece of work, but what o' that? Your Majesty, and   250
we that have free° souls, it touches us not. Let the galled
jade wince, our withers are unwrung.°
[*Enter* LUCIANUS.] This is one Lucianus, nephew to the King.

OPHELIA. You are as good as a chorus,° my lord.   255

HAMLET. I could interpret between you and your love, if I could
see the puppets dallying.°

OPHELIA. You are keen, my lord, you are keen.

HAMLET. It would cost you a groaning to take off my edge.   260

OPHELIA. Still better, and worse.

HAMLET. So you must take your husbands.° Begin, murderer.
Pox, leave thy damnable faces and begin. Come, the croaking raven doth bellow for revenge.

LUCIANUS. Thoughts black, hands apt, drugs fit, and time agreeing,   266
Confederate season, else no creature° seeing,

---

242. argument: plot. When performances were given at Court it was sometimes customary to provide a written or printed synopsis of the story for the
distinguished spectators.   247. Mousetrap: The phrase was used of a device
to entice a person to his own destruction (OED).   248. Tropically: figura-
tively, with a pun on "trap."   252. free: innocent.   252–53. galled . . . unwrung: let a nag with a sore back flinch when the saddle is put on; our shoulders (being ungalled) feel no pain.   255. chorus: the chorus sometimes introduced the characters and commented on what was to follow. See, for instance, the Chorus in *Hen V.*   257. puppets dallying: Elizabethan puppets
were crude marionettes, popular at fairs. While the figures were put through
their motions, the puppet master explained what was happening.   262. So
. . . husbands: i.e., as the marriage service expresses it, "for better, for
worse."   267. confederate . . . creature: the opportunity conspiring with
me, no other creature.

Thou mixture rank of midnight weeds collected,
With Hecate's ban° thrice blasted, thrice infected,
Thy natural magic and dire property°   270
On wholesome life usurp immediately.
       [*Pours the poison into the sleeper's ear.*]

HAMLET. He poisons him i' the garden for his estate.° His name's
    Gonzago. The story is extant, and written in very choice
    Italian. You shall see anon how the murderer gets the love
    of Gonzago's wife.

OPHELIA. The King rises.   276

HAMLET. What, frighted with false fire!°

QUEEN. How fares my lord?

POLONIUS. Give o'er the play.

KING. Give me some light. Away!   280

POLONIUS. Lights, lights, lights!
       [*Exeunt all but* HAMLET *and* HORATIO.]

HAMLET.   "Why, let the stricken deer go weep,
       The hart ungallèd play,
    For some must watch while some must sleep.
       Thus runs the world away."   285
    Would not this, sir, and a forest of feathers°—if the rest
    of my fortunes turn Turk° with me—with two Provincial
    roses° on my razed° shoes, get me a fellowship° in a cry°
    of players, sir?

HORATIO. Half a share.   290

HAMLET. A whole one, I.
       "For thou dost know, O Damon° dear,
       This realm dismantled° was
       Of Jove himself, and now reigns here
       A very, very—pajock."°   295

HORATIO. You might have rhymed.

HAMLET. O good Horatio, I'll take the ghost's word for a thou-
    sand pound. Didst perceive?

HORATIO. Very well, my lord.

HAMLET. Upon the talk of the poisoning?   300

HORATIO. I did very well note him.

HAMLET. Ah, ha! Come, some music! Come, the recorders!°

269. **Hecate's ban:** the curse of Hecate, goddess of witchcraft. 270. **property:**
nature. 273. **estate:** kingdom. 277. **false fire:** a mere show. 286. **forest of
feathers:** set of plumes, much worn by players. 287. **turn Turk:** turn heathen,
and treat me cruelly. 288. **Provincial roses:** rosettes, worn on the shoes.
razed: slashed, ornamented with cuts. 289. **fellowship:** partnership. **cry:** pack.
292. **Damon:** Damon and Pythias were types of perfect friends. 293. **dis-
mantled:** robbed. 295. **pajock:** peacock, a strutting, lecherous bird. These
verses, and the lines above, may have come from some ballad, otherwise lost.
303. **recorders:** wooden pipes.

"For if the King like not the comedy,
    Why then, belike, he likes it not, perdy."°   305
Come, some music!

[*Re-enter* ROSENCRANTZ *and* GUILDENSTERN.]

GUILDENSTERN. Good my lord, vouchsafe me a word with you.

HAMLET. Sir, a whole history.

GUILDENSTERN. The King, sir——   310

HAMLET. Aye, sir, what of him?

GUILDENSTERN. Is in his retirement marvelous distempered.°

HAMLET. With drink, sir?

GUILDENSTERN. No, my lord, rather with choler.°   315

HAMLET. Your wisdom should show itself more richer to signify
this to the doctor, for for me to put him to his purgation°
would perhaps plunge him into far more choler.   319

GUILDENSTERN. Good my lord, put your discourse into some
frame,° and start not so wildly from my affair.

HAMLET. I am tame, sir. Pronounce.

GUILDENSTERN. The Queen your mother, in most great affliction
of spirit, hath sent me to you.

HAMLET. You are welcome.   325

GUILDENSTERN. Nay, good my lord, this courtesy is not of the
right breed. If it shall please you to make me a wholesome
answer, I will do your mother's commandment. If not, your
pardon and my return shall be the end of my business.   330

HAMLET. Sir. I cannot.

GUILDENSTERN. What, my lord?

HAMLET. Make you a wholesome answer, my wit's diseased. But,
sir, such answer as I can make you shall command, or
rather, as you say, my mother. Therefore no more, but to
the matter. My mother, you say——   337

ROSENCRANTZ. Then thus she says. Your behavior hath struck
her into amazement and admiration.°

HAMLET. Oh, wonderful son that can so astonish a mother! But
is there no sequel at the heels of this mother's admiration?
Impart.   342

ROSENCRANTZ. She desires to speak with you in her closet ere
you go to bed.

HAMLET. We shall obey, were she ten times our mother. Have
you any further trade with us?

ROSENCRANTZ. My lord, you once did love me.   348

---

305. perdy: by God.   312. distempered: disturbed; but Hamlet takes the
word in its other sense of "drunk."   315. choler: anger, which Hamlet again
pretends to understand as meaning "biliousness."   317–18. put . . . purga-
tion: "give him a dose of salts."   321. frame: shape; i.e., "please talk sense."
339. admiration: wonder.

HAMLET. So I do still, by these pickers and stealers.°

ROSENCRANTZ. Good my lord, what is your cause of distemper?
You do surely bar the door upon your own liberty if you
deny your griefs° to your friend.

HAMLET. Sir, I lack advancement.°   354

ROSENCRANTZ. How can that be when you have the voice of the
King himself for your succession in Denmark?

HAMLET. Aye, sir, but "While the grass grows"°—the proverb   359
is something musty. [*Re-enter* PLAYERS *with recorders.*] Oh,
the recorders! Let me see one. To withdraw° with you——
why do you go about to recover the wind° of me, as if you
would drive me into a toil?°

GUILDENSTERN. O my lord, if my duty be too bold, my love is
too unmannerly.°   365

HAMLET. I do not well understand that. Will you play upon this
pipe?

GUILDENSTERN. My lord, I cannot.

HAMLET. I pray you.

GUILDENSTERN. Believe me, I cannot.   370

HAMLET. I do beseech you.

GUILDENSTERN. I know no touch of it, my lord.

HAMLET. It is as easy as lying. Govern these ventages° with your   374
fingers and thumb, give it breath with your mouth, and it
will discourse most eloquent music. Look you, these are the
stops.

GUILDENSTERN. But these cannot I command to any utterance of
harmony, I have not the skill.

HAMLET. Why, look you now, how unworthy a thing you make
of me! You would play upon me, you would seem to know   380
my stops, you would pluck out the heart of my mystery,
you would sound me from my lowest note to the top of my
compass—and there is much music, excellent voice, in this
little organ—yet cannot you make it speak. 'Sblood, do you
think I am easier to be played on than a pipe? Call me what

---

349. pickers . . . stealers: i.e., hands—an echo from the Christian's duty in
the catechism to keep his hands "from picking and stealing." **353. deny . . .
griefs:** refuse to tell your troubles. **354. advancement:** promotion. Hamlet
harks back to his previous interview with Rosencrantz and Guildenstern. See
II.2.258. **358. While . . . grows:** the proverb ends "the steed starves."
361. withdraw: go aside. Hamlet leads Guildenstern to one side of the stage.
362. recover . . . wind: a hunting metaphor; approach me with the wind
against you. **363. toil:** net. **364–65. if . . . unmannerly:** if I exceed my
duty by asking these questions, then my affection for you shows lack of manners; i.e., forgive me if I have been impertinent. **374. ventages:** holes, stops.

instrument you will, though you can fret° me, you cannot
play upon me. [*Re-enter* POLONIUS.] God bless you, sir!   390
POLONIUS. My lord, the Queen would speak with you, and
    presently.
HAMLET. Do you see yonder cloud that's almost in shape of a
    camel?
POLONIUS. By the mass, and 'tis like a camel indeed.   395
HAMLET. Methinks it is like a weasel.
POLONIUS. It is backed like a weasel.
HAMLET. Or like a whale?
POLONIUS. Very like a whale.
HAMLET. Then I will come to my mother by and by. Then fool   400
    me to the top of my bent.° I will come by and by.
POLONIUS. I will say so.   [*Exit* POLONIUS.]
HAMLET. "By and by" is easily said. Leave me, friends.
                          [*Exeunt all but* HAMLET.]
    'Tis now the very witching time° of night,   406
    When churchyards yawn and Hell itself breathes out
    Contagion° to this world. Now could I drink hot blood,
    And do such bitter business as the day   409
    Would quake to look on. Soft! Now to my mother.
    O heart, lose not thy nature, let not ever
    The soul of Nero° enter this firm bosom.
    Let me be cruel, not unnatural.
    I will speak daggers to her, but use none.
    My tongue and soul in this be hypocrites,   415
    How in my words soever she be shent,°
    To give them seals° never, my soul, consent!   [*Exit.*]

389. fret: annoy, with a pun on the frets or bars on stringed instruments by
which the fingering is regulated.   401. top . . . bent: See II.2.30, n.   406.
witching time: when witches perform their foul rites.   408. Contagion: infec-
tion.   412. Nero: Nero killed his own mother. Hamlet is afraid that in the
interview to come he will lose all self-control.   416. shent: rebuked.   417.
give . . . seals: ratify words by actions.

Scene 3 ✑ *A room in the castle.*

[*Enter* KING, ROSENCRANTZ, *and* GUILDENSTERN.]

KING. I like him not, nor stands it safe with us
To let his madness range.° Therefore prepare you.
I your commission will forthwith dispatch,
And he to England shall along with you.
The terms of our estate° may not endure   5
Hazard so near us as doth hourly grow
Out of his lunacies.
GUILDENSTERN.   We will ourselves provide.°
Most holy and religious fear° it is
To keep those many many bodies safe
That live and feed upon your Majesty.   10
ROSENCRANTZ. The single and peculiar° life is bound
With all the strength and armor of the mind
To keep itself from noyance,° but much more
That spirit upon whose weal° depends and rests
The lives of many. The cease of majesty°   15
Dies not alone, but like a gulf° doth draw
What's near it with it. It is a massy° wheel
Fixed on the summit of the highest mount,
To whose huge spokes ten thousand lesser things
Are mortised° and adjoined; which, when it falls,   20
Each small annexment, petty consequence,°
Attends° the boisterous ruin. Never alone
Did the King sigh but with a general groan.
KING. Arm you, I pray you, to this speedy voyage,
For we will fetters put upon this fear,   25

Sc. 3: 2. range: roam freely.   5. terms . . . estate: i.e., one in my position.
7. ourselves provide: make our preparations.   8. fear: anxiety.   11. peculiar:
individual.   13. noyance: injury.   14. weal: welfare.   15. cease of majesty:
death of a king.   16. gulf: whirlpool.   17. massy: massive.   20. mortised:
firmly fastened.   21. annexment . . . consequence: attachment, smallest
thing connected with it.   22. Attends: waits on, is involved in.

Which now goes too free-footed.

ROSENCRANTZ & GUILDENSTERN.   We will haste us.
               [*Exeunt* ROSENCRANTZ *and* GUILDENSTERN.]
                    [*Enter* POLONIUS.]

POLONIUS. My lord, he's going to his mother's closet.
     Behind the arras I'll convey myself
     To hear the process.° I'll warrant she'll tax° him home.
     And, as you said,° and wisely was it said,   30
     'Tis meet that some more audience than a mother,
     Since nature makes them partial, should o'erhear
     The speech, of vantage.° Fare you well, my liege.
     I'll call upon you ere you go to bed
     And tell you what I know.

KING.   Thanks, dear my lord.   [*Exit* POLONIUS.]   35
     Oh, my offense is rank,° it smells to Heaven.
     It hath the primal eldest curse° upon 't,
     A brother's murder. Pray can I not,
     Though inclination be as sharp as will.°
     My stronger guilt defeats my strong intent,   40
     And like a man to double business bound,
     I stand in pause where I shall first begin,
     And both neglect. What if this cursèd hand
     Were thicker than itself with brother's blood,
     Is there not rain enough in the sweet heavens   45
     To wash it white as snow? Whereto serves mercy
     But to confront the visage of offense?°
     And what's in prayer but this twofold force,
     To be forestallèd° ere we come to fall
     Or pardoned being down? Then I'll look up,   50
     My fault is past. But oh, what form of prayer
     Can serve my turn? "Forgive me my foul murder"?
     That cannot be, since I am still possessed
     Of those effects° for which I did the murder—
     My crown, mine own ambition, and my Queen.   55
     May one be pardoned and retain the offense?°
     In the corrupted currents° of this world
     Offense's gilded hand may shove by justice,
     And oft 'tis seen the wicked prize° itself

---

29. process: proceeding. **tax:** censure.   **30. as . . . said:** Actually Polonius
himself had said it (III.1.189–93).   **33. of vantage:** from a place of vantage;
i.e., concealment.   **36. rank:** foul.   **37. primal . . . curse:** the curse laid
upon Cain, the first murderer, who also slew his brother.   **39. will:** desire.
47. confront . . . offense: look crime in the face.   **49. forestalled:** prevented.
54. effects: advantages.   **56. offense:** i.e., that for which he has offended.
57. currents: courses, ways.   **59. wicked prize:** the proceeds of the crime.

Buys out the law. But 'tis not so above.   60
There is no shuffling, there the action lies
In his true nature,° and we ourselves compelled
Even to the teeth and forehead° of our faults
To give in evidence. What then? What rests?
Try what repentance can. What can it not?   65
Yet what can it when one cannot repent?
Oh, wretched state! Oh, bosom black as death!
Oh, limèd° soul, that struggling to be free
Art more engaged!° Help, angels! Make assay!°
Bow, stubborn knees, and heart with strings of steel,   70
Be soft as sinews of the newborn babe!
All may be well.   [*Retires and kneels.*]
                    [*Enter* HAMLET.]
HAMLET. Now might I do it pat, now he is praying,
    And now I'll do 't. And so he goes to Heaven,
    And so am I revenged. That would be scanned: 75
    A villain kills my father, and for that
    I, his sole son, do this same villain send
    To Heaven.
    Oh, this is hire and salary,° not revenge.
    He took my father grossly,° full of bread,   80
    With all his crimes broad blown, as flush° as May,
    And how his audit° stands who knows save Heaven?
    But in our circumstance and course of thought,°
    'Tis heavy with him. And am I then revenged,
    To take him in the purging of his soul,   85
    When he is fit and seasoned,° for his passage?
    No.
    Up, sword, and know thou a more horrid hent.°
    When he is drunk asleep, or in his rage,
    Or in the incestuous pleasure of his bed—   90
    At gaming, swearing, or about some act
    That has no relish of salvation in 't—
    Then trip him, that his heels may kick at Heaven
    And that his soul may be as damned and black
    As Hell, whereto it goes. My mother stays.   95
    This physic but prolongs thy sickly days.   [*Exit.*]

61–62. there . . . nature: in Heaven the case is tried on its own merits. **63.
teeth . . . forehead:** i.e., face to face. **68. limed:** caught as in birdlime.
69. engaged: stuck fast. **assay:** attempt. **79. hire . . . salary:** i.e., a kind
action deserving pay. **80. grossly:** i.e., when he was in a state of sin. See
I.5.74–80. **81. broad . . . flush:** in full blossom, as luxuriant. **82. audit:**
account. **93. circumstance . . . thought:** as it appears to my mind. **86.
seasoned:** ripe. **88. hent:** opportunity.

KING. [*Rising*] My words fly up, my thoughts remain below.
Words without thoughts never to Heaven go.   [*Exit*.]

Scene 4 ⤳ The QUEEN'S *closet*.

[*Enter* QUEEN *and* POLONIUS.]
POLONIUS. He will come straight. Look you lay home to° him.
Tell him his pranks have been too broad° to bear with,
And that your grace hath screened and stood between
Much heat and him. I'll sconce me° even here.
Pray you, be round with him.   5
HAMLET. [*Within*] Mother, Mother, Mother!
QUEEN.   I'll warrant you,
Fear me not. Withdraw, I hear him coming.
[POLONIUS *hides behind the arras*.]
[*Enter* HAMLET.]
HAMLET. Now, Mother, what's the matter?
QUEEN. Hamlet, thou hast thy father much offended.
HAMLET. Mother, you have my father much offended.   10
QUEEN. Come, come, you answer with an idle° tongue.
HAMLET. Go, go, you question with a wicked tongue.
QUEEN. Why, how now, Hamlet!
HAMLET.   What's the matter now?
QUEEN. Have you forgot me?
HAMLET.   No, by the rood,° not so.
You are the Queen, your husband's brother's wife,   15
And—would it were not so!—you are my mother.
QUEEN. Nay, then, I'll set those to you that can speak.
HAMLET. Come, come, and sit you down. You shall not budge,
You go not till I set you up a glass°
Where you may see the inmost part of you.   20
QUEEN. What wilt thou do? Thou wilt not murder me?

Sc. 4: 1. lay . . . to: be strict with.   2. broad: unrestrained. Polonius is
thinking of the obvious insolence of the remarks about second marriage in the
play scene.   4. sconce me: hide myself.   11. idle: foolish.   14. rood: crucifix.
19. glass: looking-glass.

Help, help, ho!
POLONIUS. [*Behind*] What ho! Help, help, help!
HAMLET. [*Drawing*] How now! A rat? Dead, for a ducat dead!
     [*Makes a pass through the arras.*]
POLONIUS. [*Behind*] Oh, I am slain!   [*Falls and dies.*]
QUEEN.   Oh me, what hast thou done?   25
HAMLET. Nay, I know not. Is it the King?
QUEEN. Oh, what a rash and bloody deed is this!
HAMLET. A bloody deed! Almost as bad, good Mother,
     As kill a king and marry with his brother.
QUEEN. As kill a king!
HAMLET.   Aye, lady, 'twas my word.   30
     [*Lifts up the arras and discovers POLONIUS.*]
     Thou wretched, rash, intruding fool, farewell!
     I took thee for thy better. Take thy fortune.
     Thou find'st to be too busy is some danger.
     Leave wringing of your hands. Peace! Sit you down,
     And let me wring your heart. For so I shall   35
     If it be made of penetrable stuff,
     If damnèd custom have not brassed° it so
     That it be proof and bulwark against sense.
QUEEN. What have I done that thou darest wag thy tongue
     In noise so rude against me?
HAMLET.   Such an act   40
     That blurs the grace and blush of modesty,
     Calls virtue hypocrite, takes off the rose
     From the fair forehead of an innocent love,
     And sets a blister° there—makes marriage vows
     As false as dicers' oaths. Oh, such a deed   45
     As from the body of contraction° plucks
     The very soul, and sweet religion makes
     A rhapsody of words.° Heaven's face doth glow,
     Yea, this solidity and compound mass,°
     With tristful visage, as against the doom,°   50
     Is thought-sick at the act.
QUEEN.   Aye me, what act
     That roars so loud and thunders in the index?°
HAMLET. Look here upon this picture,° and on this,

37. **brassed:** made brazen; i.e., impenetrable.   44. **sets a blister:** brands as a harlot; see IV.5.118, n.   46. **contraction:** the marriage contract.   48. **rhapsody of words:** string of meaningless words.   49. **solidity . . . mass:** i.e., solid earth.   50. **tristful . . . doom:** sorrowful face, as in anticipation of Dooms-day.   52. **in . . . index:** i.e., if the beginning (*index*, i.e., table of contents) is so noisy, what will follow?   53. **picture:** Modern producers usually interpret the pictures as miniatures, Hamlet wearing one of his father, Gertrude one of Claudius. In the eighteenth century, wall portraits were used.

The counterfeit presentment° of two brothers.
See what a grace was seated on this brow—   55
Hyperion's curls, the front° of Jove himself,
An eye like Mars, to threaten and command,
A station° like the herald Mercury°
New-lighted° on a heaven-kissing hill,
A combination° and a form indeed   60
Where every god did seem to set his seal°
To give the world assurance of a man.
This was your husband. Look you now what follows.
Here is your husband, like a mildewed ear,
Blasting his wholesome brother. Have you eyes?   65
Could you on this fair mountain leave to feed
And batten° on this moor? Ha! Have you eyes?
You cannot call it love, for at your age
The heyday° in the blood is tame, it's humble,
And waits upon the judgment. And what judgment   70
Would step from this to this? Sense° sure you have,
Else could you not have motion.° But sure that sense
Is apoplexed;° for madness would not err,
Nor sense to ecstasy° was ne'er so thralled°
But it reserved some quantity of choice   75
To serve in such a difference.° What devil was 't
That thus hath cozened° you at hoodman-blind?°
Eyes without feeling, feeling without sight,
Ears without hands or eyes, smelling sans° all,
Or but a sickly part of one true sense   80
Could not so mope.°
Oh, shame! Where is thy blush? Rebellious° Hell,
If thou canst mutine° in a matron's bones,
To flaming youth let virtue be as wax
And melt in her own fire. Proclaim no shame   85

54. counterfeit presentment: portrait. **56. front:** forehead. **58. station:** figure; lit., standing. **Mercury:** messenger of the gods, and one of the most beautiful. **59. New-lighted:** newly alighted. **60. combination:** i.e., of physical qualities. **61. set . . . seal:** guarantee as a perfect man. **67. batten:** glut yourself. **69. heyday:** excitement. **71. Sense:** feeling. **72. motion:** desire. **73. apoplexed:** paralyzed. **74. ecstasy:** excitement, passion. See II.1.102. **thralled:** enslaved. **76. serve . . . difference:** to enable you to see the difference between your former and your present husband. **77. cozened:** cheated. **hoodman-blind:** blind-man's-buff. **79. sans:** without. **81. mope:** be dull. **82–88. Rebellious . . . will:** i.e., if the passion (*Hell*) of a woman of your age is uncontrollable (*rebellious*), youth can have no restraints; there is no shame in a young man's lust when the elderly are just as eager and their reason (which should control desire) encourages them. **83. mutine:** mutiny.

When the compulsive ardor° gives the charge,
Since frost itself as actively doth burn,
And reason panders° will.
QUEEN.   O Hamlet, speak no more.
Thou turn'st mine eyes into my very soul,
And there I see such black and grainèd° spots   90
As will not leave their tinct.°
HAMLET.   Nay, but to live
In the rank sweat of an enseamèd° bed,
Stewed in corruption, honeying and making love
Over the nasty sty——
QUEEN.   Oh, speak to me no more,
These words like daggers enter in my ears.   95
No more, sweet Hamlet!
HAMLET.   A murderer and a villain,
A slave that is not twentieth part the tithe°
Of your precedent° lord, a vice of kings,°
A cutpurse° of the empire and the rule,
That from a shelf the precious diadem stole   100
And put it in his pocket!
QUEEN.   No more!
HAMLET. A king of shreds and patches——
[Enter GHOST] Save me, and hover o'er me with your wings,
You heavenly guards! What would your gracious figure?
QUEEN. Alas, he's mad!   105
HAMLET. Do you not come your tardy son to chide
That, lapsed in time and passion, lets go by
The important acting of your dread command?°
Oh, say!
GHOST. Do not forget. This visitation   110
Is but to whet thy almost blunted purpose.
But look, amazement on thy mother sits.
Oh, step between her and her fighting soul.
Conceit° in weakest bodies strongest works.
Speak to her, Hamlet.
HAMLET.   How is it with you, lady?   115
QUEEN. Alas, how is 't with you
That you do bend your eye on vacancy°
And with the incorporal° air do hold discourse?

86. **compulsive ardor:** compelling lust. 88. **panders:** acts as go-between.
90. **grained:** dyed in the grain. 91. **tinct:** color. 92. **enseamed:** greasy. 97.
tithe: tenth part. 98. **precedent:** former. **vice of kings:** caricature of a king.
99. **cutpurse:** thief. 107–08. **That . . . command:** who has allowed time to
pass and passion to cool, and neglects the urgent duty of obeying your dread
command. 114. **Conceit:** imagination. 117. **vacancy:** empty space. 118.
incorporal: bodiless.

Forth at your eyes your spirits wildly peep,
And as the sleeping soldiers in the alarm,   120
Your bedded° hairs, like life in excrements,°
Start up and stand an° end. O gentle son,
Upon the heat and flame of thy distemper°
Sprinkle cool patience. Whereon do you look?
HAMLET. On him, on him! Look you how pale he glares!   125
His form and cause conjoined,° preaching to stones,
Would make them capable.° Do not look upon me,
Lest with this piteous action you convert
My stern effects.° Then what I have to do
Will want true color—tears perchance for blood.   130
QUEEN. To whom do you speak this?
HAMLET.   Do you see nothing there?
QUEEN. Nothing at all, yet all that is I see.
HAMLET. Nor did you nothing hear?
QUEEN.   No, nothing but ourselves.
HAMLET. Why, look you there! Look how it steals away!
My father, in his habit as he lived!   135
Look where he goes, even now, out at the portal!
                                        [*Exit* GHOST.]
QUEEN. This is the very coinage of your brain.
This bodiless creation ecstasy°
Is very cunning in.
HAMLET.   Ecstasy!
My pulse, as yours, doth temperately keep time,   140
And makes as healthful music. It is not madness
That I have uttered. Bring me to the test
And I the matter will reword, which madness
Would gambol° from. Mother, for love of grace,
Lay not that flattering unction° to your soul,   145
That not your trespass but my madness speaks.
It will but skin and film the ulcerous place,
Whiles rank corruption, mining° all within,
Infects unseen. Confess yourself to Heaven,
Repent what's past, avoid what is to come,   150
And do not spread the compost° on the weeds
To make them ranker. Forgive me this my virtue,

121. **bedded:** evenly laid. **excrements:** anything that grows out of the body, such as hair or fingernails; here hair. **122. an:** on. **123. distemper:** mental disturbance. **126. form . . . conjoined:** his appearance and the reason for his appearance joined. **127. capable:** i.e., of feeling. **128–29. convert . . . effects:** change the stern action which should follow. **138. ecstasy:** madness. **144. gambol:** start away. **145. unction:** healing ointment. **148. mining:** undermining. **151. compost:** manure.

For in the fatness° of these pursy° times
Virtue itself of vice must pardon beg—
Yea, curb° and woo for leave to do him good.   155
QUEEN. O Hamlet, thou hast cleft my heart in twain.
HAMLET. Oh, throw away the worser part of it,
And live the purer with the other half.
Good night. But go not to my uncle's bed.
Assume a virtue if you have it not.   160
That° monster, custom, who all sense doth eat,
Of habits devil,° is angel yet in this,
That to the use° of actions fair and good
He likewise gives a frock or livery
That aptly° is put on. Refrain tonight,   165
And that shall lend a kind of easiness
To the next abstinence, the next more easy.
For use almost can change the stamp° of nature,
And either the Devil,° or throw him out
With wondrous potency. Once more, good night.   170
And when you are desirous to be blest,
I'll blessing beg of you. For this same lord,
   [*Pointing to* POLONIUS]
I do repent; but Heaven hath pleased it so,
To punish me with this, and this with me,
That I must be their scourge and minister.   175
I will bestow° him, and will answer well
The death I gave him. So again good night.
I must be cruel only to be kind.
Thus bad begins, and worse remains behind.
One word more, good lady.
QUEEN.   What shall I do?   180
HAMLET. Not this, by no means, that I bid you do.
Let the bloat° king tempt you again to bed,
Pinch wanton° on your cheek, call you his mouse,
And let him, for a pair of reechy° kisses
Or paddling in your neck with his damned fingers,   185
Make you to ravel° all this matter out,
That I essentially am not in madness,

153. **fatness:** grossness. **pursy:** bloated. 155. **curb:** bow low. 161–65. That . . . on: i.e., custom (bad habits) like an evil monster destroys all sense of good and evil, but yet can become an angel (good habits) when it makes us perform good actions as mechanically as we put on our clothes. 162. **devil:** This is the Q2 reading; the passage is omitted in F1. Probably the word should be "evil." 163. **use:** practice. 165. **aptly:** readily. 168. **stamp:** impression. 169. **either the Devil:** some verb such as "shame" or "curb" has been omitted. 176. **bestow:** get rid of. 182. **bloat:** bloated. 183. **wanton:** lewdly. 184. **reechy:** foul. 186. **ravel:** unravel, reveal.

But mad in craft. 'Twere good you let him know.
For who that's but a Queen, fair, sober, wise,
Would from a paddock,° from a bat, a gib,°   190
Such dear concernings° hide? Who would do so?
No, in despite° of sense and secrecy,
Unpeg the basket on the house's top,
Let the birds fly, and like the famous ape,°
To try conclusions,° in the basket creep   195
And break your own neck down.
QUEEN. Be thou assured if words be made of breath
And breath of life, I have no life to breathe
What thou hast said to me.
HAMLET. I must to England. You know that?
QUEEN.   Alack,   200
I had forgot. 'Tis so concluded on.
HAMLET. There's letters sealed, and my two schoolfellows,
Whom I will trust as I will adders fanged,
They bear the mandate.° They must sweep my way,
And marshal me to knavery. Let it work,   205
For 'tis the sport to have the enginer°
Hoist with his own petar.° And 't shall go hard
But I will delve one yard below their mines
And blow them at the moon: Oh, 'tis most sweet
When in one line two crafts° directly meet.   210
This man shall set me packing.
I'll lug the guts into the neighbor room.
Mother, good night. Indeed this counselor
Is now most still, most secret, and most grave
Who was in life a foolish prating knave.   215
Come, sir, to draw toward an end with you.
Good night, Mother.   [*Exeunt severally,*°
                              HAMLET *dragging in* POLONIUS.]

---

190. **paddock:** toad.   **gib:** tomcat.   191. **dear concernings:** important matters.
192. **despite:** spite.   194. **famous ape:** The story is not known, but evidently
told of an ape that let the birds out of their cage and, seeing them fly, crept
into the cage himself and jumped out, breaking his own neck.   195. **try con-**
clusions: repeat the experiment.   204. **mandate:** command.   206. **enginer:**
engineer.   207. **petar:** petard, land mine.   210. **crafts:** devices.   217. **s.d.,**
Exeunt severally: i.e., by separate exits. In F1 there is no break here. The King
enters as soon as Hamlet has dragged the body away. Q2 marks the break.
The act division was first inserted in a quarto of 1676.

ACT IV

Scene 1 ✑ *A room in the castle.*

[*Enter* KING, QUEEN, ROSENCRANTZ, *and* GUILDENSTERN.]
KING. There's matter° in these sighs, these profound heaves,
    You must translate. 'Tis fit we understand them.
    Where is your son?
QUEEN. Bestow this place° on us a little while.
                    [*Exeunt* ROSENCRANTZ *and* GUILDENSTERN.]
    Ah, mine own lord, what have I seen tonight!   5
KING. What, Gertrude? How does Hamlet?
QUEEN. Mad as the sea and wind when both contend
    Which is the mightier. In his lawless fit,
    Behind the arras hearing something stir,
    Whips out his rapier, cries "A rat, a rat!"   10
    And in this brainish apprehension° kills
    The unseen good old man.
KING.   Oh, heavy deed!
    It had been so with us had we been there.
    His liberty is full of threats to all,
    To you yourself, to us, to everyone.   15
    Alas, how shall this bloody deed be answered?
    It will be laid to us, whose providence°
    Should have kept short,° restrained and out of haunt,°
    This mad young man. But so much was our love
    We would not understand what was most fit,   20
    But, like the owner of a foul disease,
    To keep it from divulging° let it feed
    Even on the pith° of life. Where is he gone?

    Act IV, Sc. 1: 1. **matter:** something serious.   4. **Bestow . . . place:** give
place, leave us.   11. **brainish apprehension:** mad imagination.   17. **provi-**
dence: foresight.   18. **short:** confined. **out of haunt:** away from others.   22.
divulging: becoming known.   23. **pith:** marrow.

QUEEN. To draw apart the body he hath killed,
   O'er whom his very madness, like some ore   25
   Among a mineral of metals base,
   Shows itself pure. He weeps for what is done.
KING. O Gertrude, come away!
   The sun no sooner shall the mountains touch
   But we will ship him hence. And this vile deed   30
   We must, with all our majesty and skill,
   Both countenance° and excuse. Ho, Guildenstern!
            [*Re-enter* ROSENCRANTZ *and* GUILDENSTERN.]
   Friends both, go join you with some further aid.
   Hamlet in madness hath Polonius slain,
   And from his mother's closet hath he dragged him.   35
   Go seek him out, speak fair, and bring the body
   Into the chapel. I pray you, haste in this.
            [*Exeunt* ROSENCRANTZ *and* GUILDENSTERN.]
   Come, Gertrude, we'll call up our wisest friends,
   And let them know both what we mean to do
   And what's untimely done,°   40
   Whose whisper o'er the world's diameter
   As level as the cannon to his blank°
   Transports his poisoned shot, may miss our name
   And hit the woundless air. Oh, come away!
   My soul is full of discord and dismay.   [*Exeunt.*]   45

Scene 2 ⚜ *Another room in the castle.*

                    [*Enter* HAMLET.]
HAMLET. Safely stowed.
ROSENCRANTZ & GUILDENSTERN. [*Within*] Hamlet! Lord Hamlet!
HAMLET. But soft, what noise? Who calls on Hamlet?
   Oh, here they come.
            [*Enter* ROSENCRANTZ *and* GUILDENSTERN.]
ROSENCRANTZ. What have you done, my lord, with the dead body?   5

32. countenance: take responsibility for.   40. done: A half-line has been
omitted. Some editors fill the gap with "So, haply slander."   42. blank: target.

HAMLET. Compounded it with dust, whereto 'tis kin.
ROSENCRANTZ. Tell us where 'tis, that we may take it thence
   And bear it to the chapel.
HAMLET. Do not believe it.
ROSENCRANTZ. Believe what?   10
HAMLET. That I can keep your counsel and not mine own. Besides, to be demanded of a sponge! What replication° should
   be made by the son of a king?
ROSENCRANTZ. Take you me for a sponge, my lord?   15
HAMLET. Aye, sir, that soaks up the King's countenance,° his
   rewards, his authorities. But such officers do the King best
   service in the end. He keeps them, like an ape, in the corner
   of his jaw, first mouthed, to be last swallowed. When he
   needs what you have gleaned, it is but squeezing you and,
   sponge, you shall be dry again.   23
ROSENCRANTZ. I understand you not, my lord.
HAMLET. I am glad of it. A knavish speech sleeps in a foolish
   ear.°
ROSENCRANTZ. My lord, you must tell us where the body is, and
   go with us to the King.   28
HAMLET. The body is with the King, but the King is not with the
   body.° The King is a thing——
GUILDENSTERN. A thing, my lord?
HAMLET. Of nothing. Bring me to him. Hide fox, and all after.°   33
                                     [Exeunt.]

Scene 3   *Another room in the castle.*

[*Enter* KING, *attended.*]
KING. I have sent to seek him, and to find the body.
   How dangerous is it that this man goes loose!

Sc. 2: 14. **replication:** answer.   17. **countenance:** favor.   25–26. A . . .
ear: a fool never understands the point of a sinister speech.   29–30. The . . .
body: Hamlet deliberately bewilders his companions.   32–33. Hide . . .
after: a form of the game of hide-and-seek. With these words Hamlet runs
away from them.

Yet must not we put the strong law on him.
He's loved of the distracted° multitude,
Who like not in their judgment but their eyes;°   5
And where 'tis so, the offender's scourge° is weighed,
But never the offense. To bear° all smooth and even,
This sudden sending him away must seem
Deliberate pause.° Diseases desperate grown
By desperate appliance are relieved,   10
Or not at all.
[*Enter* ROSENCRANTZ.] How now! What hath befall'n?
ROSENCRANTZ. Where the dead is bestowed, my lord,
   We cannot get from him.
KING.   But where is he?
ROSENCRANTZ. Without, my lord, guarded, to know your pleasure.
KING. Bring him before us.   15
ROSENCRANTZ. Ho, Guildenstern! Bring in my lord.
                    [*Enter* HAMLET *and* GUILDENSTERN.]
KING. Now, Hamlet, where's Polonius?
HAMLET. At supper.
KING. At supper! Where?
HAMLET. Not where he eats, but where he is eaten. A certain con-   20
   vocation of politic worms° are e'en at him. Your worm is
   your only emperor for diet. We fat all creatures else to fat
   us, and we fat ourselves for maggots. Your fat king and
   your lean beggar is but variable service,° two dishes, but to
   one table. That's the end.   26
KING. Alas, alas!
HAMLET. A man may fish with the worm that hath eat of a king,
   and eat of the fish that hath fed of that worm.
KING. What dost thou mean by this?
HAMLET. Nothing but to show you how a king may go a pro-
   gress° through the guts of a beggar.
KING. Where is Polonius?   34
HAMLET. In Heaven—send thither to see. If your messenger find
   him not there, seek him i' the other place yourself. But in-
   deed if you find him not within this month, you shall nose
   him as you go up the stairs into the lobby.   39
KING. [*To some* ATTENDANTS] Go seek him there.
HAMLET. He will stay till you come.   [*Exeunt* ATTENDANTS.]

   Sc. 3: 4. distracted: bewildered. 5. like . . . eyes: whose likings are
swayed not by judgment but by looks. 6. scourge: punishment. 7. bear:
make. 9. Deliberate pause: the result of careful planning. 21. convocation
. . . worms: an assembly of political-minded worms. 25. variable service:
choice of alternatives. 33. go a progress: make a state journey.

KING. Hamlet, this deed, for thine especial safety,
  Which we do tender,° as we dearly grieve
  For that which thou hast done, must send thee hence
  With fiery quickness. Therefore prepare thyself.   45
  The bark is ready and the wind at help,°
  The associates tend,° and every thing is bent°
  For England.
HAMLET.   For England?
KING.   Aye, Hamlet.
HAMLET.   Good.
KING. So is it if thou knew'st our purposes.
HAMLET. I see a cherub that sees them. But, come, for England!
  Farewell, dear Mother.   51
KING. Thy loving father, Hamlet.
HAMLET. My mother. Father and mother is man and wife, man
  and wife is one flesh, and so, my mother. Come, for Eng-
  land!   [Exit.]
KING. Follow him at foot,° tempt° him with speed aboard.   56
  Delay it not, I'll have him hence tonight.
  Away! For everything is sealed and done
  That else leans on the affair. Pray you make haste.
              [Exeunt ROSENCRANTZ and GUILDENSTERN.]
  And, England, if my love thou hold'st at aught—   60
  As my great power thereof may give thee sense,
  Since yet thy cicatrice° looks raw and red
  After the Danish sword, and thy free awe°
  Pays homage to us—thou mayst not coldly set
  Our sovereign process,° which imports at full,   65
  By letters congruing° to that effect,
  The present° death of Hamlet. Do it, England,
  For like the hectic° in my blood he rages,
  And thou must cure me. Till I know 'tis done,
  Howe'er my haps,° my joys were ne'er begun.   [Exit.]   70

---

43. tender: regard highly. 46. at help: favorable. 47. associates tend: your
companions are waiting. bent: ready. 56. at foot: at his heels. tempt: entice.
62. cicatrice: scar. There is nothing in the play to explain this incident. 63.
free awe: voluntary submission. 64–65. coldly . . . process: hesitate to
carry out our royal command. 66. congruing: agreeing. 67. present: immediate. 68. hectic: fever. 70. Howe'er my haps: whatever may happen
to me.

Scene 4 ⤜ৡ *A plain in Denmark.*

[*Enter* FORTINBRAS, *a* CAPTAIN *and* SOLDIERS, *marching.*]

FORTINBRAS. Go, Captain, from me greet the Danish King.
Tell him that by his license Fortinbras
Craves the conveyance of a promised march°
Over his kingdom. You know the rendezvous.
If that His Majesty would aught with us,   5
We shall express our duty in his eye,°
And let him know so.
CAPTAIN.   I will do 't, my lord.
FORTINBRAS. Go softly on.
                              [*Exeunt* FORTINBRAS *and* SOLDIERS.]
          [*Enter* HAMLET, ROSENCRANTZ, GUILDENSTERN, *and others.*]
HAMLET. Good sir, whose powers° are these?
CAPTAIN. They are of Norway, sir.   10
HAMLET. How purposed, sir, I pray you?
CAPTAIN. Against some part of Poland.
HAMLET. Who commands them, sir?
CAPTAIN. The nephew to old Norway, Fortinbras.
HAMLET. Goes it against the main° of Poland, sir,   15
Or for some frontier?
CAPTAIN. Truly to speak, and with no addition,°
We go to gain a little patch of ground
That hath in it no profit but the name.
To pay five ducats, five, I would not farm it,   20
Nor will it yield to Norway or the Pole
A ranker° rate should it be sold in fee.°
HAMLET. Why, then the Polack never will defend it.
CAPTAIN. Yes, it is already garrisoned.
HAMLET. Two thousand souls and twenty thousand ducats   25
Will not debate the question of this straw.

Sc. 4: 3. Craves . . . march: asks for permission to transport his army, as
had already been promised. See II.2.76–82.   6. in . . . eye: before his eyes;
i.e., in person.   9. powers: forces.   15. main: mainland.   17. addition: exaggeration.   22. ranker: richer. in fee: with possession as freehold.

This is the imposthume of° much wealth and peace,
That inward breaks, and shows no cause without
Why the man dies. I humbly thank you, sir.
CAPTAIN. God be wi' you, sir.   [*Exit.*]
ROSENCRANTZ.   Will 't please you go, my lord?   30
HAMLET. I'll be with you straight. Go a little before.
                              [*Exeunt all but* HAMLET.]
How° all occasions do inform against° me
And spur my dull revenge! What is a man
If his chief good and market° of his time
Be but to sleep and feed? A beast, no more.   35
Sure, He that made us with such large discourse,
Looking before and after,° gave us not
That capability and godlike reason
To fust° in us unused. Now whether it be
Bestial oblivion, or some craven scruple   40
Of thinking too precisely on the event—
A thought which, quartered, hath but one part wisdom
And ever three parts coward—I do not know
Why yet I live to say "This thing's to do,"
Sith I have cause, and will, and strength, and means   45
To do 't. Examples gross° as earth exhort me.
Witness this army, of such mass and charge,°
Led by a delicate and tender Prince
Whose spirit with divine ambition puffed
Makes mouths at the invisible event,°   50
Exposing what is mortal and unsure
To all that fortune, death, and danger dare,
Even for an eggshell.° Rightly to be great
Is not to stir without great argument,
But greatly to find quarrel in a straw   55
When honor's at the stake.° How stand I then,
That have a father killed, a mother stained,
Excitements of my reason and my blood,
And let all sleep while to my shame I see
The imminent death of twenty thousand men   60
That for a fantasy and trick° of fame

27. **imposthume of:** inward swelling caused by.   **32–66. How . . . worth:**
The soliloquy and all the dialogue after the exit of Fortinbras are omitted in
F1.   **32. inform against:** accuse.   **34. market:** profit.   **36–37. such . . .
after:** intelligence that enables us to consider the future and the past.   **39.
fust:** grow musty.   **46. gross:** large.   **47. charge:** expense.   **50. Makes . . .
event:** mocks at the unseen risk.   **53. eggshell:** i.e., worthless trifle.   **53–56.
Rightly . . . stake:** true greatness is a matter of fighting not for a mighty
cause but for the merest trifle when honor is concerned.   **61. fantasy . . .
trick:** illusion and whim.

Go to their graves like beds, fight for a plot
Whereon the numbers cannot try the cause,°
Which is not tomb enough and continent°
To hide the slain? Oh, from this time forth,   65
My thoughts be bloody or be nothing worth!

                                                    [*Exit.*]

Scene 5 ◦◦◦ *Elsinore. A room in the castle.*

          [*Enter* QUEEN, HORATIO, *and a* GENTLEMAN.]
QUEEN. I will not speak with her.
GENTLEMAN. She is importunate, indeed distract.°
     Her mood will needs be pitied.
QUEEN.   What would she have?
GENTLEMAN. She speaks much of her father, says she hears
     There's tricks° i' the world, and hems° and beats her heart,   5
     Spurns enviously° at straws, speaks things in doubt
     That carry but half-sense. Her speech is nothing,
     Yet the unshaped use° of it doth move
     The hearers to collection.° They aim° at it,
     And botch° the words up fit to their own thoughts,   10
     Which, as her winks and nods and gestures yield them,
     Indeed would make one think there might be thought,
     Though nothing sure, yet much unhappily.
HORATIO. 'Twere good she were spoken with, for she may strew
     Dangerous conjectures in ill-breeding minds.   15
QUEEN. Let her come in.   [*Exit* GENTLEMAN.]
     [*Aside*] To my sick soul, as sin's true nature is,
     Each toy° seems prologue to some great amiss.°
     So full of artless jealousy° is guilt,

63. **Whereon . . . cause:** a piece of ground so small that it would not hold
the combatants. 64. **continent:** large enough to contain.
     Sc. 5: 2. **distract:** out of her mind. 5. **tricks:** trickery. **hems:** makes signifi-
cant noises. 6. **Spurns enviously:** kicks spitefully. 8. **unshaped use:** disorder. 9. **collection:** i.e., attempts to find a sinister meaning. **aim:** guess. 10.
botch: patch. 18. **toy:** trifle. **amiss:** calamity. 19. **artless jealousy:** clumsy
suspicion.

It spills itself in fearing to be spilt.°   20
        [Re-enter GENTLEMAN, *with* OPHELIA.°]
OPHELIA. Where is the beauteous Majesty of Denmark?
QUEEN. How now, Ophelia!
OPHELIA. [*Sings.*]
         "How should I your truelove know
           From another one?
         By his cockle hat° and staff   25
           And his sandal shoon."°
QUEEN. Alas, sweet lady, what imports this song?
OPHELIA. Say you? nay, pray you, mark. [*Sings.*]
         "He is dead and gone, lady,
           He is dead and gone,   30
         At his head a grass-green turf,
           At his heels a stone."
   Oh, oh!
QUEEN. Nay, but, Ophelia——
OPHELIA.   Pray you, mark. [*Sings.*]
   "White his shroud as the mountain snow——"   35
                [*Enter* KING.]
QUEEN. Alas, look here, my lord.
OPHELIA. [*Sings.*]
         "Larded° with sweet flowers,
           Which bewept to the grave did go
           With truelove showers."°
KING. How do you, pretty lady?   40
OPHELIA. Well, God 'ild° you! They say the owl was a baker's
   daughter.° Lord, we know what we are but know not what
   we may be. God be at your table!
KING. Conceit upon her father.   45
OPHELIA. Pray you let's have no words of this, but when they
   ask you what it means, say you this [*Sings*]:
         "Tomorrow is Saint Valentine's day,°
         All in the morning betime,

---

20. It . . . split: guilt reveals itself by its efforts at concealment. **20. s.d., Re-enter . . . Ophelia:** Q1 notes "Enter Ophelia playing on a lute, and her hair down, singing." **25. cockle hat:** a hat adorned with a cockleshell worn by pilgrims. **26. sandal shoon:** sandals, the proper footwear of pilgrims. **37. Larded:** garnished. **39. truelove showers:** the tears of his faithful love. **41. 'ild** (yield): reward. **41–42. owl . . . daughter:** An allusion to a legend that Christ once went into a baker's shop and asked for bread. The baker's wife gave him a piece but was rebuked by her daughter for giving him too much. Thereupon the daughter was turned into an owl. **48. Saint . . . day:** February 14, the day when birds are supposed to mate. According to the old belief the first single man then seen by a maid is destined to be her husband.

And I a maid at your window,   50
To be your Valentine.

"Then up he rose, and donned his clothes,
    And dupped° the chamber door,
Let in the maid, that out a maid
    Never departed more."   55

KING. Pretty Ophelia!

OPHELIA. Indeed, la, without an oath, I'll make an end on 't.
    [*Sings.*]

"By Gis° and by Saint Charity,
    Alack, and fie for shame!   60
Young men will do 't, if they come to 't,
    By cock, they are to blame.
Quoth she, before you tumbled me,
    You promised me to wed."

He answers:

"So would I ha' done, by yonder sun,   65
    An thou hadst not come to my bed."

KING. How long hath she been thus?

OPHELIA. I hope all will be well. We must be patient. But I can-
    not choose but weep to think they should lay him i' the cold
    ground. My brother shall know of it. And so I thank you   70
    for your good counsel. Come, my coach! Good night, ladies,
    good night, sweet ladies, good night, good night.   [*Exit.*]

KING. Follow her close,° give her good watch, I pray you.   75
                                        [*Exit* HORATIO.]
Oh, this is the poison of deep grief. It springs
All from her father's death. O Gertrude, Gertrude,
When sorrows come, they come not single spies,°
But in battalions! First, her father slain.
Next, your son gone, and he most violent author°   80
Of his own just remove. The people muddied,
Thick and unwholesome in their thoughts and whispers,
For good Polonius' death. And we have done but greenly°
In huggermugger° to inter him. Poor Ophelia
Divided from herself and her fair judgment,°   85
Without the which we are pictures,° or mere beasts.

---

53. **dupped:** opened.   **59–62. Gis . . . cock:** for "Jesus" and "God," both
words being used instead of the sacred names, like the modern "Jeez" and
"Gee."   **74. close:** closely.   **78. spies:** scouts.   **80. author:** cause.   **83. done
. . . greenly:** shown immature judgment.   **84. huggermugger:** secret haste,
"any which way."   **85. Divided . . . judgment:** no longer able to use her
judgment.   **86. pictures:** lifeless imitations.

Last, and as much containing as all these,
Her brother is in secret come from France,
Feeds on his wonder, keeps himself in clouds,
And wants not buzzers° to infect his ear   90
With pestilent speeches of his father's death,
Wherein necessity, of matter beggared,
Will nothing stick our person to arraign°
In ear and ear. O my dear Gertrude, this,
Like to a murdering piece,° in many places   95
Gives me superfluous death.   [*A noise within*]
QUEEN.   Alack, what noise is this?
KING. Where are my Switzers?° Let them guard the door.
     [*Enter another* GENTLEMAN.] What is the matter?
GENTLEMAN.   Save yourself, my lord.
The ocean, overpeering of his list,°
Eats not the flats° with more impetuous haste   100
Than young Laertes, in a riotous head,°
O'erbears your officers. The rabble call him lord,
And as the world were now but to begin,
Antiquity forgot, custom not known,
The ratifiers and props of every word,°   105
They cry "Choose we—Laertes shall be King!"
Caps, hands, and tongues applaud it to the clouds—
"Laertes shall be King, Laertes King!"
QUEEN. How cheerfully on the false trail they cry!
Oh, this is counter,° you false Danish dogs! [*Noise within*]   110
KING. The doors are broke.
          [*Enter* LAERTES, *armed*, DANES *following*.]
LAERTES. Where in this King? Sirs, stand you all without.
DANES. No, let's come in.
LAERTES.   I pray you, give me leave.
DANES. We will, we will.   [*They retire without the door*.]
LAERTES. I thank you. Keep the door. O thou vile King,   115
     Give me my father!
QUEEN.   Calmly, good Laertes.
LAERTES. That drop of blood that's calm proclaims me bastard,

---

90. buzzers: scandalmongers. 92–93. Wherein . . . arraign: in which, knowing nothing of the true facts, he must necessarily accuse us. 95. murdering piece: cannon loaded with grapeshot. 97. Switzers: Swiss bodyguard. 99. overpeering . . . list: looking over its boundary; i.e., flooding the mainland. 100. Eats . . . flats: floods not the flat country. 101. in . . . head: with a force of rioters. 104–05. Antiquity . . . word: forgetting ancient rule and ignoring old custom, by which all promises must be maintained. 110. counter: in the wrong direction of the scent.

Cries cuckold° to my father, brands the harlot°
Even here, between the chaste unsmirchèd brows
Of my true mother.
KING.   What is the cause, Laertes,   120
That thy rebellion looks so giantlike?
Let him go, Gertrude. Do not fear° our person.
There's such divinity doth hedge a king°
That treason can but peep° to what it would,
Acts little of his will. Tell me, Laertes,   125
Why thou art thus incensed. Let him go, Gertrude.
Speak, man.
LAERTES. Where is my father?
KING.   Dead.
QUEEN.   But not by him.
KING. Let him demand his fill.
LAERTES. How came he dead? I'll not be juggled with.   130
To Hell, allegiance! Vows, to the blackest devil!
Conscience and grace, to the profoundest pit!
I dare damnation. To this point I stand,
That both the worlds I give to negligence.°
Let come what comes, only I'll be revenged   135
Most throughly° for my father.
KING.   Who shall stay you?
LAERTES. My will, not all the world.
And for my means, I'll husband° them so well
They shall go far with little.
KING.   Good Laertes,
If you desire to know the certainty   140
Of your dear father's death, is 't writ in your revenge
That swoopstake,° you will draw both friend and foe,
Winner and loser?
LAERTES. None but his enemies.
KING.   Will you know them, then?
LAERTES. To his good friends thus wide I'll ope my arms,   145
And like the kind life-rendering pelican,°
Repast° them with my blood.
KING.   Why, now you speak

---

118. cuckold: a husband deceived by his wife. brands . . . harlot: Convicted
harlots were branded with a hot iron. Cf. III.4.44.   122. fear: fear for.   123.
divinity . . . king: divine protection surrounds a king as with a hedge.   124.
peep: look over, not break through.   134. That . . . negligence: I do not
care what happens to me in this world or the next.   136. throughly: thoroughly.   138. husband: use economically.   142. swoopstake: "sweeping the
board."   146. life-rendering pelican: The mother pelican was supposed to
feed her young with blood from her own breast.   147. Repast: feed.

Like a good child and a true gentleman.
That I am guiltless of your father's death,
And am most sensibly° in grief for it,   150
It shall as level° to your judgment pierce
As day does to your eye.
DANES. [*Within*]   Let her come in.
LAERTES. How now! What noise is that?
[*Re-enter* OPHELIA.] O heat, dry up my brains! Tears seven
    times salt
Burn out the sense and virtue of mine eye!   155
By Heaven, thy madness shall be paid with weight
Till our scale turn the beam.° O rose of May!°
Dear maid, kind sister, sweet Ophelia!
Oh heavens! Is 't possible a young maid's wits
Should be as mortal as an old man's life?   160
Nature is fine in love, and where 'tis fine
It sends some precious instance of itself
After the thing it loves.°
OPHELIA. [*Sings.*] "They bore him barefaced on the bier,
            Hey non nonny, nonny, hey nonny,   165
            And in his grave rained many a tear——"
Fare you well, my dove!
LAERTES. Hadst thou thy wits and didst persuade revenge,
It could not move thus.
OPHELIA. [*Sings.*]   "You must sing down a-down   170
            An you call him a-down-a."
Ah, how the wheel° becomes it! It is the false steward, that
stole his master's daughter.
LAERTES. This nothing's more than matter.°   174
OPHELIA. There's° rosemary, that's for remembrance—pray you,
love, remember. And there is pansies, that's for thoughts.

---

150. sensibly: feelingly.   **151. level:** clearly.   **157. turn . . . beam:** weigh
down the beam of the scale. **rose of May:** perfection of young beauty. See
III:1.160.   **161–63. Nature . . . loves:** i.e., her love for her father was so
exquisite that she has sent her sanity after him. Laertes, especially in moments
of emotion, is prone to use highly exaggerated speech.   **172. wheel:** explained
variously as the spinning wheel, Fortune's wheel, or the refrain. The likeliest
explanation is that she breaks into a little dance at the words "You must sing,"
and that the *wheel* is the turn as she circles round.   **174. This . . . matter:**
this nonsense means more than sense.   **175–85. There's . . . died:** In the
language of flowers, each has its peculiar meaning, and Ophelia distributes
them appropriately: for her brother rosemary (remembrance) and pansies
(thoughts); for the King fennel (flattery) and columbine (thanklessness);
for the Queen rue, called also herb o' grace (sorrow), and daisy (light of
love). Neither is worthy of violets (faithfulness).

LAERTES. A document° in madness, thoughts and remembrance
    fitted.   179
OPHELIA. There's fennel for you, and columbines. There's rue for
    you, and here's some for me—we may call it herb of grace
    o' Sundays. Oh, you must wear your rue with a difference.
    There's a daisy. I would give you some violets, but they
    withered all when my father died. They say a' made a good
    end. [*Sings.*]   186
        "For bonny sweet Robin is all my joy."
LAERTES. Thought and affliction, passion, Hell itself,
    She turns to favor° and to prettiness.
OPHELIA. [*Sings.*] "And will a' not come again?   190
        And will a' not come again?
          No, no, he is dead,
          Go to thy deathbed,
        He never will come again.

        "His beard was as white as snow,   195
        All flaxen was his poll.°
          He is gone, he is gone,
          And we cast away moan.
        God ha' mercy on his soul! "
    And of all Christian souls, I pray God. God be wi' you.
                                  [*Exit.*]
LAERTES. Do you see this, O God?   201
KING. Laertes, I must commune with your grief,
    Or you deny me right. Go but apart,
    Make choice of whom your wisest friends you will,
    And they shall hear and judge 'twixt you and me.   205
    If by direct or by collateral° hand
    They find us touched,° we will our kingdom give,
    Our crown, our life, and all that we call ours,
    To you in satisfaction. But if not,
    Be you content to lend your patience to us   210
    And we shall jointly labor with your soul
    To give it due content.
LAERTES.   Let this be so.
    His means of death, his obscure funeral,°
    No trophy, sword, nor hatchment° o'er his bones,

---

178. document: instruction.   **189. favor:** charm.   **196. flaxen . . . poll:** white
as flax was his head.   **206. collateral:** i.e., as an accessory.   **207. touched:**
implicated.   **213. obscure funeral:** Men of rank were buried with much ostentation. To bury Polonius "huggermugger" was thus an insult to his memory and to his family.   **214. hatchment:** device of the coat of arms carried
in a funeral and hung up over the tomb.

No noble rite nor formal ostentation,°   215
Cry to be heard, as 'twere from Heaven to earth,
That I must call 't in question.
KING.   So you shall,
And where the offense is let the great ax fall.
I pray you, go with me.   [*Exeunt.*]

Scene 6 ↜ *Another room in the castle.*

[*Enter* HORATIO *and a* SERVANT.]
HORATIO. What are they that would speak with me?
SERVANT. Seafaring men, sir. They say they have letters for you.
HORATIO. Let them come in.   [*Exit* SERVANT.]
I do not know from what part of the world
I should be greeted, if not from Lord Hamlet.   5
[*Enter* SAILORS.]
FIRST SAILOR. God bless you, sir.
HORATIO. Let Him bless thee too.
FIRST SAILOR. He shall, sir, an 't please Him. There's a letter for
you, sir. It comes from the ambassador that was bound for
England—if your name be Horatio, as I am let to know   10
it is.
HORATIO. [*Reads.*] "Horatio, when thou shalt have overlooked°
this, give these fellows some means° to the King. They have
letters for him. Ere we were two days old at sea, a pirate of
very warlike appointment° gave us chase. Finding ourselves   16
too slow of sail, we put on a compelled valor, and in the
grapple I boarded them. On the instant they got clear of
our ship, so I alone became their prisoner. They have dealt
with me like thieves of mercy; but they knew what they did   20
—I am to do a good turn for them. Let the King have the
letters I have sent, and repair thou to me with as much speed
as thou wouldest fly death. I have words to speak in thine

215. formal ostentation: ceremony properly ordered.
  Sc. 6: 13. overlooked: read. means: access. 16. appointment: equipment.

ear will make thee dumb, yet are they much too light for 25
the bore of the matter.° These good fellows will bring thee
where I am. Rosencrantz and Guildenstern hold their course
for England. Of them I have much to tell thee. Farewell. 30
             "He that thou knowest thine,
                       "HAMLET"

Come, I will make you way for these your letters,
And do 't the speedier that you may direct me
To him from whom you brought them.   [*Exeunt.*]

Scene 7 ⚜ *Another room in the castle.*

[*Enter* KING *and* LAERTES.]

KING. Now must your conscience my acquittance seal,°
    And you must put me in your heart for friend,
    Sith you have heard, and with a knowing ear,
    That he which hath your noble father slain
    Pursued my life.
LAERTES.   It well appears. But tell me   5
    Why you proceeded not against these feats,°
    So crimeful and so capital° in nature,
    As by your safety, wisdom, all things else,
    You mainly were stirred up.
KING.   Oh, for two special reasons,
    Which may to you perhaps seem much unsinewed,°   10
    But yet to me they're strong. The Queen his mother
    Lives almost by his looks, and for myself—
    My virtue or my plague, be it either which—
    She's so conjunctive° to my life and soul
    That as the star° moves not but° in his sphere,   15
    I could not but by her. The other motive

26. **too . . . matter:** i.e., words fall short, like a small shot fired from a cannon with too wide a bore.

    Sc. 7: 1. **my . . . seal:** acquit me. 6. **feats:** acts. 7. **capital:** deserving death. 10. **unsinewed:** weak, flabby. 14. **conjunctive:** joined inseparably.
15. **moves . . . but:** moves only in. **star:** planet.

Why to a public count° I might not go
Is the great love the general gender° bear him,
Who, dipping all his faults in their affection,°
Would, like the spring that turneth wood to stone,°   20
Convert his gyves to graces.° So that my arrows,
Too slightly timbered° for so loud a wind,
Would have reverted to my bow again
And not where I had aimed them.

LAERTES. And so have I a noble father lost,   25
A sister driven into desperate terms,°
Whose worth, if praises may go back again,°
Stood challenger on mount of all the age
For her perfections.° But my revenge will come.

KING. Break not your sleeps for that. You must not think   30
That we are made of stuff so flat and dull
That we can let our beard be shook with danger
And think it pastime. You shortly shall hear more.°
I loved your father, and we love ourself,
And that, I hope, will teach you to imagine——   35
[*Enter a* MESSENGER, *with letters.*] How now! What news?

MESSENGER.   Letters, my lord, from Hamlet.
This to your Majesty, this to the Queen.

KING. From Hamlet! Who brought them?

MESSENGER. Sailors, my lord, they say—I saw them not.
They were given me by Claudio, he received them   40
Of him that brought them.

KING. Laertes, you shall hear them.
Leave us.   [*Exit* MESSENGER.]
[*Reads*] "High and Mighty, you shall know I am set naked°
on your kingdom. Tomorrow shall I beg leave to see your   45
kingly eyes, when I shall, first asking your pardon thereunto,
recount the occasion of my sudden and more strange return.
                                        "HAMLET"
What should this mean? Are all the rest come back?
Or is it some abuse,° and no such thing?   50

17. count: trial.   18. general gender: common people.   19. dipping . . . affection: gilding his faults with their love.   20. like . . . stone: In several
places in England there are springs of water so strongly impregnated with
lime that they will quickly cover with stone anything placed under them.
21. Convert . . . graces: regard his fetters as honorable ornaments.   22. tim-
bered: shafted. A light arrow is caught by the wind and blown back.   26.
terms: condition.   27. if . . . again: if one may praise her for what she used
to be.   28–29. Stood . . . perfections: i.e., her worth challenged the whole
world to find one as perfect.   33. hear more: i.e., when news comes from
England that Hamlet is dead.   45. naked: destitute.   50. abuse: attempt to
deceive.

LAERTES. Know you the hand?

KING. 'Tis Hamlet's character.° "Naked! "
    And in a postscript here, he says "alone."
    Can you advise me?

LAERTES. I'm lost in it, my lord. But let him come.   55
    It warms the very sickness in my heart
    That I shall live and tell him to his teeth
    "Thus didest thou."

KING.   If it be so, Laertes—
    As how should it be so, how otherwise?—
    Will you be ruled by me?

LAERTES.   Aye, my lord,   60
    So you will not o'errule° me to a peace.

KING. To thine own peace. If he be now returned,
    As checking at° his voyage, and that he means
    No more to undertake it, I will work him
    To an exploit now ripe in my device,   65
    Under the which he shall not choose but fall.
    And for his death no wind of blame shall breathe,
    But even his mother shall uncharge the practice°
    And call it accident.

LAERTES.   My lord, I will be ruled,
    The rather if you could devise it so   70
    That I might be the organ.°

KING.   It falls right.
    You have been talked of since your travel much,
    And that in Hamlet's hearing, for a quality
    Wherein they say you shine. Your sum of parts°
    Did not together pluck such envy from him   75
    As did that one, and that in my regard
    Of the unworthiest siege.°

LAERTES.   What part is that, my lord?

KING. A very ribbon in the cap of youth,
    Yet needful too; for youth no less becomes
    The light and careless livery that it wears   80
    Than settled age his sables and his weeds,°
    Importing health and graveness. Two months since,
    Here was a gentleman of Normandy.
    I've seen myself, and served against, the French,

---

52. **character:** handwriting.   61. **o'errule:** command.   63. **checking at:** swerving aside from, like a hawk that leaves the pursuit of his prey.   68. **uncharge . . . practice:** not suspect that his death was the result of the plot.   71. **organ:** instrument.   74. **sum of parts:** accomplishments as a whole.   77. **siege:** seat, place.   81. **sables . . . weeds:** dignified robes. See III.2.138.

And they can well° on horseback; but this gallant   85
Had witchcraft in 't, he grew unto his seat,
And to such wondrous doing brought his horse
As had he been incorpsed and deminatured°
With the brave beast. So far he topped my thought°
That I, in forgery of shapes and tricks,°   90
Come short of what he did.
LAERTES.   A Norman was 't?
KING. A Norman.
LAERTES. Upon my life, Lamond.
KING.   The very same.
LAERTES. I know him well. He is the brooch° indeed
And gem of all the nation.   95
KING. He made confession° of you,
And gave you such a masterly report
For art and exercise in your defense,
And for your rapier most especial,
That he cried out 'twould be a sight indeed   100
If one could match you. The scrimers° of their nation.
He swore, had neither motion, guard, nor eye
If you opposed them. Sir, this report of his
Did Hamlet so envenom° with his envy
That he could nothing do but wish and beg   105
Your sudden coming o'er, to play with him.
Now, out of this——
LAERTES.   What out of this, my lord?
KING. Laertes, was your father dear to you?
Or are you like the painting° of a sorrow,
A face without a heart?
LAERTES.   Why ask you this?   110
KING. Not that I think you did not love your father,
But that I know love is begun by time,
And that I see, in passages of proof,°
Time qualifies° the spark and fire of it.
There lives within the very flame of love   115
A kind of wick or snuff° that will abate it.
And nothing is at a like goodness still,°

85. can well: can do well.   88. incorpsed . . . deminatured: of one body.
89. topped my thought: surpassed what I could imagine.   90. forgery . . .
tricks: imagination of all kinds of fancy tricks. shapes: fancies.   94. brooch:
ornament.   96. confession: report.   101. scrimers: fencers.   104. envenom:
poison.   109. painting: i.e., imitation.   113. passages of proof: experiences
which prove.   114. qualifies: diminishes.   116. snuff: Before the invention
of self-consuming wicks for candles, the wick smoldered and formed a ball
of soot which dimmed the light and gave out a foul smoke.   117. still: always.

For goodness, growing to a pleurisy,°
Dies in his own too much. That we would do
We should do when we would; for this "would" changes   120
And hath abatements and delays as many
As there are tongues, are hands, are accidents,
And then this "should" is like a spendthrift° sigh
That hurts by easing. But to the quick o' the ulcer.°
Hamlet comes back. What would you undertake   125
To show yourself your father's son in deed
More than in words?
LAERTES.   To cut his throat i' the church.°
KING. No place indeed should murder sanctuarize,°
Revenge should have no bounds. But, good Laertes,
Will you do this, keep close within your chamber.   130
Hamlet returned shall know you are come home.
We'll put on those° shall praise your excellence
And set a double varnish on the fame
The Frenchman gave you, bring you in fine° together
And wager on your heads. He, being remiss,°   135
Most generous° and free from all contriving,°
Will not peruse the foils, so that with ease,
Or with a little shuffling, you may choose
A sword unbated,° and in a pass of practice°
Requite him for your father.
LAERTES.   I will do 't,   140
And for that purpose I'll anoint my sword.
I bought an unction° of a mountebank°
So mortal that but dip a knife in it,
Where it draws blood no cataplasm° so rare,
Collected from all simples° that have virtue   145
Under the moon,° can save the thing from death
That is but scratched withal. I'll touch my point
With this contagion, that if I gall° him slightly,
It may be death.

---

118. **pleurisy:** fullness.   123. **spendthrift:** wasteful, because sighing was supposed to be bad for the blood.   124. **quick . . . ulcer:** i.e., to come to the real issue. **quick:** flesh, sensitive part.   127. **cut . . . church:** i.e., to commit murder in a holy place, which would bring Laertes in danger of everlasting damnation; no crime could be worse.   128. **sanctuarize:** give sanctuary to. 132. **put . . . those:** set on some.   134. **fine:** short.   135. **remiss:** careless. 136. **generous:** noble. **contriving:** plotting.   139. **unbated:** not blunted, with a sharp point. **pass of practice:** treacherous thrust.   142. **unction:** poison. **mountebank:** quack doctor.   144. **cataplasm:** poultice.   145. **simples:** herbs. 146. **Under . . . moon:** herbs collected by moonlight were regarded as particularly potent.   148. **gall:** break the skin.

KING.   Let's further think of this,
    Weigh what convenience both of time and means   150
    May fit us to our shape.° If this should fail,
    And that our drift look through our bad performance,°
    'Twere better not assayed. Therefore this project
    Should have a back or second, that might hold
    If this did blast in proof.° Soft! Let me see—   155
    We'll make a solemn wager on your cunnings.
    I ha 't.
    When in your motion you are hot and dry—
    As make your bouts° more violent to that end—
    And that he calls for drink, I'll have prepared him   160
    A chalice° for the nonce,° whereon but sipping,
    If he by chance escape your venomed stuck,°
    Our purpose may hold there. But stay, what noise?
    [*Enter* QUEEN.] How now, sweet Queen!
QUEEN. One woe doth tread upon another's heel,
    So fast they follow. Your sister's drowned, Laertes.   165
LAERTES. Drowned! Oh, where?
QUEEN. There is a willow grows aslant a brook
    That shows his hoar° leaves in the glassy stream.
    There with fantastic garlands did she come
    Of crowflowers, nettles, daisies, and long purples   170
    That liberal° shepherds give a grosser name,
    But our cold maids do dead-men's-fingers call them.
    There on the pendent° boughs her coronet weeds°
    Clambering to hang, an envious sliver° broke,
    When down her weedy trophies and herself   175
    Fell in the weeping brook. Her clothes spread wide,
    And mermaidlike a while they bore her up—
    Which time she chanted snatches of old tunes,
    As one incapable° of her own distress,
    Or like a creature native and indued°   180
    Unto that element. But long it could not be
    Till that her garments, heavy with their drink,

150–51. Weigh . . . shape: consider the best time and method of carrying out our plan. **152. drift . . . performance:** intention be revealed through bungling. **155. blast in proof:** break in trial, like a cannon which bursts when being tested. **159. bouts:** attacks, in the fencing match. **161. chalice:** cup. **nonce:** occasion. **162. stuck:** thrust. **168. hoar:** gray. The underside of the leaves of the willow are silver-gray. **171. liberal:** coarse-mouthed. **173. pendent:** hanging over the water. **coronet weeds:** wild flowers woven into a crown. **174. envious sliver:** malicious branch. **179. incapable:** not realizing. **180. indued:** endowed; i.e., a creature whose natural home is the water (*element*).

　　　　Pulled the poor wretch from her melodious lay°
　　　　To muddy death.
LAERTES.　　　　　　　Alas, then, she is drowned!
QUEEN. Drowned, drowned.　　　　　　　　　　　　　　　185
LAERTES. Too much of water hast thou, poor Ophelia,
　　　　And therefore I forbid my tears. But yet
　　　　It is our trick°—Nature her custom holds,
　　　　Let shame say what it will. When these° are gone,
　　　　The woman will be out.° Adieu, my lord.　　　　190
　　　　I have a speech of fire that fain° would blaze
　　　　But that this folly douts° it.　　　　　[Exit.]
KING.　　　　　　　　　　Let's follow, Gertrude.
　　　　How much I had to do to calm his rage!
　　　　Now fear I this will give it start again,
　　　　Therefore let's follow.　　　　　[Exeunt.]　195

183. lay: song.　187–88. But . . . trick: it is our habit; i.e., to break into
tears at great sorrow.　189. these: i.e., my tears.　190. woman . . . out:
I shall be a man again.　191. fain: willingly.　192. douts: puts out.

ACT V

Scene 1 ఆ§ *A churchyard.*

[*Enter two* CLOWNS,° *with spades, etc.*]

FIRST CLOWN. Is she to be buried in Christian burial° that will-
fully seeks her own salvation?

SECOND CLOWN. I tell thee she is, and therefore make her grave
straight.° The crowner° hath sat on her, and finds it Chris-
tian burial.   5

FIRST CLOWN. How can that be, unless she drowned herself in her
own defense?

SECOND CLOWN. Why, 'tis found so.

FIRST CLOWN. It must be "se offendendo,"° it cannot be else.
For here lies the point. If I drown myself wittingly,° it   10
argues an act, and an act hath three branches—it is to act,
to do, and to perform. Argal,° she drowned herself wittingly.

SECOND CLOWN. Nay, but hear you, goodman delver.°   15

FIRST CLOWN. Give me leave. Here lies the water, good. Here
stands the man, good. If the man go to this water and
drown himself, it is will he, nill he° he goes, mark you that;
but if the water come to him and drown him, he drowns not
himself. Argal, he that is not guilty of his own death
shortens not his own life.   22

SECOND CLOWN. But is this law?

Act V, Sc. 1: s.d., Clowns: countrymen. See Gen. Intro. p. xiii.   **1. Christian burial:** Suicides were not allowed burial in consecrated ground, but were
buried at crossroads. The gravediggers and the priest are professionally
scandalized that Ophelia should be allowed Christian burial solely because
she is a lady of the Court.   **4. straight:** straightway. **crowner:** coroner.   **9. se
offendendo:** for *defendendo,* in self-defense.   **11. wittingly:** with full knowledge.   **12. Argal:** for the Latin *ergo,* therefore.   **15. delver:** digger.   **18. will
he, nill he:** willy-nilly, whether he wishes or not.

FIRST CLOWN. Aye, marry, is 't, crowner's quest° law.

SECOND CLOWN. Will you ha' the truth on 't? If this had not been
a gentlewoman, she should have been buried out o' Chris-
tian burial.   28

FIRST CLOWN. Why, there thou say'st. And the more pity that
great folks should have countenance° in this world to drown
or hang themselves more than their even° Christian. Come,
my spade. There is no ancient gentlemen but gardeners,
ditchers, and gravemakers. They hold up° Adam's profes-   35
sion.

SECOND CLOWN. Was he a gentleman?

FIRST CLOWN. A' was the first that ever bore arms.°

SECOND CLOWN. Why, he had none.   39

FIRST CLOWN. What, art a heathen? How dost thou understand
the Scripture? The Scripture says Adam digged. Could
he dig without arms? I'll put another question to thee. If
thou answerest me not to the purpose, confess thyself——

SECOND CLOWN. Go to.   45

FIRST CLOWN. What is he that builds stronger than either the
mason, the shipwright, or the carpenter?

SECOND CLOWN. The gallows-maker, for that frame outlives a
thousand tenants.   50

FIRST CLOWN. I like thy wit well, in good faith. The gallows does
well, but how does it well? It does well to those that do ill.
Now thou dost ill to say the gallows is built stronger than
the church; argal, the gallows may do well to thee. To 't
again, come.   56

SECOND CLOWN. Who builds stronger than a mason, a shipwright,
or a carpenter?

FIRST CLOWN. Aye, tell me that, and unyoke.°

SECOND CLOWN. Marry, now I can tell.   60

FIRST CLOWN. To 't.

SECOND CLOWN. Mass,° I cannot tell.

            [*Enter* HAMLET *and* HORATIO, *afar off.*]

FIRST CLOWN. Cudgel thy brains no more about it, for your dull
ass will not mend his pace with beating, and when you are
asked this question next, say "A gravemaker." The houses
that he makes last till Doomsday. Go, get thee to Yaughan,°   67
fetch me a stoup° of liquor.   [*Exit* SECOND CLOWN.]
            [FIRST CLOWN *digs, and sings.*]

24. **quest:** inquest.   30. **countenance:** favor.   33. **even:** fellow.   35. **hold
up:** support.   38. **bore arms:** had a coat of arms—the outward sign of a
gentleman.   59. **unyoke:** finish the job, unyoking the plow oxen being the
end of the day's work.   62. **Mass:** by the mass.   67. **Yaughan:** apparently an
innkeeper near the Globe Theatre.   68. **stoup:** large pot.

"In youth,° when I did love, did love,
   Methought it was very sweet,
   To contract; oh, the time, for-a my behoove,°   71
   Oh, methought, there-a was nothing-a meet."

HAMLET. Has this fellow no feeling of his business, that he sings
at grave-making?

HORATIO. Custom hath made it in him a property of easiness.°

HAMLET. 'Tis e'en so. The hand of little employment hath the
daintier sense.°   78

FIRST CLOWN. [Sings.] "But age, with his stealing steps,
   Hath clawed me in his clutch,
   And hath shipped me intil the land°
   As if I had never been such."
     [Throws up a skull.]

HAMLET. That skull had a tongue in it, and could sing once. How
the knave jowls° it to the ground, as if it were Cain's jaw-   84
bone, that did the first murder! It might be the pate of a
politician which this ass now o'erreaches°—one that would
circumvent° God, might it not?

HORATIO. It might, my lord.   89

HAMLET. Or of a courtier, which could say "Good morrow, sweet
lord! How dost thou, good lord?" This might be my lord
Such-a-one that praised my lord Such-a-one's horse when he
meant to beg it, might it not?

HORATIO. Aye, my lord.   95

HAMLET. Why, e'en so. And now my Lady Worm's chapless,°
and knocked about the mazzard° with a sexton's spade.
Here's fine revolution, an we had the trick to see 't. Did
these bones cost no more the breeding but to play at log-
gats° with 'em? Mine ache to think on 't.   100

FIRST CLOWN. [Sings.] "A pickax and a spade, a spade,
   For and a shrouding sheet—
   Oh, a pit of clay for to be made
   For such a guest is meet."   105
     [Throws up another skull.]

HAMLET. There's another. Why may not that be the skull of a

69–105. In youth . . . meet: The song which the gravedigger sings without
much care for accuracy or sense was first printed in Tottel's Miscellany,
1558. 71. behoove: benefit. 75–76. property of easiness: careless habit.
77–78. hand . . . sense: those who have little to do are the most sensitive.
81. shipped . . . land: shoved me into the ground. 84. jowls: dashes. 87.
o'erreaches: gets the better of. circumvent: get around. 97. chapless: without jaws. mazzard: head, a slang word; lit., drinking-bowl. 100. loggats: a
a game in which billets of wood or bones were stuck in the ground and
knocked over by throwing at them.

lawyer?° Where be his quiddities now, his quillets, his cases,
his tenures, and his tricks? Why does he suffer this rude
knave now to knock him about the sconce° with a dirty   110
shovel, and will not tell him of his action of battery? Hum!
This fellow might be in 's time a great buyer of land, with
his statutes, his recognizances, his fines, his double vouchers,
his recoveries. Is this the fine° of his fines and the recovery   115
of his recoveries, to have his fine pate full of fine dirt? Will
his vouchers vouch him no more of his purchases, and
double ones too, than the length and breadth of a pair of
indentures? The very conveyances of his lands will hardly lie
in this box,° and must the inheritor himself have no more,   120
ha?

HORATIO. Not a jot more, my lord.

HAMLET. Is not parchment made of sheepskins?

HORATIO. Aye, my lord, and of calfskins too.

HAMLET. They are sheep and calves which seek out assurance
in that. I will speak to this fellow. Whose grave's this, sirrah?

FIRST CLOWN. Mine, sir. [Sings.]
        "Oh, a pit of clay for to be made
            For such a guest is meet."   129

HAMLET. I think it be thine indeed, for thou liest in 't.

FIRST CLOWN. You lie out on 't, sir, and therefore 'tis not yours.
For my part, I do not lie in 't, and yet it is mine.   135

HAMLET. Thou dost lie in 't, to be in 't and say it is thine. 'Tis
for the dead, not for the quick, therefore thou liest.

FIRST CLOWN. 'Tis a quick lie, sir, 'twill away again, from me to
you.   140

HAMLET. What man dost thou dig it for?

FIRST CLOWN. For no man, sir.

HAMLET. What woman, then?

FIRST CLOWN. For none, neither.

HAMLET. Who is to be buried in 't?   145

FIRST CLOWN. One that was a woman, sir, but, rest her soul, she's
dead.

HAMLET. How absolute° the knave is! We must speak by the
card,° or equivocation° will undo us. By the Lord, Horatio,   149
this three years I have taken note of it—the age is grown

107–18. lawyer . . . indentures: Hamlet strings out a number of the legal
phrases loved by lawyers: *quiddities:* subtle arguments; *quillets:* quibbles;
tenures: titles to property; *tricks:* knavery; *statutes:* bonds; *recognizances:*
obligations; *fines:* conveyances; *vouchers:* guarantors; *recoveries:* transfers;
indentures: agreements.   110. sconce: head; lit., blockhouse.   114. fine: ending.   120. box: coffin.   148. absolute: exact.   149. by . . . card: exactly.
The card is the mariner's compass. equivocation: speaking with a double
sense. The word was much discussed when *Hamlet* was written.

so picked° that the toe of the peasant comes so near the
heel of the courtier, he galls his kibe.° How long hast thou
been a gravemaker?   154

FIRST CLOWN. Of all the days i' the year, I came to 't that day
that our last King Hamlet o'ercame Fortinbras.

HAMLET. How long is that since?

FIRST CLOWN. Cannot you tell that? Every fool can tell that. It
was that very day that young Hamlet was born, he that is
mad, and sent into England.   164

HAMLET. Aye, marry, why was he sent into England?

FIRST CLOWN. Why, because a' was mad. A' shall recover his wits
there, or, if a' do not, 'tis no great matter there.

HAMLET. Why?

FIRST CLOWN. 'Twill not be seen in him there—there the men are
as mad as he.   170

HAMLET. How came he mad?

FIRST CLOWN. Very strangely, they say.

HAMLET. How "strangely"?

FIRST CLOWN. Faith, e'en with losing his wits.

HAMLET. Upon what ground?

FIRST CLOWN. Why, here in Denmark. I have been sexton here,
man and boy, thirty years.°   177

HAMLET. How long will a man lie i' the earth ere he rot?

FIRST CLOWN. I' faith, if a' be not rotten before a' die—as we
have many pocky° corses nowadays that will scarce hold
the laying in—a' will last you some eight year or nine year.
A tanner will last you nine year.

HAMLET. Why he more than another?   185

FIRST CLOWN. Why, sir, his hide is so tanned with his trade that
a' will keep out water a great while, and your water is a sore
decayer of your whoreson° dead body. Here's a skull now.   189
This skull has lain in the earth three and twenty years.

HAMLET. Whose was it?

FIRST CLOWN. A whoreson mad fellow's it was. Whose do you
think it was?

HAMLET. Nay, I know not.   195

---

151. picked: refined.   **151–53. toe . . . kibe:** i.e., the peasant follows the
courtier so closely that he rubs the courtier's heel into a blister. From about
1598 onward, writers, especially dramatists, often satirized the practice of
yeoman farmers grown rich from war profits in sending their awkward sons
to London to learn gentlemanly manners. Ben Jonson portrays two specimens
in Stephen in *Every Man in His Humour* and Sogliardo in *Every Man out of
His Humour.*   **177. thirty years:** The Clown's chronology has puzzled critics,
for the general impression is that Hamlet was much younger.   **181. pocky:**
suffering from the pox (venereal disease).   **189. whoreson:** bastard, "son
of a bitch."

FIRST CLOWN. A pestilence on him for a mad rogue! A' poured a
    flagon of Rhenish on my head once. This same skull, sir,
    was Yorick's skull, the King's jester.
HAMLET. This?
FIRST CLOWN. E'en that.
HAMLET. Let me see. [*Takes the skull.*] Alas, poor Yorick! I knew
    him, Horatio—a fellow of infinite jest, of most excellent
    fancy. He hath borne me on his back a thousand times, and   205
    now how abhorred in my imagination it is! My gorge rises°
    at it. Here hung those lips that I have kissed I know not how
    oft. Where be your gibes now? Your gambols? Your songs?
    Your flashes of merriment that were wont to set the table on
    a roar? Not one now, to mock your own grinning? Quite   210
    chopfallen?° Now get you to my lady's chamber and tell her,
    let her paint an inch thick, to his favor° she must come—
    make her laugh at that. Prithee, Horatio, tell me one thing.
HORATIO. What's that, my lord?   217
HAMLET. Dost thou think Alexander looked o' this fashion i' the
    earth?
HORATIO. E'en so.
HAMLET. And smelt so? Pah!   [*Puts down the skull.*]
HORATIO. E'en so, my lord.
HAMLET. To what base uses we may return, Horatio! Why may
    not imagination trace the noble dust of Alexander till he find
    it stopping a bunghole?°   226
HORATIO. 'Twere to consider too curiously° to consider so.
HAMLET. No, faith, not a jot, but to follow him thither with
    modesty° enough and likelihood to lead it. As thus: Alex-
    ander died, Alexander was buried, Alexander returneth into
    dust; the dust is earth; of earth we make loam;° and why of
    that loam, whereto he was converted, might they not stop a
    beer barrel?   235
        "Imperious Caesar, dead and turned to clay,
          Might stop a hole to keep the wind away.
          Oh, that that earth which kept the world in awe
          Should patch a wall to expel the winter's flaw!"°
    But soft! But soft! Aside—here comes the King.
        [*Enter* PRIESTS,° *etc., in procession; the corpse of*

206. My . . . rises: I feel sick. gorge: throat.   212. chopfallen: downcast,
with a pun on "chapless," (see l. 97).   213. favor: appearance, especially
in the face.   226. bunghole: the hole in a beer barrel.   227. curiously:
precisely.   230. with modesty: without exaggeration.   233. loam: mixture of
clay and sand, used in plastering walls.   239. flaw: blast.   240. s.d., Enter
Priests. The stage directions in early texts are less elaborate. Q2 notes, curtly,
Enter K.Q. Laertes and the corse. F1 has *Enter King, Queen, Laertes, and*

Ophelia, LAERTES *and* MOURNERS *following;*
                KING, QUEEN, *their trains, etc.*]
          The Queen, the courtiers—who is this they follow?
          And with such maimèd° rites? This doth betoken°   242
          The corse they follow did with desperate hand
          Fordo° its own life. 'Twas of some estate.°
          Couch° we awhile, and mark.   [*Retiring with* HORATIO.]
LAERTES. What ceremony else?
HAMLET. That is Laertes, a very noble youth. Mark.
LAERTES. What ceremony else?
FIRST PRIEST. Her obsequies have been as far enlarged
          As we have warranty.° Her death was doubtful,   250
          And but that great command o'ersways the order,°
          She should in ground unsanctified have lodged
          Till the last trumpet; for° charitable prayers,
          Shards,° flints, and pebbles should be thrown on her.
          Yet here she is allowed her virgin crants,°   255
          Her maiden strewments° and the bringing home
          Of bell and burial.
LAERTES. Must there no more be done?
FIRST PRIEST.   No more be done.
          We should profane the service of the dead
          To sing a requiem and such rest to her   260
          As to peace-parted souls.°
LAERTES.   Lay her i' the earth.
          And from her fair and unpolluted flesh
          May violets spring! I tell thee, churlish priest,
          A ministering angel shall my sister be
          When thou liest howling.
HAMLET.   What, the fair Ophelia!   265
QUEEN. [*Scattering flowers*] Sweets to the sweet. Farewell!
          I hoped thou shouldst have been my Hamlet's wife,
          I thought thy bride bed to have decked, sweet maid,

***

a coffin, with Lords attendant. Q1 prints *Enter King and Queen, Laertes and other lords, with a Priest after the coffin.* This probably was how the scene was originally staged. The modern directions ignore the whole significance of the "maimed rites"—Ophelia's funeral is insultingly simple. **242. maimed:** curtailed. **betoken:** indicate. **244. Fordo:** destroy. **estate:** high rank. **245. Couch:** lie down. **249–50. Her . . . warranty:** the funeral rites have been as complete as may be allowed. **251. but . . . order:** if the King's command had not overruled the proper procedure. **253. for:** instead of. **254. Shards:** pieces of broken crockery. **255. crants:** wreaths of flowers—a sign that she had died unwed. **256. maiden strewments:** the flowers strewn on the corpse of a maiden. **261. peace-parted souls:** souls which departed in peace, fortified with the rites of the Church.

And not have strewed thy grave.
LAERTES.   Oh, treble woe
Fall ten times treble on that cursèd head   270
Whose wicked deed thy most ingenious sense°
Deprived thee of! Hold off the earth a while
Till I have caught her once more in mine arms.
            [*Leaps into the grave.*]
Now pile your dust upon the quick° and dead
Till of this flat a mountain you have made   275
To o'ertop old Pelion° or the skyish° head
Of blue Olympus.
HAMLET. [*Advancing*] What is he whose grief
Bears such an emphasis? Whose phrase of sorrow
Conjures the wandering stars and makes them stand°
Like wonder-wounded hearers? This is I,   280
Hamlet the Dane.   [*Leaps into the grave.*]
LAERTES. The Devil take thy soul!   [*Grappling with him*]
HAMLET.   Thou pray'st not well.
I prithee, take thy fingers from my throat,
For though I am not splenitive° and rash,
Yet have I in me something dangerous,   285
Which let thy wisdom fear. Hold off thy hand.
KING. Pluck them asunder.
QUEEN.   Hamlet, Hamlet!
ALL.   Gentlemen——
HORATIO. Good my lord, be quiet.
            [*The* ATTENDANTS *part them, and they come out
                        of the grave.*]
HAMLET. Why, I will fight with him upon this theme
Until my eyelids will no longer wag.   290
QUEEN. O my son, what theme?
HAMLET. I loved Ophelia. Forty thousand brothers
Could not, with all their quantity of love,
Make up my sum. What wilt thou do for her?
KING. Oh, he is mad, Laertes.   295
QUEEN. For love of God, forbear him.°
HAMLET. 'Swounds,° show me what thou'lt do.

---

271. most . . . sense: lively intelligence.   274. quick: living.   276. Pelion:
When the giants fought against the gods in order to reach Heaven, they tried
to pile Mount Pelion and Mount Ossa on Mount Olympus, the highest mountain in Greece. skyish: reaching the sky.   279. stand: stand still.   284. spleni-
tive: hot-tempered.   296. forbear him: leave him alone.   297–307. 'Swounds
. . . thou: Hamlet in his excitement cries out that if Laertes wishes to make
extravagant boasts of what he will do to show his sorrow, he will be even
more extravagant.

Woo 't weep? Woo 't fight? Woo 't fast? Woo 't tear thyself?
Woo 't drink up eisel?° Eat a crocodile?
I'll do 't. Dost thou come here to whine?   300
To outface° me with leaping in her grave?
Be buried quick with her, and so will I.
And if thou prate of mountains, let them throw
Millions of acres on us, till our ground,
Singeing his pate against the burning zone,   305
Make Ossa° like a wart! Nay, an thou 'lt mouth,
I'll rant as well as thou.
QUEEN.   This is mere madness.
And thus awhile the fit will work on him.
Anon, as patient as the female dove
When that her golden couplets° are disclosed,°   310
His silence will sit drooping.
HAMLET.   Hear you, sir.
What is the reason that you use me thus?
I loved you ever. But it is no matter,
Let Hercules himself do what he may,
The cat will mew and dog will have his day.°   [Exit.]   315
KING. I pray thee, good Horatio, wait upon him. [Exit HORATIO.]
[To LAERTES] Strengthen your patience in our last night's
     speech.
We'll put the matter to the present push.°
Good Gertrude, set some watch over your son.
This grave shall have a living monument.°   320
An hour of quiet shortly shall we see,
Till then, in patience our proceeding be.   [Exeunt.]

---

299. eisel: vinegar.   301. outface: browbeat.   306. Ossa: See l. 276, n.   310.
couplets: eggs, of which the dove lays two only. disclosed: hatched.   314–15.
Let . . . day: i.e., let this ranting hero have his turn; mine will come sometime.   318. push: test; lit., thrust of a pike.   320. living monument: with
the double meaning of "lifelike memorial" and "the death of Hamlet."

Scene 2 🙒 *A hall in the castle.*

[*Enter* HAMLET *and* HORATIO.]
HAMLET. So much for this, sir. Now shall you see the other.
    You do remember all the circumstance?
HORATIO. Remember it, my lord!
HAMLET. Sir, in my heart there was a kind of fighting
    That would not let me sleep. Methought I lay   5
    Worse than the mutines in the bilboes.° Rashly,
    And praised be rashness for it, let us know,
    Our indiscretion sometime serves us well
    When our deep plots do pall.° And that should learn° us
    There's a divinity that shapes our ends,   10
    Roughhew them how we will.°
HORATIO.   That is most certain.
HAMLET. Up from my cabin,
    My sea gown° scarfed° about me, in the dark
    Groped I to find out them,° had my desire,
    Fingered their packet, and in fine withdrew   15
    To mine own room again, making so bold,
    My fears forgetting manners, to unseal
    Their grand commission where I found, Horatio—
    Oh royal knavery!—an exact command,
    Larded° with many several sorts of reasons,   20
    Importing Denmark's health and England's too,
    With, ho! such bugs° and goblins in my life°
    That, on the supervise,° no leisure bated,°
    No, not to stay the grinding of the ax,

Sc. 2: 6. **mutines . . . bilboes:** mutineers in the shackles used on board
ship. **9. pall:** fail. **learn:** teach. **10–11. There's . . . will:** though we may
make the rough beginning, God finishes our designs. **13. sea gown:** a thick
coat with a high collar worn by seamen. **scarfed:** wrapped. **14. them:** i.e.,
Rosencrantz and Guildenstern. **20. Larded:** garnished. **22. bugs:** bugbears.
in my life: so long as I was alive. **23. supervise:** reading. **bated:** allowed.

My head should be struck off.

HORATIO.   Is 't possible?   25

HAMLET. Here's the commission. Read it at more leisure
But wilt thou hear me how I did proceed?

HORATIO. I beseech you.

HAMLET. Being thus benetted round with villainies—
Ere I could make a prologue to my brains,   30
They had begun the play—I sat me down,
Devised a new commission, wrote it fair.
I once did hold it, as our statists° do,
A baseness to write fair, and labored much
How to forget that learning, but, sir, now   35
It did me yeoman's service.° Wilt thou know
The effect of what I wrote?

HORATIO.   Aye, good my lord.

HAMLET. An earnest conjuration from the King,
As England was his faithful tributary,
As love between them like the palm might flourish,   40
As peace should still her wheaten garland wear
And stand a comma 'tween their amities,°
And many suchlike "Ases"° of great charge,°
That, on the view and knowing of these contents,
Without debatement° further, more or less,   45
He should the bearers put to sudden death,
Not shriving time allowed.°

HORATIO.   How was this sealed?

HAMLET. Why, even in that was Heaven ordinant.°
I had my father's signet in my purse,
Which was the model° of that Danish seal—   50
Folded the writ° up in the form of the other,
Subscribed° it, gave 't the impression,° placed it safely,

---

33. statists: statesmen. As scholars who have had to read Elizabethan documents know, the more exalted the writer, the worse his handwriting. As a girl Queen Elizabeth wrote a beautiful script; as Queen her letters are as illegible as any. All but the most confidential documents were copied out in a fair hand by a secretary. **36. yeoman's service:** faithful service. The most reliable English soldiers were yeomen—farmers and their men. **42. stand . . . amities:** be a connecting link of their friendship. **43. "Ases":** Official documents were written in flowery language full of metaphorical clauses beginning with "As." Hamlet puns on "asses." **great charge:** "great weight" and "heavy burden." **45. debatement:** argument. **47. Not . . . allowed:** without giving them time even to confess their sins. **48. ordinant:** directing, in control. **50. model:** copy. **51. writ:** writing. **52. Subscribed:** signed. **impression:** of the seal.

The changeling° never known. Now the next day
Was our sea fight, and what to this was sequent°
Thou know'st already.   55
HORATIO. So Guildenstern and Rosencrantz go to 't.
HAMLET. Why, man, they did make love to this employment.
They are not near my conscience, their defeat°
Does by their own insinuation° grow.
'Tis dangerous when the baser nature comes   60
Between the pass and fell incensèd points
Of mighty opposites.°
HORATIO.   Why, what a King is this!
HAMLET. Does it not, think'st thee, stand me now upon—
He that hath killed my King and whored my mother.
Popped in between the election and my hopes,°   65
Thrown out his angle° for my proper° life,
And with such cozenage°—is 't not perfect conscience,
To quit° him with this arm? And is 't not to be damned,
To let this canker° of our nature come
In further evil?   70
HORATIO. It must be shortly known to him from England
What is the issue of the business there.
HAMLET. It will be short. The interim° is mine,
And a man's life's no more than to say "One."
But I am very sorry, good Horatio,   75
That to Laertes I forgot myself,
For by the image of my cause I see
The portraiture of his. I'll court his favors.
But, sure, the bravery° of his grief did put me
Into a towering passion.
HORATIO.   Peace! Who comes here?   80
                    [*Enter* OSRIC.°]
OSRIC. Your lordship is right welcome back to Denmark.
HAMLET. I humbly thank you, sir. Dost know this water fly?°

---

53. changeling: lit., an ugly child exchanged by the fairies for a fair one.   **54. sequent:** following.   **58. defeat:** destruction.   **59. by . . . insinuation:** because they insinuated themselves into this business.   **60–62. 'Tis . . . opposites:** it is dangerous for inferior men to interfere in a duel between mighty enemies. **pass:** thrust. **fell:** fierce.   **65. Popped . . . hopes:** As is from time to time shown in the play, the Danes chose their King by election.   **66. angle:** fishing rod and line. **proper:** own.   **67. cozenage:** cheating.   **68. quit:** pay back.   **69. canker:** maggot. See I.3.39.   **73. interim:** interval—between now and the news from England.   **79. bravery:** excessive show.   **80. s.d., Osric:** Osric is a specimen of the fashionable, effeminate courtier. He dresses prettily and talks the jargon of his class, which at this time affected elaborate and allusive metaphors and at all costs avoided saying plain things plainly.   **83. water fly:** a useless little creature that flits about.

HORATIO. No, my good lord.

HAMLET. Thy state is the more gracious,° for 'tis a vice to know   85
him. He hath much land, and fertile. Let a beast be lord of
beasts and his crib shall stand at the King's mess.° 'Tis a
chough,° but, as I say, spacious° in the possession of dirt.   90

OSRIC. Sweet lord, if your lordship were at leisure, I should impart a thing to you from His Majesty.

HAMLET. I will receive it, sir, with all diligence of spirit. Put
your bonnet to his right use,° 'tis for the head.   95

OSRIC. I thank your lordship, it is very hot.

HAMLET. No, believe me, 'tis very cold. The wind is northerly.

OSRIC. It is indifferent° cold, my lord, indeed.   100

HAMLET. But yet methinks it is very sultry and hot, for my complexion——

OSRIC. Exceedingly, my lord. It is very sultry, as 'twere—I cannot
tell how. But, my lord, His Majesty bade me signify to you
that he has laid a great wager on your head. Sir, this is the
matter——

HAMLET. I beseech you, remember——   108
    [HAMLET *moves him to put on his hat.*]

OSRIC. Nay, good my lord, for mine ease, in good faith. Sir, here
is newly come to Court Laertes—believe me, an absolute°
gentleman, full of most excellent differences,° of very soft
society° and great showing.° Indeed, to speak feelingly° of   114
him, he is the card or calendar of gentry,° for you shall find
in him the continent of what part a gentleman would see.°

HAMLET. Sir,° his definement suffers no perdition in you, though
I know to divide him inventorially would dizzy the arithmetic of memory, and yet but yaw neither, in respect of his

---

85. Thy . . . gracious: you are in the better state. **88–89. Let . . . mess:**
i.e., any man, however low, who has wealth enough will find a good place
at Court. **crib:** manger. **mess:** table. **89. chough:** jackdaw. **90. spacious:**
wealthy. **95. Put . . . use:** i.e., put your hat on your head. Osric is so nice-
mannered that he cannot bring himself to wear his hat in the presence of
the Prince. **100. indifferent:** moderately. **111. absolute:** perfect. **112. differences:** qualities peculiar to himself. **soft society:** gentle breeding. **112–13.
great showing:** distinguished appearance. **113. feelingly:** with proper appreciation. **114. card . . . gentry:** the very fashion plate of what a gentleman should be. **115–16. continent . . . see:** all the parts that should be
in a perfect gentleman. **117–25. Sir . . . more:** Hamlet retorts in similar
but even more extravagant language. This is too much for Osric (and for
most modern readers). Hamlet's words may be paraphrased: "Sir, the description of this perfect gentleman loses nothing in your account of him;
though I realize that if one were to try to enumerate his excellences, it would
exhaust our arithmetic, and yet"—here he changes the image to one of sailing—"we should still lag behind him as he outsails us. But in the true
vocabulary of praise, I take him to be a soul of the greatest worth, and his

quick sail. But in the verity of extolment, I take him to be a   120
soul of great article, and his infusion of such dearth and
rareness as, to make true diction of him, his semblable is his
mirror, and who else would trace him, his umbrage—noth-
ing more.   125

OSRIC. Your lordship speaks most infallibly of him.

HAMLET. The concernancy,° sir? Why do we wrap the gentleman
in our more rawer breath?°

OSRIC. Sir?°   129

HORATIO. Is 't not possible to understand in another tongue?
You will do 't, sir, really.

HAMLET. What imports the nomination° of this gentleman?   133

OSRIC. Of Laertes?

HORATIO. His purse is empty already, all's golden words are spent.

HAMLET. Of him, sir.

OSRIC. I know you are not ignorant——

HAMLET. I would you did, sir. Yet, in faith, if you did, it would
not much approve° me. Well, sir?   141

OSRIC. You are not ignorant of what excellence Laertes is——

HAMLET. I dare not confess that, lest I should compare with him
in excellence, but to know a man well were to know himself.

OSRIC. I mean, sir, for his weapon,° but in the imputation° laid
on him by them, in his meed° he's unfellowed.°   150

HAMLET. What's his weapon?

OSRIC. Rapier and dagger.

HAMLET. That's two of his weapons, but, well.

OSRIC. The King, sir, hath wagered with him six Barbary horses,
against the which he has imponed,° as I take it, six French   156
rapiers and poniards, with their assigns,° as girdle, hanger,°
and so—three of the carriages, in faith, are very dear to
fancy,° very responsive to° the hilts, most delicate carriages, and of very liberal conceit.°   160

perfume"—i.e., his personal essence—"so scarce and rare that to speak truly
of him, the only thing like him is his own reflection in his mirror, and everyone else who tries to follow him merely his shadow." yaw: fall off from the
course laid. verity . . . extolment: in true praise. infusion: essence. semblable:
resemblance. trace: follow. umbrage: shadow.   127. concernancy: i.e., what
is all this talk about?   127–28. Why . . . breath: why do we discuss the
gentleman with our inadequate voices?   129. Sir: Osric is completely baffled.   133. nomination: naming.   141. approve: commend.   148. his
weapon: i.e., skill with his weapon.   149. imputation: reputation. meed:
merit.   150. unfellowed: without an equal.   156. imponed: laid down as a
stake.   157. assigns: that which goes with them. hanger: straps by which the
scabbard was hung from the belt.   158–59. dear to fancy: of beautiful
design.   159. responsive to: matching.   160. liberal conceit: elaborately
artistic.

HAMLET. What call you the carriages?

HORATIO. I knew you must be edified by the margent° ere you had done.

OSRIC. The carriages, sir, are the hangers.   164

HAMLET. The phrase would be more germane° to the matter if we could carry a cannon by our sides. I would it might be hangers till then. But, on—six Barbary horses against six French swords, their assigns, and three liberal-conceited carriages. That's the French bet against the Danish. Why is this "imponed," as you call it?   171

OSRIC. The King, sir, hath laid, sir, that in a dozen passes between yourself and him, he shall not exceed you three hits. He hath laid on twelve for nine,° and it would come to immediate trial if your lordship would vouchsafe the answer.

HAMLET. How if I answer no?   177

OSRIC. I mean, my lord, the opposition of your person in trial.

HAMLET. Sir, I will walk here in the hall. If it please His Majesty, it is the breathing-time of day with me.° Let the foils be   182 brought, the gentleman willing, and the King hold his purpose, I will win for him an I can. If not, I will gain nothing but my shame and the odd hits.

OSRIC. Shall I redeliver you e'en so?

HAMLET. To this effect, sir, after what flourish° your nature will.   187

OSRIC. I commend my duty to your lordship.

HAMLET. Yours, yours. [*Exit* OSRIC.] He does well to commend it himself, there are no tongues else for 's turn.

HORATIO. This lapwing° runs away with the shell on his head.

HAMLET. He did comply with his dug° before he sucked it. Thus   195 has he—and many more of the same breed that I know the drossy° age dotes on—only got the tune of the time and outward habit of encounter,° a kind of yesty collection° which carries them through and through the most fond° and winnowed° opinions—and do but blow them to their trial,   200

---

162. edified . . . margent: informed by the notes. In Shakespeare's time the notes were often printed in the margin. 165. germane: related. 174–75. twelve . . . nine: i.e., Laertes will hit Hamlet twelve times before Hamlet hits him nine times. 181–82. breathing-time . . . me: time when I take exercise. 187. flourish: fanfare, elaborate phrasing. 193. lapwing: a pretty, lively little bird. It is so lively that it can run about the moment it is hatched. 195. did . . . dug: was ceremonious with the nipple; i.e., behaved in this fantastic way from his infancy. See II.2.389. 197. drossy: scummy, frivolous. 198–99. tune . . . encounter: i.e., they sing the same tune as everyone else and have the same society manners. 199. yesty collection: frothy catchwords. 200. fond: foolish. 201. winnowed: light as chaff. Winnowing in the process of fanning the chaff from the grain.

the bubbles are out.°

[*Enter a* LORD.]

LORD. My lord, His Majesty commended him to you by young
Osric, who brings back to him that you attend him in the
hall. He sends to know if your pleasure hold to play with
Laertes, or that you will take longer time.   207

HAMLET. I am constant to my purposes, they follow the King's
pleasure. If his fitness speaks, mine is ready, now or when-
soever, provided I be so able as now.

LORD. The King and Queen and all are coming down.

HAMLET. In happy time.°   214

LORD. The Queen desires you to use some gentle entertainment°
to Laertes before you fall to play.

HAMLET. She well instructs me.   [*Exit* LORD.]

HORATIO. You will lose this wager, my lord.   219

HAMLET. I do not think so. Since he went into France I have been
in continual practice, I shall win at the odds. But thou
wouldst not think how ill all's here about my heart—but it
is no matter.

HORATIO. Nay, good my lord——

HAMLET. It is but foolery, but it is such a kind of gaingiving° as   226
would perhaps trouble a woman.

HORATIO. If your mind dislike anything, obey it. I will forestall
their repair hither and say you are not fit.

HAMLET. Not a whit, we defy augury.° There's special providence   230
in the fall of a sparrow.° If it be now, 'tis not to come; if
it be not to come, it will be now; if it be not now, yet it will
come. The readiness is all. Since no man has aught of what
he leaves, what is 't to leave betimes? Let be.   235

[*Enter* KING, QUEEN, LAERTES, *and* LORDS, OSRIC *and*
other ATTENDANTS *with foils; a table and flagons of*
wine on it.]

KING. Come, Hamlet, come, and take this hand from me.

[*The* KING *puts* LAERTES' *hand into* HAMLET'S.]

HAMLET. Give me your pardon, sir. I've done you wrong,
But pardon 't, as you are a gentleman.
This presence° knows,
And you must needs have heard, how I am punished   240

201–02. do . . . out: force them to make sense of their words and they are
deflated, as Hamlet has just deflated Osric.   214. In . . . time: at a good
moment.   215–16. gentle entertainment: kindly treatment; i.e., be reconciled
after the brawl in the churchyard.   226. gaingiving: misgiving.   230. augury:
omens.   231. special . . . sparrow: The idea comes from Matthew 10:29.
"Are not two sparrows sold for a farthing? and one of them shall not fall to
the ground without your Father."   239. presence: the whole Court.

With sore distraction. What I have done
That might your nature, honor, and exception°
Roughly awake, I here proclaim was madness.
Was 't Hamlet wronged Laertes? Never Hamlet.
If Hamlet from himself be ta'en away,°   245
And when he's not himself does wrong Laertes,
Then Hamlet does it not, Hamlet denies it.
Who does it, then? His madness. If 't be so,
Hamlet is of the faction that is wronged,
His madness is poor Hamlet's enemy.   250
Sir, in this audience
Let my disclaiming from a purposed evil°
Free me so far in your most generous thoughts
That I have shot mine arrow o'er the house,
And hurt my brother.

LAERTES.   I am satisfied in nature,   255
Whose motive, in this case, should stir me most
To my revenge. But in my terms of honor
I stand aloof, and will no reconcilement
Till by some elder masters of known honor
I have a voice and precedent of peace   260
To keep my name ungored.° But till that time
I do receive your offered love like love
And will not wrong it.

HAMLET.   I embrace it freely,
And will this brother's wager frankly play.
Give us the foils. Come on.

LAERTES.   Come, one for me.   265

HAMLET. I'll be your foil,° Laertes. In mine ignorance
Your skill shall, like a star i' the darkest night,
Stick° fiery off indeed.

LAERTES.   You mock me, sir.

HAMLET. No, by this hand.

KING. Give them the foils, young Osric. Cousin Hamlet,   270
You know the wager?

HAMLET.   Very well, my lord.
Your Grace has laid the odds o' the weaker side.

242. exception: resentment.   245. If . . . away: i.e., Hamlet mad is not
Hamlet.   252. Let . . . evil: let my declaration that I did not intend any
harm.   255–61. I . . . ungored: I bear you no grudge so far as concerns
my personal feelings, which would most readily move me to vengeance; but
as this matter touches my honor, I cannot accept your apology until I have
been assured by those expert in matters of honor that I may so do without
loss of reputation.   266. foil: Hamlet puns on the other meaning of foil—tin
foil set behind a gem to give it luster.   268. Stick . . . off: shine out.

KING. I do not fear it, I have seen you both.

But since he is bettered,° we have therefore odds.

LAERTES. This is too heavy, let me see another.   275

HAMLET. This likes° me well. These foils have all a length?°

                [*They prepare to play.*]

OSRIC. Aye, my good lord.

KING. Set me the stoups° of wine upon that table.

If Hamlet give the first or second hit,

Or quit° in answer of the third exchange,   280

Let all the battlements their ordnance fire.

The King shall drink to Hamlet's better breath,

And in the cup a union° shall he throw

Richer than that which four successive kings

In Denmark's crown have worn. Give me the cups,   285

And let the kettle° to the trumpet speak,

The trumpet to the cannoneer without,

The cannon to the Heavens, the Heaven to earth,

"Now the King drinks to Hamlet." Come, begin,

And you, the judges, bear a wary eye.   290

HAMLET. Come on, sir.

LAERTES.   Come, my lord.   [*They play.*]

HAMLET.   One.

LAERTES.   No.

HAMLET.   Judgment.

OSRIC. A hit, a very palpable° hit.

LAERTES.   Well, again.

KING. Stay, give me drink. Hamlet, this pearl is thine°—

Here's to thy health.

      [*Trumpets sound, and cannon shot off within.*]

                Give him the cup.

HAMLET. I'll play this bout first. Set it by a while.   295

Come. [*They play.*] Another hit, what say you?

LAERTES. A touch, a touch, I do confess.

KING. Our son shall win.

QUEEN.   He's fat° and scant of breath.

Here, Hamlet, take my napkin, rub thy brows.

The Queen carouses to thy fortune, Hamlet.   300

HAMLET. Good madam!

KING.   Gertrude, do not drink.

QUEEN. I will, my lord, I pray you pardon me.   [*She drinks.*]

---

274. bettered: considered your superior. **276. likes:** pleases. **have . . . length:** are all of equal length. **278. stoups:** drinking-vessels. **280. quit:** strike back. **283. union:** a large pearl. **286. kettle:** kettledrum. **292. palpable:** clear. **293. this . . . thine:** With these words the King drops the poisoned pearl into the cup intended for Hamlet. **298. fat:** out of condition.

KING. [*Aside*] It is the poisoned cup, it is too late.
HAMLET. I dare not drink yet, madam—by and by.
QUEEN. Come, let me wipe thy face.   305
LAERTES. My lord, I'll hit him now.
KING.   I do not think 't.
LAERTES. [*Aside*] And yet 'tis almost against my conscience.
HAMLET. Come, for the third, Laertes. You but dally.°
    I pray you pass with your best violence,
    I am afeard you make a wanton of me.°   310
LAERTES. Say you so? Come on.   [*They play.*]
OSRIC. Nothing, neither way.
LAERTES. Have at you now!
    [LAERTES *wounds* HAMLET; *then, in scuffling, they change*
         rapiers, and HAMLET *wounds* LAERTES.]
KING.   Part them, they are incensed.
HAMLET. Nay, come, again.   [*The* QUEEN *falls.*]
OSRIC.   Look to the Queen there, ho!
HORATIO. They bleed on both sides. How is it, my lord?   315
OSRIC. How is 't, Laertes?
LAERTES. Why, as a woodcock to mine own springe,° Osric,
    I am justly killed with mine own treachery.
HAMLET. How does the queen?
KING.   She swounds to see them bleed.
QUEEN. No, no, the drink, the drink!—O my dear Hamlet—   320
    The drink, the drink! I am poisoned.   [*Dies.*]
HAMLET. Oh, villainy! Ho! Let the door be locked.
    Treachery! Seek it out.   [LAERTES *falls.*]
LAERTES. It is here, Hamlet. Hamlet, thou art slain.
    No medicine in the world can do thee good,   325
    In thee there is not half an hour of life.
    The treacherous instrument is in thy hand,
    Unbated and envenomed. The foul practice
    Hath turned itself on me. Lo, here I lie
    Never to rise again. Thy mother's poisoned.   330
    I can no more. The King, the King's to blame.
HAMLET. The point envenomed too!
    Then, venom, to thy work.   [*Stabs the* KING.]
ALL. Treason! Treason!
KING. Oh, yet defend me, friends, I am but hurt.   335
HAMLET. Here, thou incestuous, murderous, damnèd Dane,
    Drink off this potion. Is thy union° here?
    Follow my mother.   [KING *dies.*]

---

308. dally: play. **310. make . . . me:** treat me like a child by letting me
win. **317. springe:** snare. **337. union:** pearl, as in l. 283.

LAERTES.   He is justly served.
It is a poison tempered° by himself.
Exchange forgiveness with me, noble Hamlet.   340
Mine and my father's death come not upon thee,°
Nor thine on me!   [*Dies.*]
HAMLET. Heaven make thee free of it!° I follow thee.
I am dead, Horatio. Wretched Queen, adieu!
You that look pale and tremble at this chance,   345
That are but mutes or audience to this act,
Had I but time—as this fell° sergeant,° Death,
Is strict in his arrest—oh, I could tell you——
But let it be. Horatio, I am dead,
Thou livest. Report me and my cause aright   350
To the unsatisfied.°
HORATIO.   Never believe it.
I am more an antique Roman° than a Dane.
Here's yet some liquor left.
HAMLET.   As thou 'rt a man,
Give me the cup. Let go—by Heaven, I'll have 't.
O good Horatio, what a wounded name,   355
Things standing thus unknown, shall live behind me!
If thou didst ever hold me in thy heart,
Absent thee from felicity a while,
And in this harsh world draw thy breath in pain
To tell my story.   [*March afar off, and shot within*]
What warlike noise is this?   360
OSRIC. Young Fortinbras, with conquest come from Poland,
To the ambassadors of England gives
This warlike volley.
HAMLET.   Oh, I die, Horatio,
The potent poison quite o'ercrows° my spirit.
I cannot live to hear the news from England,   365
But I do prophesy the election° lights
On Fortinbras. He has my dying voice.°
So tell him, with the occurrents, more and less,
Which have solicited.° The rest is silence.   [*Dies.*]
HORATIO. Now cracks a noble heart. Good night, sweet Prince,   370
And flights of angels sing thee to thy rest!   [*March within.*]

339. tempered: mixed.   **341. come . . . thee:** are not on your head.   **343.
Heaven . . . it:** God forgive you.   **347. fell:** dread. **sergeant:** the officer of
the Court who made arrests.   **351. unsatisfied:** who do not know the truth.
352. antique Roman: like Cato and Brutus, who killed themselves rather
than survive in a world which was unpleasing to them.   **364. o'ercrows:**
overpowers.   **366. election:** as King of Denmark. See l. 65 above.   **367.
voice:** support.   **368–69. occurrents . . . solicited:** events great and small
which have caused me to act.

Why does the drum come hither?
[*Enter* FORTINBRAS, *and the* ENGLISH AMBASSADORS, *with*
drum, colors, and ATTENDANTS.]
FORTINBRAS. Where is this sight?
HORATIO.   What is it you would see?
If aught of woe or wonder, cease your search.
FORTINBRAS. This quarry cries on havoc.° O proud Death,   375
What feast is toward° in thine eternal cell
That thou so many princes at a shot
So bloodily hast struck?
FIRST AMBASSADOR.   The sight is dismal,
And our affairs from England come too late.
The ears are senseless that should give us hearing,   380
To tell him his commandment is fulfilled,
That Rosencrantz and Guildenstern are dead.
Where should we have our thanks?
HORATIO.   Not from his mouth
Had it the ability of life to thank you.
He never gave commandment for their death.   385
But since, so jump° upon this bloody question,°
You from the Polack wars, and you from England,
Are here arrived, give order that these bodies
High on a stage be placèd to the view,
And let me speak to the yet unknowing world   390
How these things came about. So shall you hear
Of carnal, bloody, and unnatural acts,
Of accidental judgments, casual slaughters,
Of deaths put on by cunning and forced cause,
And, in this upshot, purposes mistook   395
Fall'n on the inventors' heads.° All this can I
Truly deliver.
FORTINBRAS.   Let us haste to hear it,
And call the noblest to the audience.
For me, with sorrow I embrace my fortune.
I have some rights of memory° in this kingdom,   400

---

375. quarry . . . havoc: heap of slain denotes a pitiless slaughter. See *Caesar*,
III.1.273.   376. toward: being prepared.   386. jump: exactly. See I.1.65.
question: matter.   392–96. carnal . . . heads: These lines sum up the whole
tragedy: Claudius' adultery with Gertrude, his murder of his brother, the
death of Ophelia due to an accident, that of Polonius by casual chance,
Hamlet's device which caused the deaths of Rosencrantz and Guildenstern,
the plan which went awry and caused the deaths of Claudius and Laertes.
400. rights of memory: rights which will be remembered; i.e., with the dis-
appearance of all the family of the original King Hamlet the situation re-
verts to what it was before the death of Fortinbras' father. See I.1.80–95.

Which now to claim my vantage° doth invite me.
HORATIO. Of that I shall have also cause to speak,
   And from his mouth whose voice will draw on more.°
   But let this same be presently performed,
   Even while men's minds are wild, lest more mischance   405
   On plots and errors happen.
FORTINBRAS.   Let four captains
   Bear Hamlet, like a soldier, to the stage.
   For he was likely, had he been put on,°
   To have proved most royally. And for his passage
   The soldiers' music and the rites of war   410
   Speak loudly for him.
   Take up the bodies. Such a sight as this
   Becomes the field, but here shows much amiss.
   Go, bid the soldiers shoot.
                    [*A dead march. Exeunt, bearing off the bodies;
                        after which a peal of ordnance is shot off.*]

401. vantage: i.e., my advantage, there being none to dispute my claim.
403. voice . . . more: i.e., Hamlet's dying voice will strengthen your claim.
408. had . . . on: had he become King.

QUESTIONS

ACT I

1. Scene 1 provides very little information and does not introduce the
   major figures of the play. It does set the atmosphere and introduce us
   to the "world" in which the action is to occur. Examine the details
   that compose the scene—e.g., a soldier on watch, a ghost, a discussion
   of political troubles—and try to describe what kind of world is built
   up here.
2. In the second scene the action shifts from the dark battlements to the
   brilliant center of the Danish court, the King's council chamber. Contrast the two scenes and discuss the different attitudes toward the
   world and its problems shown in each.
3. It has often been remarked that Claudius is an exceptionally capable
   king and politician. How does this impression of Claudius emerge in
   his first long speech? Take into account not only the way he deals
   with problems but the *style* of his speech—his diction, images, and
   rhythms.
4. Claudius offers Hamlet some perfectly sound advice about how to

take the death of a father, but it rings false. What is there about his way of delivering these truisms that suggests they are meaningless?

5. Contrast the rhythms of Hamlet's first soliloquy, "Oh, that this too too solid flesh," with those of Claudius' first speech. How does Hamlet's speech suggest a compulsive concern? What is the compulsion?

6. At the end of the first soliloquy, what does Hamlet decide he must do about this "unweeded garden" of the world?

7. Compose a picture of old Hamlet from the information provided in Horatio and Hamlet's discussion of him and from what he tells us about himself, both directly and in his style of speaking, in his appearance on the battlements. Compare him with Claudius, the new king; with Hamlet, his son.

8. Scene 3 offers a good picture of Polonius' family, which is to play a prominent part in coming events. Look carefully at all the advice Laertes and Polonius offer on various subjects and describe their approach to the world and their understanding of human nature. Would you call them sensitive or practical? What does this scene gain in meaning by being placed between two scenes involving a ghost come back from another world to speak of the corruption in this one?

9. In lines 24–35 of Scene 4 Hamlet defines the tragic flaw, that weakness or failing supposedly found in all tragic heroes which is said to bring about their downfall. Is this applicable to Hamlet? Has any weakness of character led him into this desperate situation of being asked to kill a king and of standing in danger of his life from the clever, suspicious man who has killed his father, married his mother, and stolen his throne?

10. Compare Hamlet's attitude in Scene 5 (lines 92–112), just after the Ghost has sworn him to revenge, with his attitude in the final lines of the scene: "Oh, cursèd spite/That ever I was born to set it right!" Where else do we see this fluctuation or mixture of motives in Hamlet? What two major conflicting forces are at work deep in his mind? Are they symbolized by his two roles: prince of Denmark and student at Wittenberg?

11. During Act I several "fathers" offer advice to their children. Compare and contrast the different fathers and the kinds of advice.

ACT II

12. Polonius' description of his method for discovering truth,

> With windlasses and with assays of bias,
> By indirections find directions out,

defines very nicely the way the court in which he is chief councilor operates. Find other examples of this movement by "indirection." Why is it necessary in this world?

13. How does Hamlet "find directions out" in the events described by Ophelia (lines 87–119)? How does this differ from the practice of the court?

14. Why do Ophelia's rejection of Hamlet and the spying of his old friends Rosencrantz and Guildenstern seem to Hamlet dreadful breaches of trust? How do all three justify their actions?

15. Critics have been painfully anxious to settle the question of Hamlet's madness. Looking at the way he manages Polonius and Rosencrantz and Guildenstern in these scenes, can you see any evidence for arguing that Hamlet is truly mad? Can you see, perhaps, why in a world so practical and "sane" as Elsinore he might be considered mad?

16. How do Rosencrantz and Guildenstern betray their true motives?

17. In what ways does Hamlet's famous speech "What a piece of work is a man" (2.304–22) explain his melancholy? Compare the beliefs he once held about man and the world with the realities of Elsinore.

18. One critic has suggested that the dominant tone of *Hamlet* is set by the frequent questions asked, ranging from such apparently trivial ones as "Who's there"—the opening line of the play—to such gigantic questions as "What should such fellows as I do crawling between earth and heaven?" Select several of Hamlet's most crucial questions, discuss them, and show how the issues they raise are central to the play.

ACT III

19. Hamlet uses the play within the play to trap Claudius, and it works exceptionally well. Does this play also say certain things about human nature, human will, and man's fate that are applicable to the larger play, *Hamlet?*

20. How does Claudius' prayer (Scene 3) complicate his character?

21. Consider carefully the reason why Claudius cannot truly pray for forgiveness. Does this identify the force in life that Claudius represents? If so, does this illuminate other actions and statements of the King? Does it make understandable the things Hamlet says about him?

22. Can it be said that Hamlet sets up for his mother another little play within the play, which is intended to have the same results as *The Murder of Gonzago?*

23. What do you make of Gertrude's inability to see the Ghost and her remark "yet all that is I see"? What does this tell us about her? Does the ability to see the Ghost begin to take on special meaning?

24. In what ways does the stabbing of Polonius through the arras manifest in action what Hamlet has been attempting to do throughout the play?

ACT IV

25. Can Hamlet's jokes about the body of Polonius be understood as mere signs of madness? What state of mind has he arrived at by now?

26. Why are Fortinbras and his army so attractive to Hamlet? Does his description of them also contain criticism?

27. Ophelia is the most pitiful figure in the play, and her madness and death are the direct results of the conflict between those "mighty opposites," Claudius and Hamlet. What point do you think Shakespeare is making here about the position of innocence and dutifulness in this world?

28. Describe the ways in which Laertes' situation when he returns in Act IV parallels Hamlet's in Act I.

29. Do the parallel situations and Laertes' response to his situation in any way complicate the frequent argument that Hamlet should not have delayed a moment in seeking his revenge?

ACT V

30. Compare Hamlet's attitude when he leaves for England at the end of Act III with his attitude when he appears again at the beginning of Act V. What sort of change has he undergone?

31. How is this change reflected in his very complicated attitude toward the fact of death as it is presented in the graveyard?

32. Why does Hamlet consider Laertes' conduct at the grave of Ophelia outrageous and exaggerated? Is the gravedigger's approach to death just as exaggerated in another way?

33. How did Hamlet escape the plot the King had laid to murder him? Does this teach him to regard his life in a different way?

34. Why does Osric seem so grotesque and outrageously comic in these particular circumstances?

35. Could the Hamlet of Act I have faced the duel with Laertes and said simply, "The readiness is all"? Could it be said that "character" has ceased to be more important than "plot" once this statement is made?

36. What do you make of the irony that so long as Hamlet actively pursues his revenge and lays careful plans, he never succeeds, but once he comes to accept situations as they are offered and to meet them as best he can, he achieves his revenge?

37. Does the King's final scheme for killing Hamlet sum up his methods of operation? Consider carefully the way in which he is linked with poison throughout the play. Do the objects he poisons have any special significance?

38. Is Hamlet's death in vain? Is it an unqualified triumph?

39. Are Fortinbras and old Hamlet in any ways alike?

40. What values do the antagonists, Claudius and Hamlet, represent? Would a comparison with Creon and Antigone be at all enlightening?

PART
II

PLAYS
FOR
FURTHER READING

THE CHERRY ORCHARD

BY

ANTON CHEKHOV

The plays of Anton Chekhov (1860–1904) are likely at first glance to seem trivial, pointless, plotless—the chronicle of futile people, more than slightly mad. In fact, the plays seem at first "undramatic." This effect is largely intentional, for Chekhov wanted to write plays in which, as he said, he "let the things that happen on stage be as complex and yet as simple as they are in life. For instance, people are having a meal at the table, just having a meal, but at the same time their happiness is being created, or their lives are being smashed up." *The Cherry Orchard,* first produced in 1904, was Chekhov's greatest achievement in staging these simple, seemingly unimportant events. His earlier plays—*Ivanov* (1887), *The Sea Gull* (1896), *Uncle Vanya* (1899), and *The Three Sisters* (1901)—all show "men and life as they are," not "on stilts," but each culminates in violence, involving in every case the firing of a gun. Chekhov could boast, however, that "there is not a shot" in *The Cherry Orchard* and point out that it is not "a tragedy of blood," but a "tragedy of life's trivialities."

Chekhov was the chronicler of the breakup of a way of life, of a society that had lost its ability to act effectively because it had lost the answer to basic questions like those posed by a character in *The Three Sisters:* Why do cranes fly? Why are children born? Why do stars shine in the sky? Specifically, the social group whose aimless wanderings Chekhov dramatizes is the Russian upper class of the late nineteenth and early twentieth centuries. But the impact of his plays on people of all nations suggests that Chekhov catches not just the hopelessness of one moment of history, but the general loss in our century of answers to crucial questions. "Look out there," says one of his characters, "it's snowing. What's the meaning of that?" Many people could provide a scientific description of snow, but most would find it difficult to state the "meaning" of a snowstorm.

Chekhov's charming, melancholic people have lost their bearings because by knowing too much they have come to understand too little. They still care desperately about finding a meaning in their lives, a purpose and a relation to the world around them, and though they always fail, they still have in a curious, ironic way that tragic nobility which Wallace Stevens once defined as "a violence from within that protects from a violence without; it is imagination pressing back against the pressure of reality." Chekhov's characters don't know what they seek or where to seek it, but they do seek.

Perhaps the greatest achievement of *The Cherry Orchard* is the way Chekhov keeps before us the inner lives of his characters. Even in translation, every word spoken seems the echo of a reality deep within. The characters seem transient inhabitants of the world outside themselves. And yet this outer world is always sharply defined and ever present. There are always crops to gather, mortgages to pay, and orchards to be tended. Above all else this outer reality is the progress of time in which bills and lives inevitably come due. *The Cherry Orchard* begins in the spring, and after that no one notices the time of year; but when the play closes, fall has come and frosts are beginning.

CHARACTERS

MADAME RANEVSKY (LYUBOV ANDREYEVNA), *the owner of the cherry orchard*
ANYA, *her daughter, aged* 17
VARYA, *her adopted daughter, aged* 24
GAEV, LEONID ANDREYEVITCH, *brother of Madame Ranevsky*
LOPAHIN, YERMOLAY ALEXEYEVITCH, *a merchant*
TROFIMOV, PYOTR SERGEYEVITCH, *a student*
SEMYONOV-PISHTCHIK, *a landowner*
CHARLOTTA IVANOVNA, *a governess*
EPIHODOV, SEMYON PANTALEYEVITCH, *a clerk*
DUNYASHA, *a maid*
FIRS, *an old valet, aged* 87
YASHA, *a young valet*
A VAGRANT   A POST-OFFICE CLERK
THE STATION MASTER   VISITORS, SERVANTS

The action takes place on the estate of Madame Ranevsky.

The Cherry Orchard by Anton Chekhov, translated by Constance Garnett. Reprinted by permission of Chatto & Windus Ltd. and by the estate of Constance Garnett.

ACT I

Scene: *A room, which has always been called the nursery. One of the doors leads into* ANYA's *room. Dawn, sun rises during the scene. May, the cherry trees in flower, but it is cold in the garden with the frost of early morning. Windows closed.*

[*Enter* DUNYASHA *with a candle and* LOPAHIN *with a book in his hand.*]

LOPAHIN. The train's in, thank God. What time is it?

DUNYASHA. Nearly two o'clock (*puts out the candle*). It's daylight already.

LOPAHIN. The train's late! Two hours, at least (*yawns and stretches*). I'm a pretty one; what a fool I've been. Came here on purpose to meet them at the station and dropped asleep. . . . Dozed off as I sat in the chair. It's annoying. . . . You might have waked me.

DUNYASHA. I thought you had gone (*listens*). There, I do believe they're coming!

LOPAHIN (*listens*). No, what with the luggage and one thing and another (*a pause*). Lyubov Andreyevna has been abroad five years; I don't know what she is like now. . . . She's a splendid woman. A good-natured, kind-hearted woman. I remember when I was a lad of fifteen, my poor father—he used to keep a little shop here in the village in those days—gave me a punch in the face with his fist and made my nose bleed. We were in the yard here, I forget what we'd come about—he had had a drop. Lyubov Andreyevna— I can see her now—she was a slim young girl then—took me to wash my face, and then brought me into this very room, into the nursery. "Don't cry, little peasant," says she, "it will be well in time for your wedding day" . . . (*a pause*). Little peasant. . . .

My father was a peasant, it's true, but here am I in a white waistcoat and brown shoes, like a pig in a bun shop. Yes, I'm a rich
man, but for all my money, come to think, a peasant I was, and a
peasant I am (*turns over the pages of the book*). I've been reading
this book and I can't make head or tail of it. I fell asleep over it
(*a pause*).

DUNYASHA. The dogs have been awake all night, they feel that the mistress is coming.

LOPAHIN. Why, what's the matter with you, Dunyasha?

DUNYASHA. My hands are all of a tremble. I feel as though I should
faint.

LOPAHIN. You're a spoilt soft creature, Dunyasha. And dressed like a
lady too, and your hair done up. That's not the thing. One must
know one's place.

> [*Enter* EPIHODOV *with a nosegay; he wears a pea
> jacket and highly polished creaking topboots; he
> drops the nosegay as he comes in.*]

EPIHODOV (*picking up the nosegay*). Here! the gardener's sent this,
says you're to put it in the dining room (*gives* DUNYASHA *the nosegay*).

LOPAHIN. And bring me some kvass.

DUNYASHA. I will (*goes out*).

EPIHODOV. It's chilly this morning, three degrees of frost, though the
cherries are all in flower. I can't say much for our climate (*sighs*).
I can't. Our climate is not often propitious to the occasion. Yermolay
Alexeyevitch, permit me to call your attention to the fact that I pur-
chased myself a pair of boots the day before yesterday, and they
creak, I venture to assure you, so that there's no tolerating them.
What ought I to grease them with?

LOPAHIN. Oh, shut up! Don't bother me.

EPIHODOV. Every day some misfortune befalls me. I don't complain.
I'm used to it, and I wear a smiling face.

> [DUNYASHA *comes in, hands* LOPAHIN *the kvass.*]

EPIHODOV. I am going (*stumbles against a chair, which falls over*).
There! (*as though triumphant*). There you see now, excuse the expression, an accident like that among others. . . . It's positively
remarkable (*goes out*).

DUNYASHA. Do you know, Yermolay Alexeyevitch, I must confess,
Epihodov has made me a proposal.

LOPAHIN. Ah!

DUNYASHA. I'm sure I don't know. . . . He's a harmless fellow, but
sometimes when he begins talking, there's no making anything of
it. It's all very fine and expressive, only there's no understanding it.
I've a sort of liking for him too. He loves me to distraction. He's

an unfortunate man; every day there's something. They tease him about it—two and twenty misfortunes they call him.

LOPAHIN (*listening*). There! I do believe they're coming.

DUNYASHA. They are coming! What's the matter with me? . . . I'm cold all over.

LOPAHIN. They really are coming. Let's go and meet them. Will she know me? It's five years since I saw her.

DUNYASHA (*in a flutter*). I shall drop this very minute. . . . Ah, I shall drop.

> [*There is a sound of two carriages driving up to the house.* LOPAHIN *and* DUNYASHA *go out quickly. The stage is left empty. A noise is heard in the adjoining rooms.* FIRS, *who has driven to meet* MADAME RANEV-SKY, *crosses the stage hurriedly leaning on a stick. He is wearing old-fashioned livery and a high hat. He says something to himself, but not a word can be distinguished. The noise behind the scenes goes on increasing. A voice: "Come, let's go in here." Enter* LYUBOV ANDREYEVNA, ANYA, *and* CHARLOTTA IVAN-OVNA *with a pet dog on a chain, all in travelling dresses.* VARYA *in an outdoor coat with a kerchief over her head,* GAEV, SEMYONOV-PISHTCHIK, LOPAHIN, DUNYASHA *with bag and parasol, servants with other articles. All walk across the room.*]

ANYA. Let's come in here. Do you remember what room this is, mamma?

LYUBOV (*joyfully, through her tears*). The nursery!

VARYA. How cold it is, my hands are numb. (*To* LYUBOV ANDREYEVNA) Your rooms, the white room and the lavender one, are just the same as ever, mamma.

LYUBOV. My nursery, dear delightful room. . . . I used to sleep here when I was little . . . (*cries*). And here I am, like a little child . . . (*kisses her brother and* VARYA, *and then her brother again*). Varya's just the same as ever, like a nun. And I knew Dunyasha (*kisses* DUNYASHA).

GAEV. The train was two hours late. What do you think of that? Is that the way to do things?

CHARLOTTA (*to* PISHTCHIK). My dog eats nuts, too.

PISHTCHIK (*wonderingly*). Fancy that!

> [*They all go out except* ANYA *and* DUNYASHA.]

DUNYASHA. We've been expecting you so long (*takes* ANYA'S *hat and coat*).

ANYA. I haven't slept for four nights on the journey. I feel dreadfully cold.

DUNYASHA. You set out in Lent, there was snow and frost, and now?

My darling! (*laughs and kisses her*). I *have* missed you, my precious, my joy. I must tell you . . . I can't put it off a minute. . . .

ANYA (*wearily*). What now?

DUNYASHA. Epihodov, the clerk, made me a proposal just after Easter.

ANYA. It's always the same thing with you . . . (*straightening her hair*). I've lost all my hairpins . . . (*she is staggering from exhaustion*).

DUNYASHA. I don't know what to think, really. He does love me, he does love me so!

ANYA (*looking towards her door, tenderly*). My own room, my windows just as though I had never gone away. I'm home! Tomorrow morning I shall get up and run into the garden. . . . Oh, if I could get to sleep! I haven't slept all the journey, I was so anxious and worried.

DUNYASHA. Pyotr Sergeyevitch came the day before yesterday.

ANYA (*joyfully*). Petya!

DUNYASHA. He's asleep in the bathhouse, he has settled in there. I'm afraid of being in their way, says he. (*Glancing at her watch*) I was to have waked him, but Varvara Mihalovna told me not to. Don't you wake him, says she.

[*Enter* VARYA *with a bunch of keys at her waist.*]

VARYA. Dunyasha, coffee and make haste. . . . Mamma's asking foɪ coffee.

DUNYASHA. This very minute (*goes out*).

VARYA. Well, thank God, you've come. You're home again (*petting her*). My little darling has come back! My precious beauty has come back again!

ANYA. I have had a time of it!

VARYA. I can fancy.

ANYA. We set off in Holy Week—it was so cold then, and all the way Charlotta would talk and show off her tricks. What did you want to burden me with Charlotta for?

VARYA. You couldn't have travelled all alone, darling. At seventeen!

ANYA. We got to Paris at last, it was cold there—snow. I speak French shockingly. Mamma lives on the fifth floor, I went up to her and there were a lot of French people, ladies, an old priest with a book. The place smelt of tobacco and so comfortless. I felt sorry, oh! so sorry for mamma all at once, I put my arms round her neck, and hugged her and wouldn't let her go. Mamma was as kind as she could be, and she cried. . . .

VARYA (*through her tears*). Don't speak of it, don't speak of it!

ANYA. She had sold her villa at Mentone, she had nothing left, nothing. I hadn't a farthing left either, we only just had enough to get here. And mamma doesn't understand! When we had dinner at the stations, she always ordered the most expensive things and gave the waiters a whole rouble. Charlotta's just the same. Yasha too must have the same as we do; it's simply awful. You know Yasha is mamma's valet now, we brought him here with us.

VARYA. Yes, I've seen the young rascal.

ANYA. Well, tell me—have you paid the arrears on the mortgage?

VARYA. How could we get the money?

ANYA. Oh, dear! Oh, dear!

VARYA. In August the place will be sold.

ANYA. My goodness!

LOPAHIN (*peeps in at the door and moos like a cow*). Moo! (*disappears*).

VARYA (*weeping*). There, that's what I could do to him (*shakes her fist*).

ANYA (embracing VARYA, *softly*). Varya, has he made you an offer? (VARYA *shakes her head*). Why, but he loves you. Why is it you don't come to an understanding? What are you waiting for?

VARYA. I believe that there never will be anything between us. He has a lot to do, he has no time for me . . . and takes no notice of me. Bless the man, it makes me miserable to see him. . . . Everyone's talking of our being married, everyone's congratulating me, and all the while there's really nothing in it; it's all like a dream. (*In another tone*) You have a new brooch like a bee.

ANYA (*mournfully*). Mamma bought it. (*Goes into her own room and in a lighthearted childish tone*) And you know, in Paris I went up in a balloon!

VARYA. My darling's home again! My pretty is home again!

[DUNYASHA *returns with the coffee pot and is making the coffee.*]

VARYA (*standing at the door*). All day long, darling, as I go about look-after the house, I keep dreaming all the time. If only we could marry you to a rich man, then I should feel more at rest. Then I would go off by myself on a pilgrimage to Kiev, to Moscow . . . and so I would spend my life going from one holy place to another. . . . I would go on and on. . . . What bliss!

ANYA. The birds are singing in the garden. What time is it?

VARYA. It must be nearly three. It's time you were asleep, darling (*going into* ANYA'S *room*). What bliss!

[YASHA *enters with a rug and a travelling bag.*]

YASHA (*crosses the stage, mincingly*). May one come in here, pray?

DUNYASHA. I shouldn't have known you, Yasha. How you have changed abroad.

YASHA. H'm! . . . And who are you?

DUNYASHA. When you went away, I was that high (*shows distance from floor*). Dunyasha, Fyodor's daughter. . . . You don't remember me!

YASHA. H'm! . . . You're a peach! (*Looks round and embraces her: she shrieks and drops a saucer.* YASHA *goes out hastily.*)

VARYA (*in the doorway, in a tone of vexation*). What now?

DUNYASHA (*through her tears*). I have broken a saucer.

VARYA. Well, that brings good luck.

ANYA (*coming out of her room*). We ought to prepare mamma: Petya is here.

VARYA. I told them not to wake him.

ANYA (*dreamily*). It's six years since father died. Then only a month later little brother Grisha was drowned in the river, such a pretty boy he was, only seven. It was more than mamma could bear, so she went away, went away without looking back (*shuddering*). . . . How well I understand her, if only she knew! (*a pause*) And Petya Trofimov was Grisha's tutor, he may remind her.

[*Enter* FIRS: *he is wearing a pea jacket and a white waistcoat.*]

FIRS (*goes up to the coffee pot, anxiously*). The mistress will be served here (*puts on white gloves*). Is the coffee ready? (*Sternly to* DUN-YASHA) Girl! Where's the cream?

DUNYASHA. Ah, mercy on us! (*goes out quickly*).

FIRS (*fussing round the coffee pot*). Ech! you good-for-nothing! (*Muttering to himself*) Come back from Paris. And the old master used to go to Paris too . . . horses all the way (*laughs*).

VARYA. What is it, Firs?

FIRS. What is your pleasure? (*Gleefully*) My lady has come home! I have lived to see her again! Now I can die (*weeps with joy*).

[*Enter* LYUBOV ANDREYEVNA, GAEV *and* SEMYONOV-PISHTCHIK; *the latter is in a short-waisted full coat of fine cloth, and full trousers.* GAEV, *as he comes in, makes a gesture with his arms and his whole body, as though he were playing billiards.*]

LYUBOV. How does it go? Let me remember. Cannon off the red!

GAEV. That's it—in off the white! Why, once, sister, we used to sleep together in this very room, and now I'm fifty-one, strange as it seems.

LOPAHIN. Yes, time flies.

GAEV. What do you say?

LOPAHIN. Time, I say, flies.

GAEV. What a smell of patchouli!

ANYA. I'm going to bed. Good night, mamma (*kisses her mother*).

LYUBOV. My precious darling (*kisses her hands*). Are you glad to be home? I can't believe it.

ANYA. Good night, uncle.

GAEV (*kissing her face and hands*). God bless you! How like you are to your mother! (*To his sister*) At her age you were just the same, Lyuba.

[ANYA *shakes hands with* LOPAHIN *and* PISHTCHIK, *then goes out, shutting the door after her*.]

LYUBOV. She's quite worn out.

PISHTCHIK. Aye, it's a long journey, to be sure.

VARYA (*to* LOPAHIN *and* PISHTCHIK). Well, gentlemen? It's three o'clock and time to say good-by.

LYUBOV (*laughs*). You're just the same as ever, Varya (*draws her to her and kisses her*). I'll just drink my coffee and then we will all go and rest. (FIRS *puts a cushion under her feet*.) Thanks, friend. I am so fond of coffee, I drink it day and night. Thanks, dear old man (*kisses* FIRS).

VARYA. I'll just see whether all the things have been brought in (*goes out*).

LYUBOV. Can it really be me sitting here? (*laughs*). I want to dance about and clap my hands. (*Covers her face with her hands*) And I could drop asleep in a moment! God knows I love my country, I love it tenderly; I couldn't look out of the window in the train, I kept crying so. (*Through her tears*) But I must drink my coffee, though. Thank you, Firs, thanks, dear old man. I'm so glad to find you still alive.

FIRS. The day before yesterday.

GAEV. He's rather deaf.

LOPAHIN. I have to set off for Harkov directly, at five o'clock. . . . It is annoying! I wanted to have a look at you, and a little talk. . . . You are just as splendid as ever.

PISHTCHIK (*breathing heavily*). Handsomer, indeed. . . . Dressed in Parisian style . . . completely bowled me over.

LOPAHIN. Your brother, Leonid Andreyevitch here, is always saying that I'm a low-born knave, that I'm a money grubber, but I don't care one straw for that. Let him talk. Only I do want you to believe in me as you used to. I do want your wonderful tender eyes to look at me as they used to in the old days. Merciful God! My father was a serf of your father and of your grandfather, but you—you—did so much for me once, that I've forgotten all that; I love you as though you were my kin . . . more than my kin.

LYUBOV. I can't sit still, I simply can't . . . (*jumps up and walks about in violent agitation*). This happiness is too much for me. . . . You may laugh at me, I know I'm silly. . . . My own bookcase (*kisses the bookcase*). My little table.

GAEV. Nurse died while you were away.

LYUBOV (*sits down and drinks coffee*). Yes, the Kingdom of Heaven be hers! You wrote me of her death.

GAEV. And Anastasy is dead. Squinting Petruchka has left me and is in service now with the police captain in the town (*takes a box of caramels out of his pocket and sucks one*).

PISHTCHIK. My daughter, Dashenka, wishes to be remembered to you.

LOPAHIN. I want to tell you something very pleasant and cheering (*glancing at his watch*). I'm going directly . . . there's no time to say much . . . well, I can say it in a couple of words. I needn't tell you your cherry orchard is to be sold to pay your debts; the 22nd of August is the date fixed for the sale; but don't you worry, dearest lady, you may sleep in peace, there is a way of saving it. . . . This is what I propose. I beg your attention! Your estate is not twenty miles from the town, the railway runs close by it, and if the cherry orchard and the land along the river bank were cut up into building plots and then let on lease for summer villas, you would make an income of at least 25,000 roubles a year out of it.

GAEV. That's all rot, if you'll excuse me.

LYUBOV. I don't quite understand you, Yermolay Alexeyevitch.

LOPAHIN. You will get a rent of at least 25 roubles a year for a three-acre plot from summer visitors, and if you say the word now, I'll bet you what you like there won't be one square foot of ground vacant by the autumn, all the plots will be taken up. I congratulate you; in fact, you are saved. It's a perfect situation with that deep river. Only, of course, it must be cleared—all the old buildings, for example, must be removed, this house too, which is really good for nothing and the old cherry orchard must be cut down.

LYUBOV. Cut down? My dear fellow, forgive me, but you don't know what you are talking about. If there is one thing interesting—remarkable indeed—in the whole province, it's just our cherry orchard.

LOPAHIN. The only thing remarkable about the orchard is that it's a very large one. There's a crop of cherries every alternate year, and then there's nothing to be done with them, no one buys them.

GAEV. This orchard is mentioned in the "Encyclopædia."

LOPAHIN (*glancing at his watch*). If we don't decide on something and don't take some steps, on the 22nd of August the cherry orchard and the whole estate too will be sold by auction. Make up your minds! There is no other way of saving it, I'll take my oath on that. No, No!

FIRS. In old days, forty or fifty years ago, they used to dry the cherries, soak them, pickle them, make jam too, and they used——

GAEV. Be quiet, Firs.

FIRS. And they used to send the preserved cherries to Moscow and to Harkov by the wagon-load. That brought the money in! And the preserved cherries in those days were soft and juicy, sweet and fragrant. . . . They knew the way to do them then. . . .

LYUBOV. And where is the recipe now?

FIRS. It's forgotten. Nobody remembers it.

PISHTCHIK (*to* LYUBOV ANDREYEVNA). What's it like in Paris? Did you eat frogs there?

LYUBOV. Oh, I ate crocodiles.

PISHTCHIK. Fancy that now!

LOPAHIN. There used to be only the gentlefolks and the peasants in the country, but now there are these summer visitors. All the towns, even the small ones, are surrounded nowadays by these summer villas. And one may say for sure, that in another twenty years there'll be many more of these people and that they'll be everywhere. At present the summer visitor only drinks tea in his verandah, but maybe he'll take to working his bit of land too, and then your cherry orchard would become happy, rich and prosperous. . . .

GAEV (*indignant*). What rot!

[*Enter* VARYA *and* YASHA.]

VARYA. There are two telegrams for you, mamma (*takes out keys and opens an old-fashioned bookcase with a loud crack*). Here they are.

LYUBOV. From Paris (*tears the telegrams, without reading them*). I have done with Paris.

GAEV. Do you know, Lyuba, how old that bookcase is? Last week I pulled out the bottom drawer and there I found the date branded on it. The bookcase was made just a hundred years ago. What do you say to that? We might have celebrated its jubilee. Though it's an inanimate object, still it is a *book* case.

PISHTCHIK (*amazed*). A hundred years! Fancy that now.

GAEV. Yes. . . . It is a thing . . . (*feeling the bookcase*). Dear, honoured, bookcase! Hail to thee who for more than a hundred years hast served the pure ideals of good and justice; thy silent call to fruitful labour has never flagged in those hundred years, maintaining (*in tears*) in the generations of man, courage and faith in a brighter future and fostering in us ideals of good and social consciousness (*a pause*).

LOPAHIN. Yes. . . .

LYUBOV. You are just the same as ever, Leonid.

GAEV (*a little embarrassed*). Cannon off the right into the pocket!

LOPAHIN (*looking at his watch*). Well, it's time I was off.

YASHA (*handing* LYUBOV ANDREYEVNA *medicine*). Perhaps you will take your pills now.

PISHTCHIK. You shouldn't take medicines, my dear madam . . . they do no harm and no good. Give them here . . . honoured lady (*takes the pillbox, pours the pills into the hollow of his hand, blows on them, puts them in his mouth and drinks off some kvass*). There!

LYUBOV (*in alarm*). Why, you must be out of your mind!

PISHTCHIK. I have taken all the pills.

LOPAHIN. What a glutton! (*All laugh.*)

FIRS. His honour stayed with us in Easter week, ate a gallon and a half of cucumbers . . . (*mutters*).

LYUBOV. What is he saying?

VARYA. He has taken to muttering like that for the last three years. We are used to it.

YASHA. His declining years!

> [CHARLOTTA IVANOVNA, *a very thin, lanky figure in a white dress with a lorgnette in her belt, walks across the stage.*]

LOPAHIN. I beg your pardon, Charlotta Ivanovna, I have not had time to greet you (*tries to kiss her hand*).

CHARLOTTA (*pulling away her hand*). If I let you kiss my hand, you'll be wanting to kiss my elbow, and then my shoulder.

LOPAHIN. I've no luck today! (*All laugh.*) Charlotta Ivanovna, show us some tricks!

LYUBOV. Charlotta, do show us some tricks!

CHARLOTTA. I don't want to. I'm sleepy (*goes out*).

LOPAHIN. In three weeks' time we shall meet again (*kisses* LYUBOV ANDREYEVNA'S *hand*). Good-by till then—I must go. (*To* GAEV) Good-by. (*Kisses* PISHTCHIK) Good-by. (*Gives his hand to* VARYA, *then to* FIRS *and* YASHA) I don't want to go. (*To* LYUBOV ANDRE-YEVNA) If you think over my plan for the villas and make up your mind, then let me know; I will lend you 50,000 roubles. Think of it seriously.

VARYA (*angrily*). Well, do go, for goodness sake.

LOPAHIN. I'm going, I'm going (*goes out*).

GAEV. Low-born knave! I beg pardon, though . . . Varya is going to marry him, he's Varya's fiancé.

VARYA. Don't talk nonsense, uncle.

LYUBOV. Well, Varya, I shall be delighted. He's a good man.

PISHTCHIK. He is, one must acknowledge, a most worthy man. And my Dashenka . . . says too that . . . she says . . . various things (*snores, but at once wakes up*). But all the same, honoured lady, could you oblige me . . . with a loan of 240 roubles . . . to pay the interest on my mortgage tomorrow?

VARYA (*dismayed*). No, no.

LYUBOV. I really haven't any money.

PISHTCHIK. It will turn up (*laughs*). I never lose hope. I thought everything was over, I was a ruined man, and lo and behold—the railway passed through my land and . . . they paid me for it. And something else will turn up again, if not today, then tomorrow . . . Dashenka'll win two hundred thousand . . . she's got a lottery ticket.

LYUBOV. Well, we've finished our coffee, we can go to bed.

FIRS (*brushes* GAEV, *reprovingly*). You have got on the wrong trousers again! What am I to do with you?

VARYA (*softly*). Anya's asleep. (*Softly opens the window*) Now the sun's risen, it's not a bit cold. Look, mamma, what exquisite trees! My goodness! And the air! The starlings are singing!

GAEV (*opens another window*). The orchard is all white. You've not forgotten it, Lyuba? That long avenue that runs straight, straight as an arrow, how it shines on a moonlight night. You remember? You've not forgotten?

LYUBOV (*looking out of the window into the garden*). Oh, my childhood, my innocence! It was in this nursery I used to sleep, from here I looked out into the orchard, happiness waked with me every morning and in those days the orchard was just the same, nothing has changed (*laughs with delight*). All, all white! Oh, my orchard! After the dark gloomy autumn, and the cold winter; you are young again, and full of happiness, the heavenly angels have never left you. . . . If I could cast off the burden that weighs on my heart, if I could forget the past!

GAEV. H'm! and the orchard will be sold to pay our debts; it seems strange. . . .

LYUBOV. See, our mother walking . . . all in white, down the avenue! (*Laughs with delight.*) It is she!

GAEV. Where?

VARYA. Oh, don't, mamma!

LYUBOV. There is no one. It was my fancy. On the right there, by the path to the arbor, there is a white tree bending like a woman. . . .

[*Enter* TROFIMOV *wearing a shabby student's uniform and spectacles.*]

LYUBOV. What a ravishing orchard! White masses of blossom, blue sky. . . .

TROFIMOV. Lyubov Andreyevna! (*She looks round at him.*) I will just pay my respects to you and then leave you at once (*kisses her hand warmly*). I was told to wait until morning, but I hadn't the patience to wait any longer. . . .

[LYUBOV ANDREYEVNA *looks at him in perplexity.*]

VARYA (*through her tears*). This is Petya Trofimov.

TROFIMOV. Petya Trofimov, who was your Grisha's tutor. . . . Can I have changed so much?

[LYUBOV ANDREYEVNA *embraces him and weeps quietly.*]

GAEV (*in confusion*). There, there, Lyuba.

VARYA (*crying*). I told you, Petya, to wait till tomorrow.

LYUBOV. My Grisha . . . my boy . . . Grisha . . . my son!

VARYA. We can't help it, mamma, it is God's will.

TROFIMOV (*softly through his tears*). There . . . there.

LYUBOV (*weeping quietly*). My boy was lost . . . drowned. Why? Oh, why, dear Petya? (*More quietly*) Anya is asleep in there, and I'm talking loudly . . . making this noise. . . . But, Petya? Why have you grown so ugly? Why do you look so old?

TROFIMOV. A peasant woman in the train called me a mangy-looking gentleman.

LYUBOV. You were quite a boy then, a pretty little student, and now your hair's thin—and spectacles. Are you really a student still? (*Goes towards the door.*)

TROFIMOV. I seem likely to be a perpetual student.

LYUBOV (*kisses her brother, then* VARYA). Well, go to bed. . . . You are older too, Leonid.

PISHTCHIK (*follows her*). I suppose it's time we were asleep. . . . Ugh! my gout. I'm staying the night! Lyubov Andreyevna, my dear soul, if you could . . . tomorrow morning . . . 240 roubles.

GAEV. That's always his story.

PISHTCHIK. 240 roubles . . . to pay the interest on my mortgage.

LYUBOV. My dear man, I have no money.

PISHTCHIK. I'll pay it back, my dear . . . a trifling sum.

LYUBOV. Oh, well. Leonid will give it you. . . . You give him the money, Leonid.

GAEV. Me give it him! Let him wait till he gets it!

LYUBOV. It can't be helped, give it him. He needs it. He'll pay it back.

[LYUBOV ANDREYEVNA, TROFIMOV, PISHTCHIK *and*
FIRS *go out.* GAEV, VARYA *and* YASHA *remain.*]

GAEV. Sister hasn't got out of the habit of flinging away her money. (*To* YASHA) Get away, my good fellow, you smell of the hen house.

YASHA (*with a grin*). And you, Leonid Andreyevitch, are just the same as ever.

GAEV. What's that? (*To* VARYA) What did he say?

VARYA (*to* YASHA). Your mother has come from the village; she has been sitting in the servants' room since yesterday, waiting to see you.

YASHA. Oh, bother her!

VARYA. For shame!

YASHA. What's the hurry? She might just as well have come tomorrow (*goes out*).

VARYA. Mamma's just the same as ever, she hasn't changed a bit. If she had her own way, she'd give away everything.

GAEV. Yes (*a pause*). If a great many remedies are suggested for some disease, it means that the disease is incurable. I keep thinking and racking my brains; I have many schemes, a great many, and that really means none. If we could only come in for a legacy from somebody, or marry our Anya to a very rich man, or we might go to Yaroslavl and try our luck with our old aunt, the Countess. She's very, very rich, you know.

VARYA (*weeps*). If God would help us.

GAEV. Don't blubber. Aunt's very rich, but she doesn't like us. First, sister married a lawyer instead of a nobleman. . . .

[ANYA *appears in the doorway.*]

GAEV. And then her conduct, one can't call it virtuous. She is good, and kind, and nice, and I love her, but, however one allows for extenuating circumstances, there's no denying that she's an immoral woman. One feels it in her slightest gesture.

VARYA (*in a whisper*). Anya's in the doorway.

GAEV. What do you say? (*a pause*). It's queer, there seems to be something wrong with my right eye. I don't see as well as I did. And on Thursday when I was in the district Court . . .

[*Enter* ANYA.]

VARYA. Why aren't you asleep, Anya?

ANYA. I can't get to sleep.

GAEV. My pet (*kisses* ANYA's *face and hands*). My child (*weeps*). You are not my niece, you are my angel, you are everything to me. Believe me, believe . . .

ANYA. I believe you, uncle. Everyone loves you and respects you . . . but, uncle dear, you must be silent . . . simply be silent. What were you saying just now about my mother, about your own sister? What made you say that?

GAEV. Yes, yes . . . (*puts his hand over his face*). Really, that was awful! My God, save me! And today I made a speech to the bookcase . . . so stupid! And only when I had finished, I saw how stupid it was.

VARYA. It's true, uncle, you ought to keep quiet. Don't talk, that's all.

ANYA. If you could keep from talking, it would make things easier for you, too.

GAEV. I won't speak (*kisses* ANYA's *and* VARYA's *hands*). I'll be silent. Only this is about business. On Thursday I was in the district Court; well, there was a large party of us there and we began talking of one thing and another, and this and that, and do you know, I believe that it will be possible to raise a loan on an I.O.U. to pay the arrears on the mortgage.

VARYA. If the Lord would help us!

GAEV. I'm going on Tuesday; I'll talk of it again. (*To* VARYA) Don't blubber. (*To* ANYA) Your mamma will talk to Lopahin; of course, he won't refuse her. And as soon as you're rested you shall go to Yaroslavl to the Countess, your great-aunt. So we shall all set to work in three directions at once, and the business is done. We shall pay off arrears, I'm convinced of it (*puts a caramel in his mouth*). I swear on my honour, I swear by anything you like, the estate shan't be sold (*excitedly*). By my own happiness, I swear it! Here's my hand on it, call me the basest, vilest of men, if I let it come to an auction! Upon my soul I swear it!

ANYA (*her equanimity has returned, she is quite happy*). How good you are, uncle, and how clever! (*Embraces her uncle*.) I'm at peace now! Quite at peace! I'm happy!

[*Enter* FIRS.]

FIRS (*reproachfully*). Leonid Andreyevitch, have you no fear of God? when are you going to bed?

GAEV. Directly, directly. You can go, Firs. I'll . . . yes, I will undress myself. Come, children, by-by. We'll go into details tomorrow, but now go to bed (*kisses* ANYA *and* VARYA). I'm a man of the eighties. They run down that period, but still I can say I have had to suffer not a little for my convictions in my life. It's not for nothing that the peasant loves me. One must know the peasant! One must know how . . .

ANYA. At it again, uncle!

VARYA. Uncle dear, you'd better be quiet!

FIRS (*angrily*). Leonid Andreyevitch!

GAEV. I'm coming. I'm coming. Go to bed. Potted the shot—there's a shot for you! A beauty! (*Goes out,* FIRS *hobbling after him*.)

ANYA. My mind's at rest now. I don't want to go to Yaroslavl, I don't like my great-aunt, but still my mind's at rest. Thanks to uncle (*sits down*).

VARYA. We must go to bed. I'm going. Something unpleasant happened while you were away. In the old servants' quarters there are only the old servants, as you know—Efimyushka, Polya and Yevstigney —and Karp too. They began letting stray people in to spend the night—I said nothing. But all at once I heard they had been spreading a report that I gave them nothing but pease pudding to eat. Out of stinginess, you know. . . . And it was all Yevstigney's doing. . . . Very well, I said to myself. . . . If that's how it is, I thought, wait a bit. I sent for Yevstigney . . . (*yawns*). He comes. . . . "How's this, Yevstigney," I said, "you could be such a fool as to? . . ." (*Looking at* ANYA) Anitchka! (*a pause*). She's asleep (*puts her arm round* ANYA). Come to bed . . . come along! (*leads her*). My darling has fallen asleep! Come . . . (*They go.*)

[*Far away beyond the orchard a shepherd plays on a pipe.* TROFIMOV *crosses the stage and, seeing* VARYA *and* ANYA, *stands still*.]

VARYA. 'Sh! asleep, asleep. Come, my own.

ANYA (*softly, half asleep*). I'm so tired. Still those bells. Uncle . . . dear . . . mamma and uncle . . .

VARYA. Come, my own, come along.

[*They go into* ANYA'S *room*.]

TROFIMOV (*tenderly*). My sunshine! My spring.

ACT II

📝 Scene: *The open country. An old shrine, long abandoned and fallen out of the perpendicular; near it a well, large stones that have apparently once been tombstones, and an old garden seat. The road to* GAEV'S *house is seen. On one side rise dark poplars; and there the cherry orchard begins. In the distance a row of telegraph poles and far, far away on the horizon there is faintly outlined a great town, only visible in very fine clear weather. It is near sunset.* CHARLOTTA, YASHA *and* DUNYASHA *are sitting on the seat.* EPIHODOV *is standing near, playing something mournful on a guitar. All sit plunged in thought.* CHARLOTTA *wears an old forage cap; she has taken a gun from her shoulder and is tightening the buckle on the strap.*

CHARLOTTA (*musingly*). I haven't a real passport of my own, and I don't know how old I am, and I always feel that I'm a young thing. When I was a little girl, my father and mother used to travel about to fairs and give performances—very good ones. And I used to dance *salto-mortale* and all sorts of things. And when papa and mamma died, a German lady took me and had me educated. And so I grew up and became a governess. But where I came from, and who I am, I don't know. . . . Who my parents were, very likely they weren't married . . . I don't know (*takes a cucumber out of her pocket and eats*). I know nothing at all (*a pause*). One wants to talk and has no one to talk to . . . I have nobody.

EPIHODOV (*plays on the guitar and sings*). "What care I for the noisy world! What care I for friends or foes!" How agreeable it is to play on the mandolin!

DUNYASHA. That's a guitar, not a mandolin (*looks in a hand mirror and powders herself*).

EPIHODOV. To a man mad with love, it's a mandolin. (*Sings*) "Where her heart but aglow with love's mutual flame." (YASHA *joins in.*)

CHARLOTTA. How shockingly these people sing! Foo! Like jackals!

DUNYASHA (*to* YASHA). What happiness, though, to visit foreign lands.

YASHA. Ah, yes! I rather agree with you there (*yawns, then lights a cigar*).

EPIHODOV. That's comprehensible. In foreign lands everything has long since reached full complexion.

YASHA. That's so, of course.

EPIHODOV. I'm a cultivated man, I read remarkable books of all sorts, but I can never make out the tendency I am myself precisely inclined for, whether to live or to shoot myself, speaking precisely, but nevertheless I always carry a revolver. Here it is . . . (*shows revolver*).

CHARLOTTA. I've had enough, and now I'm going (*puts on the gun*). Epihodov, you're a very clever fellow, and a very terrible one too, all the women must be wild about you. Br-r-r! (*goes*) These clever fellows are all so stupid; there's not a creature for me to speak to. . . . Always alone, alone, nobody belonging to me . . . and who I am, and why I'm on earth, I don't know (*walks away slowly*).

EPIHODOV. Speaking precisely, not touching upon other subjects, I'm bound to admit about myself, that destiny behaves mercilessly to me, as a storm to a little boat. If, let us suppose, I am mistaken, then why did I wake up this morning, to quote an example, and look round, and there on my chest was a spider of fearful magnitude . . . like this (*shows with both hands*). And then I take up a jug of kvass, to quench my thirst, and in it there is something in the highest degree unseemly of the nature of a cockroach (*a pause*). Have you read Buckle? (*a pause*). I am desirous of troubling you, Dunyasha, with a couple of words.

DUNYASHA. Well, speak.

EPIHODOV. I should be desirous to speak with you alone (*sighs*).

DUNYASHA (*embarrassed*). Well—only bring me my mantle first. It's by the cupboard. It's rather damp here.

EPIHODOV. Certainly. I will fetch it. Now I know what I must do with my revolver (*takes guitar and goes off playing on it*).

YASHA. Two and twenty misfortunes! Between ourselves, he's a fool (*yawns*).

DUNYASHA. God grant he doesn't shoot himself! (*a pause*) I am so nervous, I'm always in a flutter. I was a little girl when I was taken into our lady's house, and now I have quite grown out of peasant ways, and my hands are white, as white as a lady's. I'm such a delicate, sensitive creature, I'm afraid of everything. I'm so frightened. And if you deceive me, Yasha, I don't know what will become of my nerves.

YASHA (*kisses her*). You're a peach! Of course a girl must never forget herself; what I dislike more than anything is a girl being flighty in her behavior.

DUNYASHA. I'm passionately in love with you, Yasha; you are a man of culture—you can give your opinion about anything (*a pause*).

YASHA (*yawns*). Yes, that's so. My opinion is this: if a girl loves anyone, that means that she has no principles (*a pause*). It's pleasant smoking a cigar in the open air (*listens*). Someone's coming this way . . . it's the gentlefolk (DUNYASHA *embraces him impulsively*). Go home, as though you had been to the river to bathe; go by that path, or else they'll meet you and suppose I have made an appointment with you here. That I can't endure.

DUNYASHA (*coughing softly*). The cigar has made my head ache . . . (*goes off*).

[YASHA *remains sitting near the shrine. Enter* LYUBOV ANDREYEVNA, GAEV *and* LOPAHIN.]

LOPAHIN. You must make up your mind once for all—there's no time to lose. It's quite a simple question, you know. Will you consent to letting the land for building or not? One word in answer: Yes or no? Only one word!

LYUBOV. Who is smoking such horrible cigars here? (*sits down*).

GAEV. Now the railway line has been brought near, it's made things very convenient (*sits down*). Here we have been over and lunched in town. Cannon off the white! I should like to go home and have a game.

LYUBOV. You have plenty of time.

LOPAHIN. Only one word! (*Beseechingly*). Give me an answer!

GAEV (*yawning*). What do you say?

LYUBOV (*looks in her purse*). I had quite a lot of money here yesterday, and there's scarcely any left today. My poor Varya feeds us all on milk soup for the sake of economy; the old folks in the kitchen get nothing but pease pudding, while I waste my money in a senseless way (*drops purse, scattering gold pieces*). There, they have all fallen out! (*annoyed*)

YASHA. Allow me, I'll soon pick them up (*collects the coins*).

LYUBOV. Pray do, Yasha. And what did I go off to the town to lunch for? Your restaurant's a wretched place with its music and the table-cloth smelling of soap. . . . Why drink so much, Leonid? And eat so much? And talk so much? Today you talked a great deal again in the restaurant, and all so inappropriately. About the era of the 'seventies, about the decadents. And to whom? Talking to waiters about decadents!

LOPAHIN. Yes.

GAEV (*waving his hand*). I'm incorrigible; that's evident. (*Irritably to* YASHA) Why is it you keep fidgeting about in front of us!

YASHA (*laughs*). I can't help laughing when I hear your voice.

GAEV (*to his sister*). Either I or he . . .

LYUBOV. Get along! Go away, Yasha.

YASHA (*gives* LYUBOV ANDREYEVNA *her purse*). Directly (*hardly able to suppress his laughter*). This minute . . . (*goes off*).

LOPAHIN. Deriganov, the millionaire, means to buy your estate. They say he is coming to the sale himself.

LYUBOV. Where did you hear that?

LOPAHIN. That's what they say in town.

GAEV. Our aunt in Yaroslavl has promised to send help; but when, and how much she will send, we don't know.

LOPAHIN. How much will she send? A hundred thousand? Two hundred?

LYUBOV. Oh, well! . . . Ten or fifteen thousand, and we must be thankful to get that.

LOPAHIN. Forgive me, but such reckless people as you are—such queer, unbusinesslike people—I never met in my life. One tells you in plain Russian your estate is going to be sold, and you seem not to understand it.

LYUBOV. What are we to do? Tell us what to do.

LOPAHIN. I do tell you every day. Every day I say the same thing. You absolutely must let the cherry orchard and the land on building leases; and do it at once, as quick as may be—the auction's close upon us! Do understand! Once make up your mind to build villas, and you can raise as much money as you like, and then you are saved.

LYUBOV. Villas and summer visitors—forgive me saying so—it's so vulgar.

GAEV. There I perfectly agree with you.

LOPAHIN. I shall sob, or scream, or fall into a fit. I can't stand it! You drive me mad! (*To* GAEV) You're an old woman!

GAEV. What do you say ?

LOPAHIN. An old woman! (*Gets up to go.*)

LYUBOV (*in dismay*). No, don't go! Do stay, my dear friend! Perhaps we shall think of something.

LOPAHIN. What is there to think of?

LYUBOV. Don't go, I entreat you! With you here it's more cheerful, anyway (*a pause*). I keep expecting something, as though the house were going to fall about our ears.

GAEV (*in profound dejection*). Potted the white! It fails—a kiss.

LYUBOV. We have been great sinners. . . .

LOPAHIN. You have no sins to repent of.

GAEV (*puts a caramel in his mouth*). They say I've eaten up my property in caramels (*laughs*).

LYUBOV. Oh, my sins! I've always thrown my money away recklessly like a lunatic. I married a man who made nothing but debts. My husband died of champagne—he drank dreadfully. To my misery I loved another man, and immediately—it was my first punishment—the blow fell upon me, here, in the river . . . my boy was drowned and I went abroad—went away for ever, never to return, not to see that river again . . . I shut my eyes, and fled, distracted, and *he* after me . . . pitilessly, brutally. I bought a villa at Mentone, for *he* fell ill there, and for three years I had no rest day or night. His illness wore me out, my soul was dried up. And last year, when my villa was sold to pay my debts, I went to Paris and there he robbed me of everything and abandoned me for another woman; and I tried to poison myself. . . . So stupid, so shameful! . . . And suddenly I felt a yearning for Russia, for my country, for my little girl . . . (*dries her tears*). Lord, Lord, be merciful! Forgive my sins! Do not chastise me more! (*Takes a telegram out of her pocket*) I got this today from Paris. He implores forgiveness, entreats me to return (*tears up the telegram*). I fancy there is music somewhere (*listens*).

GAEV. That's our famous Jewish orchestra. You remember, four violins, a flute and a double bass.

LYUBOV. That still in existence? We ought to send for them one evening, and give a dance.

LOPAHIN (*listens*). I can't hear. . . . (*Hums softly*) "For money the Germans will turn a Russian into a Frenchman." (*Laughs*) I did see such a piece at the theatre yesterday! It was funny!

LYUBOV. And most likely there was nothing funny in it. You shouldn't look at plays, you should look at yourself a little oftener. How grey your lives are! How much nonsense you talk.

LOPAHIN. That's true. One may say honestly, we live a fool's life (*pause*). My father was a peasant, an idiot; he knew nothing and taught me nothing, only beat me when he was drunk, and always with his stick. In reality I am just such another blockhead and idiot. I've learnt nothing properly. I write a wretched hand. I write so that I feel ashamed before folks, like a pig.

LYUBOV. You ought to get married, my dear fellow.

LOPAHIN. Yes . . . that's true.

LYUBOV. You should marry our Varya, she's a good girl.

LOPAHIN. Yes.

LYUBOV. She's a good-natured girl, she's busy all day long, and what's more, she loves you. And you have liked her for ever so long.

LOPAHIN. Well? I'm not against it. . . . She's a good girl (*pause*).

GAEV. I've been offered a place in the bank: 6,000 roubles a year. Did you know?

LYUBOV. You would never do for that! You must stay as you are.

[*Enter* FIRS *with overcoat.*]

FIRS. Put it on, sir, it's damp.

GAEV (*putting it on*). You bother me, old fellow.

FIRS. You can't go on like this. You went away in the morning without leaving word (*looks him over*).

LYUBOV. You look older, Firs!

FIRS. What is your pleasure?

LOPAHIN. You look older, she said.

FIRS. I've had a long life. They were arranging my wedding before your papa was born . . . (*laughs*). I was the head footman before the emancipation came. I wouldn't consent to be set free then; I stayed on with the old master . . . (*a pause*). I remember what rejoicings they made and didn't know themselves what they were rejoicing over.

LOPAHIN. Those were fine old times. There was flogging anyway.

FIRS (*not hearing*). To be sure! The peasants knew their place, and the masters knew theirs; but now they're all at sixes and sevens, there's no making it out.

GAEV. Hold your tongue, Firs. I must go to town tomorrow. I have been promised an introduction to a general, who might let us have a loan.

LOPAHIN. You won't bring that off. And you won't pay your arrears, you may rest assured of that.

LYUBOV. That's all his nonsense. There is no such general.

[*Enter* TROFIMOV, ANYA *and* VARYA.]

GAEV. Here come our girls.

ANYA. There's mamma on the seat.

LYUBOV (*tenderly*). Come here, come along. My darlings! (*Embraces* ANYA *and* VARYA.) If you only knew how I love you both. Sit beside me, there, like that. (*All sit down.*)

LOPAHIN. Our perpetual student is always with the young ladies.

TROFIMOV. That's not your business.

LOPAHIN. He'll soon be fifty, and he's still a student.

TROFIMOV. Drop your idiotic jokes.

LOPAHIN. Why are you so cross, you queer fish?

TROFIMOV. Oh, don't persist!

LOPAHIN (*laughs*). Allow me to ask you what's your idea of me?

TROFIMOV. I'll tell you my idea of you, Yermolay Alexeyevitch: you are a rich man, you'll soon be a millionaire. Well, just as in the economy of nature a wild beast is of use, who devours everything that comes in his way, so you too have your use.

[*All laugh.*]

VARYA. Better tell us something about the planets, Petya.

LYUBOV. No, let us go on with the conversation we had yesterday.

TROFIMOV. What was it about?

GAEV. About pride.

TROFIMOV. We had a long conversation yesterday, but we came to no conclusion. In pride, in your sense of it, there is something mystical. Perhaps you are right from your point of view; but if one looks at it simply, without subtlety, what sort of pride can there be, what sense is there in it, if man in his physiological formation is very imperfect, if in the immense majority of cases he is coarse, dull-witted, profoundly unhappy? One must give up glorification of self. One should work, and nothing else.

GAEV. One must die in any case.

TROFIMOV. Who knows? And what does it mean—dying? Perhaps man has a hundred senses, and only the five we know are lost at death, while the other ninety-five remain alive.

LYUBOV. How clever you are, Petya!

LOPAHIN (*ironically*). Fearfully clever!

TROFIMOV. Humanity progresses, perfecting its powers. Everything that is beyond its ken now will one day become familiar and comprehensible; only we must work, we must with all our powers aid the seeker after truth. Here among us in Russia the workers are few in number as yet. The vast majority of the intellectual people I know, seek nothing, do nothing, are not fit as yet for work of any kind. They call themselves intellectual, but they treat their servants as inferiors, behave to the peasants as though they were animals, learn little, read nothing seriously, do practically nothing, only talk about science and know very little about art. They are all serious people, they all have severe faces, they all talk of weighty matters and air their theories, and yet the vast majority of us—ninety-nine per cent. —live like savages, at the least thing fly to blows and abuse, eat piggishly, sleep in filth and stuffiness, bugs everywhere, stench and damp and moral impurity. And it's clear all our fine talk is only to divert our attention and other people's. Show me where to find the crèches there's so much talk about, and the reading rooms? They only exist in novels: in real life there are none of them. There is nothing but filth and vulgarity and Asiatic apathy. I fear and dislike very serious faces. I'm afraid of serious conversations. We should do better to be silent.

LOPAHIN. You know, I get up at five o'clock in the morning, and I work from morning to night; and I've money, my own and other people's, always passing through my hands, and I see what people are made of all round me. One has only to begin to do anything to see how few honest, decent people there are. Sometimes when I lie awake at night, I think: "Oh! Lord, thou hast given us immense forests, boundless plains, the widest horizons, and living here we ourselves ought really to be giants."

LYUBOV. You ask for giants! They are no good except in storybooks; in real life they frighten us.

[EPIHODOV *advances in the background, playing on the guitar.*]

LYUBOV (*dreamily*). There goes Epihodov.

ANYA (*dreamily*). There goes Epihodov.

GAEV. The sun has set, my friends.

TROFIMOV. Yes.

GAEV (*not loudly, but, as it were, declaiming*). O nature, divine nature, thou art bright with eternal luster, beautiful and indifferent! Thou, whom we call mother, thou dost unite within thee life and death! Thou dost give life and dost destroy!

VARYA (*in a tone of supplication*). Uncle!

ANYA. Uncle, you are at it again!

TROFIMOV. You'd much better be cannoning off the red!

GAEV. I'll hold my tongue, I will.

[*All sit plunged in thought. Perfect stillness. The only thing audible is the muttering of* FIRS. *Suddenly there is a sound in the distance, as it were from the sky— the sound of a breaking harp string, mournfully dying away.*]

LYUBOV. What is that?

LOPAHIN. I don't know. Somewhere far away a bucket fallen and broken in the pits. But somewhere very far away.

GAEV. It might be a bird of some sort—such as a heron.

TROFIMOV. Or an owl.

LYUBOV (*shudders*). I don't know why, but it's horrid (*a pause*).

FIRS. It was the same before the calamity—the owl hooted and the samovar hissed all the time.

GAEV. Before what calamity?

FIRS. Before the emancipation (*a pause*).

LYUBOV. Come, my friends, let us be going; evening is falling. (*To* ANYA) There are tears in your eyes. What is it, darling? (*Embraces her.*)

ANYA. Nothing, mamma; it's nothing.

TROFIMOV. There is somebody coming.

[*The wayfarer appears in a shabby white forage cap and an overcoat; he is slightly drunk.*]

WAYFARER. Allow me to inquire, can I get to the station this way?

GAEV. Yes. Go along that road.

WAYFARER. I thank you most feelingly (*coughing*). The weather is superb. (*Declaims*) My brother, my suffering brother! . . . Come out to the Volga! Whose groan do you hear? . . . (*To* VARYA) Mademoiselle, vouchsafe a hungry Russian thirty kopeks.

[VARYA *utters a shriek of alarm.*]

LOPAHIN (*angrily*). There's a right and a wrong way of doing everything!

LYUBOV (*hurriedly*). Here, take this (*looks in her purse*). I've no silver. No matter—here's gold for you.

WAYFARER. I thank you most feelingly! (*goes off*).

[*Laughter.*]

VARYA (*frightened*). I'm going home—I'm going . . . Oh, mamma, the servants have nothing to eat, and you gave him gold!

LYUBOV. There's no doing anything with me. I'm so silly! When we get home, I'll give you all I possess. Yermolay Alexeyevitch, you will lend me some more . . . !

LOPAHIN. I will.

LYUBOV. Come, friends, it's time to be going. And Varya, we have made a match of it for you. I congratulate you.

VARYA (*through her tears*). Mamma, that's not a joking matter.

LOPAHIN. "Ophelia, get thee to a nunnery!"

GAEV. My hands are trembling; it's a long while since I had a game of billiards.

LOPAHIN. "Ophelia! Nymph, in thy orisons be all my sins remember'd."

LYUBOV. Come, it will soon be suppertime.

VARYA. How he frightened me! My heart's simply throbbing.

LOPAHIN. Let me remind you, ladies and gentlemen: on the 22nd of August the cherry orchard will be sold. Think about that! Think about it!

[*All go off, except* TROFIMOV *and* ANYA.]

ANYA (*laughing*). I'm grateful to the wayfarer! He frightened Varya and we are left alone.

TROFIMOV. Varya's afraid we shall fall in love with each other, and for days together she won't leave us. With her narrow brain she can't grasp that we are above love. To eliminate the petty and transitory which hinders us from being free and happy—that is the aim and meaning of our life. Forward! We go forward irresistibly towards the bright star that shines yonder in the distance. Forward! Do not lag behind, friends.

ANYA (*claps her hands*). How well you speak! (*a pause*). It is divine here today.

TROFIMOV. Yes, it's glorious weather.

ANYA. Somehow, Petya, you've made me so that I don't love the cherry orchard as I used to. I used to love it so dearly. I used to think that there was no spot on earth like our garden.

TROFIMOV. All Russia is our garden. The earth is great and beautiful— there are many beautiful places in it (*a pause*). Think only, Anya, your grandfather, and great-grandfather, and all your ancestors were slave owners—the owners of living souls—and from every cherry in the orchard, from every leaf, from every trunk there are human creatures looking at you. Cannot you hear their voices? Oh, it is awful! Your orchard is a fearful thing, and when in the evening or at night one walks about the orchard, the old bark on the trees glimmers dimly in the dusk, and the old cherry trees seem to be dreaming of centuries gone by and tortured by fearful visions. Yes! We are at least two hundred years behind, we have really gained nothing yet, we have no definite attitude to the past, we do nothing but theorize or complain of depression or drink vodka. It is clear that to begin to live in the present we must first expiate our past, we must break with it; and we can expiate it only by suffering, by extraordinary unceasing labour. Understand that, Anya.

ANYA. The house we live in has long ceased to be our own, and I shall leave it, I give you my word.

TROFIMOV. If you have the house keys, fling them into the well and go away. Be free as the wind.

ANYA (*in ecstasy*). How beautifully you said that!

TROFIMOV. Believe me, Anya, believe me! I am not thirty yet, I am young, I am still a student, but I have gone through so much already! As soon as winter comes I am hungry, sick, careworn, poor as a beggar, and what ups and downs of fortune have I not known! And my soul was always, every minute, day and night, full of inexplicable forebodings. I have a foreboding of happiness, Anya. I see glimpses of it already.

ANYA (*pensively*). The moon is rising.

> [EPIHODOV *is heard playing still the same mournful
> song on the guitar. The moon rises. Somewhere near
> the poplars* VARYA *is looking for* ANYA *and calling
> "Anya! where are you?"*]

TROFIMOV. Yes, the moon is rising (*a pause*). Here is happiness—here it comes! It is coming nearer and nearer; already I can hear its footsteps. And if we never see it—if we may never know it—what does it matter? Others will see it after us.

VARYA'S VOICE. Anya! Where are you?

TROFIMOV. That Varya again! (*Angrily*) It's revolting!

ANYA. Well, let's go down to the river. It's lovely there.

TROFIMOV. Yes, let's go. (*They go.*)

VARYA'S VOICE. Anya! Anya!

ACT III

≈§ Scene: *A drawing room divided by an arch from a larger drawing room. A chandelier burning. The Jewish orchestra, the same that was mentioned in Act II, is heard playing in the anteroom. It is evening. In the larger drawing room they are dancing the grand chain. The voice of* SEMYONOV-PISHTCHIK: *"Promenade à une paire!" Then enter the drawing room in couples first* PISHTCHIK *and* CHARLOTTA IVANOVNA, *then* TROFIMOV *and* LYUBOV ANDREYEVNA, *thirdly* ANYA *with the Post Office Clerk, fourthly* VARYA *with the Station Master, and other guests.* VARYA *is quietly weeping and wiping away her tears as she dances. In the last couple is* DUNYASHA. *They move across the drawing room.* PISHTCHIK *shouts:* "Grand rond, balancez!" *and* "Les Cavaliers à genou et remerciez vos dames."

[FIRS *in a swallow-tail coat brings in seltzer water on a tray.*]

[PISHTCHIK *and* TROFIMOV *enter the drawing room.*]

PISHTCHIK. I am a full-blooded man; I have already had two strokes. Dancing's hard work for me, but as they say, if you're in the pack, you must bark with the rest. I'm as strong, I may say, as a horse. My parent, who would have his joke—may the Kingdom of Heaven be his!—used to say about our origin that the ancient stock of the Semyonov-Pishtchiks was derived from the very horse that Caligula made a member of the senate (*sits down*). But I've no money, that's where the mischief is. A hungry dog believes in nothing but meat . . . (*snores, but at once wakes up*). That's like me . . . I can think of nothing but money.

TROFIMOV. There really is something horsy about your appearance.

PISHTCHIK. Well . . . a horse is a fine beast . . . a horse can be sold.

[*There is the sound of billiards being played in an adjoining room.* VARYA *appears in the arch leading to the larger drawing room.*]

TROFIMOV (*teasing*). Madame Lopahin! Madame Lopahin!

VARYA (*angrily*). Mangy-looking gentleman!

TROFIMOV. Yes, I am a mangy-looking gentleman, and I'm proud of it!

VARYA (*pondering bitterly*). Here we have hired musicians and nothing to pay them! (*Goes out.*)

TROFIMOV (*to* PISHTCHIK). If the energy you have wasted during your lifetime in trying to find the money to pay your interest, had gone to something else, you might in the end have turned the world upside down.

PISHTCHIK. Nietzsche, the philosopher, a very great and celebrated man . . . of enormous intellect . . . says in his works, that one can make forged bank notes.

TROFIMOV. Why, have you read Nietzsche?

PISHTCHIK. What next . . . Dashenka told me. . . . And now I am in such a position, I might just as well forge bank notes. The day after tomorrow I must pay 310 roubles—130 I have procured (*feels in his pockets, in alarm*). The money's gone! I have lost my money! (*Through his tears*) Where's the money? (*Gleefully*) Why, here it is behind the lining. . . . It has made me hot all over.

[*Enter* LYUBOV ANDREYEVNA *and* CHARLOTTA IVAN-OVNA.]

LYUBOV (*hums the Lezginka*). Why is Leonid so long? What can he be doing in town? (*To* DUNYASHA) Offer the musicians some tea.

TROFIMOV. The sale hasn't taken place, most likely.

LYUBOV. It's the wrong time to have the orchestra, and the wrong time to give a dance. Well, never mind (*sits down and hums softly*).

CHARLOTTA (*gives* PISHTCHIK *a pack of cards*). Here's a pack of cards. Think of any card you like.

PISHTCHIK. I've thought of one.

CHARLOTTA. Shuffle the pack now. That's right. Give it here, my dear Mr. Pishtchik. Ein, zwei, drei—now look, it's in your breast pocket.

PISHTCHIK (*taking a card out of his breast pocket*). The eight of spades! Perfectly right! (*Wonderingly*) Fancy that now!

CHARLOTTA (*holding pack of cards in her hands, to* TROFIMOV). Tell me quickly which is the top card.

TROFIMOV. Well, the queen of spades.

CHARLOTTA. It is! (*To* PISHTCHIK) Well, which card is uppermost?

PISHTCHIK. The ace of hearts.

CHARLOTTA. It is! (*claps her hands, pack of cards disappears*). Ah! what lovely weather it is today!

[*A mysterious feminine voice which seems coming
out of the floor answers her.* "Oh, yes, it's magnificent
weather, madam."]

CHARLOTTA. You are my perfect ideal.

VOICE. And I greatly admire you too, madam.

STATION MASTER (*applauding*). The lady ventriloquist—bravo!

PISHTCHIK (*wonderingly*). Fancy that now! Most enchanting Charlotta
Ivanovna. I'm simply in love with you.

CHARLOTTA. In love? (*Shrugging shoulders*) What do you know of
love, guter Mensch, aber schlechter Musikant.

TROFIMOV (*pats* PISHTCHIK *on the shoulder*). You dear old horse. . . .

CHARLOTTA. Attention, please! Another trick! (*takes a traveling rug
from a chair*). Here's a very good rug; I want to sell it (*shaking it
out*). Doesn't anyone want to buy it?

PISHTCHIK (*wonderingly*). Fancy that!

CHARLOTTA. Ein, zwei, drei! (*quickly picks up rug she has dropped;
behind the rug stands* ANYA; *she makes a curtsey, runs to her mother,
embraces her and runs back into the larger drawing room amidst
general enthusiasm.*)

LYUBOV (*applauds*). Bravo! Bravo!

CHARLOTTA. Now again! Ein, zwei, drei! (*lifts up the rug; behind the
rug stands* VARYA, *bowing*).

PISHTCHIK (*wonderingly*). Fancy that now!

CHARLOTTA. That's the end (*throws the rug at* PISHTCHIK, *makes a
curtsey, runs into the larger drawing room*).

PISHTCHIK (*hurries after her*). Mischievous creature! Fancy! (*Goes
out.*)

LYUBOV. And still Leonid doesn't come. I can't understand what he's
doing in the town so long! Why, everything must be over by now.
The estate is sold, or the sale has not taken place. Why keep us so
long in suspense?

VARYA (*trying to console her*). Uncle's bought it. I feel sure of that.

TROFIMOV (*ironically*). Oh, yes!

VARYA. Great-aunt sent him an authorization to buy it in her name,
and transfer the debt. She's doing it for Anya's sake, and I'm sure
God will be merciful. Uncle will buy it.

LYUBOV. My aunt in Yaroslavl sent fifteen thousand to buy the estate
in her name, she doesn't trust us—but that's not enough even to pay
the arrears (*hides her face in her hands*). My fate is being sealed
today, my fate . . .

TROFIMOV (*teasing* VARYA). Madame Lopahin.

VARYA (*angrily*). Perpetual student! Twice already you've been sent
down from the University.

LYUBOV. Why are you angry, Varya? He's teasing you about Lopahin.
Well, what of that? Marry Lopahin if you like, he's a good man, and

interesting; if you don't want to, don't! Nobody compels you, darling.

VARYA. I must tell you plainly, mamma, I look at the matter seriously; he's a good man, I like him.

LYUBOV. Well, marry him. I can't see what you're waiting for.

VARYA. Mamma. I can't make him an offer myself. For the last two years, everyone's been talking to me about him. Everyone talks; but he says nothing or else makes a joke. I see what it means. He's growing rich, he's absorbed in business, he has no thoughts for me. If I had money, were it ever so little, if I had only a hundred roubles, I'd throw everything up and go far away. I would go into a nunnery.

TROFIMOV. What bliss!

VARYA (*to* TROFIMOV). A student ought to have sense! (*In a soft tone with tears*) How ugly you've grown, Petya! How old you look! (*To* LYUBOV ANDREYEVNA, *no longer crying*) But I can't do without work, mamma; I must have something to do every minute.

[*Enter* YASHA.]

YASHA (*hardly restraining his laughter*). Epihodov has broken a billiard cue! (*Goes out.*)

VARYA. What is Epihodov doing here? Who gave him leave to play billiards? I can't make these people out (*goes out*).

LYUBOV. Don't tease her, Petya. You see she has grief enough without that.

TROFIMOV. She is so very officious, meddling in what's not her business. All the summer she's given Anya and me no peace. She's afraid of a love affair between us. What's it to do with her? Besides, I have given no grounds for it. Such triviality is not in my line. We are above love!

LYUBOV. And I suppose I am beneath love. (*Very uneasily*) Why is it Leonid's not here? If only I could know whether the estate is sold or not! It seems such an incredible calamity that I really don't know what to think. I am distracted . . . I shall scream in a minute . . . I shall do something stupid. Save me, Petya, tell me something, talk to me!

TROFIMOV. What does it matter whether the estate is sold today or not? That's all done with long ago. There's no turning back, the path is overgrown. Don't worry yourself, dear Lyubov Andreyevna. You mustn't deceive yourself; for once in your life you must face the truth!

LYUBOV. What truth? You see where the truth lies, but I seem to have lost my sight, I see nothing. You settle every great problem so boldly, but tell me, my dear boy, isn't it because you're young—because you haven't yet understood one of your problems through suffering? You look forward boldly, and isn't it that you don't see and don't expect anything dreadful because life is still hidden from your young eyes? You're bolder, more honest, deeper than we are, but think, be just a little magnanimous, have pity on me. I was born here, you know, my father and mother lived here, my grandfather lived here, I love this house. I can't conceive of life without the cherry orchard, and if it really must be sold, then sell me with the orchard (*embraces* TROFIMOV, *kisses him on the forehead*). My boy was drowned here (*weeps*). Pity me, my dear kind fellow.

TROFIMOV. You know I feel for you with all my heart.

LYUBOV. But that should have been said differently, so differently (*takes out her handkerchief, telegram falls on the floor*). My heart is so heavy today. It's so noisy here my soul is quivering at every sound, I'm shuddering all over, but I can't go away; I'm afraid to be quiet and alone. Don't be hard on me, Petya . . . I love you as though you were one of ourselves. I would gladly let you marry Anya—I swear I would—only, my dear boy, you must take your degree, you do nothing—you're simply tossed by fate from place to place. That's so strange. It is, isn't it? And you must do something with your beard to make it grow somehow (*laughs*). You look so funny!

TROFIMOV (*picks up the telegram*). I've no wish to be a beauty.

LYUBOV. That's a telegram from Paris. I get one every day. One yesterday and one today. That savage creature is ill again, he's in trouble again. He begs forgiveness, beseeches me to go, and really I ought to go to Paris to see him. You look shocked, Petya. What am I to do, my dear boy, what am I to do? He is ill, he is alone and unhappy, and who'll look after him, who'll keep him from doing the wrong thing, who'll give him his medicine at the right time? And why hide it or be silent? I love him, that's clear. I love him! I love him! He's a millstone about my neck, I'm going to the bottom with him, but I love that stone and can't live without it (*presses* TROFIMOV's *hand*). Don't think ill of me, Petya, don't tell me anything, don't tell me . . .

TROFIMOV (*through his tears*). For God's sake forgive my frankness: why, he robbed you!

LYUBOV. No! No! No! You mustn't speak like that (*covers her ears*).

TROFIMOV. He is a wretch! You're the only person that doesn't know it! He's a worthless creature! A despicable wretch!

LYUBOV (*getting angry, but speaking with restraint*). You're twenty-six or twenty-seven years old, but you're still a schoolboy.

TROFIMOV. Possibly.

LYUBOV. You should be a man at your age! You should understand what love means! And you ought to be in love yourself. You ought to fall in love! (*Angrily*) Yes, yes, and it's not purity in you, you're simply a prude, a comic fool, a freak.

TROFIMOV (*in horror*). The things she's saying!

LYUBOV. I am above love! You're not above love, but simply as our Firs here says, "You are a good-for-nothing." At your age not to have a mistress!

TROFIMOV (*in horror*). This is awful! The things she is saying! (*goes rapidly into the larger drawing room clutching his head*). This is awful! I can't stand it! I'm going. (*Goes off, but at once returns.*) All is over between us! (*Goes off into the anteroom.*)

LYUBOV (*shouts after him*). Petya! Wait a minute! You funny creature! I was joking! Petya! (*There is a sound of somebody running quickly downstairs and suddenly falling with a crash.* ANYA *and* VARYA *scream, but there is a sound of laughter at once.*)

LYUBOV. What has happened?

[ANYA *runs in.*]

ANYA (*laughing*). Petya's fallen downstairs! (*Runs out.*)

LYUBOV. What a queer fellow that Petya is!

[*The Station Master stands in the middle of the larger room and reads "The Magdalene," by Alexey Tolstoy. They listen to him, but before he has recited many lines strains of a waltz are heard from the anteroom and the reading is broken off. All dance.* TROFIMOV, ANYA, VARYA *and* LYUBOV ANDREYEVNA *come in from the anteroom.*]

LYUBOV. Come, Petya—come, pure heart! I beg your pardon. Let's have a dance! (*dances with* PETYA).

[ANYA *and* VARYA *dance.* FIRS *comes in, puts his stick down near the side door.* YASHA *also comes into the drawing room and looks on at the dancing.*]

YASHA. What is it, old man?

FIRS. I don't feel well. In old days we used to have generals, barons and admirals dancing at our balls, and now we send for the post office clerk and the station master and even they're not overanxious to come. I am getting feeble. The old master, the grandfather, used to give sealing wax for all complaints. I have been taking sealing wax for twenty years or more. Perhaps that's what's kept me alive.

YASHA. You bore me, old man! (*yawns*) It's time you were done with.

FIRS. Ach, you're a good-for-nothing! (*mutters*)

[TROFIMOV *and* LYUBOV ANDREYEVNA *dance in larger room and then on to the stage.*]

LYUBOV. *Merci.* I'll sit down a little (*sits down*). I'm tired.

[*Enter* ANYA.]

ANYA (*excitedly*). There's a man in the kitchen has been saying that the cherry orchard's been sold today.

LYUBOV. Sold to whom?

ANYA. He didn't say to whom. He's gone away.

[*She dances with* TROFIMOV, *and they go off into the larger room.*]

YASHA. There was an old man gossiping there, a stranger.

FIRS. Leonid Andreyevitch isn't here yet, he hasn't come back. He has his light overcoat on, *demi-saison,* he'll catch cold for sure. Ach! Foolish young things!

LYUBOV. I feel as though I should die. Go, Yasha, find out to whom it has been sold.

YASHA. But he went away long ago, the old chap *(laughs).*

LYUBOV *(with slight vexation).* What are you laughing at? What are you pleased at?

YASHA. Epihodov is so funny. He's a silly fellow, two and twenty misfortunes.

LYUBOV. Firs, if the estate is sold, where will you go?

FIRS. Where you bid me, there I'll go.

LYUBOV. Why do you look like that? Are you ill? You ought to be in bed.

FIRS. Yes *(ironically).* Me go to bed and who's to wait here? Who's to see to things without me? I'm the only one in all the house.

YASHA *(to* LYUBOV ANDREYEVNA*).* Lyubov Andreyevna, permit me to make a request of you; if you go back to Paris again, be so kind as to take me with you. It's positively impossible for me to stay here *(looking about him; in an undertone).* There's no need to say it, you see for yourself—an uncivilized country, the people have no morals, and then the dullness! The food in the kitchen's abominable, and then Firs runs after one muttering all sorts of unsuitable words. Take me with you, please do!

[*Enter* PISHTCHIK.]

PISHTCHIK. Allow me to ask you for a waltz, my dear lady. (LYUBOV ANDREYEVNA *goes with him.*) Enchanting lady, I really must borrow of you just 180 roubles *(dances),* only 180 roubles. *(They pass into the larger room.)*

YASHA *(hums softly).* "Knowest thou my soul's emotion."

[*In the larger drawing room, a figure in a gray top hat and in check trousers is gesticulating and jumping about. Shouts of "Bravo, Charlotta Ivanovna."*]

DUNYASHA *(she has stopped to powder herself).* My young lady tells me to dance. There are plenty of gentlemen, and too few ladies, but dancing makes me giddy and makes my heart beat. Firs, the post office clerk said something to me just now that quite took my breath away.

[*Music becomes more subdued.*]

FIRS. What did he say to you?

DUNYASHA. He said I was like a flower.

YASHA *(yawns).* What ignorance! *(Goes out.)*

DUNYASHA. Like a flower. I am a girl of such delicate feelings, I am awfully fond of soft speeches.

FIRS. Your head's being turned.

[*Enter* EPIHODOV.]

EPIHODOV. You have no desire to see me, Dunyasha. I might be an insect (*sighs*). Ah! life!

DUNYASHA. What is it you want?

EPIHODOV. Undoubtedly you may be right (*sighs*). But of course, if one looks at it from that point of view, if I may so express myself, you have, excuse my plain speaking, reduced me to a complete state of mind. I know my destiny. Every day some misfortune befalls me and I have long ago grown accustomed to it, so that I look upon my fate with a smile. You gave me your word, and though I——

DUNYASHA. Let us have a talk later, I entreat you, but now leave me in peace, for I am lost in reverie (*plays with her fan*).

EPIHODOV. I have a misfortune every day, and if I may venture to express myself, I merely smile at it, I even laugh.

[VARYA *enters from the larger drawing room.*]

VARYA. You still have not gone, Epihodov. What a disrespectful creature you are, really! (*To* DUNYASHA) Go along, Dunyasha! (*To* EPIHODOV) First you play billiards and break the cue, then you go wandering about the drawing room like a visitor!

EPIHODOV. You really cannot, if I may so express myself, call me to account like this.

VARYA. I'm not calling you to account, I'm speaking to you. You do nothing but wander from place to place and don't do your work. We keep you as a counting-house clerk, but what use you are I can't say.

EPIHODOV (*offended*). Whether I work or whether I walk, whether I eat or whether I play billiards, is a matter to be judged by persons of understanding and my elders.

VARYA. You dare to tell me that! (*Firing up*) You dare! You mean to say I've no understanding. Begone from here! This minute!

EPIHODOV (*intimidated*). I beg you to express yourself with delicacy.

VARYA (*beside herself with anger*). This moment! get out! away! (*He goes towards the door, she following him.*) Two and twenty misfortunes! Take yourself off! Don't let me set eyes on you! (EPIHODOV *has gone out, behind the door his voice,* "I shall lodge a complaint against you.") What! You're coming back? (*Snatches up the stick* FIRS *has put down near the door.*) Come! Come! Come! I'll show you! What! You're coming? Then take that! (*She swings the stick, at the very moment that* LOPAHIN *comes in.*)

LOPAHIN. Very much obliged to you!

VARYA (*angrily and ironically*). I beg your pardon!

LOPAHIN. Not at all! I humbly thank you for your kind reception!

VARYA. No need of thanks for it. (*Moves away, then looks round and asks softly*) I haven't hurt you?

LOPAHIN. Oh, no! Not at all! There's an immense bump coming up, though!

VOICES FROM LARGER ROOM. Lopahin has come! Yermolay Alexeyevitch!

PISHTCHIK. What do I see and hear? (*Kisses* LOPAHIN.) There's a whiff of cognac about you, my dear soul, and we're making merry here too!

[*Enter* LYUBOV ANDREYEVNA.]

LYUBOV. Is it you, Yermolay Alexeyevitch? Why have you been so long? Where's Leonid?

LOPAHIN. Leonid Andreyevitch arrived with me. He is coming.

LYUBOV (*in agitation*). Well! Well! Was there a sale? Speak!

LOPAHIN (*embarrassed, afraid of betraying his joy*). The sale was over at four o'clock. We missed our train—had to wait till half-past nine. (*Sighing heavily*) Ugh! I feel a little giddy.

[*Enter* GAEV. *In his right hand he has purchases, with his left hand he is wiping away his tears.*]

LYUBOV. Well, Leonid? What news? (*Impatiently, with tears*) Make haste, for God's sake!

GAEV (*makes her no answer, simply waves his hand. To* FIRS, *weeping*) Here, take them; there's anchovies, Kertch herrings. I have eaten nothing all day. What I have been through! (*Door into the billiard room is open. There is heard a knocking of balls and the voice of* YASHA *saying "Eighty-seven."* GAEV'S *expression changes, he leaves off weeping*). I am fearfully tired. Firs, come and help me change my things (*goes to his own room across the larger drawing room*).

PISHTCHIK. How about the sale? Tell us, do!

LYUBOV. Is the cherry orchard sold?

LOPAHIN. It is sold.

LYUBOV. Who has bought it?

LOPAHIN. I have bought it. (*A pause.* LYUBOV *is crushed; she would fall down if she were not standing near a chair and table.*)

[VARYA *takes keys from her waistband, flings them on the floor in middle of drawing room and goes out.*]

LOPAHIN. I have bought it! Wait a bit, ladies and gentlemen, pray. My head's a bit muddled, I can't speak (*laughs*). We came to the auction. Deriganov was there already. Leonid Andreyevitch only had 15,000 and Deriganov bid 30,000, besides the arrears, straight off. I saw how the land lay. I bid against him. I bid 40,000, he bid 45,000, I said 55, and so he went on, adding 5 thousands and I adding 10. Well . . . So it ended. I bid 90, and it was knocked down to me. Now the cherry orchard's mine! Mine! (*chuckles*) My God, the cherry orchard's mine! Tell me that I'm drunk, that I'm out of my mind, that it's all a dream (*stamps with his feet*).

Don't laugh at me! If my father and my grandfather could rise from their graves and see all that has happened! How their Yermolay, ignorant, beaten Yermolay, who used to run about barefoot in winter, how that very Yermolay has bought the finest estate in the world! I have bought the estate where my father and grandfather were slaves, where they weren't even admitted into the kitchen. I am asleep, I am dreaming! It is all fancy, it is the work of your imagination plunged in the darkness of ignorance (*picks up keys, smiling fondly*). She threw away the keys; she means to show she's not the housewife now (*jingles the keys*). Well, no matter. (*The orchestra is heard tuning up.*) Hey, musicians! Play! I want to hear you. Come, all of you, and look how Yermolay Lopahin will take the axe to the cherry orchard, how the trees will fall to the ground! We will build houses on it and our grandsons and great-grandsons will see a new life springing up there. Music! Play up!

[*Music begins to play.* LYUBOV ANDREYEVNA *has sunk into a chair and is weeping bitterly.*]

LOPAHIN (*reproachfully*). Why, why didn't you listen to me? My poor friend! Dear lady, there's no turning back now. (*With tears*) Oh, if all this could be over, oh, if our miserable disjointed life could somehow soon be changed!

PISHTCHIK (*takes him by the arm, in an undertone*). She's weeping, let us go and leave her alone. Come (*takes him by the arm and leads him into the larger drawing room*).

LOPAHIN. What's that? Musicians, play up! All must be as I wish it. (*With irony*) Here comes the new master, the owner of the cherry orchard! (*Accidentally tips over a little table, almost upsetting the candelabra.*) I can pay for everything! (*Goes out with* PISHTCHIK. *No one remains on the stage or in the larger drawing room except* LYUBOV, *who sits huddled up, weeping bitterly. The music plays softly.* ANYA *and* TROFIMOV *come in quickly.* ANYA *goes up to her mother and falls on her knees before her.* TROFIMOV *stands at the entrance to the larger drawing room.*)

ANYA. Mamma! Mamma, you're crying, dear, kind, good mamma! My precious! I love you! I bless you! The cherry orchard is sold, it is gone, that's true, that's true! But don't weep, mamma! Life is still before you, you have still your good, pure heart! Let us go, let us go, darling, away from here! We will make a new garden, more splendid than this one; you will see it, you will understand. And joy, quiet, deep joy, will sink into your soul like the sun at evening! And you will smile, mamma! Come, darling, let us go!

ACT IV

⌐§ Scene: *Same as in First Act. There are neither curtains on the windows nor pictures on the walls: only a little furniture remains piled up in a corner as if for sale. There is a sense of desolation; near the outer door and in the background of the scene are packed trunks, travelling bags, etc. On the left the door is open, and from here the voices of* VARYA *and* ANYA *are audible.* LOPAHIN *is standing waiting.* YASHA *is holding a tray with glasses full of champagne. In front of the stage* EPIHODOV *is tying up a box. In the background behind the scene a hum of talk from the peasants who have come to say good-by. The voice of* GAEV: "Thanks, brothers, thanks!"*

YASHA. The peasants have come to say good-by. In my opinion, Yermo-lay Alexeyevitch, the peasants are good-natured, but they don't know much about things.
> [*The hum of talk dies away. Enter across front of stage* LYUBOV ANDREYEVNA *and* GAEV. *She is not weeping, but is pale; her face is quivering—she cannot speak.*]

GAEV. You gave them your purse, Lyuba. That won't do—that won't do!

LYUBOV. I couldn't help it! I couldn't help it!
> [*Both go out.*]

LOPAHIN (*in the doorway, calls after them*). You will take a glass at parting? Please do. I didn't think to bring any from the town, and at the station I could only get one bottle. Please take a glass (*a pause*). What? You don't care for any? (*Comes away from the door*) If I'd known, I wouldn't have bought it. Well, and I'm not

going to drink it. (YASHA *carefully sets the tray down on a chair.*)
You have a glass, Yasha, anyway.

YASHA. Good luck to the travelers, and luck to those that stay behind!
(*drinks*) This champagne isn't the real thing, I can assure you.

LOPAHIN. It cost eight roubles the bottle (*a pause*). It's devilish cold
here.

YASHA. They haven't heated the stove today—it's all the same since
we're going (*laughs*).

LOPAHIN. What are you laughing for?

YASHA. For pleasure.

LOPAHIN. Though it's October, it's as still and sunny as though it were
summer. It's just right for building! (*Looks at his watch; says in
doorway*) Take note, ladies and gentlemen, the train goes in forty-
seven minutes; so you ought to start for the station in twenty minutes. You must hurry up!

> [TROFIMOV *comes in from out of doors wearing a
> greatcoat.*]

TROFIMOV. I think it must be time to start, the horses are ready. The
devil only knows what's become of my galoshes; they're lost. (*In
the doorway*) Anya! My galoshes aren't here. I can't find them.

LOPAHIN. And I'm getting off to Harkov. I am going in the same train
with you. I'm spending all the winter at Harkov. I've been wasting
all my time gossiping with you and fretting with no work to do.
I can't get on without work. I don't know what to do with my
hands, they flap about so queerly, as if they didn't belong to me.

TROFIMOV. Well, we're just going away, and you will take up your
profitable labours again.

LOPAHIN. Do take a glass.

TROFIMOV. No, thanks.

LOPAHIN. Then you're going to Moscow now?

TROFIMOV. Yes. I shall see them as far as the town, and tomorrow I
shall go on to Moscow.

LOPAHIN. Yes, I daresay, the professors aren't giving any lectures,
they're waiting for your arrival.

TROFIMOV. That's not your business.

LOPAHIN. How many years have you been at the University?

TROFIMOV. Do think of something newer than that—that's stale and
flat (*hunts for galoshes*). You know we shall most likely never see
each other again, so let me give you one piece of advice at parting:
don't wave your arms about—get out of the habit. And another
thing, building villas, reckoning up that the summer visitors will
in time become independent farmers—reckoning like that, that's
not the thing to do either. After all, I am fond of you: you have
fine delicate fingers like an artist, you've a fine delicate soul.

LOPAHIN (*embraces him*). Good-by, my dear fellow. Thanks for everything. Let me give you money for the journey, if you need it.

TROFIMOV. What for? I don't need it.

LOPAHIN. Why, you haven't got a halfpenny.

TROFIMOV. Yes, I have, thank you. I got some money for a translation. Here it is in my pocket, (*anxiously*) but where can my galoshes be!

VARYA (*from the next room*). Take the nasty things! (*Flings a pair of galoshes on to the stage.*)

TROFIMOV. Why are you so cross, Varya? h'm! . . . but those aren't my galoshes.

LOPAHIN. I sowed three thousand acres with poppies in the spring, and now I have cleared forty thousand profit. And when my poppies were in flower, wasn't it a picture! So here, as I say, I made forty thousand, and I'm offering you a loan because I can afford to. Why turn up your nose? I am a peasant—I speak bluntly.

TROFIMOV. Your father was a peasant, mine was a chemist—and that proves absolutely nothing whatever. (LOPAHIN *takes out his pocketbook.*) Stop that—stop that. If you were to offer me two hundred thousand I wouldn't take it. I am an independent man, and everything that all of you, rich and poor alike, prize so highly and hold so dear, hasn't the slightest power over me—it's like so much fluff fluttering in the air. I can get on without you. I can pass by you. I am strong and proud. Humanity is advancing towards the highest truth, the highest happiness, which is possible on earth, and I am in the front ranks.

LOPAHIN. Will you get there?

TROFIMOV. I shall get there (*a pause*). I shall get there, or I shall show others the way to get there.

> [*In the distance is heard the stroke of an axe on a tree.*]

LOPAHIN. Good-by, my dear fellow; it's time to be off. We turn up our noses at one another, but life is passing all the while. When I am working hard without resting, then my mind is more at ease, and it seems to me as though I too know what I exist for; but how many people there are in Russia, my dear boy, who exist, one doesn't know what for. Well, it doesn't matter. That's not what keeps things spinning. They tell me Leonid Andreyevitch has taken a situation. He is going to be a clerk at the bank—6,000 roubles a year. Only, of course, he won't stick to it—he's too lazy.

ANYA (*in the doorway*). Mamma begs you not to let them chop down the orchard until she's gone.

TROFIMOV. Yes, really, you might have the tact (*walks out across the front of the stage*).

LOPAHIN. I'll see to it! I'll see to it! Stupid fellows! (*Goes out after him.*)

ANYA. Has Firs been taken to the hospital?

YASHA. I told them this morning. No doubt they have taken him.

ANYA (*to* EPIHODOV, *who passes across the drawing room*). Semyon Pantaleyevitch, inquire, please, if Firs has been taken to the hospital.

YASHA (*in a tone of offense*). I told Yegor this morning—why ask a dozen times?

EPIHODOV. Firs is advanced in years. It's my conclusive opinion no treatment would do him good; it's time he was gathered to his fathers. And I can only envy him (*puts a trunk down on a cardboard hatbox and crushes it*). There, now, of course—I knew it would be so.

YASHA (*jeeringly*). Two and twenty misfortunes!

VARYA (*through the door*). Has Firs been taken to the hospital?

ANYA. Yes.

VARYA. Why wasn't the note for the doctor taken too?

ANYA (*from the adjoining room*). Where's Yasha? Tell him his mother's come to say good-by to him.

YASHA (*waves his hand*). They put me out of all patience! (DUNYASHA *has all this time been busy about the luggage. Now, when* YASHA *is left alone, she goes up to him*).

DUNYASHA. You might just give me one look, Yasha. You're going away. You're leaving me (*weeps and throws herself on his neck*).

YASHA. What are you crying for? (*drinks the champagne*). In six days I shall be in Paris again. Tomorrow we shall get into the express train and roll away in a flash. I can scarcely believe it! *Vive la France!* It doesn't suit me here—it's not the life for me; there's no doing anything. I have seen enough of the ignorance here. I have had enough of it (*drinks champagne*). What are you crying for? Behave yourself properly, and then you won't cry.

DUNYASHA (*powders her face, looking in a pocket mirror*). Do send me a letter from Paris. You know how I loved you, Yasha—how I loved you! I am a tender creature, Yasha.

YASHA. Here they are coming!

[*Busies himself about the trunks, humming softly.*

Enter LYUBOV ANDREYEVNA, GAEV, ANYA *and* CHAR-
LOTTA IVANOVNA.]

GAEV. We ought to be off. There's not much time now (*looking at* YASHA). What a smell of herrings!

LYUBOV. In ten minutes we must get into the carriage (*casts a look about the room*). Farewell, dear house, dear old home of our fathers! Winter will pass and spring will come, and then you will be no more; they will tear you down! How much those walls have seen! (*Kisses her daughter passionately.*) My treasure, how bright you look! Your eyes are sparkling like diamonds! Are you glad? Very glad?

ANYA. Very glad! A new life is beginning, mamma.

GAEV. Yes, really, everything is all right now. Before the cherry orchard was sold, we were all worried and wretched, but afterwards,
when once the question was settled conclusively, irrevocably, we
all felt calm and even cheerful. I am a bank clerk now—I am a
financier—cannon off the red. And you, Lyuba, after all, you are
looking better; there's no question of that.

LYUBOV. Yes. My nerves are better, that's true. (*Her hat and coat are
handed to her.*) I'm sleeping well. Carry out my things, Yasha. It's
time. (*To* ANYA) My darling, we shall soon see each other again.
I am going to Paris. I can live there on the money your Yaroslavl
auntie sent us to buy the estate with—hurrah for auntie!—but that
money won't last long.

ANYA. You'll come back soon, mamma, won't you? I'll be working up
for my examination in the high school, and when I have passed
that, I shall set to work and be a help to you. We will read all
sorts of things together, mamma, won't we? (*Kisses her mother's
hands.*) We will read in the autumn evenings. We'll read lots of
books, and a new wonderful world will open out before us (*dreamily*). Mamma, come soon.

LYUBOV. I shall come, my precious treasure (*embraces her*).

[*Enter* LOPAHIN. CHARLOTTA *softly hums a song.*]

GAEV. Charlotta's happy; she's singing!

CHARLOTTA (*picks up a bundle like a swaddled baby*). By, by, my
baby. (*A baby is heard crying: "Ooah! ooah!"*) Hush, hush, my
pretty boy! (*Ooah! ooah!*) Poor little thing! (*Throws the bundle
back.*) You must please find me a situation. I can't go on like this.

LOPAHIN. We'll find you one, Charlotta Ivanovna. Don't you worry
yourself.

GAEV. Everyone's leaving us. Varya's going away. We have become of
no use all at once.

CHARLOTTA. There's nowhere for me to be in the town. I must go away.
(*Hums*) What care I . . .

[*Enter* PISHTCHIK.]

LOPAHIN. The freak of nature!

PISHTCHIK (*gasping*). Oh! . . . let me get my breath. . . . I'm worn
out . . . my most honoured . . . Give me some water.

GAEV. Want some money, I suppose? Your humble servant! I'll go
out of the way of temptation (*goes out*).

PISHTCHIK. It's a long while since I have been to see you . . . dearest
lady. (*To* LOPAHIN) You are here . . . glad to see you . . . a man
of immense intellect . . . take . . . here (*gives* LOPAHIN) 400 roubles. That leaves me owing 840.

LOPAHIN (*shrugging his shoulders in amazement*). It's like a dream.
Where did you get it?

PISHTCHIK. Wait a bit . . . I'm hot . . . a most extraordinary occurrence! Some Englishmen came along and found in my land some
sort of white clay. (*To* LYUBOV ANDREYEVNA) And 400 for you . . .
most lovely . . . wonderful (*gives money*). The rest later (*sips
water*). A young man in the train was telling me just now that a
great philosopher advises jumping off a housetop. "Jump!" says he;
"the whole gist of the problem lies in that." (*Wonderingly*) Fancy
that, now! Water, please!

LOPAHIN. What Englishmen?

PISHTCHIK. I have made over to them the rights to dig the clay for
twenty-four years . . . and now, excuse me . . . I can't stay . . .
I must be trotting on. I'm going to Znoikovo . . . to Kardamanovo.
. . . I'm in debt all round (*sips*). . . . To your very good health!
. . . I'll come in on Thursday.

LYUBOV. We are just off to the town, and tomorrow I start for abroad.

PISHTCHIK. What! (*In agitation*) Why to the town? Oh, I see the
furniture . . . the boxes. No matter . . . (*through his tears*) . . .
no matter . . . men of enormous intellect . . . these Englishmen.
. . . Never mind . . . be happy. God will succor you . . . no
matter . . . everything in this world must have an end (*kisses*
LYUBOV ANDREYEVNA'S *hand*). If the rumour reaches you that my
end has come, think of this . . . old horse, and say: "There once
was such a man in the world . . . Semyonov-Pishtchik . . . the
Kingdom of Heaven be his!" . . . most extraordinary weather . . .
yes. (*Goes out in violent agitation, but as once returns and says in
the doorway*) Dashenka wishes to be remembered to you (*goes
out*).

LYUBOV. Now we can start. I leave with two cares in my heart. The
first is leaving Firs ill. (*Looking at her watch*) We have still five
minutes.

ANYA. Mamma, Firs has been taken to the hospital. Yasha sent him
off this morning.

LYUBOV. My other anxiety is Varya. She is used to getting up early
and working; and now, without work, she's like a fish out of water.
She is thin and pale, and she's crying, poor dear! (*a pause*) You
are well aware, Yermolay Alexeyevitch, I dreamed of marrying her
to you, and everything seemed to show that you would get married
(*whispers to* ANYA *and motions to* CHARLOTTA *and both go out*).
She loves you—she suits you. And I don't know—I don't know
why it is you seem, as it were, to avoid each other. I can't understand it!

LOPAHIN. I don't understand it myself, I confess. It's queer somehow,
altogether. If there's still time, I'm ready now at once. Let's settle
it straight off, and go ahead; but without you, I feel I shan't make
her an offer.

LYUBOV. That's excellent. Why, a single moment's all that's necessary.
I'll call her at once.

LOPAHIN. And there's champagne all ready too (*looking into the glasses*). Empty! Someone's emptied them already. (YASHA *coughs.*)
I call that greedy.

LYUBOV (*eagerly*). Capital! We will go out. Yasha, *allez!* I'll call her
in. (*At the door*) Varya, leave all that; come here. Come along!
(*goes out with* YASHA).

LOPAHIN (*looking at his watch*). Yes.

> [*A pause. Behind the door, smothered laughter and
> whispering, and, at last, enter* VARYA.]

VARYA (*looking a long while over the things*). It is strange, I can't find
it anywhere.

LOPAHIN. What are you looking for?

VARYA. I packed it myself, and I can't remember (*a pause*).

LOPAHIN. Where are you going now, Varvara Mihailova?

VARYA. I? To the Ragulins. I have arranged to go to them to look after
the house—as a housekeeper.

LOPAHIN. That's in Yashnovo? It'll be seventy miles away (*a pause*).
So this is the end of life in this house!

VARYA (*looking among the things*). Where is it? Perhaps I put it in
the trunk. Yes, life in this house is over—there will be no more of it.

LOPAHIN. And I'm just off to Harkov—by this next train. I've a lot
of business there. I'm leaving Epihodov here, and I've taken him on.

VARYA. Really!

LOPAHIN. This time last year we had snow already, if you remember;
but now it's so fine and sunny. Though it's cold, to be sure—three
degrees of frost.

VARYA. I haven't looked (*a pause*). And besides, our thermometer's
broken (*a pause*).

> [*Voice at the door from the yard:* "Yermolay Alex-
> eyevitch!"]

LOPAHIN (*as though he had long been expecting this summons*). This
minute!

> [LOPAHIN *goes out quickly.* VARYA *sitting on the floor
> and laying her head on a bag full of clothes, sobs
> quietly. The door opens.* LYUBOV ANDREYEVNA *comes
> in cautiously.*]

LYUBOV. Well? (*a pause*) We must be going.

VARYA (*has wiped her eyes and is no longer crying*). Yes, mamma,
it's time to start. I shall have time to get to the Ragulins today, if
only you're not late for the train.

LYUBOV (*in the doorway*). Anya, put your things on.

> [*Enter* ANYA, *then* GAEV *and* CHARLOTTA IVANOVNA.

GAEV *has on a warm coat with a hood. Servants and cabmen come in.* EPIHODOV *bustles about the luggage.*]

LYUBOV. Now we can start on our travels.

ANYA (*joyfully*). On our travels!

GAEV. My friends—my dear, my precious friends! Leaving this house forever, can I be silent? Can I refrain from giving utterance at leave-taking to those emotions which now flood all my being?

ANYA (*supplicatingly*). Uncle!

VARYA. Uncle, you mustn't!

GAEV (*dejectedly*). Cannon and into the pocket . . . I'll be quiet. . . .

[*Enter* TROFIMOV *and afterwards* LOPAHIN.]

TROFIMOV. Well, ladies and gentlemen, we must start.

LOPAHIN. Epihodov, my coat!

LYUBOV. I'll stay just one minute. It seems as though I have never seen before what the walls, what the ceilings in this house were like, and now I look at them with greediness, with such tender love.

GAEV. I remember when I was six years old sitting in that window on Trinity Day watching my father going to church.

LYUBOV. Have all the things been taken?

LOPAHIN. I think all. (*Putting on overcoat, to* EPIHODOV) You, Epihodov, mind you see everything is right.

EPIHODOV (*in a husky voice*). Don't you trouble, Yermolay Alexeyevitch.

LOPAHIN. Why, what's wrong with your voice?

EPIHODOV. I've just had a drink of water, and I choked over something.

YASHA (*contemptuously*). The ignorance!

LYUBOV. We are going—and not a soul will be left here.

LOPAHIN. Not till the spring.

VARYA (*pulls a parasol out of a bundle, as though about to hit someone with it.* LOPAHIN *makes a gesture as though alarmed*). What is it? I didn't mean anything.

TROFIMOV. Ladies and gentlemen, let us get into the carriage. It's time. The train will be in directly.

VARYA. Petya, here they are, your galoshes, by that box. (*With tears*) And what dirty old things they are!

TROFIMOV (*putting on his galoshes*). Let us go, friends!

GAEV (*greatly agitated, afraid of weeping*). The train—the station! Double balk, ah!

LYUBOV. Let us go!

LOPAHIN. Are we all here? (*Locks the side door on left.*) The things are all here. We must lock up. Let us go!

ANYA. Good-by, home! Good-by to the old life!

TROFIMOV. Welcome to the new life!

[TROFIMOV *goes out with* ANYA. VARYA *looks round
the room and goes out slowly.* YASHA *and* CHARLOTTA
IVANOVNA, *with her dog, go out.*]

LOPAHIN. Till the spring, then! Come, friends, till we meet! (*Goes out.*)

[LYUBOV ANDREYEVNA *and* GAEV *remain alone. As
though they had been waiting for this, they throw
themselves on each other's necks, and break into
subdued smothered sobbing, afraid of being over-
heard.*]

GAEV (*in despair*). Sister, my sister!

LYUBOV. Oh, my orchard!—my sweet, beautiful orchard! My life, my
youth, my happiness, good-by! good-by!

VOICE OF ANYA (*calling gaily*). Mamma!

VOICE OF TROFIMOV (*gaily, excitedly*). Aa—oo!

LYUBOV. One last look at the walls, at the windows. My dear mother
loved to walk about this room.

GAEV. Sister, sister!

VOICE OF ANYA. Mamma!

VOICE OF TROFIMOV. Aa—oo!

LYUBOV. We are coming. (*They go out.*)

[*The stage is empty. There is the sound of the doors
being locked up, then of the carriages driving away.
There is silence. In the stillness there is the dull stroke
of an axe in a tree, clanging with a mournful lonely
sound. Footsteps are heard.* FIRS *appears in the doorway on the right. He is dressed as always—in a pea
jacket and white waistcoat with slippers on his feet.
He is ill.*]

FIRS (*goes up to the doors, and tries the handles*). Locked! They have
gone . . . (*sits down on sofa*). They have forgotten me. . . .
Never mind . . . I'll sit here a bit. . . . I'll be bound Leonid
Andreyevitch hasn't put his fur coat on and has gone off in his thin
overcoat (*sighs anxiously*). I didn't see after him. . . . These young
people . . . (*mutters something that can't be distinguished*). Life
has slipped by as though I hadn't lived. (*Lies down*) I'll lie down a
bit. . . . There's no strength in you, nothing left you—all gone!
Ech! I'm good for nothing (*lies motionless*).

[*A sound is heard that seems to come from the sky,
like a breaking harp string, dying away mournfully.
All is still again, and there is heard nothing but the
strokes of the axe far away in the orchard.*]

QUESTIONS

ACT I

1. The play begins with a series of trivial acts such as missing a train, dropping some flowers, and bumping into a chair. What do these actions, and others like them, tell us about the characters and their ability to deal with life?
2. Do the things they say correspond with their actions?
3. Ordinarily, dramatic dialogue proceeds with the different characters commenting on or developing a single subject—the topic of conversation. This is not Chekhov's way, however. Describe the manner in which his dialogue works.
4. How does this peculiar type of dialogue make real, or bring into being, the inner life of the characters?
5. Is the deaf Firs an appropriate servant for this family?
6. Would an apple orchard or a wild wood be equally effective as a symbol of the society of which these people are a part?
7. Once the characters and the orchard are identified as different forms of the same society, what information provided about the orchard tells us something about the people who own it?

ACT II

8. How is the larger world, the reality existing outside the orchard, brought into being? What is its nature?
9. The family has gathered around itself a number of friends and retainers such as Trofimov, Lopahin, and Charlotta. Do these people tell us anything about the family to which they have attached themselves?
10. Do the occupations of each of these people suggest anything about the makeup of society—about its source of energy and direction?
11. In the plays you have read so far the chief characters always have a definite motive; they want to do something desperately and their whole being is directed toward that end. Can this be said of the characters in *The Cherry Orchard*? If so, must their motives be distinguished from the usual kind of dramatic motive?
12. Most of the characters are fond of philosophizing, and in their rambling discourses they say a good deal about their understanding of life. Do they explain in these speeches what is missing in their lives? what has happened to their vitality and drive?
13. How do the characters attempt to explain the "breaking harp string" heard in the distance? Are their explanations sufficient?
14. Is Lyubov really the sinner she believes herself to be? Does sin account for her present situation?

ACT III

15. How does the play express the movement of time? Do the characters understand time correctly? Consider their tendency to reminisce.

16. How many love affairs are in the play? Take into account those that are only mentioned. What do these loves have in common?

17. Does the play contain any representatives of a "new order"? Are they encouraging omens for the future?

18. Look carefully at all the actions at the party. Would the meaning of events here and the nature of the characters still be evident if the scene were "mimed," that is, acted out without words?

19. After answering the above question look at the speeches of the characters and see how (a) they support the actions, and (b) they extend their meaning. Could the language be eliminated without loss?

20. Does the destruction of the orchard to make room for a "housing development" suggest that *The Cherry Orchard* is not only presenting the lives of a number of people but also describing a well-known historical and social change? What other evidence of this historical movement does the play offer?

ACT IV

21. What significance does the sound of the axe striking the trees have? In answering this question consider the peculiar nature of this sound.

22. There is a good deal of talk in the departure scene about beginning a new and more successful life of work and love. How is it made clear that these hopes are vain?

23. Does the abandonment of Firs at the end of the play force us to take these people somewhat more seriously? This is the last event of the play, the revelation of plot. Looking back on the play, can we say that what is shown here in striking form has really been occurring all along?

24. The final scene is made up of an image and a sound: an old man lying on a couch in a chilling house and the thud of an axe biting into a cherry tree. Are the dying man and the dying orchard connected in any way?

25. Did the family *intend* to leave Firs behind? Is this characteristic? Was the orchard "left behind" for the same reasons?

26. Chekhov sometimes referred to *The Cherry Orchard* as a tragedy, but on the title page he calls it a comedy. Can you see why he might be confused? Is it comedy or tragedy?

RIDERS
TO THE SEA

BY

JOHN MILLINGTON SYNGE

John Synge (1871–1909) was an Irishman who was educated at Trinity College, Dublin. He spent several years in France and Germany writing literary criticism and was apparently headed toward a career of writing about literature and art. But then he met the great Irish poet William Butler Yeats, who persuaded him of his destiny as a poet-dramatist and convinced him that the sources of great literature were to be found not in the sophisticated cities of Europe but in the villages and countryside of Ireland, where language was still vital and where the people still were in contact with the great powers of nature—of the sky, the earth, and the sea. Synge returned to Ireland and went to live for a while among the people of the Aran Islands, and then after a time moved to Dublin, where he devoted the remainder of his life to writing a series of plays: *In the Shadow of the Glen* (1903), his masterpiece *Riders to the Sea* (1904), *The Well of the Saints* (1905), *The Playboy of the Western World* (1907), *The Tinker's Wedding* (1908), and the unfinished *Deirdre of the Sorrows*. Along with Yeats and Lady Gregory, Synge was one of the organizers of the famous Abbey Theater and one of the stalwarts in the attempt to establish an Irish national drama and theater. Most of his plays were produced at the Abbey, and it was there during the presentation of *The Playboy of the Western World* that the patriotic audience stormed the stage and wrecked the theater in indignation at the play's humorous and sarcastic treatment of certain aspects of the Irish character.

In his poem "In Memory of Major Robert Gregory," Yeats is musing over the men he has known who are now dead when the image of Synge comes into his mind:

> And that enquiring man John Synge comes next,
> That dying chose the living world for text
> And never could have rested in the tomb
> But that, long traveling, he had come
> Towards nightfall upon certain set apart
> In a most desolate stony place,
> Towards nightfall upon a race
> Passionate and simple like his heart.

That "desolate stony place" was the Aran Islands and the setting for *Riders to the Sea,* where both the islanders and the characters are, like Synge, "passionate and simple." This mixture of passion and simplicity is exactly the effect that Synge strove for and achieved in his works. He called it a mixture of imagination and realism, and in his Preface to *The Playboy of the Western World,* he explains why this essence of great poetry is to be found in Ireland: "In countries where the imagination of the people, and the language they use, is rich and living, it is possible for a writer to be rich and copious in his words, and at the same time to give the reality, which is the root of all poetry, in a comprehensive and natural form." When manifested in dramatic speech, at once poetry and prose, this concept yields a language unbelievably simple and direct and yet resonant and full of emotion and a sense of the powers of the world: "How would he go the length of that way to the far north?" and "She's passing the green head and letting fall her sails," and "There were Stephen, and Shawn, were lost in the great wind, and found after in the Bay of Gregory of the Golden Mouth, and carried up the two of them on the one plank, and in by that door."

CHARACTERS

MAURYA, *an old woman*
BARTLEY, *her son*
CATHLEEN, *her daughter*
NORA, *a younger daughter*
MEN AND WOMEN

୫ Scene: *An island off the West of Ireland.*

Cottage kitchen, with nets, oilskins, spinning wheel, some new boards standing by the wall, etc. Cathleen, a girl of about twenty, finishes kneading cake, and puts it down in the pot-oven by the fire; then wipes her hands, and begins to spin at the wheel. Nora, a young girl, puts her head in at the door.

NORA (*in a low voice*). Where is she?

CATHLEEN. She's lying down, God help her, and may be sleeping, if she's able.

> [NORA *comes in softly, and takes a bundle from under her shawl.*]

CATHLEEN (*spinning the wheel rapidly*). What is it you have?

NORA. The young priest is after bringing them. It's a shirt and a plain stocking were got off a drowned man in Donegal.

> [CATHLEEN *stops her wheel with a sudden movement, and leans out to listen.*]

NORA. We're to find out if it's Michael's they are, some time herself will be down looking by the sea.

CATHLEEN. How would they be Michael's, Nora. How would he go the length of that way to the far north?

NORA. The young priest says he's known like of it. "If it's Michael's they are," says he, "you can tell herself he's got a clean burial by the grace of God, and if they're not his, let no one say a word about them, for she'll be getting her death," says he, "with crying and lamenting."

> [*The door which* NORA *half closed is blown open by a gust of wind.*]

CATHLEEN (*looking out anxiously*). Did you ask him would he stop
Bartley going this day with the horses to the Galway fair?

NORA. "I won't stop him," says he, "but let you not be afraid. Herself
does be saying prayers half through the night, and the Almighty
God won't leave her destitute," says he, "with no son living."

CATHLEEN. Is the sea bad by the white rocks, Nora?

NORA. Middling bad, God help us. There's a great roaring in the west,
and it's worse it'll be getting when the tide's turned to the wind.
(*She goes over to the table with the bundle.*) Shall I open it now?

CATHLEEN. Maybe she'd wake up on us, and come in before we'd
done. (*Coming to the table*) It's a long time we'll be, and the two
of us crying.

NORA (*goes to the inner door and listens*). She's moving about on the
bed. She'll be coming in a minute.

CATHLEEN. Give me the ladder, and I'll put them up in the turf-loft,
the way she won't know of them at all, and maybe when the tide
turns she'll be going down to see would he be floating from the
east.

> [*They put the ladder against the gable of the chim-
> ney;* CATHLEEN *goes up a few steps and hides the
> bundle in the turf-loft.* MAURYA *comes from the inner
> room.*]

MAURYA (*looking up at* CATHLEEN *and speaking querulously*). Isn't
it turf enough you have for this day and evening?

CATHLEEN. There's a cake baking at the fire for a short space (*throwing down the turf*) and Bartley will want it when the tide turns if he
goes to Connemara.

> [NORA *picks up the turf and puts it round the pot-
> oven.*]

MAURYA (*sitting down on a stool at the fire*). He won't go this day
with the wind rising from the south and west. He won't go this day,
for the young priest will stop him surely.

NORA. He'll not stop him, mother, and I heard Eamon Simon and
Stephen Pheety and Colum Shawn saying he would go.

MAURYA. Where is he itself?

NORA. He went down to see would there be another boat sailing in
the week, and I'm thinking it won't be long till he's here now, for
the tide's turning at the green head, and the hooker's tacking from
the east.

CATHLEEN. I hear some one passing the big stones.

NORA (*looking out*). He's coming now, and he in a hurry.

BARTLEY (*comes in and looks round the room. Speaking sadly and
quietly*). Where is the bit of new rope, Cathleen, was bought in
Connemara?

CATHLEEN (*coming down*). Give it to him, Nora; it's on a nail by the white boards. I hung it up this morning, for the pig with the black feet was eating it.

NORA (*giving him a rope*). Is that it, Bartley?

MAURYA. You'd do right to leave that rope, Bartley, hanging by the boards. (BARTLEY *takes the rope.*) It will be wanting in this place, I'm telling you, if Michael is washed up to-morrow morning, or the next morning, or any morning in the week, for it's a deep grave we'll make him by the grace of God.

BARTLEY (*beginning to work with the rope*). I've no halter the way I can ride down on the mare, and I must go now quickly. This is the one boat going for two weeks or beyond it, and the fair will be a good fair for horses I heard them saying below.

MAURYA. It's a hard thing they'll be saying below if the body is washed up and there's no man in it to make the coffin, and I after giving a big price for the finest white boards you'd find in Connemara. (*She looks round at the boards.*)

BARTLEY. How would it be washed up, and we after looking each day for nine days, and a strong wind blowing a while back from the west and south?

MAURYA. If it wasn't found itself, that wind is raising the sea, and there was a star up against the moon, and it rising in the night. If it was a hundred horses, or a thousand horses you had itself, what is the price of a thousand horses against a son where there is one son only?

BARTLEY (*working at the halter, to* CATHLEEN). Let you go down each day, and see the sheep aren't jumping in on the rye, and if the jobber comes you can sell the pig with the black feet if there is a good price going.

MAURYA. How would the like of her get a good price for a pig?

BARTLEY (*to* CATHLEEN). If the west wind holds with the last bit of the moon let you and Nora get up weed enough for another cock for the kelp. It's hard set we'll be from this day with no one in it but one man to work.

MAURYA. It's hard set we'll be surely the day you're drownd'd with the rest. What way will I live and the girls with me, and I an old woman looking for the grave?

[BARTLEY *lays down the halter, takes off his old coat, and puts on a newer one of the same flannel.*]

BARTLEY (*to* NORA). Is she coming to the pier?

NORA (*looking out*). She's passing the green head and letting fall her sails.

BARTLEY (*getting his purse and tobacco*). I'll have half an hour to go down, and you'll see me coming again in two days, or in three days, or maybe in four days if the wind is bad.

MAURYA (*turning round to the fire, and putting her shawl over her head*). Isn't it a hard and cruel man won't hear a word from an old woman, and she holding him from the sea?

CATHLEEN. It's the life of a young man to be going on the sea, and who would listen to an old woman with one thing and she saying it over?

BARTLEY (*taking the halter*). I must go now quickly. I'll ride down on the red mare, and the gray pony 'll run behind me. . . . The blessing of God on you. (*He goes out.*)

MAURYA (*crying out as he is in the door*). He's gone now, God spare us, and we'll not see him again. He's gone now, and when the black night is falling I'll have no son left me in the world.

CATHLEEN. Why wouldn't you give him your blessing and he looking round in the door? Isn't it sorrow enough is on every one in this house without your sending him out with an unlucky word behind him, and a hard word in his ear?

[MAURYA *takes up the tongs and begins raking the fire aimlessly without looking round.*]

NORA (*turning towards her*). You're taking away the turf from the cake.

CATHLEEN (*crying out*). The Son of God forgive us, Nora, we're after forgetting his bit of bread. (*She comes over to the fire.*)

NORA. And it's destroyed he'll be going till dark night, and he after eating nothing since the sun went up.

CATHLEEN (*turning the cake out of the oven*). It's destroyed he'll be, surely. There's no sense left on any person in a house where an old woman will be talking for ever.

[MAURYA *sways herself on her stool.*]

CATHLEEN (*cutting off some of the bread and rolling it in a cloth; to* MAURYA). Let you go down now to the spring well and give him this and he passing. You'll see him then and the dark word will be broken, and you can say "God speed you," the way he'll be easy in his mind.

MAURYA (*taking the bread*). Will I be in it as soon as himself?

CATHLEEN. If you go now quickly.

MAURYA (*standing up unsteadily*). It's hard set I am to walk.

CATHLEEN (*looking at her anxiously*). Give her the stick, Nora, or maybe she'll slip on the big stones.

NORA. What stick?

CATHLEEN. The stick Michael brought from Connemara.

MAURYA (*taking a stick* NORA *gives her*). In the big world the old people do be leaving things after them for their sons and children, but in this place it is the young men do be leaving things behind for them that do be old.

[*She goes out slowly.* NORA *goes over to the ladder.*]

CATHLEEN. Wait, Nora, maybe she'd turn back quickly. She's that sorry, God help her, you wouldn't know the thing she'd do.

NORA. Is she gone round the bush?

CATHLEEN (*looking out*). She's gone now. Throw it down quickly, for the Lord knows when she'll be out of it again.

NORA (*getting the bundle from the loft*). The young priest said he'd be passing to-morrow, and we might go down and speak to him below if it's Michael's they are surely.

CATHLEEN (*taking the bundle*). Did he say what way they were found?

NORA (*coming down*). "There were two men," says he, "and they rowing round with poteen before the cocks crowed, and the oar of one of them caught the body, and they passing the black cliffs of the north."

CATHLEEN (*trying to open the bundle*). Give me a knife, Nora, the string's perished with the salt water, and there's a black knot on it you wouldn't loosen in a week.

NORA (*giving her a knife*). I've heard tell it was a long way to Donegal.

CATHLEEN (*cutting the string*). It is surely. There was a man in here a while ago—the man sold us that knife—and he said if you set off walking from the rocks beyond, it would be seven days you'd be in Donegal.

NORA. And what time would a man take, and he floating?

> [CATHLEEN *opens the bundle and takes out a bit of a stocking. They look at them eagerly.*]

CATHLEEN (*in a low voice*). The Lord spare us, Nora! isn't it a queer hard thing to say if it's his they are surely?

NORA. I'll get his shirt off the hook the way we can put the one flannel on the other. (*She looks through some clothes hanging in the corner.*) It's not with them, Cathleen, and where will it be?

CATHLEEN. I'm thinking Bartley put it on him in the morning, for his own shirt was heavy with the salt in it. (*Pointing to the corner*) There's a bit of a sleeve was of the same stuff. Give me that and it will do.

> [NORA *brings it to her and they compare the flannel.*]

CATHLEEN. It's the same stuff, Nora; but if it is itself aren't there great rolls of it in the shops of Galway, and isn't it many another man may have a shirt of it as well as Michael himself?

NORA (*who has taken up the stocking and counted the stitches, crying out*). It's Michael, Cathleen, it's Michael; God spare his soul, and what will herself say when she hears this story, and Bartley on the sea?

CATHLEEN (*taking the stocking*). It's a plain stocking.

NORA. It's the second one of the third pair I knitted, and I put up three score stitches, and I dropped four of them.

CATHLEEN (*counts the stitches*). It's that number is in it. (*Crying out*) Ah, Nora, isn't it a bitter thing to think of him floating that way to the far north, and no one to keen him but the black hags that do be flying on the sea?

NORA (*swinging herself round, and throwing out her arms on the clothes*). And isn't it a pitiful thing when there is nothing left of a man who was a great rower and fisher, but a bit of an old shirt and a plain stocking?

CATHLEEN (*after an instant*). Tell me is herself coming, Nora? I hear a little sound on the path.

NORA (*looking out*). She is, Cathleen. She's coming up to the door.

CATHLEEN. Put these things away before she'll come in. Maybe it's easier she'll be after giving her blessing to Bartley, and we won't let on we've heard anything the time he's on the sea.

NORA (*helping* CATHLEEN *to close the bundle*). We'll put them here in the corner.

> [*They put them into a hole in the chimney corner.*
> CATHLEEN *goes back to the spinning-wheel.*]

NORA. Will she see it was crying I was?

CATHLEEN. Keep your back to the door the way the light'll not be on you.

> [NORA *sits down at the chimney corner, with her back
> to the door.* MAURYA *comes in very slowly, without
> looking at the girls, and goes over to her stool at the
> other side of the fire. The cloth with the bread is still
> in her hand. The girls look at each other, and* NORA
> *points to the bundle of bread.*]

CATHLEEN (*after spinning for a moment*). You didn't give him his bit of bread?

> [MAURYA *begins to keen softly, without turning
> round.*]

CATHLEEN. Did you see him riding down?

> [MAURYA *goes on keening.*]

CATHLEEN (*a little impatiently*). God forgive you; isn't it a better thing to raise your voice and tell what you seen, than to be making lamentation for a thing that's done? Did you see Bartley, I'm saying to you.

MAURYA (*with a weak voice*). My heart's broken from this day.

CATHLEEN (*as before*). Did you see Bartley?

MAURYA. I seen the fearfulest thing.

CATHLEEN (*leaves her wheel and looks out*). God forgive you; he's riding the mare now over the green head, and the gray pony behind him.

MAURYA (*starts, so that her shawl falls back from her head and shows her white tossed hair. With a frightened voice*). The gray pony behind him.

CATHLEEN (*coming to the fire*). What is it ails you, at all?

MAURYA (*speaking very slowly*). I've seen the fearfulest thing any person has seen, since the day Bride Dara seen the dead man with the child in his arms.

CATHLEEN *and* NORA. Uah.

> [*They crouch down in front of the old woman at the*
> *fire.*]

NORA. Tell us what it is you seen.

MAURYA. I went down to the spring well, and I stood there saying a
prayer to myself. Then Bartley came along, and he riding on the red
mare with the gray pony behind him. (*She puts up her hands, as if to
hide something from her eyes.*) The Son of God spare us, Nora!

CATHLEEN. What is it you seen.

MAURYA. I seen Michael himself.

CATHLEEN (*speaking softly*). You did not, mother; It wasn't Michael
you seen, for his body is after being found in the far north, and
he's got a clean burial by the grace of God.

MAURYA (*a little defiantly*). I'm after seeing him this day, and he
riding and galloping. Bartley came first on the red mare; and I
tried to say "God speed you," but something choked the words in
my throat. He went by quickly; and "the blessing of God on you,"
says he, and I could say nothing. I looked up then, and I crying,
at the gray pony, and there was Michael upon it—with fine clothes
on him, and new shoes on his feet.

CATHLEEN (*begins to keen*). It's destroyed we are from this day. It's
destroyed, surely.

NORA. Didn't the young priest say the Almighty God wouldn't leave
her destitute with no son living?

MAURYA (*in a low voice, but clearly*). It's little the like of him knows
of the sea. . . . Bartley will be lost now, and let you call in Eamon
and make me a good coffin out of the white boards, for I won't
live after them. I've had a husband, and a husband's father, and
six sons in this house—six fine men, though it was a hard birth
I had with every one of them and they coming to the world—
and some of them were found and some of them were not found,
but they're gone now the lot of them. . . . There were Stephen,
and Shawn, were lost in the great wind, and found after in the Bay
of Gregory of the Golden Mouth, and carried up the two of them
on the one plank, and in by that door.

> [*She pauses for a moment, the girls start as if they*
> *heard something through the door that is half open*
> *behind them.*]

NORA (*in a whisper*). Did you hear that, Cathleen? Did you hear a
noise in the north-east?

CATHLEEN (*in a whisper*). There's some one after crying out by the
seashore.

MAURYA (*continues without hearing anything*). There was Sheamus
and his father, and his own father again, were lost in a dark night,
and not a stick or sign was seen of them when the sun went up.
There was Patch after was drowned out of a curagh that turned

over. I was sitting here with Bartley, and he a baby, lying on my two knees, and I seen two women, and three women, and four women coming in, and they crossing themselves, and not saying a word. I looked out then, and there were men coming after them, and they holding a thing in the half of a red sail, and water dripping out of it—it was a dry day, Nora—and leaving a track to the door.

[*She pauses again with her hand stretched out towards the door. It opens softly and old women begin to come in, crossing themselves on the threshold, and kneeling down in front of the stage with red petticoats over their heads.*]

MAURYA (*half in a dream, to* CATHLEEN). Is it Patch, or Michael, or what is it at all?

CATHLEEN. Michael is after being found in the far north, and when he is found there how could he be here in this place?

MAURYA. There does be a power of young men floating round in the sea, and what way would they know if it was Michael they had, or another man like him, for when a man is nine days in the sea, and the wind blowing, it's hard set his own mother would be to say what man was it.

CATHLEEN. It's Michael, God spare him, for they're after sending us a bit of his clothes from the far north.

[*She reaches out and hands* MAURYA *the clothes that belonged to* MICHAEL. MAURYA *stands up slowly and takes them in her hands.* NORA *looks out.*]

NORA. They're carrying a thing among them and there's water dripping out of it and leaving a track by the big stones.

CATHLEEN (*in a whisper to the women who have come in*). Is it Bartley it is?

ONE OF THE WOMEN. It is surely, God rest his soul.

[*Two younger women come in and pull out the table. Then men carry in the body of* BARTLEY, *laid on a plank, with a bit of a sail over it, and lay it on the table.*]

CATHLEEN (*to the women, as they are doing so*). What way was he drowned?

ONE OF THE WOMEN. The gray pony knocked him into the sea, and he was washed out where there is a great surf on the white rocks.

[MAURYA *has gone over and knelt down at the head of the table. The women are keening softly and swaying themselves with a slow movement.* CATHLEEN *and* NORA *kneel at the other end of the table. The men kneel near the door.*]

MAURYA (*raising her head and speaking as if she did not see the people around her*). They're all gone now, and there isn't anything more the sea can do to me. . . . I'll have no call now to be up crying and praying when the wind breaks from the south, and you can hear the surf is in the east, and the surf is in the west, making a great stir with the two noises, and they hitting one on the other. I'll have no call now to be going down and getting Holy Water in the dark nights after Samhain, and I won't care what way the sea is when the other women will be keening. (*To* NORA) Give me the Holy Water, Nora, there's a small sup still on the dresser.

[NORA *gives it to her.*]

MAURYA (*drops* MICHAEL'S *clothes across* BARTLEY'S *feet, and sprinkles the Holy Water over him*). It isn't that I haven't prayed for you, Bartley, to the Almighty God. It isn't that I haven't said prayers in the dark night till you wouldn't know what I'ld be saying; but it's a great rest I'll have now, and it's time surely. It's a great rest I'll have now, and great sleeping in the long nights after Samhain, if it's only a bit of wet flour we do have to eat, and maybe a fish that would be stinking.

[*She kneels down again, crossing herself, and saying prayers under her breath.*]

CATHLEEN (*to an old man*). Maybe yourself and Eamon would make a coffin when the sun rises. We have fine white boards herself bought, God help her, thinking Michael would be found, and I have a new cake you can eat while you'll be working.

THE OLD MAN (*looking at the boards*). Are there nails with them?

CATHLEEN. There are not, Colum; we didn't think of the nails.

ANOTHER MAN. It's a great wonder she wouldn't think of the nails, and all the coffins she's seen made already.

CATHLEEN. It's getting old she is, and broken.

[MAURYA *stands up again very slowly and spreads out the pieces of* MICHAEL'S *clothes beside the body, sprinkling them with the last of the Holy Water.*]

NORA (*in a whisper to* CATHLEEN). She's quiet now and easy; but the day Michael was drowned you could hear her crying out from this to the spring well. It's fonder she was of Michael, and would any one have thought that?

CATHLEEN (*slowly and clearly*). An old woman will be soon tired with anything she will do, and isn't it nine days herself is after crying and keening, and making great sorrow in the house?

MAURYA (*puts the empty cup mouth downwards on the table, and lays her hands together on* BARTLEY'S *feet*). They're all together this time, and the end is come. May the Almighty God have mercy on Bartley's soul, and on Michael's soul, and on the souls of Sheamus and Patch, and Stephen and Shawn (*bending her head*); and may He have mercy on my soul, Nora, and on the soul of every one is left living in the world.

[*She pauses, and the keen rises a little more loudly from the women, then sinks away.*]

MAURYA (*continuing*). Michael has a clean burial in the far north, by the grace of the Almighty God. Bartley will have a fine coffin out of the white boards, and a deep grave surely. What more can we want than that? No man at all can be living for ever, and we must be satisfied.

[*She kneels down again and the curtain falls slowly.*]

QUESTIONS

1. Synge's use of colors is persistent and effective. Note the frequency with which references to colors occur and describe their function. Are the colors associated with any particular place?

2. What is the effect of the wind blowing the door open? If you were staging the play, would you consider it appropriate to use sound effects of wind and sea at certain points?

3. The play is filled with simple, ordinary objects—a black pig, a piece of rope, a few boards, a baking cake, and an old stocking—that come to have powerful emotional, even heroic, associations. How does Synge give these objects their power?

4. Why does Bartley have to go to the mainland and the fair? Why is Maurya so helpless in her opposition?

5. The title refers specifically to Bartley riding the horses down to the boat. What other meanings does it come to have?

6. How is the presence of the sea surrounding the island made real without its ever being seen? What is the nature of the sea?

7. What is the significance of the young priest's inability to understand the sea? Does the play suggest in other ways an underlayer of paganism in the life of the islanders?

8. Burial in the earth is referred to frequently. What importance does it have for these people?

9. "And isn't it a pitiful thing when there is nothing left of a man who was a great rower and fisher, but a bit of an old shirt and a plain stocking?" Does this speech focus and summarize other effects of the play? Does it suggest that the play refers to more than the hard life of a few poor islanders?

10. How does the absence of the necessary nails to build the coffin function in the total effect of the play?

11. Does the "world" or "character" control the plot of this play?

12. Although tragedy portrays loneliness, isolation, destruction of hope, and the necessity of death, it usually offers some saving remnant that makes life not entirely bleak: wisdom of a kind will come from the suffering; man will learn that in some way he has a hand in his own fate, or he will somehow manifest his own greatness in his desolation. Do you see any gain here, no matter how small, or is the play a spectacle of meaningless suffering and bottomless desolation?

THE MISANTHROPE

BY

MOLIÈRE

Molière, whose actual name was Jean-Baptiste Poquelin (1622–73), was one of the great actors of his day and the greatest of all French comic playwrights. His father was upholsterer to the French king Louis XIV, and after a half-hearted attempt to study law, Molière followed his father's trade for a brief time. He seems to have been, in modern terms, stage-struck, and around 1642 he joined a company of players. The company failed in Paris and set off for the provinces, where they toured from 1645 to 1658. During this time Molière learned the trade of actor and became the leading player of his company, but he wrote only a few short plays. On their return to Paris, Molière and his company found favor with the King as a result of a farce of Molière's presented at a royal performance. From this time on their fortune was assured, and Molière, apparently encouraged by the King's kindness, produced a series of great comedies such as *The School for Wives* (1662), *The Misanthrope* (1666), *Tartuffe* (1667), *The Miser* (1668), *The Bourgeois Gentleman* (1670), and *The Hypochondriac* (1673). He died shortly after playing the leading role in a performance of this last play.

Molière was a comic dramatist. Each of his plays celebrates the triumph of pleasure, good sense, and the socially useful over stupidity, pride, rigidity, and selfishness. Like all comedies, his plays show the value of *what works* in life. The establishment of transcendental values, the probing of ultimate moral problems, and the search for absolute truths are left to tragedy. But Molière was aware of the claim of ideals, and in *The Misanthrope* he arranges a confrontation of the tragic and comic values. Behind the two chief characters of the play, Alceste and Philinte, Molière places an obviously imperfect, perhaps even a corrupt, world. Beneath their elegant manners and polished language, the fashionable gentlemen and ladies of the Paris of Louis XIV are bores, flirts, hypocrites, clotheshorses, sycophants, and plain fools. They write bad poetry and insist on being praised for it; they ruin reputations under cover of pretended friendship; they seek their own advancement by means of bribes and flattery; they spend "three quarters of an hour spitting into a well, so as to make circles in the water." There may be a few good people in it, but on the whole Philinte's summation catches this world nicely:

> This is a low, conniving age indeed;
> Nothing but trickery prospers nowadays,
> And people ought to mend their shabby ways.
> Yes, man's a beastly creature; . . .

The question posed by the play is, "How are we to act in such a world?" and this huge problem is made dramatically manageable by narrowing it to a consideration of two crucial areas of human activity—social relationships and love.

Most of the characters are blissfully unaware of any gap between their manners and their morals, between their masks and the realities of their natures. Since they observe all the social proprieties, they are able to assume that they are proper people, even while indulging in the most vicious activities. Both Philinte and Alceste recognize these imperfections, but the conclusions they draw are quite different. The discovery of human imperfection is no surprise to Philinte. This is the way people are, always have been, and always will be. This is human nature: we might as well be shocked that the "vulture dines upon the dead." Since these are the facts of human nature, it is of no use to rail at mankind; "the world won't change, whatever you say or do." Recognizing this, Philinte adjusts his conduct accordingly. He greets effusively a man whose name he scarcely knows; he praises extravagantly the sonnet of a rhyming peer; he compliments bores on their wit and decayed belles on their beauty. Since bribes and flattery are necessary to win a judgment in court, he recommends bribes and flattery to the man engaged in lawsuits. And he does all this not for personal gain, but in the name of a realistic value: society. If everyone were absolutely frank and truthful, society would degenerate into open warfare:

> Wouldn't the social fabric come undone
> If we were wholly frank with everyone?

Philinte is a man, as he says, of "pliant rectitude," but his opposite, the man with green ribbons, Alceste, is stiff and rigid and rude. He rejects Philinte's social argument and argues for absolute standards. The basis of his conduct is quite simple: he sees the truth, that men are knaves and fools, and he acts in conformity with this truth. He will not stoop to curry favor or to flatter man or poet. Where he finds deceit he exposes it; what he feels he says; what he knows he acts upon. The man of truth is one who displays his "inmost heart" in everything he does and says. And the truth admits no paltering: right is right and wrong is wrong. His disgust with mankind is limitless. Having discovered that there is a great deal of folly in the world, he sweeps on to the conclusion that "all are corrupt." He would agree with the satirist Persius who shouts, "Who is there who has not the ears of an ass?" Rigid integrity, frankness, reliance on self—these are his most apparent and his most engaging qualities, but they get him into frequent trouble and disrupt the smooth surface of society.

CHARACTERS

ALCESTE, *in love with Célimène*
PHILINTE, *Alceste's friend*
ORONTE, *in love with Célimène*
CÉLIMÈNE, *Alceste's beloved*
ÉLIANTE, *Célimène's cousin*
ARSINOÉ, *a friend of Célimène's*
ACASTE ⎫
CLITANDRE ⎭ *marquesses*
BASQUE, *Célimène's servant*
A GUARD *of the Marshalsea*
DUBOIS, *Alceste's valet*

The scene throughout is in Célimène's house at Paris.

The Misanthrope by Molière, translated by Richard Wilbur, copyright 1954, © 1955 by Richard Wilbur. Reprinted by permission of Harcourt, Brace & World, Inc.

ACT I

Scene 1 🦢 PHILINTE, ALCESTE.

PHILINTE. Now, what's got into you?
ALCESTE (*seated*).   Kindly leave me alone.
PHILINTE. Come, come, what is it? This lugubrious tone . . .
ALCESTE. Leave me, I said; you spoil my solitude.
PHILINTE. Oh, listen to me, now, and don't be rude.
ALCESTE. I choose to be rude, Sir, and to be hard of hearing.
PHILINTE. These ugly moods of yours are not endearing;
    Friends though we are, I really must insist . . .
ALCESTE (*abruptly rising*). Friends? Friends, you say? Well, cross me
    off your list.
    I've been your friend till now, as you well know;
    But after what I saw a moment ago
    I tell you flatly that our ways must part.
    I wish no place in a dishonest heart.
PHILINTE. Why, what have I done, Alceste? Is this quite just?
ALCESTE. My God, you ought to die of self-disgust.
    I call your conduct inexcusable, Sir,
    And every man of honor will concur.
    I see you almost hug a man to death,
    Exclaim for joy until you're out of breath,
    And supplement these loving demonstrations
    With endless offers, vows, and protestations;
    Then when I ask you "Who was that?" I find
    That you can barely bring his name to mind!
    Once the man's back is turned, you cease to love him,
    And speak with absolute indifference of him!
    By God, I say it's base and scandalous
    To falsify the heart's affections thus;
    If I caught myself behaving in such a way,
    I'd hang myself for shame, without delay.
PHILINTE. It hardly seems a hanging matter to me;

    I hope that you will take it graciously
    If I extend myself a slight reprieve,
    And live a little longer, by your leave.
ALCESTE. How dare you joke about a crime so grave?
PHILINTE. What crime? How else are people to behave?
ALCESTE. I'd have them be sincere, and never part
    With any word that isn't from the heart.
PHILINTE. When someone greets us with a show of pleasure,
    It's but polite to give him equal measure,
    Return his love the best that we know how,
    And trade him offer for offer, vow for vow.
ALCESTE. No, no, this formula you'd have me follow,
    However fashionable, is false and hollow,
    And I despise the frenzied operations
    Of all these barterers of protestations,
    These lavishers of meaningless embraces,
    These utterers of obliging commonplaces,
    Who court and flatter everyone on earth
    And praise the fool no less than the man of worth.
    Should you rejoice that someone fondles you,
    Offers his love and service, swears to be true,
    And fills your ears with praises of your name,
    When to the first damned fop he'll say the same?
    No, no: no self-respecting heart would dream
    Of prizing so promiscuous an esteem;
    However high the praise, there's nothing worse
    Than sharing honors with the universe.
    Esteem is founded on comparison:
    To honor all men is to honor none.
    Since you embrace this indiscriminate vice,
    Your friendship comes at far too cheap a price;
    I spurn the easy tribute of a heart
    Which will not set the worthy man apart:
    I choose, Sir, to be chosen; and in fine,
    The friend of mankind is no friend of mine.
PHILINTE. But in polite society, custom decrees
    That we show certain outward courtesies. . . .
ALCESTE. Ah, no! we should condemn with all our force
    Such false and artificial intercourse.
    Let men behave like men; let them display
    Their inmost hearts in everything they say;
    Let the heart speak, and let our sentiments
    Not mask themselves in silly compliments.
PHILINTE. In certain cases it would be uncouth
    And most absurd to speak the naked truth;

With all respect for your exalted notions,
It's often best to veil one's true emotions.
Wouldn't the social fabric come undone
If we were wholly frank with everyone?
Suppose you met with someone you couldn't bear;
Would you inform him of it then and there?

ALCESTE. Yes.

PHILINTE.   Then you'd tell old Emilie it's pathetic
The way she daubs her features with cosmetic
And plays the gay coquette at sixty-four?

ALCESTE. I would.

PHILINTE.   And you'd call Dorilas a bore,
And tell him every ear at court is lame
From hearing him brag about his noble name?

ALCESTE. Precisely.

PHILINTE.   Ah, you're joking.

ALCESTE.   *Au contraire:*
In this regard there's none I'd choose to spare.
All are corrupt; there's nothing to be seen
In court or town but aggravates my spleen.
I fall into deep gloom and melancholy
When I survey the scene of human folly,
Finding on every hand base flattery,
Injustice, fraud, self-interest, treachery. . . .
Ah, it's too much; mankind has grown so base,
I mean to break with the whole human race.

PHILINTE. This philosophic rage is a bit extreme;
You've no idea how comical you seem;
Indeed, we're like those brothers in the play
Called *School for Husbands,* one of whom was prey . . .

ALCESTE. Enough, now! None of your stupid similes.

PHILINTE. Then let's have no more tirades, if you please.
The world won't change, whatever you say or do;
And since plain speaking means so much to you,
I'll tell you plainly that by being frank
You've earned the reputation of a crank,
And that you're thought ridiculous when you rage
And rant against the manners of the age.

ALCESTE. So much the better; just what I wish to hear.
No news could be more grateful to my ear.
All men are so detestable in my eyes,
I should be sorry if they thought me wise.

PHILINTE. Your hatred's very sweeping, is it not?

ALCESTE. Quite right: I hate the whole degraded lot.

PHILINTE. Must all poor human creatures be embraced,

Without distinction, by your vast distaste?
Even in these bad times, there are surely a few . . .
ALCESTE. No, I include all men in one dim view:
Some men I hate for being rogues; the others
I hate because they treat the rogues like brothers,
And, lacking a virtuous scorn for what is vile,
Receive the villain with a complaisant smile.
Notice how tolerant people choose to be
Toward that bold rascal who's at law with me.
His social polish can't conceal his nature;
One sees at once that he's a treacherous creature;
No one could possibly be taken in
By those soft speeches and that sugary grin.
The whole world knows the shady means by which
The low-brow's grown so powerful and rich,
And risen to a rank so bright and high
That virtue can but blush, and merit sigh.
Whenever his name comes up in conversation,
None will defend his wretched reputation;
Call him knave, liar, scoundrel, and all the rest,
Each head will nod, and no one will protest.
And yet his smirk is seen in every house,
He's greeted everywhere with smiles and bows,
And when there's any honor that can be got
By pulling strings, he'll get it, like as not.
My God! It chills my heart to see the ways
Men come to terms with evil nowadays;
Sometimes, I swear, I'm moved to flee and find
Some desert land unfouled by humankind.
PHILINTE. Come, let's forget the follies of the times
And pardon mankind for its petty crimes;
Let's have an end of rantings and of railings,
And show some leniency toward human failings.
This world requires a pliant rectitude;
Too stern a virtue makes one stiff and rude;
Good sense views all extremes with detestation,
And bids us to be noble in moderation.
The rigid virtues of the ancient days
Are not for us; they jar with all our ways
And ask of us too lofty a perfection.
Wise men accept their times without objection,
And there's no greater folly, if you ask me,
Than trying to reform society.
Like you, I see each day a hundred and one
Unhandsome deeds that might be better done,

But still, for all the faults that meet my view,
I'm never known to storm and rave like you.
I take men as they are, or let them be,
And teach my soul to bear their frailty;
And whether in court or town, whatever the scene,
My phlegm's as philosophic as your spleen.

ALCESTE. This phlegm which you so eloquently commend,
Does nothing ever rile it up, my friend?
Suppose some man you trust should treacherously
Conspire to rob you of your property,
And do his best to wreck your reputation?
Wouldn't you feel a certain indignation?

PHILINTE. Why, no. These faults of which you so complain
Are part of human nature, I maintain,
And it's no more a matter for disgust
That men are knavish, selfish and unjust,
Than that the vulture dines upon the dead,
And wolves are furious, and apes ill-bred.

ALCESTE. Shall I see myself betrayed, robbed, torn to bits,
And not . . . Oh, let's be still and rest our wits.
Enough of reasoning, now. I've had my fill.

PHILINTE. Indeed, you would do well, Sir, to be still.
Rage less at your opponent, and give some thought
To how you'll win this lawsuit that he's brought.

ALCESTE. I assure you I'll do nothing of the sort.

PHILINTE. Then who will plead your case before the court?

ALCESTE. Reason and right and justice will plead for me.

PHILINTE. Oh, Lord. What judges do you plan to see?

ALCESTE. Why, none. The justice of my cause is clear.

PHILINTE. Of course, man; but there's politics to fear. . . .

ALCESTE. No, I refuse to lift a hand. That's flat.
I'm either right, or wrong.

PHILINTE.   Don't count on that.

ALCESTE. No, I'll do nothing.

PHILINTE.   Your enemy's influence
Is great, you know . . .

ALCESTE.   That makes no difference.

PHILINTE. It will; you'll see.

ALCESTE.   Must honor bow to guile?
If so, I shall be proud to lose the trial.

PHILINTE. Oh, really . . .

ALCESTE.   I'll discover by this case
Whether or not men are sufficiently base
And impudent and villainous and perverse
To do me wrong before the universe.

PHILINTE. What a man!

ALCESTE. Oh, I could wish, whatever the cost,
Just for the beauty of it, that my trial were lost.

PHILINTE. If people heard you talking so, Alceste,
They'd split their sides. Your name would be a jest.

ALCESTE. So much the worse for jesters.

PHILINTE. May I enquire
Whether this rectitude you so admire,
And these hard virtues you're enamored of
Are qualities of the lady whom you love?
It much surprises me that you, who seem
To view mankind with furious disesteem,
Have yet found something to enchant your eyes
Amidst a species which you so despise.
And what is more amazing, I'm afraid,
Is the most curious choice your heart has made.
The honest Éliante is fond of you,
Arsinoé, the prude, admires you too;
And yet your spirit's been perversely led
To choose the flighty Célimène instead,
Whose brittle malice and coquettish ways
So typify the manners of our days.
How is it that the traits you most abhor
Are bearable in this lady you adore?
Are you so blind with love that you can't find them?
Or do you contrive, in her case, not to mind them?

ALCESTE. My love for that young widow's not the kind
That can't perceive defects; no, I'm not blind.
I see her faults, despite my ardent love,
And all I see I fervently reprove.
And yet I'm weak; for all her falsity,
That woman knows the art of pleasing me,
And though I never cease complaining of her,
I swear I cannot manage not to love her.
Her charm outweighs her faults; I can but aim
To cleanse her spirit in my love's pure flame.

PHILINTE. That's no small task; I wish you all success.
You think then that she loves you?

ALCESTE. Heavens, yes!
I wouldn't love her did she not love me.

PHILINTE. Well, if her taste for you is plain to see,
Why do these rivals cause you such despair?

ALCESTE. True love, Sir, is possessive, and cannot bear
To share with all the world. I'm here today
To tell her she must send that mob away.

PHILINTE. If I were you, and had your choice to make,
    Éliante, her cousin, would be the one I'd take;
    That honest heart, which cares for you alone,
    Would harmonize far better with your own.
ALCESTE. True, true: each day my reason tells me so;
    But reason doesn't rule in love, you know.
PHILINTE. I fear some bitter sorrow is in store;
    This love . . .

Scene 2   ORONTE, ALCESTE, PHILINTE.

ORONTE (*to* ALCESTE). The servants told me at the door
    That Éliante and Célimène were out,
    But when I heard, dear Sir, that you were about,
    I came to say, without exaggeration,
    That I hold you in the vastest admiration,
    And that it's always been my dearest desire
    To be the friend of one I so admire.
    I hope to see my love of merit requited,
    And you and I in friendship's bond united.
    I'm sure you won't refuse—if I may be frank—
    A friend of my devotedness—and rank.
        [*During this speech of* ORONTE'S, ALCESTE *is ab-
        stracted, and seems unaware that he is being spoken
        to. He only breaks off his reverie when* ORONTE *says:*]
    It was for you, if you please, that my words were intended.
ALCESTE. For me, Sir?
ORONTE.   Yes, for you. You're not offended?
ALCESTE. By no means. But this much surprises me. . . .
    The honor comes most unexpectedly. . . .
ORONTE. My high regard should not astonish you;
    The whole world feels the same. It is your due.
ALCESTE. Sir . . .
ORONTE.   Why, in all the State there isn't one
    Can match your merits; they shine, Sir, like the sun
ALCESTE. Sir . . .
ORONTE.   You are higher in my estimation
    Than all that's most illustrious in the nation.
ALCESTE. Sir . . .
ORONTE.   If I lie, may heaven strike me dead!
    To show you that I mean what I have said,
    Permit me, Sir, to embrace you most sincerely,

And swear that I will prize our friendship dearly.
Give me your hand. And now, Sir, if you choose,
We'll make our vows.

ALCESTE. Sir . . .

ORONTE. What! You refuse?

ALCESTE. Sir, it's a very great honor you extend:
But friendship is a sacred thing, my friend;
It would be profanation to bestow
The name of friend on one you hardly know.
All parts are better played when well-rehearsed;
Let's put off friendship, and get acquainted first.
We may discover it would be unwise
To try to make our natures harmonize.

ORONTE. By heaven! You're sagacious to the core;
This speech has made me admire you even more.
Let time, then, bring us closer day by day;
Meanwhile, I shall be yours in every way.
If, for example, there should be anything
You wish at court, I'll mention it to the King.
I have his ear, of course; it's quite well known
That I am much in favor with the throne.
In short, I am your servant. And now, dear friend,
Since you have such fine judgment, I intend
To please you, if I can, with a small sonnet
I wrote not long ago. Please comment on it,
And tell me whether I ought to publish it.

ALCESTE. You must excuse me, Sir; I'm hardly fit
To judge such matters.

ORONTE. Why not?

ALCESTE. I am, I fear,
Inclined to be unfashionably sincere.

ORONTE. Just what I ask; I'd take no satisfaction
In anything but your sincere reaction.
I beg you not to dream of being kind.

ALCESTE. Since you desire it, Sir, I'll speak my mind.

ORONTE. *Sonnet.* It's a sonnet. . . . *Hope* . . . The poem's addressed
To a lady who wakened hopes within my breast.
Hope . . . this is not the pompous sort of thing,
Just modest little verses, with a tender ring.

ALCESTE. Well, we shall see.

ORONTE. *Hope* . . . I'm anxious to hear
Whether the style seems properly smooth and clear,
And whether the choice of words is good or bad.

ALCESTE. We'll see, we'll see.

ORONTE. Perhaps I ought to add

　　　That it took me only a quarter-hour to write it.
ALCESTE. The time's irrelevant, Sir: Kindly recite it.
ORONTE (*reading*).

> *Hope comforts us awhile, 'tis true,*
> *Lulling our cares with careless laughter,*
> *And yet such joy is full of rue,*
> *My Phyllis, if nothing follows after.*

PHILINTE. I'm charmed by this already; the style's delightful.
ALCESTE (*sotto voce, to* PHILINTE). How can you say that? Why the
　　　thing is frightful.

ORONTE. 　　　*Your fair face smiled on me awhile,*
> *But was it kindness so to enchant me?*
> *'Twould have been fairer not to smile,*
> *If hope was all you meant to grant me.*

PHILINTE. What a clever thought! How handsomely you phrase it!
ALCESTE (*sotto voce, to* PHILINTE). You know the thing is trash. How
　　　dare you praise it?

ORONTE. 　　　*If it's to be my passion's fate*
> *Thus everlastingly to wait,*
> *Then death will come to set me free:*
> *For death is fairer than the fair;*
> *Phyllis, to hope is to despair*
> *When one must hope eternally.*

PHILINTE. The close is exquisite—full of feeling and grace.
ALCESTE (*sotto voce, aside*). Oh, blast the close; you'd better close your
　　　face
　　　Before you send your lying soul to hell.
PHILINTE. I can't remember a poem I've liked so well.
ALCESTE (*sotto voce, aside*). Good Lord!
ORONTE (*to* PHILINTE). 　　　　　　　I fear you're flattering me a
　　　bit.
PHILINTE. Oh, no!
ALCESTE (*sotto voce, aside*).
　　　　　　　What else d'you call it, you hypocrite?
ORONTE (*to* ALCESTE). But you, Sir, keep your promise now: don't
　　　shrink
　　　From telling me sincerely what you think.
ALCESTE. Sir, these are delicate matters; we all desire
　　　To be told that we've the true poetic fire.
　　　But once, to one whose name I shall not mention,
　　　I said, regarding some verse of his invention,

> That gentlemen should rigorously control
> That itch to write which often afflicts the soul;
> That one should curb the heady inclination
> To publicize one's little avocation;
> And that in showing off one's works of art
> One often plays a very clownish part.

ORONTE. Are you suggesting in a devious way
> That I ought not . . .

ALCESTE.   Oh, that I do not say.
> Further, I told him that no fault is worse
> Than that of writing frigid, lifeless verse,
> And that the merest whisper of such a shame
> Suffices to destroy a man's good name.

ORONTE. D'you mean to say my sonnet's dull and trite?

ALCESTE. I don't say that. But I went on to cite
> Numerous cases of once-respected men
> Who came to grief by taking up the pen.

ORONTE. And am I like them? Do I write so poorly?

ALCESTE. I don't say that. But I told this person, "Surely
> You're under no necessity to compose;
> Why you should wish to publish, heaven knows.
> There's no excuse for printing tedious rot
> Unless one writes for bread, as you do not.
> Resist temptation, then, I beg of you;
> Conceal your pastimes from the public view;
> And don't give up, on any provocation,
> Your present high and courtly reputation,
> To purchase at a greedy printer's shop
> The name of silly author and scribbling fop."
> These were the points I tried to make him see.

ORONTE. I sense that they are also aimed at me;
> But now—about my sonnet—I'd like to be told . . .

ALCESTE. Frankly, that sonnet should be pigeonholed.
> You've chosen the worst models to imitate.
> The style's unnatural. Let me illustrate:

> For example, *Your fair face smiled on me awhile,*
> Followed by, *'Twould have been fairer not to smile!*
> Or this: *such joy is full of rue;*
> Or this: *For death is fairer than the fair;*
> Or, *Phyllis, to hope is to despair*
> *When one must hope eternally!*

> This artificial style, that's all the fashion,
> Has neither taste, nor honesty, nor passion;
> It's nothing but a sort of wordy play,

And nature never spoke in such a way.
What, in this shallow age, is not debased?
Our fathers, though less refined, had better taste;
I'd barter all that men admire today
For one old love song I shall try to say:

> *If the King had given me for my own*
> *Paris, his citadel,*
> *And I for that must leave alone*
> *Her whom I love so well,*
> *I'd say then to the Crown,*
> *Take back your glittering town;*
> *My darling is more fair, I swear,*
> *My darling is more fair.*

The rhyme's not rich, the style is rough and old,
But don't you see that it's the purest gold
Beside the tinsel nonsense now preferred,
And that there's passion in its every word?

> *If the King had given me for my own*
> *Paris, his citadel,*
> *And I for that must leave alone*
> *Her whom I love so well,*
> *I'd say then to the Crown,*
> *Take back your glittering town;*
> *My darling is more fair, I swear,*
> *My darling is more fair.*

There speaks a loving heart. (*To* PHILINTE) You're laughing, eh?
Laugh on, my precious wit. Whatever you say,
I hold that song's worth all the bibelots
That people hail today with ah's and oh's.
ORONTE. And I maintain my sonnet's very good.
ALCESTE. It's not at all surprising that you should.
You have your reasons; permit me to have mine
For thinking that you cannot write a line.
ORONTE. Others have praised my sonnet to the skies.
ALCESTE. I lack their art of telling pleasant lies.
ORONTE. You seem to think you've got no end of wit.
ALCESTE. To praise your verse, I'd need still more of it.
ORONTE. I'm not in need of your approval, Sir.
ALCESTE. That's good; you couldn't have it if you were.
ORONTE. Come now, I'll lend you the subject of my sonnet;
I'd like to see you try to improve upon it.
ALCESTE. I might, by chance, write something just as shoddy;

But then I wouldn't show it to everybody.

ORONTE. You're most opinionated and conceited.

ALCESTE. Go find your flatterers, and be better treated.

ORONTE. Look here, my little fellow, pray watch your tone.

ALCESTE. My great big fellow, you'd better watch your own.

PHILINTE (*stepping between them*). Oh, please, please, gentlemen! This
    will never do.

ORONTE. The fault is mine, and I leave the field to you.
    I am your servant, Sir, in every way.

ALCESTE. And I, Sir, am your most abject valet.

Scene 3   PHILINTE, ALCESTE.

PHILINTE. Well, as you see, sincerity in excess
    Can get you into a very pretty mess;
    Oronte was hungry for appreciation. . . .

ALCESTE. Don't speak to me.

PHILINTE.   What?

ALCESTE.   No more conversation.

PHILINTE. Really, now . . .

ALCESTE.   Leave me alone.

PHILINTE.   If I . . .

ALCESTE.   Out of my sight!

PHILINTE. But what . . .

ALCESTE.   I won't listen.

PHILINTE.   But . . .

ALCESTE.   Silence!

PHILINTE.   Now, is it polite . . .

ALCESTE. By heaven, I've had enough. Don't follow me.

PHILINTE. Ah, you're just joking. I'll keep you company.

ACT II

Scene 1 ✤ ALCESTE, CÉLIMÈNE.

ALCESTE. Shall I speak plainly, Madam? I confess
　　Your conduct gives me infinite distress,
　　And my resentment's grown too hot to smother.
　　Soon, I foresee, we'll break with one another.
　　If I said otherwise, I should deceive you;
　　Sooner or later, I shall be forced to leave you,
　　And if I swore that we shall never part,
　　I should misread the omens of my heart.
CÉLIMÈNE. You kindly saw me home, it would appear,
　　So as to pour invectives in my ear.
ALCESTE. I've no desire to quarrel. But I deplore
　　Your inability to shut the door
　　On all these suitors who beset you so.
　　There's what annoys me, if you care to know.
CÉLIMÈNE. Is it my fault that all these men pursue me?
　　Am I to blame if they're attracted to me?
　　And when they gently beg an audience,
　　Ought I to take a stick and drive them hence?
ALCESTE. Madam, there's no necessity for a stick;
　　A less responsive heart would do the trick.
　　Of your attractiveness I don't complain;
　　But those your charms attract, you then detain
　　By a most melting and receptive manner,
　　And so enlist their hearts beneath your banner.
　　It's the agreeable hopes which you excite
　　That keep these lovers round you day and night;
　　Were they less liberally smiled upon,
　　That sighing troop would very soon be gone.
　　But tell me, Madam, why it is that lately
　　This man Clitandre interests you so greatly?
　　Because of what high merits do you deem

Him worthy of the honor of your esteem?
Is it that your admiring glances linger
On the splendidly long nail of his little finger?
Or do you share the general deep respect
For the blond wig he chooses to affect?
Are you in love with his embroidered hose?
Do you adore his ribbons and his bows?
Or is it that this paragon bewitches
Your tasteful eye with his vast German breeches?
Perhaps his giggle, or his falsetto voice,
Makes him the latest gallant of your choice?

CÉLIMÈNE. You're much mistaken to resent him so.
Why I put up with him you surely know:
My lawsuit's very shortly to be tried,
And I must have his influence on my side.

ALCESTE. Then lose your lawsuit, Madam, or let it drop;
Don't torture me by humoring such a fop.

CÉLIMÈNE. You're jealous of the whole world, Sir.

ALCESTE.   That's true,
Since the whole world is well-received by you.

CÉLIMÈNE. That my good nature is so unconfined
Should serve to pacify your jealous mind;
Were I to smile on one, and scorn the rest,
Then you might have some cause to be distressed.

ALCESTE. Well, if I mustn't be jealous, tell me, then,
Just how I'm better treated than other men.

CÉLIMÈNE. You know you have my love. Will that not do?

ALCESTE. What proof have I that what you say is true?

CÉLIMÈNE. I would expect, Sir, that my having said it
Might give the statement a sufficient credit.

ALCESTE. But how can I be sure that you don't tell
The selfsame thing to other men as well?

CÉLIMÈNE. What a gallant speech! How flattering to me!
What a sweet creature you make me out to be!
Well then, to save you from the pangs of doubt,
All that I've said I hereby cancel out;
Now, none but yourself shall make a monkey of you:
Are you content?

ALCESTE.   Why, why am I doomed to love you?
I swear that I shall bless the blissful hour
When this poor heart's no longer in your power!
I make no secret of it: I've done my best
To exorcise this passion from my breast;
But thus far all in vain; it will not go;
It's for my sins that I must love you so.

CÉLIMÈNE. Your love for me is matchless, Sir; that's clear.
ALCESTE. Indeed, in all the world it has no peer;
    Words can't describe the nature of my passion,
    And no man ever loved in such a fashion.
CÉLIMÈNE. Yes, it's a brand-new fashion, I agree:
    You show your love by castigating me,
    And all your speeches are enraged and rude.
    I've never been so furiously wooed.
ALCESTE. Yet you could calm that fury, if you chose.
    Come, shall we bring our quarrels to a close?
    Let's speak with open hearts, then, and begin . . .

Scene 2   CÉLIMÈNE, ALCESTE, BASQUE.

CÉLIMÈNE. What is it?
BASQUE.   Acaste is here.
CÉLIMÈNE.   Well, send him in.

Scene 3   CÉLIMÈNE, ALCESTE.

ALCESTE. What! Shall we never be alone at all?
    You're always ready to receive a call,
    And you can't bear, for ten ticks of the clock,
    Not to keep open house for all who knock.
CÉLIMÈNE. I couldn't refuse him: he'd be most put out.
ALCESTE. Surely that's not worth worrying about.
CÉLIMÈNE. Acaste would never forgive me if he guessed
    That I consider him a dreadful pest.
ALCESTE. If he's a pest, why bother with him then?
CÉLIMÈNE. Heavens! One can't antagonize such men;
    Why, they're the chartered gossips of the court,
    And have a say in things of every sort.
    One must receive them, and be full of charm;
    They're no great help, but they can do you harm,
    And though your influence be ever so great,
    They're hardly the best people to alienate.
ALCESTE. I see, dear lady, that you could make a case
    For putting up with the whole human race;
    These friendships that you calculate so nicely . . .

Scene 4 ᘓᕗ ALCESTE, CÉLIMÈNE, BASQUE.

BASQUE. Madam, Clitandre is here as well.
ALCESTE.   Precisely.
CÉLIMÈNE. Where are you going?
ALCESTE.   Elsewhere.
CÉLIMÈNE.   Stay.
ALCESTE.   No, no.
CÉLIMÈNE. Stay, Sir.
ALCESTE.   I can't.
CÉLIMÈNE.   I wish it.
ALCESTE.   No, I must go.
  I beg you, Madam, not to press the matter;
  You know I have no taste for idle chatter.
CÉLIMÈNE. Stay: I command you.
ALCESTE.   No, I cannot stay.
CÉLIMÈNE. Very well; you have my leave to go away.

Scene 5 ᘓᕗ ÉLIANTE, PHILINTE, ACASTE, CLITANDRE, ALCESTE,
              BASQUE.

ÉLIANTE (to CÉLIMÈNE). The Marquesses have kindly come to call.
  Were they announced?
CÉLIMÈNE.   Yes. Basque, bring chairs for all.
          [BASQUE provides the chairs, and exits.]
      (To ALCESTE.) You haven't gone?
ALCESTE.   No; and I shan't depart
  Till you decide who's foremost in your heart.
CÉLIMÈNE. Oh, hush.
ALCESTE.   It's time to choose; take them, or me.
CÉLIMÈNE. You're mad.
ALCESTE.   I'm not, as you shall shortly see.
CÉLIMÈNE. Oh?
ALCESTE.   You'll decide.
CÉLIMÈNE.   You're joking now, dear friend.
ALCESTE. No, no; you'll choose; my patience is at an end.
CLITANDRE. Madam, I come from court, where poor Cléonte
  Behaved like a perfect fool, as is his wont.
  Has he no friend to counsel him, I wonder,
  And teach him less unerringly to blunder?
CÉLIMÈNE. It's true, the man's a most accomplished dunce;

His gauche behavior charms the eye at once;
And every time one sees him, on my word,
His manner's grown a trifle more absurd.

ACASTE. Speaking of dunces, I've just now conversed
With old Damon, who's one of the very worst;
I stood a lifetime in the broiling sun
Before his dreary monologue was done.

CÉLIMÈNE. Oh, he's a wondrous talker, and has the power
To tell you nothing hour after hour:
If, by mistake, he ever came to the point,
The shock would put his jawbone out of joint.

ÉLIANTE (*to* PHILINTE). The conversation takes its usual turn,
And all our dear friends' ears will shortly burn.

CLITANDRE. Timante's a character, Madam.

CÉLIMÈNE.   Isn't he, though?
A man of mystery from top to toe,
Who moves about in a romantic mist
On secret missions which do not exist.
His talk is full of eyebrows and grimaces;
How tired one gets of his momentous faces;
He's always whispering something confidential
Which turns out to be quite inconsequential;
Nothing's too slight for him to mystify;
He even whispers when he says "good-by."

ACASTE. Tell us about Géralde.

CÉLIMÈNE.   That tiresome ass.
He mixes only with the titled class,
And fawns on dukes and princes, and is bored
With anyone who's not at least a lord.
The man's obsessed with rank, and his discourses
Are all of hounds and carriages and horses;
He uses Christian names with all the great,
And the word Milord, with him, is out of date.

CLITANDRE. He's very taken with Bélise, I hear.

CÉLIMÈNE. She is the dreariest company, poor dear.
Whenever she comes to call, I grope about
To find some topic which will draw her out,
But, owing to her dry and faint replies,
The conversation wilts, and droops, and dies.
In vain one hopes to animate her face
By mentioning the ultimate commonplace;
But sun or shower, even hail or frost
Are matters she can instantly exhaust.
Meanwhile her visit, painful though it is,
Drags on and on through mute eternities,

And though you ask the time, and yawn, and yawn,
She sits there like a stone and won't be gone.
ACASTE. Now for Adraste.
CÉLIMÈNE.   Oh, that conceited elf
Has a gigantic passion for himself;
He rails against the court, and cannot bear it
That none will recognize his hidden merit;
All honors given to others give offense
To his imaginary excellence.
CLITANDRE. What about young Cléon? His house, they say,
Is full of the best society, night and day.
CÉLIMÈNE. His cook has made him popular, not he:
It's Cléon's table that people come to see.
ÉLIANTE. He gives a splendid dinner, you must admit.
CÉLIMÈNE. But must he serve himself along with it?
For my taste, he's a most insipid dish
Whose presence sours the wine and spoils the fish.
PHILINTE. Damis, his uncle, is admired no end.
What's your opinion, Madam?
CÉLIMÈNE.   Why, he's my friend.
PHILINTE. He seems a decent fellow, and rather clever.
CÉLIMÈNE. He works too hard at cleverness, however.
I hate to see him sweat and struggle so
To fill his conversation with bons mots.
Since he's decided to become a wit
His taste's so pure that nothing pleases it;
He scolds at all the latest books and plays,
Thinking that wit must never stoop to praise,
That finding fault's a sign of intellect,
That all appreciation is abject,
And that by damning everything in sight
One shows oneself in a distinguished light.
He's scornful even of our conversations:
Their trivial nature sorely tries his patience;
He folds his arms, and stands above the battle,
And listens sadly to our childish prattle.
ACASTE. Wonderful, Madam! You've hit him off precisely.
CLITANDRE. No one can sketch a character so nicely.
ALCESTE. How bravely, Sirs, you cut and thrust at all
These absent fools, till one by one they fall:
But let one come in sight, and you'll at once
Embrace the man you lately called a dunce,
Telling him in a tone sincere and fervent
How proud you are to be his humble servant.
CLITANDRE. Why pick on us? *Madame's* been speaking, Sir,

And you should quarrel, if you must, with her.
ALCESTE. No, no, by God, the fault is yours, because
    You lead her on with laughter and applause,
    And make her think that she's the more delightful
    The more her talk is scandalous and spiteful.
    Oh, she would stoop to malice far, far less
    If no such claque approved her cleverness.
    It's flatterers like you whose foolish praise
    Nourishes all the vices of these days.
PHILINTE. But why protest when someone ridicules
    Those you'd condemn, yourself, as knaves or fools?
CÉLIMÈNE. Why, Sir? Because he loves to make a fuss.
    You don't expect him to agree with us,
    When there's an opportunity to express
    His heaven-sent spirit of contrariness?
    What other people think, he can't abide;
    Whatever they say, he's on the other side;
    He lives in deadly terror of agreeing;
    'Twould make him seem an ordinary being.
    Indeed, he's so in love with contradiction,
    He'll turn against his most profound conviction
    And with a furious eloquence deplore it,
    If only someone else is speaking for it.
ALCESTE. Go on, dear lady, mock me as you please;
    You have your audience in ecstasies.
PHILINTE. But what she says is true: you have a way
    Of bridling at whatever people say;
    Whether they praise or blame, your angry spirit
    Is equally unsatisfied to hear it.
ALCESTE. Men, Sir, are always wrong, and that's the reason
    That righteous anger's never out of season;
    All that I hear in all their conversation
    Is flattering praise or reckless condemnation.
CÉLIMÈNE. But . . .
ALCESTE.   No, no, Madam, I am forced to state
    That you have pleasures which I deprecate,
    And that these others, here, are much to blame
    For nourishing the faults which are your shame.
CLITANDRE. I shan't defend myself, Sir; but I vow
    I'd thought this lady faultless until now.
ACASTE. I see her charms and graces, which are many;
    But as for faults, I've never noticed any.
ALCESTE. I see them, Sir; and rather than ignore them,
    I strenuously criticize her for them.
    The more one loves, the more one should object

To every blemish, every least defect.
Were I this lady, I would soon get rid
Of lovers who approved of all I did,
And by their slack indulgence and applause
Endorsed my follies and excused my flaws.
CÉLIMÈNE. If all hearts beat according to your measure,
The dawn of love would be the end of pleasure;
And love would find its perfect consummation
In ecstasies of rage and reprobation.
ÉLIANTE. Love, as a rule, affects men otherwise,
And lovers rarely love to criticize.
They see their lady as a charming blur,
And find all things commendable in her.
If she has any blemish, fault, or shame,
They will redeem it by a pleasing name.
The pale-faced lady's lily-white, perforce;
The swarthy one's a sweet brunette, of course;
The spindly lady has a slender grace;
The fat one has a most majestic pace;
The plain one, with her dress in disarray,
They classify as *beauté négligée;*
The hulking one's a goddess in their eyes,
The dwarf, a concentrate of Paradise;
The haughty lady has a noble mind;
The mean one's witty, and the dull one's kind;
The chatterbox has liveliness and verve,
The mute one has a virtuous reserve.
So lovers manage, in their passion's cause,
To love their ladies even for their flaws.
ALCESTE. But I still say . . .
CÉLIMÈNE.   I think it would be nice
To stroll around the gallery once or twice.
What! You're not going, Sirs?
CLITANDRE AND ACASTE.   No, Madam, no.
ALCESTE. You seem to be in terror lest they go.
Do what you will, Sirs; leave, or linger on,
But I shan't go till after you are gone.
ACASTE. I'm free to linger, unless I should perceive
Madame is tired, and wishes me to leave.
CLITANDRE. And as for me, I needn't go today
Until the hour of the King's *coucher.*
CÉLIMÈNE (*to* ALCESTE). You're joking, surely?
ALCESTE.   Not in the least; we'll see
Whether you'd rather part with them, or me.

Scene 6 ◦୫ ALCESTE, CÉLIMÈNE, ÉLIANTE, ACASTE, PHILINTE,
CLITANDRE, BASQUE.

BASQUE (*to* ALCESTE). Sir, there's a fellow here who bids me state
  That he must see you, and that it can't wait.
ALCESTE. Tell him that I have no such pressing affairs.
BASQUE. It's a long tailcoat that this fellow wears,
  With gold all over.
CÉLIMÈNE (*to* ALCESTE). You'd best go down and see.
  Or—have him enter.

Scene 7 ◦୫ ALCESTE, CÉLIMÈNE, ÉLIANTE, ACASTE, PHILINTE,
CLITANDRE, GUARD.

ALCESTE (*confronting the* GUARD). Well, what do you want with me?
  Come in, Sir.
GUARD.   I've a word, Sir, for your ear.
ALCESTE. Speak it aloud, Sir; I shall strive to hear.
GUARD. The Marshals have instructed me to say
  You must report to them without delay.
ALCESTE. Who? Me, Sir?
GUARD.   Yes, Sir; you.
ALCESTE.   But what do they want?
PHILINTE (*to* ALCESTE). To scotch your silly quarrel with Oronte.
CÉLIMÈNE (*to* PHILINTE). What quarrel?
PHILINTE.   Oronte and he have fallen out
  Over some verse he spoke his mind about;
  The Marshals wish to arbitrate the matter.
ALCESTE. Never shall I equivocate or flatter!
PHILINTE. You'd best obey their summons; come, let's go.
ALCESTE. How can they mend our quarrel, I'd like to know?
  Am I to make a cowardly retraction,
  And praise those jingles to his satisfaction?
  I'll not recant; I've judged that sonnet rightly.
  It's bad.
PHILINTE.   But you might say so more politely. . . .
ALCESTE. I'll not back down; his verses make me sick.
PHILINTE. If only you could be more politic!
  But come, let's go.
ALCESTE.   I'll go, but I won't unsay
  A single word.
PHILINTE.   Well, let's be on our way.

ALCESTE. Till I am ordered by my lord the King
     To praise that poem, I shall say the thing
     Is scandalous, by God, and that the poet
     Ought to be hanged for having the nerve to show it.
          [*To* CLITANDRE *and* ACASTE, *who are laughing.*]
     By heaven, Sirs, I really didn't know
     That I was being humorous.
CÉLIMÈNE.   Go, Sir, go;
     Settle your business.
ALCESTE.   I shall, and when I'm through,
     I shall return to settle things with you.

ACT III

Scene 1 ⁊ CLITANDRE, ACASTE.

CLITANDRE. Dear Marquess, how contented you appear;
    All things delight you, nothing mars your cheer.
    Can you, in perfect honesty, declare
    That you've a right to be so debonair?
ACASTE. By Jove, when I survey myself, I find
    No cause whatever for distress of mind.
    I'm young and rich; I can in modesty
    Lay claim to an exalted pedigree;
    And owing to my name and my condition
    I shall not want for honors and position.
    Then as to courage, that most precious trait,
    I seem to have it, as was proved of late
    Upon the field of honor, where my bearing,
    They say, was very cool and rather daring.
    I've wit, of course; and taste in such perfection
    That I can judge without the least reflection,
    And at the theater, which is my delight,
    Can make or break a play on opening night,
    And lead the crowd in hisses or bravos,
    And generally be known as one who knows.
    I'm clever, handsome, gracefully polite;
    My waist is small, my teeth are strong and white;
    As for my dress, the world's astonished eyes
    Assure me that I bear away the prize.
    I find myself in favor everywhere,
    Honored by men, and worshiped by the fair;

And since these things are so, it seems to me
I'm justified in my complacency.
CLITANDRE. Well, if so many ladies hold you dear,
Why do you press a hopeless courtship here?
ACASTE. Hopeless, you say? I'm not the sort of fool
That likes his ladies difficult and cool.
Men who are awkward, shy, and peasantish
May pine for heartless beauties, if they wish,
Grovel before them, bear their cruelties,
Woo them with tears and sighs and bended knees,
And hope by dogged faithfulness to gain
What their poor merits never could obtain.
For men like me, however, it makes no sense
To love on trust, and foot the whole expense.
Whatever any lady's merits be,
I think, thank God, that I'm as choice as she;
That if my heart is kind enough to burn
For her, she owes me something in return;
And that in any proper love affair
The partners must invest an equal share.
CLITANDRE. You think, then, that our hostess favors you?
ACASTE. I've reason to believe that that is true.
CLITANDRE. How did you come to such a mad conclusion?
You're blind, dear fellow. This is sheer delusion.
ACASTE. All right, then: I'm deluded and I'm blind.
CLITANDRE. Whatever put the notion in your mind?
ACASTE. Delusion.
CLITANDRE.   What persuades you that you're right?
ACASTE. I'm blind.
CLITANDRE.   But have you any proofs to cite?
ACASTE. I tell you I'm deluded.
CLITANDRE.   Have you, then,
Received some secret pledge from Célimène?
ACASTE. Oh, no: she scorns me.
CLITANDRE.   Tell me the truth, I beg.
ACASTE. She just can't bear me.
CLITANDRE.   Ah, don't pull my leg.
Tell me what hope she's given you, I pray.
ACASTE. I'm hopeless, and it's you who win the day.
She hates me thoroughly, and I'm so vexed
I mean to hang myself on Tuesday next.
CLITANDRE. Dear Marquess, let us have an armistice
And make a treaty. What do you say to this?
If ever one of us can plainly prove

That Célimène encourages his love,
The other must abandon hope, and yield,
And leave him in possession of the field.
ACASTE. Now, there's a bargain that appeals to me;
     With all my heart, dear Marquess, I agree.
     But hush.

Scene 2 ⟨⟩ CÉLIMÈNE, ACASTE, CLITANDRE.

CÉLIMÈNE. Still here?
CLITANDRE.   'Twas love that stayed our feet.
CÉLIMÈNE. I think I heard a carriage in the street.
     Whose is it? D'you know?

Scene 3 ⟨⟩ CÉLIMÈNE, ACASTE, CLITANDRE, BASQUE.

BASQUE.   Arsinoé is here,
     Madame.
CÉLIMÈNE.   Arsinoé, you say? Oh, dear.
BASQUE. Éliante is entertaining her below.
CÉLIMÈNE. What brings the creature here, I'd like to know?
ACASTE. They say she's dreadfully prudish, but in fact
     I think her piety . . .
CÉLIMÈNE.   It's all an act.
     At heart she's worldly, and her poor success
     In snaring men explains her prudishness.
     It breaks her heart to see the beaux and gallants
     Engrossed by other women's charms and talents,
     And so she's always in a jealous rage
     Against the faulty standards of the age.
     She lets the world believe that she's a prude
     To justify her loveless solitude,
     And strives to put a brand of moral shame
     On all the graces that she cannot claim.
     But still she'd love a lover; and Alceste
     Appears to be the one she'd love the best.
     His visits here are poison to her pride;
     She seems to think I've lured him from her side;
     And everywhere, at court or in the town,
     The spiteful, envious woman runs me down.
     In short, she's just as stupid as can be,

Vicious and arrogant in the last degree,
And . . .

Scene 4 ᴀꞧꜱᴵɴᴏᴇ́, CÉLIMÈNE, CLITANDRE, ACASTE.

CÉLIMÈNE. Ah! What happy chance has brought you here?
    I've thought about you ever so much, my dear.
ARSINOÉ. I've come to tell you something you should know.
CÉLIMÈNE. How good of you to think of doing so!
        [CLITANDRE *and* ACASTE *go out, laughing.*]

Scene 5 ARSINOÉ, CÉLIMÈNE.

ARSINOÉ. It's just as well those gentlemen didn't tarry.
CÉLIMÈNE. Shall we sit down?
ARSINOÉ.   That won't be necessary.
    Madam, the flame of friendship ought to burn
    Brightest in matters of the most concern,
    And as there's nothing which concerns us more
    Than honor, I have hastened to your door
    To bring you, as your friend, some information
    About the status of your reputation.
    I visited, last night, some virtuous folk,
    And, quite by chance, it was of you they spoke;
    There was, I fear, no tendency to praise
    Your light behavior and your dashing ways.
    The quantity of gentlemen you see
    And your by now notorious coquetry
    Were both so vehemently criticized
    By everyone, that I was much surprised.
    Of course, I needn't tell you where I stood;
    I came to your defense as best I could,
    Assured them you were harmless, and declared
    Your soul was absolutely unimpaired.
    But there are some things, you must realize,
    One can't excuse, however hard one tries,
    And I was forced at last into conceding
    That your behavior, Madam, is misleading,
    That it makes a bad impression, giving rise
    To ugly gossip and obscene surmise,
    And that if you were more *overtly* good,

You wouldn't be so much misunderstood.
Not that I think you've been unchaste—no! no!
The saints preserve me from a thought so low!
But mere good conscience never did suffice:
One must avoid the outward show of vice.
Madam, you're too intelligent, I'm sure,
To think my motives anything but pure
In offering you this counsel—which I do
Out of a zealous interest in you.

CÉLIMÈNE. Madam, I haven't taken you amiss;
I'm very much obliged to you for this;
And I'll at once discharge the obligation
By telling you about *your* reputation.
You've been so friendly as to let me know
What certain people say of me, and so
I mean to follow your benign example
By offering you a somewhat similar sample.
The other day, I went to an affair
And found some most distinguished people there
Discussing piety, both false and true.
The conversation soon came round to you.
Alas! Your prudery and bustling zeal
Appeared to have a very slight appeal.
Your affectation of a grave demeanor,
Your endless talk of virtue and of honor,
The aptitude of your suspicious mind
For finding sin where there is none to find,
Your towering self-esteem, that pitying face
With which you contemplate the human race,
Your sermonizings and your sharp aspersions
On people's pure and innocent diversions—
All these were mentioned, Madam, and, in fact,
Were roundly and concertedly attacked.
"What good," they said, "are all these outward shows,
When everything belies her pious pose?
She prays incessantly; but then, they say,
She beats her maids and cheats them of their pay;
She shows her zeal in every holy place,
But still she's vain enough to paint her face;
She holds that naked statues are immoral,
But with a naked *man* she'd have no quarrel."
Of course, I said to everybody there
That they were being viciously unfair;
But still they were disposed to criticize you,
And all agreed that someone should advise you

To leave the morals of the world alone,
And worry rather more about your own.
They felt that one's self-knowledge should be great
Before one thinks of setting others straight;
That one should learn the art of living well
Before one threatens other men with hell,
And that the Church is best equipped, no doubt,
To guide our souls and root our vices out.
Madam, you're too intelligent, I'm sure,
To think my motives anything but pure
In offering you this counsel—which I do
Out of a zealous interest in you.

ARSINOÉ. I dared not hope for gratitude, but I
Did not expect so acid a reply;
I judge, since you've been so extremely tart,
That my good counsel pierced you to the heart.

CÉLIMÈNE. Far from it, Madam. Indeed, it seems to me
We ought to trade advice more frequently.
One's vision of oneself is so defective
That it would be an excellent corrective.
If you are willing, Madam, let's arrange
Shortly to have another frank exchange
In which we'll tell each other, *entre nous,*
What you've heard tell of me, and I of you.

ARSINOÉ. Oh, people never censure you, my dear;
It's me they criticize. Or so I hear.

CÉLIMÈNE. Madam, I think we either blame or praise
According to our taste and length of days.
There is a time of life for coquetry,
And there's a season, too, for prudery.
When all one's charms are gone, it is, I'm sure,
Good strategy to be devout and pure:
It makes one seem a little less forsaken.
Some day, perhaps, I'll take the road you've taken:
Time brings all things. But I have time aplenty,
And see no cause to be a prude at twenty.

ARSINOÉ. You give your age in such a gloating tone
That one would think I was an ancient crone;
We're not so far apart, in sober truth,
That you can mock me with a boast of youth!
Madam, you baffle me. I wish I knew
What moves you to provoke me as you do.

CÉLIMÈNE. For my part, Madam, I should like to know
Why you abuse me everywhere you go.
Is it my fault, dear lady, that your hand

Is not, alas, in very great demand?
If men admire me, if they pay me court
And daily make me offers of the sort
You'd dearly love to have them make to you,
How can I help it? What would you have me do?
If what you want is lovers, please feel free
To take as many as you can from me.
ARSINOÉ. Oh, come. D'you think the world is losing sleep
Over that flock of lovers which you keep,
Or that we find it difficult to guess
What price you pay for their devotedness?
Surely you don't expect us to suppose
Mere merit could attract so many beaux?
It's not your virtue that they're dazzled by;
Nor is it virtuous love for which they sigh.
You're fooling no one, Madam; the world's not blind;
There's many a lady heaven has designed
To call men's noblest, tenderest feelings out,
Who has no lovers dogging her about;
From which it's plain that lovers nowadays
Must be acquired in bold and shameless ways,
And only pay one court for such reward
As modesty and virtue can't afford.
Then don't be quite so puffed up, if you please,
About your tawdry little victories;
Try, if you can, to be a shade less vain,
And treat the world with somewhat less disdain.
If one were envious of your amours,
One soon could have a following like yours;
Lovers are no great trouble to collect
If one prefers them to one's self-respect.
CÉLIMÈNE. Collect them then, my dear; I'd love to see
You demonstrate that charming theory;
Who knows, you might . . .
ARSINOÉ.   Now, Madam, that will do;
It's time to end this trying interview.
My coach is late in coming to your door,
Or I'd have taken leave of you before.
CÉLIMÈNE. Oh, please don't feel that you must rush away;
I'd be delighted, Madam, if you'd stay.
However, lest my conversation bore you,
Let me provide some better company for you;
This gentleman, who comes most apropos,
Will please you more than I could do, I know.

Scene 6 ▰ ALCESTE, CÉLIMÈNE, ARSINOÉ.

CÉLIMÈNE. Alceste, I have a little note to write
Which simply must go out before tonight;
Please entertain *Madame;* I'm sure that she
Will overlook my incivility.

Scene 7 ▰ ALCESTE, ARSINOÉ.

ARSINOÉ. Well, Sir, our hostess graciously contrives
For us to chat until my coach arrives;
And I shall be forever in her debt
For granting me this little tête-à-tête.
We women very rightly give our hearts
To men of noble character and parts,
And your especial merits, dear Alceste,
Have roused the deepest sympathy in my breast.
Oh, how I wish they had sufficient sense
At court, to recognize your excellence!
They wrong you greatly, Sir. How it must hurt you
Never to be rewarded for your virtue!
ALCESTE. Why, Madam, what cause have I to feel aggrieved?
What great and brilliant thing have I achieved?
What service have I rendered to the King
That I should look to him for anything?
ARSINOÉ. Not everyone who's honored by the State
Has done great services. A man must wait
Till time and fortune offer him the chance.
Your merit, Sir, is obvious at a glance,
And . . .
ALCESTE.   Ah, forget my merit; I'm not neglected.
The court, I think, can hardly be expected
To mine men's souls for merit, and unearth
Our hidden virtues and our secret worth.
ARSINOÉ. *Some* virtues, though, are far too bright to hide;
Yours are acknowledged, Sir, on every side.
Indeed, I've heard you warmly praised of late
By persons of considerable weight.
ALCESTE. This fawning age has praise for everyone,
And all distinctions, Madam, are undone.
All things have equal honor nowadays,

And no one should be gratified by praise.
To be admired, one only need exist,
And every lackey's on the honors list.

ARSINOÉ. I only wish, Sir, that you had your eye
On some position at court, however high;
You'd only have to hint at such a notion
For me to set the proper wheels in motion;
I've certain friendships I'd be glad to use
To get you any office you might choose.

ALCESTE. Madam, I fear that any such ambition
Is wholly foreign to my disposition.
The soul God gave me isn't of the sort
That prospers in the weather of a court.
It's all too obvious that I don't possess
The virtues necessary for success.
My one great talent is for speaking plain;
I've never learned to flatter or to feign;
And anyone so stupidly sincere
Had best not seek a courtier's career.
Outside the court, I know, one must dispense
With honors, privilege, and influence;
But still one gains the right, foregoing these,
Not to be tortured by the wish to please.
One needn't live in dread of snubs and slights,
Nor praise the verse that every idiot writes,
Nor humor silly Marquesses, nor bestow
Politic sighs on Madam So-and-So.

ARSINOÉ. Forget the court, then; let the matter rest.
But I've another cause to be distressed
About your present situation, Sir.
It's to your love affair that I refer.
She whom you love, and who pretends to love you,
Is, I regret to say, unworthy of you.

ALCESTE. Why, Madam! Can you seriously intend
To make so grave a charge against your friend?

ARSINOÉ. Alas, I must. I've stood aside too long
And let that lady do you grievous wrong;
But now my debt to conscience shall be paid:
I tell you that your love has been betrayed.

ALCESTE. I thank you, Madam; you're extremely kind.
Such words are soothing to a lover's mind.

ARSINOÉ. Yes, though she *is* my friend, I say again
You're very much too good for Célimène.
She's wantonly misled you from the start.

ALCESTE. You may be right; who knows another's heart?

But ask yourself if it's the part of charity
To shake my soul with doubts of her sincerity.
ARSINOÉ. Well, if you'd rather be a dupe than doubt her,
That's your affair. I'll say no more about her.
ALCESTE. Madam, you know that doubt and vague suspicion
Are painful to a man in my position;
It's most unkind to worry me this way
Unless you've some real proof of what you say.
ARSINOÉ. Sir, say no more: all doubt shall be removed,
And all that I've been saying shall be proved.
You've only to escort me home, and there
We'll look into the heart of this affair.
I've ocular evidence which will persuade you
Beyond a doubt, that Célimène's betrayed you.
Then, if you're saddened by that revelation,
Perhaps I can provide some consolation.

ACT IV

Scene 1 ⚜ ÉLIANTE, PHILINTE.

PHILINTE. Madam, he acted like a stubborn child;
　　I thought they never would be reconciled;
　　In vain we reasoned, threatened, and appealed;
　　He stood his ground and simply would not yield.
　　The Marshals, I feel sure, have never heard
　　An argument so splendidly absurd.
　　"No, gentlemen," said he, "I'll not retract.
　　His verse is bad: extremely bad, in fact.
　　Surely it does the man no harm to know it.
　　Does it disgrace him, not to be a poet?
　　A gentleman may be respected still,
　　Whether he writes a sonnet well or ill.
　　That I dislike his verse should not offend him;
　　In all that touches honor, I commend him;
　　He's noble, brave, and virtuous—but I fear
　　He can't in truth be called a sonneteer.
　　I'll gladly praise his wardrobe; I'll endorse
　　His dancing, or the way he sits a horse;
　　But, gentlemen, I cannot praise his rhyme.
　　In fact, it ought to be a capital crime
　　For anyone so sadly unendowed
　　To write a sonnet, and read the thing aloud."
　　At length he fell into a gentler mood
　　And, striking a concessive attitude,
　　He paid Oronte the following courtesies:
　　"Sir, I regret that I'm so hard to please,
　　And I'm profoundly sorry that your lyric
　　Failed to provoke me to a panegyric."
　　After these curious words, the two embraced,
　　And then the hearing was adjourned—in haste.

ÉLIANTE. His conduct has been very singular lately;
    Still, I confess that I respect him greatly.
    The honesty in which he takes such pride
    Has—to my mind—its noble, heroic side.
    In this false age, such candor seems outrageous;
    But I could wish that it were more contagious.
PHILINTE. What most intrigues me in our friend Alceste
    Is the grand passion that rages in his breast.
    The sullen humors he's compounded of
    Should not, I think, dispose his heart to love;
    But since they do, it puzzles me still more
    That he should choose your cousin to adore.
ÉLIANTE. It does, indeed, belie the theory
    That love is born of gentle sympathy,
    And that the tender passion must be based
    On sweet accords of temper and of taste.
PHILINTE. Does she return his love, do you suppose?
ÉLIANTE. Ah, that's a difficult question, Sir. Who knows?
    How can we judge the truth of her devotion?
    Her heart's a stranger to its own emotion.
    Sometimes it thinks it loves, when no love's there;
    At other times it loves quite unaware.
PHILINTE. I rather think Alceste is in for more
    Distress and sorrow than he's bargained for;
    Were he of my mind, Madam, his affection
    Would turn in quite a different direction,
    And we would see him more responsive to
    The kind regard which he receives from you.
ÉLIANTE. Sir, I believe in frankness, and I'm inclined,
    In matters of the heart, to speak my mind.
    I don't oppose his love for her; indeed,
    I hope with all my heart that he'll succeed,
    And were it in my power, I'd rejoice
    In giving him the lady of his choice.
    But if, as happens frequently enough
    In love affairs, he meets with a rebuff—
    If Célimène should grant some rival's suit—
    I'd gladly play the role of substitute;
    Nor would his tender speeches please me less
    Because they'd once been made without success.
PHILINTE. Well, Madam, as for me, I don't oppose
    Your hopes in this affair; and heaven knows
    That in my conversations with the man
    I plead your cause as often as I can.
    But if those two should marry, and so remove

All chance that he will offer you his love,
Then I'll declare my own, and hope to see
Your gracious favor pass from him to me.
In short, should you be cheated of Alceste,
I'd be most happy to be second best.

ÉLIANTE. Philinte, you're teasing.

PHILINTE.   Ah, Madam, never fear;
No words of mine were ever so sincere,
And I shall live in fretful expectation
Till I can make a fuller declaration.

Scene 2 ⚬⚬ ALCESTE, ÉLIANTE, PHILINTE.

ALCESTE. Avenge me, Madam! I must have satisfaction,
Or this great wrong will drive me to distraction!

ÉLIANTE. Why, what's the matter? What's upset you so?

ALCESTE. Madam, I've had a mortal, mortal blow.
If Chaos repossessed the universe,
I swear I'd not be shaken any worse.
I'm ruined. . . . I can say no more. . . . My soul . . .

ÉLIANTE. Do try, Sir, to regain your self-control.

ALCESTE. Just heaven! Why were so much beauty and grace
Bestowed on one so vicious and so base?

ÉLIANTE. Once more, Sir, tell us. . . .

ALCESTE.   My world has gone to wrack;
I'm—I'm betrayed; she's stabbed me in the back:
Yes, Célimène (who would have thought it of her?)
Is false to me, and has another lover.

ÉLIANTE. Are you quite certain? Can you prove these things?

PHILINTE. Lovers are prey to wild imaginings
And jealous fancies. No doubt there's some mistake. . . .

ALCESTE. Mind your own business, Sir, for heaven's sake.
                    [To ÉLIANTE.]
Madam, I have the proof that you demand
Here in my pocket, penned by her own hand.
Yes, all the shameful evidence one could want
Lies in this letter written to Oronte—
Oronte! whom I felt sure she couldn't love,
And hardly bothered to be jealous of.

PHILINTE. Still, in a letter, appearances may deceive;
This may not be so bad as you believe.

ALCESTE. Once more I beg you, Sir, to let me be;
Tend to your own affairs; leave mine to me.

ÉLIANTE. Compose yourself; this anguish that you feel . . .
ALCESTE. Is something, Madam, you alone can heal.
My outraged heart, beside itself with grief,
Appeals to you for comfort and relief.
Avenge me on your cousin, whose unjust
And faithless nature has deceived my trust;
Avenge a crime your pure soul must detest.
ÉLIANTE. But how, Sir?
ALCESTE. Madam, this heart within my breast
Is yours; pray take it; redeem my heart from her,
And so avenge me on my torturer.
Let her be punished by the fond emotion,
The ardent love, the bottomless devotion,
The faithful worship which this heart of mine
Will offer up to yours as to a shrine.
ÉLIANTE. You have my sympathy, Sir, in all you suffer;
Nor do I scorn the noble heart you offer;
But I suspect you'll soon be mollified,
And this desire for vengeance will subside.
When some belovèd hand has done us wrong
We thirst for retribution—but not for long;
However dark the deed that she's committed,
A lovely culprit's very soon acquitted.
Nothing's so stormy as an injured lover,
And yet no storm so quickly passes over.
ALCESTE. No, Madam, no—this is no lovers' spat;
I'll not forgive her; it's gone too far for that;
My mind's made up; I'll kill myself before
I waste my hopes upon her any more.
Ah, here she is. My wrath intensifies.
I shall confront her with her tricks and lies,
And crush her utterly, and bring you then
A heart no longer slave to Célimène.

Scene 3 ⟍ᢒ CÉLIMÈNE, ALCESTE.

ALCESTE (*aside*). Sweet heaven, help me to control my passion.
CÉLIMÈNE (*aside*). Oh, Lord.
[*To* ALCESTE.]
Why stand there staring in that fashion?
And what d'you mean by those dramatic sighs,
And that malignant glitter in your eyes?

ALCESTE. I mean that sins which cause the blood to freeze
    Look innocent beside your treacheries;
    That nothing Hell's or Heaven's wrath could do
    Ever produced so bad a thing as you.
CÉLIMÈNE. Your compliments were always sweet and pretty.
ALCESTE. Madam, it's not the moment to be witty.
    No, blush and hang your head; you've ample reason,
    Since I've the fullest evidence of your treason.
    Ah, this is what my sad heart prophesied;
    Now all my anxious fears are verified;
    My dark suspicion and my gloomy doubt
    Divined the truth, and now the truth is out.
    For all your trickery, I was not deceived;
    It was my bitter stars that I believed.
    But don't imagine that you'll go scot-free;
    You shan't misuse me with impunity.
    I know that love's irrational and blind;
    I know the heart's not subject to the mind,
    And can't be reasoned into beating faster;
    I know each soul is free to choose its master;
    Therefore had you but spoken from the heart,
    Rejecting my attentions from the start,
    I'd have no grievance, or at any rate
    I could complain of nothing but my fate.
    Ah, but so falsely to encourage me—
    That was a treason and a treachery
    For which you cannot suffer too severely,
    And you shall pay for that behavior dearly.
    Yes, now I have no pity, not a shred;
    My temper's out of hand; I've lost my head;
    Shocked by the knowledge of your double-dealings,
    My reason can't restrain my savage feelings;
    A righteous wrath deprives me of my senses,
    And I won't answer for the consequences.
CÉLIMÈNE. What does this outburst mean? Will you please explain?
    Have you, by any chance, gone quite insane?
ALCESTE. Yes, yes, I went insane the day I fell
    A victim to your black and fatal spell,
    Thinking to meet with some sincerity
    Among the treacherous charms that beckoned me.
CÉLIMÈNE. Pooh. Of what treachery can you complain?
ALCESTE. How sly you are, how cleverly you feign!
    But you'll not victimize me any more.
    Look: here's a document you've seen before.
    This evidence, which I acquired today,

Leaves you, I think, without a thing to say.
CÉLIMÈNE. Is this what sent you into such a fit?
ALCESTE. You should be blushing at the sight of it.
CÉLIMÈNE. Ought I to blush? I truly don't see why.
ALCESTE. Ah, now you're being bold as well as sly;
    Since there's no signature, perhaps you'll claim . . .
CÉLIMÈNE. I wrote it, whether or not it bears my name.
ALCESTE. And you can view with equanimity
    This proof of your disloyalty to me!
CÉLIMÈNE. Oh, don't be so outrageous and extreme.
ALCESTE. You take this matter lightly, it would seem.
    Was it no wrong to me, no shame to you,
    That you should send Oronte this billet-doux?
CÉLIMÈNE. Oronte! Who said it was for him?
ALCESTE.   Why, those
    Who brought me this example of your prose.
    But what's the difference? If you wrote the letter
    To someone else, it pleases me no better.
    My grievance and your guilt remain the same.
CÉLIMÈNE. But need you rage, and need I blush for shame,
    If this was written to a *woman* friend?
ALCESTE. Ah! Most ingenious. I'm impressed no end;
    And after that incredible evasion
    Your guilt is clear. I need no more persuasion.
    How dare you try so clumsy a deception?
    D'you think I'm wholly wanting in perception?
    Come, come, let's see how brazenly you'll try
    To bolster up so palpable a lie:
    Kindly construe this ardent closing section
    As nothing more than sisterly affection!
    Here, let me read it. Tell me, if you dare to,
    That this is for a woman . . .
CÉLIMÈNE.   I don't care to.
    What right have you to badger and berate me,
    And so highhandedly interrogate me?
ALCESTE. Now, don't be angry; all I ask of you
    Is that you justify a phrase or two . . .
CÉLIMÈNE. No, I shall not. I utterly refuse,
    And you may take those phrases as you choose.
ALCESTE. Just show me how this letter could be meant
    For a woman's eyes, and I shall be content.
CÉLIMÈNE. No, no, it's for Oronte; you're perfectly right.
    I welcome his attentions with delight,
    I prize his character and his intellect,
    And everything is just as you suspect.

Come, do your worst now; give your rage free rein;
But kindly cease to bicker and complain.

ALCESTE (*aside*). Good God! Could anything be more inhuman?
Was ever a heart so mangled by a woman?
When I complain of how she has betrayed me,
She bridles, and commences to upbraid me!
She tries my tortured patience to the limit;
She won't deny her guilt; she glories in it!
And yet my heart's too faint and cowardly
To break these chains of passion, and be free,
To scorn her as it should, and rise above
This unrewarded, mad, and bitter love.
                    [*To* CÉLIMÈNE.]
Ah, traitress, in how confident a fashion
You take advantage of my helpless passion,
And use my weakness for your faithless charms
To make me once again throw down my arms!
But do at least deny this black transgression;
Take back that mocking and perverse confession;
Defend this letter and your innocence,
And I, poor fool, will aid in your defense.
Pretend, pretend, that you are just and true,
And I shall make myself believe in you.

CÉLIMÈNE. Oh, stop it. Don't be such a jealous dunce,
Or I shall leave off loving you at once.
Just why should I *pretend*? What could impel me
To stoop so low as that? And kindly tell me
Why, if I loved another, I shouldn't merely
Inform you of it, simply and sincerely!
I've told you where you stand, and that admission
Should altogether clear me of suspicion;
After so generous a guarantee,
What right have you to harbor doubts of me?
Since women are (from natural reticence)
Reluctant to declare their sentiments,
And since the honor of our sex requires
That we conceal our amorous desires,
Ought any man for whom such laws are broken
To question what the oracle has spoken?
Should he not rather feel an obligation
To trust that most obliging declaration?
Enough, now. Your suspicions quite disgust me;
Why should I love a man who doesn't trust me?
I cannot understand why I continue,
Fool that I am, to take an interest in you.

I ought to choose a man less prone to doubt,
And give you something to be vexed about.
ALCESTE. Ah, what a poor enchanted fool I am;
These gentle words, no doubt, were all a sham;
But destiny requires me to entrust
My happiness to you, and so I must.
I'll love you to the bitter end, and see
How false and treacherous you dare to be.
CÉLIMÈNE. No, you don't really love me as you ought.
ALCESTE. I love you more than can be said or thought;
Indeed, I wish you were in such distress
That I might show my deep devotedness.
Yes, I could wish that you were wretchedly poor,
Unloved, uncherished, utterly obscure;
That fate had set you down upon the earth
Without possessions, rank, or gentle birth;
Then, by the offer of my heart, I might
Repair the great injustice of your plight;
I'd raise you from the dust, and proudly prove
The purity and vastness of my love.
CÉLIMÈNE. This is a strange benevolence indeed!
God grant that I may never be in need. . . .
Ah, here's Monsieur Dubois, in quaint disguise.

Scene 4   CÉLIMÈNE, ALCESTE, DUBOIS.

ALCESTE. Well, why this costume? Why those frightened eyes?
What ails you?
DUBOIS.   Well, Sir, things are most mysterious.
ALCESTE. What do you mean?
DUBOIS.   I fear they're very serious.
ALCESTE. What?
DUBOIS.   Shall I speak more loudly?
ALCESTE.   Yes; speak out.
DUBOIS. Isn't there someone here, Sir?
ALCESTE.   Speak, you lout!
Stop wasting time.
DUBOIS.   Sir, we must slip away.
ALCESTE. How's that?
DUBOIS.   We must decamp without delay.
ALCESTE. Explain yourself.
DUBOIS.   I tell you we must fly.

ALCESTE. What for?

DUBOIS.   We mustn't pause to say good-by.

ALCESTE. Now what d'you mean by all of this, you clown?

DUBOIS. I mean, Sir, that we've got to leave this town.

ALCESTE. I'll tear you limb from limb and joint from joint
     If you don't come more quickly to the point.

DUBOIS. Well, Sir, today a man in a black suit,
     Who wore a black and ugly scowl to boot,
     Left us a document scrawled in such a hand
     As even Satan couldn't understand.
     It bears upon your lawsuit, I don't doubt;
     But all hell's devils couldn't make it out.

ALCESTE. Well, well, go on. What then? I fail to see
     How this event obliges us to flee.

DUBOIS. Well, Sir: an hour later, hardly more,
     A gentleman who's often called before
     Came looking for you in an anxious way.
     Not finding you, he asked me to convey
     (Knowing I could be trusted with the same)
     The following message. . . . Now, what *was* his name?

ALCESTE. Forget his name, you idiot. What did he say?

DUBOIS. Well, it was one of your friends, Sir, anyway.
     He warned you to begone, and he suggested
     That if you stay, you may well be arrested.

ALCESTE. What? Nothing more specific? Think, man, think!

DUBOIS. No, Sir. He had me bring him pen and ink,
     And dashed you off a letter which, I'm sure,
     Will render things distinctly less obscure.

ALCESTE. Well—let me have it!

CÉLIMÈNE.   What *is* this all about?

ALCESTE. God knows; but I have hopes of finding out.
     How long am I to wait, you blitherer?

DUBOIS (*after a protracted search for the letter*). I must have left it on
     your table, Sir.

ALCESTE. I ought to . . .

CÉLIMÈNE.   No, no, keep your self-control;
     Go find out what's behind his rigmarole.

ALCESTE. It seems that fate, no matter what I do,
     Has sworn that I may not converse with you;
     But, Madam, pray permit your faithful lover
     To try once more before the day is over.

ACT V

Scene 1 ❧ ALCESTE, PHILINTE.

ALCESTE. No, it's too much. My mind's made up, I tell you.
PHILINTE. Why should this blow, however hard, compel you . . .
ALCESTE. No, no, don't waste your breath in argument;
    Nothing you say will alter my intent;
    This age is vile, and I've made up my mind
    To have no further commerce with mankind.
    Did not truth, honor, decency, and the laws
    Oppose my enemy and approve my cause?
    My claims were justified in all men's sight;
    I put my trust in equity and right;
    Yet, to my horror and the world's disgrace,
    Justice is mocked, and I have lost my case!
    A scoundrel whose dishonesty is notorious
    Emerges from another lie victorious!
    Honor and right condone his brazen fraud,
    While rectitude and decency applaud!
    Before his smirking face, the truth stands charmed,
    And virtue conquered, and the law disarmed!
    His crime is sanctioned by a court decree!
    And not content with what he's done to me,
    The dog now seeks to ruin me by stating
    That I composed a book now circulating,
    A book so wholly criminal and vicious
    That even to speak its title is seditious!
    Meanwhile Oronte, my rival, lends his credit
    To the same libelous tale, and helps to spread it!
    Oronte! a man of honor and of rank,
    With whom I've been entirely fair and frank;
    Who sought me out and forced me, willy-nilly,
    To judge some verse I found extremely silly;
    And who, because I properly refused

To flatter him, or see the truth abused,
Abets my enemy in a rotten slander!
There's the reward of honesty and candor!
The man will hate me to the end of time
For failing to commend his wretched rhyme!
And not this man alone, but all humanity
Do what they do from interest and vanity;
They prate of honor, truth, and righteousness,
But lie, betray, and swindle nonetheless.
Come then: man's villainy is too much to bear;
Let's leave this jungle and this jackal's lair.
Yes! treacherous and savage race of men,
You shall not look upon my face again.

PHILINTE. Oh, don't rush into exile prematurely;
Things aren't as dreadful as you make them, surely.
It's rather obvious, since you're still at large,
That people don't believe your enemy's charge.
Indeed, his tale's so patently untrue
That it may do more harm to him than you.

ALCESTE. Nothing could do that scoundrel any harm:
His frank corruption is his greatest charm,
And, far from hurting him, a further shame
Would only serve to magnify his name.

PHILINTE. In any case, his bald prevarication
Has done no injury to your reputation,
And you may feel secure in that regard.
As for your lawsuit, it should not be hard
To have the case reopened, and contest
This judgment . . .

ALCESTE.   No, no, let the verdict rest.
Whatever cruel penalty it may bring,
I wouldn't have it changed for anything.
It shows the times' injustice with such clarity
That I shall pass it down to our posterity
As a great proof and signal demonstration
Of the black wickedness of this generation.
It may cost twenty thousand francs; but I
Shall pay their twenty thousand, and gain thereby
The right to storm and rage at human evil,
And send the race of mankind to the devil.

PHILINTE. Listen to me. . . .

ALCESTE.   Why? What can you possibly say?
Don't argue, Sir; your labor's thrown away.
Do you propose to offer lame excuses
For men's behavior and the times' abuses?

PHILINTE. No, all you say I'll readily concede:
  This is a low, conniving age indeed;
  Nothing but trickery prospers nowadays,
  And people ought to mend their shabby ways.
  Yes, man's a beastly creature; but must we then
  Abandon the society of men?
  Here in the world, each human frailty
  Provides occasion for philosophy,
  And that is virtue's noblest exercise;
  If honesty shone forth from all men's eyes,
  If every heart were frank and kind and just,
  What could our virtues do but gather dust
  (Since their employment is to help us bear
  The villainies of men without despair)?
  A heart well-armed with virtue can endure. . . .
ALCESTE. Sir, you're a matchless reasoner, to be sure;
  Your words are fine and full of cogency;
  But don't waste time and eloquence on me.
  My reason bids me go, for my own good.
  My tongue won't lie and flatter as it should;
  God knows what frankness it might next commit,
  And what I'd suffer on account of it.
  Pray let me wait for Célimène's return
  In peace and quiet. I shall shortly learn,
  By her response to what I have in view,
  Whether her love for me is feigned or true.
PHILINTE. Till then, let's visit Éliante upstairs.
ALCESTE. No, I am too weighed down with somber cares.
  Go to her, do; and leave me with my gloom
  Here in the darkened corner of this room.
PHILINTE. Why, that's no sort of company, my friend;
  I'll see if Éliante will not descend.

Scene 2 ⤫ CÉLIMÈNE, ORONTE, ALCESTE.

ORONTE. Yes, Madam, if you wish me to remain
  Your true and ardent lover, you must deign
  To give me some more positive assurance.
  All this suspense is quite beyond endurance.
  If your heart shares the sweet desires of mine,
  Show me as much by some convincing sign;
  And here's the sign I urgently suggest:

That you no longer tolerate Alceste,
But sacrifice him to my love, and sever
All your relations with the man forever.

CÉLIMÈNE. Why do you suddenly dislike him so?
You praised him to the skies not long ago.

ORONTE. Madam, that's not the point. I'm here to find
Which way your tender feelings are inclined.
Choose, if you please, between Alceste and me,
And I shall stay or go accordingly.

ALCESTE (*emerging from the corner*). Yes, Madam, choose; this gen-
tleman's demand
Is wholly just, and I support his stand.
I too am true and ardent; I too am here
To ask you that you make your feelings clear.
No more delays, now; no equivocation;
The time has come to make your declaration.

ORONTE. Sir, I've no wish in any way to be
An obstacle to your felicity.

ALCESTE. Sir, I've no wish to share her heart with you;
That may sound jealous, but at least it's true.

ORONTE. If, weighing us, she leans in your direction . . .

ALCESTE. If she regards you with the least affection . . .

ORONTE. I swear I'll yield her to you there and then.

ALCESTE. I swear I'll never see her face again.

ORONTE. Now, Madam, tell us what we've come to hear.

ALCESTE. Madam, speak openly and have no fear.

ORONTE. Just say which one is to remain your lover.

ALCESTE. Just name one name, and it will all be over.

ORONTE. What! Is it possible that you're undecided?

ALCESTE. What! Can your feelings possibly be divided?

CÉLIMÈNE. Enough: this inquisition's gone too far:
How utterly unreasonable you are!
Not that I couldn't make the choice with ease;
My heart has no conflicting sympathies;
I know full well which one of you I favor,
And you'd not see me hesitate or waver.
But how can you expect me to reveal
So cruelly and bluntly what I feel?
I think it altogether too unpleasant
To choose between two men when both are present;
One's heart has means more subtle and more kind
Of letting its affections be divined,
Nor need one be uncharitably plain
To let a lover know he loves in vain.

ORONTE. No, no, speak plainly; I for one can stand it.

I beg you to be frank.
ALCESTE.   And I demand it.
The simple truth is what I wish to know,
And there's no need for softening the blow.
You've made an art of pleasing everyone,
But now your days of coquetry are done:
You have no choice now, Madam, but to choose,
For I'll know what to think if you refuse;
I'll take your silence for a clear admission
That I'm entitled to my worst suspicion.
ORONTE. I thank you for this ultimatum, Sir,
And I may say I heartily concur.
CÉLIMÈNE. Really, this foolishness is very wearing:
Must you be so unjust and overbearing?
Haven't I told you why I must demur?
Ah, here's Éliante; I'll put the case to her.

Scene 3 ⤳ ÉLIANTE, PHILINTE, CÉLIMÈNE, ORONTE, ALCESTE.

CÉLIMÈNE. Cousin, I'm being persecuted here
By these two persons, who, it would appear,
Will not be satisfied till I confess
Which one I love the more, and which the less,
And tell the latter to his face that he
Is henceforth banished from my company.
Tell me, has ever such a thing been done?
ÉLIANTE. You'd best not turn to me; I'm not the one
To back you in a matter of this kind:
I'm all for those who frankly speak their mind.
ORONTE. Madam, you'll search in vain for a defender.
ALCESTE. You're beaten, Madam, and may as well surrender.
ORONTE. Speak, speak, you must; and end this awful strain.
ALCESTE. Or don't, and your position will be plain.
ORONTE. A single word will close this painful scene.
ALCESTE. But if you're silent, I'll know what you mean.

Scene 4 ⤳ ARSINOÉ, CÉLIMÈNE, ÉLIANTE, ALCESTE, PHI-
                LINTE, ACASTE, CLITANDRE, ORONTE.

ACASTE (to CÉLIMÈNE). Madam, with all due deference, we two
Have come to pick a little bone with you.

CLITANDRE (*to* ORONTE *and* ALCESTE). I'm glad you're present, Sirs; as
    you'll soon learn,
  Our business here is also your concern.
ARSINOÉ (*to* CÉLIMÈNE). Madam, I visit you so soon again
  Only because of these two gentlemen,
  Who came to me indignant and aggrieved
  About a crime too base to be believed.
  Knowing your virtue, having such confidence in it,
  I couldn't think you guilty for a minute,
  In spite of all their telling evidence;
  And, rising above our little difference,
  I've hastened here in friendship's name to see
  You clear yourself of this great calumny.
ALCESTE. Yes, Madam, let us see with what composure
  You'll manage to respond to this disclosure.
  You lately sent Clitandre this tender note.
CLITANDRE. And this one, for Acaste, you also wrote.
ACASTE (*to* ORONTE *and* ALCESTE). You'll recognize this writing, Sirs,
    I think;
  The lady is so free with pen and ink
  That you must know it all too well, I fear.
  But listen: this is something you should hear.

> *How absurd you are to condemn my lightheartedness in so-*
> *ciety, and to accuse me of being happiest in the company of*
> *others. Nothing could be more unjust; and if you do not come*
> *to me instantly and beg pardon for saying such a thing, I shall*
> *never forgive you as long as I live. Our big bumbling friend the*
> *Viscount . . .*

What a shame that he's not here.

> *Our big bumbling friend the Viscount, whose name stands first*
> *in your complaint, is hardly a man to my taste; and ever since*
> *the day I watched him spend three-quarters of an hour spitting*
> *into a well, so as to make circles in the water, I have been unable*
> *to think highly of him. As for the little Marquess . . .*

In all modesty gentlemen, that is I.

> *As for the little Marquess, who sat squeezing my hand for such*
> *a long while yesterday, I find him in all respects the most trifling*
> *creature alive; and the only things of value about him are his*
> *cape and his sword. As for the man with the green ribbons . . .*

[*To* ALCESTE.]
It's your turn now, Sir.

As for the man with the green ribbons, he amuses me now and then with his bluntness and his bearish ill-humor; but there are many times indeed when I think him the greatest bore in the world. And as for the sonneteer . . .

[*To* ORONTE.]

Here's your helping.

And as for the sonneteer, who has taken it into his head to be witty, and insists on being an author in the teeth of opinion, I simply cannot be bothered to listen to him, and his prose wearies me quite as much as his poetry. Be assured that I am not always so well-entertained as you suppose; that I long for your company, more than I dare to say, at all these entertainments to which people drag me; and that the presence of those one loves is the true and perfect seasoning to all one's pleasures.

CLITANDRE. And now for me.

Clitandre, whom you mention, and who so pesters me with his saccharine speeches, is the last man on earth for whom I could feel any affection. He is quite mad to suppose that I love him, and so are you, to doubt that you are loved. Do come to your senses; exchange your suppositions for his; and visit me as often as possible, to help me bear the annoyance of his unwelcome attentions.

It's a sweet character that these letters show,
And what to call it, Madam, you well know.
Enough. We're off to make the world acquainted
With this sublime self-portrait that you've painted.
ACASTE. Madam, I'll make you no farewell oration;
No, you're not worthy of my indignation.
Far choicer hearts than yours, as you'll discover,
Would like this little Marquess for a lover.

Scene 5 ⟅ CÉLIMÈNE, ÉLIANTE, ARSINOÉ, ALCESTE, ORONTE,
PHILINTE.

ORONTE. So! After all those loving letters you wrote,
You turn on me like this, and cut my throat!
And your dissembling, faithless heart, I find,
Has pledged itself by turns to all mankind!
How blind I've been! But now I clearly see;

I thank you, Madam, for enlightening me.
My heart is mine once more, and I'm content;
The loss of it shall be your punishment.
                    [*To* ALCESTE.]
Sir, she is yours; I'll seek no more to stand
Between your wishes and this lady's hand.

Scene 6 ⚬ CÉLIMÈNE, ÉLIANTE, ARSINOÉ, ALCESTE, PHILINTE.

ARSINOÉ (*to* CÉLIMÈNE). Madam, I'm forced to speak. I'm far too stirred
  To keep my counsel, after what I've heard.
  I'm shocked and staggered by your want of morals.
  It's not my way to mix in others' quarrels;
  But really, when this fine and noble spirit,
  This man of honor and surpassing merit,
  Laid down the offering of his heart before you,
  How *could* you . . .
ALCESTE.   Madam, permit me, I implore you,
  To represent myself in this debate.
  Don't bother, please, to be my advocate.
  My heart, in any case, could not afford
  To give your services their due reward;
  And if I chose, for consolation's sake,
  Some other lady, 'twould not be you I'd take.
ARSINOÉ. What makes you think you could, Sir? And how dare you
  Imply that I've been trying to ensnare you?
  If you can for a moment entertain
  Such flattering fancies, you're extremely vain.
  I'm not so interested as you suppose
  In Célimène's discarded gigolos.
  Get rid of that absurd illusion, do.
  Women like me are not for such as you.
  Stay with this creature, to whom you're so attached;
  I've never seen two people better matched.

Scene 7 ⚬ CÉLIMÈNE, ÉLIANTE, ALCESTE, PHILINTE.

ALCESTE (*to* CÉLIMÈNE). Well, I've been still throughout this exposé,
  Till everyone but me has said his say.

Come, have I shown sufficient self-restraint?
And may I now . . .
CÉLIMÈNE.   Yes, make your just complaint.
Reproach me freely, call me what you will;
You've every right to say I've used you ill.
I've wronged you, I confess it; and in my shame
I'll make no effort to escape the blame.
The anger of those others I could despise;
My guilt toward you I sadly recognize.
Your wrath is wholly justified, I fear;
I know how culpable I must appear,
I know all things bespeak my treachery,
And that, in short, you've grounds for hating me.
Do so; I give you leave.
ALCESTE.   Ah, traitress—how,
How should I cease to love you, even now?
Though mind and will were passionately bent
On hating you, my heart would not consent.
              [*To* ÉLIANTE *and* PHILINTE.]
Be witness to my madness, both of you;
See what infatuation drives one to;
But wait; my folly's only just begun,
And I shall prove to you before I'm done
How strange the human heart is, and how far
From rational we sorry creatures are.
              [*To* CÉLIMÈNE.]
Woman, I'm willing to forget your shame,
And clothe your treacheries in a sweeter name;
I'll call them youthful errors, instead of crimes,
And lay the blame on these corrupting times.
My one condition is that you agree
To share my chosen fate, and fly with me
To that wild, trackless, solitary place
In which I shall forget the human race.
Only by such a course can you atone
For those atrocious letters; by that alone
Can you remove my present horror of you,
And make it possible for me to love you.
CÉLIMÈNE. What! *I* renounce the world at my young age,
And die of boredom in some hermitage?
ALCESTE. Ah, if you really loved me as you ought,
You wouldn't give the world a moment's thought;
Must you have me, and all the world beside?
CÉLIMÈNE. Alas, at twenty one is terrified
Of solitude. I fear I lack the force

And depth of soul to take so stern a course.
But if my hand in marriage will content you,
Why, there's a plan which I might well consent to,
And . . .
ALCESTE.   No, I detest you now. I could excuse
Everything else, but since you thus refuse
To love me wholly, as a wife should do,
And see the world in me, as I in you,
Go! I reject your hand, and disenthrall
My heart from your enchantments, once for all.

Scene 8 ⁓ ÉLIANTE, ALCESTE, PHILINTE.

ALCESTE (*to* ÉLIANTE). Madam, your virtuous beauty has no peer;
Of all this world, you only are sincere;
I've long esteemed you highly, as you know;
Permit me ever to esteem you so,
And if I do not now request your hand,
Forgive me, Madam, and try to understand.
I feel unworthy of it; I sense that fate
Does not intend me for the married state,
That I should do you wrong by offering you
My shattered heart's unhappy residue,
And that in short . . .
ÉLIANTE.   Your argument's well taken:
Nor need you fear that I shall feel forsaken.
Were I to offer him this hand of mine,
Your friend Philinte, I think, would not decline.
PHILINTE. Ah, Madam, that's my heart's most cherished goal,
For which I'd gladly give my life and soul.
ALCESTE (*to* ÉLIANTE *and* PHILINTE). May you be true to all you now
     profess,
And so deserve unending happiness.
Meanwhile, betrayed and wronged in everything,
I'll flee this bitter world where vice is king,
And seek some spot unpeopled and apart
Where I'll be free to have an honest heart.
PHILINTE. Come, Madam, let's do everything we can
To change the mind of this unhappy man.

QUESTIONS

ACT I

1. What basic attitudes toward society are voiced by Alceste and Philinte?
2. What arguments are presented by each to support his understanding of proper social conduct? Which argument of Philinte's is the most convincing?
3. Consider Alceste's line "The friend of mankind is no friend of mine." Does it suggest that Alceste's reasons for criticizing Philinte's behavior are more complicated than he himself is aware? Can you find other lines that suggest an ambivalence of motive?
4. Is Philinte also suspect in this way? Do any lines suggest that he is something more than charitable and agreeable?
5. In what way is Scene 2 an *acting out* of certain theories of conduct discussed in Scene 1?
6. Oronte's poem is a conventional seventeenth-century love poem, which expresses all the standard sentiments and employs the typical devices of that poetry. As it stands, however, is it a remarkably bad poem? Why is its "conventionality" alone enough to damn it in Alceste's eyes?
7. Examine Alceste's specific criticism of Oronte's sonnet and try to define the type of critic he is. Does his literary criticism parallel his social criticism?
8. What kind of poetry does Alceste prefer? Is the poem he recites noticeably better than Oronte's? In what ways? Can it be argued that it is just as false an image of human nature?

ACT II

9. How does Alceste's attitude toward love resemble his attitude toward society and literature?
10. Having answered the preceding question, can you describe the principle on which the plot is constructed?
11.
> I fall into deep gloom and melancholy
> When I survey the scene of human folly,
> Finding on every hand base flattery,
> Injustice, fraud, self-interest, treachery.

This is Alceste's description (I.1) of the social world in which he lives. How does Molière manage to present this scene to us without actually introducing a great number of characters and a wide variety of actions on stage? Is Alceste's estimation of his society accurate?

12. In what ways does Éliante's description of the ways in which the lover sees his beloved ("the swarthy one's a sweet brunette," etc.) ally her with Philinte?

ACT III

13. Does Arsinoé resemble Alceste in any way? Does she differ? What do the resemblances and differences tell us about Alceste?

14. Wilbur's verse form (the heroic couplet) in this translation does not exactly catch the tone of the original, but it is close enough so that we can talk with reasonable assurance about the effect of the verse. Is it appropriate in this play that everyone should make use of the *same* verse form, and in most places the same meter? What does the constant use of the heroic couplet suggest about the nature of the characters who speak in this form? To answer this last question adequately it will be necessary to define the outstanding features of the heroic couplet.

15. Does Alceste's reaction to Arsinoé prove anything that Célimène has previously said about him? Logically, shouldn't he agree with Arsinoé's view of a world blind to merit?

ACT IV

16. No question troubles Alceste more than whether or not Célimène loves him. Is it possible to answer this question from the play? Is it perhaps characteristic of Alceste that he asks it and expects an absolute answer?

17. Consider carefully Éliante's opinion about whether or not Célimène loves Alceste (IV.1) in the speech beginning, "How can we judge the truth of her devotion?" Does Éliante have a truer understanding of human nature than Alceste? Is her understanding "dramatic"?

18. Contrast Éliante and Philinte's opinions about the nature of love with those of Célimène and Alceste.

19. Do you find instances in which Alceste's language betrays him? Is his style often too high for the subject he is dealing with?

20. "The true center of *The Misanthrope* is Célimène. She embodies all the contradictions, the confusions, the weaknesses, and the glories of human nature. She is a dreadful scandalmonger who needs only be given a name to dissect the character; she is a flirt who cannot resist captivating any man who comes near her, only to make a joke of him in turn for the next man she encounters; she is an outrageous liar; and she is a vicious infighter in the drawing room, never hesitating to use the low verbal blow to cripple her opponent. All of this is no doubt bad, but Célimène is also alive and attractive: she is beautiful; she has spirit and style; she is witty; and she is courageous. Whatever she does,

she does with breathtaking elegance. In her person she sums up the world that comedy always presents—amoral, energetic, intensely vital, and filled with promise for those who understand her rightly." Do you agree with this statement about Célimène? If so, how does her character help us understand all the other characters in the play?

21. What bearing does the comic exchange between Alceste and his servant at the end of Act IV have on the previous discussion between Alceste and Célimène?

22. In the discussion between Célimène and Alceste about love are there any indications that Alceste's love is not so pure as he believes, that he "unconsciously" seeks in his relationship with Célimène satisfaction of some other needs than are usual in a lover? If you find evidence of such darker motivations, can you tie them to the ambivalent motives that appear in his attitude toward society in Act I?

ACT V

23. Does Alceste actually enjoy losing his law case?

24. At the end of Act V, Scene 1, Alceste removes himself to a dark corner of the room to sit alone. In what ways does this "visual imagery" define his nature and relations with the world?

25. Is Célimène being truthful when she tells Oronte and Alceste, "I know full well which one of you I favor"?

26. In what ways is the condition Alceste attaches to his offer to marry Célimène typical of him? How are we to understand her refusal?

27. At the end of the play Alceste leaves to "seek some spot unpeopled and apart," some "wild, trackless, solitary place/In which I shall forget the human race." This desert is Molière's one symbol used to represent the "world" that exists outside the polished society of court and town. Describe the contrast between the social and natural worlds and discuss the meaning of this juxtaposition.

28. Does Molière present any way of life or any person as perfect?

29. Critics from Molière's day to the present have been passionately divided on the question of the hero of the play. Some have seen Alceste as a man of courage and sensitivity caught in a morally corrupt world that he cannot change. Others have seen Alceste as something of a fool and have taken the urbane and reasonable Philinte as the true hero. Which view is correct in your opinion? In answering this question the most important consideration is that you decide *how* it can be *meaningfully* answered. What grounds are provided by Molière for making a decision?

30. Dramatic characters often are expressions of single, isolated tendencies or attitudes that in actual people exist in combination, and often in opposition, with other tendencies. What two common human tendencies do Alceste and Philinte represent?

TIGER
AT THE GATES

BY

JEAN GIRAUDOUX

Jean Giraudoux (1882–1944), the son of a minor French official, after distinguished accomplishments as a student seemed destined for a career of teaching and letters. He traveled widely in Europe, taught at Harvard for a year, worked as an editor, and wrote a number of articles and short stories. But circumstances, chiefly financial, forced him to take up another profession, and shortly before the First World War he entered the French diplomatic service. During the war he served with the French army and was wounded twice. The second and more serious wound he received at the Dardanelles, not far from the site of ancient Troy.

After the war Giraudoux returned to diplomacy and worked, with distinction, in the Foreign Office until 1940, when, after the defeat of France, he retired. During his years as a diplomat he continued to write, first a number of novels, and then, beginning in the late 1920's, a long series of popular and distinguished plays—*Siegfried* (1928), *Amphitryon 38* (1929), *Judith* (1931), *La Guerre de Troie n'aura pas lieu* (1935), translated as *Tiger at the Gates*, *Electra* (1937), *Ondine* (1939), *Sodom and Gomorrah* (1943), and *The Madwoman of Chaillot* (written during the war but first performed and published in 1945), to mention only the best known.

Tiger at the Gates is Giraudoux's most distinguished play and is well on its way to becoming one of the classics of the modern repertory. Though modern in his viewpoint, Giraudoux continued to write in the classical French manner. His subjects are most often the great myths of the past reinterpreted; his language and construction are precise, orderly, and logical; his dialogue is witty and filled with paradox; and the substance of his plays is speech and argument rather than action and movement. The foreground of *Tiger at the Gates* is filled with people talking, arguing, explaining their views, reasoning with others, exploring the meaning of their situations, opening truth with a flash of wit, analyzing the meaning of history, philosophy, love, war, sex, marriage, poetry—and always speaking in balanced and lucid prose. Man in Giraudoux's world is a talking and reasoning creature, and he talks and reasons beautifully. Much of the delight of the play comes from the brilliance of its language and thought, but its ultimate power comes from the presence in and behind the talk of some ominous energy—destiny, or the tiger—relentlessly moving to its necessary conclusion, oblivious to and undeterred by all the talk and reasoning. The juxtaposition of talking man and blind fate gives us a curiously ironic view of man in history. These Trojans and Greeks are not innocents going blindly to the slaughter, but competent, sophisticated, intelligent people, who are fully aware of the forces swirling through and about them and are determined to control the future; but they are also utterly helpless.

In the historians' view the Trojan War was, if it took place at all, either a modest affair, as wars go, or a mere pirate raid on a trading post. But the poets, chiefly Homer and Shakespeare, have fixed these ancient events in the Western imagination, made Priam more real for us than Haile Selassie, and the burning of Troy more real than the destruction of Rotterdam. The long, ten-year struggle between the sea and the walls of Troy, the cunning of Ulysses, the pride of Achilles, the brute strength of Ajax, the nobility of Hector, the suffering of Hecuba and Andromache, these have all become symbols of the greatness and the suffering of countless men and women in mankind's endless, dreary little wars—wars fought without reason and without hope of victory. Giraudoux is but the latest in a long line of poets who have found in the Trojan War an image of man's tragic condition and who have sought to explain in their retelling of the old tale how man with all his potentiality for happiness and greatness becomes tangled in the destruction of everything he loves.

CHARACTERS

ANDROMACHE	PEACE
CASSANDRA	TROILUS
LAUNDRESS	ABNEOS
HECTOR	BUSIRIS
PARIS	AJAX
PRIAM	ULYSSES
FIRST OLD MAN	A TOPMAN
SECOND OLD MAN	IRIS
DEMOKOS	OLPIDES
HECUBA	SERVANT
MATHEMATICIAN	SENATOR
SERVANT	SAILORS
POLYXENE	MESSENGERS
HELEN	GUARDS

CROWD

ACT I

ANDROMACHE. There's not going to be a Trojan War, Cassandra!

CASSANDRA. I shall take that bet, Andromache.

ANDROMACHE. The Greeks are quite right to protest. We are going to receive their ambassador very civilly. We shall wrap up his little Helen and give her back to him.

CASSANDRA. We shall receive him atrociously. We shall refuse to give Helen back. And there *will* be a Trojan War.

ANDROMACHE. Yes, if Hector were not here. But he is here, Cassandra, he is home again. You can hear the trumpets. At this moment he is marching into the city, victorious. And Hector is certainly going to have something to say. When he left, three months ago, he promised me this war would be the last.

CASSANDRA. It is the last. The next is still ahead of him.

ANDROMACHE. Doesn't it ever tire you to see and prophesy only disasters?

CASSANDRA. I see nothing. I prophesy nothing. All I ever do is to take account of two great stupidities: the stupidity of men, and the wild stupidity of the elements.

ANDROMACHE. Why should there be a war? Paris and Helen don't care for each other any longer.

CASSANDRA. Do you think it will matter if Paris and Helen don't care for each other any longer? Has destiny ever been interested in whether things were still true or not?

ANDROMACHE. I don't know what destiny is.

CASSANDRA. I'll tell you. It is simply the relentless logic of each day we live.

ANDROMACHE. I don't understand abstractions.

CASSANDRA. Never mind. We can try a metaphor. Imagine a tiger. You can understand that? It's a nice, easy metaphor. A sleeping tiger.

ANDROMACHE. Let it sleep.

CASSANDRA. There's nothing I should like better. But certain cocksure statements have been prodding him out of his sleep. For some considerable time Troy has been full of them.

ANDROMACHE. Full of what?

CASSANDRA. Of cocksure statements, a confident belief that the world, and the supervision of the world, is the province of mankind in general, and Trojan men and women in particular.

ANDROMACHE. I don't follow you.

CASSANDRA. Hector at this very moment is marching into Troy?

ANDROMACHE. Yes. Hector at this very moment has come home to his wife.

CASSANDRA. And Hector's wife is going to have a child?

ANDROMACHE. Yes; I am going to have a child.

CASSANDRA. Don't you call these statements a little overconfident?

ANDROMACHE. Don't frighten me, Cassandra.

[*A* YOUNG LAUNDRESS *goes past with an armful of linen.*]

LAUNDRESS. What a beautiful day, miss!

CASSANDRA. Does it seem so, indeed?

LAUNDRESS. It's the most beautiful Spring day Troy has seen this year.
(*Exit.*)

CASSANDRA. Even the laundrymaid is confident!

ANDROMACHE. And so she should be, Cassandra. How can you talk of a war on a day like this? Happiness is falling on us out of the sky.

CASSANDRA. Like a blanket of snow.

ANDROMACHE. And beauty, as well. Look at the sunshine. It is finding more mother-of-pearl on the rooftops of Troy than was ever dragged up from the bed of the sea. And do you hear the sound coming up from the fishermen's houses, and the movement of the trees, like the murmuring of sea shells? If ever there were a chance to see men finding a way to live in peace, it is today. To live in peace, in humility. And to be immortal.

CASSANDRA. Yes, I am sure those cripples who have been carried out to lie in their doorways feel how immortal they are.

ANDROMACHE. And to be good. Do you see that horseman, in the advance-guard, leaning from his saddle to stroke a cat on the battlements? Perhaps this is also going to be the first day of true fellowship between men and the animals.

CASSANDRA. You talk too much. Destiny, the tiger, is getting restive, Andromache!

ANDROMACHE. Restive, maybe, in young girls looking for husbands; but not otherwise.

CASSANDRA. You are wrong. Hector has come home in triumph to the wife he adores. The tiger begins to rouse, and opens one eye. The incurables lie out on their benches in the sun and feel immortal. The tiger stretches himself. Today is the chance for peace to enthrone herself over all the world. The tiger licks his lips. And Andromache is going to have a son! And the horsemen have started leaning from their saddles to stroke tom-cats on the battlements! The tiger starts to prowl.

ANDROMACHE. Be quiet!

CASSANDRA. He climbs noiselessly up the palace steps. He pushes open the doors with his snout. And here he is, here he is!

[HECTOR'S *voice:* Andromache!]

ANDROMACHE. You are lying! It is Hector!

CASSANDRA. Whoever said it was not?

[*Enter* HECTOR.]

ANDROMACHE. Hector!

HECTOR. Andromache!

[*They embrace.*]

And good morning to you, too, Cassandra. Ask Paris to come to me, if you will. As soon as he can.

[CASSANDRA *lingers.*]

Have you something to tell me?

ANDROMACHE. Don't listen to her! Some catastrophe or other!

HECTOR. Tell me.

CASSANDRA. Your wife is going to have a child. (*Exit* CASSANDRA.)

[HECTOR *takes* ANDROMACHE *in his arms, leads her to a stone bench, and sits beside her. A short pause.*]

HECTOR. Will it be a son or a daughter?

ANDROMACHE. Which did you want to create when you called it into life?

HECTOR. A thousand boys. A thousand girls.

ANDROMACHE. Why? Because it would give you a thousand women to hold in your arms? You are going to be disappointed. It will be a son, one single son.

HECTOR. That may very well be. Usually more boys are born than girls at the end of a war.

ANDROMACHE. And before a war? Which, before a war?

HECTOR. Forget wars, Andromache, even this war. It's over. It lost you a father and a brother, but it gave you back a husband.

ANDROMACHE. It has been too kind. It may think better of it presently.

HECTOR. Don't worry. We won't give it the chance. Directly I leave you I shall go into the square, and formally close the Gates of War. They will never open again.

ANDROMACHE. Close them, then. But they will open again.

HECTOR. You can even tell me the day, perhaps?

ANDROMACHE. I can even tell you the day: the day when the cornfields are heavy and golden, when the vines are stooping, ready for harvest, and every house is sheltering a contented couple.

HECTOR. And peace, no doubt, at its very height?

ANDROMACHE. Yes. And my son is strong and glowing with life.

[HECTOR *embraces her.*]

HECTOR. Perhaps your son will be a coward. That's one possible safeguard.

ANDROMACHE. He won't be a coward. But perhaps I shall have cut off the index finger of his right hand.

HECTOR. If every mother cut off her son's right-hand index finger, the armies of the world would fight without index fingers. And if they cut off their sons' right legs, the armies would be one-legged. And if they put out their eyes, the armies would be blind, but there would still be armies: blind armies groping to find the fatal place in the enemy's groin, or to get at his throat.

ANDROMACHE. I would rather kill him.

HECTOR. There's a truly maternal solution to war!

ANDROMACHE. Don't laugh. I can still kill him before he is born.

HECTOR. Don't you want to see him at all, not even for a moment? After that, you would think again. Do you mean never to see your son?

ANDROMACHE. It is your son that interests me. Hector, it's because he is yours, because he is you, that I'm so afraid. You don't know how like you he is. Even in this no-man's-land where he is waiting, he already has everything, all those qualities you brought to this life we live together. He has your tenderness, your silences. If you love war, he will love it. Do you love war?

HECTOR. Why ask such a question?

ANDROMACHE. Admit, sometimes you love it.

HECTOR. If a man can love what takes away hope, and happiness, and all those nearest to his heart.

ANDROMACHE. And you know it can be so. Men do love it.

HECTOR. If they let themselves be fooled by that little burst of divinity the gods give them at the moment of attack.

ANDROMACHE. Ah, there, you see! At the moment of attack you feel like a god.

HECTOR. More often not as much as a man. But sometimes, on certain mornings, you get up from the ground feeling lighter, astonished, altered. Your whole body, and the armour on your back, have a different weight, they seem to be made of a different metal. You are invulnerable. A tenderness comes over you, submerging you, a kind of tenderness of battle: you are tender because you are pitiless; what, in fact, the tenderness of the gods must be. You advance towards the enemy slowly, almost absent-mindedly, but lovingly. And you try not to crush a beetle crossing your path.

You brush off the mosquito without hurting it. You never at any time had more respect for the life you meet on your way.

ANDROMACHE. And then the enemy comes?

HECTOR. Then the enemy comes, frothing at the mouth. You pity him; you can see him there, behind the swollen veins and the whites of his eyes, the helpless, willing little man of business, the well-meaning husband and son-in-law who likes to grow his own vegetables. You feel a sort of love for him. You love the wart on his cheek and the cast in his eye. You love him. But he comes on; he is insistent. Then you kill him.

ANDROMACHE. And you bend over the wretched corpse as though you are a god; but you are not a god; you can't give back his life again.

HECTOR. You don't wait to bend over him. There are too many more waiting for you, frothing at the mouth and howling hate. Too many more unassuming, law-abiding family men.

ANDROMACHE. Then you kill them.

HECTOR. You kill them. Such is war.

ANDROMACHE. All of them: you kill them all?

HECTOR. This time we killed them all. Quite deliberately. They belonged to an incorrigibly warlike race, the reason why wars go on and multiply in Asia. Only one of them escaped.

ANDROMACHE. In a thousand years time, there the warlike race will be again, descended from that one man. His escape made all that slaughter futile after all. My son is going to love war, just as you do.

HECTOR. I think, now that I've lost my love for it, I hate it.

ANDROMACHE. How do you come to hate what you once worshipped?

HECTOR. You know what it's like when you find out a friend is a liar? Whatever he says, after that, sounds false, however true it may be. And strangely enough, war used to promise me many kinds of virtue: goodness, generosity, and a contempt for anything base and mean. I felt I owed it all my strength and zest for life, even my private happiness, you, Andromache. And until this last campaign there was no enemy I haven't loved.

ANDROMACHE. Very soon you will say you only kill what you love.

HECTOR. It's hard to explain how all the sounds of war combined to make me think it was something noble. The galloping of horse in the night, the clatter of bowls and dishes where the cooks were moving in and out of the firelight, the brush of silk and metal against your tent as the night-patrol went past, and the cry of the falcon wheeling high above the sleeping army and their unsleeping captain: it all seemed then so right, marvellously right.

ANDROMACHE. But not this time: this time war had no music for you?

HECTOR. Why was that? Because I am older? Or was it just the kind of weariness with your job which, for instance, a carpenter will be sud-

denly seized by, with a table half finished, as I was seized one morning, standing over an adversary of my own age, about to put an
end to him? Up to that time, a man I was going to kill had always
seemed my direct opposite. This time I was kneeling on a mirror,
the death I was going to give was a kind of suicide. I don't know
what the carpenter does at such a time, whether he throws away his
hammer and plane, or goes on with it. I went on with it. But after
that nothing remained of the perfect trumpet note of war. The
spear as it slid against my shield rang suddenly false; so did the
shock of the killed against the ground, and, some hours later, the
palace crumbling into ruin. And, moreover, war knew that I understood, and gave up any pretence of shame. The cries of the dying
sounded false. I had come to that.

ANDROMACHE. But it all still sounded right for the rest of them.

HECTOR. The rest of them heard it as I did. The army I brought back
hates war.

ANDROMACHE. An army with poor hearing.

HECTOR. No. When we first came in sight of Troy, an hour ago, you
can't imagine how everything in that moment sounded true for them.
There wasn't a regiment which didn't halt, racked to the heart by
this sense of returning music. So much so, we were afraid to march
boldly in through the gates: we broke up into groups outside the
walls. It feels like the only job worthy of a good army, laying
peaceful siege to the open cities of your own country.

ANDROMACHE. You haven't understood, this is where things are falser
than anywhere. War is here, in Troy, Hector. That is what welcomed
you at the gates.

HECTOR. What do you mean?

ANDROMACHE. You haven't heard that Paris has carried off Helen?

HECTOR. They told me so. What else?

ANDROMACHE. Did you know that the Greeks are demanding her back?
And their ambassador arrives today? And if we don't give her up,
it means war.

HECTOR. Why shouldn't we give her up? I shall give her back to them
myself.

ANDROMACHE. Paris will never agree to it.

HECTOR. Paris will agree, and very soon. Cassandra is bringing him
to me.

ANDROMACHE. But Paris can't agree. His honour, as you all call it,
won't let him. Nor his love either, he may tell you.

HECTOR. Well, we shall see. Run and ask Priam if he will let me speak
to him at once. And set your heart at rest. All the Trojans who have
been fighting, or who can fight, are against a war.

ANDROMACHE. There are still the others, remember.

[*As* ANDROMACHE *goes* . . . CASSANDRA *enters with*
PARIS.]

CASSANDRA. Here is Paris.

HECTOR. Congratulations, Paris. I hear you have been very well occupied while we were away.

PARIS. Not badly. Thank you.

HECTOR. What is this story they tell me about Helen?

PARIS. Helen is a very charming person. Isn't she, Cassandra?

CASSANDRA. Fairly charming.

PARIS. Why these reservations today? It was only yesterday you said you thought she was extremely pretty.

CASSANDRA. She is extremely pretty, and fairly charming.

PARIS. Hasn't she the ways of a young, gentle gazelle?

CASSANDRA. No.

PARIS. But you were the one who first said she was like a gazelle.

CASSANDRA. I made a mistake. Since then I have seen a gazelle again.

HECTOR. To hell with gazelles! Doesn't she look any more like a woman than that?

PARIS. She isn't the type of woman we know here, obviously.

CASSANDRA. What is the type of woman we know here?

PARIS. Your type, my dear sister. The fearfully unremote sort of woman.

CASSANDRA. When your Greek makes love she is a long way off, I suppose?

PARIS. You know perfectly well what I'm trying to say. I have had enough of Asiatic women. They hold you in their arms as though they were glued there, their kisses are like battering-rams, their words chew right into you. The more they undress the more elaborate they seem, until when they're naked they are more overdressed than ever. And they paint their faces to look as though they mean to imprint themselves on you. And they do imprint themselves on you. In short, you are definitely *with* them. But Helen is far away from me, even held in my arms.

HECTOR. Very interesting! But, one wonders, is it really worth a war, to allow Paris to make love at a distance?

CASSANDRA. With distance. He loves women to be distant but right under his nose.

PARIS. To have Helen with you not with you is worth anything in the world.

HECTOR. How did you fetch her away? Willingly, or did you compel her?

PARIS. Listen, Hector! You know women as well as I do. They are only willing when you compel them, but after that they're as enthusiastic as you are.

HECTOR. On horseback, in the usual style of seducers, leaving a heap of horse manure under the windows.

PARIS. Is this a court of enquiry?

HECTOR. Yes, it is. Try for once to answer precisely and accurately. Have you insulted her husband's house, or the Greek earth?

PARIS. The Greek water, a little. She was bathing.

CASSANDRA. She is born of the foam, is she? This cold one is born of the foam, like Venus.

HECTOR. You haven't disfigured the walls of the palace with offensive drawings, as you usually do? You didn't shout to the echoes any word which they would at once repeat to the betrayed husband?

PARIS. No. Menelaus was naked on the river bank, busy removing a crab from his big toe. He watched my boat sail past as if the wind were carrying his clothes away.

HECTOR. Looking furious?

PARIS. The face of a king being nipped by a crab isn't likely to look beatific.

HECTOR. No onlookers?

PARIS. My crew.

HECTOR. Perfect!

PARIS. Why perfect? What are you getting at?

HECTOR. I say perfect, because you have done nothing irrevocable. In other words: she was undressed, so neither her clothes nor her belongings have been insulted. Nothing except her body, which is negligible. I've enough acquaintance with the Greeks to know they will concoct a divine adventure out of it, to their own glory, the story of this little Greek queen who goes down into the sea, and quietly comes up again a few months later, with a look on her face of perfect innocence.

CASSANDRA. We can be quite sure of the look on her face.

PARIS. You think that I'm going to take Helen back to Menelaus?

HECTOR. We don't ask so much of you, or of her. The Greek ambassador will take care of it. He will put her back in the sea himself, like a gardener planting water-lilies, at a particular chosen spot. You will give her into his hands this evening.

PARIS. I don't know whether you are allowing yourself to notice how monstrous you are being, to suppose that a man who has the prospect of a night with Helen will agree to giving it up.

CASSANDRA. You still have an afternoon with Helen. Surely that's more Greek?

HECTOR. Don't be obstinate. We know you of old. This isn't the first separation you've accepted.

PARIS. My dear Hector, that's true enough. Up to now I have always accepted separations fairly cheerfully. Parting from a woman, however well you love her, induces a most pleasant state of mind, which

I know how to value as well as anybody. You come out of her arms
and take your first lonely walk through the town, and, the first little
dressmaker you meet, you notice with a shock of surprise how fresh
and unconcerned she looks, after that last sight you have had of the
dear face you parted from, her nose red with weeping. Because
you have come away from such broken, despairing farewells, the
laundrygirls and the fruitsellers laughing their heads off, more than
make up for whatever you've lost in the parting. By losing one
person your life has become entirely re-peopled. All the women in
the world have been created for you afresh; they are all your own,
in the liberty, honour, and peace of your conscience. Yes, you're
quite right: when a love-affair is broken off it reaches its highest
point of exaltation. Which is why I shall never be parted from Helen,
because with Helen I feel as though I had broken with every other
woman in the world, and that gives me the sensation of being free
a thousand times over instead of once.

HECTOR. Because she doesn't love you. Everything you say proves it.

PARIS. If you like. But, if I had to choose one out of all the possible
ways of passion, I would choose the way Helen doesn't love me.

HECTOR. I'm extremely sorry. But you will give her up.

PARIS. You are not the master here.

HECTOR. I am your elder brother, and the future master.

PARIS. Then order me about in the future. For the present, I obey my
father.

HECTOR. That's all I want! You're willing that we should put this to
Priam and accept his judgment?

PARIS. Perfectly willing.

HECTOR. On your solemn word? We both swear to accept that?

CASSANDRA. Mind what you're doing, Hector! Priam is mad for Helen.
He would rather give up his daughters.

HECTOR. What nonsense is this?

PARIS. For once she is telling the truth about the present instead of
the future.

CASSANDRA. And all our brothers, and all our uncles, and all our great-
great uncles! Helen has a guard-of-honour which includes every old
man in the city. Look there. It is time for her walk. Do you see,
there's a fringe of white beards draped all along the battlements?

HECTOR. A beautiful sight. The beards are white, and the faces red.

CASSANDRA. Yes; it's the blood pressure. They should be waiting at the
Scamander Gate, to welcome the victorious troops. But no; they are
all at the Scean Gate, waiting for Helen.

HECTOR. Look at them, all leaning forward as one man, like storks
when they see a rat going by.

CASSANDRA. The rat is Helen.

PARIS. Is it?

CASSANDRA. There she is: on the second terrace, standing to adjust her sandal, and giving careful thought to the crossing of her legs.

HECTOR. Incredible. All the old men of Troy are there looking down at her.

CASSANDRA. Not all. There are certain crafty ones looking up at her.

[*Cries offstage:* Long live Beauty!]

HECTOR. What are they shouting?

PARIS. They're shouting 'Long live Beauty!'

CASSANDRA. I quite agree with them, if they mean that they themselves should die as quickly as possible.

[*Cries offstage:* Long live Venus!]

HECTOR. And what now?

CASSANDRA. 'Long live Venus.' They are shouting only words without R's in them because of their lack of teeth. Long live Beauty, long live Venus, long live Helen. At least they imagine they're shouting, though, as you can hear, all they are doing is simply increasing a mumble to its highest power.

HECTOR. What has Venus to do with it?

CASSANDRA. They imagine it was Venus who gave us Helen. To show her gratitude to Paris for awarding her the apple on first sight.

HECTOR. That was another brilliant stroke of yours.

PARIS. Stop playing the elder brother!

[*Enter* TWO OLD MEN.]

FIRST OLD MAN. Down there we see her better.

SECOND OLD MAN. We had a very good view.

FIRST OLD MAN. But she can hear us better from up here. Come on. One, two, three!

BOTH. Long live Helen!

SECOND OLD MAN. It's a little tiring, at our age, to have to climb up and down these impossible steps all the time, according to whether we want to look at her or to cheer her.

FIRST OLD MAN. Would you like us to alternate? One day we will cheer her? Another day we will look at her?

SECOND OLD MAN. You are mad! One day without looking at Helen, indeed! Goodness me, think what we've seen of her today! One, two, three!

BOTH. Long live Helen!

FIRST OLD MAN. And now down we go again!

[*They run off.*]

CASSANDRA. You see what they're like, Hector. I don't know how their poor lungs are going to stand it.

HECTOR. But our father can't be like this.

PARIS. Hector, before we have this out in front of my father, I suppose you wouldn't like to take just one look at Helen.

HECTOR. I don't care a fig about Helen. Ah: greetings to you, father!

[PRIAM *enters, with* HECUBA, ANDROMACHE, *the poet*
DEMOKOS *and another old man.* HECUBA *leads by the*
hand little POLYXENE.]

PRIAM. What was it you said?

HECTOR. I said that we should make haste to shut the Gates of War,
father, see them bolted and padlocked, so that not even a gnat can
get between them.

PRIAM. I thought what you said was somewhat shorter.

DEMOKOS. He said he didn't care a fig about Helen.

PRIAM. Look over here.

[HECTOR *obeys.*]

Do you see her?

HECUBA. Indeed he sees her. Who, I ask myself, doesn't see her, or
hasn't seen her? She takes the road which goes the whole way
round the city.

DEMOKOS. It is Beauty's perfect circle.

PRIAM. Do you see her?

HECTOR. Yes, I see her. What of it?

DEMOKOS. Priam is asking you what you see.

HECTOR. I see a young woman adjusting her sandal.

CASSANDRA. She takes some time to adjust her sandal.

PARIS. I carried her off naked; she left her clothes in Greece. Those are
your sandals, Cassandra. They're a bit big for her.

CASSANDRA. Anything's too big for these little women.

HECTOR. I see two charming buttocks.

HECUBA. He sees what all of you see.

PRIAM. I'm sorry for you!

HECTOR. Why?

PRIAM. I had no idea that the young men of Troy had come to this.

HECTOR. What have they come to?

PRIAM. To being impervious to beauty.

DEMOKOS. And, consequently, ignorant of love. And, consequently, unrealistic. To us who are poets reality is love or nothing.

HECTOR. But the old men, you think, can appreciate love and beauty?

HECUBA. But of course. If you make love, or if you are beautiful, you
don't need to understand these things.

HECTOR. You come across beauty, father, at every street corner. I'm not
alluding to Helen, though at the moment she condescends to walk our
streets.

PRIAM. You are being unfair, Hector. Surely there have been occasions
in your life when a woman has seemed to be more than merely herself, as though a radiance of thoughts and feelings glowed from her
flesh, taking a special brilliance from it.

DEMOKOS. As a ruby represents blood.

HECTOR. Not to those who have seen blood. I have just come back from a close acquaintance with it.

DEMOKOS. A symbol, you understand. Soldier though you are, you have surely heard of symbolism? Surely you have come across women who as soon as you saw them seemed to you to personify intelligence, harmony, gentleness, whatever it might be?

HECTOR. It has happened.

DEMOKOS. And what did you do?

HECTOR. I went closer, and that was the end of it. And what does this we see here personify?

DEMOKOS. We have told you before: Beauty.

HECUBA. Then send her quickly back to the Greeks if you want her to personify that for long. Blonde beauty doesn't usually last for ever.

DEMOKOS. It's impossible to talk to these women!

HECUBA. Then don't talk *about* women. You're not showing much gallantry, I might say; nor patriotism either. All other races choose one of their own women as their symbol, even if they have flat noses and lips like two fishes on a plate. It's only you who have to go outside your own country to find it.

HECTOR. Listen, father: we are just back from a war, and we have come home exhausted. We have made quite certain of peace on our continent for ever. From now on we mean to live in happiness, and we mean our wives to be able to love us without anxiety, and to bear our children.

DEMOKOS. Wise principles, but war has never prevented wives from having children.

HECTOR. So explain to me why we have come back to find the city transformed, all because of Helen? Explain to me what you think she has given to us, worth a quarrel with the Greeks?

MATHEMATICIAN. Anybody will tell you! I can tell you myself!

HECUBA. Listen to the mathematician!

MATHEMATICIAN. Yes, listen to the mathematician! And don't think that mathematicians have no concern with women! We're the land-surveyors of your personal landscape. I can't tell you how we mathematicians suffer to see any slight disproportion of the flesh, on the chin or the thigh, any infringement of your geometrical desirability. Well now, until this day mathematicians have never been satisfied with the countryside surrounding Troy. The line linking the plain with the hills seemed to us too slack: the line from the hills to the mountains too taut. Now, since Helen came, the country has taken on meaning and vigour. And, what is particularly evident to true mathematicians, space and volume have now found in Helen a common denominator. We can abolish all the instruments we have invented to reduce the universe to a manageable equation. There are no more feet and inches, ounces, pounds, milligrams or leagues. There is only the weight of Helen's footfall, the length of Helen's arm, the range of Helen's look or voice; and the movement of the air as she goes past is the measure of the winds. That is what the mathematicians will tell you.

HECUBA. The old fool is crying.

PRIAM. My dear son, you have only to look at this crowd, and you will understand what Helen is. She is a kind of absolution. To each one of these old men, whom you can see now like a frieze of grotesque heads all round the city walls: to the old swindler, the old thief, the old pandar, to all the old failures, she has shown they always had a secret longing to rediscover the beauty they had lost. If throughout their lives beauty had always been as close at hand as Helen is today, they would never have tricked their friends, or sold their daughters, or drunk away their inheritance. Helen is like a pardon to them: a new beginning for them, their whole future.

HECTOR. These old men's ancient futures are no concern of mine.

DEMOKOS. Hector, as a poet I approach things by the way of poetry. Imagine if beauty, never, at any time, touched our language. Imagine there being no such word as 'delight.'

HECTOR. We should get on well enough without it. I get on without it already. 'Delight' is a word I use only when I'm absolutely driven to it.

DEMOKOS. Well, then the word 'desirable': you could get on without that as well, I suppose?

HECTOR. If it could be bought only at the cost of war, yes, I could get on without the word 'desirable.'

DEMOKOS. One of the most beautiful words there are was found only at the cost of war: the word 'courage.'

HECTOR. It has been well paid for.

HECUBA. And the word 'cowardice' was inevitably found at the same time.

PRIAM. My son, why do you so deliberately not understand us?

HECTOR. I understand you very well. With the help of a quibble, by pretending to persuade us to fight for beauty you want to get us to fight for a woman.

PRIAM. Would you never go to war for any woman?

HECTOR. Certainly not!

HECUBA. And he would be unchivalrously right.

CASSANDRA. If there were only one woman, then perhaps he would go to war for her. But we have exceeded that number, quite extravagantly.

DEMOKOS. Wouldn't you go to war to rescue Andromache?

HECTOR. Andromache and I have already made our secret plans for escaping from any prison in the world, and finding our way back to each other again.

DEMOKOS. Even if there's no hope of it on earth?

HECTOR. Even then.

HECUBA. You have done well to unmask them, Hector. They want you to make war for the sake of a woman; it's the kind of lovemaking men believe in who are past making love in any other way.

DEMOKOS. And doesn't that make you all the more valuable?

HECUBA. Ah yes! You may say so!

DEMOKOS. Excuse me, but I can't agree with you. The sex which gave me my mother will always have my respect, even its least worthy representatives.

HECUBA. We know that. You have, as we know, shown your respect for instance to——

[*The* SERVANTS *who have stood by to hear the argument burst out laughing.*]

PRIAM. Hecuba! Daughters! What can this mean? Why on earth are you all so up in arms? The Council are considering giving the city a public holday in honour of one of your sex.

ANDROMACHE. I know of only one humiliation for a woman: injustice.

DEMOKOS. It's painful to say so, but there's no one knows less what a woman is than a woman.

[*The* YOUNG SERVANT, *passing:* Oh, dear! dear!]

HECUBA. We know perfectly well. I will tell you myself what a woman is.

DEMOKOS. Don't let them talk, Priam. You never know what they might say.

HECUBA. They might tell the truth.

PRIAM. I have only to think of one of you, my dears, to know what a woman is.

DEMOKOS. In the first place, she is the source of our energy. You know that, Hector. The soldiers who haven't a portrait of a woman in their kit aren't worth anything.

CASSANDRA. The source of your pride, yes, I agree.

HECUBA. Of your vices.

ANDROMACHE. She is a poor bundle of uncertainty, a poor mass of fears, who detests whatever is difficult, and adores whatever is vulgar and easy.

HECTOR. Dear Andromache!

HECUBA. It's very simple. I have been a woman for fifty years, and I've never yet been able to discover precisely what it is I am.

DEMOKOS. Secondly, whether she likes it or not, she's the only reward for courage. Ask any soldier. To kill a man is to merit a woman.

ANDROMACHE. She loves cowards and libertines. If Hector were a coward or a libertine I shouldn't love him less; I might even love him more.

PRIAM. Don't go too far, Andromache. You will prove the very opposite of what you want to prove.

POLYXENE. She is greedy. She tells lies.

DEMOKOS. So we're to say nothing of her fidelity, her purity: we are not to mention them?

THE SERVANT. Oh, dear! dear!

DEMOKOS. What did you say?

THE SERVANT. I said 'Oh dear! dear!' I say what I think.

POLYXENE. She breaks her toys. She puts them headfirst into boiling water.

HECUBA. The older we women grow, the more clearly we see what men really are: hypocrites, boasters, he-goats. The older men grow, the more they doll us up with every perfection. There isn't a slut you've hugged behind a wall who isn't transformed in your memories into a loved and lovely creature.

PRIAM. Have you ever deceived me, Hecuba?

HECUBA. Only with yourself; scores of times with yourself.

DEMOKOS. Has Andromache ever deceived Hector?

HECUBA. You can leave Andromache out of this. There is nothing she could recognize in the sad histories of erring women.

ANDROMACHE. But I know if Hector were not my husband, if he were a club-footed, bandy-legged fisherman I should run after him and find him in his hovel, and lie down on the pile of oyster-shells and seaweed, and give him a son in adultery.

POLYXENE. She pretends to go to sleep at night, but she's really playing games in her head with her eyes shut.

HECUBA (to POLYXENE). You may well say so! It's dreadful! You know how I scold you for it!

THE SERVANT. The only thing worse than a woman is a man; there are no words to describe him.

DEMOKOS. Then more's the pity if a woman deceives us! More's the pity if she scorns her own value and dignity! If she can't be true to a pattern of perfection which would save her from the ravages of conscience, we have to do it for her.

THE SERVANT. Oh, the kind guardian angel!

PARIS. One thing they've forgotten to say of themselves: they are never jealous.

PRIAM. My dear daughters, the fact that you're so furious is a proof in itself that we are right. I can't conceive of any greater unselfishness than the way you now fight for peace, when peace will give you idle, feeble, chicken-hearted husbands, and war would turn them into men.

DEMOKOS. Into heroes.

HECUBA. Yes, we know the jargon. In war-time a man is called a hero. It doesn't make him any braver, and he runs for his life. But at least it's a hero who is running away.

ANDROMACHE. Father, I must beg you to listen. If you have such a fondness for women, listen to what they have to say to you, for I can promise I speak for all the women in the world. Let us keep our husbands as they are. The gods took care to see they were surrounded with enough obstacles and dangers to keep them brave and vigorous. Quite enough if they had nothing to cope with except floods and storms! Or only wild animals! The small game, foxes and hares and pheasants, which a woman can scarcely distinguish from the heather they hide in, prove a man's quickness of eye far better than this target you propose: the enemy's heart hiding in flesh and metal. Whenever I have seen a man kill a stag or an eagle, I have offered up thanks to them. I know they died for Hector. Why should you want me to owe Hector to the deaths of other men?

PRIAM. I don't want it, my dear child. But why do you think you are here now, all looking so beautiful, and valiantly demanding peace? Why: because your husbands and your fathers, and their fathers, and theirs, were fighting men. If they had been too lazy and self-indulgent to spring to arms, if they hadn't known how this dull and stupid business we call life suddenly leaps into flame and justifies itself through the scorn men have for it, you would find *you* were the cowards now, and you would be clamouring for war. A man has only one way of being immortal on this earth: he has to forget he is mortal.

ANDROMACHE. Why, exactly so, father: you're only too right. The brave men die in war. It takes great luck or judgment not to be killed. Once at least the head has to bow and the knee has to bend to danger. The soldiers who march back under the triumphal arches are death's deserters. How can a country increase in strength and honour by sending them both to their graves?

PRIAM. Daughter, the first sign of cowardice in a people is their first moment of decay.

ANDROMACHE. But which is the worse cowardice? To appear cowardly to others, and make sure of peace? Or to be cowardly in your own eyes, and let loose a war?

DEMOKOS. Cowardice is not to prefer death on every hand rather than the death of one's native land.

HECUBA. I was expecting poetry at this point. It never lets us down.

ANDROMACHE. Everyone always dies for his country. If you have lived in it, well and wisely and actively, you die for it too.

HECUBA. It would be better if only the old men fought the wars. Every country is the country of youth. When its youth dies it dies with them.

DEMOKOS. All this nonsense about youth! In thirty years time youth is nothing but these old men you talk about.

CASSANDRA. Wrong.

HECUBA. Wrong! When a grown man reaches forty we change him for an old one. He has completely disappeared. There's only the most superficial resemblance between the two of them. Nothing is handed on from one to the other.

DEMOKOS. I still take a serious concern in my fame as a poet.

HECUBA. Yes, that's quite true. And your rheumatism.

[*Another outburst of laughter from the* SERVANTS.]

HECTOR. And you can listen to all this without saying a word, Paris? Can you still not decide to give up an adventure to save us from years of unhappiness and massacre?

PARIS. What do you want me to say? My case is an international problem.

HECTOR. Are you really in love with Helen, Paris?

CASSANDRA. They've become now a kind of symbol of love's devotion. They don't still have to love each other.

PARIS. I worship Helen.

CASSANDRA (*at the rampart*). Here she is.

HECTOR. If I persuade her to set sail, will you agree?

PARIS. Yes, I'll agree.

HECTOR. Father, if Helen is willing to go back to Greece, will you hold her here by force?

PRIAM. Why discuss the impossible?

HECTOR. Do you call it impossible? If women are a tenth of what you say they are, Helen will go of her own free will.

PARIS. Father, now *I'm* going to ask you to let him do what he wants. You have seen what it's like. As soon as the question of Helen cropped up, this whole tribe royal turned itself into a family conclave of all the poor girl's sisters-in-law, mother- and father-in-law, brother-in-law, worthy of the best middle-class tradition. I doubt if there's anything more humiliating than to be cast for the part of the seducer son in a large family. I've had quite enough of their insinuations. I accept Hector's challenge.

DEMOKOS. Helen's not only yours, Paris. She belongs to the city. She belongs to our country.

MATHEMATICIAN. She belongs to the landscape.

HECUBA. You be quiet, mathematician.

CASSANDRA. Here's Helen; here she is.

HECTOR. Father, I must ask you to let me handle this. Listen; they are calling us to go to the ceremony, to close the Gates of War. Leave this to me. I'll join you soon.

PRIAM. Do you really agree to this, Paris?

PARIS. I'm eager for it.

PRIAM. Very well, then; let it be so. Come along, the rest of you; we will see that the Gates of War are made ready.

CASSANDRA. Those poor gates. They need more oil to shut them than to open them.

[PARIS *and the rest withdraw.* DEMOKOS *stays.*]

HECTOR. What are you waiting for?

DEMOKOS. The visitation of my genius.

HECTOR. Say that again?

DEMOKOS. Every time Helen walks my way I am thrown into a transport of inspiration. I shake all over, break into sweat, and impro-
vise. Good heavens, here it is! (*He declaims:*)

> Beautiful Helen, Helen of Sparta,
> Singular as the evening star,
> The gods forbid that we should part a
> Pair as fair as you and Paris are.

HECTOR. Your line-endings give me a headache.

DEMOKOS. It's an invention of mine. I can obtain effects even more
surprising. Listen: (*declaims*)

> Face the great Hector with no qualm,
> Troy's glory though he be, and the world's terror:
> He is the storm, and you the after-calm,
> Yours is the right, and his the boist'rous error.

HECTOR. Get out!

DEMOKOS. What are you glaring at? You look as though you have as
little liking for poetry as you have for war.

HECTOR. They make a pretty couple! Now vanish. (*Exit* DEMOKOS.)

[*Enter* CASSANDRA.]

CASSANDRA. Helen!

[*Enter* HELEN *and* PARIS.]

PARIS. Here he is, Helen darling; this is Hector. He has a proposition
to make to you, a perfectly simple proposition. He wants to hand
you over to the Greeks, and prove to you that you don't love me.
Tell me you do love me, before I leave you with him. Tell me in
your own words.

HELEN. I adore you, my sweet.

PARIS. Tell me how beautiful the wave was which swept you away
from Greece.

HELEN. Magnificent! A magnificent wave! Where did you see a wave?
The sea was so calm.

PARIS. Tell me you hate Menelaus.

HELEN. Menelaus? I hate him.

PARIS. You haven't finished yet. I shall never again return to Greece.
Say that.

HELEN. You will never again return to Greece.

PARIS. No, no, this is about you, my darling.

HELEN. Oh, of course! How silly I am! I shall never again return to
Greece.

PARIS. I didn't make her say it.—Now it's up to you. (*He goes off.*)

HECTOR. Is Greece a beautiful country?

HELEN. Paris found it ravishing.

HECTOR. I meant is Greece itself beautiful, apart from Helen?

HELEN. How very charming of you.

HECTOR. I was simply wondering what it is really like.

HELEN. Well, there are quite a great many kings, and a great many goats, dotted about on marble.

HECTOR. If the kings are in gold, and the goats angora, that would look pretty well when the sun was rising.

HELEN. I don't get up very early.

HECTOR. And a great many gods as well, I believe? Paris tells me the sky is crawling with them; he tells me you can see the legs of goddesses hanging down from the clouds.

HELEN. Paris always goes about with his nose in the air. He may have seen them.

HECTOR. But you haven't?

HELEN. I am not gifted that way. I will look out for them when I go back there again.

HECTOR. You were telling Paris you would never be going back there.

HELEN. He asked me to tell him so. I adore doing what Paris wants me to do.

HECTOR. I see. Is that also true of what you said about Menelaus? Do you not, after all, hate him?

HELEN. Why should I hate him?

HECTOR. For the one reason which might certainly make for hate. You have seen too much of him.

HELEN. Menelaus? Oh, no! I have never seen Menelaus. On the contrary.

HECTOR. You have never seen your husband?

HELEN. There are some things, and certain people, that stand out in bright colours for me. They are the ones I can see. I believe in them. I have never been able to see Menelaus.

HECTOR. Though I suppose he must have come very close to you sometimes.

HELEN. I have been able to touch him. But I can't honestly tell you I saw him.

HECTOR. They say he never left your side.

HELEN. Apparently. I must have walked across him a great many times without knowing it.

HECTOR. Whereas you have seen Paris.

HELEN. Vividly; in the clearest outline against the sky and the sun.

HECTOR. Does he still stand out as vividly as he did? Look down there: leaning against the rampart.

HELEN. Are you sure that's Paris, down there?

HECTOR. He is waiting for you.

HELEN. Good gracious! He's not nearly as clear as usual!

HECTOR. And yet the wall is freshly whitewashed. Look again: there he is in profile.

HELEN. It's odd how people waiting for you stand out far less clearly than people you are waiting for.

HECTOR. Are you sure that Paris loves you?

HELEN. I don't like knowing about other people's feelings. There is nothing more embarrassing. Just as when you play cards and you see your opponent's hand. You are sure to lose.

HECTOR. What about yourself? Do you love him?

HELEN. I don't much like knowing my own feelings either.

HECTOR. But, listen: when you make love with Paris, when he sleeps in your arms, when you are circled round with Paris, overwhelmed with Paris, haven't you any thoughts about it?

HELEN. My part is over. I leave any thinking to the universe. It does it much better than I do.

HECTOR. Have there been many others, before Paris?

HELEN. Some.

HECTOR. And there will be others after him, wouldn't you say, as long as they stand out in clear relief against the sky, or the wall, or the white sheets on the bed? It is just as I thought it was. You don't love Paris particularly, Helen; you love men.

HELEN. I don't dislike them. They're as pleasant as soap and a sponge and warm water; you feel cleansed and refreshed by them.

HECTOR. Cassandra! Cassandra!

CASSANDRA (*entering*). What do you want?

HECTOR. Cassandra, Helen is going back this evening with the Greek ambassador.

HELEN. I? What makes you think so?

HECTOR. Weren't you telling me that you didn't love Paris particularly?

HELEN. That was your interpretation. Still, if you like.

HECTOR. I quote my authority. You have the same liking for men as you have for a cake of soap.

HELEN. Yes; or pumice stone perhaps is better. What about it?

HECTOR. Well, then, you're not going to hesitate in your choice between going back to Greece, which you don't mind, and a catastrophe as terrible as war?

HELEN. You don't understand me at all, Hector. Of course I'm not hesitating. It would be very easy to say 'I will do this or that, so that this can happen or that can happen.' You've discovered my weakness and you are overjoyed. The man who discovers a woman's weakness is like the huntsman in the heat of the day who finds a cool spring. He wallows in it. But you mustn't think, because you have convinced me, you've convinced the future, too. Merely by making children behave as you want them to, you don't alter the course of destiny.

HECTOR. I don't follow your Greek shades and subtleties.

HELEN. It's not a question of shades and subtleties. It's no less than a question of monsters and pyramids.

HECTOR. Do you choose to leave here, yes or no?

HELEN. Don't bully me. I choose what happens in the way I choose men, or anything else. I choose whatever is not indefinite and vague. I choose what I see.

HECTOR. I know, you said that: what you see in the brightest colours. And you don't see yourself returning to Menelaus in a few days' time?

HELEN. No. It's very difficult.

HECTOR. We could no doubt persuade your husband to dress with great brilliance for your return.

HELEN. All the purple dye from all the murex shells in the sea wouldn't make him visible to me.

HECTOR. Here you have a rival, Cassandra. Helen can read the future, too.

HELEN. No, I can't read the future. But when I imagine the future some of the pictures I see are coloured, and some are dull and drab. And up to now it has always been the coloured scenes which have happened in the end.

HECTOR. We are going to give you back to the Greeks at high noon, on the blinding sand, between the violet sea and the ochre-coloured wall. We shall all be in golden armour with red skirts; and my sisters, dressed in green and standing between my white stallion and Priam's black mare, will return you to the Greek ambassador, over whose silver helmet I can imagine tall purple plumes. You see that, I think?

HELEN. No, none of it. It is all quite sombre.

HECTOR. You are mocking me, aren't you?

HELEN. Why should I mock you? Very well, then. Let us go, if you like! Let us go and get ready to return me to the Greeks. We shall see what happens.

HECTOR. Do you realize how you insult humanity, or is it unconscious?

HELEN. I don't know what you mean.

HECTOR. You realize that your coloured picture-book is holding the world up to ridicule? While we are all battling and making sacrifices to bring about a time we can call our own, there are you, looking at your pictures which nothing in all eternity can alter. What's wrong? Which one has made you stop and stare at it with those blind eyes? I don't doubt it's the one where you are standing here on the ramparts, watching the battle going on below. Is it the battle you see?

HELEN. Yes.

HECTOR. And the city is in ruins or burning, isn't that so?

HELEN. Yes. It's a vivid red.

HECTOR. And what about Paris? You are seeing his body dragged behind a chariot?

HELEN. Oh, do you think that is Paris? I see what looks like a flash of sunlight rolling in the dust. A diamond sparkling on his hand. Yes, it is! Often I don't recognize faces, but I always recognize the jewellery. It's his ring, I'm quite certain.

HECTOR. Exactly. Do I dare to ask you about Andromache, and myself, the scene of Andromache and Hector? You are looking at us. Don't deny it. How do you see us? Happy, grown old, bathed in light?

HELEN. I am not trying to see it.

HECTOR. The scene of Andromache weeping over the body of Hector, does that shine clearer?

HELEN. You seem to know. But sometimes I see things shining, brilliantly shining, and they never happen. No one is infallible.

HECTOR. You needn't go on. I understand. There is a son between the weeping mother and the father stretched on the ground?

HELEN. Yes. He is playing with his father's tangled hair. He is a sweet boy.

HECTOR. And these scenes are there in your eyes, down in the depths of them. Could I see them there?

HELEN. I don't know. Look.

HECTOR. Nothing. Nothing except the ashes of all those fires, the gold and the emerald in dust. How innocent it is, this crystal where the future is waiting. But there should be tears bathing it, and where are they? Would you cry, Helen, if you were going to be killed?

HELEN. I don't know. But I should scream. And I feel I shall scream if you go on at me like this, Hector. I am going to scream.

HECTOR. You will leave for Greece this evening, Helen, otherwise I shall kill you.

HELEN. But I want to leave! I'm prepared to leave. All that I'm trying to tell is that I simply can't manage to distinguish the ship that is going to carry me there. Nothing is shining in the least, neither the metal on the mast, nor the ring in the captain's nose, nor the cabin-boy's eyes, nor anything.

HECTOR. You will go back on a grey sea under a grey sun. But we must have peace.

HELEN. I cannot see peace.

HECTOR. Ask Cassandra to make her appear for you. Cassandra is a sorceress. She can summon up shapes and spirits.

A MESSENGER (*entering*). Hector, Priam is asking for you. The priests are opposed to our shutting the Gates of War. They say the gods will consider it an insult.

HECTOR. It is curious how the gods can never speak for themselves in these difficult matters.

MESSENGER. They have spoken for themselves. A thunderbolt has fallen on the temple, several men have been killed, the entrails of the victims have been consulted, and they are unanimously against Helen's return to Greece.

HECTOR. I would give a good deal to be able to consult the entrails of the priests . . . I'll follow you.

[*The* MESSENGER *goes.*]

Well, now, Helen, do we agree about this?

HELEN. Yes.

HECTOR. From now on you will say what I tell you to say? You will do what I tell you to do?

HELEN. Yes.

HECTOR. When we come in front of Ulysses you won't contradict me, you will bear out everything I say?

HELEN. Yes.

HECTOR. Do you hear this, Cassandra? Listen to this solid wall of negation which says Yes! They have all given in to me. Paris has given in to me, Priam has given in to me, Helen has given in to me. And yet I can't help feeling that in each of these apparent victories I have been defeated. You set out, thinking you are going to have to wrestle with giants; you brace yourself to conquer them, and you find yourself wrestling with something inflexible reflected in a woman's eye. You have said yes beautifully, Helen, and you're brimful of a stubborn determination to defy me!

HELEN. That's possible. But how can I help it? It isn't my own determination.

HECTOR. By what peculiar vagary did the world choose to place its mirror in this obtuse head?

HELEN. It's most regrettable, obviously. But can you see any way of defeating the obstinacy of a mirror?

HECTOR. Yes. I've been considering that for the past several minutes.

ANOTHER MESSENGER (*entering*). Hector, make haste. They are in a turmoil of revolt down on the beach. The Greek ships have been sighted, and they have hoisted their flag not masthead but hatchway. The honour of our navy is at stake. Priam is afraid the ambassador may be murdered as soon as he lands.

HECTOR. I leave you in charge of Helen, Cassandra. I must go and give my orders.

HELEN. If you break the mirror, will what is reflected in it cease to exist?

HECTOR. That is the whole question. (*Exit* HECTOR.)

CASSANDRA. I never see anything at all, you know, either coloured or not. But I can feel the weight on me of every person who comes towards me. I know what is in store for them by the sensation of suffering which flows into my veins.

HELEN. Is it true that you are a sorceress? Could you really make Peace take shape and appear for us?

CASSANDRA. Peace? Very easily? She is always standing in her beggarly way on every threshold. Wait . . . you will see her now.

[PEACE *appears.*]

HELEN. Oh, how pretty she is!

PEACE. Come to my rescue, Helen: help me!

HELEN. But how pale and wan she is.

PEACE. Pale and wan? What do you mean? Don't you see the gold shining in my hair?

HELEN. Gold? Well, perhaps a golden grey. It's very original.

PEACE. Golden grey? Is my gold now grey? (*She disappears.*)

CASSANDRA. I think she means to make herself clearer.

[PEACE *re-appears, outrageously painted.*]

PEACE. Is that better now?

HELEN. I don't see her as well as I did before.

PEACE. Is that better?

CASSANDRA. Helen doesn't see you as well as she did.

PEACE. But you can see me: you are speaking to me.

CASSANDRA. It's my speciality to speak to the invisible.

PEACE. What is going on, then? Why are all the men in the city and along the beach making such a pandemonium?

CASSANDRA. Apparently their gods are insulted, and their honour is at stake.

PEACE. Their gods! Their honour!

CASSANDRA. Yes . . . You are ill!

ACT II

꿍 Scene: *A palace enclosure. At each corner a view of the sea. In the middle a monument, the Gates of War. They are wide open.*

[HELEN. *The young* TROILUS.]

HELEN. You, you, hey! You down there! Yes, it's you I'm calling. Come here.

TROILUS. No.

HELEN. What is your name?

TROILUS. Troilus.

HELEN. Come here.

TROILUS. No.

HELEN. Come here, Troilus!

[TROILUS *draws near.*]

That's the way. You obey when you're called by your name: you are still very like a puppy. It's rather beguiling. Do you know you have made me call out to a man for the first time in my life. They keep so close to my side I have only usually to move my lips. I have called out to sea-gulls, to dogs, to the echoes, but never before to a man. You will pay for that. What's the matter? Are you trembling?

TROILUS. No, I'm not.

HELEN. You tremble, Troilus.

TROILUS. Yes, I do.

HELEN. Why are you always just behind me? If I walk with my back to the sun and suddenly stop, the head of your shadow stubs itself against my feet. That doesn't matter, as long as it doesn't overshoot them. Tell me what you want.

TROILUS. I don't want anything.

HELEN. Tell me what you want, Troilus!

TROILUS. Everything! I want everything!

HELEN. You want everything. The moon?

TROILUS. Everything! Everything and more!

HELEN. You're beginning to talk like a real man already; you want to kiss me!

TROILUS. No!

HELEN. You want to kiss me, isn't that it, Troilus?

TROILUS. I would kill myself directly afterwards!

HELEN. Come nearer. How old are you?

TROILUS. Fifteen. Alas!

HELEN. Bravo that alas. Have you kissed girls of your own age?

TROILUS. I hate them.

HELEN. But you have kissed them?

TROILUS. Well, yes, you're bound to kiss them, you kiss them all. I would give my life not to have kissed any of them.

HELEN. You seem prepared to get rid of quite a number of lives. Why haven't you said to me frankly: Helen, I want to kiss you! I don't see anything wrong in your kissing me. Kiss me.

TROILUS. Never.

HELEN. And then, when the day came to an end, you would have come quietly to where I was sitting on the battlements watching the sun go down over the islands, and you would have turned my head towards you with your hands—from golden it would have become dark, only shadow now, you would hardly have been able to see me —and you would have kissed me, and I should have been very happy. Why this is Troilus, I should have said to myself: young Troilus is kissing me! Kiss me.

TROILUS. Never.

HELEN. I see. You think, once you have kissed me, you would hate me?

TROILUS. Oh! Older men have all the luck, knowing how to say what they want to!

HELEN. You say it well enough.

　　　　　　　　　　[*Enter* PARIS.]

PARIS. Take care Helen, Troilus is a dangerous fellow.

HELEN. On the contrary. He wants to kiss me.

PARIS. Troilus, you know that if you kiss Helen, I shall kill you?

HELEN. Dying means nothing to him; no matter how often.

PARIS. What's the matter with him? Is he crouching to spring? Is he going to take a leap at you? He's too nice a boy. Kiss Helen, Troilus. I'll let you.

HELEN. If you can make up his mind to it you're cleverer than I am.

　　　　　[TROILUS *who was about to hurl himself on* HELEN
　　　　　　　　　immediately draws back.]

PARIS. Listen, Troilus! Here's a committee of our revered elders coming to shut the Gates of War. Kiss Helen in front of them; it will make you famous. You want to be famous, don't you, later on in life?

TROILUS. No. I want nobody to have heard of me.

PARIS. You don't want to be famous? You don't want to be rich and powerful?

TROILUS. No. Poor. Ugly.

PARIS. Let me finish! So that you can have all the women you want.

TROILUS. I don't want any, none at all, none.

PARIS. Here come the senators! Now you can choose: either you kiss Helen in front of them, or I shall kiss her in front of you. Would you rather I did it? All right! Look! . . . Why, this was a new version of kiss you gave me, Helen. What was it?

HELEN. The kiss I had ready for Troilus.

PARIS. You don't know what you're missing, my boy! Are you leaving us? Goodbye, then.

HELEN. We shall kiss one another, Troilus. I'll answer for that.

[TROILUS *goes.*]

Troilus!

PARIS (*slightly unnerved*). You called very loudly, Helen.

[*Enter* DEMOKOS.]

DEMOKOS. Helen, one moment! Look me full in the face. I've got here in my hand a magnificent bird which I'm going to set free. Are you looking? Here it is. Smooth back your hair, and smile a beautiful smile.

PARIS. I don't see how the bird will fly any better if Helen smooths her hair and gives a beautiful smile.

HELEN. It can't do me any harm, anyway.

DEMOKOS. Don't move. One! Two! Three! There! It's all over, you can go now.

HELEN. Where was the bird?

DEMOKOS. It's a bird who knows how to make himself invisible.

HELEN. Ask him next time to tell you how he does it. (*She goes.*)

PARIS. What is this nonsense?

DEMOKOS. I am writing a song on the subject of Helen's face. I needed to look at it closely, to engrave it, smiling, on my memory.

[*Enter* HECUBA, POLYXENE, ABNEOS, *the* MATHEMA-TICIAN, *and some* OLD MEN.]

HECUBA. Well, are you going to shut these Gates for us?

DEMOKOS. Certainly not. We might well have to open them again this very evening.

HECUBA. It is Hector's wish. And Hector will persuade Priam.

DEMOKOS. That is as we shall see. And what's more I have a surprise in store for Hector.

POLYXENE. Where do the Gates lead to, mama?

ABNEOS. To war, my child. When they are open it means there is war.

DEMOKOS. My friends . . .

HECUBA. War or not, it's an absurd symbolism, your Gateway, and those two great doors always left open look very unsightly. All the dogs stop there.

MATHEMATICIAN. This is no domestic matter. It concerns war and the Gods.

HECUBA. Which is just as I said: the Gods never remember to shut their doors.

POLYXENE. I remember to shut them very well, don't I, mama?

PARIS. And you even include your fingers in them, don't you, my pretty one?

DEMOKOS. May I ask for a moment of silence, Paris? Abneos, and you, Mathematician, and you, my friends: I asked you to meet here earlier than the time fixed for the ceremony so that we could hold our first council. And it promises well that this first council of war should be, not a council of generals, but a council of intellectuals. For it isn't enough in war-time to have our soldiers drilled, well-armed, and spectacular. It is absolutely necessary to bring their enthusiasm up to fever pitch. The physical intoxication which their officers will get from them by a generous allowance of cheap wine supplied at the right moment, will still be ineffective against the Greeks, unless it is reinforced by the spiritual and moral intoxication which the poets can pour into them. If we are too old to fight we can at least make sure that the fighting is savage. I see you have something to say on the subject, Abneos.

ABNEOS. Yes. We must make a war-song.

DEMOKOS. Very proper. A war requires a war-song.

PARIS. We have done without one up to now.

HECUBA. War itself sings quite loud enough.

ABNEOS. We have done without one because up to now we were fighting only barbarians. It was nothing more than a hunt, and the hunting horn was all we needed. But now with the Greeks we're entering a different region of war altogether.

DEMOKOS. Exactly so, Abneos. The Greeks don't fight with everybody.

PARIS. We already have a national anthem.

ABNEOS. Yes. But it's a song of peace.

PARIS. If you sing a song of peace with enough gestures and grimaces it becomes a war-song. What are the words we have already?

ABNEOS. You know them perfectly well. There's no spirit in them:

> We cut and bind the harvest,
> We tread the vineyard's blood.

DEMOKOS. At the very most it's a war-song against farm produce. You won't frighten the Spartans by threatening a wheatfield.

PARIS. Sing it with a spear in your hand, and a dead body at your feet, you will be surprised.

HECUBA. It includes the word 'blood,' there's always that.

PARIS. The word 'harvest' as well. War rather approves of the word 'harvest.'

ABNEOS. Why discuss it, when Demokos can invent an entirely new one in a couple of hours.

DEMOKOS. A couple of hours is rather short.

HECUBA. Don't be afraid; it's more than you need for it. And after the song will come the hymn, and after the hymn the cantata. As soon as war is declared it will be impossible to hold the poets back. Rhyme is still the most effective drum.

DEMOKOS. And the most useful, Hecuba: you don't know how wisely you speak. I know war. As long as war isn't with us, and the Gates are shut, each of us is free to insult it and execrate it as we will. But once war comes, its pride and autocracy is huge. You can gain its goodwill only by flattery and adoration. So the mission of those who understand how to speak and write is to compliment and praise war ceaselessly and indiscriminately, otherwise we shut ourselves out from his favour.

PARIS. Have you got an idea for your song already?

DEMOKOS. A marvellous idea, which no one will understand better than you. War must be tired of the mask we always give it, of Medusa's venomous hair and a Gorgon's lips. I have had the notion to compare War's face with Helen's. It will be enchanted by the comparison.

POLYXENE. What does War look like, mama?

HECUBA. Like your Aunt Helen.

POLYXENE. She is very pretty.

DEMOKOS. Then the discussion is closed. You can expect the war-song. Why are you looking worried, Mathematician?

MATHEMATICIAN. Because there are other things far more urgent than this war-song, far more urgent!

DEMOKOS. You think we should discuss the question of medals, false information, atrocity stories, and so on?

MATHEMATICIAN. I think we should discuss the insulting epithets.

HECUBA. The insulting epithets?

MATHEMATICIAN. Before they hurl their spears the Greek fighting-men hurl insults. You third cousin of a toad, they yell! You son of a sow!—They insult each other, like that! And they have a good reason for it. They know that the body is more vulnerable when self-respect has fled. Soldiers famous for their composure lose it immediately when they're treated as warts or maggots. We Trojans suffer from a grave shortage of insults.

DEMOKOS. The Mathematician is quite right. We are the only race in the world which doesn't insult its enemies before it kills them.

PARIS. You don't think it's enough that the civilians insult the enemy civilians?

MATHEMATICIAN. The armies have to show the same hatred the civilians do. You know what dissemblers armies can be in this way. Leave them to themselves and they spend their time admiring each other. Their front lines very soon become the only ranks of real brotherhood in the world. So naturally, when the theatre of war is so full of mutual consideration, hatred is driven back on to the schools, the salons, the tradespeople. If our soldiers aren't at least equal to the Greeks in the fury of their epithets, they will lose all taste for insults and calumny, and as a natural consequence all taste for war.

DEMOKOS. Suggestion adopted! We will organize a cursing parade this evening.

PARIS. I should have thought they're big enough to find their own curses.

DEMOKOS. What a mistake! Could you, adroit as you are, find your own effective curses?

PARIS. I believe so.

DEMOKOS. You fool yourself. Come and stand face to face with Abneos and begin.

PARIS. Why Abneos?

DEMOKOS. Because he lends himself to this sort of thing, with his corpulence and one thing and another.

ABNEOS. Come on, then, speak up, you piece of pie-crust!

PARIS. No. Abneos doesn't inspire me. I'll start with you, if you don't mind.

DEMOKOS. With me? Certainly. You can let fly at ten paces. There we are. Begin.

HECUBA. Take a good look at him. You will be inspired.

PARIS. You old parasite! You filthy-footed iambic pentameter!

DEMOKOS. Just one second. To avoid any mistake you had better say who it is you're addressing.

PARIS. You're quite right! Demokos! Bloodshot bullock's eye! You fungus-ridden plum-tree!

DEMOKOS. Grammatically reasonable, but very naive. What is there in a fungus-ridden plum-tree to make me rise up foaming at the lips?

HECUBA. He also called you a bloodshot bullock's eye.

DEMOKOS. Bloodshot bullock's eye is better. But you see how you flounder, Paris? Search for something that can strike home to me. What are my faults, in your opinion?

PARIS. You are cowardly: your breath smells, and you have no talent.

DEMOKOS. You're asking for trouble!

PARIS. I was trying to please you.

POLYXENE. Why are we scolding Uncle Demokos, mama?

HECUBA. Because he is a cuckoo, dearest!

DEMOKOS. What did you say, Hecuba?

HECUBA. I was saying that you're a cuckoo, Demokos. If cuckoos

had the absurdity, the affectation, the ugliness and the stench of
vultures, you would be a cuckoo.

DEMOKOS. Wait a bit, Paris! Your mother is better at this than you
are. Model yourselves on her. One hour's exercise each day for
each soldier, and Hecuba has given us the superiority in insults
which we badly need. As for the war-song, I'm not sure it wouldn't
be wiser to entrust that to her as well.

HECUBA. If you like. But if so, I shouldn't say that war looks like
Helen.

DEMOKOS. What would you say it looks like, in your opinion?

HECUBA. I will tell you when the Gates have been shut.

> [*Enter* PRIAM, HECTOR, ANDROMACHE, *and presently*
> HELEN. *During the closing of the Gates,* ANDROMACHE
> *takes little* POLYXENE *aside and whispers a secret or
> an errand to her.*]

HECTOR. As they nearly are.

DEMOKOS. One moment, Hector!

HECTOR. Aren't we ready to begin the ceremony?

HECUBA. Surely? The hinges are swimming in oil.

HECTOR. Well, then.

PRIAM. What our friends want you to understand, Hector, is that war
is ready, too. Consider carefully. They're not mistaken. If you
shut these Gates, in a minute we may have to open them again.

HECUBA. Even one minute of peace is worth taking.

HECTOR. Father, you should know what peace means to men who
have been fighting for months. It's like solid ground to someone
who was drowning or sinking in the quicksands. Do let us get our
feet on to a few inches of peace, touch it, if only with the tips of
our toes.

PRIAM. Hector: consider: inflicting the word peace on to the city today is as ruthless as though you gave it poison. You will take her
off her guard, undermine her iron determination, debase, with the
word peace, the accepted values of memory, affection, and hope.
The soldiers will rush to buy the bread of peace, to drink the wine
of peace, to hold in their arms the woman of peace, and in an hour
you will put them back to face a war.

HECTOR. The war will never take place!

> [*The sound of clamour near the Gates.*]

DEMOKOS. No? Listen!

HECTOR. Shut the Gates. This is where we shall meet the Greeks.
Conversation will be bitter enough as it is. We must receive them in
peace.

PRIAM. My son, are we even sure we should let the Greeks disembark?

HECTOR. Disembark they shall. This meeting with Ulysses is our last
chance of peace.

DEMOKOS. Disembark they shall not. Our honour is at stake. We shall be the laughing-stock of the whole world.

HECTOR. And you're taking it upon yourself to recommend to the Senate an action which would certainly mean war?

DEMOKOS. Upon myself? No, not at all. Will you come forward now, Busiris. This is where your mission begins.

HECTOR. Who is this stranger?

DEMOKOS. He is the greatest living expert on the rights of nations. It's a lucky chance he should be passing through Troy today. You can't say that he's a biased witness. He is neutral. Our Senate is willing to abide by his decision, a decision which all other nations will agree with tomorrow.

HECTOR. And what is your opinion?

BUSIRIS. My opinion, Princes, based on my own observation and further enquiry, is that the Greeks, in relation to Troy, are guilty of three breaches of international law. If you give them permission to disembark you will have sacrificed your position as the aggrieved party, and so lost the universal sympathy which would certainly have been yours in the conflict to follow.

HECTOR. Explain yourself.

BUSIRIS. Firstly, they have hoisted their flag hatchway and not mast-head. A ship of war, my dear Princes and colleagues, hoists its flag hatchway only when replying to a salute from a boat carrying cattle. Clearly, then, so to salute a city and a city's population is an insult. As it happens, we have a precedent. Last year the Greeks hoisted their flag hatchway when they were entering the port of Orphea. The reply was incisive. Orphea declared war.

HECTOR. And what happened?

BUSIRIS. Orphea was beaten. Orphea no longer exists, nor the Orpheans either.

HECUBA. Perfect.

BUSIRIS. But the annihilation of a people doesn't alter in the least their superior moral position.

HECTOR. Go on.

BUSIRIS. Secondly, on entering your territorial waters the Greeks adopted the formation known as frontal. At the last congress there was some talk of including this formation in the paragraph of measures called defensive-aggressive. I was very happy to be able to get it restored under its proper heading of aggressive-defensive: so without doubt it is now one of the subtle forms of naval manœuvre which is a disguised form of blockade: that is to say, it constitutes a fault of the first degree! We have a precedent for this, as well. Five years ago the Greek navy adopted the frontal formation when they anchored outside Magnesia. Magnesia at once declared war.

HECTOR. Did they win it?

BUSIRIS. They lost it. There's not one stone of Magnesia still standing on another. But my redraft of the paragraph is still standing.

HECUBA. I congratulate you. We were beginning to be anxious.

HECTOR. Go on.

BUSIRIS. The third fault is not so serious. One of the Greek triremes has crept close in to shore without permission. Its captain, Ajax, the most unruly and impossible man among the Greeks, is climbing up towards the city, shouting scandal and provocation, and swearing he would like to kill Paris. But this is a very minor matter, from the international point of view; because it isn't, in any way, a formal breach of the law.

DEMOKOS. You have your information. The situation can only be resolved in one of two ways. To swallow an outrage, or return it. Choose.

HECTOR. Oneah, go and find Ajax. Head him off in this direction.

PARIS. I'm waiting here for him.

HECTOR. You will be good enough to stay in the Palace until I call for you. As for you, Busiris, you must understand that our city has no intention of being insulted by the Greeks.

BUSIRIS. I am not surprised. Troy's incorruptible pride is a legend all the world over.

HECTOR. You are going to provide me, here and now, with an argument which will allow our Senate to say that there has been no fault whatever on the part of our visitors, and with our pride untouched we welcome them here as our guests.

DEMOKOS. What nonsense is this?

BUSIRIS. It isn't in keeping with the facts, Hector.

HECTOR. My dear Busiris, all of us here know there's no better way of exercising the imagination than the study of law. No poet ever interpreted nature as freely as a lawyer interprets truth.

BUSIRIS. The Senate asked me for an opinion: I gave it.

HECTOR. And I ask you for an interpretation. An even subtler point of law.

BUSIRIS. It goes against my conscience.

HECTOR. Your conscience has seen Orphea destroyed, Magnesia destroyed: is it now contemplating, just as lightheartedly, the destruction of Troy?

HECUBA. Yes. He comes from Syracuse.

HECTOR. I do beg of you, Busiris. The lives of two countries depend on this. Help us.

BUSIRIS. Truth is the only help I can give you.

HECTOR. Precisely. Discover a truth which saves us. What is the use of justice if it doesn't hammer out a shield for innocent people? Forge us a truth. If you can't, there is one thing I can tell you, quite simply: we shall hold you here for as long as the war goes on.

BUSIRIS. What are you saying?

DEMOKOS. You're abusing your position, Hector!

HECUBA. During war we imprison the rights of man. There seems no reason why we shouldn't imprison a lawyer.

HECTOR. I mean what I say, Busiris. I've never failed yet to keep my promises, or my threats. And now either these guards are going to take you off to prison for a year or two, or else you leave here, this evening, heaped with gold. With this in mind, you can dispassionately examine the evidence once again.

BUSIRIS. Actually there are certain mitigating arguments.

HECTOR. I was sure there were.

BUSIRIS. In the case of the first fault, for instance, when the cattle-boat salute is given in certain seas where the shores are fertile, it could be interpreted as a salute from the sailors to the farmers.

HECTOR. That would be, in fact, the logical interpretation. The salute of the sea to the earth.

BUSIRIS. Not to mention that the cargo of cattle might easily be a cargo of bulls. In that case the homage would verge on flattery.

HECTOR. There you are. You've understood what I meant. We've arrived at our point of view.

BUSIRIS. And as to the frontal formation, that could as easily mean a promise as a provocation. Women wanting children give themselves not from the side but face to face.

HECTOR. Decisive argument.

BUSIRIS. Then, again, the Greek ships have huge carved nymphs for figureheads. A woman who comes towards you naked and open-armed is not a threat but an offer. An offer to talk, at any rate.

HECTOR. So there we have our honour safe and sound, Demokos. The next step is to make this consultation with Busiris public. Meanwhile, Minos, tell the port authorities to let Ulysses disembark without any loss of time.

DEMOKOS. It's no use even trying to discuss honour with these fighting men. They trade on the fact that you can't treat them as cowards.

MATHEMATICIAN. At any rate, Hector, deliver the Oration for the Dead. That will make you think again.

HECTOR. There's not going to be an Oration for the Dead.

PRIAM. But it's a part of the ceremony. The victorious general must always speak in honour of the dead when the Gates are closed.

HECTOR. An Oration for the Dead of a war is a hypocritical speech in defence of the living, a plea for acquittal. I am not so sure of my innocence.

DEMOKOS. The High Command is not responsible.

HECTOR. Alas, no one is: nor the Gods either. Besides, I have given my oration for the dead already. I gave it to them in their last minute of life, when they were lying on the battlefield, on a little slope of olive-trees, while they could still attend me with what was left of their sight and hearing. I can tell you what I said to them. There was one, disembowelled, already turning up the whites of his eyes, and I said to him: 'It's not so bad, you know, it's not so bad; you will do all right, old man.' And one with his skull split in two; I said: 'You look pretty comical with that broken nose.' And my little equerry, with his left arm hanging useless and his last blood flowing out of him; and I said, 'It's a good thing for you it's the left arm you've splintered.' I am happy I gave them one final swig of life; it was all they asked for; they died drinking it. And there's nothing else to be said. Shut the Gates.

POLYXENE. Did the little equerry die, as well?

HECTOR. Yes, puss-cat. He died. He stretched out his right arm. Some-one I couldn't see took him by his perfect hand. And then he died.

DEMOKOS. Our general seems to confuse remarks made to the dying with the Oration for the Dead.

PRIAM. Why must you be so stubborn, Hector?

HECTOR. Very well: you shall have the Oration. (*He takes a position below the Gates.*)—You who cannot hear us, who cannot see us, listen to these words, look at those who come to honour you. We have won the war. I know that's of no moment to you. You are the victors, too. But we are victorious, and still live. That's where the difference is between us and why I'm ashamed. I don't know whether, among the crowd of the dead, any privilege is given to men who died victorious. But the living, whether victorious or not, have privilege enough. We have our eyes. We see the sun. We do what all men do under the sun. We eat. We drink. By the moon, we sleep with our wives. And with yours, now you have gone.

DEMOKOS. You insult the dead!

HECTOR. Do you think so?

DEMOKOS. Either the dead or the living.

HECTOR. There is a distinction.

PRIAM. Come to the peroration, Hector. The Greeks are coming ashore.

HECTOR. I will come to it now . . . Breathe in this incense, touch these offerings, you who can neither smell nor touch. And under-stand, since I speak to you sincerely, I haven't an equal tenderness and respect for all of you. Though all of you are the dead, with you as with us who survive there are men of courage and men of fear, and you can't make me confuse, for the sake of a ceremony, the dead I admire with those I can't admire. But what I have to say to you today is that war seems to me the most sordid, hypocritical way of making all men equal: and I accept death neither as a pun-ishment or expiation for the coward, nor as a reward to the living.

So, whatever you may be, absent, forgotten, purposeless, unresting, without existence, one thing is certain when we close these Gates: we must ask you to forgive us, we, the deserters who survive you, who feel we have stolen two great privileges, I hope the sound of their names will never reach you: the warmth of the living body, and the sky.

POLYXENE. The gates are shutting, mama!

HECUBA. Yes, darling.

POLYXENE. The dead men are pushing them shut.

HECUBA. They help, a little.

POLYXENE. They're helping quite a lot, especially over on the right.

HECTOR. Is it done? Are they shut?

GUARD. Tight as a clam.

HECTOR. We're at peace, father, we're at peace.

HECUBA. We're at peace!

POLYXENE. It feels much better, doesn't it, mama?

HECTOR. Indeed it does.

POLYXENE. I feel much better, anyway.

[*The sound of the* GREEKS' *music.*]

A MESSENGER. The Greeks have landed, Priam!

DEMOKOS. What music! What frightful music! It's the most anti-Trojan music there could possibly be! Let's go and give them a welcome to match it.

HECTOR. Receive them royally, bring them here safely. You are responsible.

MATHEMATICIAN. At any rate we ought to counter with some Trojan music. Hector, if we can't be indignant any other way, you can authorize a battle of music.

CROWD. The Greeks! The Greeks!

MESSENGER. Ulysses is on the landing-stage, Priam. Where are we to take him?

PRIAM. Conduct him here. Send word to us in the palace when he comes. Keep with us, Paris. We don't want you too much in evidence just yet.

HECTOR. Let's go and prepare what we shall say to the Greeks, father.

DEMOKOS. You'd better prepare it somewhat better than your speech for the dead; you're likely to meet more contradiction.

[*Exeunt* PRIAM *and his sons.*]

If you are going with them, tell us before you go, Hecuba, what it is you think war looks like.

HECUBA. You insist on knowing?

DEMOKOS. If you've seen what it looks like, tell us.

HECUBA. Like the bottom of a baboon. When the baboon is up in a tree, with its hind end facing us, there is the face of war exactly: scarlet, scaley, glazed, framed in a clotted, filthy wig.

DEMOKOS. So he has two faces: this you describe, and Helen's. (*Exit.*)

ANDROMACHE. Here is Helen now. Polyxene, you remember what you have to say to her?

POLYXENE. Yes.

ANDROMACHE. Go to her, then.

[*Enter* HELEN.]

HELEN. Do you want to talk to me, darling?

POLYXENE. Yes, Aunt Helen.

HELEN. It must be important, you're so very tense.

POLYXENE. Yes, Aunt Helen.

HELEN. Is it something you can't tell me without standing so stiffly?

POLYXENE. No, Aunt Helen.

HELEN. Do tell me, then; you make me feel terrible when you stand there like a little stick.

POLYXENE. Aunt Helen, if you love anyone, please go away.

HELEN. Why should I go away, darling?

POLYXENE. Because of the war.

HELEN. Do you know about war already, then?

POLYXENE. I don't exactly know about it. I think it means we have to die.

HELEN. And do you know what dying is?

POLYXENE. I don't exactly. I think it means we don't feel anything any more.

HELEN. What exactly was it that Andromache told you to ask me?

POLYXENE. If you love us at all, please to go away.

HELEN. That doesn't seem to me very logical. If you loved someone you wouldn't leave them?

POLYXENE. Oh, no! Never!

HELEN. Which would you rather do: go right away from Hecuba, or never feel anything any more?

POLYXENE. Oh, never feel anything! I would rather stay, and never feel anything any more.

HELEN. You see how badly you put things to me. If I'm to leave you, I mustn't love you. Would you rather I didn't love you?

POLYXENE. Oh, no! I want you to love me.

HELEN. In other words, you didn't know what you were saying, did you?

POLYXENE. No.

HECUBA (*offstage*). Polyxene! (*Enter* HECUBA.) Are you deaf, Polyxene? Why did you shut your eyes when you saw me? Are you playing at being a statue? Come with me.

HELEN. She is teaching herself not to feel anything. But she has no gift for it.

HECUBA. Can you hear me, Polyxene? And see me?

POLYXENE. Yes, I can hear you. I can see you, too.

HECUBA. Why are you crying? Don't you like to see and hear me?

POLYXENE. If I do, you will go away.

HECUBA. I think it would be better, Helen, if you left Polyxene alone. She is too sensitive to touch the insensitive, even through your beautiful dress and your beautiful voice.

HELEN. I quite agree with you. I advise Andromache to carry her own messages. Kiss me, Polyxene. I shall go away this evening, since that is what you would like.

POLYXENE. Don't go! Don't go!

HELEN. Bravo! You are quite loosened up again!

HECUBA. Are you coming with us, Andromache?

ANDROMACHE. No: I shall wait here.

[*Exeunt* HECUBA *and* POLYXENE.]

HELEN. You want an explanation?

ANDROMACHE. I believe it's necessary.

HELEN. Listen to the way they're shouting and arguing down below. Isn't that enough? Do you and I have to have explanations, too? And what explanations, since I'm leaving here anyway?

ANDROMACHE. Whether you go or stay isn't any longer the problem.

HELEN. Tell Hector that. You will make his day easier.

ANDROMACHE. Yes, Hector is obsessed by the thought of getting you away. All men are the same. They take no notice of the stag in the thicket because they're already chasing the hare. Perhaps men can hunt like that. But not the gods.

HELEN. If you have discovered what the gods are after in this affair, I congratulate you.

ANDROMACHE. I don't know that the gods are after anything. But there is something the universe is after. Ever since this morning, it seems to me, everything has begged and cried out for it, men, animals, even the leaves on the trees and my own child, not yet born.

HELEN. Cried out for what?

ANDROMACHE. That you should love Paris.

HELEN. If they know so certainly that I don't love Paris, they are better informed than I am.

ANDROMACHE. But you don't love him! You could love him, perhaps. But, at present, you are both living in a misunderstanding.

HELEN. I live with him happily, amicably, in complete agreement. We understand each other so well, I don't really see how this can be called a misunderstanding.

ANDROMACHE. Agreement is never reached in love. The life of a wife and husband who love each other is never at rest. Whether the marriage is true or false, the marriage portion is the same: elemental discord. Hector is my absolute opposite. He shares none of my tastes. We pass our days either getting the better of one another, or sacrificing ourselves. There is no tranquillity for lovers.

HELEN. And if I went pale whenever I saw Paris: and my eyes filled
with tears, and the palms of my hands were moist, you think Menelaus would be delighted, and the Greeks pleased and quite satisfied?
ANDROMACHE. It wouldn't much matter then what the Greeks thought.
HELEN. And the war would never happen?
ANDROMACHE. Perhaps, indeed, it would never happen. Perhaps if you
loved him, love would call to the rescue one of its own equals:
generosity or intelligence. No one, not even destiny itself, attacks
devotion lightheartedly. And even if the war did happen, why, I
think even then——
HELEN. Then it wouldn't be the same war, I suppose.
ANDROMACHE. Oh, no, Helen! You know what this struggle is going
to be. Fate would never take so many precautions for an ordinary
quarrel. It means to build the future on this war, the future of our
countries and our peoples, and our ways of thinking. It won't be so
bad if our thoughts and our future are built on the story of a man
and a woman who truly love each other. But fate hasn't noticed yet
that you are lovers only on paper, officially. To think that we're
going to suffer and die only for a pair of theoretical lovers: and the
splendour and calamity of the age to come will be founded on a
trivial adventure between two people who don't love each other—
that's what is so horrible.
HELEN. If everybody thinks that we love each other, it comes to the
same thing.
ANDROMACHE. They don't think so. But no one will admit that he
doesn't. Everyone, when there's war in the air, learns to live in a
new element: falsehood. Everybody lies. Our old men don't worship
beauty: they worship themselves, they worship ugliness. And this
indignation the Greeks are showing us is a lie. God knows, they're
amused enough at what you can do with Paris! Their boats, in the
bay, with their patriotic anthems and their streamers flying, are a
falsehood of the sea. And Hector's life and my son's life, too, are
going to be played out in hypocrisy and pretence.
HELEN. So?
ANDROMACHE. I beg of you, Helen. You see how I'm pressed against
you as though I were begging you to love me. Love Paris! Or tell
me that I'm mistaken! Tell me that you would kill yourself if Paris
were to die! Tell me that you would even let yourself be disfigured
if it would keep him alive. Then the war will only be a scourge,
not an injustice.
HELEN. You are being very difficult. I don't think my way of loving
is as bad as all that. Certainly I don't get upset and ill when Paris
leaves me to play bowls or go fishing for eels. But I do feel commanded by him, magnetically attracted. Magnetism is a kind of love,
as much as devotion. And it's an old and fruitful passion in its own

way, as desperate devotion and passionate weeping are in theirs. I'm as content in this love as a star in a constellation. It's my own centre of gravity; I shine there; it's the way I breathe, and the way I take life in my arms. And it's easy to see what sons this love can produce: tall, clear-cut boys, of great distinction, with fine fingers and short noses. What will it all become if I fill it with jealousy, with emotion, and anxiety? The world is nervous enough already: look at yourself!

ANDROMACHE. Fill it with pity, Helen. That's the only help the world needs.

HELEN. There we are; I knew it would come; the word has been said.

ANDROMACHE. What word?

HELEN. The word 'pity.' You must talk to someone else. I'm afraid I'm not very good at pity.

ANDROMACHE. Because you don't know unhappiness.

HELEN. Maybe. It could also be that I think of unhappy people as my equals, I accept them, and I don't think of my health and my position and beauty as any better than their misery. It's a sense of brotherhood I have.

ANDROMACHE. You're blaspheming, Helen.

HELEN. I am sure people pity others to the same extent that they would pity themselves. Unhappiness and ugliness are mirrors they can't bear to look into. I haven't any pity for myself. You will see, if war breaks out. I'll put up with hunger and pain better than you will. And insults, too. Do you think I don't hear what the Trojan women say when I'm going past them? They treat me like a slut. They say that the morning light shows me up for what they think me. It may be true, or it may not be. It doesn't matter to me, one way or the other.

ANDROMACHE. Stop, Helen!

HELEN. And of course I can see, in what your husband called the coloured picture-book in my head, pictures of Helen grown old, flabby, toothless, sitting hunched-up in the kitchen, sucking sweets. I can see the white enamel I've plastered over my wrinkles, and the bright colours the sweets are, very clearly. But it leaves me completely indifferent.

ANDROMACHE. I am lost.

HELEN. Why? If you're content with one perfect couple to make the war acceptable, there is always you and Hector, Andromache.

[*Enter* AJAX, *then* HECTOR.]

AJAX. Where is he? Where's he hiding himself? A coward! A typical Trojan!

HECTOR. Who are you looking for?

AJAX. I'm looking for Paris.

HECTOR. I am his brother.

AJAX. Beautiful family! I am Ajax! What's your name?

HECTOR. My name's Hector!

AJAX. It ought to be pimp!

HECTOR. I see that Greece has sent over her diplomats. What do you want?

AJAX. War.

HECTOR. Not a hope. Why do you want it?

AJAX. Your brother carried off Helen.

HECTOR. I am told she was willing.

AJAX. A Greek woman can do what she likes. She doesn't have to ask permission from you. He carried her off. It's a reason for war.

HECTOR. We can offer our apologies.

AJAX. What's a Trojan apology? We're not leaving here without your declaration of war.

HECTOR. Declare it yourselves.

AJAX. All right, we will. As from this evening.

HECTOR. That's a lie. You won't declare war. There isn't an island in the archipelago that will back you if we aren't in any way responsible. And we don't intend to be.

AJAX. Will you declare it yourself, personally, if I call you a coward?

HECTOR. That is a name I accept.

AJAX. I've never known such unmilitary reaction! Suppose I tell you what the people of Greece think of Troy, that Troy is a cess-pit of vice and stupidity?

HECTOR. Troy is obstinate. You won't get your war.

AJAX. Suppose I spit on her?

HECTOR. Spit.

AJAX. Suppose I strike you, you, one of her princes?

HECTOR. Try it.

AJAX. Suppose I slap your face, you disgusting example of Troy's conceit and her spurious honour?

HECTOR. Strike.

AJAX (*striking him*). There. If this lady's your wife she must be proud of you.

HECTOR. I know her. She is proud.

[*Enter* DEMOKOS.]

DEMOKOS. What's all the noise about? What does this drunkard want, Hector?

HECTOR. He has got all he wants.

DEMOKOS. What is going on, Andromache?

ANDROMACHE. Nothing.

AJAX. Two times nothing. A Greek hits Hector, and Hector puts up with it.

DEMOKOS. Is this true, Hector?

HECTOR. Completely false, isn't it, Helen?

HELEN. The Greeks are great liars. Greek men, I mean.

AJAX. Is it natural for him to have one cheek redder than the other?

HECTOR. Yes. I am healthier on that side.

DEMOKOS. Tell the truth, Hector. Has he dared to raise his hand against you?

HECTOR. That is my concern.

DEMOKOS. It's the concern of war. You are the figurehead of Troy.

HECTOR. Exactly. No one is going to slap a figurehead.

DEMOKOS. Who are you, you brute? I am Demokos, second son of Achichaos!

AJAX. The second son of Achichaos? How do you do? Tell me: is it as serious to slap a second son of Achichaos as to strike Hector?

DEMOKOS. Quite as serious, you drunk. I am the head of the senate. If you want war, war to the death, you have only to try.

AJAX. All right. I'll try. (*He slaps* DEMOKOS.)

DEMOKOS. Trojans! Soldiers! To the rescue!

HECTOR. Be quiet, Demokos!

DEMOKOS. To arms! Troy's been insulted! Vengeance!

HECTOR. Be quiet, I tell you.

DEMOKOS. I *will* shout! I'll rouse the city!

HECTOR. Be quiet! If you won't. I shall hit you, too!

DEMOKOS. Priam! Anchises! Come and see the shame of Troy burning on Hector's face!

> [HECTOR *strikes* DEMOKOS. AJAX *laughs. During the scene,* PRIAM *and his lords group themselves ready to receive* ULYSSES.]

PRIAM. What are you shouting for, Demokos?

DEMOKOS. I have been struck.

AJAX. Go and complain to Achichaos!

PRIAM. Who struck you?

DEMOKOS. Hector! Ajax! Ajax! Hector!

PARIS. What is he talking about? He's mad!

HECTOR. Nobody struck him, did they, Helen?

HELEN. I was watching most carefully, and I didn't notice anything.

AJAX. Both his cheeks are the same colour.

PARIS. Poets often get upset for no reason. It's what they call their inspiration. We shall get a new national anthem out of it.

DEMOKOS. You will pay for this, Hector.

VOICES. Ulysses! Here is Ulysses!

> [AJAX *goes amicably to* HECTOR.]

AJAX. Well done. Plenty of pluck. Noble adversary. A beautiful hit.

HECTOR. I did my best.

AJAX. Excellent method, too. Straight elbow. The wrist on an angle. Safe position for the carpus and metacarpus. Your slap must be stronger than mine is.

HECTOR. I doubt it.

AJAX. You must be able to throw a javelin magnificently with this iron forearm and this shoulder-bone for a pivot.

HECTOR. Eighty yards.

AJAX. My deepest respect! My dear Hector, forgive me. I withdraw my threats, I take back my slap. We have enemies in common, in the sons of Achichaos. I won't fight with anybody who shares with me an enmity for the sons of Achichaos. Not another mention of war. I don't know what Ulysses has got in mind, but count on me to arrange the whole thing.

[*He goes towards* ULYSSES *and comes back with him.*]

ANDROMACHE. I love you, Hector.

HECTOR (*showing his cheek*). Yes; but don't kiss me just yet.

ANDROMACHE. You have won this round, as well. Be confident.

HECTOR. I win every round. But still with each victory the prize escapes me.

ULYSSES. Priam and Hector?

PRIAM. Yes. And behind us, Troy, and the suburbs of Troy, and the land of Troy, and the Hellespont.

ULYSSES. I am Ulysses.

PRIAM. This is Anchises.

ULYSSES. There are many people here for a diplomatic conversation.

PRIAM. And here is Helen.

ULYSSES. Good morning, my queen.

HELEN. I've grown younger here, Ulysses. I've become a princess again.

PRIAM. We are ready to listen to you.

AJAX. Ulysses, you speak to Priam. I will speak to Hector.

ULYSSES. Priam, we have come to take Helen home again.

AJAX. You do understand, don't you, Hector? We can't have things happening like this.

ULYSSES. Greece and Menelaus cry out for vengeance.

AJAX. If deceived husbands can't cry out for vengeance, what can they do?

ULYSSES. Deliver Helen over to us within an hour. Otherwise it means war.

HECTOR. But if we give Helen back to you give us your assurance there will be peace.

AJAX. Utter tranquillity.

HECTOR. If she goes on board within an hour, the matter is closed.

AJAX. And all is forgotten.

HECTOR. I think there's no doubt we can come to an understanding, can we not, Helen?

HELEN. Yes, no doubt.

ULYSSES. You don't mean to say that Helen is being given back to us?

HECTOR. Exactly that. She is ready.

AJAX. What about her baggage? She is sure to have more to take back than when she came.

HECTOR. We return her to you, bag and baggage, and you guarantee peace. No reprisals, no vengeance!

AJAX. A woman is lost, a woman is found, and we're back where we were. Perfect! Isn't it, Ulysses?

ULYSSES. Just wait a moment. I guarantee nothing. Before we say there are going to be no reprisals we have to be sure there has been no cause for reprisals. We have to make sure that Menelaus will find Helen exactly as she was when she was taken from him.

HECTOR. How is he going to discover any difference?

ULYSSES. A husband is very perceptive when a world-wide scandal has put him on his guard. Paris will have had to have respected Helen. And if that isn't so . . .

CROWD. Oh, no! It isn't so!

ONE VOICE. Not exactly!

HECTOR. And if it is so?

ULYSSES. Where is this leading us, Hector?

HECTOR. Paris has not touched Helen. They have both taken me into their confidence.

ULYSSES. What is this absurd story?

HECTOR. The true story, isn't it, Helen?

HELEN. Why does it seem to you so extraordinary?

A VOICE. It's terrible! It puts us to shame!

HECTOR. Why do you have to smile, Ulysses? Do you see the slightest indication in Helen that she has failed in her duty?

ULYSSES. I'm not looking for one. Water leaves less mark on a duck's back than dishonour does on a woman.

PARIS. You're speaking to a queen.

ULYSSES. Present queens excepted, naturally. So, Paris, you have carried off this queen, carried her off naked; and I imagine that you didn't go into the water wearing all your armour; and yet you weren't seized by any taste or desire for her?

PARIS. A naked queen is dressed in her dignity.

HELEN. She has only to remember to keep it on.

ULYSSES. How long did the voyage last? I took three days with my ships, which are faster than yours.

VOICES. What are these intolerable insults to the Trojan navy?

A VOICE. Your winds are faster! Not your ships!

ULYSSES. Let us say three days, if you like. Where was the queen during those three days?

PARIS. Lying down on the deck.

ULYSSES. And Paris was where? In the crow's nest?

HELEN. Lying beside me.

ULYSSES. Was he reading as he lay beside you? Or fishing for goldfish?

HELEN. Sometimes he fanned me.

ULYSSES. Without ever touching you?

HELEN. One day, the second day, I think it was, he kissed my hand.

ULYSSES. Your hand! I see. An outbreak of the animal in him.

HELEN. I thought it was more dignified to take no notice.

ULYSSES. The rolling of the ship didn't throw you towards each other? I don't think it's an insult to the Trojan navy to suggest that its ships roll?

A VOICE. They roll much less than the Greek ships pitch!

AJAX. Pitch? Our Greek ships? If they seem to be pitching it's because of their high prows and their scooped-out sterns!

A VOICE. Oh, yes! The arrogant face and the flat behind, that's Greek all right.

ULYSSES. And what about the three nights you were sailing? The stars appeared and vanished again three times over the pair of you. Do you remember nothing of those three nights?

HELEN. I don't know. Oh, yes! I'd forgotten. I learnt a lot more about the stars.

ULYSSES. While you were asleep, perhaps, he might have taken you . . .

HELEN. A mosquito can wake me.

HECTOR. They will both swear to you, if you like, by our goddess Aphrodite.

ULYSSES. We can do without that. I know what Aphrodite is. Her favourite oath is a perjury.—It's a curious story you're telling me: and it will certainly destroy the idea that the rest of the Archipelago has always had of the Trojans.

PARIS. Why, what do they think of us in the Archipelago?

ULYSSES. You're thought of as less accomplished at trading than we are, but handsome and irresistible. Go on with your story, Paris. It's an interesting contribution to the study of human behaviour. What good reason could you have possibly had for respecting Helen when you had her at your mercy?

PARIS. I . . . I loved her.

HELEN. If you don't know what love is, Ulysses, I shouldn't venture on the subject.

ULYSSES. You must admit, Helen, you would never have followed him if you had known the Trojans were impotent.

VOICES. Shame! Muzzle him! Bring your women here, and you'll soon see! And your grandmother!

ULYSSES. I expressed myself badly. I meant that Paris, the handsome Paris, is impotent.

A VOICE. Why don't you say something, Paris? Are you going to make us the laughing-stock of the world?

PARIS. Hector, you can see, this is a most unpleasant situation for me!

HECTOR. You have to put up with it only a few minutes longer. Good-
bye, Helen. And I hope your virtue will become as proverbial as
your frailty might have done.

HELEN. That doesn't worry me. The centuries always give us the recognition we deserve.

ULYSSES. Paris the impotent, that's a very good surname! If you care
to, Helen, you can kiss him for once.

PARIS. Hector!

FIRST TOPMAN. Are you going to tolerate this farce, commander?

HECTOR. Be quiet! I am in charge here!

TOPMAN. And a rotten job you make of it! We've stood quite enough.
We'll tell you, we, Paris's own seamen, we'll tell you what he did
with your queen!

VOICES. Bravo! Tell him!

TOPMAN. He's sacrificing himself on his brother's orders. I was an
officer on board his ship. I saw everything.

HECTOR. You were quite wrong.

TOPMAN. Do you think a Trojan sailor doesn't know what he sees?
I can tell the sex of a seagull thirty yards off. Come over here,
Olpides. Olpides was up in the crow's nest. He saw everything from
on top. I was standing on the stairs in the hatchway. My head was
exactly on a level with them, like a cat on the end of a bed. Shall
I tell him, Trojans?

HECTOR. Silence!

VOICES. Tell him! Go on and tell him!

TOPMAN. And they hadn't been on board more than two minutes,
wasn't that true, Olpides?

OLPIDES. Only time enough for the queen to dry herself, being just
come up out of the water, and to comb the parting into her hair
again. I could see her parting, from her forehead over to the nape
of her neck, from where I was.

TOPMAN. And he sent us all down into the hold, except the two of us
who he couldn't see.

OLPIDES. And without a pilot, the ship drifted due north. There was
no wind, and yet the sails were bellied out full.

TOPMAN. And when I looked out from where I was hiding, what I
should have seen was the outline of one body, but what I did see
was in the shape of two, like a wheaten loaf and rye bread, baking
in the oven together.

OLPIDES. But from up where I was, I more often saw one body than
two, but sometimes it was white, and sometimes it was golden
brown.

TOPMAN. So much for impotence! And as for respectful, inexpressive
love, and unspoken affection, you tell him, Olpides, what you heard
from your ledge up there! Women's voices carry upwards, men's

voices stay on the ground. I shall tell you what Paris said.

OLPIDES. She called him her ladybird, her little ewe-lamb.

TOPMAN. And he called her his lion, his panther. They reversed the sexes. Because they were being so affectionate. It's not unusual.

OLPIDES. And then she said: 'You are my darling oak-tree, I put my arms round you as if you were an oak-tree.' When you're at sea you think about trees, I suppose.

TOPMAN. And he called her his birch-tree: 'My trembling silver birch-tree!' I remember the word birch-tree very well. It's a Russian tree.

OLPIDES. And I had to stay up in the crow's nest all night. You don't half get thirsty up there, and hungry, and everything else.

TOPMAN. And when at last they got up from the deck to go to bed they swayed on their feet. And that's how your wife Penelope would have got on with Trojan impotence.

VOICES. Bravo! Bravo!

A WOMAN'S VOICE. All praise to Paris.

A JOVIAL MAN. Render to Paris what belongs to Paris!

HECTOR. This is a pack of lies, isn't it, Helen?

ULYSSES. Helen is listening enraptured.

HELEN. I forgot they were talking about me. They sound so wonderfully convincing.

ULYSSES. Do you dare to say they are lying, Paris?

PARIS. In some of the particulars, yes, I think they are.

TOPMAN. We're not lying, either in the general or the particular. Are we, Olpides? Do you deny the expressions of love you used? Do you deny the word panther?

PARIS. Not especially the word panther.

TOPMAN. Well, birch-tree, then? I see. It's the phrase 'trembling silver birch-tree' that embarrasses you. Well, like it or not, you used it. I swear you used it, and anyway what is there to blush about in the word 'birch-tree'? I have seen these silver birch-trees trembling against the snow in wintertime, by the shores of the Caspian, with their rings of black bark apparently separated by rings of space, so that you wondered what was carrying the branches. And I've seen them at the height of summer, beside the canal at Astrakhan, with their white rings like fresh mushrooms. And the leaves talked and made signs to me. To see them quivering, gold above and silver underneath, it makes your heart melt! I could have wept like a woman, isn't that true, Olpides? That's how I feel about the birch-tree.

CROWD. Bravo! Bravo!

ANOTHER SAILOR. And it wasn't only the topman and Olpides who saw them, Priam. The entire crew came wriggling up through the hatches and peering under the handrails. The whole ship was one great spy-glass.

THIRD SAILOR. Spying out love.

ULYSSES. There you have it, Hector!

HECTOR. Be quiet, the lot of you.

TOPMAN. Well, keep this quiet, if you can!

　　　　　　　　　[IRIS *appears in the sky.*]

PEOPLE. Iris! Iris!

PARIS. Has Aphrodite sent you?

IRIS. Yes, Aphrodite sent me, and told me that I should say to you that love is the world's chief law. Whatever strengthens love becomes in itself sacred, even falsehood, avarice, or luxury. She takes all lovers under her protection, from the king to the goat-herd. And she forbids both of you, Hector and Ulysses, to separate Paris from Helen. Or else there will be war.

PARIS *and* THE OLD MEN. Thank you, Iris.

HECTOR. Is there any message from Pallas Athene?

IRIS. Yes; Pallas Athene told me that I should say to you that reason is the chief law of the world. All who are lovers, she wishes me to say, are out of their minds. She would like you to tell her quite frankly what is more ridiculous than the mating of cocks with hens or flies with flies. And she orders both of you, Hector, and Ulysses, to separate Helen from this Paris of the curly hair. Or else there will be war.

HECTOR *and* THE WOMEN. Thank you, Iris!

PRIAM. Oh, my son, it isn't Aphrodite nor Pallas Athene who rules the world. What is it Zeus commands us to do in this time of uncertainty?

IRIS. Zeus, the master of the Gods, told me that I should say to you that those who see in the world nothing but love are as foolish as those who cannot see it at all. It is wise, Zeus, master of the Gods informs you, it is wise sometimes to make love, and at other times not to make love. The decision he gives to Hector and Ulysses, is to separate Helen and Paris without separating them. He orders all the rest of you to go away and leave the negotiators to face each other. And let them so arrange matters that there will be no war. Or else—he swears to you: he swears there will be war. (*Exit* IRIS.)

HECTOR. At your service, Ulysses!

ULYSSES. At your service.

　　　　　[*All withdraw. A great rainbow is seen in the sky.*]

HELEN. How very like Iris to leave her scarf behind.

HECTOR. Now we come to the real tussle, Ulysses.

ULYSSES. Yes: out of which either war or peace is going to come.

HECTOR. Will war come of it?

ULYSSES. We shall know in five minutes time.

HECTOR. If it's to be a battle of words, my chances are small.

ULYSSES. I believe it will be more a battle of weight. It's as though we were one on each side of a pair of scales. How we weigh in the balance will be what counts in the end.

HECTOR. How we weigh in the balance? And what is my weight, Ulysses? My weight is a young man, a young woman, an unborn child. Joy of life, belief in life, a response to whatever's natural and good.

ULYSSES. And my weight is the mature man, the wife thirty-five years old, the son whose height I measure each month with notches against the doorpost of the palace. My weight is the pleasures of living, and a mistrust of life.

HECTOR. Hunting, courage, loyalty, love.

ULYSSES. Circumspection in the presence of the gods, of men, and everything else.

HECTOR. The Phrygian oak-tree, all the leafy, thick-set oak-trees that grow on our hills with our curly-coated oxen.

ULYSSES. The power and wisdom of the olive-tree.

HECTOR. I weigh the hawk, I look straight into the sun.

ULYSSES. I weigh the owl.

HECTOR. I weigh the whole race of humble peasants, hard-working craftsmen, thousands of ploughs and looms, forges and anvils . . . Why is it, when I put all these in the scale in front of you, all at once they seem to me to weigh so light?

ULYSSES. I am the weight of this incorruptible, unpitying air of these coasts and islands.

HECTOR. Why go on? The scales have tipped.

ULYSSES. To my side? Yes, I think so.

HECTOR. And you want war?

ULYSSES. I don't want it. But I'm less sure whether war may not want us.

HECTOR. Our peoples have brought us together to prevent it. Our meeting itself shows that there is still some hope.

ULYSSES. You are young, Hector! It's usual on the eve of every war, for the two leaders of the peoples concerned to meet privately at some innocent village, on a terrace in a garden overlooking a lake. And they decide together that war is the world's worst scourge, and as they watch the rippling reflections in the water, with magnolia petals dropping on to their shoulders, they are both of them peace-loving, modest and friendly. They study one another. They look into each other's eyes. And, warmed by the sun and mellowed by the claret, they can't find anything in the other man's face to justify hatred, nothing, indeed, which doesn't inspire human affection, nothing incompatible in their languages any more, or in their particular way of scratching the nose or drinking wine. They really are exuding peace, and the world's desire for peace. And when their meeting is over, they shake hands in a most sincere brotherly fashion, and turn to smile and wave as they drive away. And the next day war breaks out. And so it is with us both at this moment. Our peoples, who have drawn aside, saying nothing while we have this interview, are not expecting us to win a victory over the inevitable. They have merely given us full powers, isolated here together, to stand above the catastrophe and taste the essential brotherhood of enemies. Taste it. It's a rare dish. Savour it. But that is all. One of the privileges of the great is to witness catastrophes from a terrace.

HECTOR. Do you think this is a conversation between enemies we are having?

ULYSSES. I should say a duet before the full orchestra. Because we have been created sensible and courteous, we can talk to each other, an hour or so before the war, in the way we shall talk to each other long after it's over, like old antagonists. We are merely having our reconciliation before the struggle instead of after it. That may be unwise. If one day one of us should have to kill the other, it might be as well if it wasn't a friend's face we recognize as the body dropped to the ground. But, as the universe well knows, we are going to fight each other.

HECTOR. The universe might be mistaken. One way to recognize error is the fact that's it's universal.

ULYSSES. Let's hope so. But when destiny has brought up two nations, as for years it has brought up yours and mine, to a future of similar invention and authority, and given to each a different scale of values (as you and I saw just now, when we weighed pleasure against pleasure, conscience against conscience, even nature itself against nature): when the nation's architects and poets and painters have created for them opposing kingdoms of sound, and form, and subtlety, when we have a Trojan tile roof, a Theban arch, Phrygian red, Greek blue: the universe knows that destiny wasn't preparing alternative ways for civilization to flower. It was contriving the dance of death, letting loose the brutality and human folly which is all that the gods are really contented by. It's a mean way to contrive things, I agree. But we are Heads of State, you and I; we can say this between ourselves: it is Destiny's way of contriving things, inevitably.

HECTOR. And this time it has chosen to match Greece with Troy?

ULYSSES. This morning I was still in doubt. As soon as I stepped on to your landing stage I was certain of it.

HECTOR. You mean you felt yourself on enemy soil?

ULYSSES. Why will you always harp on the word enemy? Born enemies don't fight. Nations you would say were designed to go to war against each other—by their skins, their language, their smell: always jealous of each other, always hating each other—they're not

the ones who fight. You will find the real antagonists in nations
fate has groomed and made ready for the same war.

HECTOR. And you think we have been made ready for the Greek war?

ULYSSES. To an astonishing extent. Just as nature, when she foresees
a struggle between two kinds of insects, equips them with weaknesses and weapons which correspond, so we, living well apart, unknown to ourselves, not even suspecting it, have both been gradually
raised up to the level where war begins. All our weapons and habits
correspond with each other and balance against each other like the
beams of a gable. No other women in the world excite less brutality
in us, or less desire, than your wives and daughters do; they give
us a joy and an anguish of heart which is a sure sign of impending
war between us. Doom has transfigured everything here with the
colour of storm: your grave buildings shaking with shadow and fire,
the neighing horses, figures disappearing into the dark of a colon-
nade: the future has never impressed me before with such startling
clarity. There is nothing to be done. You're already living in the
light of the Greek war.

HECTOR. And do the rest of the Greeks think this?

ULYSSES. What they think is no more reassuring. The rest of the Greeks
think Troy is wealthy, her warehouses bulging, her soil prolific.
They think that they, on the other hand, are living cramped on a
rock. And your golden temples and golden wheatfields flashed from
your promontories a signal our ships will never forget. It isn't very
wise to have such golden gods and vegetables.

HECTOR. This is more like the truth, at last. Greece has chosen Troy
for her prey. Then why a declaration of war? It would have been
simpler to have taken Troy by surprise when I was away with the
army. You would have had her without striking a blow.

ULYSSES. There's a kind of permission for war which can be given only
by the world's mood and atmosphere, the feel of its pulse. It would
have been madness to undertake a war without that permission.
We didn't have it.

HECTOR. But you have it now.

ULYSSES. I think we do.

HECTOR. But why against us? Troy is famous for her arts, her justice,
her humanity.

ULYSSES. A nation doesn't put itself at odds with its destiny by its
crimes, but by its faults. Its army may be strong, its treasury well
filled, its poets at the height of inspiration. But one day, why it is
no one knows, because of some simple event, such as the citizens
wantonly cutting down the trees, or their prince wickedly making
off with a woman, or the children getting out of hand, the nation
is suddenly lost. Nations, like men, die by imperceptible disorders.
We recognize a doomed people by the way they sneeze or pare

their nails. There's no doubt you carried off Helen badly.

HECTOR. What fairness of proportion can you see between the rape of one woman, and the possible destruction of a whole people, yours or mine, in war?

ULYSSES. We are speaking of Helen. You and Paris have made a great mistake about Helen. I've known her fifteen years, and watched her carefully. There's no doubt about it: she is one of the rare creatures destiny puts on the earth for its own personal use. They're apparently quite unimportant. It might be not even a person, but a small town, or a village: a little queen, or a child; but if you lay hands on them, watch out! It's very hard to know how to recognize one of these hostages of fate among all the other people and places. You haven't recognized it. You could have laid hands with impunity on our great admirals or one of our kings. Paris could have let himself go with perfect safety in a Spartan bed, or a Theban bed, with generous returns twenty times over; but he chose the shallowest brain, the hardest heart, the narrowest understanding of sex. And so you are lost.

HECTOR. We are giving Helen back to you.

ULYSSES. The insult to destiny can't be taken back.

HECTOR. What are we discussing, then? I'm beginning to see what is really behind your words. Admit it. You want our wealth! You had Helen carried off to give you an honourable pretext for war! I blush for Greece. She will be responsible and ashamed for the rest of time.

ULYSSES. Responsible and ashamed? Do you think so? The two words hardly agree. Even if we believed we were responsible for the war, all our generation would have to do would be to deny it, and lie, to appease the conscience of future generations. And we shall lie. We'll make that sacrifice.

HECTOR. Ah, well, the die is cast, Ulysses. On with the war! The more I hate it, the more I find growing in me an irresistible need to kill. If you won't help me, it were better you should leave here.

ULYSSES. Understand me, Hector; you have my help. Don't ask me to interpret fate. All I have tried to do is to read the world's hand, in the great lines of desert caravans, the wake of ships, and the track of migrant birds and wandering peoples. Give me your hand. There are lines there, too. We won't search to see if their lesson tells the same story. We'll suppose that these three little lines at the base of Hector's hand contradict the waves, the wings, and the furrows. I am inquisitive by nature, and not easily frightened. I'm quite willing to join issue with fate. I accept your offer of Helen. I will take her back to Menelaus. I've more than enough eloquence to convince a husband of his wife's virtue. I will even persuade Helen to believe it herself. And I'll leave at once, to avoid any chance of disturbance. Once back on my ship perhaps we can take the risk of running war on to the rocks.

HECTOR. Is this part of Ulysses' cunning, or his greatness?

ULYSSES. In this particular instance, I'm using my cunning against destiny, not against you. It's my first attempt, so I deserve some credit for it. I am sincere, Hector. If I wanted war, I should have asked for a ransom more precious to you than Helen. I am going now. But I can't shake off the feeling that the road from here to my ship is a long way.

HECTOR. My guard will escort you.

ULYSSES. As long as the road of a visiting king, when he knows there has been a threat against his life. Where are the assassins hiding? We're lucky if it's not in the heavens themselves. And the distance from here to the corner of the palace is a long way. A long way, taking this first step. Where is it going to carry me among all these perils? Am I going to slip and kill myself? Will part of the cornice fall down on me? It's all new stonework here; at any moment a stone may be dislodged. But courage. Let us go. (*He takes a first step.*)

HECTOR. Thank you, Ulysses.

ULYSSES. The first step is safely over. How many more?

HECTOR. Four hundred and sixty.

ULYSSES. Now the second! You know what made me decide to go, Hector?

HECTOR. Yes. Your noble nature.

ULYSSES. Not precisely. Andromache's eyelashes dance as my wife Penelope's do.

[*Enter* ANDROMACHE *and* CASSANDRA.]

HECTOR. Were you there all the time, Andromache?

ANDROMACHE. Let me take your arm. I've no more strength.

HECTOR. Did you hear what we said?

ANDROMACHE. Yes. I am broken.

HECTOR. You see, we needn't despair.

ANDROMACHE. We needn't despair for ourselves, perhaps. But for the world, yes. That man is terrible. All the unhappiness of the world is in me.

HECTOR. A moment or two more, and Ulysses will be on board. You see how fast he is travelling. You can follow his progress from here. There he is, on a level with the fountains. What are you doing?

ANDROMACHE. I haven't the strength any longer to hear any more. I am covering up my ears. I won't take my hands away until we know what our fate is to be.

HECTOR. Find Helen, Cassandra!

[AJAX *enters, more drunk than ever. He sees* ANDROM-
ACHE. *Her back is towards him.*]

CASSANDRA. Ulysses is waiting for you down at the harbour, Ajax. Helen will be brought to you there.

AJAX. Helen! To hell with Helen! This is the one I want to get my arms around.

CASSANDRA. Go away, Ajax. That is Hector's wife.

AJAX. Hector's wife! Bravo! I've always liked my friends' wives, my best friends' wives!

CASSANDRA. Ulysses is already half-way there. Hurry.

AJAX. Don't worry, my dear. She's got her hands over her ears. I can say what I like, she can't hear me. If I touched her, now, if I kissed her, certainly! But words she can't hear, what's the matter with that?

CASSANDRA. Everything is the matter with that. Go away, Ajax!

[AJAX, *while* CASSANDRA *tries to force him away from* ANDROMACHE *and* HECTOR, *slowly raises his javelin.*]

AJAX. Do you think so? Then I might as well touch her. Might as well kiss her. But chastely, always chastely, with your best friends' wives! What's the most chaste part of your wife, Hector, her neck? So much for her neck. Her ear has a pretty little look of chastity to me. So much for her ear. I'll tell you what I've always found the chastest thing about a woman . . . Let me alone, now; let me alone! She can't even hear when I kiss her . . . You're so cursed strong! All right, I'm going, I said I was going. Goodbye. (*He goes.*)

[HECTOR *imperceptibly lowers his javelin. At this moment* DEMOKOS *bursts in.*]

DEMOKOS. What's this cowardice? You're giving Helen back? Trojans, to arms! They've betrayed us. Fall in! And your war-song is ready! Listen to your war-song!

HECTOR (*striking him*). Have that for your war-song!

DEMOKOS (*falling*). He has killed me!

HECTOR. The war isn't going to happen, Andromache!

[*He tries to take* ANDROMACHE'S *hands from her ears: she resists, her eyes fixed on* DEMOKOS. *The curtain which had begun to fall is lifted little by little.*]

ABNEOS. They have killed Demokos! Who killed Demokos?

DEMOKOS. Who killed me? Ajax! Ajax! Kill him!

ABNEOS. Kill Ajax!

HECTOR. He's lying. I am the man who struck him.

DEMOKOS. No. It was Ajax.

ABNEOS. Ajax has killed Demokos. Catch him! Punish him!

HECTOR. I struck you, Demokos, admit it! Admit it, or I'll put an end to you!

DEMOKOS. No, my dear Hector, my good dear Hector. It was Ajax. Kill Ajax!

CASSANDRA. He is dying, just as he lived, croaking like a frog.

ABNEOS. There. They have taken Ajax. There. They have killed him!

HECTOR (*drawing* ANDROMACHE'S *hands away from her ears*). The
    war will happen.
        [*The Gates of War slowly open, to show* HELEN *kiss-
            ing* TROILUS.]
CASSANDRA. The Trojan poet is dead. And now the Grecian poet will
    have his word.

QUESTIONS

1. Is the image of the tiger a better representation of what is going to
    happen than the abstract word "destiny"?
2. What is the meaning of making the tiger metamorphose into Hector
    coming on stage? Consider the ending of the play in answering.
3. How does the play manage to give war reality and power quite inde-
    pendent of any of the people who want or don't want it?
4. Giraudoux writes dialogue in the classical French manner: quick, sharp,
    and witty. Look at several examples of his wit and see if you can ana-
    lyze the way in which it achieves its effects.
5. There is a good deal of the mock-heroic in the play. Characters with
    noble associations are presented in a realistic, humorous fashion, and
    the great events of the past are scaled down, even burlesqued at times.
    How does this mock-heroic technique relate to the wit?
6. What forces in men and society make for war? for peace?
7. Why does Paris find Helen's Greek beauty particularly attractive in
    contrast to that of the Asiatic women?
8. Demokos the poet asks Hector if he has ever seen perfect beauty;
    Hector replies that he has, but then "went closer." The two men here
    represent two views of reality that are fundamental to the play: one
    the abstract, distant view; the other the close-up, involved, felt view.
    Look for other instances of the way in which Hector continually goes
    closer to things to look at them carefully, while Demokos continu-
    ally withdraws to take the distant view. Consider the styles of the
    two men.
9. Why is a mathematician introduced to plead for beauty and for war?
10. Compare Demokos and Giraudoux as poets.
11. When Helen looks at or thinks about things and people, some stand
    out in vivid colors for her, while others remain vague, dull, and drab.
    What kind of things does she see vividly? Why do these come true
    while the others do not?
12. Both Helen and Cassandra are prophets. Compare their prophetic
    methods.
13. What is the meaning of making the intellectuals favor war, while the
    soldier and the women try to prevent it?

14. Throughout the play, Hector wins every argument and everyone either agrees or is forced to act in the way he wishes. Nevertheless, war comes closer and closer. Why? Does "world" or "character" make the plot?

15. Hector agrees that no one, including the High Command and the gods, is responsible for the deaths of men in battle. Does the play support this view or does it assign responsibility for war?

16. What is the nature of the "love" between Helen and Paris? Why does Andromache feel that it is so desperately important that Helen truly love Paris? Is the Helen-Paris affair a key to, a central image of, the nature of this war-directed world?

17. Contrast the love of Hector and Andromache to that of Helen and Paris.

18. What function do the voices from the crowd of Trojans perform in the meeting between Ulysses and Hector to discuss the return of Helen?

19. Sexual pride plays a large part in making the war inevitable. Does sex underlie other warlike attitudes in the play? Does Giraudoux distinguish between sex and love?

20. Are the gods of much help in resolving the problem? What is the meaning of making the gods give contradictory advice and orders that are impossible for men to carry out?

21. What other peace conferences are evoked by Ulysses' description of the meeting of heads of state on the eve of war? How does Giraudoux arrange to make the events in Troy remind us of so many other historical and political events, even, in an uncanny way, of those that have happened since the date of the play, 1935?

22. In the "weighing scene," what are the Greek values? the Trojan? Does this conflict run through the play?

23. "One of the privileges of the great is to witness catastrophes from a terrace," says Ulysses. Does this extraordinarily powerful image summarize other "long-range" views in the play?

24. In Ulysses' view of history, war is inevitable in certain situations. Why? What kind of issues or places have a peculiar fatefulness? What kind of nations fight one another?

25. Look at what happens in the final scene, where Hector strikes Demokos, and see if it recapitulates in terms of action the events that have led to it. Consider carefully the irony: in an attempt to prevent war Hector strikes Demokos and thereby makes war certain.

26. As the curtain falls, the Gates of War swing open and reveal Helen kissing Troilus. Is this appropriate? What has been Helen's relationship to the young throughout the play?

PICNIC ON THE BATTLEFIELD

BY

FERNANDO ARRABAL

Picnic on the Battlefield exemplifies that certain combination of subject matter and dramatic style that has come to be known as Theater of the Absurd. Philosophically, "absurd" refers to the situation of man, with his longings for truth, justice, and personal meaning, adrift in a vast, indifferent, mechanical universe, which by its nature denies not only the satisfaction of his desires but even the *possibility* of their satisfaction. In the writings of the existential philosophers, this is the inescapable human situation, the basis of human tragedy; but the concept of absurdity has undergone subtle shifts in emphasis in the plays of such writers as Jean Genet, Samuel Beckett, Eugene Ionesco, and Fernando Arrabal. In their plays, tragedy becomes irony or satire: what is stressed is not the suffering of a creature who seeks truth in the world where there is no such thing as truth, but the ridiculousness of a creature who continues to speak confidently and certainly of traditional truths and values in a context that reveals them to be nonsense. Arrabal's solidly middle-class family, uttering platitudes and completely incapable of thought, out for a Sunday ride and a picnic on a battlefield, is a perfect image of this kind of absurdity. Not serious enough to be tragic, but too serious to be comic; not important enough to be taken seriously, but so serious as to be catastrophic; banal to the point of tediousness and frightening to the point of terror—these are the ironies on which the drama of the absurd is built.

The style of the drama of the absurd is an extension and realization of these ironies. The most ordinary people, saying the most ordinary things, in the most ordinary tone of voice, are placed in the midst of situations that are utterly bizarre—situations whose bizarreness they somehow fail to notice. Thus, the extremes of realism and expressionism are mixed, and the result is the unsettling effect of reality's being turned topsy-turvy. What begins as strange comes to seem quite realistic, believable, while what at first seems realistic becomes strange, fantastic. "How," these plays force us to ask, "can people go on talking and acting in such an odd way and be so blind to where they really are and what they really are doing?" The enormous gap in the drama of the absurd between the situation and the way the characters act, between the battlefield and the picnic in Arrabal's play, ultimately reveals man to be stupid, blind, mechanical, indifferent. Hedda Gabler's failure to perceive the difference between what she thought she was doing and what she was actually doing is understandable—and tragic —because in Ibsen's realism the difference between what seems and what is, is so difficult to perceive. But the failure of the Tépan family to see that their picnic spot—and, by extension, their world—is a battlefield, their failure to understand the reality of a battlefield, is both ridiculous and frightening.

Fernando Arrabal (b. 1932) is one of the younger and more experimental second-generation dramatists of the absurd. Born and raised in Franco's Spain, he went to Paris to live in 1955. He writes his plays in French; several of them have been translated into English: *The Automobile Graveyard,* in which the world with all its luxuries and pretensions to virtue and value is figured as a junk yard filled with wrecked cars, *The Two Executioners,* and *Picnic on the Battlefield,* which was written in the late 1950's. His more recent work has been the center of considerable controversy because of its extraordinary sexual frankness.

CHARACTERS

ZAPO, *a soldier*
MONSIEUR TÉPAN, *the soldier's father*
MADAME TÉPAN, *the soldier's mother*
ZÉPO, *an enemy soldier*
FIRST CORPSMAN
SECOND CORPSMAN

~~& Scene: *A battlefield. Barbed wire stretches from one end of the stage to the other, with sandbags piled against it.*

Battle is in full swing. We hear bombs bursting, rifle shots and machine-gun fire.

Alone on stage, hidden flat on his belly among the sandbags, ZAPO *is very frightened.*

The fighting stops. Silence.

From a knitting-bag, ZAPO *takes out a ball of wool, knitting needles, and starts knitting a sweater that is already quite well along. The field telephone beside him suddenly rings.*

ZAPO. Hello . . . hello . . . yes, sir, Captain. . . . Yes, this is the sentry in Section 47. . . . Nothing new, Captain. . . . Excuse me, Captain, when are we going to start fighting again? . . . And what am I supposed to do with the grenades? Should I send them on up front or to the rear? . . . Don't get annoyed, I didn't say that to upset you. . . . And, Captain, I'm really feeling pretty lonesome. Couldn't you send me a companion out here? . . . Even the goat. (*Evidently the Captain gives him a good dressing down.*) Yes sir, Captain, yes sir! (ZAPO *hangs up. We hear him grumbling to himself. Silence.*)

> [*Enter* MONSIEUR *and* MADAME TÉPAN, *carrying baskets as though they are off on a picnic. Their son, who is sitting with his back turned, does not see them arriving.*]

M. TÉPAN (*ceremoniously*). My boy, get up and kiss your mother on the forehead.

> [*Taken by surprise,* ZAPO *gets up and, with a great deal of respect, gives his mother a kiss on the forehead. He is about to speak, but his father beats him to it.*]

Now give *me* a kiss.

ZAPO. My dear sweet parents, how did you ever dare come all the way out to a dangerous spot like this? You must leave here right away.

M. TÉPAN. Are you trying to tell your father what war and danger are all about? For me, all this is only a game. How many times do you think I've jumped off the subway while it was still moving?

MME. TÉPAN. We thought you were probably bored, so we came to pay you a little visit. After all, this war business must get pretty tiresome.

ZAPO. It all depends.

M. TÉPAN. I know perfectly well what goes on. In the beginning, it's all new and exciting. You enjoy the killing and throwing grenades and wearing a helmet; it's quite the thing, but you end up bored as hell. In my day, you'd have really seen something. Wars were a lot livelier, much more colorful. And then best of all, there were horses, lots of horses. It was a real pleasure: if the captain said "Attack!" before you could shake a stick we were all assembled on horseback in our red uniforms. That was something to see. And then we'd go galloping forward, sword in hand, and suddenly find ourselves hard against the enemy. And they'd be at their finest too, with their horses—there were always loads and loads of beautifully round-bottomed horses and their polished boots, and their green uniforms.

MME. TÉPAN. No, the enemy uniform wasn't green. It was blue. I remember perfectly well it was blue.

M. TÉPAN. And I say it was green.

MME. TÉPAN. When I was little I went out on the balcony any number of times to watch the battle, and I'd say to the little boy next door, "I'll bet you a gumdrop the Blues win." And the Blues were our enemies.

M. TÉPAN. All right, so you win.

MME. TÉPAN. I always loved battles. When I was little, I always said that when I grew up I wanted to be a Colonel in the Dragoons. But Mama didn't want me to. You know what a stickler she is.

M. TÉPAN. Your mother's a real nincompoop.

ZAPO. Forgive me, but you've got to leave. You can't go walking into a war when you're not a soldier.

M. TÉPAN. I don't give a damn. We're here to have a picnic with you in the country and spend a nice Sunday.

MME. TÉPAN. I even made a lovely meal. Sausage, hard-boiled eggs, I know how much you like them! Ham sandwiches, red wine, some salad and some little cakes.

ZAPO. O.K., we'll do whatever you say. But if the Captain comes along he'll throw a fit. Plus the fact that he doesn't much go for the idea of visiting the battlefront. He keeps telling us: "War calls for discipline and grenades, but no visits."

M. TÉPAN. Don't you worry about it, I'll have a few words with your Captain.

ZAPO. And what if we have to start fighting again?

M. TÉPAN. You think that scares me, I've seen worse. Now if it was only cavalry battles! Times have changed, that's something you don't understand. (*A pause.*) We came on motorcycle. Nobody said anything.

ZAPO. They probably thought you were arbitrators.

M. TÉPAN. We did have some trouble getting through, though. With all those jeeps and tanks.

MME. TÉPAN. And the very minute we arrived, you remember that bottleneck because of the cannon?

M. TÉPAN. During wartime, you've got to be prepared for anything. Everybody knows that.

MME. TÉPAN. Well now, we're ready to start eating.

M. TÈPAN. Right you are, I could eat a horse. It's the smell of gunpowder that does it.

MME. TÉPAN. We'll eat sitting down on the blanket.

ZAPO. All right to eat with my rifle?

MME. TÉPAN. Let your rifle alone. It's bad manners to bring your rifle to the table. (*A pause.*) Why, child, you're filthy as a little pig. How did you manage to get in such a mess? Let's see your hands.

ZAPO. (*Ashamed, he shows them.*) I had to crawl along the ground during maneuvers.

MME. TÉPAN. How about your ears?

ZAPO. I washed them this morning.

MME. TÉPAN. That should do then. Now how about your teeth? (*He shows them.*) Very good. Now who's going to give his little boy a great big kiss for brushing his teeth so nicely? (*To her husband.*) Well, give your son a kiss for brushing his teeth so nicely. (M. TÉPAN *gives his son a kiss.*) Because, you know, one thing I just won't allow is not washing, and blaming it on the war.

ZAPO. Yes, Mama

[*They eat.*]

M. TÉPAN. Well, my boy, have you been keeping up a good shooting score?

ZAPO. When?

M. TÉPAN. Why, the last few days.

ZAPO. Where?

M. TÉPAN. Right here and now. After all, you *are* fighting a war.

ZAPO. No, no great shakes. I haven't kept up a very good score. Practically no bull's-eyes.

M. TÉPAN. Well, what have you been scoring best with in your shooting, enemy horses or soldiers?

ZAPO. No, no horses. There aren't any horses any more.

M. TÉPAN. Well, soldiers then?

ZAPO. Could be.

M. TÉPAN. Could be? Aren't you sure?

ZAPO. It's just that I . . . I fire without taking aim (*a pause*) and when I fire I say an *Our Father* for the guy I shot.

M. TÉPAN. You've got to show more courage. Like your father.

MME. TÉPAN. I'm going to put a record on the phonograph. (*She puts on a record: a Spanish pasodoble. Sitting on the ground, they all three listen.*)

M. TÉPAN. Now that's real music. Yes, ma'am. I tell you. *Olé!*

> [*As the music continues, an enemy soldier,* ZÉPO
> *enters. He is dressed like* ZAPO. *Only the color of his
> uniform is different.* ZÉPO *wears green;* ZAPO *wears
> gray.*
> *Standing unseen behind the family, his mouth
> agape,* ZÉPO *listens to the music. The record comes
> to an end.* ZAPO, *getting up, spots* ZÉPO. *Both raise
> their hands in the air, while* M. *and* MME. TÉPAN *look
> at them, startled.*]

M. TÉPAN. What's going on?

> [ZAPO *seems about to act, but hesitates. Then, very
> decisively, he points his rifle at* ZÉPO.]

ZAPO. Hands up!

> [ZÉPO, *more terrified than ever, raises his hands still
> higher.* ZAPO *doesn't know what to do. All of a sud-
> den, he hurriedly runs toward* ZÉPO *and taps him
> gently on the shoulder, saying*]

ZAPO. You're it! (*Pleased as punch, to his father.*) There you are! A prisoner!

M. TÉPAN. That's fine. Now what are you going to do with him?

ZAPO. I don't know. But could be they'll make me a corporal.

M. TÉPAN. In the meantime, tie him up.

ZAPO. Tie him up? What for?

M. TÉPAN. That's what you do with prisoners, you tie 'em up!

ZAPO. How?

M. TÉPAN. By his hands.

MME. TÉPAN. Oh yes, you've definitely got to tie his hands. That's the way I've always seen it done.

ZAPO. All right. (*To the prisoner.*) Please put your hands together.

ZÉPO. Don't do it too hard.

ZAPO. Oh, no.

ZÉPO. Ouch! You're hurting me.

M. TÉPAN. Come on now, don't mistreat your prisoner.

MME. TÉPAN. Is that the way I brought you up? Haven't I told you over and over again that you've got to be considerate of your fellow man?

ZAPO. I didn't do it on purpose. (*To* ZÉPO.) Does it hurt the way it is now?

ZÉPO. No, like this it doesn't hurt.

M. TÉPAN. Speak right up and tell him if it does. Just pretend we're not here.

ZÉPO. This way it's O.K.

M. TÉPAN. Now his feet.

ZAPO. His feet too? How long does this go on?

M. TÉPAN. Didn't they teach you the rules?

ZAPO. Sure.

M. TÉPAN. Well?

ZAPO (*to* ZÉPO, *very politely*). Would you kindly be good enough to please sit down on the ground?

ZÉPO. All right, but don't hurt me.

MME. TÉPAN. See! Now he's taking a dislike to you.

ZAPO. No. No he's not. I'm not hurting you, am I?

ZÉPO. No, this is fine.

ZAPO (*out of nowhere*). Papa, suppose you took a snapshot with the prisoner down there on the ground and me standing with my foot on his stomach?

M. TÉPAN. Say, yes! That'll look classy.

ZÉPO. Oh, no you don't. Not that.

MME. TÉPAN. Let him. Don't be so stubborn.

ZÉPO. No. I said no and I mean no.

MME. TÉPAN. Just a little old snip of a snapshot. What difference could that possibly make to you? Then we could put it in the dining room right next to the Lifesaving Certificate my husband got thirteen years ago.

ZÉPO. No, you'll never talk me into it.

ZAPO. But why should you refuse?

ZÉPO. I've got a fiancée. And if she ever sees the snapshot, she'll say I don't know how to fight a war.

ZAPO. No, all you have to do is tell her it isn't you at all, it's a panther.

MME. TÉPAN. C'mon, say yes.

ZÉPO. All right, but I'm only doing it to please you.

ZAPO. Stretch all the way out.

> [ZÉPO *stretches all the way out.* ZAPO *puts one foot on his stomach and grabs his rifle with a military air.*]

MME. TÉPAN. Throw your chest out more.

ZAPO. Like this?

MME. TÉPAN. Yes, that's it. Don't breathe.

M. TÉPAN. Make like a hero.

ZAPO. How do you mean a hero, like this?

M TÉPAN. It's a cinch. Make like the butcher when he was telling us what a lady-killer he is.

ZAPO. Like so?

M. TÉPAN. Yes, that's it.

MME. TÉPAN. Just be sure your chest is puffed way out, and don't breathe.

ZÉPO. Are you about finished?

M. TÉPAN. Have a little patience. One . . . two . . . three.

ZAPO. I hope I'll come out all right.

MME. TÉPAN. Oh yes, you looked very military.

M. TÉPAN. You were fine.

MME. TÉPAN. That makes me want to have my picture taken, too.

M. TÉPAN. Now there's a good idea.

ZAPO. All right. I'll take it if you want me to.

MME. TÉPAN. Give me your helmet so I'll look like a soldier.

ZÉPO. I don't want any more pictures. Even one was too much.

ZAPO. Don't feel that way. Come right down to it, what difference could it make?

ZÉPO. That's my final say.

M. TÉPAN (*to his wife*). Don't push him. Prisoners are always very touchy. If we keep it up, he'll get mad and spoil all our fun.

ZAPO. Well now, what are we going to do with him?

MME. TÉPAN. We could ask him to eat with us. What do you think?

M. TÉPAN. I don't see any reason why not.

ZAPO (*to* ZÉPO). All right then, how'd you like to eat with us?

ZÉPO. Uh . . .

M. TÉPAN. We brought along a nice bottle of wine.

ZÉPO. Well, in that case O.K.

MME. TÉPAN. Make yourself right at home. Don't be afraid to ask for things.

ZÉPO. Fine.

M. TÉPAN. Well now, how about you, have you been keeping up a good shooting score?

ZÉPO. When?

M. TÉPAN. Why, the last few days.

ZÉPO. Where?

M. TÉPAN. Right here and now. After all, you *are* fighting a war.

ZÉPO. No, no great shakes. I haven't kept up a very good score. Practically no bull's-eyes.

M. TÉPAN. Well, what have you been scoring best with in your shooting, enemy horses or soldiers?

ZÉPO. No, no horses. There aren't any horses any more.

M. TÉPAN. Well, soldiers then?

ZÉPO. Could be.

M. TÉPAN. Could be? Aren't you sure?

ZÉPO. It's just that I . . . I fire without taking aim (*a pause*) and when I fire I say a *Hail Mary* for the guy I shot.

ZAPO. A *Hail Mary?* I'd have thought you'd say an *Our Father.*

zÉPO. No. Always a *Hail Mary. (A pause.)* It's shorter.

M. TÉPAN. Come, my boy, you have to be courageous.

MME. TÉPAN *(to* zÉPO*).* If you like, we can untie you.

zÉPO. No, leave me this way. It doesn't matter.

M. TÉPAN. You're not going to start putting on airs with us? If you want us to untie you, just say the word.

MME. TÉPAN. Please feel free.

zÉPO. Well, if you really mean it, untie my feet. But it's just to please you people.

M. TÉPAN. Zapo, untie him.

> [zAPO *unties him.*]

MME. TÉPAN. Well now, feel better?

zÉPO. Sure do. But listen, maybe I'm causing you too much trouble.

M. TÉPAN. Not at all. Make yourself right at home. And if you want us to undo your hands, just say so.

zÉPO. No, not my hands, too. I don't want to overdo it.

M. TÉPAN. Not at all, my boy, not at all. I tell you, you don't disturb us one bit.

zÉPO. All right, go ahead and untie my hands then. But just while we eat, huh? I don't want you to think when you give me an inch I'm going to take a mile.

M. TÉPAN. Untie his hands, sonny.

MME. TÉPAN. Well, since our honorable prisoner is so nice, we're going to have a lovely day out here in the country.

zÉPO. Don't call me "honorable" prisoner. Just say "prisoner" plain and simple.

MME. TÉPAN. You're sure that won't make you feel bad?

zÉPO. No, not at all.

M. TÉPAN. Well, you're certainly unpretentious, anyway.

> [*Sound of airplanes.*]

zAPO. Airplanes. They're going to bomb us for sure.

> [zAPO *and* zÉPO *dive for the sandbags and hide.*]

zAPO *(to his parents).* Run for cover! The bombs are going to land right on you.

> [*The sound of the planes drowns out everything. Im-
> mediately bombs start falling. Shells explode nearby.
> Deafening racket.* zAPO *and* zÉPO *are crouching
> among the sandbags.* M. TÉPAN *goes on calmly talk-
> ing to his wife, who answers him with equal calm.
> Because of the bombardment we cannot hear their
> conversation.*
>
> MME. TÉPAN *heads for one of the picnic baskets,
> from which she takes an umbrella. She opens it. The*
> TÉPANS *take shelter under the umbrella as though it
> were raining. Standing there, they shift from one foot
> to the other, in rhythm, all the while discussing per-*

sonal matters. The bombardment continues.
At last, the airplanes take off. Silence.
M. TÉPAN *stretches one arm out from under the*
umbrella to make certain there is no longer anything
coming down from the sky.]

M. TÉPAN. You can close your umbrella now.

[MME. TÉPAN *closes it. Together they go over to their*
son and prod him on the behind a couple of times
with the umbrella.]

M. TÉPAN. All right, come on out. The bombing's over.

[ZAPO *and* ZÉPO *come out of their hiding place.*]

ZAPO. They didn't get you?

M. TÉPAN. You don't expect anything to happen to your father, do you? (*Proudly.*) Little bombs like that? Don't make me laugh.

[*From the left, a pair of Red Cross* CORPSMEN *enter,*
carrying a stretcher.]

FIRST CORPSMAN. Any bodies?

ZAPO. No, none here.

FIRST CORPSMAN. You're sure you took a good look?

ZAPO. Absolutely.

FIRST CORPSMAN. And there's not one single body?

ZAPO. Didn't I just say so?

FIRST CORPSMAN. Not even someone wounded?

ZAPO. Not even.

SECOND CORPSMAN. Well, we're really up the creek! (*To* ZAPO, *persuasively.*) Take a good look all around here, see if you don't turn up a stiff someplace.

FIRST CORPSMAN. Don't press the issue. They told you once and for all there aren't any.

SECOND CORPSMAN. What a lousy deal!

ZAPO. I'm really very sorry. I swear I didn't plan it that way.

SECOND CORPSMAN. That's what they all say. That there aren't any corpses, and that they didn't plan it that way.

FIRST CORPSMAN. So let the man alone!

M. TÉPAN (*obligingly*). If we can help you at all, we'd be delighted to. At your service.

SECOND CORPSMAN. Well, I don't know. If we keep on like this, I really don't know what the Captain's going to say to us.

M. TÉPAN. What seems to be the trouble?

SECOND CORPSMAN. Just that the others are all getting sore wrists carrying out the dead and wounded, while we still haven't come up with anything. And it's not because we haven't been looking.

M. TÉPAN. I see. That really is a bore. (*To* ZAPO.) You're quite sure there are no corpses?

ZAPO. Obviously, Papa.

M. TÉPAN. You looked under the sandbags?

ZAPO. Yes, Papa.

M. TÉPAN (*angrily*). Why don't you come right out and say you don't want to have any part in helping these good gentlemen?

FIRST CORPSMAN. Don't jump on him like that. Leave him alone. We'll just hope we have better luck in some other trench where maybe everybody'll be dead.

M. TÉPAN. I'd be delighted for you.

MME. TÉPAN. So would I. Nothing pleases me more than to see people who take their work seriously.

M. TÉPAN (*indignantly, to anyone within hearing*). Well, isn't anyone going to do anything for these gentlemen?

ZAPO. If it was up to me, it'd be good as done.

ZÉPO. Same here.

M. TÉPAN. Look here now, isn't one of you at least wounded?

ZAPO (*ashamed*). No, not me.

M. TÉPAN (*to* ZÉPO). What about you?

ZÉPO (*ashamed*). Me either. I never was lucky.

MME. TÉPAN (*delighted*). I just remembered! This morning, while I was peeling onions, I cut my finger. How's that?

M. TÉPAN. Why of course! (*Really in the swing of things.*) They'll put you on the stretcher and carry you right off!

FIRST CORPSMAN. Sorry, it's no good. Women don't count.

M. TÉPAN. Well, that didn't get us anywhere.

FIRST CORPSMAN. It doesn't matter.

SECOND CORPSMAN. Maybe we can get our fill in the other trenches. (*They start to go off.*)

M. TÉPAN. Don't you worry, if we find a corpse, we'll hang onto it for you. There's not a chance we'd give it to anybody but you.

SECOND CORPSMAN. Thank you very much, sir.

M. TÉPAN. It's nothing, my boy. It's the very least I could do.

[*The* CORPSMEN *make their goodbyes. All four of the others reply in kind. The* CORPSMEN *exit.*]

MME. TÉPAN. That's what's so pleasant about spending Sunday out in the battlefield. You always run into such nice folks. (*A pause.*) Come to think of it, why is it you're enemies?

ZÉPO. I don't know. I'm not too well educated.

MME. TÉPAN. I mean is it from birth, or did you become enemies after?

ZÉPO. I don't know. I don't know a thing about it.

M. TÉPAN. Well then, how did you come to go to war?

ZÉPO. One day I was home fixing my mother's iron and a man came by and said to me: "Are you Zépo?" . . . "Yes." . . . "Good, you've got to go to war." So I asked him, "What war?" And he said to me: "Don't you read the newspapers? You *are* a hick!" So I told him yes I did, but not all that war stuff . . .

ZAPO. That's just what happened to me; exactly what happened to me.

M. TÉPAN. Sure, they came after you, too.

MME. TÉPAN. No, it's not the same. You weren't fixing the iron that day, you were repairing the car.

M. TÉPAN. I was talking about the rest of it. (*To* ZÉPO.) Go on. Then what happened?

ZÉPO. Well, then I told him that I had a fiancée, and if I didn't take her to the movies on Sunday, she wouldn't know what to do with herself. He said that that didn't matter.

ZAPO. Same as me. Exactly the same as me.

ZÉPO. Well, then my father came down and he said I couldn't go to war because I didn't have a horse.

ZAPO. Like my father said.

ZÉPO. The man said they didn't use horses any more, and I asked him if I could take along my fiancée. He said no. Then I asked him could I take along my aunt to make me custard every Thursday. I like custard.

MME. TÉPAN (*realizing that she has forgotten something*). Oh! The custard!

ZÉPO. Again he said no.

ZAPO. The way he did to me.

ZÉPO. And ever since then, here I am, nearly always all alone in the trench here.

MME. TÉPAN. As long as you're so much alike, and both so bored, I think you and your honorable prisoner might play together this afternoon.

ZAPO. Oh no, Mama! I'm too scared. He's an enemy.

M. TÉPAN. Oh come on now, don't be scared.

ZAPO. If you knew what the general told us about the enemy.

MME. TÉPAN. What did he tell you?

ZAPO. He said the enemy soldiers are very mean. When they take prisoners, they put pebbles in their socks so it hurts when they walk.

MME. TÉPAN. How horrible! What savages!

M. TÉPAN (*indignantly, to* ZÉPO). Aren't you ashamed to be part of an army of criminals?

ZÉPO. I didn't do anything. I'm not mad at anybody.

MME. TÉPAN. He's trying to put one over on us, acting like a little saint.

M. TÉPAN. We should never have untied him. Probably all we have to do is have our backs turned for him to go putting pebbles in our socks.

ZÉPO. Don't be so mean to me.

M. TÉPAN. How do you expect us to be? I'm shocked. I know just what I'm going to do. I'm going to find the Captain and ask him to let me go into battle.

ZAPO. He won't let you. You're too old.

M. TÉPAN. Well then I'll go buy a horse and a saber and I'll go to war on my own.

ZÉPO. Please, madame, don't treat me like this. Besides, I was just going to tell you, *our* general said the same thing about you people.

MME. TÉPAN. How could he dare tell such a lie?

ZAPO. The very same thing, honest?

ZÉPO. Yes, the very same thing.

M. TÉPAN. Maybe it's the same one who talked to both of you.

MME. TÉPAN. Well, if it is the same general, the least he could do is use a different speech. Imagine telling everybody the same thing.

M. TÉPAN (*to* ZÉPO, *changing his tone*). Can I fill your glass again?

MME. TÉPAN. I hope you enjoyed our little lunch.

M. TÉPAN. It was better than last Sunday, anyway.

ZÉPO. What happened then?

M. TÉPAN. Well, we went out to the country and laid all our chow out on the blanket. While we had our backs turned, a cow came along and ate the whole lunch, including the napkins.

ZÉPO. What a glutton, that cow!

M. TÉPAN. Yes, but then to get even, we ate the cow.

[*They laugh.*]

ZAPO (*to* ZÉPO). I bet they weren't hungry after that.

M. TÉPAN. To your health!

[*They all drink.*]

MME. TÉPAN (*to* ZÉPO). Tell me something, what do you do for amusement in the trenches?

ZÉPO. Just to pass the time and keep myself amused, I take odds and ends of rags and make little flowers out of them. See, I get bored a lot.

MME. TÉPAN. And what do you do with these rag flowers?

ZÉPO. At first I used to send them to my fiancée, but one day she told me that the cellar and the greenhouse were already filled with them, that she didn't know what to do with them any more, and would I mind sending her something else for a change?

MME. TÉPAN. And what did you do?

ZÉPO. I tried learning something else, but I couldn't do it. So, to pass the time, I just go on making my rag flowers.

MME. TÉPAN. And then do you throw them away?

ZÉPO. No, now I've found a way to make use of them: I furnish one flower for each of my buddies who dies. That way, I know that even if I make a whole lot, there'll never be enough.

M. TÉPAN. You found a good way out.

ZÉPO (*timidly*). Yes.

ZAPO. Well, you know what I do so's not to get bored is knit.

MME. TÉPAN. But tell me, do all the soldiers get bored the way you two do?

ZÉPO. That depends on what they do for relaxation.

ZAPO. Same thing over on our side.

M. TÉPAN. Well then, let's stop the war.

ZÉPO. But how?

M. TÉPAN. Very easy. You tell your buddies that the enemy doesn't want to fight, and you tell the same thing to your comrades. And everybody goes home.

ZAPO. Terrific!

MME. TÉPAN. That way you can finish fixing the iron.

ZAPO. How come nobody ever thought of that before?

MME. TÉPAN. It takes your father to come up with ideas like that. Don't forget he's a Normal School graduate, and a philatelist, too.

ZÉPO. But what will all the field-marshals and the corporals do?

M. TÉPAN. We'll give 'em guitars and castanets to keep 'em quiet.

ZÉPO. Excellent idea.

M. TÉPAN. See how easy it is? It's all settled.

ZÉPO. We'll wow 'em.

ZAPO. Boy, will my buddies be glad!

MME. TÉPAN. What do you say we celebrate and put on that pasodoble we were listening to before?

ZÉPO. Wonderful!

ZAPO. Yes, put on the record, Mama.

> [MME. TÉPAN *puts on the record. She winds the phonograph and waits. Not a sound is heard.*]

M. TÉPAN. You can't hear anything.

MME. TÉPAN (*going to the phonograph*). Oh! . . . I made a boo-boo! Instead of putting on a record, I put on a beret.

> [*She puts the record on. A lively pasodoble is heard.*
> ZAPO *dances with* ZÉPO; MME. TÉPAN *with her husband.*
>
> *The field telephone rings. None of the group hears it. They go on dancing in a lively manner.*
>
> *The phone rings again. The dancing continues. Battle breaks out once more with a great din of bombs, rifle fire and the crackle of machine-guns. Having noticed nothing, the two couples keep on dancing gaily.*
>
> *A sudden machine-gun blast mows them all down. They fall to the ground, stone dead. One bullet seems to have nicked the phonograph: the music keeps repeating the same strain over and over, like a record with a scratch in it. We hear this repeated strain for the remainder of the play.*
>
> *From the left, the two* CORPSMEN *enter, carrying the empty stretcher.*]

FAST CURTAIN

QUESTIONS

1. What is the meaning of having all the forces that kill—the orders, the bombs, the bullets—come from unseen sources?

2. "Absurdity" here is achieved by the juxtaposition and interweaving of incongruities, which, though at first apparently nonsensical, come to have a strange aptness. Work out a number of these incongruities as they appear in (a) setting and action, (b) language (both ways of speaking and subject matter), and (c) what is said and what is done.

3. How does Arrabal manage to implicate his characters in their own fate? Consider the ways in which the characters are at once very helpless and yet somehow very ferocious, appealing clowns *and* frightening, faceless energies.

4. How is the view of the causes of war established? Is it a simple or complex view?

5. The language of the characters is extraordinarily simple, flat, uncharged with complex meaning or irony; their beliefs and values are also alarmingly ordinary. What kind of minds are revealed by these ways of speaking? Do you detect any changes in their thought or any growth of understanding during the course of the play?

6. What is the meaning of the Tépan family's out-of-date view of the ways war is fought?

7. What function does the subdued but fairly continuous arguing of the senior Tépans serve? Can you relate Madame Tépan's surprising desire to have her picture taken with the prisoner to other things she says and does?

8. The play takes a number of conventional attitudes that are quite acceptable in the context of ordinary life and brings out their latent "absurd" meanings by putting them in the unexpected context of the war. What attitudes and values are being exposed in the incident of the stretcher-bearers? Can you find other instances of the same device?

9. Why are Zapo and Zépo made so similar?

10. In what ways does the scene in which the Tépans stand talking under an umbrella while bombs rain down serve as an image of the entire play?

11. As in most drama of the absurd, the characters of this play have little psychological depth, but they do display one noticeable psychic quality—sudden radical shifts from one set of mind and feeling to the exact opposite (e.g. from hatred to sympathy). Under what conditions do these changes occur, and what do they suggest about the characters?

12. What makes the Tépans decide to stop the war?

13. Does the confusion of the beret and the record have any significance?

14. What comment does the nicked record make on the action? Is it a meaningful comment on what *has* happened as well as what *will* happen?

PART III

GLOSSARY

Glossary

I THEATERS

The only requirements of a theater are that it provide a place for the actors to work and that it permit the audience to see and hear the play. Yet every great culture has built its own particular theater. Radical changes in belief about the function of the drama seem to be accompanied by radical changes in the physical construction and arrangement of theaters. It would appear from this that the shape of a theater and the arrangement of its parts in some way reflects, or gives physical form to, the view of life offered in the plays written for that theater. The theater, we might say, is part of the symbolic statement made about man and his world in any play performed in it; and it follows that in reading plays it is helpful to have some idea of the theater for which they were planned.

Evidence about the theaters of the past is often sketchy, and the descriptions that follow are not to be taken as precise re-creations of any particular theater. Instead, what is offered is a description of a *type* of theater, a listing of the major features that would have been found in some form in most of the theaters of a given age.

THE GREEK THEATER: Greek drama apparently originated in religious festivals that celebrated and attempted to ensure the fertility of the land and the well-being of its people. These rituals were originally connected with the worship of the god Dionysus, a nature god who, like the fields, died and was reborn each year. The details of these festivals are extremely obscure, but most authorities speculate that they involved singing and dancing by a chorus, but did not employ individual actors until a very late date. Thespis—from whom our word *thespian* comes—is said to have been the first to

introduce the individual actor in performances of plays in the sixth
century B.C. About 534 B.C. the Athenian ruler Pisistratus instituted
a competition among playwrights at the annual festival of Dionysus
held during March and April. (There was another Dionysiac festival, the
Lenaea, held earlier in the year, at which only comedies were presented
originally.) At this festival three days were given to showing tragedies.
The cost of these performances was shared by the state and by a
prominent citizen, chosen by lot, called the *choregus.* First, second,
and third prizes were awarded the dramatists whose works were considered the best. Aeschylus, Sophocles, and Euripides—the three tragic
authors whose works have, in part, survived—were apparently the
most frequent winners during the fifth century, the great age of
Athenian drama.

From these few facts emerges a concept of theater that seems
strange to the modern reader accustomed to thinking of plays as private ventures put on to make money by providing entertainment and,
sometimes, instruction. Athenian theatrical productions were civic
occasions attended by nearly the entire free population of the city.
The prizes and the method of financing the productions suggest an
attempt to encourage artistic excellence, as if the greatness and health
of the state depended to some degree on the writing of great drama.
Beyond this, the fact that the plays were presented during a religious
celebration hints that, in origin at least, plays were considered semi-
religious rites dealing with the relations of men and the gods.

The physical theater in which these plays were performed consisted
basically of three parts: the auditorium, the orchestra, and the stage.
The auditorium was semicircular and built up of tiers of seats, first
of wood and later of stone, cut into a hillside. At the bottom of the
semicircle and within its arms was the orchestra, a round space in
which the chorus danced and sang. Behind the orchestra—and somewhat later in development—was a rectangular building known as the
skene. In front of the skene was a row of pillars, the proscenium.
Scholars differ on whether the actors performed in front of the
proscenium (between the orchestra and the row of pillars), or whether
a raised stage was supported by the pillars of the proscenium and the
front of the upper portion of the skene.

This was a very simple theater, yet it provided everything needed
for performance. It also dictated the fundamentals of Greek drama:
a chorus between the audience and one or more actors moving before
a scene suggesting the town square and palace of a Greek city-state.

Closest to the audience was the chorus, at one time a group of fifty
men, but ordinarily in the fifth century not more than twelve. The
chorus usually chanted and moved in unison, but in most plays there
was a chorus leader who had individual lines and addressed the actors

directly. When the chorus was not speaking it remained in the orchestra watching the actors. The function of the chorus varies from playwright to playwright—Euripides nearly eliminated it from any serious part in his plays—and even from play to play, but ordinarily this group represented the people or, more specifically, the elders of the city. Theirs was the voice of bewilderment in times of trouble, of caution in times of prosperity, of traditional wisdom, and of helpless sorrow for the suffering that was taking place on the stage beyond them.

At the farthest reach of the theater stood those isolated individuals, the two or three actors who played all the single parts. Their heroic size was magnified by the *cothurnus,* the elevated shoe or "tragic boot," worn in tragedy; their expressions of pain and determination were fixed and exaggerated by startling masks; and their proportions and magnificence were extended by padded, brilliantly colored costumes. Behind them was first the palace, the symbol of the earthly authority and rule they exercised, and then the open sky where dwelt those mysterious powers controlling human fate with which the hero, as the representative of his people, had to struggle.

THE MEDIEVAL THEATER : Medieval drama originated in the church; all over Europe in the eleventh and twelfth centuries brief liturgical plays presenting the events of the Resurrection and the birth of Christ were performed at Easter and Christmas for the instruction of the laity. During the next few hundred years religious drama spread beyond the church to the town squares, to wagon-stages hauled through the streets of the cities, and to other suitable playing places; at the same time, the subject matter of these plays expanded to include dramatizations of the principal events of the Bible—*mystery plays;* the events of saints' lives—*miracle plays;* and, ultimately, allegorical presentations of moral problems and religious doctrine— *morality plays. Everyman* belongs to this last category, which marks the most advanced stage of medieval drama before it gave way to the secular, professional drama of the Renaissance.

Though medieval "theaters" were set up anywhere a suitable playing space could be found—the aisles and chapels of a cathedral, the open square of a town, the elevated platform of a pageant wagon and the adjacent street, or even a flat field—these theaters do have certain common features. The first and most striking is the use of *mansions* or small houses placed around the edge of the "stage." These were basically small canvas booths of some sort; they could be either very plain or elaborately constructed to resemble the places they represented (e.g., the Temple in Jerusalem, Heaven, or the Mouth of Hell). These were the *loci,* or *places,* the locales, representing some specific region or condition of being, and every character in a play had his particular

mansion. In *Everyman*, though we have no exact information on how
the play was staged, there were presumably several of these mansions,
perhaps lined up side by side at the back of the playing area, and
each was designated as the house of a particular character. From this
house he came onto the stage for his dealings with Everyman, and
into it he retired when his business was finished. The grave into which
Everyman goes at the end of the play was probably another mansion,
rather than a simulated grave.

The open area between or in front of the mansions—aisle, street,
or square—was neutral ground, unlocalized in space or time. Across
it the devils moved from Hell to collect their victims, here Herod
raged and ranted, and here the Wise Men from the East traveled
from their mansion to the manger at Bethlehem. The chief point to
be made about this open playing area is that it was all places at all
times and could, therefore, be turned into any given place and time
when a particular character walked onto it. At one moment God
might create the world on it, and in the next moment it would become
the field in which Cain slew Abel.

This theater is characteristically medieval in its mingling of the
specific and the timeless, the specific mansions and the open, unlocalized stage. The same kind of mingling is to be found in the stage
effects. This theater was not pale and abstract but lively and spectacular. The Holy Ghost was represented by a container of flaming spirits
lowered on stage; tree leaves and flowers were designed to open at
the word of God; the grotesque monster's mouth representing the entrance to Hell opened and closed and belched smoke; realistic and
bloody tortures were simulated on stage; heads appeared to be struck
off and to spurt blood; and the costumes of the actors were elaborate
and highly colored. Yet these intensely realistic effects, which suggest
an awareness of the objective world so powerful and immediate
that it gives even the mysteries of the Christian religion flamboyant,
substantial forms, existed together in a most unrealistic arrangement
of space and time. The Garden of Eden and the Throne of God on
Judgment Day would appear on the same stage simultaneously, and
the Creation and the Crucifixion, presented as realistically as possible,
could take place on the same ground in a short space of time. This
blending of the ideal and the actual worlds is duplicated also in the
characterization and language of the plays. The man who drives the
nails through Christ's hands speaks with the voice of a Yorkshire
carpenter and grumbles about the poor workmen who made the cross.
An abstract personification of some quality such as Mercy speaks in
the familiar and earthy tones of a good-hearted neighbor woman. In
the medieval theater, as in the medieval world, the abstract ideal and
the solid, immediate world were equally real, and they fitted neatly

together in drama, as in philosophy, since both were expressions on
different levels of being of the same ultimate, unchanging reality.

THE ELIZABETHAN THEATER: The first Elizabethan
public theater, designed and erected solely for the purpose of producing
plays, was built as a private, money-making enterprise in 1576, north of
London. Although we know the names of many Elizabethan theaters,
our information about their exact dimensions, their seating capacity,
and their stage features is very limited. Most of what we do know
comes from a copy of a drawing of the Swan Theater made by a
Dutch traveler, from two builders' contracts for the erection of
theaters, and from the plays themselves, which often suggest the type
of stage necessary for their production. Out of these diverse materials
emerge a few general facts that the modern reader—who is likely to
think that any theater built before our own century must have been
crude and small—needs to know. All references to Elizabethan theaters suggest that they were very ornate and richly decorated buildings.
Second, they were in many cases quite large buildings, providing
standing and seating room for between two and three thousand
people. Third, the audience was made up of a cross section of the
citizens of London, not just the apprentices and lower classes. The
Elizabethan theater, like the Greek, was a truly public theater where
the central values of the nation and the concerns of all classes of
citizens were staged.

The outer frame of the theater was circular or many-sided. On
one side was a gate through which the playgoer could pass by paying
a penny. Once inside, he could stand in what was known as the "pit,"
an unroofed open area in the center of the building. Around him,
forming the interior of the walls, rose three or four galleries of seats.
These were, of course, more comfortable places from which to see the
play, and they were roofed. Entrance to the gallery required an additional payment of a penny or two. At the front of the pit, and project-
ing out into it, was the platform stage, supported on trestles or posts
covered with cloth or palings. This stage was quite large; the one
contract we have that supplies dimensions stipulates that the stage
be 43 feet wide and 27½ feet deep. One or more traps opened from
the stage into the space below, which was called the "cellarage" or
"hell." Above the stage, supported by pillars resting on the stage or
cantilevered out from the roof, was a cover known as the "shadow"
or the "heavens." The first function of this shadow was to protect the
players and their expensive costumes from the English rain, but it was
also painted underneath with elaborate representations of the stars,
the planets, and the signs of the zodiac.

At the rear of the stage rose the front wall of the "tiring (attiring) house," or what would now be called "backstage." The front wall of the tiring house had one or more doors to allow the actors to enter and exit. Available evidence suggests that in the center of this wall there was some provision for a small "inner stage." Whether this was a built-in recess or some temporary tent-like arrangement, we do not know for certain. The one drawing we have of the interior of an Elizabethan theater shows nothing on this wall but two large doors. Some plays, however, make it clear that a small curtained area at stage rear was often required for production. Above this area, and connected with the platform stage by some sort of stairs or ladder, was the "upper stage," a narrow gallery running the width of the stage, which was used for balcony and battlement scenes. Above this was the "musicians' gallery," a small balcony for the orchestra, which provided the frequent music required in Elizabethan plays. Somewhere above or to the rear of the musicians' gallery was the sound-effects and machinery room. Here cannonballs were rolled down wooden troughs to create the sound of thunder, fireworks were set off to suggest lightning, and the pulleys and ropes that were used for such spectacular effects as lowering gods to the stage and sending spirits flying through the air were housed.

Add to all these features of the Elizabethan stage the gorgeous and expensive costumes the actors wore, and it becomes clear that this theater, far from being crude and improvised, was in fact extremely advanced and sophisticated. But it was not a realistic theater. It used little scenery, and it made no attempt to recreate an exact illusion of life. The stage was unlocalized (not restricted to any particular place or time), so any part of the eternal human drama might be presented without concern for the limitations imposed by common-sense notions about time, space, and probability. On this stage a thirteen-year-old girl, Juliet, could rise to the heights of love and idealism; an entire life could pass during the two hours playing time; and blank verse could magically shift the scene in a moment's time from the coast of England to a battlefield in France.

To understand what the Elizabethan theater was truly like, we need to turn away from maps, building contracts, and sketches, and try to discover the symbolic values of the details of that theater—how it looked not to the literal eye, but to the eye of the imagination that sees in the parts suggestions of the whole and in imperfect material matter the rough shape of ideal forms. Fortunately, we can see the Elizabethan theater in just this way. The voice is Hamlet's:

. . . this goodly frame the earth seems to me a sterile promontory. This most excellent canopy, the air, look you, this brave o'erhanging firmament, this majestical roof fretted with golden fire—why, it appears no other thing to me than a foul and pestilent congregation of vapors. What a piece of work is a man! How noble in reason! How infinite in faculty! In form and moving how express and admirable! In action how like an angel! In apprehension how like a god! The beauty of the world! The paragon of animals!

As Hamlet speaks these words, his finger travels from one part of the theater to the other, and he calls out their symbolic values. "This goodly frame" is "the earth"—frame was the technical term used for the outer walls of the auditorium. He moves next to the shadow, or heavens, overhead, "this most excellent canopy, the air," and details the beauty of the constellations painted on it. Then he descends to the stage itself, pointing to the richly costumed, graceful actors, "What a piece of work is a man! . . . In form and moving how express and admirable! In action how like an angel!" Below him, and unmentioned, is hell, from which he has already, perhaps, had a visitor, and into which, as to the heavens above, a quick passage was always available in the Elizabethan theater. The name of the theater in which Hamlet first spoke these lines was the Globe, and in each of its details, like other Elizabethan theaters, it was a little globe mirroring the great globe on which it was modeled.

THE THEATER OF MODERN REALISM: This type of theater is not a descendant of the Elizabethan theater with its unlocalized stage, but the product of a separate line of development that began in Italy in the late Renaissance. Its form was stabilized during the nineteenth century, and it is ideally suited for the presentation of realistic drama, such as Ibsen's *Hedda Gabler,* where the illusion is carefully maintained that the play shows life exactly as it appears to the eyes of common sense.

Since this theater is still the standard type, only a brief description of its physical features is necessary. The auditorium is covered—in contrast to the Greek and Elizabethan theaters—and seats are provided for the entire audience. The stage does not extend out into the audience but is entirely recessed into the back wall. Its front is framed by what is known as the proscenium arch. Perspective scenery is used in back of the arch to give the set a realistic appearance, usually of the inside of a room furnished appropriately. The effect achieved is one of a "real" room with the fourth wall cut away. Since the audience sits in darkness with only the stage lighted, the illusion is furthered that the events on stage are "a slice of life," which the spectators are privileged to witness without themselves being seen. In other words, the theater of modern realism tries to deny the fact that it is a *theater,* a place of pretense and show. Instead it attempts to be a "candid camera," which catches real people doing real things in real settings.

Realistic acting styles in which the actor *becomes* the character he plays, sets in which walls are realistically solid and water actually flows from faucets, technical effects that reproduce on stage the phenomena of life, costumes that are historically accurate down to the last button, and lifelike makeup—all have grown up in the last hundred years to intensify the impression that what we see on stage is not an image of reality, but reality itself.

During the same time that the theater of realism was being perfected, some men of the theater who wished to return once more to a frankly illusionistic stage conducted a series of experiments with different types of nonrealistic techniques. The revolt against realism has so far not succeeded—the realistic theater is still standard—but it continues, and it is not unusual today to find stages that project out into the audience; theaters in the round, where the actors are surrounded by auditors; bare stages with no scenery at all; and scenery that is symbolic rather than realistic. Our own age, it would seem, is in the process of constructing a new type of theater in response to its changed sense of the world, but it is not clear yet just what form this theater will take.

II TYPES OF DRAMA

A L L E G O R Y : A work in which abstract qualities and values are presented as characters and a definite system of thought is dramatized. In *Everyman* Death and Fellowship, for example, become characters, and the play works out in dramatic terms the Christian doctrine of salvation. It is sometimes difficult to tell at just what point an allegorical figure becomes a true "character," since every personage in all plays represents to some degree a general quality of human nature.

B U R L E S Q U E : A satiric treatment of some well-known play, or a style of play, in which themes and conventions are treated in such a way as to make them ridiculous. High burlesque results when something is shown in a form to which it aspires but which is obviously grander than it deserves—the ward politician in the robes of a king. Low burlesque works in the opposite way—a great general dressed as a butcher. *Picnic on the Battlefield* is an extended low burlesque treatment of realistic, bourgeois drama.

C O M E D Y : A form concerned not so much with the individual as with the welfare of society and the human race. It envisions a benefi-

cent world and a nature that, while tricky, is ultimately bounteous
and rewarding. Man's function in comedy is to adjust himself to the
world and to enjoy it. The marks of comedy are (1) a tendency to
present rather simple, straightforward characters given to a few traditional vices or virtues; (2) the classification of characters into a few
types—lawyer, doctor, merchant, chief—who do the same things over
and over; (3) concentration on man as a social creature by showing
him usually as part of a group—seldom alone as in tragedy; (4) the
use of a familiar type of story, usually involving love, which suggests
that what has happened before is still happening and will happen
again; (5) a plot that is rather loosely put together and that is apt
to involve unexpected and unprepared-for events; (6) a pursuit not
of truth but of some very worldly goal such as wealth, pleasure, or
sex; (7) an eventual triumph of youth over age, flexibility and wit
over rigidity and dogmatism, life over death; (8) a happy conclusion,
which usually is expressed in a wedding, a feast, or a dance—all symbols of social agreement.

D R A M A : A serious play that cannot properly be called tragedy.
The French term for this type of play is *drame*.

E X P R E S S I O N I S M : The opposite of naturalism. While naturalism concentrates on the external details of reality and environment
to reflect the naturalistic belief that these are the shaping forces in
life, expressionism presents directly the internal life of man and shows
the world as he experiences it. The term was first used to describe
plays written in the late nineteenth century but can be applied to any
play—*Everyman,* for example—in which mental experience is openly
staged. In expressionism the primary fact of life becomes the world
as it is subjectively rather than objectively perceived.

F A R C E : Ludicrous exaggeration of comic actions. Usually defined
as "highly improbable actions and situations," farce is better understood as a dramatic technique that permits the author to show,
without concern for realism, human foolishness and ineffectiveness. It
is quite closely related to parody and burlesque.

M E L O D R A M A : What farce is to comedy, melodrama is to
tragedy. The distinguishing marks of melodrama are an excess of
pathetic situations and a thinness of characterization. In melodrama
the plot is stressed at the expense of character, which means that the
persons of the play have little effect on their destiny. They suffer without acting.

M I M E : What the Elizabethans called a "dumb show." A good example occurs in *Hamlet* where the play within the play is introduced with a dumb show. Essentially, miming is acting without words; every actor mimes, and every playwright makes use of this "language of the body."

M I R A C L E   P L A Y : A type of medieval play dramatizing a saint's life or some miraculous event of Christian history.

M O R A L I T Y   P L A Y : Any allegorical drama, most popular in England in the fifteenth and sixteenth centuries, written to dramatize Christian moral problems. See ALLEGORY.

M Y S T E R Y   P L A Y : A medieval dramatization of the events of the Bible. They were presented in a series beginning with Creation and ending with the Last Judgment. The craft guilds undertook the expense and labor of constructing the wagons on which the plays were performed and of acting them out; hence the name "mystery plays," *mystery* being a synonym for *craft* or *skill*.

N A T U R A L I S M : The opposite of expressionism. The term was first employed in the late nineteenth century to describe such plays as Strindberg's *The Father* and Zola's *Thérèse Raquin,* which reproduced the realistic appearance of the world and dramatized the theories of naturalistic philosophy. But any play that shows men as the victims of their environment, the creations of their social and natural world, may properly be called naturalistic.

P R O B L E M   P L A Y : Thesis play, propaganda play, play with a message, or social drama are variant terms. The common denominator here is an attempt on the part of the author to set up some specific contemporary problem and provide, explicitly or implicitly, a solution to it by recommending a course of action. In contrast to a play like *The Misanthrope,* which dramatizes a continuing human problem without advising us on what to do to find a solution, a problem play is constructed to persuade us to think and act in a particular manner.

R E A L I S M : A difficult term, which should always be handled with a great deal of care. After all, what is reality? Since every work of art is an imitation of the real and not itself real, realism can only be a relative term when applied to plays, pictures, and poems. But realism can be a useful descriptive term if we remember that it refers only to approximations of the world. Generally, it applies to works that present us with an image of what we ordinarily see and hear. No poetic play, for example, can strictly be called realistic since people do not ordinarily speak in verse.

S Y M B O L I S M : Generally speaking, the antithesis of realism, because in it objects, actions, and characters are not created to give the illusion of immediate reality, but to reflect or define some truth that lies below the surface of things as we usually see them. Poetic drama is thus one kind of symbolism; expressionism is another. More recently the term symbolism has been restricted in dramatic criticism to the endowing of various objects in a play with particular, but unspecified, significance. The pistols and the portrait of the General in *Hedda Gabler* are examples of symbolism in this narrow sense.

T R A G E D Y : Commonly taken to refer to any unhappy or painful situation, particularly if it involves death. But while pain, suffering, and death are prominent parts of literary tragedy, the tragic experience as it is presented in great art is much more complicated. Essentially, literary tragedy deals with a great individual at war with himself, with his society, and with the world around him. He seeks the fulfillment of an intensely personal, essentially human, need—a need he knows he must satisfy in order to fulfill himself—and he persists in his search while more ordinary men give in. In pursuit of his goal, he must commit himself to some course of action, he must *do* something; and once he commits himself, he releases certain powers, brings himself into conflict with forces whose existence he had hitherto not suspected, and he necessarily abides the consequences. And so he stumbles forward into his suffering, holding to an ideal which has by now become so qualified and complex that the hero himself is no longer certain of it. In the end he usually achieves something of value by his struggles. He may in the most optimistic of tragedies bring about the reformation of a kingdom or free an entire people from terror and plague. In darker tragedies he may do no more than discover the truth about himself or by some final, desperate act validate his own worth and freedom. But no matter what he discovers, the price the tragic man pays for the discovery is almost impossibly high—usually it is his life. Tragedy celebrates our lives as individuals, those hopes and ideals that comprise our personal selves; it shows the difficulty of realizing this individuality and accepts the double nature of enlightenment—at once the price and the reward of man's struggle with his limitations. On the other hand, comedy, to which tragedy should be contrasted, shows man as a member of society, of the human race, of life itself, and submerges his individuality in the pattern of a continuing world.

T R A G I C O M E D Y : The mixing of comedy and tragedy. Formal Renaissance critics insisted that tragedy and comedy should not properly be mixed, that kings and clowns did not belong on the same stage. But playwrights have quite happily joined the two forms in a single play—as in *The Skin of Our Teeth,* or even *Tiger at the Gates.* The immediate reason for doing so is probably to provide the audience with the pleasures of both comedy and tragedy; but more serious authors mix the two forms because they wish to show life as being both comic and tragic at once.

III   CRITICAL TERMS

A N T I C L I M A X : Failure of conflicting forces to come into open confrontation or to arrive at a conclusive decision. The anticlimax is popularly believed to be a sign of poor plotting, but *The Cherry Orchard* presents a series of anticlimaxes. The skillful dramatist can always use this device to mirror a world in which people never press on to logical or emotional conclusions.

A S I D E : Lines spoken by an actor that are by convention heard only by the audience, not by the other actors on stage. The aside is basically a device for presenting thought.

A T M O S P H E R E : A vague term used to describe the "quality" built up in a play by language, scenery, costumes, and so on. For example, we might say that the series of unanswered questions coupled with the cold, dark battlements in the first scene of *Hamlet* build up an atmosphere of mystery and fear. It would be more precise and useful to say that the characters live in a mysterious world in which they grope for information.

B A T H O S : A descent from the sublime to the ridiculous. A plot is bathetic when it tumbles from the serious to the ridiculous: when for example, in *The Misanthrope,* two ladies begin by offering one another the highest moral advice in the most elevated tones and end up squabbling.

C A T A S T R O P H E : A word that usually means disaster of any kind, but which technically refers to that point in the play where one of the conflicting forces or persons triumphs over the other. This ordinarily occurs near or at the end of the play. *Dénouement* is a synonym, but more neutral in its implications, for catastrophe, which means literally, "to turn downwards."

CATHARSIS: A term used by Aristotle in his *Poetics* to describe the purging of the feelings of pity and fear that, according to him, the audience should experience at the conclusion of a tragedy. Aristotle argued that the production of this effect was the proper end of tragedy. The term has been extended to cover any release of emotion experienced by the audience.

CHORUS: The group of dancers and singers, usually representing the elders of the community, used in Greek tragedy and comedy. Their number varied from twelve to fifty at different times.

CLIMAX: The high point of the play's action, toward which events have been building throughout; the point at which the character sees that what he thinks he has been doing is not what he has *in fact* been doing.

COMIC RELIEF: A device by which the dramatist, who has presented very serious and tragic matters for some time, affords his audience a rest by inserting a comic scene; this is how affective critics—those who try to describe a play by the feelings it creates in the audience—account for comic relief. But in well-constructed plays the comic scenes usually handle in a different way the same themes and problems dealt with in the preceding "serious" scenes. Comic perspective would be an apter term for this dramatic technique.

CONTRAST: One of the artist's principal techniques for establishing meaning. Basically, contrast is the juxtaposition of unlikes so that each will question the other and thereby emphasize it. Black and white, hate and love, Hamlet and Claudius, Alceste and Philinte—these are all effective contrasts.

CONVENTIONS: Abbreviated ways of saying things, present in every art, which, because we are accustomed to them, we take for granted and often fail to notice. The Japanese theatergoer has no trouble accepting the convention of his theater that hopping up and down on one leg represents running a considerable distance. In the same way we accept the conventions of our theater: we can accept the passage of several days in the space of three hours playing time; we pretend that the characters speaking their thoughts aloud in asides and soliloquies are thinking rather than speaking; and we allow one scene to be changed to another while we wait.

DÉNOUEMENT : Literally, the untying or unraveling of the plot. The point at which the meaning of past events becomes clear. See CATASTROPHE.

DEUS EX MACHINA : The "god from the machine"; the term is used in dramatic criticism for the unanticipated intervention of some outside force or person to tie up the plot. The term derives from the occasional practice in the Greek theater of solving the problems of the plot and bringing the play to a conclusion by lowering a god onto the stage by some mechanical device. The god then dispensed justice and brought the play to an end. The term now is used to refer to the use of any person or piece of information hitherto unmentioned in the play to bring it to an end. A rich uncle returning unexpectedly in the last act, the discovery of an unknown will, a fortunate coincidence, or some quirk of fate—these are all instances of the *deus ex machina*. Plays using this device are said to be badly plotted, since the conclusion is supposed to grow, properly, out of character and past events. But comedy frequently ends with the introduction of some variety of *deus ex machina* because it presents a world in which there are always fortuitous happenings.

DRAMATIS PERSONAE : The persons of the drama. A useful term for distinguishing the characters of the play from real people.

EPISODIC PLOT : A type of plot in which events are not part of a cause and effect pattern, but are related in some other manner, or not related at all. *Mother Courage* is a good example of a play with an episodic plot: twelve different scenes in which the same thing happens again and again in different ways, but one event does not cause the next. Yet the play has unity. It is a serial representation of the same view of life.

EXPOSITION : Technically, the opening part of the play, devoted to introducing the characters and providing the necessary background information about them. Exposition can, however, take place at any point in the play or throughout it. But the term as it is ordinarily used suggests that a playwright mechanically stops his action for a time while he contrives some way of providing necessary information. A skillful playwright, however, will keep his play in movement at all times, and the statement of background material by the characters will be used as continuing demonstrations of their motives. When Hedda Gabler tells us about her earlier relationship with Eilert Lövborg, she is providing background information that helps us understand what is taking place, but she is also acting out her desire for freedom by proxy from the restraints imposed by polite society.

F A B L E : The traditional English name for the story of the play, or the plot. Aristotle's term for the fable was *mythos*, the myth.

F A L L I N G   A C T I O N : That section of the play which comes between the catastrophe and the conclusion.

F O R E S H A D O W I N G   (*prolepsis*) : Traditionally, obvious hints of what will come. *Tiger at the Gates* is made up of a continuing series of foreshadowings. In most plays of the first order, some kind of foreshadowing is omnipresent. Every act of Hedda Gabler's, for example, tells us what she will eventually do. If a character is consistent, then his end is contained, foreshadowed, in his beginning. Heavy use of foreshadowing emphasizes the role of fate in a play.

I M A G E R Y : The general term for comparisons: metaphor, simile, personification, analogue, symbol, and so on. Since all art is an attempt to find a suitable image for an unnamed quality, the subject of imagery is as wide as art itself. But ordinarily, dramatic critics use the term to mean only those comparisons that are made in the language of the play.

I R O N Y : A device by which what seems to be and what is are in some way opposed. Dramatists use irony frequently to portray situations in which men pretend to be something they are not, or in which they think they are doing something when in fact they are doing something else. At any time irony appears, character becomes complicated because irony creates two levels of being: "seems" and "is."

O B L I G A T O R Y   S C E N E : A relic of nineteenth-century French dramatic criticism. This term originally referred to a mechanical, contrived scene that the audience was led to expect. If at the beginning of a play, for example, a man seduced a woman and then left her, the audience would expect that there would inevitably be a child and that ultimately the child and the father would meet. The meeting would be the obligatory scene. This describes the mechanical plotting of many so-called well-made plays. More usefully, the obligatory scene is the event compelled by the logic of the play, the full and clear expression of motives and conflicts that have been present in the play in one form or another from the outset. Hedda Gabler's suicide is an obligatory scene. It should be noticed that comedy often refuses to supply the obligatory scene since in comedy, as its spirit Puck says,

> Those things best please me
> That befall preposterously.

PATHOS: A word that originally meant, in Greek, "enduring" or "suffering." It is correctly applied to circumstances in which characters are forced to accept, helplessly, a fate that they did not intend—Hector at the end of *Tiger at the Gates*. Excessive pathos exploited for its own sake is usually termed *sentimentality*.

PERSONIFICATION: A character in a play who merely represents some idea or aspect of life—Good Works and Fellowship in *Everyman*, for example. Personifications lack individuality and seem to have no life of their own. It is often extremely difficult, however, to decide whether a figure is a personification or a "character." All dramatic characters are to some degree personifications.

POINT OF ATTACK: That point in time at which the playwright picks up events and begins his play. Earlier details necessary to an understanding of the events dramatized are introduced in the dialogue.

PROBABILITY: Aristotle's recommendation that events in tragedy should follow one another in a probable and necessary manner. That is, if a character begins as courageous he should not be shown later as cowardly. Probability is perhaps better understood as consistency: what is shown in the beginning should still be there at the end. The characters and events of tragedy are usually, though not always, consistent; but comedy is less likely to deal in the probable.

RECOGNITION: That point at which a character suddenly sees himself and understands his position truly. Hedda Gabler's recognition occurs when Brack tells her of the manner of Lövborg's death and shows that he intends to use this knowledge for his own benefit. Recognition will usually, though not necessarily, involve a reversal and will occur at the dénouement. But the term *recognition* focuses attention not only on the change of fortune described by reversal and dénouement, but also on the apprehension of that change and its moral implications by the chief character. Recognition is, very simply, the point of full awareness.

REVERSAL: An Aristotelian critical term (*peripety*), which refers to the point in a play where affairs turn in an unexpected direction. The reversal occurs in *Oedipus* when it becomes clear that the murderer Oedipus is tracking down is himself, and in *Antigone* when it becomes clear that Creon's actions have destroyed his family and his city rather than saving them. In this book, reversal has been treated as one form of dramatic irony.

RISING ACTION: The traditional way of describing the events that come between the joining of the conflict and its climax. In this book, rising action is handled as the increasingly overt expression of the central motives.

SETTING: The equivalent of the "world" of the play. The environment of the characters of the drama created with the physical set, lighting, sound effects, and language.

SOLILOQUY: Monologue. A speech delivered by a character alone on stage, which is, by convention, accepted as voiced thought.

SUSPENSE: A useful critical term only if we assume that the playwright designs his play to hold the attention of the audience by raising questions and anticipations and then delaying their answers and fulfillments. If we assume, however, as most modern critics do, that a good play is not so much concerned with its effect on the audience as it is with staging some truth about life, then the interval between the opening of a line of action and its completion must be understood as some part of the playwright's strategy for giving form to his sense of life. It is a part of what is in this book called the *rhythm of action.*

TEMPO: The timing or over-all plot rhythm of the play. Do events move swiftly or slowly? Is the action maintained at a high level? Does it rise and fall?

THEME: A word used to describe the "meaning" or "central idea" of a play. There is a danger involved in its use, however, for it suggests that the entire play can be reduced to one abstract statement: its theme. In fact, every detail in a well-constructed play contributes to its theme. Statements about the theme of a play should only be thought of as working tools, ways of getting closer to the heart of a play.

TRAGIC FLAW: The weakness or moral failing—pride, envy, temper—that blemishes the tragic hero's otherwise perfect character and causes his difficulties. Since he is "flawed," it follows that his downfall is to some degree just, and that the operation of the universe is therefore moral. This concept of the tragic flaw was believed to have originated with Aristotle, but he actually spoke not of a flaw but of "some human failing or weakness." In other words, the characteristic that involves the tragic hero in his painful destiny need not be a moral failing but simply some limitation common to all men, such as inability to foresee the future or imperfect knowledge of his own nature. Furthermore, there are a great many tragic heroes, Hamlet for example, who are thrust into tragedy for no reason except that they were born. Even in heroes who do seem to be morally culpable in some way, the "flaw" is often the very source of their greatness. Only a god could speak without sounding impossibly smug of the moral flaws of Antigone or Mother Courage.

THE UNITIES: Time, place, and action. Renaissance critics, believing that they were following Aristotle, laid down the rule that plays must observe these unities. That is, a play must limit the time portrayed to twenty-four hours, the place to an area which could reasonably be covered in that time, and the action to the events of one story only.